1100s	1000s	900s	800s	700s	600s	500s	400s		200s	100s

. 1547 B.C.)

47 B.C.)

after the 40 years of wandering (ca. 1507 B.C.)

ses (ca. 1507 B.C.)

the death of Joshua (ca. 1427 B.C.)

death of Joshua to the birth of Samuel (just before 1125 B.C.)

likely during the middle part of the 12th century B.C.

1 Samuel birth of Samuel to the death of Saul

2 Samuel death of Saul to the death of David (ca. 1015 B.C.)

1 Kings end of David's reign to the transition from Elijah to Elisha (ca. 851 B.C.)

2 Kings Elisha to Babylonian captivity (ca. 857 B.C.)

Adam to the death of David and the reign of Solomon (ca. 1015 B.C.)

2 Chronicles Solomon to the decree of Cyrus (537 B.C.)

Ezra Cyrus to the repatriation (ca. 459 B.C.)

Nehemiah perhaps ca. 444 B.C.

Esther ca. 479 B.C.

Psalms King David to ca. 1015 B.C.

Proverbs reign of Solomon (ca. 1015 B.C.–ca. 975 B.C.)

Ecclesiastes traditionally 1015 B.C. to 975 B.C., though perhaps 300 B.C.–250 B.C.

Isaiah 740 B.C.–701 B.C.

Jeremiah 626 B.C.–585 B.C.

Lamentations ca. 587 B.C.–585 B.C.

Ezekiel ca. 592 B.C.–570 B.C.

Daniel ca. 604 B.C.–562 B.C.

Hosea 8th century B.C., probably just prior to the ministry of Isaiah

Joel approx. 9th century B.C.

Amos reigns of King Jeroboam II of Israel and King Uzziah of Judah

Obadiah probably 587 B.C.

Jonah ca. 790 B.C.–749 B.C.

Micah ca. 728 B.C.

Nahum late 8th century B.C. or the mid- to late 7th century B.C.

Habakkuk possibly ca. 600 B.C.

Zephaniah 639 B.C.–608 B.C.

Haggai ca. 520 B.C.

Zechariah ca. 520 B.C.–518 B.C.

Malachi ca. 430 B.C.

1 & 2 Nephi first year of the reign of Zedekiah (ca. 598 B.C.) to the last decades of 6th century B.C.

S0-AQL-622

TEACHINGS AND COMMENTARIES

on the

OLD TESTAMENT

ALSO BY ED J. PINEGAR AND RICHARD J. ALLEN:

Living by the Word
Teachings and Commentary on the Book of Mormon
Teachings and Commentary on the Doctrine and Covenants
(with Karl R. Anderson)
Your Patriarchal Blessing
Come unto Me
Press Forward, Saints
Choose Ye This Day
Words of Wisdom for Missionaries

ALSO BY ED J. PINEGAR

Latter-day Commentary on the New Testament: The Four Gospels
(with K. Douglas Bassett and Ted L. Earl)
The Ultimate Missionary Companion
A Prophet's Voice

TEACHINGS AND COMMENTARIES

on the

OLD TESTAMENT

ED J. PINEGAR *and* RICHARD J. ALLEN

Covenant Communications, Inc.

Cover painting *The Prophet Ezekiel* by Lyle Beddes © Intellectual Reserve, Inc.

Cover and book design © 2005 by Covenant Communications, Inc.

Published by Covenant Communications, Inc.
American Fork, Utah

Printed in Canada
First Printing: October 2005

11 10 09 08 07 06 05   10 9 8 7 6 5 4 3 2 1

ISBN 1-59811-014-4

PREFACE

In this volume we offer a comprehensive array of resources and learning materials designed to enhance the experience of approaching and understanding the word of God as memorialized in the Old Testament. This priceless scripture is an essential part of the sacred canon. Through the teachings of the Old Testament and the associated texts of the books of Moses and Abraham in the Pearl of Great Price, we gain precious insights into the plan of salvation and the transcendent blessings of following the principles and procedures of the Lord's covenant program "to bring to pass the immortality and eternal life of" His children (Moses 1:39).

Teachings and Commentary on the Old Testament is organized in a straightforward way to simplify the process of applying these materials to daily life and to teaching opportunities of diverse kinds. We open with an introductory section containing ideas and strategies—based on counsel from noted authorities—on how to enhance our understanding and appreciation of the Old Testament. Then follows a section called "Portrait of the Old Testament," comprising an overview of each book in the Old Testament (plus Moses and Abraham), giving author, position within the sacred record, time period, purpose, and key sections.

The central part of the book is a detailed treatment of the central theme of the Old Testament—the glorious mission and personality of the Savior, the Mediator of the sacred covenant with the Father, so richly chronicled and explicated in these ancient records.

Following this portrait, we offer a section called "Spiritual Oases," a collection of 35 separate entries giving the major themes, stories, doctrines, and applications from the Old Testament and Pearl of Great Price arranged in chronological order. Across the vast landscape of the Old Testament lands, we see a panoramic view of mixed scenes, encompassing alternately both a wasteland patchwork of wilderness as well as fertile pastures of verdure and splendor. Likewise, in the Old Testament chronicle, we see the wasteland of man' prideful intemperance and sin as well as the pastures of penitence, humility, and covenant devotion. Both are present, intermingled in the experiences of the human condition.

As travelers across this terrain, we labor in grief and sorrow (as did Enoch in Moses 7:20–40) through the accounts of Israel's travail under the burdens of wickedness, but we also rejoice from time to time through our encounters along the way with scenes of grandeur and triumph as the Lord's prophets and disciples, leaders and saints, rise on eagle's wings to the potential of their God-given destiny. Such are the spiritual oases that beckon the anxious traveler seeking the fountains of living water to quench the thirst for truth, truth that is embedded in the sacred chronicles of the Lord's dealings with His children.

The final section of the book contains teachings and commentary on the Old Testament to coincide with the weekly Sunday School lessons. The approach used is thematic, each major theme in the reading selection being addressed in a consistent pattern of study that includes relevant scriptural passages, a "moment of truth" giving the historical context of pertinent chapters from the Old Testament and Pearl of Great Price, selected statements from the Lord's modern-day prophets, and one or more illustrations and applications for our time. The appendix then provides a comparative chronology to help the reader place the elements of the Old Testament and Pearl of Great Price into more meaningful juxtaposition with one another and with synchronisms from secular history.

The following reference works were particularly helpful in determining chronological dates: (1) *The World History Chart: A Chronology of World History According to R. H. Carling,* 8th ed. (International Timeline, 2004); "Chronology," in the Bible Dictionary (635–45); and "The Shepherd's Page Chronology of Time According to Scripture" (a service of www.abdicate.net). Many other reference sources were also consulted to ensure that the dates cited were as accurate as possible.

It is our earnest hope that this resource book will be of assistance to all those who wish to apply the teachings of the Old Testament and Pearl of Great Price to their lives. We give sincere thanks to those who have helped us complete this undertaking through their encouragement and counsel—particularly Pat Pinegar and Carol Lynn Allen. In addition, we wish to thank the editors of Covenant Communications, especially Shauna Humphreys, for their devoted help and collaboration in structuring and refining this project.

Ed J. Pinegar
Richard J. Allen

ABBREVIATIONS

AGQ   Joseph Fielding Smith. *Answers to Gospel Questions.* 5 vols. Salt Lake City: Deseret Book, 1957–66.

CR   Conference Report. Salt Lake City: The Church of Jesus Christ of Latter-day Saints.

Discourses   John A. Widtsoe, sel. *Discourses of Brigham Young.* Salt Lake City: Deseret Book, 1954.

DS   Joseph Fielding Smith. *Doctrines of Salvation.* Ed. Bruce R. McConkie. 3 vols. Salt Lake City: Bookcraft, 1954–56.

HC   Joseph Smith. *History of the Church of Jesus Christ of Latter-day Saints.* Ed. B. H. Roberts. 7 vols. Salt Lake City: The Church of Jesus Christ of Latter-day Saints, 1932–51.

JD   Brigham Young and others. *Journal of Discourses.* 26 vols. Liverpool: George Q. Cannon, 1855–86.

MD   Bruce R. McConkie. *Mormon Doctrine.* 2nd ed. Salt Lake City: Bookcraft, 1966.

TETB   Ezra Taft Benson. *The Teachings of Ezra Taft Benson.* Salt Lake City: Bookcraft, 1988.

TGBH   Gordon B. Hinckley. *Teachings of Gordon B. Hinckley.* Salt Lake City: Deseret Book, 1997.

THWH   Howard W. Hunter. *The Teachings of Howard W. Hunter.* Ed. Clyde J. Williams. Salt Lake City: Bookcraft, 1997.

TPJS   Joseph Smith. *Teachings of the Prophet Joseph Smith.* Comp. Joseph Fielding Smith. Salt Lake City: Deseret Book, 1976.

TSWK   Spencer W. Kimball. *The Teachings of Spencer W. Kimball.* Ed. Edward L. Kimball. Salt Lake City: Bookcraft, 1982.

TABLE OF CONTENTS

TEACHINGS AND COMMENTARY

"This Is My Work and My Glory"
    Moses 1

"Thou Wast Chosen Before Thou Wast Born"
    Abraham 3; Moses 4:1–4

"And Behold, All Things Which I Had Made Were Very Good"
    Moses 1:27–42; 2–3

"This Is the Place of Salvation Unto All Men"
    Moses 4; 5:1–15; 6:48–62

"If Thou Doest Well, Thou Shalt Be Accepted"
    Moses 5–7

"Noah . . . Prepared an Ark to the Saving of His House"
    Moses 8:19–30; Genesis 6–9; 11:1–9

"I Will Make My Covenant Between Me and Thee"
    Abraham 1:1–4; 2:1–11; Genesis 12:1–8; 17:1–9

UNDERSTANDING *and* APPRECIATING *the* OLD TESTAMENT

A BOOK OF LIGHT

From the divine dawning of the Creation to the glories of Sinai to the pervasive flame of prophecy illuminating the mission of the coming Redeemer, the Old Testament is a book of light. "It is written, Man shall not live by bread alone, but by every word that proceedeth out of the mouth of God" (Matt. 4:4). Thus responded the mortal Messiah, quoting from Deuteronomy 8:3, to the temptations of Satan, over whom He had already prevailed in the pre-mortal councils of heaven (Abr. 3:27–28). And so it is. The banquet of endowed truth is incomplete without the spiritual nourishment provided by the Old Testament, the foundational library of the holy canon. Through the power and light of the Old Testament, we gain precious and enduring benefits: a deeper understanding of the origin and nature of God's design for the immortality and eternal life of man, life-sustaining insights into the covenant process of sanctification and purification, a treasured witness of the verity of Christ's calling and atonement, and a greater abundance of strength and courage to "seek the face of the Lord always," as we are reminded in the Doctrine and Covenants, "that in patience ye may possess your souls, and ye shall have eternal life" (D&C 101:38).

But the radiance of the Old Testament does not flow to us without our devoted effort and humble dependence upon the inspiration of the Holy Ghost. By study and faith, we can drink from the refreshing well of truth that awaits us. By prayer and pondering, we can avail ourselves of the message of the Old Testament, which John A. Widtsoe has summarized eloquently as follows:

> What is the message of the Old Testament? From the first to the last, in the Pentateuch, in the historical books, in the poetical books, and in the prophets, it teaches the existence of a personal God, the Maker of the heavens and the earth, the Father of the human race. It teaches that the earth and all things upon it are

provided for man's benefit but that man must obey law, divine law, to secure the blessings he desires. It teaches that obedience to the moral law, given by God for human conduct, involving faith in God, not to be compared with man-made, ethical, selfish codes of action, is the most important concern of man. It is the message of messages for humankind. (*Evidences and Reconciliations* [Salt Lake City: Improvement Era], 135)

This "message of messages" is centered in the atoning mission of Jesus Christ as our Redeemer and Savior. That is the primary purpose of the Old Testament: to provide a divine witness of the Son of God, the great Jehovah, and show us how we can move forward to be more like Him through covenant fidelity and obedience. Indeed, our view of the Savior in His sacred role as Jehovah, Messiah, Christ, Creator, Emmanuel, Jesus, and King provides a lens for us to perceive more fully the divine truth that is presented to us in the Old Testament record.

Edward J. Brandt brings to us the insight that we must look *to* Christ and *for* Christ in the Law of Moses if we are to develop an understanding of the message of the Old Testament. He describes this process as follows:

"But their minds were blinded: for until this day remaineth the same vail untaken away in the reading of the old testament; which vail is done away in Christ." When Christ is recognized in the Old Testament, then comes understanding and a love of it! But even to this day when Moses (or the Old Testament) is read, "the vail is upon their heart." Paul gave us the key that removes the veil from one's mind: "Nevertheless when it shall turn to the Lord, the vail shall be taken away." The Joseph Smith Translation adds two words that give a clearer focus: their heart. Nevertheless, "when their heart shall turn to the Lord, the vail shall be taken away." In other words, there must be humility, teachableness, meekness, and obedience. To have the veil removed makes it possible for the individual to repent and come unto Christ. That was the true spirit of the law of Moses. (in Richard D. Draper, ed., *A Witness of Jesus Christ: The 1989 Sperry Symposium on the Old Testament* [Salt Lake City: Deseret Book, 1990], 34)

By making the Savior the central focus of our study of the Old Testament, we can look forward to rich blessings of wisdom in applying the Lord's doctrines and commandments in righteousness.

HOW TO UNDERSTAND THE OLD TESTAMENT

The Old Testament is part of the divine canon of truth delivered to us by the Lord through His prophets. Understanding that the canon provides a standard for spiritual progress in keeping with covenant measures and obligations allows us to inquire how we can achieve a deeper understanding of the Old Testament and its eternal message. Here are eight suggestions:

1. Study and Pray

2. Follow the Spirit

3. Look at the Big Picture

4. Look upon the Old Testament as a "Family Matter"

5. Read the Old Testament on Its Own Terms

6. Become Accustomed to the Figurative and Symbolic Language of the Old Testament

7. Cross-Illumination: Turn to Latter-day Revelation

8. Look for Practical Themes and Applications

Study and Pray
Daniel H. Ludlow has reminded us of ways to understand the Old Testament through a process of spiritual discovery:

> Actually the Old Testament is not an extremely hard or difficult book to understand. It is a relatively simple book if you understand how and why the book is put together the way it is. Remember the words from Brigham Young: "The Bible, *when it is understood,* is one of the simplest books in the world, for, as far as it is translated correctly, it is nothing but truth, and in truth there is no mystery *save to the ignorant.*" This statement gives us a clue to understanding the Old Testament: We must remove our *ignorance* concerning it. In other words, we must study and ponder the book, become acquainted with its makeup and format, and learn its doctrines and teachings.
>
> A statement in the Book of Mormon also gives us a hint about how we should study the scriptures. In Alma 17:2 we read that the sons of Mosiah "had waxed strong in the knowledge of the truth; for they were men of a sound understanding and they had *searched* the scriptures *diligently,* that they might know the word of God" (italics added).
>
> Note again the principle: The scriptures must be *searched diligently.*

The reason why the scriptures should be searched diligently is in the statement by the Savior in John 5:39, "They are they which testify of me." (in Richard D. Draper, ed., *A Witness of Jesus Christ: The 1989 Sperry Symposium on the Old Testament* [Salt Lake City: Deseret Book, 1990], 118)

Follow the Spirit

Accompanying our diligent searching and pondering of the scriptures is the need to seek and listen to the promptings of the Spirit of the Lord. Nephi taught of the power of combining the word of God with the guidance of the Holy Spirit:

> Feast upon the words of Christ; for behold, the words of Christ will tell you all things what ye should do.
>
> Wherefore, now after I have spoken these words, if ye cannot understand them it will be because ye ask not, neither do ye knock; wherefore, ye are not brought into the light, but must perish in the dark.
>
> For behold, again I say unto you that if ye will enter in by the way, and receive the Holy Ghost, it will show unto you all things what ye should do. (2 Ne. 32:3–5)

We need the Spirit to better understand more fully the message of the Old Testament, as Ellis T. Rasmussen points out:

> The individuals and the peoples of the Old Testament experienced hopes and fears, aspirations and disappointments, achievements and failings in all of which we can find examples of good or evil, to be emulated or avoided. Indeed, as we see Old Testament accounts of our spiritual forebears and sense their faith, reverence, hope and joy—or feel their doubt, infidelity, despair, and misery—we may find ways to avoid pitfalls ourselves, reach our ideals, and attain more joy. But it must here be declared that the most important aid to understanding the Old Testament, or any other book of scripture, is the inspiration from the Holy Spirit, which is promised to us in those scriptures. (*A Latter-day Saint Commentary on the Old Testament* [Salt Lake City: Deseret, 1993], vii–viii)

Look at the Big Picture

Whether we are focusing our attention on a specific scriptural passage in the Old Testament or on a broader sweep of events and developments, it is helpful to begin our consideration by examining things from a higher perspective. By looking at the big picture—the structure and purpose of an entire book or series of books—we can often acquire a framework for understanding and interpreting individual passages or events. Charles W. Penrose counsels us, "In reading the scriptures, whether the Old

Testament or the New Testament, in order to understand them properly we should not take one isolated text, but read it in conjunction with the context, then we get the meaning of the writer or speaker" (*CR,* April 1911, 33).

Often the use of the Bible Dictionary is helpful in understanding the bigger picture. Victor Ludlow gives us some specific recommendations of this kind: "The reader should study the following items in the Bible Dictionary to better understand the Old Testament as a whole: Scripture, Bible, Canon, Italics, Joseph Smith Translation, Writing, Scroll, Roll, Codex, Lost Books, Apocrypha, Pseudepigrapha, Hagiographa, Masoretic Text, Septuagint, Vulgate, Dead Sea Scrolls, Tell el-Amarna Letters, Talmud" (*Unlocking the Old Testament* [Salt Lake City: Deseret Book, 1981], 2).

Look upon the Old Testament as a "Family Matter"
The scriptures deal with the Lord's relationship to and interaction with His "family"—the vast congregations of mankind that constitute His progeny. In this sense, all scripture is family history. This is especially true of the Old Testament, which lays down the foundation of the origins of mankind and the progress of several branches thereof that have been given the particular responsibility for bringing the blessings of the gospel to the world under the aegis of the Abrahamic covenant. Daniel H. Ludlow provides some interesting details in connection with this view of scripture:

> The Old Testament is primarily a record of a series of families. In order to understand and appreciate the Old Testament, you will need to understand the major events, beliefs, customs, and traditions of the families discussed.
>
> The family of Adam is introduced first, but by chapter six of the first book (Genesis), the family of Noah appears. In only six more chapters (Genesis 12), the family of Abraham is featured, next Isaac (whose birth is recorded in chapter 21), and then Jacob (Israel), whose story begins in chapter 25 and whose descendants dominate the remainder of the Old Testament. Thus, of the 929 chapters in the thirty-nine books in the Old Testament, only 24 chapters do not deal directly with Jacob and his descendants, and these first 24 chapters provide the background for the coming forth of the family of Israel.
>
> The last part of the Old Testament is primarily concerned with a specific segment of Jacob's family—the Jews, descendants of Jacob's fourth son (Judah), and also citizens of the kingdom of Judah. Thus, sometimes the entire Old Testament is referred to as the "record of the Jews."
>
> Other titles associated with the heads of major families might be used to indicate that the Old Testament is also the record of—
>
> 1. The Semites (descendants of Shem, the son of Noah).

2. The Hebrews (descendants of Abraham).

3. The Israelites (descendants of Jacob/Israel).

The problem of using these terms to refer to the major peoples of the Bible is that the terms are not synonymous—thus, the speaker must be certain he is using each term correctly. All Jews (descendants of Judah) are Israelites (descendants of Jacob/Israel), but not all Israelites are Jews. (There are many descendants of the other sons of Jacob who are not descendants of Judah.)

All Israelites (descendants of Jacob/Israel) are Hebrews (descendants of Abraham), but not all Hebrews are Israelites. (The descendants of Ishmael and of the six sons of Abraham through Keturah are Hebrews, but they are not descendants of Jacob.)

All Hebrews (descendants of Abraham) are Semites (descendants of Shem), but not all Semites are Hebrews.

One reason the world is confused about these terms is that essentially the only Israelites the world has known about for over 2,700 years (from 722 B.C., when the ten tribes were taken captive, to the present) are the Jews. Most people, therefore, think the terms *Jew* and *Israelite* are synonymous, but they are not. (*A Companion to Your Study of the Old Testament* [Salt Lake City: Deseret Book, 1981], 5–6)

Read the Old Testament on Its Own Terms

Like all scripture, the Old Testament blossomed from the seedbed of its own culture and time frame. Thus it conveys both the signature of its own setting and environment as well as the signature of divine principle and truth valid in all dispensations and time frames. It is prudent, then, to approach the Old Testament with a willingness to understand the cultural imprint of its originators—responding to the challenges and circumstances of a given time frame—as well as to seek and appreciate the timeless truths that are conveyed across the generations. Rather than impose our own agenda upon the scripture, we should let it project its own message in its own way.

Lowell L. Bennion has given us valuable advice for understanding the Old Testament on its own terms:

Why is the Old Testament so little read and appreciated? One reason is that its very age creates problems. To understand it presupposes some knowledge of the time and circumstances of its writing and of the authors and their audience and purpose. The prophets were speaking in their own century to their own people in critical historical situations. Some of their teachings have local and temporary meaning only; others have universal and enduring value. It is not always easy to distinguish between the two, but the Old Testament cannot be understood apart from the times and circumstances in which its writings were produced. This does not require a specialist's knowledge, of course; many excellent commentaries will provide a perfectly adequate introduction.

A second problem with understanding the Old Testament is its structure. People habitually read a book from cover to cover, from beginning to end; but the Old Testament was not written as a single book. Instead, it is a collection of thirty-nine separate writings brought together into a single volume centuries after they were written. It is more like a shelf of books in a library, arranged neither chronologically nor alphabetically. Proverbs and Psalms are themselves collections of writings composed over centuries. . . .

Some Christians have not been interested in the Old Testament for its own sake but only because it predicts the coming of Jesus Christ. Although this interest is legitimate, it can be so powerful that they may relate passages to the Savior that do not apply to him. This might be called "Christianizing" the Old Testament, a practice understandably disturbing to Jewish scholars. Certainly some passages in the Old Testament that predict the coming of a Messiah are admirably fulfilled by Christ. Moreover, Jesus, Peter, and Paul quote the Old Testament to establish the Christian faith. But looking only for Christian-related passages in the Old Testament will divert our attention from many other religious concepts that are unique to that scripture and of great importance and value. . . .

Each scripture is unique. Each has its original and special contribution to make. Each should be studied and appreciated for what it is. Each should be respected for its own integrity. . . .

In short, much of the Old Testament is valid for us today, but some of it is an expression of different conditions, attitudes, and a more limited understanding of the will of God. . . .

The law of Moses is a splendid achievement for its day. Much of it, such as the Decalogue, or Ten Commandments, is equally valid for us. Other parts—dietary laws, hygienic rules, and sacrifices—are much less relevant, even among modern Jews.

The Old Testament is a wonderfully honest and human record as well as inspired of God. Its humanity and divinity co-mingle in a fascinating record. It works best when it is read for its own sake, not as something it is not. (*The Unknown Testament* [Salt Lake City: Deseret Book, 1988], 4–6)

Similarly, we need to remember that the Old Testament was formulated within a linguistic context very different from our own. If we were to seek an intimate understanding of the basic text of the Old Testament, we would likely want to acquire a knowledge of Hebrew. It is well-known that the Prophet Joseph Smith arranged for Hebrew to be taught to the early elders of the Church at the school in Kirtland (see *HC* 2:318, 355–56,

376–77, 391), the Prophet himself being among the most ardent of the students. Though most of us do not have the time to become expert in Hebrew, we can still turn to a Hebrew dictionary or lexicon from time to time to assist in understanding the text.

Become Accustomed to the Figurative and Symbolic Language of the Old Testament

The ancient prophets frequently turned to figurative or symbolic language and often expressed themselves in poetic imagery to convey their inspired messages. Gerald Lund gives the following counsel concerning the symbolic or figurative elements of the Old Testament text:

> The question comes to mind, then, When is an act or object recorded in scripture to be taken literally and when should it be interpreted figuratively? Symbols can be taken too literally, and their true meaning lost in a grotesque parody of reality. On the other hand, sometimes one can explain away the actual meaning of a passage by saying it is only figurative. The following guidelines may be helpful as one tries to decide how to interpret correctly the symbols used in the Old Testament:
>
> 1. Look for the interpretation of the symbol in the scriptures themselves.
>
> 2. Look for Christ in the symbols and imagery of the scriptures.
>
> 3. Let the nature of the object used as a symbol contribute to your understanding of its spiritual meaning.
>
> 4. Seek the reality behind the symbol. . . .
>
> The reality behind the Old Testament is Jesus Christ and his teachings of salvation. The better we understand him, the more clearly we will see the meaning of the symbols. (*Jesus Christ, Key to the Plan of Salvation* [Salt Lake City: Deseret Book, 1991], 54–56)

D. Kelly Ogden gives these additional insights into the figurative language of the Old Testament:

> While figurative language may thus be used to disguise some messages, it can also be used to enhance the meaning for those who understand. Figurative language is poetic; it is a unique use of language. It uses words that, if they were understood literally, could obscure the actual intent of the expression. Figurative language is saying one thing that represents another. The rib of Adam used in creating a woman

(Gen. 2:22), the burning coal used in cleansing Isaiah (Isaiah 6:6–7), and the scrolls or books that Ezekiel and John were to eat (Ezek. 3:1; Rev. 10:9) were all symbolic expressions. The woman was formed to be "one" with Adam, but she was not necessarily formed from his rib. Isaiah's cleansing was literal, but it was spiritual rather than physical. Ezekiel and John took to heart and performed their missions to the people of Israel, but not by literally eating written words. (*Doctrines of the Book of Mormon: 1991 Sperry Symposium on the Book of Mormon* [Salt Lake City: Deseret Book, 1992], 158)

We are well counseled to allow the poetic nature of some Old Testament discourse to lift the message upward with increased eloquence and power of expression. In this regard, Victor L. Ludlow makes these observations:

Do not be concerned if you have a hard time understanding Old Testament poetry the first time you read it. Your understanding of the poetry in the Bible (especially in Isaiah) will increase as you read more of the scriptures. Most of Psalms and Proverbs, and Isaiah and other prophetic books are written in the poetic pattern of parallelism, and you will soon recognize the beauty and strength it gives to these writings and the rest of the Old Testament.

Old Testament poetry is hard to recognize and understand for the following reasons:

1. We usually do not know the Hebrew forms of speech, the Israelite cultural settings, or the symbolisms found in the writings.

2. The poet or prophet usually does not explain everything. He leaves much interpretive work to us.

3. When a poetic work is highly structured (such as in chiastic or acrostic patterns) the material is sometimes stilted, stretched, or forced by the author to fit the pattern.

4. Sometimes we want to read into the material more than the author originally tried to present. However, this potential for many, varied interpretations is what gives the scriptures much of their richness and lasting value.

5. We are usually unfamiliar with the parallelistic poetic style, and only as we read and study it can we better recognize and appreciate it. (*Unlocking the Old Testament* [Salt Lake City: Deseret Book, 1981], 135)

It is surely not an exaggeration to assume that the visions of eternity, as proffered to the Lord's anointed prophets, can often be conveyed to others only through a loftier, more expressive language, even a poetic medium. The prophets of the Old Testament, especially Isaiah, often felt inspired to project the message of divine purpose and love through such poetic formulations.

Cross-Illumination: Turn to Latter-day Revelation

We are extremely fortunate to be able to enrich our understanding of the Old Testament through insights and guidance derived from latter-day scripture. There are many illustrations of how this process of cross-illumination works. Robert J. Matthews provides the following insights in this regard:

> It is evident that the Old Testament, as it has come to us today, is not as clear and not as complete as it was anciently. Many plain and precious things have been taken from it, even entire books have been removed, and also many deletions have occurred in the books that we do have. Thus we need the benefit of latter-day revelation, such as the Book of Mormon, the Doctrine and Covenants, the Joseph Smith Translation, the Pearl of Great Price, and the teachings of the Prophet Joseph Smith, to give us a perspective and understanding of the Old Testament. Without latter-day revelation, a correct and thorough viewpoint of the Old Testament cannot be achieved, and hence I am bold to declare that the Latter-day Saints can have a more correct understanding of the Old Testament than anyone else upon the face of the earth. We may not always have as much cultural and linguistic appreciation, but we have a clearer doctrinal and spiritual perception of the Old Testament than anyone else. Without these latter-day scriptures and the personal witness of the Holy Ghost, the Old Testament is a sealed book. (*Selected Writings of Robert J. Matthews: Gospel Scholars Series* [Salt Lake City: Deseret Book, 1999], 109)

And again:

> The point is that we study the Old Testament not alone for the history but for the application we can make from it. Knowing those things from the Old Testament helps us understand the New Testament. And knowing those things in the Old and New Testament helps us understand the Book of Mormon. And knowing things from ancient scripture enables us more perfectly to understand the Doctrine and Covenants. And understanding the Doctrine and Covenants enables us to see more clearly what is happening in the earth today in the Church and what is yet to happen. (180)

Sidney B. Sperry, the noted Bible scholar, makes this observation concerning cross-illumination of texts:

Like the Book of Mormon, the Doctrine and Covenants is another unique source for the study of the Old Testament. It is not in many respects as valuable and prolific a source as the Nephite record which fact we should rather expect since it deals mainly with problems incident to the restoration of the Church of Christ in our own age. Nevertheless, it does contain materials of the greatest importance for the understanding of certain parts of the Old Testament. Nearly sixty sections of the Doctrine and Covenants would be recognized by close students of the Old Testament as having some bearing on that scripture. And of these sections the following would be acknowledged as being outstanding in importance: D&C 2, 13, 20, 27, 29, 45, 68, 76, 84, 91, 98, 107, 110, 113, 116, 124, 128, 132, 133.

Some of the subjects dealt with in the Doctrine and Covenants that illumine the Old Testament are these: (1) The ancient patriarchs from Adam to Moses and Aaron, (2) the Aaronic and Melchizedek priesthoods, (3) the work and mission of Elijah as referred to in Mal. 4:5–6, (4) the origin and nature of Israel's religion including the law of Moses (cf. D&C 84:6–28), (5) the nature of the fall and the atonement, (6) the gospel given to man from the beginning, (7) the nature of the relationship existing between ancient and modern Israel, (8) the reason for plural marriage among the ancient Hebrews, (9) the Urim and Thummim, (10) the lost tribes of Israel, (11) temples and their uses. (*The Spirit of the Old Testament* [Salt Lake City: Deseret Book, 1980], 17–18)

Look for Practical Themes and Applications

Our study of the Old Testament can be rendered more productive if we will seek to draw out themes and applications that can assist us in cultivating a more spiritual nature in our daily lives. One writer identified seven such themes in the Old Testament:

> First, it is the old testament of Jesus Christ. The word "testament" implies a witness. This is the oldest written witness of the Savior's divine mission. The ancient prophets saw His coming and understood His ministry. The promise of the Messiah permeated the stories, ordinances, and prophecies that they chose to preserve. . . .
>
> Second, the message of the Old Testament is [that] the gospel is eternal. It was the same for the ancient patriarchs as it is for Latter-day Saints. . . .
>
> Third, the Old Testament is a book about covenants. The ancients entered into covenants throughout their history. They were a covenant people. Our study of this ancient book of scripture helps us learn how to make and keep covenants. We also learn the horrible consequences of breaking our oaths to God. . . .
>
> Fourth, the Old Testament is a key to unlocking other scriptures. For instance, we can better appreciate the latter-day reference to steadying the ark (D&C 85:8) if we remember Uzza's attempt to steady the ark (1 Chr. 13:9). We can better understand

Peter's reluctance to eat unclean animals (Acts 10:14) if we are familiar with the Law of Moses. We are able to see that Abinadi's mention of Moses' luster (Mosiah 13:5) is not a coincidence when he is also filled with the same light as he rebukes the priests of Noah.

Fifth, the Old Testament is the record of our spiritual and physical ancestors. These are not nameless strangers who once lived on the earth, but our forefathers. The Old Testament is our family journal. We are covenant Israel in the latter-days. We are literal descendants of the Old Testament patriarchs. Their lives and struggles have been preserved so we can learn. This is the reason we have a feeling of coming home as we read the Old Testament. It is the journal account of our own ancestors' struggles to live the gospel.

Sixth, we come to better appreciate temples through the Old Testament. Our own Latter-day Saint temple heritage gives us an appreciation of why the children of Israel would sacrifice to build a temple to the Lord. We have a greater appreciation for our own temples as we see how the ancients cared for their desert temple, known as the tabernacle.

We also gain a deeper understanding into the symbolism and typology that saturates our own Latter-day Saint temple experience. . . .

Seventh, we gain a greater appreciation for the laws of God in the Old Testament. We watch our ancestors spend a great deal of effort and time meticulously obeying God's commandments. The Hebrew word for law is torah. The torah or the law took a very special place in the hearts of the people. In one of the most touching scenes of the Old Testament, the people gathered into the streets to hear their prophet read them the law. . . .

These are a few of the reasons why I have found the Old Testament so compelling. There are familiar tones of eternal principles in this testament of Christ. Its message is so familiar to Latter-day Saints because it is the same gospel. One can embrace this book because reading it is like coming home to an old friend. (Lee Donaldson, "Record of a Loving God and His People," *LDS Church News,* January 1, 1994)

By allowing the Old Testament to enter into our daily lives in a practical, applied manner, we can more readily derive the spiritual blessings that await us from our study of this portion of the Lord's word. It is our prayer that the resources provided in this volume will aid you in achieving a deeper understanding of the Old Testament and its eternal message.

Genesis

In the beginning God created the heaven and the earth. (Genesis 1:1)

Author: Moses (see confirmation of authorship from latter-day revelation: 1 Ne. 5:10–11; 2 Ne. 3:17; Moses 1:40–41).

Position: First book of the Pentateuch. The Pentateuch includes the five books of Moses: Genesis, Exodus, Leviticus, Numbers, and Deuteronomy.

Time Span: The Creation to the death of Joseph (around 1671 B.C.).

Purpose: To set forth an introductory account of the design and purpose of God's plan of salvation for mankind, beginning with the Creation and then moving forward through the dispensations of Adam and Noah to the origins of the Abrahamic generations of God's covenant people—Abraham, Isaac, Jacob (Israel), and their posterity.

Length: 50 chapters

Key Sections:
- Creation, Adam and Eve—Chapters 1–4

- Noah—Chapters 5–9

- Abraham—Chapters 11–23

- Isaac—Chapters 23–26

- Jacob and Jacob's family—Chapters 27–50

Cross References:
- Moses

- Abraham

- JST, Genesis 14:25–40 (Melchizedek)

- 2 Nephi 3 (the words of Joseph of Egypt)

Let my people go, that they may serve me. (Exodus 8.1; also 8:20; 9:1, 13; 10:3)

Author: Moses (see confirmation of authorship from latter-day revelation: 1 Ne. 5:10–11; 2 Ne. 3:17; Moses 1:40–41).

Position: Second book of the Pentateuch. The Pentateuch includes the five books of Moses: Genesis, Exodus, Leviticus, Numbers, and Deuteronomy.

Time Span: The death of Joseph (around 1671 B.C.) until the period just after the Exodus (around 1547 B.C.).

Purpose: To recount the emergence of the chosen nation as the Israelites are freed by the Lord from bondage in Egypt, through the guidance of the prophet Moses, and then receive the word of the Lord for daily living (Ten Commandments, code of laws, worship practices, Tabernacle).

Length: 40 chapters

Key Sections:
- Historical account—Chapters 1–18

- Commandments and governing practices—Chapters 19–40

Cross References:
- Moses 1

- JST, Exodus 34:1–2 (removal of the higher priesthood)

Leviticus

And ye shall be holy unto me: for I the Lord am holy, and have severed you from other people, that ye should be mine. (Leviticus 20:26)

Author: Moses (see confirmation of authorship from latter-day revelation: 1 Ne. 5:10–11; 2 Ne. 3:17; Moses 1:40–41). Much of the book consists of the words of the Lord given to Moses.

Position: Third book of the Pentateuch. The Pentateuch includes the five books of Moses: Genesis, Exodus, Leviticus, Numbers, and Deuteronomy.

Time Span: Shortly after the Exodus (around 1547 B.C.).

Purpose: To present a comprehensive statement about the laws, rites, and practices of the priests of Israel (the Levites). The governing theme is that of a Holy God whose presence is felt among a holy covenant people dwelling in a hold land. The thrust of the book is that each individual is to draw nearer to God through a process of atonement and sanctification facilitated by a program of rituals and ordinances designed to help tune the mind and spirit to ultimate truths, especially the truths concerning the Redeemer and the plan of salvation.

Length: 27 chapters

Key Sections:
- Presentation of the procedures used in Israel for religious worship, the performance of ordinances, and priestly consecration—Chapters 1–16

- Laws governing religious practices (the law of holiness) and social ceremonies and observances—Chapters 17–26

- Supplement on vows and redemption of "devoted" things—Chapter 27

Cross References:
- Hebrews 5, 9 (summarizes the principles for understanding Leviticus)

Numbers

But as truly as I live, all the earth shall be filled with the glory of the Lord.
(Numbers 14:21)

Author: Moses (see confirmation of authorship from latter-day revelation: 1 Ne. 5:10–11; 2 Ne. 3:17; Moses 1:40–41).

Position: Fourth book of the Pentateuch. The Pentateuch includes the five books of Moses: Genesis, Exodus, Leviticus, Numbers, and Deuteronomy.

Time Span: The second year after the Exodus (around 1547 B.C.) plus some events that took place at the conclusion of the 40 years of wandering in the wilderness.

Purpose: To recount the experiences of the Israelites in the wilderness and their preparations to enter into the Promised Land. The title of the book derives from the census taken of the people during their sojourn, first at Sinai and then later at Moab.

Length: 36 chapters

Cross References:
- Alma 33:19–22 (the Brass Serpent; see also Hel. 8:14–15; John 3:14–15)

Hear, O Israel: The Lord our God is one Lord: And thou shalt love the Lord thy God with all thine heart, and with all thy soul, and with all thy might. (Deuteronomy 6:4–5)

Author: Moses (see confirmation of authorship from latter-day revelation: 1 Ne. 5:10–11; 2 Ne. 3:17; Moses 1:40–41).

Position: Fifth book of the Pentateuch. The Pentateuch includes the five books of Moses: Genesis, Exodus, Leviticus, Numbers, and Deuteronomy.

Time Span: Just prior to the death (translation) of Moses at the end of the 40-year period of wandering in the wilderness.

Purpose: The meaning of the word Deuteronomy is "repetition of the law" or "second statement of the law." The book covers a review and exposition of the law of God as given through Moses during the wilderness period. The format of the book is chiefly the last three discourses delivered by Moses prior to his passing (translation).

Length: 34 chapters

Key Sections:
- The first of the three final discourses of Moses, serving as an introduction to the book as a whole—Chapters 1–4

- The second of the discourses of Moses, covering the Ten Commandments and the comprehensive Israelite code of special laws and practices—Chapters 5–26

- The third of the discourses of Moses, comprising a renewal of the covenant with the Lord and setting forth the blessings of obedience and the consequences of disobedience—Chapters 27–30

- An appendix to the book, including exhortations to Joshua and a final celebratory occasion before the departure of Moses—Chapters 31–34

Cross References:
- Deuteronomy is quoted frequently in the New Testament. For example: Matt. 4:4/Deut. 8:3; Matt. 4:7/Deut. 6:16; Matt. 4:10/Deut. 6:13; Mark 12:30/Deut. 6:5; 2 Cor. 13:1/Deut. 19:15.

Joshua

Now therefore fear the Lord, and serve him in sincerity and in truth: and put away the gods which your fathers served on the other side of the flood, and in Egypt; and serve ye the Lord. And if it seem evil unto you to serve the Lord, choose you this day whom ye will serve; whether the gods which your fathers served that were on the other side of the flood, or the gods of the Amorites, in whose land ye dwell: but as for me and my house, we will serve the Lord. (Joshua 24:14–15)

Author: Traditionally, the authorship is assigned to Joshua with the exception of the concluding section (24:29–33), which was added by another writer.

Position: Historical sequel to Deuteronomy. The Pentateuch (Genesis, Exodus, Leviticus, Numbers, and Deuteronomy) constitutes the "Law" in terms of Jewish tradition. The book of Joshua stands as the first of the "Prophets" in this continuing tradition.

Time Span: Just after the passing (translation) of Moses until the death of Joshua (ca. 1427 B.C.).

Purpose: To provide a chronicle of the fulfillment of the Lord's promise to lead Israel to the Promised Land and provide for them an inheritance. The historical account is then overlaid with teachings and exhortations to the Israelites to honor their covenant vows and choose to worship and follow the true and eternal God.

Length: 24 chapters

Key Sections:
- History of the conquest of Canaan—Chapters 1–12

- Allotment of the land to the various tribes of Israel—Chapters 13–21

- Farewell address of Joshua and the account of his death—Chapters 22–24

*And when the Lord raised them up judges, then the Lord was with the judge, and deliv-
ered them out of the hand of their enemies all the days of the judge.* (Judges 2:18)

Author: Anonymous compiler. The prophet Samuel might have participated in the
formulation.

Position: The books of Judges and Ruth present all of the Jewish history available in
the turbulent period of time commencing with the death of Joshua and extending to
the birth of Samuel.

Time Span: The death of Joshua (ca. 1427 B.C.) to the birth of Samuel (shortly before
1095 B.C.).

Purpose: To present a cyclical pattern of sin and bondage followed by repentance and
devotion. The threshold of the decline is typically marked by a statement such as:
"Then the sons of Israel again did evil in the sight of the Lord" (see Judg. 2:11; 3:7,
12; 4:1; 6:1; 10:6; 13:1). The Israelites would remember their covenants when there
stood before them a valiant leader who would foster obedience and righteousness;
however, when the leader died, the Israelites would again wander into the murky
bypaths of idolatry and sin until the Lord allowed their enemies to rise up to scourge
and persecute them so that they became humble and penitent once again.

Length: 21 chapters

Key Sections:
- Introduction—Chapters 1–3

- History of the judges—Chapters 3–16

- Narratives that reveal and summarize the disposition of the Israelites
  toward idolatry and disobedience—Chapters 17–21

Cross References:
- The pattern of decline and recovery in the book of Judges—based on the degree of faithfulness and spirituality that prevailed—presents a strong parallel to the experiences of the tribes and nations in the Book of Mormon as they passed through a relentless undulation of prosperity and depravity, based on the degree of obedience they cultivated.

And Ruth said, Intreat me not to leave thee, or to return from following after thee: for whither thou goest, I will go; and where thou lodgest, I will lodge: thy people shall be my people, and thy God my God. (Ruth 1:16)

Author: Unnamed compiler.

Position: The books of Judges and Ruth present all of the Jewish history available in the turbulent period of time commencing with the death of Joshua and extending to the birth of Samuel. Ruth is also one of the 11 books of the Old Testament that belong to the Hagiographa ("sacred writings") of the Jewish canon, along with the books of Chronicles (counted as one book), Ezra-Nehemiah (also counted as one book), Esther, Job, Psalms, Proverbs, Ecclesiastes, Song of Solomon, Lamentations, and Daniel.

Time Span: Likely the middle part of the twelfth-century B.C.

Purpose: The book of Ruth is a story of unsurpassed beauty and tenderness illustrating loyalty and devotion within the family—especially in the context of the integration of a non-Israelite into the fold of Israel. As such, the story is an emblem of conversion, of setting aside one's former ways in favor of a new and higher pattern of living aligned with the spiritual laws of Jehovah. Moreover, the book provides a serene contrast to the pattern of turbulence and disorder that prevailed in cycles during the time of the judges.

Length: 4 chapters

Key Sections:
- Move of the family of Elimelech to Moab; marriages and deaths; return to Bethlehem—Chapter 1

- Courtship of Boaz and Ruth—Chapters 2–3

- New marriage—Chapter 4

Cross References:
- Matthew 1:5–17 (genealogy of Christ)

Then said David to the Philistine, Thou comest to me with a sword, and with a spear, and with a shield: but I come to thee in the name of the Lord of hosts, the God of the armies of Israel, whom thou hast defied. (1 Samuel 17:45)

Author: Unknown.

Position: The books of First and Second Samuel are combined as one in the Hebrew Bible but are separated in the Greek Bible. The chronicle constitutes the beginning of the historical account of the kings of Israel.

Time Span: The birth of Samuel (ca. 1125 B.C.) to the death of Saul and his sons.

Purpose: To set forth the commencement of the history of Israel under King Saul and his successor, King David.

Length: 31 chapters

Key Sections:
- The rise of Samuel as a great prophet of the Lord—Chapters 1–8

- The reign of Saul as the first king in Israel—Chapters 9–15

- The rise of David as the succeeding king in Israel —Chapters 16–31

Cross References:
- Samuel adjured the people to relent in demanding that a king be placed over them and rehearsed before them the burdens such a ruler can impose when the people choose a worldly sovereign rather than the Lord (1 Sam. 8:6–18). The Book of Mormon is the peerless textbook of the destruction that can follow in the wake of royal evil and unrighteousness (see Mosiah 23:7; 29).

2 Samuel

And when thy days be fulfilled, and thou shalt sleep with thy fathers, I will set up thy
seed after thee, which shall proceed out of thy bowels, and I will establish his kingdom.
(2 Samuel 7:12)

Author: Unknown.

Position: The books of First and Second Samuel are combined as one in the Hebrew Bible but are separated in the Greek Bible. The chronicle constitutes the beginning of the historical account of the kings of Israel.

Time Span: The death of Saul and his sons to just prior to the death of David (ca. 1015 B.C.).

Purpose: The book of Second Samuel provides a detailed portrait of David as King of Israel—his towering strengths of leadership and magnanimity as well as his devastating weakness in succumbing to carnal temptation.

Length: 24 chapters

Key Sections:
- David's ascension to the thrown and his early successes as Israel's leader—Chapters 1–10

- The personal sorrows and governmental tribulations and perturbations following David's sin with Bath-Sheba and against Uriah and extending to the end of his reign as king—Chapters 11–21

- David's psalm of praise, his pronouncements under inspiration, and his final acts—Chapters 22–24

Cross References:
- D&C 132:39 (David's wives)

And Elijah came unto all the people, and said, How long halt ye between two opinions?
if the Lord be God, follow him: but if Baal, then follow him. And the people answered
him not a word. (1 Kings 18:21)

Author: Unknown.

Position: The books of First and Second Kings are combined as one in the Hebrew Bible but are separated in the Greek Bible, a convention retained in the Latin and English versions.

Time Span: The time of the rebellion of Adonijah (fourth son of David—see 2 Sam. 3:4) (ca. 1015 B.C.) to the transition of prophetic leadership from Elijah to Elisha (ca. 851 B.C.).

Purpose: To depict the panorama of kingly ascent and descent as a function of the degree of truth and righteousness cultivated by the sovereign. As a backdrop, the spiritual leadership of Elijah serves as a stark contrast to the unsteadiness of royal leadership by providing a standard of enduring faith, undeviating devotion, uncompromising righteousness, and the invocation and implementation of priesthood power.

Length: 22 chapters

Key Sections:
- The rise and fall of King Solomon—Chapters 1–11

- Turmoil, conspiracy, intrigue, and idolatry reign unchecked in the Kingdom—Chapters 12–16

- The ministry of the prophet Elijah (and later the calling of Elisha)—Chapters 17–22

Cross References:
- D&C 110:14–16 (role of Elijah in the last days; see also Mal. 4:5–6; 3 Ne. 25:5–6; D&C 2:1–2; 27:9; 35:4; 128:17; 133:55; 138:46–47; JS—H 1:38–39).

And when the servant of the man of God was risen early, and gone forth, behold, an host compassed the city both with horses and chariots. And his servant said unto him, Alas, my master! how shall we do? And he answered, Fear not: for they that be with us are more than they that be with them. And Elisha prayed, and said, Lord, I pray thee, open his eyes, that he may see. And the Lord opened the eyes of the young man; and he saw: and, behold, the mountain was full of horses and chariots of fire round about Elisha. (2 Kings 6:15–17)

Author: Unknown.

Position: The books of First and Second Kings are combined as one in the Hebrew Bible but are separated in the Greek Bible, a convention retained in the Latin and English versions.

Time Span: The time of transition of prophetic leadership from Elijah to Elisha (ca. 851 B.C.) to the destruction of Jerusalem by Nebuchadnezzar of Babylon (around 587 B.C.).

Purpose: As in First Kings, to provide a contrast of the pervasive wickedness of the people and their kings (with the notable exceptions of Hezekiah and Josiah) and the glorious devotion and righteousness of the prophets of God—Elijah, Elisha, and Isaiah.

Length: 25 chapters

Key Sections:
- The transition of leadership from Elijah to Elisha; Elisha's ministry—Chapters 1–13

- Diverse kings and administrations contend for supremacy until the Ten Tribes are carried away captive into Assyria—Chapters 13–17

- Reformation under the righteous leadership of Hezekiah and then Josiah in Judah—Chapters 18–23

- The rule of Zedekiah and the Babylonian captivity—Chapters 24–25

Cross References:
- The destruction of Jerusalem and the captivity of Judah by the Babylonians corresponds to the period of time when the Book of Mormon account begins (1 Ne. 1:4; 5:12–13; Omni 1:15; Hel. 6:10; 8:21).

1 Chronicles

Glory ye in his holy name: let the heart of them rejoice that seek the Lord. Seek the Lord and his strength, seek his face continually. (1 Chronicles 16:10–11)

Author: Unknown.

Position: First and Second Chronicles were counted as one book in the Hebrew scriptures. These records preserve and communicate Israelite history in broad strokes, particularly religious history.

Time Span: Adam to the death of David and the assumption of the throne by Solomon (ca. 1015 B.C.).

Purpose: With Second Chronicles, to provide a concise history of the Lord's peoples from Adam down to the return of the Jews to Palestine, with an emphasis on religious events and themes, especially temple worship. First and Second Chronicles (counted as one book) are also one of the 11 books of the Old Testament that belong to the Hagiographa ("sacred writings") of the Jewish canon, along with the books of Ruth, Ezra-Nehemiah (also counted as one book), Esther, Job, Psalms, Proverbs, Ecclesiastes, Song of Solomon, Lamentations, and Daniel.

Length: 29 chapters

Key Sections:
- Genealogies of the various leading families from the beginning—Chapters 1–9

- Defeat of Israel by the Philistines and the end of Saul's reign—Chapter 10

- The reign of David—Chapters 11–22

- The beginning of Solomon's reign—Chapters 23–29

Cross References:
- The material parallels in many points the accounts in First and Second Samuel.

2 Chronicles

And thus did Hezekiah throughout all Judah, and wrought that which was good and right and truth before the Lord his God. And in every work that he began in the service of the house of God, and in the law, and in the commandments, to seek his God, he did it with all his heart, and prospered. (2 Chronicles 31:20–21)

Author: Unknown.

Position: First and Second Chronicles were counted as one book in the Hebrew scriptures. These records preserve and communicate Israelite history in broad strokes, particularly religious history. First and Second Chronicles (counted as one book) are also one of the 11 books of the Old Testament that belong to the Hagiographa ("sacred writings") of the Jewish canon, along with the books of Ruth, Ezra-Nehemiah (also counted as one book), Esther, Job, Psalms, Proverbs, Ecclesiastes, Song of Solomon, Lamentations, and Daniel.

Time Span: The death of David and the assumption of the throne by Solomon (ca. 1015 B.C.) to the Babylonian conquest and subsequent decree of Cyrus authorizing the Jews to return to Palestine (537 B.C.).

Purpose: With First Chronicles, to provide a concise history of the Lord's peoples from Adam down to the return of the Jews to Palestine, with an emphasis on religious events and themes, especially temple worship. Second Chronicles more specifically recounts the reign of Solomon—in particular the building of the temple—and the division of the kingdom into two parts (Judah and Israel).

Length: 36 chapters

Key Sections:
- The reign of Solomon and the building of the temple—Chapters 1–9

- Division of the kingdom into two parts, Judah and Israel, with subsequent dislocations and contentions—Chapters 10–28

- Righteous reign of Hezekiah—Chapters 29–32

- Decline under Manasseh and restoration under Josiah—Chapters 33–35

- Babylonian conquest of Judah and subsequent decree of Cyrus permitting Judah to return to rebuild Jerusalem and the temple—Chapter 36

Cross References:
- The material parallels in many points the accounts in First and Second Samuel.

Ezra

And now for a little space grace hath been shewed from the Lord our God, to leave us a remnant to escape, and to give us a nail in his holy place, that our God may lighten our eyes, and give us a little reviving in our bondage. For we were bondmen; yet our God hath not forsaken us in our bondage, but hath extended mercy unto us in the sight of the kings of Persia, to give us a reviving, to set up the house of our God, and to repair the desolations thereof, and to give us a wall in Judah and in Jerusalem. (Ezra 9:8–9)

Author: Ezra.

Position: Ezra provides an account of the return of a second wave of Jewish people from the Babylonian captivity for resettlement in Jerusalem. Nehemiah is a sequel to Ezra, the two being regarded as one in the Jewish canon. Together, they are also one of the 11 books of the Old Testament that belong to the Hagiographa ("sacred writings") of the Jewish canon, along with the books of Ruth, Chronicles (counted as one book), Esther, Job, Psalms, Proverbs, Ecclesiastes, Song of Solomon, Lamentations, and Daniel.

Time Span: The decree of Cyrus authorizing the Jews to return to Palestine (537 B.C.) to the ministry of Ezra and the repatriation of many more of the Jewish people (around 459 B.C.).

Purpose: To extol the process of recovery, rebuilding, repentance, and reform based on faith and devotion to the statues of the Lord.

Length: 10 chapters

Key Sections:
- Historical summary as a backdrop to the ministry of Ezra—Chapters 1–6

- Mission and service of Ezra—Chapters 7–10

Cross References:
- D&C 85:11–12

Nehemiah

Remember, I beseech thee, the word that thou commandedst thy servant Moses, saying, If ye transgress, I will scatter you abroad among the nations: But if ye turn unto me, and keep my commandments, and do them; though there were of you cast out unto the uttermost part of the heaven, yet will I gather them from thence, and will bring them unto the place that I have chosen to set my name there. (Nehemiah 1:8–9)

Author: Nehemiah is considered to be the author of most of the book.

Position: Nehemiah covers the project of rebuilding the walls of Jerusalem. Nehemiah is a continuation of Ezra, the two being regarded as one in the Jewish canon. Together, they are also one of the 11 books of the Old Testament that belong to the Hagiographa ("sacred writings") of the Jewish canon, along with the books of Ruth, Chronicles (counted as one book), Esther, Job, Psalms, Proverbs, Ecclesiastes, Song of Solomon, Lamentations, and Daniel.

Time Span: Either contemporaneous with the later ministry of Ezra or shortly thereafter, beginning perhaps around 444 B.C. This book closes the historical account of the Old Testament, Malachi being a contemporary with Nehemiah.

Purpose: To continue the cause of the book of Ezra to extol the process of recovery, rebuilding, repentance, and reform based on faith and devotion to the statutes of the Lord.

Length: 13 chapters

Key Sections:
- A record of the rebuilding of the wall of Jerusalem; account of the register Nehemiah discovered of those who had returned from Babylon—Chapters 1–7

- A record of the manner of religious practice being conducted among the Jews of this period, including the remarkable and precedent-setting public reading of the law of God by the priest Ezra—Chapters 8–10

- Reforms and civic practices among the people; dedication of the wall of Jerusalem—Chapters 11–13

Cross References:

The story of Nehemiah's leadership in organizing the Israelites to rebuild the walls of Jerusalem, often under threat of attack from enemy forces round about, is a reminder of an incident from Church history that occurred on Wednesday, January 8, 1834, in Kirtland, Ohio. On that day, guards were placed to protect the Kirtland temple as a result of persecution by detractors and the threat of violence at the hands of the gathering mob. Some workmen were seen armed with a hammer in one hand and a rifle in the other. Joseph Smith recorded in his journal: "On the morning of the 8th of January, about 1 o'clock, the inhabitants of Kirtland were alarmed by the firing of about thirteen rounds of cannon, by the mob, on the hill about half a mile northwest of the village" (*HC* 2:2). However, with the coming of dawn, it was determined that the temple wasn't damaged. Of this period, Heber C. Kimball wrote in the *Times and Seasons:* "We had to guard ourselves night after night, and for weeks were not permitted to take off our clothes, and were obliged to lay with our fire locks [rifles] in our arms" (*HC* 2:2).

And who knoweth whether thou art come to the kingdom for such a time as this?
(Esther 4:14)

Author: Unknown.

Position: Esther is one of the late historical books (along with Ezra and Nehemiah). Esther is also one of the 11 books of the Old Testament that belong to the Hagiographa ("sacred writings") of the Jewish canon, along with the books of Ruth, Chronicles (counted as one book), Ezra-Nehemiah (also counted as one book), Job, Psalms, Proverbs, Ecclesiastes, Song of Solomon, Lamentations, and Daniel.

Time Span: Around 479 B.C., some 52 years after the return from Babylonian captivity.

Purpose: To present the historical context and the religious/moral foundation for the establishment of the Jewish feast of Purim. Purim is the Hebrew word for *lot*—a reference to the plan of Haman, chief officer at the court of the king of Persia Ahasuerus (most likely Xerxes), to cast lots for determining a good omen relative to his plan for putting all the Jews of the captivity to death. The king had decided to divorce his wife Vashti when she refused to display her beauty before the people and the princes and had selected as successor the beautiful Esther (whose name is a Syro-Arabian modification of "satarah," a Persian word meaning *star*). However, Esther was the adopted daughter of the Jew Mordecai, whom Haman despised—hence his plan to exterminate all the Jews. Esther courageously came before the king and had the decree reversed, thus saving the Jews and providing the historical context for the annual holiday of Purim.

Length: 10 chapters

Key Sections:
- The king of Persia divorces his wife Vashti and selects Esther as his queen—Chapters 1–2

- Haman's plot to kill all the Jews of the kingdom—Chapter 3

- Esther's intervention to reverse the extermination decree and deliver all the Jews from peril—Chapters 4–8

- The Jews enjoy greater stature and security; the Feast of Purim established—Chapters 9–10

Job

For I know that my redeemer liveth, and that he shall stand at the latter day upon the earth: And though after my skin worms destroy this body, yet in my flesh shall I see God.
(Job 19:25–26)

Author: Unknown.

Position: Job is one of the 11 books of the Old Testament that belong to the Hagiographa ("sacred writings") of the Jewish canon, along with the books of Ruth, Chronicles (counted as one book), Ezra-Nehemiah (also counted as one book), Esther, Psalms, Proverbs, Ecclesiastes, Song of Solomon, Lamentations, and Daniel.

Time Span: Unspecified.

Purpose: The book of Job provides a poetic drama of unsurpassed intensity and meaning concerning the human condition: the misery and lowliness of man in comparison with the majesty and supremacy of God; the trials of life as a test of man's integrity and loyalty to his Creator (and not necessarily as evidence of unrighteousness); and the divine spark of testimony within man that God lives and guides man toward a better state based on his obedience, patience, and willingness to endure to the end.

Length: 42 chapters

Key Sections:
- Opening prologue and framework—Chapters 1–3

- Job's three friends (Eliphaz, Bildad, and Zophar) discuss with him the implications of his suffering—Chapters 4–18

- Job declares his faith in God's design and confirms his enduring testimony—Chapter 19

- Job continues his dialogue with his friends—Chapters 20–28

- Job reviews his condition—Chapters 29–31

- Elihu intervenes with a sermon on man's weakness and God's majesty—Chapters 31–37

- God speaks with Job and teaches him truths from the divine perspective—Chapters 38–41

- Job repents and is blessed—Chapter 42

Cross References:
- D&C 121–23

- James 5:10–11

Psalms

I will praise the Lord according to his righteousness: and will sing praise to the name of the Lord most high. (Psalm 7:17)

Author: 73 of the Psalms in the collection are ascribed to David personally.

Position: Psalms is one of the 11 books of the Old Testament that belong to the Hagiographa ("sacred writings") of the Jewish canon, along with the books of Ruth, Chronicles (counted as one book), Ezra-Nehemiah (also counted as one book), Esther, Job, Proverbs, Ecclesiastes, Song of Solomon, Lamentations, and Daniel.

Time Span: Written during the reign of King David (his tenure in Jerusalem was generally the third quarter of the eleventh century B.C.).

Purpose: To express a genuine poetic sentiment that captures much of the essence of the gospel and its enduring truths.

Length: 150 chapters (or psalms)

Key Sections: Though complex in structure and rich in theme, these 150 psalms reflect perhaps three main subjects:

- *Messiah, the Good Shepherd.* David captures the chief moments of the Redeemer's mission as the poet looks forward with a prophetic eye to the coming of the Savior in the meridian of time and His eventual return in glory and majesty at the end of the world's history and the beginning of the millennium.

- What is man, that thou art mindful of him: and the son of man, that thou visitest him? Thou hast made him a little lower than the angels, and hast crowned him with glory and honour. (8:4–5)

- I have said, Ye are gods; and all of you are children of the most High. (82:6)

- And I will make him my firstborn, higher than the kings of the earth. (89:27)

- The stone which the builders refused is become the head stone of the corner. (118:22)

- *Redeeming the Soul.* David's prayers are rooted in his sense of sin, guilt, remorse, fear, anguish, and isolation—all emotions anchored in the experience of carnal weakness. But his prayers turn into songs of praise for the mercy, forgiveness, peace, freedom, healing, and atonement associated with the Master's touch and the Redeemer's craft.

- Preserve me, O God: for in thee do I put my trust. (16:1)

- Who shall ascend into the hill of the Lord? or who shall stand in his holy place? He that hath clean hands, and a pure heart. (24:3–4)

- Create in me a clean heart, O God. (51:11)

- *Defending and Building Up Zion.* As David regards the situation of the Lord's covenant people, his prayers are rooted in a sense of oppression, iniquity within enemy ranks, ensnarement, captivity, pride, arrogance, affliction, reproach, and contempt—all emotions that flow from the burdens of Zion at the hands of her enemies. However, David's prayers turn to songs of praise as he celebrates God's gifts to Zion: His protection, defense, liberation, foundation, light, glory, blessings—all associated with love and compassion.

- The Lord is my rock, and my fortress, and my deliverer; my God, my strength in whom I will trust. (18:2)

- Let all those that seek thee rejoice and be glad in thee: and let such as love thy salvation say continually, Let God be magnified. (70:4)

Cross References:
- The Psalms have a pervasive presence in the subsequent canon of scripture, being cited countless times. For example, of the 283 direct citations of Old Testament material in the New Testament, 116 stem from Psalms. Note, also, how the Psalms are memorialized in many of our current hymns, such as "The Lord Is My Shepherd" (Hymn 108; Ps. 23), "The Lord Is My Light" (Hymn 89; Ps. 27:1), "How Great Thou Art" (Hymn 86; Ps. 8:3–9; 9:1–2), and "Praise to the Lord, the Almighty" (Hymn 72; Ps. 23:6; 150).

The fear of the Lord is the beginning of wisdom: and the knowledge of the holy is understanding. (Proverbs 9:10; compare Proverbs 1:7)

Author: Solomon and successors who imitated his craft.

Position: Proverbs is one of the 11 books of the Old Testament that belong to the Hagiographa ("sacred writings") of the Jewish canon, along with the books of Ruth, Chronicles (counted as one book), Ezra-Nehemiah (also counted as one book), Esther, Job, Psalms, Ecclesiastes, Song of Solomon, Lamentations, and Daniel.

Time Span: The reign of Solomon extended from around 1015 B.C. until his death around 975 B.C.

Purpose: The Proverbs of Solomon (together with the pronouncements of the "Preacher" in the Book of Ecclesiastes) include a veritable garden of wisdom in the form of cogent maxims, exhortations, and poems for governing one's life. Solomon was enormously prolific: "And he spake three thousand proverbs: and his songs were a thousand and five" (1 Kgs. 4:32).

Length: 31 chapters

Key Sections:
- An exposition concerning wisdom of the genuine kind—Chapters 1–9

- A collection of maxims and sentences contrasting the right and wrong ways to conduct one's life—Chapters 10–24

- Proverbs of Solomon that were copied out by scribes during the administration of Hezekiah, king of Judah—Chapters 25–29

- Writings of Agur and Lemuel, including the latter's portrait of the ideal wife—Chapters 30–31

There are, in general, four principal themes running through the Proverbs:

- Trusting in God is the foundation of wisdom.

The fear of the Lord is the beginning of wisdom. (1:7)

Every word of God is pure: he is a shield unto them that put their trust in him. (30:5)

- A willingness to be entreated is the key to cultivating wisdom.

For whom the Lord loveth he correcteth; even as a father the son in whom he delighteth. (3:12)

For the commandment is a lamp; and the law is light; and reproofs of instruction are the way of life. (6:23)

- The flowering of wisdom is to bring forth good fruit unto the Lord.

Wisdom is the principal thing; therefore get wisdom: and with all thy getting get understanding. (4:7)

- Pride leads to folly.

Pride goeth before destruction, and a haughty spirit before a fall. (16:18)

Cross References:
- The Proverbs are frequently quoted in the New Testament.

Ecclesiastes

Let us hear the conclusion of the whole matter: Fear God, and keep his commandments: for this is the whole duty of man. For God shall bring every work into judgment, with every secret thing, whether it be good, or whether it be evil. (Ecclesiastes 12:13–14)

Author: A traditional view has been to interpret "The words of the Preacher, the son of David, king in Jerusalem" (Eccl. 1:1) and "I the Preacher was king over Israel in Jerusalem" (Eccl. 1:12) as referring to Solomon, son of David. However, this attribution could refer to a successor king as well.

Position: Ecclesiastes is one of the 11 books of the Old Testament that belong to the Hagiographa ("sacred writings") of the Jewish canon, along with the books of Ruth, Chronicles (counted as one book), Ezra-Nehemiah (also counted as one book), Esther,

Job, Psalms, Proverbs, Song of Solomon, Lamentations, and Daniel. The word *ecclesiastes* is based on the Greek rendering of the Hebrew word *koheleth,* meaning *preacher.*

Time Span: The reign of Solomon extended from around 1015 B.C. until his death around 975 B.C. The writing of Ecclesiastes, however, appears to have occurred much later (around 300 B.C. to 250 B.C.).

Purpose: To provide a cogent and soul-searching contrast between a worldly perspective marked by impermanence and a godly view, in which the eternal destiny of man is anchored in the fear of God and obedience to His commandments.

Length: 12 chapters

Key Sections:
- An intricate exploration of the theme "all is vanity" (Eccl. 1:2)— Chapters 1–10

- The summum bonum of life: to do good, fear God, and keep his commandments—Chapters 11–12

Representative Sayings:
- Vanity of vanities, saith the Preacher, vanity of vanities; all is vanity. (1:2)

- The thing that hath been, it is that which shall be; and that which is done is that which shall be done: and there is no new thing under the sun. (1:9)

- To every thing there is a season, and a time to every purpose under the heaven. (3:1)

- Two are better than one; because they have a good reward for their labour. For if they fall, the one will lift up his fellow: but woe to him that is alone when he falleth; for he hath not another to help him up. (4:9–10)

- Be not rash with thy mouth, and let not thine heart be hasty to utter any thing before God: for God is in heaven, and thou upon earth: therefore let thy words be few. (5:2)

- I returned, and saw under the sun, that the race is not to the swift, nor the battle to the strong, neither yet bread to the wise, nor yet riches to men of understanding, nor yet favour to men of skill; but time and chance happeneth to them all. (9:11)

- Rejoice, O young man, in thy youth; and let thy heart cheer thee in the days of thy youth, and walk in the ways of thine heart, and in the sight of thine eyes: but know thou, that for all these things God will bring thee into judgment. (11:9)

- Let us hear the conclusion of the whole matter: Fear God, and keep his commandments: for this is the whole duty of man. (12:13)

Cross References:
- Sentiments from Ecclesiastes are echoed on occasion in the New Testament.

Song of Solomon

Many waters cannot quench love, neither can the floods drown it.
(Song of Solomon 8:7)

Author: It is doubtful that Solomon was the author.

Position: Song of Solomon is one of the 11 books of the Old Testament that belong to the Hagiographa ("sacred writings") of the Jewish canon, along with the books of Ruth, Chronicles (counted as one book), Ezra-Nehemiah (also counted as one book), Esther, Job, Psalms, Proverbs, Ecclesiastes, Lamentations, and Daniel.

Time Span: Uncertain.

Purpose: From a religious perspective, the Song of Solomon can be interpreted as an allegory of God's love for Israel and/or for His church. Note, however, that the Joseph Smith Translation manuscript states that "The Songs of Solomon are not inspired writings."

Length: 8 chapters

Key Sections:
- The book is a continuous sequence of pronouncements, images, metaphors, and similes concerning the love relationship.

Isaiah

And now, behold, I say unto you, that ye ought to search these things. Yea, a commandment I give unto you that ye search these things diligently; for great are the words of Isaiah. For surely he spake as touching all things concerning my people which are of the house of Israel; therefore it must needs be that he must speak also to the Gentiles. And all things that he spake have been and shall be, even according to the words which he spake. (3 Nephi 23:1–3)

Author: Isaiah.

Position: The book of Isaiah is one of the major prophetic books of the Old Testament, along with Jeremiah, Lamentations (by Jeremiah), Ezekiel, and Daniel.

Time Span: Isaiah's ministry was in the time frame of 740 B.C. to 701 B.C. He was chief advisor to Hezekiah, King of Judah.

Purpose: In his prophetic and inspired discourse, Isaiah captures the grand and sweeping contours of the Lord's plan for mankind. Isaiah is unequalled in his ability to speak as if viewing a panoramic vista encompassing the entire range of the Lord's plan of salvation—from the pre-mortal existence to the meridian of time to the millennial reign and the ultimate consummation of covenant blessings. Often Isaiah will span the entire range of man's existence in the space of a verse or two, always returning to the central theme of the Messiah, the Savior of mankind.

Length: 66 chapters

Key Sections:
- The Lord's design for His covenant children and their eventual salvation—Chapters 1–5

- The Lord calls Isaiah as His prophet—Chapter 6

- Messianic prophecies and exhortations to Israel—Chapters 7–35

- Counsel to King Hezekiah—Chapters 36–39

- Messianic prophecies and counsel for Israel concluded—Chapters 40–66

Representative Sayings:

- Though your sins be as scarlet, they shall be as white as snow; though they be red like crimson, they shall be as wool. (1:18)

- And it shall come to pass in the last days, that the mountain of the Lord's house shall be established in the top of the mountains, and shall be exalted above the hills; and all nations shall flow unto it. (2:2)

- And the Lord will create upon every dwelling place of mount Zion, and upon her assemblies, a cloud and smoke by day, and the shining of a flaming fire by night: for upon all the glory shall be a defence. (4:5)

- And he will lift up an ensign to the nations from far, and will hiss unto them from the end of the earth: and, behold, they shall come with speed swiftly. (5:26)

- Then said I, Here am I; send me. (6:8)

- Behold, a virgin shall conceive, and bear a son, and shall call his name Immanuel. (7:14)

- For unto us a child is born, unto us a son is given: and the government shall be upon his shoulder: and his name shall be called Wonderful, Counsellor, The mighty God, The everlasting Father, The Prince of Peace. (9:6)

- Behold, God is my salvation; I will trust, and not be afraid: for the Lord Jehovah is my strength and my song; he also is become my salvation. (12:2)

- How art thou fallen from heaven, O Lucifer, son of the morning! (14:12)

- And I will fasten him as a nail in a sure place; and he shall be for a glorious throne to his father's house. (22:23)

- For precept must be upon precept, precept upon precept; line upon line, line upon line; here a little, and there a little. (28:10)

- Therefore, behold, I will proceed to do a marvellous work among this people, even a marvellous work and a wonder. (29:14)

- The desert shall rejoice, and blossom as the rose. (35:1)

- But they that wait upon the Lord shall renew their strength; they shall mount up with wings as eagles; they shall run, and not be weary; and they shall walk, and not faint. (40:31)

- I, even I, am the Lord; and beside me there is no saviour. (43:11)

- I have sworn by myself, the word is gone out of my mouth in righteousness, and shall not return, That unto me every knee shall bow, every tongue shall swear. (45:23)

- Behold, I have refined thee, but not with silver; I have chosen thee in the furnace of affliction. (48:10)

- And he hath made my mouth like a sharp sword; in the shadow of his hand hath he hid me, and made me a polished shaft; in his quiver hath he hid me; And said unto me, Thou art my servant, O Israel, in whom I will be glorified. (49:2–3)

- Behold, I will lift up mine hand to the Gentiles, and set up my standard to the people: and they shall bring thy sons in their arms, and thy daughters shall be carried upon their shoulders. And kings shall be thy nursing fathers, and their queens thy nursing mothers. (49:22–23)

- I gave my back to the smiters, and my cheeks to them that plucked off the hair: I hid not my face from shame and spitting. (50:6)

- For the Lord shall comfort Zion: he will comfort all her waste places; and he will make her wilderness like Eden, and her desert like the garden of the Lord. (51:3)

- How beautiful upon the mountains are the feet of him that bringeth good tidings, that publisheth peace; that bringeth good tidings of good, that publisheth salvation; that saith unto Zion, Thy God reigneth! (52:7)

- Be ye clean, that bear the vessels of the Lord. (52:11)

- Surely he hath borne our griefs, and carried our sorrows: yet we did esteem him stricken, smitten of God, and afflicted. (53:4)

- Enlarge the place of thy tent, and let them stretch forth the curtains of thine habitations: spare not, lengthen thy cords, and strengthen thy stakes. (54:2)

- For my thoughts are not your thoughts, neither are your ways my ways, saith the Lord. For as the heavens are higher than the earth, so are my ways higher than your ways, and my thoughts than your thoughts. (55:8–9)

- The sun shall be no more thy light by day; neither for brightness shall the moon give light unto thee: but the Lord shall be unto thee an everlasting light, and thy God thy glory. (60:19)

- The Spirit of the Lord God is upon me; because the Lord hath anointed me to preach good tidings unto the meek; he hath sent me to bind up the brokenhearted, to proclaim liberty to the captives, and the opening of the prison to them that are bound. (61:1)

- For since the beginning of the world men have not heard, nor perceived by the ear, neither hath the eye seen, O God, beside thee, what he hath prepared for him that waiteth for him. (64:4)

Cross References:
- Of all the prophets in the Old Testament, Isaiah is the most often cited in the other scriptures of the canon. Modern-day scripture, in numerous instances, sheds valuable light on the inspired words of Isaiah and constitutes the most dependable source for clarifying and understanding the magnificent words of this singularly important prophet of the Lord.

Jeremiah

But this shall be the covenant that I will make with the house of Israel; After those days, saith the Lord, I will put my law in their inward parts, and write it in their hearts; and will be their God, and they shall be my people. And they shall teach no more every man his neighbour, and every man his brother, saying, Know the Lord: for they shall all know me, from the least of them unto the greatest of them, saith the Lord; for I will forgive their iniquity, and I will remember their sin no more. (Jeremiah 31:33–34)

Author: Jeremiah.

Position: The book of Jeremiah is one of the major prophetic books of the Old Testament, along with Isaiah, Lamentations (also written by Jeremiah), Ezekiel, and Daniel.

Time Span: 626 to 585 B.C.

Purpose: To declare the basic and governing principles of the gospel—that peace and happiness depend on obedience and honoring the covenants of the Lord; that the consequences of sin are destruction and war, dislocation and scattering, misery and woe; that the Lord will chasten His people until they learn to be virtuous and righteous; and that He will eventually establish a new covenant with His faithful children and gather them in from the four quarters of the earth to be their King.

Length: 52 chapters

Key Sections:
- Prophecies during the reign of Josiah (626 B.C. to 608 B.C.)—Chapters 1–6

- Prophecies during the reign of Jehoiakim (608 B.C. to 597 B.C.)—Chapters 7–20

- Prophecies during the reign of Zedekiah (597 B.C. to 586 B.C.)—Chapters 21–38

- History of Jeremiah and other happenings after the fall of Jerusalem around 586 B.C.—Chapters 39–45

- Prophecies concerning foreign nations—Chapters 46–51

- Historical conclusion—Chapter 52

Cross References:
- Jeremiah was a contemporary of the prophet Lehi, along with Ezekiel and the younger Daniel. Jeremiah's prophecies, in part, were included in the brass plates of Laban (see 1 Ne. 5:10–13; also 1 Ne. 7:14; Hel. 8:20).

Let us search and try our ways, and turn again to the Lord. Let us lift up our heart with our hands unto God in the heavens. (Lamentations 3:40–41)

Author: Jeremiah.

Position: The book of Lamentations is one of the major prophetic books of the Old Testament, along with Isaiah, Jeremiah, Ezekiel, and Daniel. Lamentations is also one of the 11 books of the Old Testament that belong to the Hagiographa ("sacred writings") of the Jewish canon, along with the books of Ruth, Chronicles (counted as one book), Ezra-Nehemiah (also counted as one book), Esther, Job, Psalms, Proverbs, Ecclesiastes, Song of Solomon, and Daniel.

Time Span: Jeremiah prophesied from 626 B.C. to 585 B.C. The book of Lamentations must post-date the fall of Jerusalem (587 B.C.).

Purpose: Jeremiah laments the pitiful state of the great fallen city and bewails the fate of her lost citizens—but he does so in the spirit of a prophetic messenger commissioned to both cry repentance as well as confirm the mercies of a tender Lord. The people have brought upon themselves the judgments of God; still, despite the hardness of their hearts, He will remember them in His own due time following their chastening. We see in the panorama of Jeremiah's view an awful scene of the darkest catastrophe below; yet above is the faintly discerned scene of godly order. Man may fall; but God is in charge, and goodness and mercy and peace will eventually prevail.

Length: 5 chapters

Key Sections:
- Jeremiah's lamentation over the fallen city and nation—Chapters 1–4

- His prayer for the eventual recovery of the people—Chapter 5

Ezekiel

A new heart also will I give you, and a new spirit will I put within you: and I will take away the stony heart out of your flesh, and I will give you an heart of flesh. And I will put my spirit within you, and cause you to walk in my statutes, and ye shall keep my judgments, and do them. And ye shall dwell in the land that I gave to your fathers; and ye shall be my people, and I will be your God. (Ezekiel 36:26–28)

Author: Ezekiel.

Position: The book of Ezekiel is one of the major prophetic books of the Old Testament, along with Isaiah, Jeremiah, Lamentations, and Daniel.

Time Span: 592 B.C. to 570 B.C.; Ezekiel was a contemporary of Jeremiah and Daniel, and also a younger contemporary of Lehi.

Purpose: The prophet Ezekiel was granted extraordinary visions that establish the principles of the gospel pertaining to the house of Israel, then and now.

Length: 48 chapters

Key Sections:
- Prophecies of God's judgment against Jerusalem and the nations in proximity—Chapters 1–24

- Prophecies concerning the gathering and restoration—Chapters 25–39

- Visions of the temple of the Lord, its reconstruction, and its sacred function—Chapters 40–48

Cross References:
- D&C 29:21; 138:43

And in the days of these kings shall the God of heaven set up a kingdom, which shall never be destroyed: and the kingdom shall not be left to other people, but it shall break in pieces and consume all these kingdoms, and it shall stand for ever. Forasmuch as thou sawest that the stone was cut out of the mountain without hands, and that it brake in pieces the iron, the brass, the clay, the silver, and the gold; the great God hath made known to the king what shall come to pass hereafter: and the dream is certain, and the interpretation thereof sure. (Daniel 2:44–45)

Author: Daniel.

Position: The book of Daniel is one of the major prophetic books of the Old Testament, along with Isaiah, Jeremiah, Lamentations, and Ezekiel. Daniel is also one of the 11 books of the Old Testament that belong to the Hagiographa ("sacred writings") of the Jewish canon, along with the books of Ruth, Chronicles (counted as one book), Ezra-Nehemiah (also counted as one book), Esther, Job, Psalms, Proverbs, Ecclesiastes, Song of Solomon, and Lamentations.

Time Span: During the Babylonian conquest of Jerusalem shortly before the turn of the sixth century B.C. Daniel prophesied in the same general time frame as Jeremiah and Ezekiel, and was a younger contemporary of Lehi.

Purpose: To confirm by prophetic pronouncements that the Lord is in charge of the destiny of humankind and that righteousness will ultimately prevail over the forces of worldly pride and power. Daniel is a prominent example of "apocalyptic" writing (from the Greek word meaning "revealed" or "uncovered", as in the Revelation of John) where great and symbolic visions of the ultimate consummation of God's work are presented.

Length: 12 chapters

Key Sections:
- The experiences of Daniel and his three companions in the court of Nebuchadnezzar—Chapters 1–6

- Visions concerning the grand design of the Lord for the unfolding of His gospel plan among the nations of the world and the ultimate restoration and glorious triumph of His Kingdom in the latter days—Chapters 7–12

Cross References:
- Ezekiel 14:14, 20; 28:3

- Heb. 11:33 (Daniel's faith)

- D&C 116; 128:21 (identifies the "Ancient of Days" as Adam)

- D&C 65:2 (reference to Daniel's vision of the stone cut from the mountain)
  Note that the story of Daniel, with his gift of interpreting dreams, and his rise to leadership in a foreign nation, is similar to the story of Joseph of Egypt (see Gen. 39–41).

Hosea

Who is wise, and he shall understand these things? prudent, and he shall know them? for the ways of the Lord are right, and the just shall walk in them: but the transgressors shall fall therein. (Hosea 14:9)

Author: Hosea.

Position: One of the twelve prophets of the Old Testament with shorter books (though by no means reflecting messages of lesser import). Hosea is the only prophet of the Northern Kingdom whose writings have been handed down to us as part of the canon.

Time Span: Hosea prophesied in the eighth century B.C., probably during the latter reign of Jeroboam II and just prior to the ministry of Isaiah.

Purpose: God is holy and supreme, and happiness and joy can flow to mankind only through obedience to His laws and commandments.

Length: 14 chapters

Key Sections:
- The calling of Hosea as a prophet—Chapter 1

- The vision of the ultimate restoration of Israel, despite her current decline and iniquity—Chapters 2–3

- The House of Israel, in her current state, destined to fall—Chapters 4–5

- Hosea's message of repentance and exhortation—Chapter 6

- Israel's unfortunate pathway of punishment and captivity for wrong-doing—Chapters 7–10

- The love of the Lord to bring about a dawning of redemption for the Lord's people—Chapters 11–14

Representative Sayings:
- When Israel was a child, then I loved him, and called my son out of Egypt. . . . I taught Ephraim also to go, taking them by their arms; but they knew not that I healed them. I drew them with cords of a man, with bands of love. (11:1, 3–4)

Cross References:
Hosea had a strong influence on later prophets (see Isa. 40–66; Ezek. 16:33).

And it shall come to pass afterward, that I will pour out my spirit upon all flesh; and your sons and your daughters shall prophesy, your old men shall dream dreams, your young men shall see visions: And also upon the servants and upon the handmaids in those days will I pour out my spirit. And I will shew wonders in the heavens and in the earth, blood, and fire, and pillars of smoke. The sun shall be turned into darkness, and the moon into blood, before the great and the terrible day of the Lord come. And it shall come to pass, that whosoever shall call on the name of the Lord shall be delivered: for in mount Zion and in Jerusalem shall be deliverance, as the Lord hath said, and in the remnant whom the Lord shall call. (Joel 2:28–32)

Author: Joel.

Position: One of the twelve prophets of the Old Testament with shorter books (though by no means reflecting messages of lesser import). Joel is a prophet of Judah.

Time Span: Unknown—as early as the ninth century or as late as the return from the Babylonian captivity following the decree of liberation of the Jews issued by Cyrus in 537 B.C.

Purpose: Joel uses an occasion of dire famine and suffering to reflect on the perennial famine of truth among the unrighteous down through the generations of time. Such a famine will be relieved through the eventual restoration of the Lord's Kingdom on earth—a day when vision and prophesy will again be made manifest among the faithful and penitent and the Lord will reign supreme.

Length: 3 chapters

Cross References:
- Acts 2:17

- JS—H 1:41 (Joel is cited by Moroni in his visitation to the Prophet Joseph Smith)

Amos

Surely the Lord God will do nothing, but he revealeth his secret unto his servants the prophets. (Amos 3:7)

Author: Amos.

Position: Amos was one of the twelve prophets of the Old Testament with shorter books (though by no means reflecting messages of lesser import). He was a shepherd from a community south of Jerusalem, but his ministry was among those of the Northern Kingdom of Israel.

Time Span: Amos prophesied during the reigns of Uzziah, king of Judah (who died around 740 B.C.), and Jeroboam II, king of Israel (who died around 750 B.C.).

Purpose: Amos discerns the evils around him and invokes the spirit of divine exhortation to lift the people from their shackles of sin and motivate them to rise to their godly potential.

Length: 9 chapters

Key Sections:
- The Lord's judgments to be poured out upon the wicked—Chapters 1–2

- The Lord always acts through His prophets to bring about his eternal purposes—Chapter 3

- Wickedness inexorably evokes the call to repent and return to the Lord— Chapters 4–6

- The calling of Amos as prophet—Chapter 7

- Prophecies about the imminent scattering and eventual gathering of Israel—Chapters 8–9

Representative Sayings:
- Behold, the days come, saith the Lord God, that I will send a famine in the land, not a famine of bread, nor a thirst for water, but of hearing the words of the Lord: And they shall wander from sea to sea, and from the north even to the east, they shall run to and fro to seek the word of the Lord, and shall not find it. (8:11–12)

Cross References:
- The Joseph Smith Translation renders Amos 3:7 thus: "Surely the Lord God will do nothing, until he revealeth his secret unto his servants the prophets."

Obadiah

And saviours shall come up on mount Zion to judge the mount of Esau; and the kingdom shall be the Lord's. (Obadiah 1:21)

Author: Obadiah.

Position: Obadiah was one of the twelve prophets of the Old Testament with shorter books (though by no means reflecting messages of lesser import). Nothing is known of Obadiah's personal life.

Time Span: The time is not known with certainty; however, the book was written in the context of the capture of Jerusalem, probably referring to the capture by the Chaldeans in 587 B.C.

Length: 1 chapter

Key Sections:
- The shame of Edom for participating in the program to attack Jerusalem and destroy the Lord's covenant people—Verses 1–16

- The ultimate victory of truth and right associated with the Second Coming; the fall of Edom and the triumph of the Lord's work and glory for the salvation and exaltation of the faithful—Verses 17–21

Cross References:
- Isaiah 63:1–4

- D&C 1:36

- In a discourse on May 16, 1841, the Prophet Joseph Smith made reference to the passage in Obadiah concerning "saviours on mount Zion" (verse 21) as follows: "The election of the promised seed still continues, and in the last day, they shall have the Priesthood restored unto them, and they shall be the 'saviors on Mount Zion,' the ministers of our God; if it were not for the remnant which was left, then might men now be as Sodom and Gomorrah" (*TPJS,* 189). See also the Prophet's additional words on this subject:

> And now as the great purposes of God are hastening to their accomplishment, and the things spoken of in the Prophets are fulfilling, as the kingdom of God is established on the earth, and the ancient order of things restored, the Lord has manifested to us this day and privilege, and we are commanded to be baptized for our dead, thus fulfilling the words of Obadiah, when speaking of the glory of the latter-day: "And saviors shall come up on Mount Zion to judge the remnant of Esau, and the kingdom shall be the Lord's." A view of these things reconciles the Scriptures of truth, justifies the ways of God to man, places the human family upon an equal footing, and harmonizes with every principle of righteousness, justice and truth. We will conclude with the words of Peter: "For the time past of our life may suffice us to have wrought the will of the Gentiles." "For, for this cause was the Gospel preached also to them that are dead, that they might be judged according to men in the flesh, but live according to God in the Spirit." (*TPJS,* 223)

Compare the article by Monte S. Nyman on the interpretation of Obadiah 1:21: "Restoring 'Plain and Precious Parts': The Role of Latter-day Scriptures in Helping

Us Understand the Bible," *Ensign,* Dec. 1981, 19; see also the article by Russell M. Nelson, "The Spirit of Elijah," *Ensign,* Nov. 1994, 84.

But I will sacrifice unto thee with the voice of thanksgiving; I will pay that that I have vowed. Salvation is of the Lord. (Jonah 2:9)

Author: An unknown later writer who is describing a series of related episodes from the prophet's life.

Position: Jonah was one of the twelve prophets of the Old Testament with shorter books (though by no means reflecting messages of lesser import) and one of several books, like Job, that are poetic in structure.

Time Span: Jonah lived during the reign of Jeroboam II of Israel (around 790 B.C. to around 749 B.C.). During this same period, the prophets Hosea and Amos were active.

Purpose: To confirm the Lord's universal love for His children of all nationalities and origins.

Length: 4 chapters

Key Sections:
- Jonah's commission of the Lord and the consequences of his failure to obey—Chapter 1–2

- Jonah's mission to Nineveh—Chapter 3

- Jonah's coming to terms with the mercy of the Lord—Chapter 4

Representative Sayings:
- Salvation is of the Lord. (2:9)

Cross References:
- During His earthly ministry, the Savior made specific mention of Jonah, using the episode with the whale as a symbol of the death and resurrection of the Messiah (Matt. 12:38–41; compare Luke 11:29–30; see also Matt. 16:4).

Micah

He hath shewed thee, O man, what is good; and what doth the Lord require of thee, but to do justly, and to love mercy, and to walk humbly with thy God? (Micah 6:8)

Author: Micah.

Position: Micah was one of the twelve prophets of the Old Testament with shorter books (though by no means reflecting messages of lesser import).

Time Span: Micah, a prophet of Judah, prophesied during the reign of King Hezekiah (Hezekiah ascended the throne around 728 B.C. and reigned for 29 years). Thus Micah was a contemporary of Isaiah, whose ministry extended from 740 B.C. to 701 B.C.

Purpose: The Lord will bring judgment upon evildoers while showing mercy and forgiveness to those who repent and follow His statutes and remember His covenants.

Length: 7 chapters

Key Sections:
- Prophecies of judgment and destruction because of idolatry and sinfulness—Chapters 1–3

- Prophecies concerning the restoration and the Messianic mission—Chapters 4–5

- Prophetic statements concerning the goodness of the Lord and His expectations of the covenant people—Chapters 6–7

Representative Sayings:
- But in the last days it shall come to pass, that the mountain of the house of the Lord shall be established in the top of the mountains, and it shall be exalted above the hills; and people shall flow unto it. And many nations shall come, and say, Come, and let us go up to the mountain of the Lord, and to the house of the God of Jacob; and he will teach us of his ways, and we will walk in his paths: for the law shall go forth of Zion, and the word of the Lord from Jerusalem. (4:1–2)

- But thou, Beth-lehem Ephratah, though thou be little among the thousands of Judah, yet out of thee shall he come forth unto me that is to be ruler in Israel; whose goings forth have been from of old, from everlasting. (5:2)

Cross References:
- Isaiah 2:2–3 (compare Ezek. 20:40); 2 Nephi 12:2–3; D&C 133:12 ("mountain of the house of the Lord" Micah 4:1–2)

Behold upon the mountains the feet of him that bringeth good tidings, that publisheth peace! O Judah, keep thy solemn feasts, perform thy vows: for the wicked shall no more pass through thee; he is utterly cut off. (Nahum 1:15)

Author: Nahum.

Position: Nahum was one of the twelve prophets of the Old Testament with shorter books (though by no means reflecting messages of lesser import).

Time Span: Scholarly opinion varies concerning the date of composition by this prophet of Judah, some judging that it was written during the latter part of the eighth century B.C. (during the reign of Hezekiah) and others concluding that it was written in the mid- to late-seventh century B.C. In any case, the book refers to the collapse of Nineveh, capital of the Assyrian empire, which fell around 606 B.C.

Purpose: To prophesy the destruction of Nineveh as the seat of the Assyrian empire and elevate this image as a symbol for the defeat of all evil in opposition to the triumph of the Kingdom of the Lord at the Second Coming.

Length: 3 chapters

Key Sections:
- The Lord's design in bringing mercy to the righteous and judgment to the wicked—Chapter 1

- The fate of Nineveh as an archetype of the degenerate kingdom of pride and idolatry—Chapters 2–3

Cross References:
- Compare the merciful designs of the Lord toward a repentant Nineveh at the time of Jonah's ministry (first half of the eighth century B.C.), as recorded in the Book of Jonah (written by a later writer).

- Isaiah 52:7; Mosiah 15:13–18; D&C 128:19 (imagery recorded in Nahum 1)

But the Lord is in his holy temple: let all the earth keep silence before him.
(Habakkuk 2:20)

Author: Habakkuk.

Position: Habakkuk was one of the twelve prophets of the Old Testament with shorter books (though by no means reflecting messages of lesser import).

Time Span: It is uncertain when this prophet of Judah ministered—possibly around 600 B.C., concurrent with the activities of Lehi in Jerusalem and contemporary with the work of Jeremiah, Daniel, and Ezekiel.

Purpose: God punishes the wicked through the incursions of the wicked. His plan of salvation will prevail unto the blessing of all who remember His commandments.

Length: 3 chapters

Key Sections:
- The land of Israel to be overrun by the invading Chaldeans—Chapter 1

- The Chaldeans, in turn, to feel the wrath of the Lord for their idolatry—Chapter 2

Representative Sayings:
- For the earth shall be filled with the knowledge of the glory of the Lord, as the waters cover the sea. (2:14)

Cross References:
- Mormon 4:5 (the Lord's design for punishing the wicked)

Zephaniah

The Lord thy God in the midst of thee is mighty; he will save, he will rejoice over thee with joy; he will rest in his love, he will joy over thee with singing. (Zephaniah 3:17)

Author: Zephaniah.

Position: Zephaniah was one of the twelve prophets of the Old Testament with shorter books (though by no means reflecting messages of lesser import).

Time Span: Written during the reign of Josiah (639–608 B.C.) and contemporary with Lehi, Jeremiah, Daniel, and Ezekiel.

Purpose: To proclaim severe judgments against the unrighteous and to confirm hope and joy for the righteous at the Second Coming.

Length: 3 chapters

Key Sections:
- The judgments of the Lord to be poured out upon an unrighteous Judah—Chapter 1

- The Lord's counsel to His people to avoid the hand of destruction decreed against their enemies—Chapter 2

- A panoramic view of the affairs of the righteous and the wicked at the Second Coming—Chapter 3

Cross References:
- The "minor" prophets of the Old Testament often provide cogent and compelling warnings for modern-day readers concerning the difficulties and dislocations of the last days:

> We must not underestimate, however, the difficulty of the last days. Joel and Zephaniah both speak of the last days as being "a day of . . . gloominess." The coming decades will be times of despair. Why? Because, as Moroni said, despair comes of iniquity. The more iniquity, the more despair. And unless there is widespread repentance, despair will both deepen and spread—except among those who have gospel gladness. (Neal A. Maxwell, "Be of Good Cheer," *Ensign*, Nov. 1982, 67)

And be strong, all ye people of the land, saith the Lord, and work: for I am with you, saith the Lord of hosts: According to the word that I covenanted with you when ye came out of Egypt, so my spirit remaineth among you: fear ye not. (Haggai 2:4–5)

Author: Haggai.

Position: Haggai was one of the twelve prophets of the Old Testament with shorter books (though by no means reflecting messages of lesser import).

Time Span: Written around 520 B.C., shortly after the return of Judah from exile in Babylon.

Purpose: To energize the people to devoted action in building the temple of the Lord and to cause them to look forward in hope to the last days when the Lord will return in glory to reign in peace among the righteous.

Length: 2 chapters

Key Sections:
- Exhortation to build the temple—Chapter 1

- Vision of the Second Coming and the establishment of the future temple of unsurpassed glory—Chapter 2

Representative Sayings:
- The glory of this latter house shall be greater than of the former, saith the Lord of hosts: and in this place will I give peace, saith the Lord of hosts. (2:9)

Zechariah

Thus saith the Lord of hosts; Let your hands be strong, ye that hear in these days these words by the mouth of the prophets, which were in the day that the foundation of the house of the Lord of hosts was laid, that the temple might be built. (Zechariah 8:9)

Author: Zechariah.

Position: Zechariah was one of the twelve prophets of the Old Testament with shorter books (though by no means reflecting messages of lesser import).

Time Span: 520–518 B.C.—shortly after the return of Judah from exile in Babylon under authority of Cyrus. Contempory of the prophet Haggai.

Purpose: To unfold the vision of the Lord's plan of salvation for His people, using contemporary events as symbolic leverage for capturing the scope and grandeur of the ultimate restoration and sublimation of Israel's faithful at the Second Coming.

Length: 14 chapters

Key Sections:
- Visions concerning the future of the chosen people of the Lord—Chapters 1–8

- Additional prophecies concerning the unfolding of the Lord's plan for defeating the wicked and sustaining and redeeming the righteous in the final days—Chapters 9–14

Representative Sayings:
- Rejoice greatly, O daughter of Zion; shout, O daughter of Jerusalem: behold, thy King cometh unto thee: he is just, and having salvation; lowly, and riding upon an ass, and upon a colt the foal of an ass. (9:9)

- When I have bent Judah for me, filled the bow with Ephraim, and raised up thy sons, O Zion, against thy sons, O Greece, and made thee as the sword of a mighty man. And the Lord shall be seen over them, and his arrow shall go forth as the lightning: and the Lord God shall blow the trumpet, and shall go with whirlwinds of the south. . . . And the Lord their God shall save them in that day as the flock of his people: for they shall be as the stones of a crown, lifted up as an ensign upon his land. For how great is his goodness, and how great is his beauty! (9:13–14, 16–17)

- And I said unto them, If ye think good, give me my price; and if not, forbear. So they weighed for my price thirty pieces of silver. (11:12)

- And one shall say unto him, What are these wounds in thine hands? Then he shall answer, Those with which I was wounded in the house of my friends. (13:6)

Cross References:
The Prophet Joseph Smith invoked the words of Zechariah (among others) in explaining the final gathering as a manifestation of the love of the Lord:

> In speaking of the gathering, we mean to be understood as speaking of it according to scripture, the gathering of the elect of the Lord out of every nation on earth, and bringing them to the place of the Lord of Hosts, when the city of righteousness shall be built, and where the people shall be of one heart and one mind, when the Savior comes: yea, where the people shall walk with God like Enoch, and be free from sin. The word of the Lord is precious; and when we read that the veil spread over all nations will be destroyed, and the pure in heart see God, and reign with Him a thousand years on earth, we want all honest men to have a chance to gather and build up a city of righteousness, where even upon the bells of the horses shall be written *"Holiness to the Lord."* (*TPJS*, 93)

Behold, I will send you Elijah the prophet before the coming of the great and dreadful day of the Lord: And he shall turn the heart of the fathers to the children, and the heart of the children to their fathers, lest I come and smite the earth with a curse.
(Malachi 4:5–6)

Author: Malachi.

Position: Malachi was one of the twelve prophets of the Old Testament with shorter books (though by no means reflecting messages of lesser import).

Time Span: Around 430 B.C.

Purpose: To call the people and their priests to repentance for gross shortcomings and remind them to prepare for the Second Coming and the judgments of the Lord.

Length: 4 chapters

Key Sections:
- The Lord's people called to repentance for unrighteous service and offerings—Chapter 1

- The Lord's priests reproved for their failings—Chapter 2

- Events preceding the Second Coming; law of tithing explained—Chapter 3

- Final judgment at the Second Coming; Elijah to return before that "great and dreadful day"—Chapter 4

Representative Sayings:
- Behold, I will send my messenger, and he shall prepare the way before me: and the Lord, whom ye seek, shall suddenly come to his temple, even the messenger of the covenant, whom ye delight in: behold, he shall come, saith the Lord of hosts. (3:1)

- Bring ye all the tithes into the storehouse, that there may be meat in mine house, and prove me now herewith, saith the Lord of hosts, if I will not open you the windows of heaven, and pour you out a blessing, that there shall not be room enough to receive it. (3:10)

Cross References:
- Matthew 11:10; see also Mark 1:2; 1 Nephi 11:27; D&C 35:4; 45:9 (the Lord speaking of John the Baptist)

- 3 Nephi 24:1

- D&C 110:14; 128:17; 133:64; 138:46 (the mission of Elijah and his return before the Second Coming)

- JS—H 1:36–39

Moses

For behold, this is my work and my glory—to bring to pass the immortality and eternal life of man. (Moses 1:39)

Author: Moses.

Position: The precise title given in the current edition of the Pearl of Great Price is "Selections from the Book of Moses: An extract from the translation of the Bible as revealed to Joseph Smith the Prophet, June 1830—February 1831." Professor Robert J. Matthews summarizes the origin of this sacred material as follows:

The material constituting the eight chapters of the book of Moses is an extract from Joseph Smith's translation of the Bible. More precisely, chapter one of Moses is an account of a revelation given to the Prophet Joseph just prior to, or at the commencement of, the translation, while Moses chapters two through eight constitute his translation of Genesis from chapter one through chapter six, verse thirteen. The Joseph Smith translation of the Bible (hereafter identified as JST) began with Genesis and continued through the entire Bible to the book of Revelation. The initial draft of his Bible translation was made between June 1830 and July 1833. However, the short excerpt that we recognize as the book of Moses, being the early part of Genesis, was completed in its first draft by February 1831. (Robert J. Matthews, "How We Got the Book of Moses," *Ensign,* Jan. 1986, 43)

Time Span: The work originated during the ministry of the prophet Moses, the essential time marker being the Exodus (around 1547 B.C.).

Purpose: To provide an inspired and correct account of the calling and preparation of the prophet Moses as well as excerpts from the record of the Creation and subsequent ministries of the prophets of the Lord, especially Adam and Enoch.

Length: 8 chapters

Key Sections:
- The calling and enlightenment of Moses—Chapter 1

- The Creation—Chapters 2–3

- The Fall—Chapter 4

- The dispensation of Adam and the establishment of the family of Adam and Eve—Chapter 5

- An account of the ministry and visions of Enoch—Chapter 6–7

- The ministries of Methuselah and Noah—Chapter 8

Cross References:
- The Book of Moses in the Pearl of Great Price provides added enlightenment and clarification beyond the record given in Genesis with regard to several doctrinal principles. For more details on the significant role of the book of Moses in restoring truth and light to the existing canon, refer to Robert J.

Matthews, "How We Got the Book of Moses," *Ensign,* Jan. 1986, 43; Robert J. Matthews, "Plain and Precious Things Restored," *Ensign,* July 1982, 15; Richard D. Draper, "The Remarkable Book of Moses," *Ensign,* Feb. 1997, 14.

Abraham

And there stood one among them that was like unto God, and he said unto those who were with him: We will go down, for there is space there, and we will take of these materials, and we will make an earth whereon these may dwell; And we will prove them herewith, to see if they will do all things whatsoever the Lord their God shall command them; And they who keep their first estate shall be added upon; and they who keep not their first estate shall not have glory in the same kingdom with those who keep their first estate; and they who keep their second estate shall have glory added upon their heads for ever and ever. (Abraham 3:24–26)

Author: Abraham.

Position: The precise title given in the current edition of the Pearl of Great Price is "The Book of Abraham: Translated from the Papyrus, by Joseph Smith." The Prophet Joseph Smith reports the origins of the book of Abraham in his journal:

> On the 3rd of July, Michael H. Chandler came to Kirtland to exhibit some Egyptian mummies. There were four human figures, together with some two or more rolls of papyrus covered with hieroglyphic figures and devices. As Mr. Chandler had been told I could translate them, he brought me some of the characters, and I gave him the interpretation, and like a gentleman, he gave me the following certificate:
>
> Kirtland, July 6, 1835.
>
> This is to make known to all who may be desirous, concerning the knowledge of Mr. Joseph Smith, Jun., in deciphering the ancient Egyptian hieroglyphic characters in my possession, which I have, in many eminent cities, showed to the most learned; and, from the information that I could ever learn, or meet with, I find that of Mr. Joseph Smith, Jun., to correspond in the most minute matters.
>
> Michael H. Chandler,
>
> Traveling with, and proprietor of, Egyptian mummies. (*HC* 2:235)

The Prophet Joseph continues his account of the coming forth of the Book of Abraham:

Soon after this, some of the Saints at Kirtland purchased the mummies and papyrus, a description of which will appear hereafter, and with W. W. Phelps and Oliver Cowdery as scribes, I commenced the translation of some of the characters or hieroglyphics, and much to our joy found that one of the rolls contained the writings of Abraham, another the writings of Joseph of Egypt, etc.,—a more full account of which will appear in its place, as I proceed to examine or unfold them. Truly we can say, the Lord is beginning to reveal the abundance of peace and truth. (*HC* 2:236)

The Prophet published the Book of Abraham (or that portion that he had translated) in the *Times and Seasons* in March, 1842. The material was included in a small volume called the "Pearl of Great Price," published in 1951 in England to support the missionary effort there. It was this volume that was used as the basis for the scriptural book of the same name that was accepted into the canon by the Church in 1880.

Time Span: The work originated during the ministry of the prophet Abraham, whose long and productive life of some 175 years encompassed the span of time from approximately 2052 B.C. to 1877 B.C.

Purpose: To provide truths for understanding the divine origins and beneficent designs of the Abrahamic covenant as a means for carrying the gospel message to the world and blessing all of mankind. The book also gives insight into the premortal experience of man in the presence of God and illuminates the purposes for earth life as an essential component of the process of perfection. The calling of the Savior from before the foundations of the earth is also explained, with commentary on His mission as Son, Creator, and Redeemer.

Length: 5 chapters

Key Sections:
- The origins of Abraham and his divine rescue from murderous idolaters—Chapters 1–2

- The Lord's instructions to Abraham concerning the divine governance of the universe and implementation of the plan of salvation—Chapter 3

- The Creation—Chapters 4–5

Cross References:
- The Book of Abraham sheds much additional light on the history and calling of the patriarch Abraham as found in the Old Testament (see Genesis 11–25) as well as on the Creation itself (Genesis 1–2).

- The Book of Mormon speaks frequently of the Abrahamic covenant as explained in the Book of Abraham (see especially 1 Ne. 15:18; 17:40; 22:9; 2 Ne. 29:14; 3 Ne. 20:25–27; Mormon 5:20; Ether 13:11).

- References to the Abrahamic covenant or the sacred nature thereof are also found in the Doctrine and Covenants 110:12; 124:58; 131:1–4; 132:19, 29–31, 51.

- Galatians 3:8–9, 29

- There is a traditionally enigmatic passage in Jude (1:6) that is clarified by a reference in Abraham.

PORTRAIT *of the* SAVIOR *in the* OLD TESTAMENT *and* PEARL *of* GREAT PRICE

Magnificent in scope and detail, inspiring in thematic content, and riveting in its anecdotal abundance, the Old Testament is the foundational scripture of the divine canon. Above all else in terms of mission and purpose, the Old Testament—supported by the books of Moses and Abraham from the Pearl of Great Price—constitutes a grand and glorious exposition of the character, qualities, and mission of Jesus Christ, the Messiah and Mediator of the sacred covenant with the Father. The thoughtful and prayerful reader cannot read these passages of scripture concerning the Savior without being touched spiritually with the profound significance of His love, the mercy of His longsuffering, and the majesty of His divine intercession on behalf of mankind.

Among the numerous offices and titles of the Lord revealed through the scriptural record, the following six might be considered the principal and predominant ones: *Jehovah* ("Unchangeable One"), *Messiah* or *Christ* ("Anointed One"), *Creator, Emmanuel* ("God Among Us"), *Jesus* ("God is help" or "Savior"), and *King.* These six transcendent offices or titles are illustrated in the chart below and are described in the subsequent material.

Understanding the interrelated matrix of spiritual agendas that constitute the mission of the Lord serves as a kind of lens through which to view the unfolding panorama of God's dealings with His people during the dispensations of time recorded in the Old Testament and the Pearl of Great Price. The overarching theme of these and all other scriptures of the sacred canon is the Lord Jesus Christ and His central role in the plan of salvation. As Nephi declared: "This is the way; and there is none other way nor name given under heaven whereby man can be saved in the kingdom of God. And now, behold, this is the doctrine of Christ, and the only and true doctrine of the Father, and of the Son, and of the Holy Ghost, which is one God, without end" (2 Ne. 31:21; compare Moses 6:51–52).

OFFICES & TITLES OF THE SON OF GOD

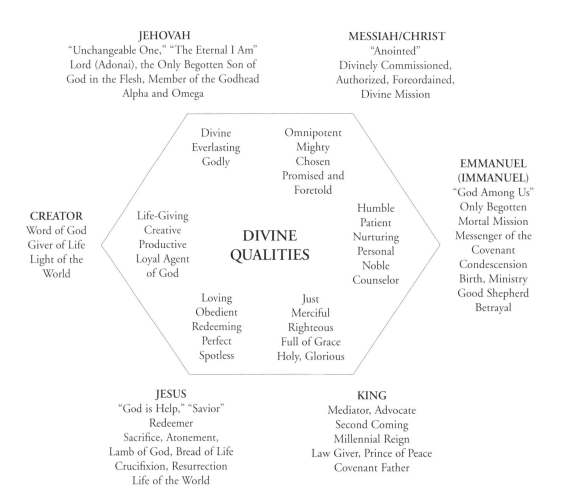

JEHOVAH
"Unchangeable One," "The Eternal I Am"
Lord (Adonai), the Only Begotten Son of
God in the Flesh, Member of the Godhead
Alpha and Omega

MESSIAH/CHRIST
"Anointed"
Divinely Commissioned,
Authorized, Foreordained,
Divine Mission

Divine
Everlasting
Godly

Omnipotent
Mighty
Chosen
Promised and
Foretold

**EMMANUEL
(IMMANUEL)**
"God Among Us"
Only Begotten
Mortal Mission
Messenger of the
Covenant
Condescension
Birth, Ministry
Good Shepherd
Betrayal

CREATOR
Word of God
Giver of Life
Light of the
World

Life-Giving
Creative
Productive
Loyal Agent
of God

**DIVINE
QUALITIES**

Humble
Patient
Nurturing
Personal
Noble
Counselor

Loving
Obedient
Redeeming
Perfect
Spotless

Just
Merciful
Righteous
Full of Grace
Holy, Glorious

JESUS
"God is Help," "Savior"
Redeemer
Sacrifice, Atonement,
Lamb of God, Bread of Life
Crucifixion, Resurrection
Life of the World

KING
Mediator, Advocate
Second Coming
Millennial Reign
Law Giver, Prince of Peace
Covenant Father

Jehovah

In the King James Version of the Old Testament, the word Lord signifies that the original text upon which the translation into English was based contained at that point the name Jehovah, which means "Unchangeable One." Out of respect for Deity, Jewish readers did not speak aloud the name Jehovah or any of its variants but instead substituted a Hebrew word such as Adonai, meaning "Lord." The name Jehovah signifies everlasting, endless, and eternal God, a reflection of the supernal constancy of Deity, the Word of God—"The grass withereth, the flower fadeth: but the word of our God shall stand for ever" (Isa. 40:8). In latter-day scripture, this everlasting state of being is confirmed: "Listen to the voice of the Lord your God, even Alpha and

Omega, the beginning and the end, whose course is one eternal round, the same today as yesterday, and forever" (D&C 35:1; compare Heb. 13:8; 2 Ne. 2:4; 27:23; 29:9; Alma 31:17; Morm. 9:9; Moro. 10:19; D&C 20:12).

It was under the auspices of this transcendent function of everlasting and unchanging God—the Eternal I Am—that Jehovah conversed with Moses on the mount:

> And Moses said unto God, Behold, when I come unto the children of Israel, and shall say unto them, The God of your fathers hath sent me unto you; and they shall say to me, What is his name? what shall I say unto them?
>
> And God said unto Moses, I AM THAT I AM: and he said, Thus shalt thou say unto the children of Israel, I AM hath sent me unto you.
>
> And God said moreover unto Moses, Thus shalt thou say unto the children of Israel, The Lord God of your fathers, the God of Abraham, the God of Isaac, and the God of Jacob, hath sent me unto you: this is my name for ever, and this is my memorial unto all generations. (Ex. 3:13–15)

For further examples of the use of the word Lord (meaning Jehovah) in the Old Testament, see Genesis 2:4–25; 4:25–26; 22:14; 28:13; Exodus 3:6; Psalm 96:13; Isaiah 6:1–5; 41:4, 13–14; 43:3–11; 44:6, 24; 45:17, 21; 60:16; 63:7–14.

Note also the following illustrations in which the specific name Jehovah (or a variant) is used:

> Exodus 6:3—And I appeared unto Abraham, unto Isaac, and unto Jacob, by the name of God Almighty, but by my name Jehovah was I not known to them.
>
> Psalm 68:4—Sing unto God, sing praises to his name: extol him that rideth upon the heavens by his name Jah, and rejoice before him.
>
> Psalm 83:18—That men may know that thou, whose name alone is Jehovah, art the most high over all the earth.
>
> Isaiah 12:2–5—Behold, God is my salvation; I will trust, and not be afraid: for the Lord Jehovah is my strength and my song; he also is become my salvation. Therefore with joy shall ye draw water out of the wells of salvation. And in that day shall ye say, Praise the Lord, call upon his name, declare his doings among the people, make mention that his name is exalted. Sing unto the Lord; for he hath done excellent things: this is known in all the earth.
>
> Isaiah 26:4—Trust ye in the Lord for ever: for in the Lord Jehovah is everlasting strength.

The nature of Jehovah as an eternal, unchanging, and everlasting being derives from His relationship to and grounding in the Father, Elohim. Jehovah is in very deed the Son of God, even the First Born: "I will declare the decree: the Lord hath said unto me, Thou art my Son; this day have I begotten thee" (Ps. 2:7). Furthermore: "Also I will make him my firstborn, higher than the kings of the earth. My mercy will I keep for him for evermore, and my covenant shall stand fast with him. His seed also will I make to endure for ever, and his throne as the days of heaven" (Ps.89:27–29). Isaiah confirmed the same truth: "Who hath wrought and done it, calling the generations from the beginning? I the Lord, the first, and with the last; I am he" (Isa. 41:4). In the New Testament, Book of Mormon, and Doctrine and Covenants, this defining position as the First as well as the Last was applied to Jesus Christ and is embodied in the appellation "Alpha and Omega" (see Rev. 1:8, 11; 21:6; 22:13; 3 Ne. 9:18; D&C 19:1; 35:1; 38:1; 45:7; 54:1; 61:1; 63:60; 68:35; 75:1; 81:7; 84:120; 112:34; 132:66).

Qualities of Jehovah

Not only is Jehovah endless and eternal, He also serves everlastingly as a member of the Godhead under the direction of the Father and in conjunction with the Holy Ghost. The qualities of the Son that radiate from this magnificent position of grace and truth are divinity, everlasting nature, and godliness. These are the same qualities of Jehovah to which His disciples are to aspire through obedience to His gospel plan of exaltation and by enduring in faith and honor to the end. What a glorious blessing it is to have a resplendent and perfected personage—even Jehovah—as our spiritual model and eternal guide: "Therefore, what manner of men ought ye to be? Verily I say unto you, even as I am" (3 Ne. 27:27).

Messiah/Christ

"Messiah" is an Aramaic word meaning "the Anointed." Aramaic belongs to the Semitic language group (which also includes Hebrew and Arabic) and became the official language of the Assyrian and later the Babylonian and Persian empires. Aramaic was, for centuries, the dominant language in Jewish worship and daily life; Jesus himself spoke Aramaic.

The Greek equivalent of Messiah was Christ. The word "Christ" does not appear in the King James Version of the Old Testament, but it does appear in the book of Moses from the Pearl of Great Price in four verses, as follows:

> Moses 6:52—And he [God] also said unto him [Adam]: If thou wilt turn unto me, and hearken unto my voice, and believe, and repent of all thy transgressions, and be baptized, even in water, in the name of mine Only Begotten Son, who is full of grace and truth, which is Jesus Christ, the only name which shall be given under heaven, whereby salvation shall come unto the children of men, ye shall receive the gift of the Holy Ghost, asking all things in his name, and whatsoever ye shall ask, it shall be given you.

Moses 6:57—Wherefore teach it unto your children, that all men, everywhere, must repent, or they can in nowise inherit the kingdom of God, for no unclean thing can dwell there, or dwell in his presence; for, in the language of Adam, Man of Holiness is his name, and the name of his Only Begotten is the Son of Man, even Jesus Christ, a righteous Judge, who shall come in the meridian of time.

Moses 7: 50—And it came to pass that Enoch continued his cry unto the Lord, saying: I ask thee, O Lord, in the name of thine Only Begotten, even Jesus Christ, that thou wilt have mercy upon Noah and his seed, that the earth might never more be covered by the floods.

Moses 8: 24—Believe and repent of your sins and be baptized in the name of Jesus Christ, the Son of God, even as our fathers, and ye shall receive the Holy Ghost, that ye may have all things made manifest; and if ye do not this, the floods will come in upon you; nevertheless they hearkened not.

The title "Messiah" appears only twice in the Old Testament (Dan. 9:25–26) and once in the Pearl of Great Price (Moses 7:53).

What is important about the terms "Messiah" and "Christ" is the underlying meaning of these titles as "the Anointed," signifying that Jesus was divinely commissioned of the Father to carry out the work of redemption and atonement on behalf of all mankind. He was foreordained to His supernal mission: "And the Lord said: Whom shall I send? And one answered like unto the Son of Man: Here am I, send me. And another answered and said: Here am I, send me. And the Lord said: I will send the first" (Abr. 3:27; compare Job 19:25; 38:1–7; Isa. 25:8–9). Jesus—as the Messiah and the Christ—is the authorized and empowered agent of the Father with the express calling to carry out the divine mission of saving and exalting mankind in keeping with the eternal principles of truth and spiritual deliverance. Isaiah expresses this divine mission of the "Anointed One" in the following terms:

The Spirit of the Lord God is upon me; because the Lord hath anointed me to preach good tidings unto the meek; he hath sent me to bind up the brokenhearted, to proclaim liberty to the captives, and the opening of the prison to them that are bound;

To proclaim the acceptable year of the Lord, and the day of vengeance of our God; to comfort all that mourn;

To appoint unto them that mourn in Zion, to give unto them beauty for ashes, the oil of joy for mourning, the garment of praise for the spirit of heaviness; that they might be called trees of righteousness, the planting of the Lord, that he might be glorified. (Isa. 61:1–3)

The Old Testament confirms the divine authority of Jesus in a variety of additional passages, including this memorable one from Isaiah:

> For unto us a child is born, unto us a son is given: and the government shall be upon his shoulder: and his name shall be called Wonderful, Counsellor, The mighty God, The everlasting Father, The Prince of Peace.
>
> Of the increase of his government and peace there shall be no end, upon the throne of David, and upon his kingdom, to order it, and to establish it with judgment and with justice from henceforth even for ever. (Isa. 9:6–7; see also Gen. 49:10; Isa. 10:27; 11:1–9)

Jeremiah also confirms the stature of Jesus as being commissioned (i.e., anointed) of the Father:

> Behold, the days come, saith the Lord, that I will raise unto David a righteous Branch, and a King shall reign and prosper, and shall execute judgment and justice in the earth.
>
> In his days Judah shall be saved, and Israel shall dwell safely: and this is his name whereby he shall be called, THE LORD OUR RIGHTEOUSNESS.
>
> Therefore, behold, the days come, saith the Lord, that they shall no more say, The LORD liveth, which brought up the children of Israel out of the land of Egypt;
>
> But, The Lord liveth, which brought up and which led the seed of the house of Israel out of the north country, and from all countries whither I had driven them; and they shall dwell in their own land. (Jer. 23:5–8)

In addition, Daniel was privileged to see in vision the nobility and divine agency of the Son:

> I saw in the night visions, and, behold, one like the Son of man came with the clouds of heaven, and came to the Ancient of days, and they brought him near before him.
>
> And there was given him dominion, and glory, and a kingdom, that all people, nations, and languages, should serve him: his dominion is an everlasting dominion, which shall not pass away, and his kingdom that which shall not be destroyed. (Dan. 7:13–14; compare Zech. 14:4–9)

Qualities of Messiah/Christ

To officiate in this singularly indispensable and lofty capacity as the Anointed One, Jesus must necessarily be omnipotent, chosen, and mighty to effect change for good.

We would expect the prophets of God throughout successive dispensations to have promised and foretold the work and ministry of Jesus in this respect. And such is the case, as the following Old Testament excerpts demonstrate (arranged, in general, according to the chronology of the prophetic utterances):

Triumph over evil (Genesis 3:15, see also Num. 24:17)—And I will put enmity between thee and the woman, and between thy seed and her seed; it shall bruise thy head, and thou shalt bruise his heel.

Reign as the Eternal Lawgiver (Genesis 49:10; compare JST, Gen. 50:24; Ezek. 21:27)—The sceptre shall not depart from Judah, nor a lawgiver from between his feet, until Shiloh [the Messiah] come; and unto him shall the gathering of the people be.

Arise as the great Prophet (Deuteronomy 18:15, 18–19)—The Lord thy God will raise up unto thee a Prophet [Messiah] from the midst of thee, of thy brethren, like unto me; unto him ye shall hearken . . . I will raise them up a Prophet from among their brethren, like unto thee [Moses], and will put my words in his mouth; and he shall speak unto them all that I shall command him. And it shall come to pass, that whosoever will not hearken unto my words which he shall speak in my name, I will require it of him.

Prevail over earthly kingdoms (Psalm 2:6–12; see also Ps. 68:18)—Yet have I set my king upon my holy hill of Zion. I will declare the decree: the Lord hath said unto me, Thou art my Son; this day have I begotten thee. Ask of me, and I shall give thee the heathen for thine inheritance, and the uttermost parts of the earth for thy possession. Thou shalt break them with a rod of iron; thou shalt dash them in pieces like a potter's vessel. Be wise now therefore, O ye kings: be instructed, ye judges of the earth. Serve the Lord with fear, and rejoice with trembling. Kiss the Son, lest he be angry, and ye perish from the way, when his wrath is kindled but a little. Blessed are all they that put their trust in him.

Be crucified (Psalm 22:1, 16, 18; see also Zech. 13:6; compare Ps. 69:20–21; Isa. 50:5–9; 53:1–12; Zech. 11:12)—My God, my God, why hast thou forsaken me? why art thou so far from helping me, and from the words of my roaring? . . . the assembly of the wicked have inclosed me: they pierced my hands and my feet. . . . They part my garments among them, and cast lots upon my vesture.

Be the Chief Cornerstone (Psalm 118:22–23; compare Isa. 28:16)—The stone which the builders refused is become the head stone of the corner. This is the Lord's doing; it is marvellous in our eyes.

Be born of a virgin (Isaiah 7:14)—Therefore the Lord himself shall give you a sign; Behold, a virgin shall conceive, and bear a son, and shall call his name Immanuel.

Be the Prince of Peace (Isaiah 9:6–7; compare Isa. 11:1–5)—For unto us a child is born, unto us a son is given: and the government shall be upon his shoulder: and his name shall be called Wonderful, Counsellor, The mighty God, The everlasting Father, The Prince of Peace. Of the increase of his government and peace there shall be no end, upon the throne of David, and upon his kingdom, to order it, and to establish it with judgment and with justice from henceforth even for ever. The zeal of the Lord of hosts will perform this.

Reign as Glorious Sovereign (Isaiah 22:21–23)—And I will clothe him with thy robe, and strengthen him with thy girdle, and I will commit thy government into his hand: and he shall be a father to the inhabitants of Jerusalem, and to the house of Judah. And the key of the house of David will I lay upon his shoulder; so he shall open, and none shall shut; and he shall shut, and none shall open. And I will fasten him as a nail in a sure place; and he shall be for a glorious throne to his father's house.

Overcome death (Isaiah 25:8–9)—He will swallow up death in victory; and the Lord GOD will wipe away tears from off all faces; and the rebuke of his people shall he take away from off all the earth: for the LORD hath spoken it. And it shall be said in that day, Lo, this is our God; we have waited for him, and he will save us: this is the Lord; we have waited for him, we will be glad and rejoice in his salvation.

Reveal the glory of the Lord (Isaiah 40:4–5)—Every valley shall be exalted, and every mountain and hill shall be made low: and the crooked shall be made straight, and the rough places plain: And the glory of the LORD shall be revealed, and all flesh shall see it together: for the mouth of the LORD hath spoken it.

Liberate (Isaiah 42:1, 6–7; see also Isa. 61:1–3)—Behold my servant, whom I uphold; mine elect, in whom my soul delighteth; I have put my spirit upon him: he shall bring forth judgment to the Gentiles. . . . I the Lord have called thee in righteousness, and will hold thine hand, and will keep thee, and give thee for a covenant of the people, for a light of the Gentiles; To open the blind eyes, to bring out the prisoners from the prison, and them that sit in darkness out of the prison house.

Redeem (Isaiah 59:20; compare Ezek. 37:1–28; Hosea 13:4, 14)—And the Redeemer shall come to Zion, and unto them that turn from transgression in Jacob, saith the LORD.

Atone (Daniel 9:24–25; compare Dan. 9:26)—Seventy weeks are determined upon thy people and upon thy holy city, to finish the transgression, and to make an end of sins, and to make reconciliation for iniquity, and to bring in everlasting righteousness, and to seal up the vision and prophecy, and to anoint the most Holy. Know therefore and understand, that from the going forth of the commandment to restore and to build Jerusalem unto the Messiah the Prince shall be seven weeks, and threescore and two weeks: the street shall be built again, and the wall, even in troublous times.

Save (Hosea 13:4; see also Jonah 2:9)—Yet I am the LORD thy God from the land of Egypt, and thou shalt know no god but me: for there is no saviour beside me.

Judge (Habakkuk 3:3–4, 18)—His glory covered the heavens, and the earth was full of his praise. And his brightness was as the light; he had horns coming out of his hand: and there was the hiding of his power. . . . Yet I will rejoice in the LORD, I will joy in the God of my salvation.

Build the Temple of the Lord (Zechariah 6:12–13; see also Zech. 3:8–9)—Thus speaketh the LORD of hosts, saying, Behold the man whose name is The BRANCH; and he shall grow up out of his place, and he shall build the temple of the LORD: Even he shall build the temple of the LORD; and he shall bear the glory, and shall sit and rule upon his throne; and he shall be a priest upon his throne: and the counsel of peace shall be between them both.

Appear in the latter-day temple (Malachi 3:1)—Behold, I will send my messenger, and he shall prepare the way before me: and the Lord, whom ye seek, shall suddenly come to his temple, even the messenger of the covenant, whom ye delight in: behold, he shall come, saith the LORD of hosts.

Just these few samples of prophetic discourse concerning the divine mission of the Messiah indicate the extraordinarily pervasive presence of the Messianic theme throughout the Old Testament. It is the office, function, and blessings of "the Anointed One" that form the fabric of sacred revelation preserved by the hand of God through the ages. It is from Jehovah, acting as the agent of the Father, that salvation and redemption flow to those who believe and honor the covenants of the Lord.

Creator

The Unchangeable and Anointed One served as the principal divine agent in laying the foundation of the world through the Creation itself. When God directed by His word that the Creation should proceed (Gen. 1–2; Moses 2–3; Deut. 4:32), it was through the Word of God (Jehovah, Messiah, Christ) that this divine process was initiated and completed:

By the word of the Lord were the heavens made; and all the host of them by the breath of his mouth. (Ps. 33:6)

Thus saith the Lord, thy redeemer, and he that formed thee from the womb, I am the LORD that maketh all things; that stretcheth forth the heavens alone; that spreadeth abroad the earth by myself. (Isa. 44:24)

That they may see, and know, and consider, and understand together, that the hand of the LORD hath done this [governed and sustained the vitality of nature], and the Holy One of Israel hath created it. (Isa. 41:20)

Thus the Word of God was Creation incarnate. John the Apostle rendered this verity using the following celebrated language:

> In the beginning was the Word, and the Word was with God, and the Word was God.
>
> The same was in the beginning with God.
>
> All things were made by him; and without him was not any thing made that was made.
>
> In him was life; and the life was the light of men.
>
> And the light shineth in darkness; and the darkness comprehended it not. (John 1:1–5; compare also Col. 1:16; Rev. 10:6; 2 Ne. 2:14; 29:7; Mosiah 4:2, 9; 5:15; Alma 18:28–29; 22:10; Hel. 14:12; 3 Ne. 9:15; Morm. 9:11, 17; D&C 14:9)

What greater symbolic representation could there be of the office and function of the Creator and Life-Giver than the image of being the "Light of the World"? "And God said, Let there be light: and there was light. And God saw the light, that it was good: and God divided the light from the darkness" (Gen. 1:3–4; see also Moses 2:3–4). In keeping with the essence of this divine capacity, the Psalmist celebrated the Word of God as follows: "The LORD is my light and my salvation; whom shall I fear? the LORD is the strength of my life; of whom shall I be afraid?" (Ps. 27:1). Furthermore, Isaiah counseled: "O house of Jacob, come ye, and let us walk in the light of the LORD" (Isa. 2:5; see also Isa. 9:2), and then looked beyond the objects of the Creation to assert: "The sun shall be no more thy light by day; neither for brightness shall the moon give light unto thee: but the Lord shall be unto thee an everlasting light, and thy God thy glory" (Isa. 60:19; see also Micah 7:8–9).

In modern scripture, this process of light-giving (enlightenment) is further elucidated:

> And the light which shineth, which giveth you light, is through him who enlighteneth your eyes, which is the same light that quickeneth your understandings;
>
> Which light proceedeth forth from the presence of God to fill the immensity of space—
>
> The light which is in all things, which giveth life to all things, which is the law by which all things are governed, even the power of God who sitteth upon his throne, who is in the bosom of eternity, who is in the midst of all things. (D&C 88:11–13)

In terms of spiritual illumination, this light of Christ has profound implications for the covenant relationship that we have with God:

> For the word of the Lord is truth, and whatsoever is truth is light, and whatsoever is light is Spirit, even the Spirit of Jesus Christ.
>
> And the Spirit giveth light to every man that cometh into the world; and the Spirit enlighteneth every man through the world, that hearkeneth to the voice of the Spirit.
>
> And every one that hearkeneth to the voice of the Spirit cometh unto God, even the Father.
>
> And the Father teacheth him of the covenant which he has renewed and confirmed upon you, which is confirmed upon you for your sakes, and not for your sakes only, but for the sake of the whole world. (D&C 84:45–48; see also Moro. 7:13–19)

Many additional references from the Old Testament confirm and expand on the mission of the Word of God as Creator. For example, the Lord asked Job, in his adversity:

> Where wast thou when I laid the foundations of the earth? declare, if thou hast understanding.
>
> Who hath laid the measures thereof, if thou knowest? or who hath stretched the line upon it?
>
> Whereupon are the foundations thereof fastened? or who laid the corner stone thereof;
>
> When the morning stars sang together, and all the sons of God shouted for joy? (Job 38:4–7; see also Job 10:8–12; 26:12–13)

Clearly the one most capable of understanding our plight as mortals and rendering succor and solace concerning our privation and suffering is the Lord Himself, the Creator of heaven and earth: "And Hezekiah prayed before the Lord, and said, O Lord God of Israel, which dwellest between the cherubims, thou art the God, even thou alone, of all the kingdoms of the earth: thou hast made heaven and earth" (2 Kgs. 19:15).

Isaiah speaks in prophetic terms of the role of the Son of God in the Creation:

> To whom then will ye liken me, or shall I be equal? saith the Holy One.
>
> Lift up your eyes on high, and behold who hath created these things, that bringeth out their host by number: he calleth them all by names by the greatness of his might, for that he is strong in power; not one faileth.

> Why sayest thou, O Jacob, and speakest, O Israel, My way is hid from the
> LORD, and my judgment is passed over from my God?
>
> Hast thou not known? hast thou not heard, that the everlasting God, the LORD,
> the Creator of the ends of the earth, fainteth not, neither is weary? there is no search-
> ing of his understanding. (Isa. 40:25–28; compare Isa. 42:5; 45:11–14, 18; 65:17)

Similarly, Jeremiah proclaims, through the voice of inspiration, the mighty process of the Creation at the hands of the Son of God:

> He hath made the earth by his power, he hath established the world by his wisdom,
> and hath stretched out the heaven by his understanding.
>
> When he uttereth his voice, there is a multitude of waters in the heavens; and
> he causeth the vapours to ascend from the ends of the earth: he maketh lightnings
> with rain, and bringeth forth the wind out of his treasures. (Jer. 51:15–16)

The identity of the Creator is made clear by the prophet Amos: "For, lo, he that formeth the mountains, and createth the wind, and declareth unto man what is his thought, that maketh the morning darkness, and treadeth upon the high places of the earth, The LORD, The God of hosts, is his name" (Amos 4:13).

Qualities of the Creator

As Creator, Jehovah embodies specific qualities of office and character. He is life-giving, creative, productive, and a loyal agent of God. These are among the very qualities that go to define discipleship for the faithful who are committed to follow in the footsteps of the Savior by emulating His exemplary mode of living.

Using these same qualities, the Son of God governed and governs the vital process of generating and preserving life itself—beginning with the Creation and continuing with the unfolding of the process of dynamic growth of all living things pertaining to this world and all other worlds: "And worlds without number have I created; and I also created them for mine own purpose; and by the Son I created them, which is mine Only Begotten" (Moses 1:33). The Gatekeeper of the eternal realm (2 Ne. 9:41) is also the Gatekeeper of life itself—the Curator of the principles and processes of enlivenment and growth for all creation. Jehovah oversees and administers the transition between the potential and the real, between the spiritual creation (as described in Moses 3:5) and the actual, emerging (natural) creation.

The Greeks had a word for this magnificent process of emergence—*entelechy*, meaning "completion" or the "realization of the essence of a thing." In this sense, the predominant quality of Jesus Christ as Creator is "One who completes," or One who—through faith, obedience, power, and divine light—generates and sustains life unto salvation. What an extraordinary Being is this Creator to generate as the Word of God all the conditions and processes by which we, as sons and daughters of God, can enjoy mortal life and look forward with hope, faith, and covenant valor to the time when we shall inherit immortality and eternal life in the mansions of the Father and the Son. In that joyous hour, the faithful shall meet once again the very Creator of our being, look upon His face with rapture, and speak His name in love: "And he shall be called Jesus Christ, the Son of God, the Father of heaven and earth, the Creator of all things from the beginning" (Mosiah 3:8; see also Moses 6:63; 7:56; Abr. 4:20).

Emmanuel (Immanuel)

One of the greatest of all the miracles of the gospel is the condescension of God, that the great Jehovah—the "Unchangeable One," the "Anointed One" (being Messiah and Christ), even the grand Creator of heaven and earth—should deem it to be His essential mission to do the will of the Father and come among mortals to bring to pass for all mankind the effectual conditions of faith, salvation, and redemption. In this capacity, His office and title is known as "Emmanuel" (also rendered "Immanuel")—that is, "God Among Us." As the Only Begotten of the Father, He accepted His mortal mission to serve as the Messenger of the Covenant and experienced birth, grew to manhood, completed His ministry as the Good Shepherd, and suffered betrayal and death as the "author of eternal salvation" (see Heb. 5:8–9).

The chronicle of Emmanuel's mortal experience is woven through prophetic utterance into the fabric of the Old Testament. The Psalmist foresaw the work of the mortal Messiah:

> The Lord is high above all nations, and his glory above the heavens.
>
> Who is like unto the Lord our God, who dwelleth on high,
>
> Who humbleth himself to behold the things that are in heaven, and in the earth! (Ps. 113:4–6)

Isaiah envisioned the infinite humility of the Son in submitting Himself willingly to His detractors: "The Lord God hath opened mine ear, and I was not rebellious, neither turned away back. I gave my back to the smiters, and my cheeks to them that plucked off the hair: I hid not my face from shame and spitting" (Isa. 50:5–6). Continuing his inspired pronouncement, Isaiah articulates with consummate and unforgettable eloquence the pains of the Lord in doing the will of the Father upon the earth:

> Who hath believed our report? and to whom is the arm of the Lord revealed?
>
> For he shall grow up before him as a tender plant, and as a root out of a dry ground: he hath no form nor comeliness; and when we shall see him, there is no beauty that we should desire him.

He is despised and rejected of men; a man of sorrows, and acquainted with grief: and we hid as it were our faces from him; he was despised, and we esteemed him not.

Surely he hath borne our griefs, and carried our sorrows: yet we did esteem him stricken, smitten of God, and afflicted.

But he was wounded for our transgressions, he was bruised for our iniquities: the chastisement of our peace was upon him; and with his stripes we are healed.

All we like sheep have gone astray; we have turned every one to his own way; and the Lord hath laid on him the iniquity of us all.

He was oppressed, and he was afflicted, yet he opened not his mouth: he is brought as a lamb to the slaughter, and as a sheep before her shearers is dumb, so he openeth not his mouth.

He was taken from prison and from judgment: and who shall declare his generation? for he was cut off out of the land of the living: for the transgression of my people was he stricken.

And he made his grave with the wicked, and with the rich in his death; because he had done no violence, neither was any deceit in his mouth.

Yet it pleased the LORD to bruise him; he hath put him to grief: when thou shalt make his soul an offering for sin, he shall see his seed, he shall prolong his days, and the pleasure of the Lord shall prosper in his hand.

He shall see of the travail of his soul, and shall be satisfied: by his knowledge shall my righteous servant justify many; for he shall bear their iniquities.

Therefore will I divide him a portion with the great, and he shall divide the spoil with the strong; because he hath poured out his soul unto death: and he was numbered with the transgressors; and he bare the sin of many, and made intercession for the transgressors. (Isa. 53:1–12)

The pathway of the Christ into mortality via the lineage of Abraham (the Davidic descent) is abundantly accounted for in the pages of the sacred record: "I have made a covenant with my chosen, I have sworn unto David my servant, Thy seed will I establish for ever, and build up thy throne to all generations" (Ps. 89:3–4; see also 1 Sam. 16:1; 17:12; 2 Sam. 7:12–17; Ps. 132:11–18; Isa. 9:6–7; 11:1–10: Jer. 23:5–6; 33:14–16; Zech. 3:8–9; 6:10–15; 12:7–12).

The earthly mission of the Lord is likewise a central theme throughout the Old Testament record:

Messenger of God (Isaiah 61:1)—The Spirit of the Lord GOD is upon me; because the LORD hath anointed me to preach good tidings unto the meek; he hath sent me to bind up the brokenhearted, to proclaim liberty to the captives, and the opening of the prison to them that are bound.

Betrayal (Psalm 22:15–18; compare Psa. 41:9; Zech. 11:12–14)—And thou hast brought me into the dust of death. For dogs have compassed me: the assembly of the wicked have inclosed me: they pierced my hands and my feet. I may tell all my bones: they look and stare upon me. They part my garments among them, and cast lots upon my vesture.

Suffering (Zechariah 13:6)—And one shall say unto him, What are these wounds in thine hands? Then he shall answer, Those with which I was wounded in the house of my friends.

Victory over death (Isaiah 25:8)—He will swallow up death in victory; and the Lord God will wipe away tears from off all faces; and the rebuke of his people shall he take away from off all the earth: for the Lord hath spoken it.

Enoch, too, saw in vision the entry of the Lord into mortality: "And behold, Enoch saw the day of the coming of the Son of Man, even in the flesh; and his soul rejoiced, saying: The Righteous is lifted up, and the Lamb is slain from the foundation of the world; and through faith I am in the bosom of the Father, and behold, Zion is with me" (Moses 7:47).

The all-encompassing view of the condescension of the Only Begotten is that of the Good Shepherd who tends His flocks personally as "the shepherd, the stone of Israel" (Gen. 49:24). This role is most memorably expressed in the twenty-third Psalm—"The Lord is my shepherd; I shall not want" (v. 1)—but is also encapsulated in several other prophetic passages of great beauty and tenderness:

Give ear, O Shepherd of Israel, thou that leadest Joseph like a flock; thou that dwellest between the cherubims, shine forth. Before Ephraim and Benjamin and Manasseh stir up thy strength, and come and save us.

Turn us again, O God, and cause thy face to shine; and we shall be saved. (Ps. 80:2–3)

For he is our God; and we are the people of his pasture, and the sheep of his hand. To day if ye will hear his voice. (Ps. 95:7; see also Zech. 13:7)

Perhaps the most detailed view of the Good Shepherd Emmanuel is given in Ezekiel 34:11–19:

For thus saith the Lord God; Behold, I, even I, will both search my sheep, and seek them out.

As a shepherd seeketh out his flock in the day that he is among his sheep that are scattered; so will I seek out my sheep, and will deliver them out of all places where they have been scattered in the cloudy and dark day.

And I will bring them out from the people, and gather them from the countries, and will bring them to their own land, and feed them upon the mountains of Israel by the rivers, and in all the inhabited places of the country.

I will feed them in a good pasture, and upon the high mountains of Israel shall their fold be: there shall they lie in a good fold, and in a fat pasture shall they feed upon the mountains of Israel.

I will feed my flock, and I will cause them to lie down, saith the Lord GOD.

I will seek that which was lost, and bring again that which was driven away, and will bind up that which was broken, and will strengthen that which was sick: but I will destroy the fat and the strong; I will feed them with judgment.

And as for you, O my flock, thus saith the Lord GOD; Behold, I judge between cattle and cattle, between the rams and the he goats.

Seemeth it a small thing unto you to have eaten up the good pasture, but ye must tread down with your feet the residue of your pastures? and to have drunk of the deep waters, but ye must foul the residue with your feet?

And as for my flock, they eat that which ye have trodden with your feet; and they drink that which ye have fouled with your feet.

Qualities of Emmanuel

The Good Shepherd, by nature of His divine calling and commission, radiates the qualities of being humble, patient, nurturing, personal, and exhibit the characteristics of the long-suffering, noble counselor.

The scriptures illustrate abundantly the manner in which the Lord works one-on-one, in mercy and kindness, with His faithful servants. According to the Old Testament account, the Lord appeared *in person* to Abraham (Gen. 12:7), Jacob (Gen. 32:30), Moses (Ex. 32:30–31; Num. 12:6–8; Deut. 5:24), Isaiah (Isa. 6:1), Ezekiel (Ezek. 1:26–28), and Amos (Amos 9:1). He no doubt appeared to many other prophets as well.

The extraordinary record in the Pearl of Great Price concerning Moses' interaction with the Lord on the mount confirms the personal nature of God's interaction with his servants:

The words of God, which he spake unto Moses at a time when Moses was caught up into an exceedingly high mountain,

And he saw God face to face, and he talked with him, and the glory of God was upon Moses; therefore Moses could endure his presence.

And God spake unto Moses, saying: Behold, I am the Lord God Almighty, and Endless is my name; for I am without beginning of days or end of years; and is not this endless?

> And, behold, thou art my son; wherefore look, and I will show thee the workmanship of mine hands; but not all, for my works are without end, and also my words, for they never cease.
>
> Wherefore, no man can behold all my works, except he behold all my glory; and no man can behold all my glory, and afterwards remain in the flesh on the earth.
>
> And I have a work for thee, Moses, my son; and thou art in the similitude of mine Only Begotten; and mine Only Begotten is and shall be the Savior, for he is full of grace and truth; but there is no God beside me, and all things are present with me, for I know them all. (Moses 1:1–6)

It was during the course of this personal dialogue that the Lord shared with Moses the true nature of His divine mission: "For behold, this is my work and my glory—to bring to pass the immortality and eternal life of man" (Moses 1:39). An inherent part of this mission is to prepare the sons and daughters of God to come into His presence once again and partake of His glory as heirs to all the celestial blessings. The Psalmist reminds us to cultivate an openness to the Lord's invitation to achieve a personal relationship with Him:

> O come, let us worship and bow down: let us kneel before the LORD our maker.
>
> For he is our God; and we are the people of his pasture, and the sheep of his hand. To day if ye will hear his voice,
>
> Harden not your heart, as in the provocation, and as in the day of temptation in the wilderness:
>
> When your fathers tempted me, proved me, and saw my work.
>
> Forty years long was I grieved with this generation, and said, It is a people that do err in their heart, and they have not known my ways:
>
> Unto whom I sware in my wrath that they should not enter into my rest. (Ps. 95:6–11)

This provocation (which Paul also cites in Hebrews 3:7–19) occurred when the Israelites, despite the impassioned exhortations of Moses, refused to rise to the occasion of preparing to meet the Lord their God *personally* (Num. 14:1–23) as He had commanded them. Thus He removed from among them the higher priesthood and denied them the privilege of entering into His rest and partaking of the joys of the Promised Land. In the Book of Mormon, both Jacob and Alma implore the people to avoid a second provocation of this kind (Jacob 1:7; Alma 12:36). In latter-day scripture, the Lord re-emphasizes the counsel that all should seek a personal relationship with Him in order to enjoy the blessings of eternity: "And seek the face of the Lord always, that in patience ye may possess your souls, and ye shall have eternal life" (D&C 101:38).

Thus we are to honor in all diligence the commandment to follow the Good Shepherd in humility and patience, cultivating with Him personally an enduring and liberating relationship as between a faithful and grateful son or daughter and a loving Father.

Jesus

The name "Jesus" is the Greek form of the name Joshua or Jeshua, meaning "God is Help" (or "Jehovah is Help"), i.e., "Savior." The name implies the sacred office of Redeemer, Lamb of Life, Bread of Life, the One who brings about the atonement through the sacrificial crucifixion, the One who ushers in the process of the resurrection, the One who is therefore, in all respects, the Life of the World. In this capacity as Savior, the Son of God is the means for rescuing all mankind from the effects of the temporal death and enabling the faithful and obedient to escape the clutches of the second (or spiritual) death through compliance with the principles and ordinances of the gospel.

The Old Testament is a vibrant and compelling witness of the office of Savior and Redeemer as consummated in the crucifixion and resurrection of Jesus. The Psalmist anticipated the express words of the sacrificial Lamb of God—"My God, my God, why hast thou forsaken me?" (Ps. 22:1)—and discerned in prophetic vision the process of the crucifixion: "the assembly of the wicked have inclosed me: they pierced my hands and my feet. I may tell all my bones: they look and stare upon me. They part my garments among them, and cast lots upon my vesture. But be not thou far from me, O Lord: O my strength, haste thee to help me" (Psalm 22:16–19).

Isaiah foresaw in great detail the travail of the Lord on the cross:

> But he was wounded for our transgressions, he was bruised for our iniquities: the chastisement of our peace was upon him; and with his stripes we are healed.
>
> All we like sheep have gone astray; we have turned every one to his own way; and the Lord hath laid on him the iniquity of us all.
>
> He was oppressed, and he was afflicted, yet he opened not his mouth: he is brought as a lamb to the slaughter, and as a sheep before her shearers is dumb, so he openeth not his mouth.
>
> He was taken from prison and from judgment: and who shall declare his generation? for he was cut off out of the land of the living: for the transgression of my people was he stricken.
>
> And he made his grave with the wicked, and with the rich in his death; because he had done no violence, neither was any deceit in his mouth.
>
> Yet it pleased the Lord to bruise him; he hath put him to grief: when thou shalt make his soul an offering for sin, he shall see his seed, he shall prolong his days, and the pleasure of the Lord shall prosper in his hand.
>
> He shall see of the travail of his soul, and shall be satisfied: by his knowledge shall my righteous servant justify many; for he shall bear their iniquities.

Therefore will I divide him a portion with the great, and he shall divide the spoil with the strong; because he hath poured out his soul unto death: and he was numbered with the transgressors; and he bare the sin of many, and made intercession for the transgressors. (Isa. 53:5–12)

Likewise, Zechariah was blessed to spiritually view the crucifixion and atonement from the perspective of the Savior, saying: "And I will pour upon the house of David, and upon the inhabitants of Jerusalem, the spirit of grace and of supplications: and they shall look upon me whom they have pierced, and they shall mourn for him, as one mourneth for his only son, and shall be in bitterness for him, as one that is in bitterness for his firstborn" (Zech. 12:10).

The redeeming death of the Savior secured the faith and hope of His followers in all ages:

And thus he shall bring salvation to all those who shall believe on his name; this being the intent of this last sacrifice, to bring about the bowels of mercy, which overpowereth justice, and bringeth about means unto men that they may have faith unto repentance.

And thus mercy can satisfy the demands of justice, and encircles them in the arms of safety, while he that exercises no faith unto repentance is exposed to the whole law of the demands of justice; therefore only unto him that has faith unto repentance is brought about the great and eternal plan of redemption. (Alma 34:15–16)

A number of Old Testament scriptures echo this principle:

Proverbs 14:32—But the righteous hath hope in his death.

Isaiah 25:8—He will swallow up death in victory; and the Lord GOD will wipe away tears from off all faces; and the rebuke of his people shall he take away from off all the earth: for the Lord hath spoken it.

Isaiah 53:7, 9—He was oppressed, and he was afflicted, yet he opened not his mouth: he is brought as a lamb to the slaughter, and as a sheep before her shearers is dumb, so he openeth not his mouth. . . . And he made his grave with the wicked, and with the rich in his death; because he had done no violence, neither was any deceit in his mouth.

Hosea 13:14—I will ransom them from the power of the grave; I will redeem them from death: O death, I will be thy plagues; O grave, I will be thy destruction: repentance shall be hid from mine eyes.

Jonah 1:17—Now the LORD had prepared a great fish to swallow up Jonah. And Jonah was in the belly of the fish three days and three nights. (compare with Matt. 12:38–40; see also Matt. 16:4; Luke 11:29–30)

The concept of Jesus as the Lamb of God was made a regular part of the worship of ancient Israel through the ritual sacrifice of a lamb "without blemish" (Ex. 12:5)—one per household—during the Passover:

> And the blood shall be to you for a token upon the houses where ye are: and when I see the blood, I will pass over you, and the plague shall not be upon you to destroy you, when I smite the land of Egypt.
>
> And this day shall be unto you for a memorial; and ye shall keep it a feast to the Lord throughout your generations; ye shall keep it a feast by an ordinance for ever. (Ex. 12:13–14)

Isaiah celebrated the symbolism of the Lamb of God with these words:

> He is brought as a lamb to the slaughter, and as a sheep before her shearers is dumb, so he openeth not his mouth. . . . when thou shalt make his soul an offering for sin, he shall see his seed, he shall prolong his days, and the pleasure of the Lord shall prosper in his hand. (Isa. 53:7, 10)

The glorious atonement and resurrection of the Savior was the crowning triumph of His ministry. In Hannah's song of praise, we hear: "The LORD killeth, and maketh alive: he bringeth down to the grave, and bringeth up" (1 Sam. 2:6). Job extols the divine gift of the restoration of life: "And though after my skin worms destroy this body, yet in my flesh shall I see God: Whom I shall see for myself, and mine eyes shall behold, and not another; though my reins be consumed within me" (Job 19:26–27). The Psalmist foresees the eventual purification and enlivenment of the soul: "Therefore my heart is glad, and my glory rejoiceth: my flesh also shall rest in hope. For thou wilt not leave my soul in hell; neither wilt thou suffer thine Holy One to see corruption" (Ps. 16:9–10). Isaiah prophesies of the Lord's conquest over death: "He will swallow up death in victory; and the Lord GOD will wipe away tears from off all faces; and the rebuke of his people shall he take away from off all the earth: for the LORD hath spoken it" (Isa. 25:8). And again, "Thy dead men shall live, together with my dead body shall they arise. Awake and sing, ye that dwell in dust: for thy dew is as the dew of herbs, and the earth shall cast out the dead" (Isa. 26:19). Hosea likewise celebrates the Savior's eventual supremacy over the forces of destruction: "I will ransom them from the power of the grave; I will redeem them from death: O death, I will be thy plagues; O grave, I will be thy destruction: repentance shall be hid from mine eyes" (Hosea 13:14).

Out of the shadowy abyss of divine suffering emerged triumphant the glory of the redemption and the atonement. The Old Testament account repeatedly celebrates this eternal victory:

For the life of the flesh is in the blood: and I have given it to you upon the altar to make an atonement for your souls: for it is the blood that maketh an atonement for the soul. (Lev. 17:11; compare Lev. 4:20–35)

For I know that my redeemer liveth, and that he shall stand at the latter day upon the earth. (Job 19:25)

Fear not, thou worm Jacob, and ye men of Israel; I will help thee, saith the Lord, and thy redeemer, the Holy One of Israel. (Isa. 41:14)

He hath poured out his soul unto death: and he was numbered with the transgressors; and he bare the sin of many, and made intercession for the transgressors. (Isa. 53:12)

For thy Maker is thine husband; the Lord of hosts is his name; and thy Redeemer the Holy One of Israel; The God of the whole earth shall he be called. (Isa. 54:5)

I will mention the lovingkindnesses of the Lord, and the praises of the LORD, according to all that the LORD hath bestowed on us, and the great goodness toward the house of Israel, which he hath bestowed on them according to his mercies, and according to the multitude of his lovingkindnesses.

For he said, Surely they are my people, children that will not lie: so he was their Saviour.

In all their affliction he was afflicted, and the angel of his presence saved them: in his love and in his pity he redeemed them; and he bare them, and carried them all the days of old. (Isa. 63:7–9; see also Hosea 13:4–14; Hab. 3:2–18)

Thus the Old Testament prophets expressed their inspired witness of the coming work of the Redeemer of mankind.

In the same exultant spirit, the ancient prophets confirmed Jesus as the Savior who would at a future time be born into the world. Consider these passages:

Exodus 15:2—The LORD is my strength and song, and he is become my salvation: he is my God, and I will prepare him an habitation; my father's God, and I will exalt him.

Psalm 27:1—The LORD is my light and my salvation; whom shall I fear? the Lord is the strength of my life; of whom shall I be afraid?

Isaiah 43:3, 11—For I am the Lord thy God, the Holy One of Israel, thy Saviour: . . . I, even I, am the LORD; and beside me there is no saviour.

Isaiah 43:25—I, even I, am he that blotteth out thy transgressions for mine own sake, and will not remember thy sins.

Isaiah 45:15—Verily thou art a God that hidest thyself, O God of Israel, the Saviour.

Joel 2:23, 26–27, 32—Be glad then, ye children of Zion, and rejoice in the LORD your God . . . And ye shall eat in plenty, and be satisfied, and praise the name of the LORD your God, that hath dealt wondrously with you: and my people shall never be ashamed. And ye shall know that I am in the midst of Israel, and that I am the LORD your God, and none else: and my people shall never be ashamed. . . . And it shall come to pass, that whosoever shall call on the name of the LORD shall be delivered: for in mount Zion and in Jerusalem shall be deliverance, as the LORD hath said, and in the remnant whom the LORD shall call.

Qualities of Jesus

Jesus the Atoning One is the singularly most potent prototype of the set of qualities that belong to "Saviorhood": loving, obedient, redeeming, perfect, spotless. He is so loving that He verily weeps when we fall short of our potential: "Wherefore, he suffereth for their sins; inasmuch as they will repent in the day that my Chosen shall return unto me, and until that day they shall be in torment; Wherefore, for this shall the heavens weep, yea, and all the workmanship of mine hands" (Moses 7:39–40). At the same time, He rejoices when we repent and follow in His footsteps: "For, behold, the Lord your Redeemer suffered death in the flesh; wherefore he suffered the pain of all men, that all men might repent and come unto him. And he hath risen again from the dead, that he might bring all men unto him, on conditions of repentance. And how great is his joy in the soul that repenteth!" (D&C 18:11–13).

King

Jehovah, the "Unchangeable One," was anointed in the premortal realm as Messiah and Christ to lay the foundation of the world through the Creation and serve as the author of eternal salvation by coming to live among mortals in obedience to the will of the Father, for the purpose of completing His atoning mission as Jesus, thus becoming the Savior to all the world. In the final chapter of the history of this world, Jesus Christ will return in glory as King, Judge, Lawgiver, Mediator, Advocate, and Prince of Peace to usher in the Millennial Reign and take His place as the covenant Father of all the righteous and redeemed.

With great clarity, the Old Testament account confirms this divine design of consummation and the ultimate royal ascension of the Son to the throne of glory. The return of the Redeemer at the Second Coming is anticipated by the voices of many prophets:

Job—For I know that my redeemer liveth, and that he shall stand at the latter day upon the earth. (Job 19:25)

David—Lift up your heads, O ye gates; and be ye lift up, ye everlasting doors; and the King of glory shall come in. Who is this King of glory? The LORD strong and mighty, the LORD mighty in battle. Lift up your heads, O ye gates; even lift them up, ye everlasting doors; and the King of glory shall come in. Who is this King of glory? The LORD of hosts, he is the King of glory. (Ps. 24:7–10)

When the LORD shall build up Zion, he shall appear in his glory. (Ps. 102:16)

Isaiah—The voice of him that crieth in the wilderness, Prepare ye the way of the LORD, make straight in the desert a highway for our God. Every valley shall be exalted, and every mountain and hill shall be made low: and the crooked shall be made straight, and the rough places plain: And the glory of the Lord shall be revealed, and all flesh shall see it together: for the mouth of the LORD hath spoken it" (Isa. 40:3–5).

How beautiful upon the mountains are the feet of him that bringeth good tidings, that publisheth peace; that bringeth good tidings of good, that publisheth salvation; that saith unto Zion, Thy God reigneth! Thy watchmen shall lift up the voice; with the voice together shall they sing: for they shall see eye to eye, when the LORD shall bring again Zion. Break forth into joy, sing together, ye waste places of Jerusalem: for the LORD hath comforted his people, he hath redeemed Jerusalem. The LORD hath made bare his holy arm in the eyes of all the nations; and all the ends of the earth shall see the salvation of our God. (Isa. 52:7–10; compare Isa. 45:23; 49:10–12; 60:1–3, 19–21; 63:1–4)

Ezekiel—I will overturn, overturn, overturn, it [iniquity]: and it shall be no more, until he come whose right it is; and I will give it him. (Ezek. 21:27)

Daniel—I saw in the night visions, and, behold, one like the Son of man came with the clouds of heaven, and came to the Ancient of days, and they brought him near before him. (Dan. 7:13)

Joel—The sun and the moon shall be darkened, and the stars shall withdraw their shining. The LORD also shall roar out of Zion, and utter his voice from Jerusalem; and the heavens and the earth shall shake: but the LORD will be the hope of his people, and the strength of the children of Israel. So shall ye know that I am the LORD your God dwelling in Zion, my holy mountain: then shall Jerusalem be holy, and there shall no strangers pass through her any more. (Joel 3:15–17)

Micah—For, behold, the Lord cometh forth out of his place, and will come down, and tread upon the high places of the earth. And the mountains shall be molten under him, and the valleys shall be cleft, as wax before the fire, and as the waters that are poured down a steep place. (Micah 1:3–4)

Haggai—For thus saith the LORD of hosts; Yet once, it is a little while, and I will shake the heavens, and the earth, and the sea, and the dry land; And I will shake all nations, and the desire of all nations shall come: and I will fill this house with glory, saith the LORD of hosts. (Hag. 2:6–7)

Zechariah—And it shall come to pass in that day, that I will seek to destroy all the nations that come against Jerusalem. And I will pour upon the house of David, and upon the inhabitants of Jerusalem, the spirit of grace and of supplications: and they shall look upon me whom they have pierced, and they shall mourn for him, as one mourneth for his only son, and shall be in bitterness for him, as one that is in bitterness for his firstborn. (Zech. 12:9–10)

And his feet shall stand in that day upon the mount of Olives, which is before Jerusalem on the east, and the mount of Olives shall cleave in the midst thereof toward the east and toward the west, and there shall be a very great valley; and half of the mountain shall remove toward the north, and half of it toward the south. . . . And it shall be in that day, that living waters shall go out from Jerusalem; half of them toward the former sea, and half of them toward the hinder sea: in summer and in winter shall it be. And the LORD shall be king over all the earth: in that day shall there be one LORD, and his name one. (Zech. 14:4, 8–9)

Malachi—Behold, I will send my messenger, and he shall prepare the way before me: and the Lord, whom ye seek, shall suddenly come to his temple, even the messenger of the covenant, whom ye delight in: behold, he shall come, saith the LORD of hosts. But who may abide the day of his coming? and who shall stand when he appeareth? for he is like a refiner's fire, and like fullers' soap: And he shall sit as a refiner and purifier of silver: and he shall purify the sons of Levi, and purge them as gold and silver, that they may offer unto the Lord an offering in righteousness. (Mal. 3:1–3)

The Millennial Reign of the Lord is predicted with prophetic certainty throughout the ancient record and described as having the following characteristics:

Everlasting—I will sing of the mercies of the Lord for ever: with my mouth will I make known thy faithfulness to all generations. For I have said, Mercy shall be built up for ever: thy faithfulness shalt thou establish in the very heavens. I have made a covenant with my chosen, I have sworn unto David my servant, Thy seed will I establish for ever, and build up thy throne to all generations. (Ps. 89:2–4)

Theocratic—For unto us a child is born, unto us a son is given: and the government shall be upon his shoulder: and his name shall be called Wonderful, Counsellor, The mighty God, The everlasting Father, The Prince of Peace. Of the increase of his government and peace there shall be no end, upon the throne of David, and upon his kingdom, to order it, and to establish it with judgment and with justice from henceforth even for ever. The zeal of the Lord of hosts will perform this. (Isa. 9:6–7)

Merciful—And in mercy shall the throne be established: and he shall sit upon it in truth in the tabernacle of David, judging, and seeking judgment, and hasting righteousness. (Isa. 16:5, see also Isa 40:9–11)

Righteous—Behold, the days come, saith the LORD, that I will raise unto David a righteous Branch, and a King shall reign and prosper, and shall execute judgment and justice in the earth. In his days Judah shall be saved, and Israel shall dwell safely: and this is his name whereby he shall be called, THE LORD OUR RIGHTEOUSNESS. (Jer. 23:5–6; compare Zeph. 3:15)

All-Consuming—I saw in the night visions, and, behold, one like the Son of man came with the clouds of heaven, and came to the Ancient of days, and they brought him near before him. And there was given him dominion, and glory, and a kingdom, that all people, nations, and languages, should serve him: his dominion is an everlasting dominion, which shall not pass away, and his kingdom that which shall not be destroyed. (Dan. 7:13–14; compare Dan. 2:44; Zech. 14:1–9)

Joyful—Sing and rejoice, O daughter of Zion: for, lo, I come, and I will dwell in the midst of thee, saith the LORD. And many nations shall be joined to the LORD in that day, and shall be my people: and I will dwell in the midst of thee, and thou shalt know that the LORD of hosts hath sent me unto thee. And the LORD shall inherit Judah his portion in the holy land, and shall choose Jerusalem again. Be silent, O all flesh, before the LORD: for he is raised up out of his holy habitation. (Zech. 2:10–13)

Glorious—Who is this King of glory? The LORD of hosts, he is the King of glory. (Ps. 24:10; compare Ex. 33:18–23; 40:34–35; Isa. 6:3; 40:5; 60:1–2; Ezek. 1:26–28; Zech. 2:5)

The ushering in of the Millennial Reign is a time of universal judgment, as the scriptural record confirms:

The adversaries of the LORD shall be broken to pieces; out of heaven shall he thunder upon them: the LORD shall judge the ends of the earth; and he shall give strength unto his king, and exalt the horn of his anointed. (1 Sam. 2:10; compare Gen. 18:25; Deut. 32:36; Judg. 11:27)

And he shall judge the world in righteousness, he shall minister judgment to the people in uprightness. (Ps. 9:8; see also Pss. 7:8–11; 50:6; 58:11; 72:2–19; 82:8; 94:2; 96:10–13; Eccl. 3:17; 12:14; Isa. 2:4; 3:14; 5:16)

And he shall not judge after the sight of his eyes, neither reprove after the hearing of his ears: But with righteousness shall he judge the poor, and reprove with equity for the meek of the earth: and he shall smite the earth with the rod of his mouth, and with the breath of his lips shall he slay the wicked. (Isa. 11:3–4)

For the LORD is our judge, the LORD is our lawgiver, the LORD is our king; he will save us. (Isa. 33:22; compare Isa. 51:5; see also Jer. 23:2–8; Joel 3:12)

All the prophets down through the ages have spoken of the final judgment and the responsibility of man—according to his God-given agency and stewardship—to account for his every thought and deed. The Savior Himself declared to the Nephites:

And it shall come to pass, that whoso repenteth and is baptized in my name shall be filled; and if he endureth to the end, behold, him will I hold guiltless before my Father at that day when I shall stand to judge the world.

And he that endureth not unto the end, the same is he that is also hewn down and cast into the fire, from whence they can no more return, because of the justice of the Father. (3 Ne. 27:16–17)

Qualities of the King

As presented in the scriptural account of the Millennial Reign, the Great Jehovah will consummate the final judgment and disposition of mankind by being just, merciful, righteous, full of grace, holy, and glorious. These are the qualities of His royal office. Alma provides perhaps the most compelling summary of the implementation of these qualities by the Savior as part of the plan of salvation:

And thus he shall bring salvation to all those who shall believe on his name; this being the intent of this last sacrifice, to bring about the bowels of mercy, which overpowereth justice, and bringeth about means unto men that they may have faith unto repentance.

And thus mercy can satisfy the demands of justice, and encircles them in the arms of safety, while he that exercises no faith unto repentance is exposed to the whole law of the demands of justice; therefore only unto him that has faith unto repentance is brought about the great and eternal plan of redemption. (Alma 34:15–16)

Our joy and peace in this world and the world to come will depend on the degree to which we can cultivate these qualities within our character, together with all others that pertain to the mission of the Lord as our eternal exemplar.

Summary

The overarching reach of divine influence in the lives of God's children traces a pattern of magnanimous grace and love on the part of the Lord. From Jehovah (the "Unchangeable One" and First Born), to Messiah or Christ ("Anointed"), to Creator, to Emmanuel ("God Among Us") to Jesus ("Jehovah is Help" or Savior), and finally to King, we can trace the means of which He sustains and perfects His immortal sovereignty as our Master and Redeemer, having glorified the Father through uncompromising obedience.

By using the portrait of the Savior that is unfolded to our view in the ancient canon of scripture and expanded and augmented through modern-day revelation, we can bring to our study of the gospel a guiding lens through which we can discern the truth of God's design for our spiritual growth and perfection. In the final analysis, we perceive in His divine career many titles and offices, but only one Lord; many qualities, but only one unified manifestation of divine love; many influences and interactions with mankind, but only one cause: "to bring to pass the immortality and eternal life of man" (Moses 1:39).

From the days of Adam, it was made known unto the children of men that all things pertaining to this mission of salvation and exaltation must be accomplished through the name of Jesus Christ, our Lord, and through His name alone:

> And he called upon our father Adam by his own voice, saying: I am God; I made the world, and men before they were in the flesh. And he also said unto him: If thou wilt turn unto me, and hearken unto my voice, and believe, and repent of all thy transgressions, and be baptized, even in water, in the name of mine Only Begotten Son, who is full of grace and truth, which is Jesus Christ, the only name which shall be given under heaven, whereby salvation shall come unto the children of men, ye shall receive the gift of the Holy Ghost, asking all things in his name, and whatsoever ye shall ask, it shall be given you. (Moses 6:51–52; compare 2 Ne. 31:21; Mosiah 3:17)

"LET THERE BE LIGHT": CREATION

MOMENT OF TRUTH

President J. Reuben Clark Jr. gives a brief synopsis of the first days of the Creation:

> First, formless, voidless matter and darkness; the coming of light, its division from darkness into day and night; the division of the waters, below and above the firmament (clouds of watery vapor); the gathering together of the waters below the firmament into the seas; the appearance of the dry land; the coming of vegetable life; the unveiling of the sun and moon and the appearance of the stars as the skies cleared; the full shining of the sun and moon, along with the stars, now showing in their places in the heavens in the great already existing galactic firmament where there was yet space that existed possibly eons before; and so on down to the final creations of all things in orderly progression,—all indescribably glorious, clothed with the eternal beauty of the divine creation, all down where there were space and materials. (*Behold the Lamb of God* [Salt Lake City: Deseret Book, 1991], 37)

Then followed the creation of the animals and lastly of man—the crowning glory of God's eternal design.

MODERN PROPHETS SPEAK

Bruce R. McConkie:
> We are frank to admit that our knowledge of the creation of the universe, of this earth, of man, and of all living things is meager—perhaps almost miniscule—as compared to what there is to learn. But the Lord has revealed to us as much about the mystery of creation as is necessary for us in our probationary estate.

He has revealed to us the basic verities which enable us to understand the true doctrine of creation. This doctrine is that the Lord Jesus Christ is both the Creator and the Redeemer of this earth and all that on it is, save only man. It is that the Lord God himself, the Father of us all, came down and created man, male and female, in his own image and likeness. It is that the earth and all else were created in a paradisaical state so there could be a fall. It is that the Great Creator became the Redeemer so he could ransom men from the effects of the Fall, thereby bringing to pass the immortality and eternal life of man. It is that the Creation, the Fall, and the Atonement are the three pillars of eternity. It is that all who accept him as both the Creator and the Redeemer have power to become joint-heirs with him and thereby inherit all that his Father hath. ("Christ and the Creation," *Ensign,* June 1982, 15)

DOCTRINES AND PRINCIPLES

Robert J. Matthews describes the purpose for this magnificent act:

The Creation was done for a specific purpose. Latter-day revelation shows that the purpose of the earth is (1) to provide a place for our spirits to get a body of flesh and bones, (2) to provide a place for embodied spirits to live in a probationary state, and (3) to provide eventually an eternal celestial sphere upon which those beings who lived on this earth may dwell—a sanctified place which even God the Father will visit. The scriptures explain that the earth was deliberately formed or organized for these very definite purposes. (Robert J. Matthews, *A Bible! A Bible!* [Salt Lake City: Bookcraft, 1990], 171)

FAMILY *of* GOD: ADAM *and* EVE *and the* FALL

MOMENT OF TRUTH

The stage for the unfolding of this famous story is set, following the Creation, with God's action relative to the man created in His own image and likeness:

> And I, the Lord God, took the man, and put him into the Garden of Eden, to dress it, and to keep it.
>
> And I, the Lord God, commanded the man, saying: Of every tree of the garden thou mayest freely eat,
>
> But of the tree of the knowledge of good and evil, thou shalt not eat of it, nevertheless, thou mayest choose for thyself, for it is given unto thee; but, remember that I forbid it, for in the day thou eatest thereof thou shalt surely die. (Moses 3:15–17)

When Satan came on the scene, having been cast out of the pre-mortal realm as a rebel through the power of the Only Begotten (Moses 4:3), he initiated the work of evil in the world by tempting Eve:

> And he said unto the woman: Yea, hath God said—Ye shall not eat of every tree of the garden? (And he spake by the mouth of the serpent.)
>
> And the woman said unto the serpent: We may eat of the fruit of the trees of the garden;
>
> But of the fruit of the tree which thou beholdest in the midst of the garden, God hath said—Ye shall not eat of it, neither shall ye touch it, lest ye die.
>
> And the serpent said unto the woman: Ye shall not surely die;
>
> For God doth know that in the day ye eat thereof, then your eyes shall be opened, and ye shall be as gods, knowing good and evil.

> And when the woman saw that the tree was good for food, and that it became pleasant to the eyes, and a tree to be desired to make her wise, she took of the fruit thereof, and did eat, and also gave unto her husband with her, and he did eat.
>
> And the eyes of them both were opened, and they knew that they had been naked. And they sewed fig-leaves together and made themselves aprons. (Moses 4:7–13)

The Fall was a pivotal point in the development of mankind. Because of the transgression of Adam and Eve, they were expelled from the Garden of Eden:

> And unto Adam, I, the Lord God, said: Because thou hast hearkened unto the voice of thy wife, and hast eaten of the fruit of the tree of which I commanded thee, saying—Thou shalt not eat of it, cursed shall be the ground for thy sake; in sorrow shalt thou eat of it all the days of thy life.
>
> Thorns also, and thistles shall it bring forth to thee, and thou shalt eat the herb of the field.
>
> By the sweat of thy face shalt thou eat bread, until thou shalt return unto the ground—for thou shalt surely die—for out of it wast thou taken: for dust thou wast, and unto dust shalt thou return. (Moses 4:23–25)

The Lord caused that cherubim and a flaming sword should be deployed to prevent Adam and Eve from partaking of the tree of life:

> And I, the Lord God, said unto mine Only Begotten: Behold, the man is become as one of us to know good and evil; and now lest he put forth his hand and partake also of the tree of life, and eat and live forever,
>
> Therefore I, the Lord God, will send him forth from the Garden of Eden, to till the ground from whence he was taken;
>
> For as I, the Lord God, liveth, even so my words cannot return void, for as they go forth out of my mouth they must be fulfilled.
>
> So I drove out the man, and I placed at the east of the Garden of Eden, cherubim and a flaming sword, which turned every way to keep the way of the tree of life. (Moses 4:28–31; compare Gen. 3:22–24.)

Instead of granting access to the Garden of Eden once more, the Lord instituted the plan to impart to Adam and Eve and their posterity the plan of salvation, that they might understand and enjoy the blessings of the atonement brought about by the sacrifice of the Savior on the cross—another kind of "tree of life" that ensured immortality for all and eternal life for the faithful and obedient (see Moses 5).

MODERN PROPHETS SPEAK

Bruce R. McConkie:

> The Lord expects us to believe and understand the true doctrine of the Creation—the creation of this earth, of man, and of all forms of life. Indeed, as we shall see, an understanding of the doctrine of creation is essential to salvation. Unless and until we gain a true view of the creation of all things we cannot hope to gain that fulness of eternal reward which otherwise would be ours.
>
> God himself, the Father of us all, ordained and established a plan of salvation whereby his spirit children might advance and progress and become like him. It is the gospel of God, the plan of Eternal Elohim, the system that saves and exalts, and it consists of three things. These three are the very pillars of eternity itself. They are the most important events that ever have or will occur in all eternity. They are the Creation, the Fall, and the Atonement.
>
> Before we can even begin to understand the temporal creation of all things, we must know how and in what manner these three eternal verities—the Creation, the Fall, and the Atonement—are inseparably woven together to form one plan of salvation. No one of them stands alone; each of them ties into the other two; and without a knowledge of all of them, it is not possible to know the truth about any one of them. ("Christ and the Creation," *Ensign,* June 1982, 9)

DOCTRINES AND PRINCIPLES

Our understanding about the Fall comes primarily from modern-day scriptures, in particular the Book of Mormon and the book of Moses. The Fall was part of the plan of redemption brought about "in the wisdom of him who knoweth all things" (2 Ne. 2:24). Robert J. Matthews makes this observation:

> If Adam and Eve had been created mortal, they would have been denied one of the steps in the process that they were capable of performing themselves. As we read in the Book of Mormon, man "brought upon himself" his own fall (Alma 42:12). Since the Fall was a necessary part of the plan of salvation, and since man was capable of bringing about the fallen condition himself, he was required—or rather it was his privilege—to take the necessary steps. (*A Bible! A Bible!* [Salt Lake City: Bookcraft, 1990], 186)

Prior to the Fall, Adam and Eve were in a state of innocence, knowing no joy or misery (see 2 Ne. 2:23). Conflicting commandments were given to Adam and Eve. They were commanded not to partake of the fruit of the tree of knowledge of good and evil (Moses 3:17). At the same time, they were told to multiply and replenish the earth (Moses 2:28). They could not keep the first commandment without breaking the second (2 Ne. 2:25; Moses 5:11). Joseph Fielding Smith comments on this paradox:

> Just why the Lord would say to Adam that he forbade him to partake of the fruit of that tree is not made clear in the Bible account, but in the original as it comes to us in the Book of Moses it is made definitely clear. It is that the Lord said to Adam that if he wished to remain as he was in the garden, then he was not to eat the fruit, but if he desired to eat it and partake of death he was at liberty to do so. So really it was not in the true sense a transgression of a divine commandment. Adam made the wise decision, in fact the only decision that he could make.
>
> It was the divine plan from the very beginning that man should be placed on the earth and be subject to mortal conditions and pass through a probationary state as explained in the Book of Mormon where he and his posterity would be subject to all mortal conditions. It was part of the divine plan that man should have this period of mortality where he would be shut out of the presence of God and be subject to all the vicissitudes of mortality, the temptations and trials of the flesh, thus gaining experience and being placed in a position of trial, temptation, and be purified by passing through the trials and tribulations of the flesh, or mortality, as Paul has described it. This life is a very brief part of our existence, but is the most critical, for it is in mortality where we are tried and figuratively placed in the fire and tested, proved to see what kind of material we are made of, whether we will be worthy of an exaltation in the kingdom of God or be assigned to some other kingdom. (*AGQ,* 4:81–82)

Clearly, as the Fall came by free choice of man, so salvation through the Atonement must come in the same manner.

Eve was beguiled by Satan and partook of the fruit of the tree of knowledge of good and evil and then gave it to Adam (see Moses 4:12). Their eyes were opened, and they realized that they were naked and made aprons for themselves (see Moses 4:13). The Lord God appeared, and Adam and Eve confessed to their transgression. They were cast out of the garden (see Moses 4:29–31).

In the world, Adam and Eve prayed, and the Lord commanded them to offer the firstlings of the flock as an offering unto the Lord (see Moses 5:4–5). Adam was faithfully obedient to the Lord's commandments, not fully understanding why he was to offer a sacrifice (see Moses 5:6). In this context, Bruce R. McConkie taught:

> Baptism and sacrifice both began with Adam. We have seen how the angelic ministrant revealed to him that his sacrificial performances were in "similitude of the sacrifice of the Only Begotten of the Father" (Moses 5:7). We must also remember that God, "by his own voice," taught Adam about faith, repentance, baptism, and the gift

of the Holy Ghost, and "that Adam cried unto the Lord, and he was caught away by the Spirit of the Lord, and was carried down into the water, and was laid under the water, and was brought forth out of the water. And thus he was baptized, and the Spirit of God descended upon him, and thus he was born of the Spirit, and became quickened in the inner man. And he heard a voice out of heaven, saying: "Thou art baptized with fire, and with the Holy Ghost" (Moses 6:51–66). (*The Mortal Messiah: From Bethlehem to Calvary* [Salt Lake City: Deseret Book, 1981], 1:395)

Robert L. Millet and Kent P. Jackson go on to explain the antiquity of the gospel:

One of the powerful contributions of the Pearl of Great Price is an insight into the nature of Christ's Eternal Gospel, the revelation to the Church and the world that Christian doctrine and Christian ordinances have been taught by Christian prophets since the days of Adam. Much of what has been delivered through Joseph Smith and his successors is a restoration—not alone of the first century Christian Church—but of those matters which pertain to the ancient of days and have their origins in the earth's primeval period of temporal existence. Adam was told by an angel that he was to do all that he did in the name of the Son, and that he and his posterity were to repent and call upon the Father in the name of the Son forevermore (Moses 5:8). Adam was further instructed—four thousand years before the time of the Master— that Jesus Christ is "the only name which shall be given under heaven, whereby salvation shall come unto the children of men" (Moses 6:52). In like fashion, Enoch, looking down through the stream of time, "saw the day of the coming of the Son of Man, even in the flesh; and his soul rejoiced, saying: The Righteous is lifted up, and the Lamb is slain from the foundation of the world" (Moses 7:47). (*Studies in Scripture: The Pearl of Great Price* [Salt Lake City, Randall Book: 1985], 8)

Adam and Eve blessed God and began to teach the plan of redemption to their children (see Moses 5:12). Bruce C. Hafen and Marie K. Hafen comment:

As the descendants of Adam and Eve then become accountable for their own sins at the age of eight, they all taste sin to one degree or another as the result of their curiosity and their experiences with temptation in a free environment. Those whose cumulative experience leads them to love "Satan more than God" (Moses 5:28) will to that degree become "carnal, sensual, and devilish" (Moses 5:13; 6:49) by nature— "natural men." On the other hand, those who accept Christ's grace by their faith, repentance, baptism, and continued striving will yield to the "enticings of the Holy Spirit," put off "the natural man," and become "saint[s] through the atonement of Christ the Lord" (Mosiah 3:19). Thus, after taking the initiative by faith to accept the grace made available by the Atonement, one may then nourish one's faith by obedience that interacts with grace until one "becomes a saint" by nature, thereby enjoy-ing eternal or godlike life. (*The Belonging Heart: The Atonement and Relationships with God and Family* [Salt Lake City: Deseret Book, 1994], 111–12)

The plan requires opposition (see 2 Ne. 2:11). The law of opposition in all things is an eternal verity. Larry E. Dahl demonstrates it well:

> There just have to be exalted purposes in all this testing. The scriptures help to iden-tify some. Lehi explained that without opposition, neither righteousness nor happi-ness could be brought about (2 Ne. 2:11). In a revelation to Joseph Smith the Lord said, "If they never should have the bitter they could not know the sweet" (D&C 29:39; see also Moses 6:55). To Brigham Young came the word that "my people must be tried in all things, that they may be prepared to receive the glory that I have for them, even the glory of Zion," though just how it prepares them is not said (D&C 136:31). The Lord indicates that being chastened and tried is a prerequisite to being sanctified (D&C 101:4–5). James taught that the "trying of your faith worketh patience" (James 1:3). We learn from 2 Chronicles 32:31 that being tried exposes the heart: "God left him, to try him, that he might know all that was in his heart." Note what Christ's suffering did for him, in addition to all that it did for us. Alma taught, "And he will take upon him their infirmities, that his bowels may be filled with mercy, according to the flesh, that he may know according to the flesh how to succor his peo-ple according to their infirmities" (Alma 7:12). Paul wrote, "For in that he himself hath suffered being tempted, he is able to succour them that are tempted" (Heb. 2:18). In Abraham's case, his trial, being "a similitude of God and his Only Begotten Son" (Jacob 4:5), brought to him a piercing understanding of Another's feelings. The same is true for all of us—experiencing trials can bring deep empathy. (Richard D. Draper, ed., *A Witness of Jesus Christ: The 1989 Sperry Symposium on the Old Testament* [Salt Lake City: Deseret Book, 1990], 63–64)

We are free to choose eternal life through the Lord Jesus Christ or captivity and death according to the devil (see 2 Ne. 2:27).

Neal A. Maxwell reminds us of the power of our choices and how our choices (or the lack of them) eternally affect our fate. He said:

> Individuals who thus excuse themselves from joy do so by measurable and on-the-record acts of free will. These acts are, alas, demonstrably adverse to their own interests. We are, "according to the flesh," free to choose (2 Ne. 2:27), free to act for ourselves, or we can merely wait passively to be acted upon: "And now remem-ber, remember, my brethren, that whosoever perisheth, perisheth unto himself; and

whosoever doeth iniquity, doeth it unto himself; for behold, ye are free; ye are permitted to act for yourselves; for behold, God hath given unto you a knowledge and he hath made you free" (Hel. 14:30; see also 2 Ne. 10:23). (*Meek and Lowly* [Salt Lake City: Deseret Book, 1987], 90–91)

ATONEMENT: THE SYMBOLISM *of* ADAM'S SACRIFICE

MOMENT OF TRUTH

One of the great stories in the ancient record of God's dealings with man is the incident in the life of Adam and Eve where they are obedient to the voice of the Lord in offering sacrifices. Because they had been evicted from the Garden of Eden as a result of transgression, they were no longer in the presence of God, but they still heard His voice speaking to them from the direction of the Garden, giving them counsel and instructions on how to conduct their lives. The account of this singularly important incident and the subsequent experiences of Adam and Eve is contained in Moses:

> And Adam and Eve, his wife, called upon the name of the Lord, and they heard the voice of the Lord from the way toward the Garden of Eden, speaking unto them, and they saw him not; for they were shut out from his presence.
>
> And he gave unto them commandments, that they should worship the Lord their God, and should offer the firstlings of their flocks, for an offering unto the Lord. And Adam was obedient unto the commandments of the Lord.
>
> And after many days an angel of the Lord appeared unto Adam, saying: Why dost thou offer sacrifices unto the Lord? And Adam said unto him: I know not, save the Lord commanded me.
>
> And then the angel spake, saying: This thing is a similitude of the sacrifice of the Only Begotten of the Father, which is full of grace and truth.
>
> Wherefore, thou shalt do all that thou doest in the name of the Son, and thou shalt repent and call upon God in the name of the Son forevermore.
>
> And in that day the Holy Ghost fell upon Adam, which beareth record of the Father and the Son, saying: I am the Only Begotten of the Father from the beginning, henceforth and forever, that as thou hast fallen thou mayest be redeemed, and all mankind, even as many as will. (Moses 5:4–9)

This moment of truth constituted the birth of the process by means of which the Lord, in His mercy and grace, taught the gospel of salvation to His children. Adam had acted in faith to obey the commandment to worship the Lord and offer up the firstlings of the flock. He was taught by the angel of the Lord the principle of repentance. His mind was focused now on the Savior as the central aim of his faith and worship—for the Savior alone could bring about the means for overcoming the Fall through the atonement. Then Adam received the Holy Ghost as a spiritual confirmation of these verities.

In the next episode of this story we observe how Adam and Eve responded to this extraordinary lesson:

> And in that day Adam blessed God and was filled, and began to prophesy concerning all the families of the earth, saying: Blessed be the name of God, for because of my transgression my eyes are opened, and in this life I shall have joy, and again in the flesh I shall see God.
>
> And Eve, his wife, heard all these things and was glad, saying: Were it not for our transgression we never should have had seed, and never should have known good and evil, and the joy of our redemption, and the eternal life which God giveth unto all the obedient.
>
> And Adam and Eve blessed the name of God, and they made all things known unto their sons and their daughters. (Moses 5:10–12)

Thus was inaugurated the process through which the mighty change of heart could take place for those who respond to the invitation of the Lord to follow Him and keep His commandments (compare Mosiah 5:2–3; Alma 5:13–14).

MODERN PROPHETS SPEAK

Gordon B. Hinckley:

> I cannot be grateful enough for the Atonement wrought by my Savior and my Redeemer. Through His sacrifice at the culmination of a life of perfection—that sacrifice offered in pain unspeakable—the bonds of death were broken, and the resurrection of all became assured. Beyond this, the doors of celestial glory have been opened to all who will accept divine truth and obey its precepts. ("My Testimony," *Ensign,* November 1993, 52)

Gordon B. Hinckley:

> I sense in a measure the meaning of His atonement. I cannot comprehend it all. It is so vast in its reach and yet so intimate in its effect that it defies comprehension. When all is said and done, when all of history is examined, when the deepest depths of the human mind have been explored, there is nothing so wonderful, so majestic,

so tremendous as this act of grace when the Son of the Almighty, the prince of His Father's royal household, . . . gave his life in ignominy and pain so that all of the sons and daughters of God, of all generations of time, every one of whom must die, might walk again and live eternally. (*TGBH*, 28)

James E. Talmage:

The individual effect of the atonement makes it possible for any and every soul to obtain absolution from the effect of personal sins, through the mediation of Christ; but such saving intercession is to be invoked by individual effort as manifested through faith, repentance, and continued works of righteousness. The laws under which individual salvation is obtainable have been prescribed by Christ, whose right it is to say how the blessings made possible by His own sacrifice shall be administered. All men are in need of the Savior's mediation, for all are transgressors. So taught the apostles of old: "For all have sinned, and come short of the glory of God." And again: "If we say that we have no sin, we deceive ourselves, and the truth is not in us." That the blessing of redemption from individual sins, while open for all to attain, is nevertheless conditioned on individual effort, is as plainly declared as is the truth of unconditional redemption from death as an effect of the fall. There is a judgment ordained for all, and all will be judged "according to their works." The free agency of man enables him to choose or reject, to follow the path of life or the road that leads to destruction; therefore it is but just that he be held to answer for the exercise of his power of choice and that he meet the results of his acts. (*Articles of Faith* [Salt Lake City: Deseret Book, 1981], 81)

DOCTRINES AND PRINCIPLES

Understanding the atonement of Christ and its relationship to our eternal existence is the greatest knowledge we can have in support of our quest to return to God. The atonement is the center of the gospel of Jesus Christ. When we diligently apply its principles to our lives through the covenant process—faith unto repentance, baptism, and receiving the gift of the Holy Ghost—we become liberated from the fallen state we are in. We become free through Christ by obedience. Yet it is by the grace of God that we are saved, after all we can do (2 Ne. 25:23). It is by such means that the atonement will draw us to the Lord. The reality of the atonement demonstrates the tender mercy and the goodness of God, who gave His Only Begotten Son for the salvation of mankind.

The following Old Testament scriptures symbolize or refer to the future atonement that would be wrought for the salvation of mankind through the Lord.

Leviticus 9:7—And Moses said unto Aaron, Go unto the altar, and offer thy sin offering, and thy burnt offering, and make an atonement for thyself, and for the people: and offer the offering of the people, and make an atonement for them; as the Lord commanded.

Leviticus 17:11—For the life of the flesh is in the blood: and I have given it to you upon the altar to make an atonement for your souls: for it is the blood that maketh an atonement for the soul.

Isaiah 53:6—All we like sheep have gone astray; we have turned every one to his own way; and the Lord hath laid on him the iniquity of us all.

Zechariah 9:11—As for thee also, by the blood of thy covenant I have sent forth thy prisoners out of the pit wherein is no water.

The Book of Mormon speaks plainly and clearly of the atonement prior to the coming of the Messiah and His future redeeming ministry:

1 Nephi 11:32–33—And it came to pass that the angel spake unto me again, saying: Look! And I looked and beheld the Lamb of God, that he was taken by the people; yea, the Son of the everlasting God was judged of the world; and I saw and bear record. And I, Nephi, saw that he was lifted up upon the cross and slain for the sins of the world.

2 Nephi 2:6–9—Wherefore, redemption cometh in and through the Holy Messiah; for he is full of grace and truth. Behold, he offereth himself a sacrifice for sin, to answer the ends of the law, unto all those who have a broken heart and a contrite spirit; and unto none else can the ends of the law be answered. Wherefore, how great the importance to make these things known unto the inhabitants of the earth, that they may know that there is no flesh that can dwell in the presence of God, save it be through the merits, and mercy, and grace of the Holy Messiah, who layeth down his life according to the flesh, and taketh it again by the power of the Spirit, that he may bring to pass the resurrection of the dead, being the first that should rise. Wherefore, he is the firstfruits unto God, inasmuch as he shall make intercession for all the children of men; and they that believe in him shall be saved.

2 Nephi 2:26—And the Messiah cometh in the fulness of time, that he may redeem the children of men from the fall. And because that they are redeemed from the fall they have become free forever, knowing good from evil; to act for themselves and not to be acted upon, save it be by the punishment of the law at the great and last day, according to the commandments which God hath given.

The list continues concerning the prophetic statements of the plan of redemption through the atonement of the Lord Jesus Christ: 2 Ne. 9:7–53; 11:5–6; 31:17–20; Jacob 4:11; Mosiah 3:1–9, 12–18; 15:18–28; Alma 7:11–13; 34:8–16; 42:15; Hel. 5:9–12. A beautiful treatise on the atonement is also given in the Bible Dictionary, "Atonement," 617.

PURE *in* HEART: ENOCH

MOMENT OF TRUTH

The story of the prophet Enoch and his ministry (Moses 6–7) is a perennial favorite, for he was truly exemplary as an effective teacher of righteousness. Enoch was taught by his father, Jared, "in all the ways of God" (Moses 6:21). All the prophets in the line of descent from Adam preached righteousness, prophesied, and called the people to repent and exercise faith (see Moses 6:23). Enoch did the same, for he was blessed with the Spirit of God and was called by God to his prophetic office:

> And he heard a voice from heaven, saying: Enoch, my son, prophesy unto this people, and say unto them—Repent, for thus saith the Lord: I am angry with this people, and my fierce anger is kindled against them; for their hearts have waxed hard, and their ears are dull of hearing, and their eyes cannot see afar off;
>
> And for these many generations, ever since the day that I created them, have they gone astray, and have denied me, and have sought their own counsels in the dark; and in their own abominations have they devised murder, and have not kept the commandments, which I gave unto their father, Adam.
>
> Wherefore, they have foresworn themselves, and, by their oaths, they have brought upon themselves death; and a hell I have prepared for them, if they repent not;
>
> And this is a decree, which I have sent forth in the beginning of the world, from my own mouth, from the foundation thereof, and by the mouths of my servants, thy fathers, have I decreed it, even as it shall be sent forth in the world, unto the ends thereof. (Moses 6:27–30)

Enoch was humbled and wondered why he was called, for he was slow of speech. The Lord reassured him saying,

Go forth and do as I have commanded thee, and no man shall pierce thee. Open thy mouth, and it shall be filled, and I will give thee utterance, for all flesh is in my hands, and I will do as seemeth me good.

Say unto this people: Choose ye this day, to serve the Lord God who made you.

Behold my Spirit is upon you, wherefore all thy words will I justify; and the mountains shall flee before you, and the rivers shall turn from their course; and thou shalt abide in me, and I in you; therefore walk with me. (Moses 6:32–34)

Enoch surely was a chosen vessel of the Lord. He received mighty visions and the people recognized that he was a seer. Enoch was enthusiastic in his calling, crying with a loud voice for the people to repent. Because of that, many were offended. Word was circulated that a seer was prophesying and indeed "a wild man hath come among us" (Moses 6:38). The people feared him, and no one dared lay a hand upon him for he "walked with God" (Moses 6:39).

Enoch explained to the people that he had been sent by the Lord to preach to them. He taught them the word of God concerning the Fall and the results of succumbing to the temptations of Satan. He explained to them the commandments given to Adam. He emphasized the coming of Jesus Christ and His mission of redemption and salvation. He admonished them to repent and be baptized and teach these things freely to their children.

Enoch quoted to the people what the Lord had taught Adam:

That by reason of transgression cometh the fall, which fall bringeth death, and inasmuch as ye were born into the world by water, and blood, and the spirit, which I have made, and so became of dust a living soul, even so ye must be born again into the kingdom of heaven, of water, and of the Spirit, and be cleansed by blood, even the blood of mine Only Begotten; that ye might be sanctified from all sin, and enjoy the words of eternal life in this world, and eternal life in the world to come, even immortal glory;

For by the water ye keep the commandment; by the Spirit ye are justified, and by the blood ye are sanctified;

Therefore it is given to abide in you; the record of heaven; the Comforter; the peaceable things of immortal glory; the truth of all things; that which quickeneth all things, which maketh alive all things; that which knoweth all things, and hath all power according to wisdom, mercy, truth, justice, and judgment.

And now, behold, I say unto you: This is the plan of salvation unto all men, through the blood of mine Only Begotten, who shall come in the meridian of time. . . .

And it came to pass, when the Lord had spoken with Adam, our father, that Adam cried unto the Lord, and he was caught away by the Spirit of the Lord, and was carried down into the water, and was laid under the water, and was brought forth out of the water.

And thus he was baptized, and the Spirit of God descended upon him, and thus he was born of the Spirit, and became quickened in the inner man. (Moses 6:59–62, 64–65)

Enoch continued to preach unto the people and tell them of the mighty visions that the Lord continued to open up to his view. So strong was his faith and so miraculous his power of speech that the people heeded his word and followed in the paths of righteousness:

> And the Lord called his people ZION, because they were of one heart and one mind, and dwelt in righteousness; and there was no poor among them.
> And Enoch continued his preaching in righteousness unto the people of God. And it came to pass in his days, that he built a city that was called the City of Holiness, even ZION. (Moses 7:18–19)

The spirit of the city was the Spirit of truth and grace centered in the Holy One of Israel, Jesus Christ, whom Enoch was privileged to see in the unfolding visions with which the Lord blessed him as the prophet/leader of his dispensation. The conclusion of the extraordinary story of Enoch's ministry is summarized in this verse: "And Enoch and all his people walked with God, and he dwelt in the midst of Zion; and it came to pass that Zion was not, for God received it up into his own bosom; and from thence went forth the saying, ZION IS FLED" (Moses 7:69). It is this same city that will again return at the Second Coming to join with the congregations of Saints caught up in the cloud to meet the returning Savior and King (see JST Gen. 9:21–25; D&C 45:12).

MODERN PROPHETS SPEAK

Bruce R. McConkie:
> Those who receive the gospel and join The Church of Jesus Christ of Latter-day Saints have power given them to become the sons of God (D&C 11:30; 35:2; 39:1–6; 45:8; John 1:12). Sonship does not come from church membership alone, but admission into the Church opens the door to such high status, if it is followed by continued faith and devotion (Rom. 8:14–18; Gal. 3:26–29; 4:1–7). The sons of God are members of his family and, hence, are joint-heirs with Christ, inheriting with him the fulness of the Father (D&C 93:17–23). Before gaining entrance to that glorious household, they must receive the higher priesthood (Moses 6:67–68), magnify their callings therein (D&C 84:33–41), enter into the new and everlasting covenant of marriage (D&C 131:1–4; 132), and be obedient in all things (*Doctrines of Salvation*, 2:8–9, 37–41, 59, 64–65). Those who become the sons of God in this life (1 Jn. 3:1–3) are the ones who by enduring in continued righteousness will be gods in eternity (D&C 76:58). (*MD*, 745)

DOCTRINES AND PRINCIPLES

Through the eyes and ministry of Enoch we learn grand truths concerning the power of the priesthood to gather people to holy places and plant in their hearts the commitment to cultivate lasting purity and spirituality.

Enoch was allowed to see all the nations of the earth and their wickedness and the sorrow and weeping of the Lord. He saw into the future and became saddened and wept over his brethren, and he could not be comforted until he saw the coming of the Lord. Enoch witnessed the Savior and His crucifixion and resurrection, and then the Savior gave him a great promise:

> Blessed is he through whose seed Messiah shall come; for he saith—I am Messiah, the King of Zion, the Rock of Heaven, which is broad as eternity; whoso cometh in at the gate and climbeth up by me shall never fall; wherefore, blessed are they of whom I have spoken, for they shall come forth with songs of everlasting joy. (Moses 7:53)

Enoch was then shown the mighty events that would transpire in the future: the Lord's Second Coming, the gathering of His elect, the preparation of a Holy City— "my tabernacle, and it shall be called Zion, a New Jerusalem" (Moses 7:62). Enoch's Zion city will then meet the Lord and the Saints of the New Jerusalem, and there shall be a thousand years of peace.

And thus we see that it is possible to be a Zion people—pure in heart. This is the grand lesson of the story of Enoch. The latter-day prophets have since spoken about the pure in heart with great specificity:

Joseph Smith:

> They [the brethren who leave their families to serve missions] pray our heavenly Father that you may be very prayerful, very humble, and very charitable; working diligently, spiritually and temporally for the redemption of Zion, that the pure in heart may return with songs of everlasting joy to build up her waste places, and meet the Lord when He comes in His glory. Brethren, in the name of Jesus Christ, we entreat you to live worthy of the blessings that shall follow, after much tribulation, to satiate the souls of them that hold out faithful to the end. (*TPJS,* 77)

Brigham Young:

> The Lord has declared it to be his will that his people enter into covenant, even as Enoch and his people did, which of necessity must be before we shall have the privilege of building the Center Stake of Zion, for the power and glory of God will be there, and none but the pure in heart will be able to live and enjoy it. (*Discourses,* 178)

John Taylor:

We ought to have a heaven upon earth—to be really the Zion of our God, the pure in heart, each one seeking another's welfare. "Thou shalt love the Lord thy God with all thy heart, with all thy might, with all thy soul, with all thy strength, and thy neighbor as thyself." (*The Gospel Kingdom: Selections from the Writings and Discourses of John Taylor* [Salt Lake City: Bookcraft, 1944], 72)

Lorenzo Snow:

Let us try to build up Zion. Zion is the pure in heart. Zion cannot be built up except on the principles of union required by the celestial law. It is high time for us to enter into these things. It is more pleasant and agreeable for the Latter-day Saints to enter into this work and build up Zion, than to build up ourselves and have this great competition which is destroying us. (*The Teachings of Lorenzo Snow* [Salt Lake City: Bookcraft, 1984], 181)

Joseph F. Smith:

We firmly believe that Zion—which is the pure in heart—shall escape, if she observes to do all things whatsoever God has commanded; but, in the opposite event, even Zion shall be visited "with sore affliction, with pestilence, with plague, with sword, with vengeance, and with devouring fire" (D&C 97:26). All this that her people may be taught to walk in the light of truth and in the way of the God of their salvation. (*Gospel Doctrine: Selections from the Sermons and Writings of Joseph F. Smith* [Salt Lake City: Deseret Book, 1919], 55)

George Albert Smith:

He [the Lord] has told us in great plainness that the world will be in distress, that there will be warfare from one end of the world to the other, that the wicked shall slay the wicked and that peace shall be taken from the earth. And He has said, too, that the only place where there will be safety will be in Zion. Will we make this Zion? Will we keep it to be Zion, because Zion means the pure in heart? (Daniel H. Ludlow, ed., *Latter-day Prophets Speak: Selections from the Sermons and Writings of Church Presidents* [Salt Lake City: Bookcraft, 1948], 249)

David O. McKay:

Zion is the pure in heart, we have been told, and the strength of this Church lies in the purity of the thoughts and lives of its members, then the testimony of Jesus abides in the soul, and strength comes to each individual to withstand the evils of the world. (*Gospel Ideals: Selections from the Discourses of David O. McKay* [Salt Lake City: The Improvement Era, 1953], 153)

Joseph Fielding Smith:

Temples are sanctified for the purpose of performing rites for and making covenants with the pure in heart, who have proved themselves by faithful service worthy of the blessings of exaltation. (*DS,* 2:231)

Spencer W. Kimball:

Zion can be built up only among those who are the pure in heart, not a people torn by covetousness or greed, but a pure and selfless people. Not a people who are pure in appearance, rather a people who are pure in heart. Zion is to be in the world and not of the world not dulled by a sense of carnal security, nor paralyzed by material- ism. No, Zion is not things of the lower, but of the higher order, things that exalt the mind and sanctify the heart.

Zion is "every man seeking the interest of his neighbor, and doing all things with an eye single to the glory of God" (D&C 82:19). As I understand these mat- ters, Zion can be established only by those who are pure in heart, and who labor for Zion, for "the laborer in Zion shall labor for Zion; for if they labor for money they shall perish" (2 Ne. 26:31). (*TSWK,* 363)

Ezra Taft Benson:

Love and mutual confidence must be safeguarded to strengthen parent-children rela- tionships. Home must become the abiding place of the Spirit of God because the pure in heart dwell therein. (*TETB,* 525)

Howard W. Hunter:

We must be prepared to qualify for revelation. To qualify for revelation, we must learn to recognize the spirit of revelation, prepare our minds for spiritual things, and be virtuous and pure in heart. (*THWH,* 265)

Gordon B. Hinckley:

And beyond all of this is the unfailing promise of God to those who walk in virtue. Declared Jesus of Nazareth, speaking on the mountain, "Blessed are the pure in heart: for they shall see God" (Matt. 5:8). That is a promise, made by him who has the power to fulfill. (*TGBH,* 679)

PEACE *through* RIGHTEOUSNESS: MELCHIZEDEK

MOMENT OF TRUTH

The story of Melchizedek is the story of peace, for it represents an extraordinary trans-formation of a wayward society through the redemptive power of spiritual principles of faith, repentance, and committed righteousness. When Melchizedek assumed the office of prophet/leader, Salem (later called Jerusalem) was under a veil of spiritual darkness and rebellion—"yea, they had all gone astray" (Alma 13:17). But Melchizedek was well prepared for his mission: "Now Melchizedek was a man of faith, who wrought righteousness; and when a child he feared God, and stopped the mouths of lions, and quenched the violence of fire. And thus, having been approved of God, he was ordained an high priest after the order of the covenant which God made with Enoch" (JST, Gen. 14:26–27). What Melchizedek accomplished was nothing short of a miracle, for his influence on the people had the astounding effect of bringing them all back into the fold:

> But Melchizedek having exercised mighty faith, and received the office of the high priesthood according to the holy order of God, did preach repentance unto his peo-ple. And behold, they did repent; and Melchizedek did establish peace in the land in his days; therefore he was called the prince of peace, for he was the king of Salem; and he did reign under his father.
>
> Now, there were many before him, and also there were many afterwards, but none were greater; therefore, of him they have more particularly made mention. (Alma 13:18–19)

So great was Melchizedek's office and stature that he was also placed in charge of the abundance of the Lord's kingdom:

And he lifted up his voice, and he blessed Abram, being the high priest, and the keeper of the storehouse of God;

Him whom God had appointed to receive tithes for the poor.

Wherefore, Abram paid unto him tithes of all that he had, of all the riches which he possessed, which God had given him more than that which he had need. (JST, Gen. 14:37–39)

Were it not for modern-day revelation, we would enjoy only a narrow glimpse into the life of this distinguished and noble prophet. The Apostle Paul shared with us only a few of the particulars of Melchizedek's life:

For this Melchisedec, king of Salem, priest of the most high God, who met Abraham returning from the slaughter of the kings, and blessed him;

To whom also Abraham gave a tenth part of all; first being by interpretation King of righteousness, and after that also King of Salem, which is, King of peace;

Without father, without mother, without descent, having neither beginning of days, nor end of life; but made like unto the Son of God; abideth a priest continually.

Now consider how great this man was, unto whom even the patriarch Abraham gave the tenth of the spoils. (Heb. 7:1–4)

The Joseph Smith Translation records for Hebrews 7:3 the following changes:

For this Melchizedek was ordained a priest after the order of the Son of God, which order was without father, without mother, without descent, having neither beginning of days, nor end of life. And all those who are ordained unto this priesthood are made like unto the Son of God, abiding a priest continually. (JST, Heb. 7:3)

Through this restorative change in the text, we can understand much better the magnificence of the Holy Priesthood, its eternal nature, its relationship to the Son of God, and how we too can become the Sons of God by obtaining this priesthood. Melchizedek was honored to have the priesthood called after his own name:

Why the first is called the Melchizedek Priesthood is because Melchizedek was such a great high priest.

Before his day it was called *the Holy Priesthood, after the Order of the Son of God.*

But out of respect or reverence to the name of the Supreme Being, to avoid the too frequent repetition of his name, they, the church, in ancient days, called that priesthood after Melchizedek, or the Melchizedek Priesthood. (D&C 107:2–4)

MODERN PROPHETS SPEAK

Gordon B. Hinckley:

> The satisfying thing is that obedience brings happiness; it brings peace; it brings growth—all of these to the individual, and his good example brings respect for the institution of which he is a part. (*Be Thou an Example* [Salt Lake City: Deseret Book, 1981], 12)

DOCTRINES AND PRINCIPLES

The Savior: Prince of Peace

Melchizedek is a type of the Savior, the divine Prince of Peace. Rex C. Reeve, Jr., states:

> We can look to Joseph Smith and the Doctrine and Covenants for revelations concerning Melchizedek, one of God's ancient high priests of whom "none were greater" (see Alma 13:10, 19). Melchizedek conferred the priesthood upon Abraham and received his tithing (see D&C 84:14; Alma 13:15). Melchizedek was honored by having his name used to identify the Holy Priesthood after the Order of the Son of God, thus enabling men to avoid the too frequent repetition of the name of Deity (see D&C 107:2–4). In the eyes of his people Melchizedek stood as a prototype of the Son of God: both bore the title "Prince of Peace," and both were joint heirs of the Father's kingdom. ("A Latter-day Testament of Biblical Truth," *Ensign*, Jan. 2001, 26)

Tithing

The depth of understanding concerning Melchizedek's role is magnified in his relationship to Father Abraham, as we learn again from the Prophet Joseph's translation of the Bible:

> And Melchizedek, king of Salem, brought forth bread and wine; and he brake bread and blest it; and he blest the wine, he being the priest of the most high God, And he gave to Abram, and he blessed him, and said, Blessed Abram, thou art a man of the most high God, possessor of heaven and of earth; And blessed is the name of the most high God, which hath delivered thine enemies into thine hand. And Abram gave him tithes of all he had taken. (JST, Gen. 14:17–20)

The same principle is confirmed in the Book of Mormon, where we learn the following from Alma:

Yea, humble yourselves even as the people in the days of Melchizedek, who was also a high priest after this same order which I have spoken, who also took upon him the high priesthood forever.

And it was this same Melchizedek to whom Abraham paid tithes; yea, even our father Abraham paid tithes of one-tenth part of all he possessed.

Now these ordinances were given after this manner, that thereby the people might look forward on the Son of God, it being a type of his order, or it being his order, and this that they might look forward to him for a remission of their sins, that they might enter into the rest of the Lord. (Alma 13:14–16)

Repentance

Melchizedek was a righteous and noble prophet of God, as Alma stated: "Now, there were many before him, and also there were many afterwards, but none were greater; therefore, of him they have more particularly made mention" (Alma 13:19). What made him so great? What did he do? Why was he so honored to have the Lord's priesthood named after him? The answer is that he "exercised mighty faith" (Alma 13:18), magnified his holy office in the priesthood, and preached repentance. Preaching repentance is the commission given of God to all His holy prophets since the world began, and it will continue to be so until the end. There is no doctrine taught or preached more frequently than the doctrine of repentance. Repent and come unto Christ is the message of the Kingdom of God. From Adam to Joseph Smith to the present day, it has ever been the same message. Nephi gives a particularly compelling encapsulation of the prophetic message:

And we talk of Christ, we rejoice in Christ, we preach of Christ, we prophesy of Christ, and we write according to our prophecies, that our children may know to what source they may look for a remission of their sins.

Wherefore, we speak concerning the law that our children may know the deadness of the law; and they, by knowing the deadness of the law, may look forward unto that life which is in Christ, and know for what end the law was given. And after the law is fulfilled in Christ, that they need not harden their hearts against him when the law ought to be done away.

And now behold, my people, ye are a stiffnecked people; wherefore, I have spoken plainly unto you, that ye cannot misunderstand. And the words which I have spoken shall stand as a testimony against you; for they are sufficient to teach any man the right way; for the right way is to believe in Christ and deny him not; for by denying him ye also deny the prophets and the law.

And now behold, I say unto you that the right way is to believe in Christ, and deny him not; and Christ is the Holy One of Israel; wherefore ye must bow down before him, and worship him with all your might, mind, and strength, and your whole soul; and if ye do this ye shall in nowise be cast out.

And, inasmuch as it shall be expedient, ye must keep the performances and ordinances of God until the law shall be fulfilled which was given unto Moses. (2 Ne 25:26–30)

Yes, the eternal message of the gospel of Jesus Christ is to have mighty faith unto repentance, that all might come unto Christ. That is the message that all of the great prophets have given. There can be no greater service than to help people repent. Alma reflected this kind of commitment when he said,

Yea, and from that time even until now, I have labored without ceasing, that I might bring souls unto repentance; that I might bring them to taste of the exceeding joy of which I did taste; that they might also be born of God, and be filled with the Holy Ghost.

Yea, and now behold, O my son, the Lord doth give me exceedingly great joy in the fruit of my labors. (Alma 36:24–25)

Peace

Alma was given joy in his labors. Melchizedek's success in bringing his people to repentance is reflected in the outcomes of his labors: peace. His people became a holy people like unto the people of Enoch, for that is what Melchizedek sought: "And his people wrought righteousness, and obtained heaven, and sought for the city of Enoch which God had before taken, separating it from the earth, having reserved it unto the latter days, or the end of the world; . . . And this Melchizedek, having thus established righteousness, was called the king of heaven by his people, or, in other words, the King of peace" (JST, Gen. 14:34, 36).

In a unique way, the kind of peace characteristic of Melchizedek's Jerusalem is also aligned with the peace of the temples of God. Frank F. Judd, Jr., who has conducted research into the details of Melchizedek's reign, gives this report concerning information derived from Josephus, an early Jewish historian:

As Melchizedek and his people established their city of Zion, it seems that they, too, enjoyed temple blessings. Josephus, a Jewish historian who lived in the first century after Christ, knew of a tradition that Melchizedek, not Solomon, was the first person to build a temple of the Lord in Palestine. "Its [Salem's] original founder was a Canaanite chief, called in the native tongue "Righteous King" [or Melchizedek]; for such indeed he was. In virtue thereof he was the first to officiate as priest of God and, being the first to build the temple, gave the city, previously called Solyma [or

Salem], the name of Jerusalem. (*Thy People Shall Be My People and Thy God My God* [Salt Lake City: Deseret Book, 1994], 41)

This seems to clearly indicate, as previously noted, that much of the goodness of Melchizedek was simply lost in the transmission of accounts in the Old Testament down through time. The Prophet Joseph's revelation concerning Moses indicates this as well: "And in a day when the children of men shall esteem my words as naught and take many of them from the book which thou shalt write, behold, I will raise up another like unto thee; and they shall be had again among the children of men—among as many as shall believe" (Moses 1:41).

OBEDIENCE: ABRAHAM *and* ISAAC

MOMENT OF TRUTH

Abraham was commanded to offer up the thing most dear to his heart—his own son:

> Take now thy son, thine only son Isaac, whom thou lovest, and get thee into the
> land of Moriah; and offer him there for a burnt offering. (Gen. 22:2)

Abraham then took Isaac and two other young men on the journey to Moriah, where
he was to offer Isaac as a burnt offering—a sacrifice—to the Lord. On the third day,
Abraham and Isaac went to worship. Isaac carried the wood as they journeyed. Isaac
asked about the sacrifice, and Abraham replied, "My son, God will provide himself a
lamb for a burnt offering" (Gen. 22:8). Abraham then bound Isaac and laid him on
the altar, preparing for the ultimate sacrifice. As Abraham took the knife, an angel of
the Lord forbade him and said, "For now I know that thou fearest [i.e., shows unyielding reverence to] God, seeing thou hast not withheld thy son" (Gen. 22:12). A ram
was subsequently provided, and the Lord promised Abraham, "In thy seed shall all the
nations of the earth be blessed" (Gen. 22:18).

It was a moment in time when Abraham was put to the supreme test. Would he
shrink from the awesome task, or would he rise in majesty as a figure of unforgettable
valor and unshakeable obedience? He obeyed—and the Lord stayed his hand. Such
was a prefiguring of the coming sacrifice of the Only Begotten for the sake of
mankind. Only through a commitment to sacrifice all that we have, if required to do
so, can we manifest to the Lord that our enduring love for Him and His divine cause
is perfect.

MODERN PROPHETS SPEAK

Thomas S. Monson:

> How exceedingly difficult it must have been for Abraham, in obedience to God's command, to take his beloved Isaac into the land of Moriah there to present him as a burnt offering. Can you imagine the heaviness of his heart as he gathered the wood for the fire and journeyed to the appointed place? Surely pain must have racked his body and tortured his mind as he bound Isaac and laid him on the altar upon the wood and stretched forth his hand and took the knife to slay his son. How glorious was the pronouncement, and with what wondered welcome did it come, "Lay not thine hand upon the lad, neither do thou any thing unto him: for now I know that thou fearest God seeing thou has not withheld thy son, thine only son from me" (Gen. 22:12). (*CR,* October 1965, 142)

Gordon B. Hinckley:

> Now, the Lord has said something about that. He said, "Be not weary in well-doing, for ye are laying the foundation of a great work. And out of small things proceedeth that which is great. Behold, the Lord requireth the heart and a willing mind" (D&C 64:33–34). That's what it takes: the heart and a willing mind. These are the words of the Lord. You are laying the foundation of a great work, and the power lies within you to accomplish it. (*TGBH,* 361–62)

DOCTRINES AND PRINCIPLES

We can see reflected in the life of Abraham the exemplary pattern of spiritual growth that all of God's righteous children can strive for as part of the mortal experience. From his early youth, Abraham's faith and devotion were schooled on experiences of adversity and oppression, and the lessons of obedience and valor he learned carried him through life on the wings of divine support and blessing. Never losing the vision of his destined calling as a key participant in the grand design of the Lord, he set an unequalled example of one willing to do everything asked of him by God, without hesitation and without question.

In many ways, the life journey of Abraham shows that our mortal experience is very cyclical: the trials we encounter in life lead to opportunities for exerting our faith through obedience and godly behavior, which in turn lead to an outpouring of blessings from our Father in Heaven and a multiplicity of valuable lessons learned. Then the whole sequence is repeated once more. As we go through this cycle again and again, our progress is traced by a spiral that carries us higher and higher, according to our diligence and willingness to keep the commandments. The motion is an upward cycle, ever closer to the objective of being more like our Father in Heaven and His Son, Jesus Christ. We see in the scriptural account three of Abraham's spiritual cycles: the preparations of his youth, the challenge that he and his wife faced in their old age to fulfill the Lord's promise for a son, and the requested sacrifice of Isaac. All of these experiences taught Abraham, as they teach us, that the Lord will provide a way for us to follow His will in all things.

Stories from the scriptures testify of the goodness of God in preserving and blessing His children so that the work of salvation could go forward—the blessing of His children that they might have immortality and eternal life. The question begs to be asked: How often has the Lord provided for us means whereby we not only obey, but we can actually *live* so that we might obey? Does He not provide all things, including our very breath (see Mosiah 2:21)? We simply must have eyes and hearts of gratitude to be aware of His goodness.

Without trials and adversity, faith could not flourish. Without the shadows of life's burdens and tests, the light of hope could not expand to its full luster. The Lord made a covenant with Abraham and his posterity, as He had done earlier with the great prophets before him. In exchange for obedience and leadership in blessing the nations of the world, the people were promised a great lineage now and eternal increase in the hereafter, places of refuge on earth and mansions in heaven, gospel truth here, and salvation in the world to come. Abraham passed all tests given. He stands across the centuries as a beacon of obedience and valiant service. No matter what trials were encountered, he exerted faith and stood for principle. The Lord blessed him mightily through lessons of truth and priesthood power. As the "father of the faithful" (D&C 138:41), he is even now enthroned in heaven, along with Isaac and Jacob. Already these three ancient prophets, according to revelation, "are not angels but are gods" (D&C 132:37). We are told that the Saints "must needs be chastened and tried, even as Abraham" (D&C 101:4). The lesson is clear: "Go ye, therefore, and do the works of Abraham; enter ye into my law and ye shall be saved" (D&C 132:32).

VALOR: JACOB *and* ESAU

MOMENT OF TRUTH

Every child needs to live up to the divine lineage of being a son or daughter of God, created in His image. In a special way, all those who participate in the Abrahamic covenant must be true to their birthright and calling as servants of the Lord, commissioned to be exemplars of obedience and righteousness in carrying the gospel to the world.

In ancient Israel, the birthright was the right and privilege of the oldest son. However, Esau, son of Isaac, gave up his birthright to his brother Jacob.

> And Esau said, Behold, I am at the point to die: and what profit shall this birthright do to me?
>
> And Jacob said, Swear to me this day; and he sware unto him: and he sold his birthright unto Jacob.
>
> Then Jacob gave Esau bread and pottage of lentiles; and he did eat and drink, and rose up, and went his way: thus Esau despised his birthright. (Gen. 25:32–34)

Esau later lamented his decision. He had confused his priorities and valued his temporal comforts above his spiritual birthright. Thus the Lord saw to it that the birthright blessings fell to Jacob, the younger son. The lesson is clear: We must have the faith and the humility to follow the Lord's counsel by seeking first His kingdom, and then He will bless us and multiply our gifts in righteousness and justice.

MODERN PROPHETS SPEAK

Wilford Woodruff:

> We should be men and women of faith, valiant for the truth as it has been revealed and committed into our hand. We should be men and women of integrity to God, and to his Holy Priesthood, true to him and true to one another. We should not

permit houses and land, gold and silver, nor any of this world's goods to draw us aside from pursuing the great object which God has sent us to perform. Our aim is high, our destiny is high, and we should never disappoint our Father, nor the heavenly hosts who are watching over us. We should not disappoint the millions in the spirit world who, too, are watching over us with an interest and anxiety that have hardly entered into our hearts to conceive of. These are great and mighty things which God requires of us. (*JD*, 22:233)

DOCTRINES AND PRINCIPLES

Everyone, no matter how old, has the responsibility to fight the ongoing struggle to cultivate and maintain self-control. The true expression of self-control is temperance. In the pedagogy of taking upon oneself the divine nature of Christ (see 2 Pet. 1:1–10), we gain knowledge prior to taking on temperance or exercising self-control. In doing so, we show forbearance. We demonstrate restraint. We become the master of our soul as we become submissive to the will of God. This humility helps us overcome selfishness and pride—we don't seek physical pleasures or aggrandizement but seek to live a higher law. The trial and test in life is making the body subject to the Spirit instead of to the flesh. This is the essence of gaining self-mastery.

Jacob was valiant according to his values, knowing that which was most important. When we understand and appreciate the value of any doctrine or possession, we seek to preserve it. We become valiant in the preservation of that which is of most worth. This is why it is essential for us to have our values aligned with the gospel and commandments of God.

ENVY *and* JEALOUSY:
JOSEPH SOLD *into* EGYPT

MOMENT OF TRUTH

In the contrast between the character of Joseph and the character of his brothers, we see played out in the starkest terms the preeminence of integrity over envy, honesty over jealousy, and (in the case of some of the brothers) virtue over moral laxity. Joseph built his life upon a foundation of enduring principles and a commitment to follow the guidance of the Spirit. As such, his moral courage and leadership reflect the kind of strength, discipline, and stability that a great leader must always have. By way of contrast, those who operate out of unchecked greed or lust display a wavering instability from which harmony, peace, and lasting happiness can never flow.

MODERN PROPHETS SPEAK

Joseph B. Wirthlin:

> I believe happiness comes from a clear conscience and from being without guile or deception. It means avoiding jealousy and envy. It means cultivating peace in our homes and enjoying the peace in our hearts that righteousness brings. It comes from a knowledge and assurance, given by the Spirit, that the life we are pursuing is in accord with God's will and is acceptable to him. The Prophet Joseph's oft-quoted statement remains in force: "Happiness is the object and design of our existence; and will be the end thereof, if we pursue the path that leads to it; and this path is virtue, uprightness, faithfulness, holiness, and keeping all the commandments of God." We need not feel depressed or discouraged about conditions in the world, for the Lord will help us find the good that will lead us to happiness. (*Finding Peace in Our Lives* [Salt Lake City: Deseret Book, 1995], 133)

DOCTRINES AND PRINCIPLES

In the case of the brothers of Joseph, we learn the devastating effect of envy and jealousy. Envy is one of the most devastating feelings one can have. When you feel discontent or ill will concerning another's prosperity or success, you suffer from envy. Envy, which often leads to unrighteous actions, should be avoided at all costs. Envious activities literally take captive those who participate in them, and they become prisoners of themselves—never free, for they are chained by their faults, always wanting more material goods, power, or status. Being captive to envy not only destroys the mind and heart but, allowed to fester and grow, destroys the freedom of the individual, because it can lead to serious transgression and sin. When envy moves to jealous actions, it creates an unrighteous desire or ambition for things one does not possess.

It is so ironic, as we seek for happiness, that we should become jealous of another's prosperity and happiness. Happiness is from within, yet envy and jealousy seek it from without—externally—and that is a mistake. It is for many individuals most difficult to learn that having the things of the world or the gifts of another do not inherently lead to joy or happiness, for even if we were to possess these things, there will always be others who have more. Often envy and finding "faults" in those who have more are simply masks of a hidden jealousy within. Envy and jealousy separate us from Deity. They create negative feelings and are truly debilitating to those who succumb to those feelings. In place of envy and jealousy one should foster both a spirit of gratitude for one's blessings and gifts as well as a willingness to rejoice with others in the blessings and gifts that are theirs. Indeed, it is charity and love that swallow up envy and jealousy. True love cheers for success of others and their well-being just as Alma did for the success of the Sons of Mosiah (see Alma 29:14).

INTEGRITY: JOSEPH *in* EGYPT

MOMENT OF TRUTH

Joseph's example of integrity and moral uprightness in Egypt is among the most celebrated instances of strength of character in all of Holy Writ. Joseph had made the Lord his God and the Lord was with him. We learn from the scriptural account:

> And the Lord was with Joseph, and he was a prosperous man; and he was in the house of his master the Egyptian.
>
> And his master saw that the Lord was with him, and that the Lord made all that he did to prosper in his hand.
>
> And Joseph found grace in his sight, and he served him: and he made him overseer over his house, and all that he had he put into his hand. (Gen. 39:2–4)

Joseph's devoted effort and performance with his assigned duties brought favor with Potiphar. Joseph was a faithful servant, yet his allegiance was to the Lord. As the story unfolds, Joseph was accosted and tempted by Potiphar's wife. In response, Joseph said, "How then can I do this great wickedness, and sin against God?" (Gen. 39:9). Because of his sterling character and moral strength, Joseph took immediate action "and fled, and got him out" (Gen. 39:12).

Potiphar's wife accused him falsely and reported him to her husband. As a consequence, Joseph was put in prison. But again the hand of the Lord preserved him. He invoked the power of the Lord to interpret the dreams of Pharaoh concerning the seven years of plenty followed by the seven years of famine (Gen. 41). Pharaoh was pleased, as the following confirms:

> And Pharaoh said unto his servants, Can we find such a one as this is, a man in whom the Spirit of God is?

And Pharaoh said unto Joseph, Forasmuch as God hath shewed thee all this, there is none so discreet and wise as thou art:

Thou shalt be over my house, and according unto thy word shall all my people be ruled: only in the throne will I be greater than thou.

And Pharaoh said unto Joseph, See, I have set thee over all the land of Egypt.

And Pharaoh took off his ring from his hand, and put it upon Joseph's hand, and arrayed him in vestures of fine linen, and put a gold chain about his neck;

And he made him to ride in the second chariot which he had; and they cried before him, Bow the knee: and he made him ruler over all the land of Egypt. (Gen. 41:39–43)

Joseph's strength of character and his dependence upon the Lord were buoyant forces for good in his life and opened up the gateway to future service. Joseph's flight at the adulterous overtures of Potiphar's wife stands in stark contrast with the moral weakness of some of his brothers. The story of his integrity is a beacon of light that still shines today in our world of moral relativity characterized by the loss of the anchor of enduring principles. Moreover, Joseph's resiliency, positive leadership and creative problem-solving caused him to be elevated in stature and office in his Egyptian setting, thus laying the groundwork for his future role of preserver of his heritage under the Abrahamic covenant.

MODERN PROPHETS SPEAK

Brigham Young:

The sooner an individual resists temptation to do, say, or think wrong, while he has light to correct his judgment, the quicker he will gain strength and power to overcome every temptation to evil. (*Discourses,* 266)

Russell M. Nelson:

Cardiac surgeons speak of the heart in terms of its structural integrity. The word *integrity* is related to the word *integer,* which means "entire" or "whole." Integrity may be defined as "the state of being unimpaired." Integrity also means "incorruptibility"—a firm adherence to a code of values. Integrity denotes a state of completeness. If any component of the heart loses its integrity, the heart is impaired and a vicious cycle ensues. An anatomical flaw leads to improper function, and improper function leads to further failure. Therefore, the ultimate objective of any cardiac operation is to restore structural integrity to the heart. . . .

Integrity safeguards love, and love makes family life rich and zestful—now and forever. But none of us is immune to temptation, and the adversary knows it. He would deceive, connive, or contrive any means to deprive us of potential joy and exaltation. He knows that if one little cord of control can be snapped, others likely will weaken later under increased strain. The result would be no integrity, no eternal life. Satan's triumph would be assured. If this domino-like deterioration causes a run in our spiritual stocking, qualities of character are lost and our cherished integrity is gone.

The Apostle Paul warned of the lethal wages of sin, but the Savior didn't limit His caution to major transgression. He specifically warned against breaking "one of these least commandments." His admonitions were meant to protect and preserve our precious integrity.

A surgeon can repair or replace a mitral valve that has lost its integrity. But no surgical procedure can be performed for loss of spiritual integrity of heart. Such breakdown is under individual control. (*Perfection Pending, and Other Favorite Discourses* [Salt Lake City: Deseret Book, 1998], 21, 23–24)

DOCTRINES AND PRINCIPLES

Integrity becomes the basis of all relationships and eventually forms the foundation of your capacity to prove yourself worthy of returning to the presence of our Heavenly Father. The little exaggerations, the silent tongue when things need to be said, the so-called misrepresentations—all of these militate against integrity and undermine honesty.

President Hinckley exhorts us, "Simple honesty is so remarkable a quality. It is of the very essence of integrity. It demands that we be straightforward, unequivocal, in walking the straight and narrow line of what is right and true. It is so easy to cheat. At times it is so enticing to do so. Better a poor grade than a dishonest act" (*TGBH,* 269).

FORGIVENESS: JOSEPH SAVES HIS FAMILY *in* EGYPT

MOMENT OF TRUTH

Joseph's forgiving attitude and understanding of the necessity of his role in preserving Israel through dire circumstances are made evident as we read the details of the story when Joseph's brothers came to Egypt for food during the acute famine:

> Then Joseph could not refrain himself before all them that stood by him; and he cried, Cause every man to go out from me. And there stood no man with him, while Joseph made himself known unto his brethren.
>
> And he wept aloud: and the Egyptians and the house of Pharaoh heard.
>
> And Joseph said unto his brethren, I am Joseph; doth my father yet live? And his brethren could not answer him; for they were troubled at his presence.
>
> And Joseph said unto his brethren, Come near to me, I pray you. And they came near. And he said, I am Joseph your brother, whom ye sold into Egypt.
>
> Now therefore be not grieved, nor angry with yourselves, that ye sold me hither: for God did send me before you to preserve life.
>
> For these two years hath the famine been in the land: and yet there are five years, in the which there shall neither be earing nor harvest.
>
> And God sent me before you to preserve you a posterity in the earth, and to save your lives by a great deliverance.
>
> So now it was not you that sent me hither, but God: and he hath made me a father to Pharaoh, and lord of all his house, and a ruler throughout all the land of Egypt.
>
> Haste ye, and go up to my father, and say unto him, Thus saith thy son Joseph, God hath made me lord of all Egypt: come down unto me, tarry not:
>
> And thou shalt dwell in the land of Goshen, and thou shalt be near unto me, thou, and thy children, and thy children's children, and thy flocks, and thy herds, and all that thou hast:

And there will I nourish thee; for yet there are five years of famine; lest thou, and thy household, and all that thou hast, come to poverty.

And, behold, your eyes see, and the eyes of my brother Benjamin, that it is my mouth that speaketh unto you.

And ye shall tell my father of all my glory in Egypt, and of all that ye have seen: and ye shall haste and bring down my father hither.

And he fell upon his brother Benjamin's neck, and wept; and Benjamin wept upon his neck.

Moreover he kissed all his brethren, and wept upon them: and after that his brethren talked with him. (Gen. 45:1–15)

Later, following the death of Jacob (Israel), Joseph's forgiving nature had preserved his love for his brothers, who, not understanding, still feared that he might show retribution toward them:

And they sent a messenger unto Joseph, saying, Thy father did command before he died, saying,

So shall ye say unto Joseph, Forgive, I pray thee now, the trespass of thy brethren, and their sin; for they did unto thee evil: and now, we pray thee, forgive the trespass of the servants of the God of thy father. And Joseph wept when they spake unto him.

And his brethren also went and fell down before his face; and they said, Behold, we be thy servants.

And Joseph said unto them, Fear not: for am I in the place of God?

But as for you, ye thought evil against me; but God meant it unto good, to bring to pass, as it is this day, to save much people alive.

Now therefore fear ye not: I will nourish you, and your little ones. And he comforted them, and spake kindly unto them. (Gen. 50:16–21)

MODERN PROPHETS SPEAK

David E. Sorensen:

Joseph's brothers jealously hated him. They plotted to take his life and finally sold him as a slave. Joseph was carried into Egypt and struggled for years to rise from slavery. During these challenging times, Joseph might have condemned his brothers and sworn revenge. He might have soothed his pain by scheming to get even someday. But he did not.

In time, Joseph became ruler over all of Egypt, second in command only to Pharaoh. During a devastating famine, Joseph's brothers traveled to Egypt for food. Not recognizing Joseph, they bowed down to him because of his high position.

Surely at that moment Joseph had the power to exact revenge. He might have put his brethren in prison or sentenced them to death. Instead he confirmed his forgiveness. He said: "I am Joseph your brother, whom ye sold into Egypt. Now therefore be not grieved, nor angry with yourselves, that ye sold me hither. . . . And God sent me before you to preserve you a posterity . . . and to save your lives by a great deliverance. So now it was not you that sent me hither, but God" (Gen. 45:4–5, 7–8). Joseph's will to forgive changed bitterness to love. ("Forgiveness Will Change Bitterness to Love," *Ensign,* May 2003, 12)

Gordon B. Hinckley:

I know of no more beautiful story in all literature than that found in the fifteenth chapter of Luke. It is the story of a repentant son and a forgiving father. It is the story of a son who wasted his inheritance in riotous living, rejecting his father's counsel, spurning those who loved him. When he had spent all, he was hungry and friendless, and "when he came to himself" (Luke 15:17), he turned back to his father, who, on seeing him afar off, "ran, and fell on his neck, and kissed him" (Luke 15:20).

I ask you to read that story. Every parent ought to read it again and again. It is large enough to encompass every household, and enough larger than that to encompass all mankind, for are we not all prodigal sons and daughters who need to repent and partake of the forgiving mercy of our Heavenly Father and then follow His example?

His Beloved Son, our Redeemer, reaches out to us in forgiveness and mercy, but in so doing he commands repentance. A true and magnanimous spirit of forgiveness will become an expression of that required repentance. ("Of You It Is Required to Forgive," *Ensign,* June 1991, 5)

DOCTRINES AND PRINCIPLES

The great principles of character exhibited by Joseph were his willingness to forgive and his visionary understanding of the destiny of the House of Israel and his own posterity. The scriptures report the blessing that Jacob gave to Joseph and his posterity:

Joseph is a fruitful bough, even a fruitful bough by a well; whose branches run over the wall:

The archers have sorely grieved him, and shot at him, and hated him:

But his bow abode in strength, and the arms of his hands were made strong by the hands of the mighty God of Jacob; (from thence is the shepherd, the stone of Israel:)

> Even by the God of thy father, who shall help thee; and by the Almighty, who shall bless thee with blessings of heaven above, blessings of the deep that lieth under, blessings of the breasts, and of the womb:
>
> The blessings of thy father have prevailed above the blessings of my progenitors unto the utmost bound of the everlasting hills: they shall be on the head of Joseph, and on the crown of the head of him that was separate from his brethren. (Gen. 49:22–26)

Surely Joseph was one of the great prophets of the House of Israel, who indeed saw our day as Nephi recorded, concerning the inspired insights of his father Lehi:

> Wherefore, Joseph truly saw our day. And he obtained a promise of the Lord, that out of the fruit of his loins the Lord God would raise up a righteous branch unto the house of Israel; not the Messiah, but a branch which was to be broken off, nevertheless, to be remembered in the covenants of the Lord that the Messiah should be made manifest unto them in the latter days, in the spirit of power, unto the bringing of them out of darkness unto light—yea, out of hidden darkness and out of captivity unto freedom.
>
> For Joseph truly testified, saying: A seer shall the Lord my God raise up, who shall be a choice seer unto the fruit of my loins.
>
> Yea, Joseph truly said: Thus saith the Lord unto me: A choice seer will I raise up out of the fruit of thy loins; and he shall be esteemed highly among the fruit of thy loins. And unto him will I give commandment that he shall do a work for the fruit of thy loins, his brethren, which shall be of great worth unto them, even to the bringing of them to the knowledge of the covenants which I have made with thy fathers.
>
> And I will give unto him a commandment that he shall do none other work, save the work which I shall command him. And I will make him great in mine eyes; for he shall do my work. (2 Ne. 3:5–8)

Lehi goes on to say,

> But a seer will I raise up out of the fruit of thy loins; and unto him will I give power to bring forth my word unto the seed of thy loins—and not to the bringing forth my word only, saith the Lord, but to the convincing them of my word, which shall have already gone forth among them.
>
> Wherefore, the fruit of thy loins shall write; and the fruit of the loins of Judah shall write; and that which shall be written by the fruit of thy loins, and also that which shall be written by the fruit of the loins of Judah, shall grow together, unto the confounding of false doctrines and laying down of contentions, and establishing

peace among the fruit of thy loins, and bringing them to the knowledge of their fathers in the latter days, and also to the knowledge of my covenants, saith the Lord.

And out of weakness he shall be made strong, in that day when my work shall commence among all my people, unto the restoring thee, O house of Israel, saith the Lord.

And thus prophesied Joseph, saying: Behold, that seer will the Lord bless; and they that seek to destroy him shall be confounded; for this promise, which I have obtained of the Lord, of the fruit of my loins, shall be fulfilled. Behold, I am sure of the fulfilling of this promise;

And his name shall be called after me; and it shall be after the name of his father. And he shall be like unto me; for the thing, which the Lord shall bring forth by his hand, by the power of the Lord shall bring my people unto salvation.

Yea, thus prophesied Joseph: I am sure of this thing, even as I am sure of the promise of Moses; for the Lord hath said unto me, I will preserve thy seed forever. (2 Ne. 3:11–16)

The scriptures make clear that the descendents of Joseph shall indeed have a great role to play in the gathering of Israel in these the last days. Robert L. Millet and Kent Jackson explain:

Again using Old Testament prophecies, the Lord declared that the assignment of the Saints was to "push the people together from the ends of the earth" (D&C 58:45). Students of the Old Testament will recognize this phrase as a blessing of Moses on the descendants of Joseph (Deut. 33:13–17). The land given to Joseph's descendants was America (3 Ne. 15:12–13). In order for the wilderness to blossom, the children of Ephraim and Manasseh must be gathered together on the entire land of the Americas, not only in Missouri. This was to be accomplished through the preaching of the gospel in the regions round about. Since the house of Israel had been scattered among the Gentiles (Hosea 8:8–10; Amos 9:8–9), the preaching of the gospel among the Gentiles in the surrounding regions would be the process of gathering together "the ten thousands of Ephraim and . . . the thousands of Manasseh" (Deut. 33:17). Ephraim, being the birthright holder of all of Israel, would of necessity be gathered first. But included also would be thousands of the children of Manasseh, Joseph's other son, because America was given to all of Joseph's children. (*Studies in Scripture: The Doctrine and Covenants* [Salt Lake City: Deseret Book, 1989], 239–240)

DELIVERANCE: MOSES LIBERATES *the* ISRAELITES

MOMENT OF TRUTH

The story of Moses is legendary. Rescued from the bulrushes by a princess, he grew up as a child in the court of Pharoah but was called to deliver the Israelites from their crushing burdens of slavery. In the course of his preparation, Moses went up into Mount Horeb and there had the extraordinary experience of the burning bush and received his call from the Lord:

> Come now therefore, and I will send thee unto Pharaoh, that thou mayest bring forth my people the children of Israel out of Egypt.
>
> And Moses said unto God, Who am I, that I should go unto Pharaoh, and that I should bring forth the children of Israel out of Egypt?
>
> And he said, Certainly I will be with thee; and this shall be a token unto thee, that I have sent thee: When thou hast brought forth the people out of Egypt, ye shall serve God upon this mountain.
>
> And Moses said unto God, Behold, when I come unto the children of Israel, and shall say unto them, The God of your fathers hath sent me unto you; and they shall say to me, What is his name? what shall I say unto them?
>
> And God said unto Moses, I AM THAT I AM: and he said, Thus shalt thou say unto the children of Israel, I AM hath sent me unto you.
>
> And God said moreover unto Moses, Thus shalt thou say unto the children of Israel, The Lord God of your fathers, the God of Abraham, the God of Isaac, and the God of Jacob, hath sent me unto you: this is my name for ever, and this is my memorial unto all generations.
>
> Go, and gather the elders of Israel together, and say unto them, The Lord God of your fathers, the God of Abraham, of Isaac, and of Jacob, appeared unto me, saying, I have surely visited you, and seen that which is done to you in Egypt:

> And I have said, I will bring you up out of the affliction of Egypt unto the land
> of the Canaanites, and the Hittites, and the Amorites, and the Perizzites, and the
> Hivites, and the Jebusites, unto a land flowing with milk and honey.
>
> And they shall hearken to thy voice: and thou shalt come, thou and the elders
> of Israel, unto the king of Egypt, and ye shall say unto him, The Lord God of the
> Hebrews hath met with us: and now let us go, we beseech thee, three days' journey
> into the wilderness, that we may sacrifice to the Lord our God. (Ex. 3:10–18)

Moses approached Pharaoh to petition the Israelites' freedom, but Pharaoh
refused and increased their daily quota of required bricks, including the gathering of
their own straw. Moses was disheartened, and the Lord said,

> Wherefore say unto the children of Israel, I am the Lord, and I will bring you out
> from under the burdens of the Egyptians, and I will rid you out of their bondage,
> and I will redeem you with a stretched out arm, and with great judgments:
>
> And I will take you to me for a people, and I will be to you a God: and ye shall
> know that I am the Lord your God, which bringeth you out from under the bur-
> dens of the Egyptians. (Ex. 6:6–7)

The Israelites would not hearken to Moses, but the Lord had a design to show the
Egyptians as well as the Israelites that He was God over all the earth and had power
to do all things. As time proceeded, the signs and plagues were sent upon the
Egyptians, thus showing the might and power of the God of Israel: the Nile river—
the Egyptians' material god and source of sustenance—was turned to blood, and the
fish died (Ex. 7:14–21), frogs were sent upon the land (Ex. 8:1–15), lice came upon
the people (Ex. 8:16–19), flies were everywhere (Ex. 8:22–32), the animals of the
Egyptians died (Ex. 9:1–7), sores came upon the Egyptians, and a mighty hailstorm
killed all those who were exposed (Ex. 9:8–35), grasshoppers came and devoured all
their plants (Ex. 10:4–20), and darkness covered the land for three days (Ex.
10:21–27). Each time, the Pharaoh promised to let them go if Moses would stop the
plague, but he then went back on his word.

Finally, the Lord told Moses that the firstborn child in every Egyptian home was
to die. The Israelites were to take a lamb without blemish, kill it, and administer the
blood as follows:

> And ye shall take a bunch of hyssop, and dip it in the blood that is in the bason, and
> strike the lintel and the two side posts with the blood that is in the bason; and none
> of you shall go out at the door of his house until the morning.
>
> For the Lord will pass through to smite the Egyptians; and when he seeth the
> blood upon the lintel, and on the two side posts, the Lord will pass over the door,
> and will not suffer the destroyer to come in unto your houses to smite you.

And ye shall observe this thing for an ordinance to thee and to thy sons for ever. (Ex. 12:22–24)

In the Egyptians' homes, the firstborn child was taken by the destroying angel of the Lord. That was the crucial intervening act that caught Pharaoh's attention in earnest. Pharaoh told Moses and Aaron to take the children of Israel and leave (Ex. 12:30–38), and the Lord led the Israelites to freedom. Still desirous to regain the slavery of the Israelites, Pharaoh followed after them with his hosts. Moses, endowed with the power of the Lord, parted the Red Sea, and the Israelites walked across on dry ground. The Egyptians followed, only to be swallowed by the resurging waters (Ex.14:5–30).

The Israelites were finally free. In gratitude, Moses led the Israelites in praises of their God of deliverance (Ex. 15). Thus ends the story of the bondage and liberation of the Israelites through the power of God and His merciful dealings with His covenant people. In remembrance of the liberation, the "Passover" became a day of celebration and gratitude to the Lord for deliverance from Egyptian bondage, for the angel of destruction had passed over the homes of the righteous.

MODERN PROPHETS SPEAK

Russell M. Nelson:

> For both the Israelites and the Saints, their travail forged great spiritual strength. They both endured trials of their faith, during which the weak were winnowed away and the strong were empowered to endure to the end (see Ether 12:6; D&C 101:4–5; D&C 105:19). They had to leave their homes and earthly possessions and learn to rely wholly upon God. Protection was provided for ancient Israel by the Lord, who "went before them by day in a pillar of a cloud, to lead them the way; and by night in a pillar of fire" (Ex. 13:21; see also Ex. 13:22; Num. 14:14; Deut. 1:33; Neh. 9:19). The same has been said of the divine watchcare afforded to the pioneers (see *HC,* 3:xxxiv; see also Thomas S. Monson, *CR,* Apr. 1967, 56).
>
> Scriptures given to both societies speak of the strength of the Lord's hand in their deliverance. To those of ancient Israel, Moses said, "Remember this day, in which ye came out from Egypt, out of the house of bondage; for by strength of hand the Lord brought you out from this place" (Ex. 13:3).
>
> To the Latter-day Saints, a comparable scripture was revealed: "For I, the Lord, have put forth my hand to exert the powers of heaven; ye cannot see it now, yet a little while and ye shall see it, and know that I am" (D&C 84:119).
>
> The children of Israel had a portable tabernacle wherein covenants were made and ordinances were performed to strengthen them on their journey. Many Latter-day Saints were endowed in the Nauvoo Temple before their arduous trek westward.
>
> The Israelites gratefully celebrated their exodus from Egypt. The Latter-day Saints commemorated their exodus with the establishment of the world headquarters

of the restored Church in the tops of the mountains. All celebrants acclaimed their deliverance by God (see Jer. 23:7–8). ("The Exodus Repeated," *Ensign,* July 1999, 9–10)

DOCTRINES AND PRINCIPLES

Just as the Lord liberated the captive Israelites from Egyptian bondage, He has also put in place the saving truths, ordinances, and powers to bless our lives with redeeming grace through the atonement of Jesus Christ. "Let my people go" was the watchword for the Exodus (Ex. 5:1). Similarly, the gospel of Jesus Christ provides the means and power to "let people go" from the bondage of sin and pass through the waters of baptism toward a new life following in the footsteps of the Lord.

PREPARATION: ISRAELITES *in the* WILDERNESS

MOMENT OF TRUTH

As the Israelites journeyed through the wilderness, trials and tests of their faith in God were ongoing. They found that the garden of the Lord was not without its challenges. There was no water to be found for three days. When they found water, it was bitter to the taste, and the people began to murmur. Moses was their representative before the Lord:

> And he cried unto the Lord; and the Lord shewed him a tree, which when he had cast into the waters, the waters were made sweet: there he made for them a statute and an ordinance, and there he proved them,
>
> And said, If thou wilt diligently hearken to the voice of the Lord thy God, and wilt do that which is right in his sight, and wilt give ear to his commandments, and keep all his statutes, I will put none of these diseases upon thee, which I have brought upon the Egyptians: for I am the Lord that healeth thee. (Ex. 15:25–26)

This became the covenant with the Lord—if they obeyed they would be blessed. They continued to travel in the wilderness and struggled for food and became angry with Moses, but when they humbled themselves, the Lord blessed them with food.

MODERN PROPHETS SPEAK

Ezra Taft Benson:
> Let us live the gospel fully, and may we recognize the infallibility of God's inspired word—whether by his "own voice" or the "voice of [his] servants, it is the same." The days ahead are sobering and challenging. Oh, may we be prepared spiritually and temporally! (*God, Family, Country: Our Three Great Loyalties* [Salt Lake City: Deseret Book, 1974], 273)

Neal A. Maxwell:

> There are many who suffer so much more than the rest of us: some go agonizingly; some go quickly; some are healed; some are given more time; some seem to linger. There are variations in our trials but no immunities. Thus, the scriptures cite the fiery furnace and fiery trials (see Dan. 3:6–26; 1 Pet. 4:12). Those who emerge successfully from their varied and fiery furnaces have experienced the grace of the Lord, which He says is sufficient (see Ether 12:27). . . .
>
> The redeeming presence of our loving Father-God in the universe is the grand fact pertaining to the human condition. It is the supernal truth which, along with His plan of happiness, reigns preeminent and imperial over all other realities. Other truths, by comparison, are merely fleeting factoids about which we may be "ever learning" without coming to a knowledge of the grand truths (2 Tim. 3:7).
>
> Mortal experience points evermore to the Atonement of Jesus Christ as the central act of all human history. The more I learn and experience, the more unselfish, stunning, and encompassing His Atonement becomes! ("From Whom All Blessings Flow," *Ensign,* May 1997, 11–12)

DOCTRINES AND PRINCIPLES

The "Manna from Heaven" given to the Israelites during their sojourn in the wilderness typifies the allotment or gift from God embodied in salvation and exaltation. He will provide this transcendent gift if we but believe and act according to His commands. We live by His gifts—in particular the word of God (see D&C 84:43–46). He is the Bread of Life (see John 6:35, 48–51). He is the Atoning Sacrifice. We shall ever be indebted to the Lord (see Mosiah 2:21). Like the ancient Israelites, we also have to obey with exactness to merit the Lord's blessings.

We can recall when the people again became angry with Moses for the lack of water. The Lord, as always after fervent prayer, instructed His prophet:

> Behold, I will stand before thee there upon the rock in Horeb; and thou shalt smite the rock, and there shall come water out of it, that the people may drink. And Moses did so in the sight of the elders of Israel. (Ex. 17:5–6)

The water in the wilderness is analogous to the "living waters" of the gospel (Jer. 17:13; John 4:10; 7:38; 1 Ne. 11:25; D&C 63:23). The wilderness was a preparatory time for the Israelites to progress to become worthy of the law of the Lord. Similarly, we are going through our own preparatory time day-by-day as we progress on the pathways of mortality, endeavoring to live the laws of the Lord and seek His face always (D&C 101:38).

COMMANDMENTS: THE TEN COMMANDMENTS

MOMENT OF TRUTH

The story of the giving of the Ten Commandments is one of the great episodes in all of human history. Joseph Fielding Smith explained how the two sets of tables Moses brought down from Mount Sinai relate to the Law of Moses and the Priesthood:

> Question: *There has been a discussion among members of the ward concerning Moses and his receiving the Ten Commandments. One side of the discussion says that when Moses came down from the mount the first time with the tables and found the people had made them a golden calf to worship, Moses threw down the tables and broke them. These tables contained the gospel, and the people were not ready to accept the gospel, so Moses returned to the mount and received from the Lord the carnal commandments—"Thou shalt not."*
>
> *The other side of the discussion claims that both sets of the tables, the ones he broke and the ones he brought back the second time, were the same, the Ten Commandments on both sets.*
>
> *Please advise, giving references from both ancient and modern scriptures.*
>
> Answer: When Israel came out of Egypt it was the intention of the Lord to make of Israel a royal priesthood. That is to say, that he was to give them the Melchizedek Priesthood and the principles of exaltation. When Moses went up into the mount and was gone forty days, Israel sinned a very serious sin and turned back to the worship of the Egyptians and had Aaron make for them a golden calf. When Moses came down from the mountain, in his anger, he threw down the tables and broke them. Then at the command of the Lord he went back into the mountain, and the Lord gave him other tables on which he wrote with his finger.
>
> The Lord did not write the same things on the second tables that were on the first, but confined Israel to the Aaronic Priesthood and denied the Melchizedek Priesthood to the tribes of Israel except in special cases with certain prophets like

Isaiah, Jeremiah and others. These prophets had the Melchizedek Priesthood by special appointment. The Lord gave to Israel the carnal law and said that they should not enter into his rest while they were in the wilderness.

The Ten Commandments were in existence long before Moses' time, and the Lord only renewed them in the days of Moses, just as he has done in our day.

Now we do not find in the Bible the full history of these things. We do learn that the Lord withdrew from Israel the right to the Melchizedek Priesthood and confined them largely to the Aaronic Priesthood. The full reason for this is not clearly stated. This is due to the fact that the Bible has lost much in translations and copying by the scribes. In the Doctrine and Covenants the Lord has restored some of this history as in D&C 84:19–27. I refer you to the revision given by the Prophet Joseph Smith which tells more about this action.

"And the Lord said unto Moses, Hew thee two other tables of stone, like unto the first, and I will write upon them also, the words of the law, according as they were written at the first on the tables which thou brakest; but it shall not be according to the first, for I will take away the priesthood out of their midst; therefore my holy order, and the ordinances thereof, shall not go before them; for my presence shall not go up in their midst lest I destroy them." (*AGQ*, 3:154–56)

Bruce R. McConkie explained the situation of two sets of tables or tablets in the following manner:

Moses received the Ten Commandments twice (Ex. 20; Deut. 5). Both times they were written by the finger of the Lord on tablets of stone. The first time they were revealed as part of the fulness of the gospel, but when Moses, returning with the sacred tablets, found Israel reveling in idolatrous worship, he broke the tablets. Thereafter, "The Lord said unto Moses, Hew thee two other tables of stone, like unto the first, and I will write upon them also, the words of the law, according as they were written at the first on the tables which thou brakest; *but it shall not be according to the first, for I will take away the priesthood out of their midst;* therefore my holy order, and the ordinances thereof, shall not go before them; for my presence shall not go up in their midst, lest I destroy them. But I will give unto them the law as at the first, *but it shall be after the law of a carnal commandment;* for I have sworn in my wrath, that they shall not enter into my presence, into my rest, in the days of their pilgrimage" (*Inspired Version*, Ex. 34:1–2).

Thus the 2nd revelation to Moses of the Ten Commandments was as part of the law of carnal commandments, rather than of the gospel itself. In both instances, however, the same unchanging, eternal standards of worship and moral conduct were revealed. The two accounts differ in only one major respect and that is in the reason assigned for honoring the Sabbath day. While they lived under the law, the

Sabbath was to Israel an occasion to commemorate their deliverance from Egyptian bondage (Deut. 5:12–15) rather than to point their attention back to the hallowed period of rest that followed the six days of creative work when the earth was made (Ex. 20:8–11). (*MD,* 783)

MODERN PROPHETS SPEAK

Hugh B. Brown:

Sometimes men speak of breaking the Ten Commandments, but as Cecil B. DeMille observed, "Men do not break the Ten Commandments, they only break themselves against them." In the same sense laws of nature cannot be broken, though we may try to ignore them; for instance, we cannot break the law of gravity. One may try to defy it by jumping off a cliff, but whether he be prince or pauper, and however repentant he may be on the way down, there will be no mitigation of consequences. He will be broken by the law through his own folly. (*Continuing the Quest* [Salt Lake City: Deseret Book, 1961], 225)

George Albert Smith:

It was a long time ago that the Lord gave to Moses the Ten Commandments. If the people of the world had observed the Ten Commandments from that time until now, we would have a different world. There would be millions of people who would live longer than they have lived and be happier. The Ten Commandments are in force today, and if we are good Latter-day Saints and are observing what the Lord has advised, among other things, we will honor the Sabbath day and not make it a day of pleasure. The Constitution guarantees us liberty that no other nation enjoys. Most of the nations are losing the liberties they have had because they have not kept the commandments of the Lord. (*The Teachings of George Albert Smith* [Salt Lake City: Deseret Book, 2004], 97)

Harold B. Lee:

Order and peace come from keeping the two great commandments. When asked by critical questioners, one of which was a lawyer, "Master, which is the great commandment in the law? Jesus said unto him, Thou shalt love the Lord thy God with all thy heart, and with all thy soul, and with all thy mind. This is the first and great commandment. And the second is like unto it, Thou shalt love thy neighbour as thyself. On these two commandments hang all the law and the prophets" (Matt. 22:36–40). . . .

A moment's reflection with reference to the Master's statement in regard to these two greatest commandments will be a realization that the first five of the Ten Commandments could be obeyed if men were to observe the first of the two great commandments, "to love the Lord thy God with heart, soul, and mind." If this commandment were obeyed, men would have no other gods before Him; they would make no graven image of Him; they would not worship any other god; there would be no taking of the name of God in vain; all would keep the Sabbath day holy.

Likewise, if the second of the Master's greatest commandments were obeyed, men would honor their fathers and mothers; there would be no murders, no adultery, no stealing; they could not bear false witness against their neighbors; they would not covet that which was their neighbor's. Thus declared is the profound truth that if men would love God and their neighbors as themselves there would be order—there would be peace. (*The Teachings of Harold B. Lee* [Salt Lake City: Bookcraft, 1996], 84–85)

Ezra Taft Benson:

We must put God in the forefront of everything else in our lives. He must come first, just as He declares in the first of His Ten Commandments: "Thou shalt have no other gods before me" (Exodus 20:3).

When we put God first, all other things fall into their proper place or drop out of our lives. Our love of the Lord will govern the claims of our affection, the demands on our time, the interests we pursue, and the order of our priorities. (*TETB,* 349–50)

Neal L. Maxwell:

Once we remove belief in God from the center of our lives, as the source of truth and as a determiner of justice, a tremendous vacuum is created into which selfishness surges, a condition that governments delight in managing.

Tens of thousands of regulations emerging from governments receive attention not given the Ten Commandments, perhaps because the Ten Commandments, which are so much a part of our Judeo-Christian heritage, are not flexible; they resist rationalization. Any amendments to the Ten Commandments could come only from the original Source. We cannot amend the seventh commandment to read, for instance, "Thou shalt not commit adultery except between consenting adults."

We are, of course, free to obey or not to obey those commandments discarding the lamp noted in Proverbs. But we cannot get that lamp to make light by using a substitute fuel. We may, by legislation and regulation, vainly try to create a zone of private morality. But there is, ultimately, no such thing as private morality; there are not an indoor set and an outdoor set of Ten Commandments.

Those who disavow the existence of certain absolute truths must forever forgo disapproving of anything on moral grounds. They may try to evoke a social or political response by using the old words that went with the old values, but they will soon learn that words cannot, for long, be appropriated productively minus their moral content. (*Notwithstanding My Weakness* [Salt Lake City: Deseret Book, 1981], 34–35)

HOLINESS *to the* LORD: THE TABERNACLE

MOMENT OF TRUTH

Since the beginning of time the Lord has desired to come to His people in His House that He might bless them. The Lord commanded Moses, "And let them make me a sanctuary; that I may dwell among them" (Ex. 25:8). The Lord revealed to Moses how to build His Tabernacle. The Lord said:

> And there I will meet with the children of Israel, and [the tabernacle] shall be sanctified by my glory.
>
> And I will sanctify the tabernacle of the congregation, and the altar: I will sanctify also both Aaron and his sons, to minister to me in the priest's office.
>
> And I will dwell among the children of Israel, and will be their God.
>
> And they shall know that I am the Lord their God, that brought them forth out of the land of Egypt, that I may dwell among them: I am the Lord their God. (Ex. 29:43–46)

The children of Israel obeyed the Lord and sacrificed their precious things for the building of the Tabernacle. Moses truly was joyful with the building of the Tabernacle and blessed it and those who helped in its construction. Then the power, glory, and blessing of the Lord were manifested and continued with the Israelites as they traveled:

> Then a cloud covered the tent of the congregation, and the glory of the Lord filled the tabernacle.
>
> And Moses was not able to enter into the tent of the congregation, because the cloud abode thereon, and the glory of the Lord filled the tabernacle.
>
> And when the cloud was taken up from over the tabernacle, the children of Israel went onward in all their journeys:

But if the cloud were not taken up, then they journeyed not till the day that it was taken up.

For the cloud of the Lord was upon the tabernacle by day, and fire was on it by night, in the sight of all the house of Israel, throughout all their journeys. (Ex. 40:34–38)

Just as the Lord commanded Moses, He also commanded the Prophet Joseph concerning His holy house, as is recorded:

For, for this cause I commanded Moses that he should build a tabernacle, that they should bear it with them in the wilderness, and to build a house in the land of promise, that those ordinances might be revealed which had been hid from before the world was.

Therefore, verily I say unto you, that your anointings, and your washings, and your baptisms for the dead, and your solemn assemblies, and your memorials for your sacrifices by the sons of Levi, and for your oracles in your most holy places wherein you receive conversations, and your statutes and judgments, for the beginning of the revelations and foundation of Zion, and for the glory, honor, and endowment of all her municipals, are ordained by the ordinance of my holy house, which my people are always commanded to build unto my holy name.

And verily I say unto you, let this house be built unto my name, that I may reveal mine ordinances therein unto my people;

For I deign to reveal unto my church things which have been kept hid from before the foundation of the world, things that pertain to the dispensation of the fulness of times.

And I will show unto my servant Joseph all things pertaining to this house, and the priesthood thereof, and the place whereon it shall be built.

And ye shall build it on the place where you have contemplated building it, for that is the spot which I have chosen for you to build it.

If ye labor with all your might, I will consecrate that spot that it shall be made holy. (D&C 124:38–44)

MODERN PROPHETS SPEAK

Joseph Fielding Smith:

The Lord required haste in the building of the tabernacle by Moses so that he might reveal himself therein. It was in this portable, but costly sanctuary, that the Lord instructed Moses after it was built. For several centuries the tabernacle served the people of Israel and was known as the temple of God. (*DS,* 2:235)

Gordon B. Hinckley:

> The Lord has made it possible for us in these holy houses to receive our own [ordinances]. Then we have the opportunity and responsibility of extending these same blessings to those who have passed on without the privilege. But in the very process there comes into our own lives a refinement of character, together with increased spirituality. It is interesting to reflect on the fact that although many on the other side may not receive the ordinances done for them here, those who perform these ordinances will be blessed in the very process of doing so. (*TGBH*, 622–23)

Gordon B. Hinckley:

> This vicarious work constitutes an unprecedented labor of love on the part of the living in behalf of the dead. It makes necessary a vast undertaking of genealogical research to find and identify those who have gone before. (*Be Thou an Example* [Salt Lake City: Deseret Book, 1981], 131)

DOCTRINES AND PRINCIPLES

Surely it is in the temple that the blessings of the eternities are given to the children of God if they are but worthy. Temples are sacred. They are "The House of the Lord." They are erected and dedicated as sacred precincts where we can worship God and receive sacred ordinances of exaltation. Temple work and family history is all about families. Families can be forever. Family history and temple work are key in regard to having eternal families—without this work, families could not be forever. The restoration of the Priesthood and sealing power through Elijah has truly caused the children and their fathers to turn toward each other (see D&C 2). This power makes possible the eternal family. As we search out our ancestors and do their temple work, we can be made perfect with them, and they in us (see D&C 128:15). Developing and studying family history brings appreciation and gratitude for the past and all the sacrifices that were made. The process brings families closer together. The histories serve as inspiration and motivation for the descendants to live righteous lives. Part of our family history work is in doing genealogical research to identify family members who need temple ordinances, and then in ensuring that these ordinances are performed. Truly the temple serves as the transcendent beacon of light drawing families toward their promised eternal covenant destiny.

SUCCOR HIS PEOPLE: ISRAEL *in the* WILDERNESS

MOMENT OF TRUTH

The Lord's people must be tried. It is in the trials and tribulations that we are humbled and turn to the Lord so that He can nurture and succor us in all of our afflictions (see Alma 7:11–12). The wilderness sojourn for the Israelites after the Exodus from Egypt was indeed a difficult experience. They struggled. They murmured. The Lord sent them manna; they grew tired of manna and wanted meat. The Lord sent them quail; they were still anxious and desirous for better conditions. Finally, they came to the land of Canaan. Moses sent a spy delegation consisting of a leader from each of the twelve tribes. The report came back: Canaan was indeed a land of milk and honey, but the inhabitants were too strong for the Israelites to defeat. Once more the seeds of doubt were sown, and the people, lacking in faith, again became angry with Moses. The record gives the Lord's reaction:

> And the Lord spake unto Moses and unto Aaron, saying,
>
> How long shall I bear with this evil congregation, which murmur against me? I have heard the murmurings of the children of Israel, which they murmur against me.
>
> Say unto them, As truly as I live, saith the Lord, as ye have spoken in mine ears, so will I do to you:
>
> Your carcases shall fall in this wilderness; and all that were numbered of you, according to your whole number, from twenty years old and upward, which have murmured against me,
>
> Doubtless ye shall not come into the land, concerning which I sware to make you dwell therein, save Caleb the son of Jephunneh, and Joshua the son of Nun.
>
> But your little ones, which ye said should be a prey, them will I bring in, and they shall know the land which ye have despised.
>
> But as for you, your carcases, they shall fall in this wilderness.
>
> And your children shall wander in the wilderness forty years, and bear your whoredoms, until your carcases be wasted in the wilderness. (Num. 14:26–33)

After all the Lord had done for them, Israel feared for their lives and lacked faith and trust in the God of Israel—and thus began the 40 years in the wilderness: "And the Lord's anger was kindled against Israel, and he made them wander in the wilderness forty years, until all the generation, that had done evil in the sight of the Lord, was consumed" (Num. 32:13).

The Lord will have a humble people. He will have a people willing to follow His commandments and prove themselves worthy of the Promised Land: "And thou shalt remember all the way which the Lord thy God led thee these forty years in the wilderness, to humble thee, and to prove thee, to know what was in thine heart, whether thou wouldest keep his commandments, or no" (Deut. 8:2; see also Josh. 5:6).

Let us remember that all among the Israelites died off who were "twenty years old and upward," save Joshua and Caleb. Traditions die hard. Traditions have power—for good or bad—and the Israelites suffered because of their wicked traditions. Hence a new generation came about. A new generation born of righteousness was required in order to enter the Promised Land.

MODERN PROPHETS SPEAK

Neal A. Maxwell:

> The Lord has also clearly promised to succor us in the midst of our temptations: "Behold, and hearken, O ye elders of my church, saith the Lord your God, even Jesus Christ, your advocate, who knoweth the weakness of man and how to succor them who are tempted" (D&C 62:1). Such divine, close-in support as is promised in the scriptures means that God's grace will be sufficient for us if we are humble.
>
> However, we must turn ourselves over to the Lord, so that we can be succored by Him and so that our weaknesses can even become strengths.
>
> It is also required of us, however, that we help others along the way. The counsel given to Frederick G. Williams when he was called to be a counselor in the First Presidency applies to us all: "Wherefore, be faithful; stand in the office which I have appointed unto you; succor the weak, lift up the hands which hang down, and strengthen the feeble knees" (D&C 81:5).
>
> Those are second-commandment duties. Job was praised for doing them: "Behold, thou hast instructed many, and thou hast strengthened the weak hands. Thy words have upholden him that was falling, and thou hast strengthened the feeble knees" (Job 4:3–4).
>
> Clearly, we are to help each other in the journey along the straight and narrow path. Even though such helping seems to drain us of energy and surely takes precious time, it will actually strengthen us. We will become more like Him whose followers we are. (Neal A. Maxwell, *Notwithstanding My Weakness* [Salt Lake City: Deseret Book, 1981], 14–15)

AGENCY: JOSHUA

MOMENT OF TRUTH

As the Israelites prepared to end their 40 years' sojourn in the wilderness and enter the Promised Land, Joshua was called of the Lord and reminded: "There shall not any man be able to stand before thee all the days of thy life: as I was with Moses, so I will be with thee: I will not fail thee, nor forsake thee" (Josh. 1:5).

The Lord assured Joshua that Israel would possess the Promised Land as their inheritance. The priests carrying the Ark of the Covenant touched the Jordan River banks, and the water was stopped up, and the Israelites crossed on dry ground. Again, the power of the Lord was manifest on behalf of the Israelites. After following the Lord's instructions to bring down the walls of Jericho, Joshua divided the land among the tribes of Israel and promised them, so long as they were righteous, that they could enjoy the fruits of the Promised Land.

As Joshua came to the end of his life, he cautioned the people about worshipping false Gods and enjoined them to keep the commandments. Then he made this bold and memorable declaration:

> Now therefore fear the Lord, and serve him in sincerity and in truth: and put away the gods which your fathers served on the other side of the flood, and in Egypt; and serve ye the Lord.
>
> And if it seem evil unto you to serve the Lord, choose you this day whom ye will serve; whether the gods which your fathers served that were on the other side of the flood, or the gods of the Amorites, in whose land ye dwell: but as for me and my house, we will serve the Lord. (Josh. 24:14–15)

MODERN PROPHETS SPEAK

Gordon B. Hinckley:

> I should like to suggest three standards by which to judge each of the decisions that determine the behavior patterns of your lives. These standards are so simple as to appear elementary, but I believe their faithful observance will provide a set of moral imperatives by which to govern without argument or equivocation each of our actions and which will bring unmatched rewards. They are: 1. Does it enrich the mind? 2. Does it discipline and strengthen the body? 3. Does it nourish the spirit?" ("Caesar, Circus, or Christ?" *BYU Speeches of the Year,* October 26, 1965, 4)

DOCTRINES AND PRINCIPLES

We should make the same decision that Joshua made. We are free to choose. We have moral agency as a gift—with consequences or blessings according to our choices (see 2 Ne. 2:27).

Agency is supreme. We are a result of the use of our agency. Our choices and decisions determine our blessings or the consequences of our actions. Agency can operate because there is (1) opposition in all things, (2) knowledge of good and evil, (3) laws and commandments given by God, and (4) the freedom to choose. This free gift is really moral agency, which connotes responsibility and accountability in regard to our choices.

Satan seeks to take away our agency by making us think that our decisions have no consequences. He does his insidious work through subtlety, lies, and half-truths (see 2 Ne. 28:7–9; Moses 4:4; 3 Ne. 2:2; Alma 12:4).

LOYALTY: RUTH *and* NAOMI

MOMENT OF TRUTH

The book of Ruth demonstrates many of the building blocks of the abundant life, including the loyalty and devotion of Ruth, the kindness and love of Boaz, the effulgent joy that the hopeful Naomi experienced to see her emptied home filled again with loved ones, and the tolerance and respect that the Israelites learned to cultivate for one of their Moabite adoptees. These building blocks of the abundant life are still efficacious in our day and age. The same principles apply to our challenges and tests as applied to these people in ancient times, for abundance is a gift of the Spirit and comes through principles of righteousness.

MODERN PROPHETS SPEAK

Thomas S. Monson:

> A model of ideal womanhood is Ruth. Sensing the grief-stricken heart of her mother-in-law Naomi—who suffered the loss of each of her two fine sons—feeling perhaps the pangs of despair and loneliness that plagued the very soul of Naomi, Ruth uttered what has become that classic statement of loyalty: "Intreat me not to leave thee, or to return from following after thee: for whither thou goest, I will go; and where thou lodgest, I will lodge: thy people shall be my people, and thy God my God" (Ruth 1:16). Ruth's actions demonstrated the sincerity of her words.
>
> Through Ruth's undeviating loyalty to Naomi, she was to marry Boaz, by which she—the foreigner and Moabite convert—became a great-grandmother of David and, therefore, an ancestor of our Savior Jesus Christ. ("Models to Follow," *Ensign,* Nov. 2002, 61)

DOCTRINES AND PRINCIPLES

A transcending truth unfolds when we recognize that Ruth was of the Moabite lineage, one of the indigenous cultures remaining in the Holy Land after the return of

Israel from Egypt. The original Moab was the son of Lot's oldest daughter (see Gen. 19:37), and thus the Moabites were akin to the Israelites but represented a different way of life and religion. Ruth represented the local culture at its best, being a pure and virtuous individual with the highest aspirations and character, and she embraced wholeheartedly the Israelite way of life. She was welcomed into her new environment and became instrumental in continuing the promised lineage via David to the Savior himself. What a fitting unfolding of history that the Author of universal salvation should have come from a line that combined in Ruth and Boaz the confluence of two cultures—one Israelite and the other non-Israelite—but both from the same Maker and Creator. It is a reminder that converts to the Church and Kingdom of God are welcome from all kindreds, nations, tongues, and peoples.

The traits of kindness and love, so enduringly reflected in the story of the relationship of Boaz and Ruth, add a glow of the divine to our temporal lives of challenge and trial: "And now my daughter, fear not; I will do to thee all that thou requirest: for all the city of my people doth know that thou art a virtuous woman" (Ruth 3:11); "Blessed be the Lord, which hath not left thee this day without a kinsman, that his name may be famous in Israel. And he shall be unto thee a restorer of thy life, and a nourisher of thine old age" (Ruth 4:14–15).

Ruth gave up many personal things because of her devotion and loyalty to Naomi—her family, her friends, and her homeland with all of its cultural surroundings. Because of her strong family ties, she was faithful to Naomi. This lesson brings to light the character traits of true Saints. Devotion and loyalty rank high among those attributes we should seek.

Loyalty must be anchored in correct principles. We should be loyal to enduring values, we should be honorable, and we should base our loyalty on love. Loyalty is an active trait. It is the first line of defense. It lifts and encourages. Loyalty is wise. We should establish priorities as to where we put our loyalties. We should build strong relationships—loyalty to a person is only as strong as the bonds of the relationship, and loyalty to a cause is only as strong as the conversion to that cause. You earn loyalty through loyalty. Loyalty is ultimately spiritual. One cannot be loyal to one's fellows without being loyal to the Father of us all.

One of the difficult decisions in loyalty arises when torn between loyalty to the person and loyalty to the cause. If all were perfect, this conflict might never exist. The importance of people far outweighs that of a program or project or cause—so long as we are loyal to our God and so long as others do not suffer unnecessarily as a result of one's choice. People truly matter most.

The story of Ruth exemplifies so many truly Christ-like attributes. We can see why Thomas S. Monson declared: "There is place for her name in the Hall of Fame" ("My Personal Hall of Fame," *Ensign*, Jul. 1991, 4).

PRAYER: SAMUEL

MOMENT OF TRUTH

Samuel came into the care of the priest Eli. During the night, Samuel heard a voice. Samuel inquired of Eli who it might be, but Eli had him return to his bed. When this scene repeated itself twice more, Eli told him to listen, for it was the Lord calling. Samuel continued in righteousness and became the prophet of the Lord:

> And Samuel grew, and the Lord was with him, and did let none of his words fall to the ground.
>
> And all Israel from Dan even to Beersheba knew that Samuel was established to be a prophet of the Lord. (1 Sam 3:19–20)

MODERN PROPHETS SPEAK

Gordon B. Hinckley:

> Be prayerful. You can't do it alone. You know that. You cannot make it alone and do your best. You need the help of the Lord . . . and the marvelous thing is that you have the opportunity to pray, with the expectation that your prayers will be heard and answered. . . . The marvelous thing about prayer is that it is personal, it's individual, it's something that no one else gets into, in terms of your speaking with your Father in Heaven in the name of the Lord Jesus Christ. Be prayerful. Ask the Lord to forgive your sins. Ask the Lord for help. Ask the Lord to bless you. Ask the Lord to help you realize your righteous ambitions. . . . Ask the Lord for all of the important things that mean so much to you in your lives. He stands ready to help. Don't ever forget it. (*TGBH,* 468)

DOCTRINES AND PRINCIPLES

The Lord hears and answers prayers of righteousness, even as He heard Hannah's. The blessings of prayer truly empower us to do all things. We can preach and teach with the power and authority of God (see Alma 17:3), seek forgiveness of sins (see Enos 1:4), gain knowledge of the truth (see Alma 5:46), help people who know not God (see Alma 6:6), bless others through our righteous prayers (see Mosiah 27:14; Alma 10:23), counsel with the Lord and receive direction in or lives (see Alma 37:37), become stronger in our humility and firmer in our faith (see Hel. 3:35), and receive the blessings of charity when praying with all the energy of our heart (see Moro. 7:48). In all things, we shall be blessed as we call upon God.

PRIDE: KING SAUL

MOMENT OF TRUTH

Just as in the case of the young Saul, the Lord favors the humble and spiritually malleable, and blesses them in their callings by giving them a transformed and rejuvenated heart. However, we must work to maintain that humility throughout our lives.

When we begin to govern our lives according to our own desires and judgment rather than acting in the spirit of our commission as servants of God, then we begin to falter and lose favor with the Lord. Only by obedience to the commandments and will of God can we hope to have the blessings of heaven and prosper in our duties and service. We learn this great lesson from the scriptures when Saul pridefully asserted his own will rather than follow the commandments of God. Samuel reminded him: "Hath the Lord as great delight in burnt offerings and sacrifices, as in obeying the voice of the Lord? Behold, to obey is better than sacrifice, and to hearken than the fat of rams" (1 Sam. 15:22).

Then came the divine verdict: "And Samuel said unto Saul, I will not return with thee: for thou hast rejected the word of the Lord, and the Lord hath rejected thee from being king over Israel" (1 Sam. 15:26). Samuel then sought out a future King to replace Saul—one who would not be dominated by pride but would heed the counsels of the Lord.

MODERN PROPHETS SPEAK

Ezra Taft Benson:

> In the scriptures there is no such thing as righteous pride. It is always considered as a sin. We are not speaking of a wholesome view of self-worth, which is best established by a close relationship with God. But we are speaking of pride as the universal sin, as someone has described it. Mormon writes that "the pride of this nation,

or the people of the Nephites, hath proven their destruction" (Moro. 8:27). The Lord says in the Doctrine and Covenants, "Beware of pride, lest ye become as the Nephites of old" (D&C 38:39). Essentially, pride is a "my will" rather than "thy will" approach to life. The opposite of pride is humbleness, meekness, submissiveness, or teachableness (see Alma 13:28). (*TETB,* 435)

Ezra Taft Benson:

> Pride is . . . the universal sin, the great vice. It manifests itself in competition, selfishness, contention, power-seeking, backbiting, living beyond our means, coveting, climbing the ladder of worldly success at the expense of others, and in a multitude of ways that "pit our will against God's" and limit our progression. Pride affects all of us at various times and in various degrees. . . . Pride is the stumbling block to Zion. The antidote for pride is humility—meekness, submissiveness. Members can choose to humble themselves by conquering enmity toward others, receiving counsel and chastisement, forgiving others, rendering selfless service, going on missions and preaching the word that can humble others, going to the temple more frequently, and by confessing and forsaking sins and being born of God. ("Beware of Pride," *Ensign,* May 1989, 4)

DOCTRINES AND PRINCIPLES

A sad but oft repeated phenomenon occurred in the life of King Saul. It started out well, with Samuel telling Saul, "And the Spirit of the Lord will come upon thee, and thou shalt prophesy with them, and shalt be turned into another man" (1 Sam. 10:6). But things went into decline. Pride and arrogance of the type that consumed King Saul are the fuels of lethal envy and jealousy. Only by cultivating a life of humility and penitence can we hope to avoid such an insidious state of pride and greed and qualify for the spirit of harmony, peace, and joy in this life and eternal rest in the life to come.

Saul was an eye-witness to the process of his own dethronement: "And Saul saw and knew that the Lord was with David . . . And Saul was yet the more afraid of David; and Saul became David's enemy continually" (1 Sam. 18:28–29). Saul was plagued by the spirit of jealousy and continually plotted for the death of David. But David deftly followed the course of safety opened up for him by the Lord and thus repeatedly escaped harm. Saul had been abandoned by the Lord—or rather he had abandoned the Lord—just as David had been taken into the Lord's favor, thus it was inevitable that David would ultimately ascend the throne of Israel.

Saul had now turned entirely to his own ways, doing his own will and being full of pride. How often have we seen this same scenario play out in the Book of Mormon:

humility brings blessings; blessings bring prosperity; prosperity brings pride; and pride leads to downfall. The cycle of pride was demonstrated time and time again. We too are subject to that same cycle—individually and collectively—unless we continually humble ourselves before God in gratitude and thanksgiving on a daily basis as we have been taught. Failing to do so invites pride to creep into our patterns of living. Pride is at the crux of most sins. It is a sin that is universal in nature. Most are afflicted to one degree or another with elements of pride. Pride is expressed in arrogance, haughtiness, self-love, vanity, and egotism. Pride creates enmity between God and man.

It is not only an attitudinal problem; prideful thoughts are so powerful that they lead to sinful behavior—sins of commission as well as omission. Pride brings with it other sins that are all too easily expressed, such as selfishness, greed, lust, jealousy, power-seeking, envy, and a whole host of trailing problems that will tempt us and lead us to sin. This is why the Lord continually counsels us against pride (see Prov. 16:18; D&C 23:1).

STRENGTH *in* *the* LORD: DAVID *and* GOLIATH

MOMENT OF TRUTH

The classic story of David and Goliath teaches many truths. David showed humility, trust, faith, and strength in the Lord. By way of contrast, Goliath's boastful nature and trust in the arm of the flesh were evident, as we learn from the scriptures.

> And the Philistine said to David, Come to me and I will give thy flesh unto the fowls of the air, and to the beasts of the field.
>
> Then said David to the Philistine, Thou comest to me with a sword, and with a spear, and with a shield: but I come to thee in the name of the Lord of hosts, the God of the armies of Israel, whom thou hast defied.
>
> This day will the Lord deliver thee into mine hand. (1 Sam. 17:44–46)

The Lord will truly fight our battles and provide a way for us to accomplish His righteous purposes (see 1 Ne. 3:7; D&C 105:14).

MODERN PROPHETS SPEAK

Harold B. Lee:

> Stand therefore, having your loins girt about with truth, and having on the breastplate of righteousness;
>
> And your feet shod with the preparation of the gospel of peace.
>
> And take the helmet of salvation (Eph. 6:14–15, 17).
>
> Did you note carefully the four main parts of your bodies to be guarded:
>
> 1. A girdle about your loins.
>
> 2. A breastplate over your heart.

3. Your feet shod.

4. A helmet on your head.

These instructions take on full significance when it is remembered the loins are those portions of the body between the lower ribs and the hips in which are located the vital generative organs, and also that in the scriptures and other inspired writings the loins symbolize virtue or moral purity and vital strength. The heart suggests our daily conduct in life, for as the Master taught:

"Out of the abundance of the heart the mouth speaketh. A good man . . . bringeth forth good things: and an evil man . . . bringeth forth evil things." (Matt. 12:34–35)

The feet typify the course you chart in the journey of life. The head, of course, represents your intellect.

But now pay careful heed to the fabric from which the various parts of your armor are to be fashioned.

Truth is to be the substance of which the girdle about your loins is to be formed if your virtue and vital strength are to be safeguarded. (*Stand Ye in Holy Places* [Salt Lake City: Deseret Book, 1974], 330–31)

Spencer W. Kimball:

Now, my young brothers, remember that every David has a Goliath to defeat, and every Goliath can be defeated. He may not be a bully who fights with fists or sword or gun. He may not even be flesh and blood. He may not be nine feet tall; he may not be armor-protected, but every boy has his Goliaths. And every boy has access to the brook with its smooth stones.

You will meet Goliaths who threaten you. Whether your Goliath is a town bully or is the temptation to steal or to destroy or the temptation to rob or the desire to curse and swear; if your Goliath is the desire to wantonly destroy or the temptation to lust and to sin, or the urge to avoid activity, whatever is your Goliath, he can be slain. But remember, to be the victor, one must follow the path that David followed:

"David behaved himself wisely in all his ways; and the Lord was with him" (1 Sam. 18:14). (*TSWK,* 154)

DOCTRINES AND PRINCIPLES

The Lord can transform our weaknesses into strengths. By all appearances, David was no match for Goliath, but the young lad prevailed for the cause of Israel because he acted in the strength of the Lord. Once more, the record gives evidence of the power of God to do all things—to deliver David (see 1 Sam. 17:37), to strengthen Paul (see 2 Cor. 12:9), to empower Ammon (see Alma 26:12), to guide the missionaries of today as we proclaim the gospel (see D&C 1:23)—and the list goes on ad infinitum with many examples of the Lord strengthening His children.

The power of the story of David and Goliath lies within being humble and relying on the Lord in all things. Lest we forget, as to ourselves we are nothing, but in the strength of the Lord we can do all things (see 1 Ne. 21:5; Alma 20:4; 26:12; Ether 12:27).

REPENTANCE: KING DAVID

MOMENT OF TRUTH

David's temptation did not end with sexual sin, but extended to further evil machinations beyond his lasciviousness:

> And it came to pass in the morning, that David wrote a letter to Joab, and sent *it* by the hand of Uriah.
>
> And he wrote in the letter, saying, Set ye Uriah in the forefront of the hottest battle, and retire ye from him, that he may be smitten, and die. (2 Sam. 11:14–15)

In acting upon his lust, David committed a greater crime in arranging for the death of Uriah. David then married Bath-sheba, but God knew his sin. Nathan, the prophet, came to David and said, "Wherefore hast thou despised the commandment of the Lord, to do evil in his sight? thou hast killed Uriah the Hittite with the sword, and hast taken his wife to be thy wife, and hast slain him with the sword of the children of Ammon" (2 Sam. 12:9).

This bleak and treacherous circumstance lead David to the devastating insight that he had committed gross sin. The seeds of repentance sprouted slowly but surely: "And David said unto Nathan, I have sinned against the Lord. And Nathan said unto David, The Lord also hath put away thy sin; thou shalt not die" (2 Sam 12:13).

MODERN PROPHETS SPEAK

Joseph Fielding Smith:

> Question: *Some time ago the question came up as to the standing of King David because of his sin as pertaining to Uriah. Because we understand there is no forgiveness for murder some of the class felt he lost his priesthood and retrogressed from the time of this inci-*

dent. Others felt that inasmuch as David repented and abhorred his sin and indicated his sorrow, that he did not lose his priesthood. Would you please enlighten us? What is the teaching of the Church on this point? What is his status?

Answer: David sorely repented all his life, but his sin was so great that he lost everything and the Prophet Joseph Smith has given us this information. Speaking of the Jews whom Peter addressed as recorded in the third chapter of Acts, they could not receive forgiveness for their sins, although they repented, until Christ comes, and the same is true of David. These are the words of the Prophet to the Jews:

"A murderer, for instance, one that sheds innocent blood, cannot have forgiveness. David sought repentance at the hand of God carefully with tears, for the murder of Uriah; but he could only get it through hell; he got a promise that his soul should not be left in hell.

"Although David was a king, he never did obtain the spirit and power of Elijah and the fulness of the priesthood; and the priesthood that he received, and the throne and kingdom of David is to be taken from him and given to another by the name of David in the last days, raised up out of his lineage. . . ."

"Repent ye therefore, and be converted, that your sins may be blotted out, when the times of refreshing (redemption) shall come from the presence of the Lord, and he shall send Jesus Christ, which before was preached unto you," &c. (Acts 3:19–21). The time of redemption here had reference to the time when Christ should come; then and not till then, would their sins be blotted out. Why? Because they were murderers, and no murderer hath eternal life. Even David must wait for those times of refreshing, before he can come forth and his sins be blotted out. For Peter, speaking of him says, "David hath not yet ascended into heaven, for his sepulchre is with us to this day" (Acts 2:29). His remains were then in the tomb. Now, we read that many bodies of the Saints arose at Christ's resurrection, probably all the Saints, but it seems that David did not (Matt. 27:52–53). Why? Because he had been a murderer. (*AGQ*, 3:145–46)

DOCTRINES AND PRINCIPLES

In considering our own sins, we need to realize that an unrighteous thought and/or action—or the lack of action (omission) that might be called for in keeping with righteous principles—is usually considered as a sin when one is accountable. It is transgressing the law of God (see 1 Jn. 3:4). The devil "inviteth and enticeth to sin" (Moro. 7:12). When we sin, we do withdraw ourselves from the Spirit (see Mosiah 2:36) and become more easily influenced by the devil and his temptations (see D&C 29:40). All have sinned (see 1 Jn. 1:8–10), but we are free to choose righteousness rather than sin (see 2 Ne. 2:27). The test of life is to make good choices and to repent of our sins by exercising faith unto repentance (see Alma 34:15–17), and when we confess and forsake our sins, the Lord remembers them no more (see D&C 58:42–43). The Lord makes no allowance for sin, but He is compassionate and merciful to the repentant sinner (see D&C 1:31–32)—for we cannot be saved in our sins (see Alma 11:37).

When we succumb to sin, we subject ourselves to the consequences of the sin according to the natural law that applies—we lose the Spirit, and then we lose all the blessings associated with keeping the commandment.

WISDOM: KING SOLOMON

MOMENT OF TRUTH

And God gave Solomon wisdom and understanding exceeding much, and largeness of heart, even as the sand that is on the sea shore.

And Solomon's wisdom excelled the wisdom of all the children of the east country, and all the wisdom of Egypt.

For he was wiser than all men; than Ethan the Ezrahite, and Heman, and Chalcol, and Darda, the sons of Mahol: and his fame was in all nations round about.

And he spake three thousand proverbs: and his songs were a thousand and five.

And he spake of trees, from the cedar tree that is in Lebanon even unto the hyssop that springeth out of the wall: he spake also of beasts, and of fowl, and of creeping things, and of fishes.

And there came of all people to hear the wisdom of Solomon, from all kings of the earth, which had heard of his wisdom. (1 Kgs. 4:29–34)

Solomon's wisdom is recounted in the often told story of the two women who each claimed to be the mother of a baby boy. Solomon discerned the truth and replied with an order to cut the baby in half and give half to each mother. "Then spake the woman whose the living child was unto the king, for her bowels yearned upon her son, and she said, O my lord, give her the living child, and in no wise slay it. But the other said, Let it be neither mine nor thine, but divide it. Then the king answered and said, Give her the living child, and in no wise slay it: she is the mother thereof" (1 Kgs. 3:26–27).

Despite his enormous wisdom and his triumph in building the great temple, Solomon eventually allowed his interests to shift unwisely to behaviors that violated his sacred trust, for he married outside Israel and his heart turned to idolatry (1 Kgs. 11). In his example, we can perceive with clarity the opposing principles of wisdom and worldliness. Through his example, we can learn important lessons about seeking to make wise choices and avoiding the pitfalls of temptation.

MODERN PROPHETS SPEAK

Bruce R. McConkie:

> That wisdom which leads to salvation comes from God by revelation. Every person on earth, in or out of the Church, can gain wisdom from the Lord, who is the source and font of all truth and righteousness. Those outside the Church who diligently seek will be led to the gospel of salvation where perfect wisdom resides; those in the Church, when they seek righteousness with all their hearts, will be led along the path of truth and revelation until they know all things and have all wisdom. (*Doctrinal New Testament Commentary,* [Salt Lake City: Bookcraft, 1965–73], 3:245)

Gordon B. Hinckley:

> We need not look far in the world to know that "the wisdom of the wise has perished and that the understanding of the prudent has come to naught." That wisdom for which the world should seek is the wisdom which comes from God. The only understanding that will save the world is divine understanding. (*TGBH,* 500)

DOCTRINES AND PRINCIPLES

One of the greatest tests of character is how we use the talents, gifts, and means with which the Lord has blessed us. The better part of wisdom is to aspire to outcomes of service and honor that will merit the judgment cited by the Savior in His parable of the talents: "Well done, thou good and faithful servant; thou hast been faithful over a few things, I will make thee ruler over many things: enter into the joy of thy lord" (Matt. 25:21, 23). Few in the history of the world have been blessed with gifts and means to exceed those of Solomon, the son of David. As long as he used these resources to bless the lives of others and further God's purposes—such as rendering sound judgment among the people and erecting the Temple of the Lord—he prospered and enjoyed the blessings of heaven. When he lost balance in his life and elevated worldly goods and honors above the principles of heaven, he was supplanted.

Wisdom is the ability to make wise choices based on truth. Truth that is based upon the principles of the gospel of Jesus Christ is the truth on which we can build a foundation for making wise decisions and good choices. We recognize that those who make good choices are enlightened by the light of Christ and inspired by the Holy Ghost. We can and will be wise as we live worthy of the Holy Ghost. The Holy Ghost will testify of all truth (see Moro. 10:5) and show us all things to do (see 2 Ne. 32:5). Living by the Spirit will indeed make one wise.

Wisdom is a gift of the Spirit (see 1 Cor. 12:8). We should seek the best gifts, for in wisdom we can be happy and get understanding as well (see Prov. 3:13). Wisdom is better than rubies; there is nothing to compare it with because it brings so many blessings (see Prov. 8:11).

Secular learning and things of the world are not eternal verities. They are changing and are not absolute like unto the truth and wisdom of God.

GLORY: THE TEMPLE

MOMENT OF TRUTH

The temple was made from wood, stone, gold, and other precious materials, using meticulous craftsmanship, and included a baptismal font upheld by twelve oxen. The construction took seven long years. When Solomon dedicated the temple to the Lord as His dwelling place, he also sought forgiveness for his people. The Lord accepted the temple and encouraged the people to keep His commandments:

> And the Lord said unto him, I have heard thy prayer and thy supplication, that thou hast made before me: I have hallowed this house, which thou hast built, to put my name there for ever; and mine eyes and mine heart shall be there perpetually.
>
> And if thou wilt walk before me, as David thy father walked, in integrity of heart, and in uprightness, to do according to all that I have commanded thee, and wilt keep my statutes and my judgments. (1 Kgs. 9:3–4)

MODERN PROPHETS SPEAK

Joseph Fielding Smith:
> When you go to the house of the Lord, and make covenants, and enter into ordinances, and receive the blessings of that house, it is expected that you observe and keep those instructions and commandments as they are given unto you; and it is not within your power when you come out to alter or change. . . .
>
> Do you think for one minute that we can go through the temple and make covenants that we will do certain things, with the promise made to us that if we will do these things the Lord will receive us into his kingdom—not as aliens, not as strangers, not as servants, but he will receive us into that kingdom with open arms, as sons and daughters in very deed—and then we can go off, after receiving these covenants from

the house of the Lord, and alter and change and break those covenants to suit our fancy and what we consider our convenience because we desire to follow the customs and fashions of a sinful world, and then expect the promised blessing? (*DS*, 2:256)

Howard W. Hunter:

Let us truly be a temple-attending and a temple-loving people. We should hasten to the temple as frequently, yet prudently, as our personal circumstances allow. We should go not only for our kindred dead but also for the personal blessing of temple worship, for the sanctity and safety that are within those hallowed and consecrated walls. As we attend the temple, we learn more richly and deeply the purpose of life and the significance of the atoning sacrifice of the Lord Jesus Christ. Let us make the temple, with temple worship and temple covenants and temple marriage, our ultimate earthly goal and the supreme mortal experience. (*THWH*, 236)

Gordon B. Hinckley:

The Lord has made it possible for us in these holy houses to receive our own [ordinances]. Then we have the opportunity and responsibility of extending these same blessings to those who have passed on without the privilege. But in the very process there comes into our own lives a refinement of character, together with increased spirituality. It is interesting to reflect on the fact that although many on the other side may not receive the ordinances done for them here, those who perform these ordinances will be blessed in the very process of doing so. (*TGBH*, 622–23)

DOCTRINES AND PRINCIPLES

We are to act upon the feelings of our hearts that the Lord has planted there through the restored keys and powers of Elijah. This power that Elijah restored truly has changed the hearts of all mankind. It has affected us to turn back to those who have gone before and seek after them. In another special way, it has made family members turn to their immediate family in compassion and love. Let us never forget that the earth would be wasted if there were not a link from the children to their fathers. The question remains: Do we have the spirit of Elijah in our hearts? Can we do more to further this celestial cause with greater faith and devotion?

Lest we forget, our exaltation is dependent upon our vicarious temple service:

And now, my dearly beloved brethren and sisters, let me assure you that these are principles in relation to the dead and the living that cannot be lightly passed over, as pertaining to our salvation. For their salvation is necessary and essential to our salvation, as Paul says concerning the fathers—that they without us cannot be made perfect—neither can we without our dead be made perfect. (D&C 128:15)

The vicarious work we do for those who have gone before is recorded in our temples. This is "the Book" that is our offering unto the Lord in righteousness—our vicarious temple work. This is the work of exaltation for the souls of mankind (see D&C 128:24).

SCATTERING *of* ISRAEL: THE DIVIDED KINGDOM

MOMENT OF TRUTH

We learn graphic lessons from unrighteous leaders as demonstrated by Rehoboam and Jeroboam. Rehoboam's words are recorded as follows: "And spake to them after the counsel of the young men, saying, My father made your yoke heavy, and I will add to your yoke: my father also chastised you with whips, but I will chastise you with scorpions" (1 Kgs. 12:14). Jeroboam returned to idol worship and wouldn't listen to the prophets of God; thus the House of Israel became wicked and idolatrous. The Northern and Southern Kingdoms made war one with another for many years, as is the case when people ripen in iniquity. In consequence of wicked and nefarious leadership, the Northern Kingdom of Israel under Jeroboam became wicked like unto the Kingdom of Judah: "I exalted thee out of the dust, and made thee prince over my people Israel; and thou hast walked in the way of Jeroboam, and hast made my people Israel to sin, to provoke me to anger with their sins" (1 Kgs. 16:2).

As so often with a wayward people, the Lord's response was to scatter them: "And again: Hearken, O ye house of Israel, all ye that are broken off and are driven out because of the wickedness of the pastors of my people; yea, all ye that are broken off, that are scattered abroad, who are of my people, O house of Israel. Listen, O isles, unto me, and hearken ye people from far" (1 Ne. 21:1). The call of the Lord is always to repent, that the people may once again be gathered to worship the Lord in unity and faith:

> And then, O house of Israel, behold, these shall come from far; and lo, these from the north and from the west; and these from the land of Sinim [i.e., a most distant country].
>
> Sing, O heavens; and be joyful, O earth; for the feet of those who are in the east shall be established; and break forth into singing, O mountains; for they shall be

smitten no more; for the Lord hath comforted his people, and will have mercy upon his afflicted. (1 Ne. 21:12–13; compare Isa. 49:12–13)

MODERN PROPHETS SPEAK

Ezra Taft Benson:

> You can become courageous leaders! Who can better fulfill this need of our times than you who have been so favored by heritage, home, and Church? You must not fail. Forget not that each of you has been endowed with the priceless gift of free agency. You need not be the "victims of circumstance," for unto you it is given to achieve and become "perfect, even as your father which is in heaven is perfect" (Matt. 5:48). (*TETB*, 370)

Ezra Taft Benson:

> A love of people is essential to effective leadership. Do you love those whom you work with? Do you realize the worth of souls is great in the sight of God (see D&C 18:10)? Do you have faith in youth? Do you find yourself praising their virtues, commending them for their accomplishments? Or do you have a critical attitude toward them because of their mistakes? (*TETB*, 370)

DOCTRINE AND PRINCIPLES

From the story of the scattering of Israel, we see the results of wicked kings leading their people astray and into grievous sins. Throughout the history of the world, mankind has suffered from misguided or heinous leadership. As individuals and groups, we have an obligation and responsibility for the welfare of all mankind. We are to take action. If no action is taken, apathy results in torpidity of conscience, and lives suffer. The consequences are real for sins of both omission as well as commission. As in the case of King Noah of the Book of Mormon, the sins of the people will come to rest upon their leaders.

Leadership is a dynamic force for good or bad—depending upon the leader. By way of contrast to the wicked kings among the promised people, the great-grandson of Rehoboam, Jehoshaphat, provides a marked contrast to the leadership style of his wicked predecessors (see 1 Kgs. 15:24; 22). He eliminated idolatry in his nation (Judah), sent Levite teachers among the people to teach the principles of the gospel from the scriptures, sought the Lord's advice in defending the land, and united the people against their common enemies from without. As a result, the Lord was willing to fight their battles for them and preserve their independence.

POWER *of* GOD:
ELIJAH *and* *the* PRIESTS *of* BAAL

MOMENT OF TRUTH

The power of God is manifested unto the children of men through prophets of God such as Elijah. And so it is throughout the scriptures. The principle is always the same. The Brother of Jared explains it clearly with respect to his commission:

> And I know, O Lord, that thou hast all power, and can do whatsoever thou wilt for the benefit of man; therefore touch these stones, O Lord, with thy finger, and prepare them that they may shine forth in darkness; and they shall shine forth unto us in the vessels which we have prepared, that we may have light while we shall cross the sea. (Ether 3:4)

When we come to know and appreciate the power and goodness of God, our faith in Him increases. The prophets always invoke these divine qualities when the people begin to have doubts or stray from the truth. They remind them of the power and goodness of God. Such was the case with Elijah throughout his life and in particular with the priests of Baal.

Remember that God is all-powerful (omnipotent—see Ether 3:4). He is all-knowing (omniscient—see 2 Ne. 9:20). He is in and through all things (omnipresent—see D&C 88:41). As we come to know God and His goodness and power, we come to understand His love for us as His children and His eternal purposes regarding His children.

MODERN PROPHETS SPEAK

Bruce R. McConkie:

> The issue is not what men purport to believe; it is whether, having believed the truth, they also get the power of God into their lives. Salvation does not come by

reading about religion, by learning that holy men in former days had spiritual experiences. It is not found through research in musty archives; it does not spring forth as the result of intellectual dialogues about religious matters. Salvation is born of obedience to the laws and ordinances of the gospel; salvation comes to those who obey the statutes and judgments of that God who created it and ordained the laws whereby it might be gained.

Salvation comes by getting Christ into our hearts today, by being born again, by becoming new creatures of the Holy Ghost, by receiving personal revelation, by exercising the gifts of the Spirit, by having the power of God manifest in our lives. (*CR,* Oct. 1968, 135)

Heber C. Kimball:

The Spirit of the Lord, the mighty power of God, was with us, and we felt greatly strengthened, and a determination to go forward, come life or death, honor or reproach, was manifested by us all. (*Journal of Heber C. Kimball,* [Nauvoo, IL: Robinson and Smith, 1840], 17)

Harold B. Lee:

What is priesthood? Well, we've had the definition—it's the power of the Lord given to man to act for Him in things pertaining to salvation. But I have a different definition that to me seems more accurate. Priesthood is the power by which the power of the Almighty works through man. The priesthood is the center, the core, the power by which all the activities of the Church are to be directed. (*The Teachings of Harold B. Lee,* [Salt Lake City: Bookcraft, 1996], 482)

Neal A. Maxwell:

To magnify one's calling means seeing "with the eye of faith" the enlarged and detailed possibilities of service to one's family, flock, friends, and others. After all, the same power of God that brought into existence "worlds without number" (Moses 1:33) can surely watch over our little universes of individual experience! (*Lord, Increase Our Faith* [Salt Lake City: Bookcraft, 1994], 48)

Bruce R. McConkie:

Salvation comes only when the power of God is received and used; and this power is the power of the priesthood and the power of the Holy Ghost. These must operate in the lives of men; otherwise their souls cannot be cleansed; they cannot be born again; they cannot become new creatures of the Holy Ghost; they cannot put off the natural man and become saints; they cannot be sanctified by the Spirit. In this sense the gospel cannot be written, except in the bones and sinews and tissues of a human body. When it is so written, the record is then found in the Book of Life of the converted believer. And it will be out of what is written in this Book of Life that men shall be judged (Rev. 20:12–13).

Anyone can claim to have the gospel and can in fact have it in the intellectual sense of knowing what the doctrines of salvation are. But only those who receive the power of God in their lives have the fulness of the gospel; they only are candidates for salvation. To identify this power, God has ordained that certain signs and gifts shall follow those that believe. By faith they cast out devils, heal the sick, raise the dead, work miracles, gain testimonies, receive revelations, entertain angels, and view the visions of eternity. Where these signs are, there is the power of the gospel; and where the power is, there is the fulness of the everlasting gospel (Mark 16:16–20; Morm. 9:7–27). (*Doctrinal New Testament Commentary* [Salt Lake City: Bookcraft, 1965–73], 3:43)

DOCTRINES AND PRINCIPLES

The scriptures are replete with references to the power of God:

2 Samuel 22:33—God is my strength and power: and he maketh my way perfect.

Luke 1:37—For with God nothing shall be impossible.

JST, Romans 1:16—For I am not ashamed of the gospel of Christ; for it is the power of God unto salvation to every one that believeth; to the Jew first, and also to the Greek.

1 Nephi 14:14—And it came to pass that I, Nephi, beheld the power of the Lamb of God, that it descended upon the saints of the church of the Lamb, and upon the covenant people of the Lord, who were scattered upon all the face of the earth; and they were armed with righteousness and with the power of God in great glory.

Alma 57:26—And now, their preservation was astonishing to our whole army, yea, that they should be spared while there was a thousand of our brethren who were slain. And we do justly ascribe it to the miraculous power of God, because of their exceeding faith in that which they had been taught to believe—that there was a just God, and whosoever did not doubt, that they should be preserved by his marvelous power.

Mormon 7:9—For behold, this is written for the intent that ye may believe that; and if ye believe that ye will believe this also; and if ye believe this ye will know concerning your fathers, and also the marvelous works which were wrought by the power of God among them.

Moroni 10:31—Yea, come unto Christ, and be perfected in him, and deny yourselves of all ungodliness; and if ye shall deny yourselves of all ungodliness, and love God with all your might, mind and strength, then is his grace sufficient for you, that by his grace ye may be perfect in Christ; and if by the grace of God ye are perfect in Christ, ye can in nowise deny the power of God.

D&C 61:1—Behold, and hearken unto the voice of him who has all power, who is from everlasting to everlasting, even Alpha and Omega, the beginning and the end.

D&C 68:4—And whatsoever they shall speak when moved upon by the Holy Ghost shall be scripture, shall be the will of the Lord, shall be the mind of the Lord, shall be the word of the Lord, shall be the voice of the Lord, and the power of God unto salvation.

HUMILITY *of the* FAST: ELIJAH TALKS *with the* LORD

MOMENT OF TRUTH

After Elijah called down fire to consume the idolatrous priests of Baal (1 Kgs. 18), the prophet went into hiding to avoid the treacherous hand of Queen Jezebel. He was sustained by an angel and then fasted for forty days and forty nights and went to Mount Horeb to speak with the Lord:

> And he came thither unto a cave, and lodged there; and, behold, the word of the Lord came to him, and he said unto him, What doest thou here, Elijah?
>
> And he said, I have been very jealous for the Lord God of hosts: for the children of Israel have forsaken thy covenant, thrown down thine altars, and slain thy prophets with the sword; and I, even I only, am left; and they seek my life, to take it away.
>
> And he said, Go forth, and stand upon the mount before the Lord. And, behold, the Lord passed by, and a great and strong wind rent the mountains, and brake in pieces the rocks before the Lord; but the Lord was not in the wind: and after the wind an earthquake; but the Lord was not in the earthquake:
>
> And after the earthquake a fire; but the Lord was not in the fire: and after the fire a still small voice.
>
> And it was so, when Elijah heard it, that he wrapped his face in his mantle, and went out, and stood in the entering in of the cave. (1 Kgs. 19:9–13)

The Lord then instructed Elijah:

> And the Lord said unto him, Go, return on thy way to the wilderness of Damascus: and when thou comest, anoint Hazael to be king over Syria:

> And Jehu the son of Nimshi shalt thou anoint to be king over Israel: and Elisha the son of Shaphat of Abel-meholah shalt thou anoint to be prophet in thy room.
>
> And it shall come to pass, that him that escapeth the sword of Hazael shall Jehu slay: and him that escapeth from the sword of Jehu shall Elisha slay.
>
> Yet I have left me seven thousand in Israel, all the knees which have not bowed unto Baal, and every mouth which hath not kissed him. (1 Kgs. 19:15–18)

The story of Elijah's humble way of approaching the Lord through fasting and prayer is exemplary for our own patterns of living.

MODERN PROPHETS SPEAK

Bruce R. McConkie:

> Fasting, with prayer as its companion, is designed to increase spirituality; to foster a spirit of devotion and love of God; to increase faith in the hearts of men, thus assuring divine favor; to encourage humility and contrition of soul; to aid in the acquirement of righteousness to teach man his nothingness and dependence upon God; and to hasten those who properly comply with the law of fasting along the path to salvation.
>
> Many specific reasons for fasting are found in the scriptures. It is a general obligation imposed by revelation upon church members in good standing (D&C 59:13–14; 88:76; Luke 5:33–35; 2 Cor. 6:5; 11: 27). It is itself a form of the true worship of God (Luke 2:37; Acts 9:9; Alma 45:1; 4 Ne. 12). It is proper to fast for the sick (2 Sam. 12:16); for special blessings (Mosiah 27:22–23); to gain a testimony (Alma 5:46); to gain revelation (Alma 17:3; 3 Ne. 27:1; Ex. 34:28; Deut. 9:9, 18); for the conversion of nonmembers to the truth (Alma 6:6; 17:9); for guidance in the choice of church officers (Acts 13: 3); as an accompaniment of righteous mourning and sorrow (Alma 28:2–6; 30:2; Hela. 9:10); as a means of sanctifying one's soul (Hela. 3: 35); and for guidance along the path leading to salvation (Omni 26). Temples are houses of fasting (D&C 88:119; 95:16; 109:8, 16). To be acceptable fasting must conform to the Lord's law and not be done for hypocritical reasons (Matt. 6:16–18; 3 Ne. 13:16–18). (*MD,* 276)

DOCTRINES AND PRINCIPLES

Great blessings flow from God to the faithful who sincerely practice a prayerful fast, whether it be strengthening, healing, or an increase of understanding. The blessings of the Spirit and the power to teach by that same Spirit come through fasting and prayer (see Alma 17:3, 9).

We are to act with faith and bring an offering of sincere fasting and prayer in order to have a more contrite disposition in accordance with heavenly principles.

There are additional blessings that come from fasting and prayer: "Nevertheless they did fast and pray oft, and did wax stronger and stronger in their humility, and firmer and firmer in the faith of Christ, unto the filling their souls with joy and consolation, yea, even to the purifying and the sanctification of their hearts, which sanctification cometh because of their yielding their hearts unto God" (Hel. 3:35).

The law of the fast, when practiced sincerely, empowers the individual with spiritual power. One literally overcomes the flesh. When we pay our fast offerings, we practice the great commandment of love. The Lord is explicit that we must care for the needy. The Lord has said through his servant Amulek:

> And now behold, my beloved brethren, I say unto you, do not suppose that this is all; for after ye have done all these things, if ye turn away the needy, and the naked, and visit not the sick and afflicted, and impart of your substance, if ye have, to those who stand in need—I say unto you, if ye do not any of these things, behold, your prayer is vain, and availeth you nothing, and ye are as hypocrites who do deny the faith. (Alma 34:28)

The Lord in His almighty power stands waiting to bless mankind. It is His agenda that governs the flow of life upon the earth. Through fasting and prayer we can learn of His will and see His hand at work as He manifests Himself and blesses His children. We can literally call down the power of Heaven through fasting and prayer.

The regular practice of fasting and prayer is a dynamic power in our lives, for it allows us to tap into the power of God to enrich our lives and make us more valiant servants. The power of prayer and fasting is demonstrated in the following references:

Overcoming and avoiding temptation (3 Ne. 18:15, 18)

To restore health (Mosiah 27:22)

As a form of thanksgiving and worship (Alma 45:1)

To know the things of God (Alma 5:46)

To enjoy the Spirit of revelation and prophecy (Alma 17:3)

To help those who know not God (Alma 6:6)

To gain faith and humility (Hel. 3:35)

To become sanctified (Hel. 3:35)

SUCCESSION: ELIJAH *and* ELISHA

MOMENT OF TRUTH

Elijah is a singularly imposing figure in a long line of extraordinary prophetic servants of the Lord. His influence was felt with compelling force among the Israelites and non-Israelites of his day, was called forth again on the Mount of Transfiguration (see Matt. 17:1–11), and touches countless lives today through the restored keys of the sealing power for temple work placed in his charge (see D&C 110:13–16). The story of Elijah is a dramatic confirmation of the fact that the Lord's work is always founded on prophetic ministry. As we take upon ourselves the assignment of being about the Lord's errand, we need to live worthy of all the blessings that attend faithful service, including the sustaining support of miracles both seen and unseen, the power of God unto salvation, and the omnipresent guiding hand of the Lord that directs and facilitates the course of events leading to the time when all children of God will once more be called home to account for their sojourn on earth and receive the glory to which they are entitled based on their level of obedience and service.

MODERN PROPHETS SPEAK

Ezra Taft Benson:

> We declare that God has not left man to grope in darkness as to His mind and will. By succession and ordination, there stands on earth today a prophet of God, whom we sustain and revere as president of the Church—prophet, seer, and revelator—the same as Moses of ancient days.
>
> This is our message. It is intended for all mankind. The Church proclaims that God spoke in times past through His prophets, has spoken again in this dispensation, and speaks now through His appointed servants. (*Come unto Christ* [Salt Lake City: Deseret Book, 1983], 78)

Spencer W. Kimball:

> Never again will the sun go down; never again will all men prove totally unworthy of communication with their Maker; never again will God be totally hidden from his children on earth. Revelation is here to remain. Prophets will follow each other in a never-ending succession, and the secrets of the Lord will be revealed without measure. (*TSWK,* 433)

George F. Richards:

> In all this work we have the evidence that God has not forsaken his people since the death of the Prophet Joseph Smith. Those who have come after, who have succeeded him to the presidency, have received the mantle of the Prophet, each in succession, and his administration has been attended with the power of God for the growth and the development and onward progress of his work in the earth. As we see the work today, we have a living evidence of God's power that is in this work, and with his people. We do know that the truth will ultimately triumph, that this Church and kingdom is established never to be thrown down or to be given to another people. (*CR,* Oct. 1921, 184)

DOCTRINES AND PRINCIPLES

The Lord, according to His will, provides prophets for His people. The prophets will call them to repentance and lead them in righteousness as required. Today, as in times past, the Lord prepares and calls prophets to succeed one another to direct His work here upon the earth. Well spoke Amos when he said: "Surely the Lord God will do nothing, but he revealeth his secret unto his servants the prophets" (Amos 3:7).

MIRACLES: ELISHA *the* PROPHET

MOMENT OF TRUTH

Elisha, with the mantle of the prophet upon him, proceeded to perform miracles. He parted the Jordan River and walked through on dry ground, and the Israelites meeting him on the other side knew that he indeed was the prophet. He, through the priesthood and power of God, multiplied the woman's oil that she might pay her debts. He prophesied of a couple being able to finally have a son who later became ill and died. Elisha called down the power of God, and the boy was brought back to life. The most-told miracle of Elisha is the healing of Naaman the leper (see 2 Kgs. 2–6). These miracles exemplified Elisha's righteousness (see 3 Ne. 8:1; Mosiah 8:18) as well as the faith of the people (see Ether 12:16, 18).

MODERN PROPHETS SPEAK

Spencer W. Kimball:

> A question often asked is: If miracles are a part of the gospel program, why do we not have such today?
>
> The answer is a simple one: We do have miracles today—beyond imagination! If all the miracles of our own lifetime were recorded, it would take many library shelves to hold the books which would contain them.
>
> What kinds of miracles do we have? All kinds—revelations, visions, tongues, healings, special guidance and direction, evil spirits cast out. Where are they recorded? In the records of the Church, in journals, in news and magazine articles and in the minds and memories of many people.
>
> The rationalist continues: Many people are administered to and are not healed. That is true, as it has been in all times. It was never intended that all should be healed or that all should be raised from the dead, else the whole program of mortality and death and resurrection and exaltation would be frustrated.

However, the Lord does make specific promises: Signs will follow them that believe. He makes no promise that signs will create belief nor save nor exalt. Signs are the product of faith. They are born in the soil of unwavering sureness. They will be prevalent in the Church in about the same degree to which the people have true faith. (*TSWK,* 499–500)

Gordon B. Hinckley:

I have seen miracles in my time, my brothers and sisters. The greatest miracle of all, I believe, is the transformation that comes into the life of a man or a woman who accepts the restored gospel of Jesus Christ and tries to live it in his or her life. (*TGBH,* 340)

Gordon B. Hinckley:

If you move with faith, keeping in touch with Him and building around you people of faith, you can accomplish anything. I believe that with all my heart. I have seen miracle after miracle after miracle across this world. I once thought that the best people in the world are in East Millcreek [where I presided as stake president] and I still believe that. But there are millions of others just like you wherever you go in Hong Kong, Korea, Taiwan, Bangkok, Singapore, Bombay, Sydney, Edinburgh, Wellington, Christchurch, Nuku'alofa, São Paulo, Buenos Aires, Santiago, Lima, Stockholm, Copenhagen, London, Birmingham, everywhere there are wonderful people in this Church. This is an age of miracles. We are part of a miracle as this work moves across the world in fulfillment of the great destiny which the Lord has set for us. (*TGBH,* 340)

Gordon B. Hinckley:

The history of this Church is replete with miracles of healing. I know that. I am confident of that. I recall once when I arrived in Hong Kong I was asked if I would visit a woman in the hospital whose doctors had told her she was going blind and would lose her sight within a week. She asked if we would administer to her and we did so, and she states that she was miraculously healed. I have a painting in my home that she gave me which says on the back of it, "To Gordon B. Hinckley in grateful appreciation for the miracle of saving my sight." I said to her, "I didn't save your sight. Of course, the Lord saved your sight. Thank Him and be grateful to Him." (*TGBH,* 343)

DOCTRINES AND PRINCIPLES

Miracles are wrought according to the patterns established by our Father in Heaven. Bruce R. McConkie summarizes the key points:

In the gospel sense, *miracles are those occurrences wrought by the power of God which are wholly beyond the power of man to perform.* Produced by a supernatural power, they are marvels, wonders, and signs which cannot be duplicated by man's present powers or by any powers which he can obtain by scientific advancements. Miracles in the gospel sense are gifts of the Spirit; they take place when the Lord on his own motion manifests his powers or when man by faith prevails upon Deity to perform supernatural events. . . . As gifts of the Spirit (D&C 46:21; 1 Cor. 12:10, 29; Moro. 10:12), miracles are always performed among people who have faith (D&C 45:8). . . . *Faith and righteousness are the powers by which miracles are wrought* (2 Ne. 26:13; Mosiah 8:18), and miracles are not manifest until after the foundation of faith has been securely built (Ether 12:15–16, 18). Miracles cease when wickedness prevails among a people (Morm. 1:13). . . . *Miracles are one of the great evidences of the divinity of the Lord's work.* They are the signs which always follow the true believers (Mark 16:14–20; Morm. 9:20–25). (*MD*, 506–7)

COURAGE: ESTHER

MOMENT OF TRUTH

The story of Esther is one of courage and faith. She was blessed with great beauty, and King Ahasuerus, who was king over all the land in Persia, invited many young women to come to his house, for he sought to have a new queen. He chose Esther, who was of Jewish descent. Haman, who was over all the king's princes, demanded that all the Jews should bow and show reverence to Haman. Mordecai, Esther's cousin, would not bow down. Haman told the king that the Jews would not obey the laws, and so letters were sent throughout the land to kill all the Jews. They fasted and prayed for deliverance, and Mordecai warned Esther. She encouraged the Jews to fast and pray for three days.

Then Esther, full of courage and faith, went to the king and explained Haman's plan and revealed that she was a Jew. King Ahasuerus became angry with Haman and had him executed. We learn, as the Lord has shown us throughout the scriptures, how He rewards the faith and courage of His people.

MODERN PROPHETS SPEAK

President Thomas S. Monson:

> The call for courage comes constantly to each of us. It has ever been so, and so shall it ever be. The battlefields of war witness acts of courage. Some are printed on pages of books or contained on rolls of film, while others are indelibly impressed on the human heart. (*Live the Good Life* [Salt Lake City: Deseret Book, 1988], 66)

Joseph F. Smith:

> Leaders must be courageous. One of the highest qualities of all true leadership is a high standard of courage. When we speak of courage and leadership we are using terms that stand for the quality of life by which men determine consciously the

proper course to pursue and stand with fidelity to their convictions. There has never been a time in the Church when its leaders were not required to be courageous men; not alone courageous in the sense that they were able to meet physical dangers, but also in the sense that they were steadfast and true to a clear and upright conviction.
(Boyd K. Packer, *The Holy Temple* [Salt Lake City: Bookcraft, 1980], 179)

DOCTRINES AND PRINCIPLES

Courage is the power to act in difficult situations. It can be an act of bravery in every sense of the word, whether in battle or in the personal trials of life. Courage, when fueled by faith, is the attribute of character that brings about the greatest growth and blessings from God. It is akin to sacrifice. Courageous deeds are often an act of spontaneity on a grand scale, but there are millions of patient, quiet, and enduring acts of courage going on in our homes, schools, and workplaces every day. Courage to honor our covenants before the Lord is the test of life and brings with it the joy of knowing that we are doing the will of God.

Courage is an expression of faith, for we put aside fear and doubt and move forward in the strength of the Lord. Each act of courage in dealing with a difficult situation will result in increased power to act and to do good.

The stripling warriors were courageous. Why? They knew that God was with them. They thought more about the liberty of others than themselves, because they were taught by their mothers that if they acted in faith, nothing doubting, God would deliver them (see Alma 56:46–48).

ADVERSITY: JOB

MOMENT OF TRUTH

There is no treatise or prose that plumbs the depths of man, his relationships, and his integrity of heart, like the book of Job. We learn much in these pages concerning the relationship between God and man as well as the interrelationships among human beings and the test of life with all its growth and suffering. Job surely passed the test. He was a perfect and just man, always true to his God. From him, we learn great lessons of life about the role of afflictions and trials in life and how to understand God's dealings with mankind.

Job surely fulfilled the spirit of King Benjamin's words when he said:

> For the natural man is an enemy to God, and has been from the fall of Adam, and will be, forever and ever, unless he yields to the enticings of the Holy Spirit, and putteth off the natural man and becometh a saint through the atonement of Christ the Lord, and becometh as a child, submissive, meek, humble, patient, full of love, willing to submit to all things which the Lord seeth fit to inflict upon him, even as a child doth submit to his father. (Mosiah 3:19)

Job indeed did submit to all the tests placed before him, beginning with the loss of all his property, possessions, servants, and children—and yet he still praised and blessed the name of the Lord. He was afflicted with boils and lost his health. His wife complained to him to curse God and die, and still Job could say no evil thing. Friends came to comfort him to no avail and later would be inconsistent in their "comforting" of Job and accuse him unjustly. Job, as would anyone, wondered as to the cause and the why of it all and sought release from his afflictions, even if it should be through death. Yet Job, a perfect man and full of faith and trust in God, had confidence in God in regard to all things. He said: "For I know that my redeemer liveth, and that he shall stand at the latter day upon the earth: And though after my skin worms destroy this body, yet in my flesh shall I see God" (Job 19:25–26).

Then Job, as a man of God, realized he was being tested and that he would come forth in righteousness. He uttered, "But he knoweth the way that I take: when he hath tried me, I shall come forth as gold. My foot hath held his steps, his way have I kept, and not declined" (Job 23:10–11). Job, like the Prophet Joseph, proclaimed in faith that his life was in harmony with the will of God, for he knew of his own integrity—the true test of all things.

The story of Job reminds us to ask ourselves if we too are true to our God and to His commandments.

MODERN PROPHETS SPEAK

Thomas S. Monson:

> Perhaps there has never occurred such a demonstration of patience as that exemplified by Job, who was described in the Holy Bible as being perfect and upright and one who feared God and eschewed evil (Job 1:1). He was blessed with great wealth and riches in abundance. Satan obtained leave from the Lord to try to tempt Job. How great was Job's misery, how terrible his loss, how tortured his life. He was urged by his wife to curse God and die. His later reply bespoke his faith: "I know that my redeemer liveth, and that he shall stand at the latter day upon the earth: And though after my skin worms destroy this body, yet in my flesh shall I see God" (Job 19:25–26). What faith, what courage, what trust. Job lost possessions—all of them. Job lost his health—all of it. Job honored the trust given him. Job personified patience. ("Patience, a Heavenly Virtue," *Ensign,* Sept. 2002, 4)

Robert D. Hales:

> The story of Job in the Old Testament relates three of the great tests we all should be prepared to face at some period in our lives. First, temporal setbacks. Job lost all he owned. Second, physical illness that will test our faith and testimony. And third, depression. Job said, "Why died I not from the womb?" (Job 3:11). "My soul is weary of my life" (Job 10:1). But the great lesson of Job is that, "in all this Job sinned not, nor charged God foolishly" (Job 1:22). Too often when adversity strikes, we use it as a justification to commit sin and turn away from the teachings of Jesus Christ, the prophets who lead us, and our family and friends. Job maintained his testimony and was blessed for his unwavering faith that God lived and that he would dwell in God's presence. ("Examples from the Life of a Prophet," *Ensign,* Nov. 1981, 19)

DOCTRINES AND PRINCIPLES

This testing and trial of Job was referred to by the Lord when Joseph Smith was in Liberty Jail: "Thou art not yet as Job; thy friends do not contend against thee, neither charge thee with transgression, as they did Job" (D&C 121:10). The Lord went on to express supernal truths concerning our testing and of its necessity:

> And if thou shouldst be cast into the pit, or into the hands of murderers, and the sentence of death passed upon thee; if thou be cast into the deep; if the billowing surge conspire against thee; if fierce winds become thine enemy; if the heavens gather blackness, and all the elements combine to hedge up the way; and above all, if the very jaws of hell shall gape open the mouth wide after thee, know thou, my son, that all these things shall give thee experience, and shall be for thy good. (D&C 122:7)

Truly this mortal experience is a testing time, a time to prove ourselves to see if we will submit to the will of God and keep His commandments:

> And we will prove them herewith, to see if they will do all things whatsoever the Lord their God shall command them;
>
> And they who keep their first estate shall be added upon; and they who keep not their first estate shall not have glory in the same kingdom with those who keep their first estate; and they who keep their second estate shall have glory added upon their heads for ever and ever. (Abr. 3:25–26)

STANDARDS: DANIEL *and* HIS FRIENDS

MOMENT OF TRUTH

During the siege and captivity of the House of Judah by the Babylonians, exceptional courage and spiritual strength was shown by Daniel and his young friends. It was in the strength of the Lord, which they sought and obtained through mighty prayer and fasting, that they were able to perform their missions with exemplary valor. Character is always measured in the context of adversity and challenge.

King Nebuchadnezzar brought some of the promising Jewish young men into his palace that they might be taught in the Babylonian language and culture (see Dan. 1). Daniel and his friends refused to eat the king's meat or drink the wine and sought the king's servant to give them pulse (vegetables) and water and see how they would fare in ten days. At the end of the test, their countenance was fairer than in the case of those who ate of the king's meat and wine. In three years, they were taken before the king, having learned the local language and increased in their knowledge:

> And the king communed with them; and among them all was found none like Daniel, Hananiah, Mishael, and Azariah: therefore stood they before the king.
>
> And in all matters of wisdom and understanding, that the king enquired of them, he found them ten times better than all the magicians and astrologers that were in all his realm. (Dan. 1:19–20)

Surely the Lord magnifies his obedient servants in all things. Holding true to our beliefs and standards brings down the blessings of Heaven, as described by the Lord: "There is a law, irrevocably decreed in heaven before the foundations of this world, upon which all blessings are predicated—And when we obtain any blessing from God, it is by obedience to that law upon which it is predicated" (D&C 130:20–21).

MODERN PROPHETS SPEAK

Gordon B. Hinckley:

> We live in a day of shifting values, of changing standards, of will-o'-the-wisp programs that blossom in the morning and die in the evening. We see this in government, we see it in public and private morality, we see it in the homes of the people; we see it in the churches, and we even see it among some of our own members who are led away by the sophistry of men. Men everywhere seem to be groping as men in darkness, casting aside the traditions that were the strength of our society, yet unable to find a new star to guide them. . . .
>
> While standards generally may totter, we of the Church are without excuse if we drift in the same manner. We have standards—sure, tested, and effective. To the extent that we observe them, we shall go forward. To the extent that we neglect them, we shall hinder our own progress and bring embarrassment to the work of the Lord. . . .
>
> The satisfying thing is that obedience brings happiness. It brings peace; it brings growth—all of these to the individual, and his good example brings respect for the institution of which he is a part.
>
> Our adherence to these divinely given standards need never be an offensive thing to those about us. We need not contend with them. But if we will pursue a steady course, our very example will become the most effective argument we could ever advance for the virtues of the cause with which we are associated. ("Contend Not with Others, But Pursue a Steady Course," *Improvement Era,* Jun. 1970, 40)

Gordon B. Hinckley:

> It is not always easy to live in the world and not be a part of it. We cannot live entirely with our own or unto ourselves, nor would we wish to. We must mingle with others. In so doing, we can be gracious. We can be inoffensive. We can avoid any spirit or attitude of self-righteousness. But we can maintain our standards. The natural tendency will be otherwise, and many have succumbed to it. . . .
>
> I do not advocate a retreat from society. On the contrary, we have a responsibility and a challenge to take our places in the world of business, science, government, medicine, education, and every other worthwhile and constructive vocation. We have an obligation to train our hands and minds to excel in the work of the world for the blessing of all mankind. In so doing we must work with others. But this does not require a surrender of standards. (*TGBH,* 611–12)

DOCTRINES AND PRINCIPLES

Think of the courage and trust of these young men—surrounded as they were by the daunting opulence of a foreign palace—as they took a firm and principled stand on the principles in which they believed. Their experience is an early echo of the truths that the Lord gave unto His restored church in this dispensation through the Word of Wisdom:

> And all saints who remember to keep and do these sayings, walking in obedience to the commandments, shall receive health in their navel and marrow to their bones;
>> And shall find wisdom and great treasures of knowledge, even hidden treasures;
>> And shall run and not be weary, and shall walk and not faint.
>> And I, the Lord, give unto them a promise, that the destroying angel shall pass by them, as the children of Israel, and not slay them. (D&C 89:18–21)

REVELATION: DANIEL *and* *the* KING'S DREAMS

MOMENT OF TRUTH

God's chosen prophets and seers are, from time to time, granted access to sacred spiritual views of how the Kingdom of Heaven unfolds through successive dispensations for the blessing of mankind. In keeping with this revelatory commission, the young prophet Daniel—like his ancient predecessor, Joseph of Egypt—was endowed with a visionary understanding of dreams. Nebuchadnezzar, King of the Babylonian Empire, had taken Daniel and several of his colleagues captive around the turn of the century—a few years ahead of the siege and destruction of Jerusalem in 587 B.C. One night, the king had a troubling dream about a stone hewn from the mountain without hands that destroyed a mighty image in human form. Daniel counseled with his three young companions—renamed Shadrach, Meshach, and Abed-nego by their hosts—and as a team, they sought the "mercies of the God of heaven concerning this secret" (Dan. 2:18). The answer was given to the grateful Daniel "in a night vision" (v. 19), and he subsequently disclosed to the king the interpretation of the dream. What the king beheld, the prophet revealed, was a representation of history portending the coming of the restored Kingdom of Heaven—an inexorably expanding kingdom that was destined to prevail over a sequence of mighty worldly empires and become "a great mountain" that would fill "the whole earth" (v. 35).

Some twenty-five hundred years later, the promised Restoration took place according to the design of heaven and as announced through all previous dispensations by the prophets of the Lord—including Daniel. In regard to this Kingdom of God, we are counseled in modern-day revelation as follows: "Prepare ye the way of the Lord, make his paths straight. The keys of the kingdom of God are committed unto man on the earth, and from thence shall the gospel roll forth unto the ends of the earth, as the stone which is cut out of the mountain without hands shall roll forth, until it has filled the whole earth" (D&C 65:1–2).

MODERN PROPHETS SPEAK

Joseph Smith:

> The spirit of revelation is in connection with these blessings. A person may profit by noticing the first intimation of the spirit of revelation; for instance, when you feel pure intelligence flowing into you, it may give you sudden strokes of ideas, so that by noticing it, you may find it fulfilled the same day or soon; (i.e.) those things that were presented unto your minds by the Spirit of God, will come to pass; and thus by learning the Spirit of God and understanding it, you may grow into the principle of revelation, until you become perfect in Christ Jesus. (*HC,* 3:381)

Joseph B. Wirthlin:

> In our own lives today, we receive revelation through the still, small voice that whispers "Yes, that applies to me." The Prophet Joseph Smith received this kind of revelation when he read in James 1:5 that he should pray and ask God. It was in a similar circumstance that President Joseph F. Smith, after reading and contemplating the scriptures, had the vision of the redemption of the dead (D&C 138) opened to his mind. Regular study of the scriptures and meditating upon them are essential for continual revelation. (*Finding Peace in Our Lives* [Salt Lake City: Deseret Book, 1995], 173)

DOCTRINES AND PRINCIPLES

Revelation is the communication from God to His children. This is given in many ways: personal visitations of Deity, angels, or the Holy Ghost; open visions; voices from above; dreams; a whispering in your mind and heart; or any similar inspiration from the Holy Ghost. Revelation can be of universal significance, as given through the prophets, or of personal application, as given to us in our personal lives and Church callings. We as children of our Heavenly Father have the privilege to receive inspiration and direction in our lives, for God is no respecter of persons (see D&C 38:16). The Holy Ghost is the Revelator, and we can receive revelation and direction according to our need and worthiness (see 2 Ne. 32:5; Moro. 10:5). We can know God (see D&C 67:10). The blessings of revelation can be ours as we ask in faith, believing (see D&C 8:1–3).

Let us remember these things concerning revelation:

We can trust in our prophets because they do in fact receive revelations from our Heavenly Father to direct the Church (see D&C 1:38; 4–6; 107:92).

Revelation is the pattern by which mankind has been shown the things of God and in particular the plan of salvation. It is the rock upon which the Church and Kingdom of God is built (see Matt.16:18). Continuing revelation sets us apart from other religions.

The Revelator is the Holy Ghost. He will show us all things to do (see 2 Ne. 32:5), the things to say (see D&C 100:5–6), and the truth of all things (see Moro. 10:5). We must live worthy of the Spirit by increasing our faith (see 1 Ne. 10:17), being full of love, purifying ourselves before God (see D&C 76:116), and cultivating exact, immediate, and courageous obedience as we keep the commandments (see D&C 20:77, 79). The Lord will provide a way to do this if we but try in faith and humility (see 1 Ne. 3:7).

It is our right, along with the prophets, to know the things of God (see D&C 42:61; 76:7). There is a price to pay in order to know the things of God, as Oliver Cowdery learned (see D&C 9:7). We are to do our part: study the word of God, fast and pray, exercise our faith, and have a righteous reason as to the purpose of our asking (see Alma 17:2–3).

Continuous revelation is absolutely essential for the Church to bless the lives of Heavenly Father's children. We live by the word of God (see D&C 84:43–46). For revelation in the form of inspiration, it is imperative for us as individuals to keep the commandments and do the things that the Lord would have us do.

WORSHIP: SHADRACH, MESHACH, *and* ABED-NEGO

MOMENT OF TRUTH

King Nebuchadnezzar, idolatrous in his worship, built a huge golden idol and commanded, "That at what time ye hear the sound of the cornet, flute, harp, sackbut, psaltery, dulcimer, and all kinds of musick, ye fall down and worship the golden image that Nebuchadnezzar the king hath set up" (Dan. 3:5). And the decree went forth: "And whoso falleth not down and worshippeth shall the same hour be cast into the midst of a burning fiery furnace" (Dan. 3:6).

Shadrach, Meshach, and Abed-nego, true to their God, would not bow down to the idol. The king was informed of their disobedience and, being angry, commanded that they should be put into the fiery furnace. The Lord was with them, and they were protected from harm. The king, being very astonished, called them to come forth, having seen a fourth person in the furnace with them, and announced:

> Blessed be the God of Shadrach, Meshach, and Abed-nego, who hath sent his angel, and delivered his servants that trusted in him, and have changed the king's word, and yielded their bodies, that they might not serve nor worship any god, except their own God.
>
> Therefore I make a decree, That every people, nation, and language, which speak any thing amiss against the God of Shadrach, Meshach, and Abed-nego, shall be cut in pieces, and their houses shall be made a dunghill: because there is no other God that can deliver after this sort. (Dan. 3:28–29)

From this lesson we learn a great message about the indispensability of always worshipping our God in truth and light.

MODERN PROPHETS SPEAK

Gordon B. Hinckley:

> Strange as it seems, we alone, among all the great organizations that worship God, have a true description and a true definition of him. The experience of Joseph Smith in a few moments in the grove on a spring day in 1820, brought more light and knowledge and understanding of the personality and reality and substance of God and his Beloved Son than men had arrived at during centuries of speculation. (*TGBH,* 236)

DOCTRINES AND PRINCIPLES

To worship is to show reverence, honor, devotion, homage, love, and admiration. It is more than just a feeling or attitude. It should be accompanied by an offering of self and service. We worship Heavenly Father through our Savior Jesus Christ by the Holy Spirit (see D&C 20:29).

Unfortunately, we are often inclined, at the same time, to worship things of the world. This dichotomy is the source of a great many problems in the world today. We often care more about things than we do about our God and our brothers and sisters, and in so doing, we forget God, the source of all life and its accompanying blessings. The commandments are clear: "Ye cannot serve God and mammon" (Matt. 6:24); "Thou shalt have no other gods before me" (Ex. 20:3); "worship God, in whatsoever place ye may be in, in spirit and in truth" (Alma 34.38); "Master, which is the great commandment in the law? Jesus said unto him, Thou shalt love the Lord thy God with all thy heart, and with all thy soul, and with all thy mind. This is the first and great commandment" (Matt. 22:36–38). We are to worship God with an eye single to His glory (see Morm. 8:15; D&C 4:5; 27:2; 55:1; 59:1; 82:19; 88:67). That is a what is expected of the Saints of God.

The Ten Commandments have never been revoked or changed. They are still in effect. The first four have to do with worshipping God, and the others have to do with dealing with our fellowman. "No other gods" means that no other thing or entity should in any way be put ahead of, or in place of, our Heavenly Father. We are to live a life focused upon our Heavenly Father and His commandments that He has given us through our Savior Jesus Christ.

We worship God through the Spirit at all times, not just when we are in church or in the temple. We acknowledge His truth (His laws and commandments) and we worship Him by acknowledging His Son—and His glorious atoning sacrifice—and by keeping the commandments.

PROTECTION *through* PRAYER: DANIEL *and* *the* LIONS' DEN

MOMENT OF TRUTH

Darius, like some of the previous kings in Persia, placed Daniel in a prominent leadership role. Those with whom Daniel worked were jealous and sought a cause against him. They knew Daniel prayed to God, and so they convinced the king to enact a law forbidding one to pray. If the decree were disobeyed, the offender would be thrown into the lions' den.

Daniel, as a righteous man, prayed three times daily. He was observed at prayer and reported to the king. The conspirators reminded Darius that his decrees could not be changed and had to be enforced. The king lamented his edict, yet the king had faith in Daniel's God: "Then the king commanded, and they brought Daniel, and cast him into the den of lions. Now the king spake and said unto Daniel, Thy God whom thou servest continually, he will deliver thee" (Daniel 6:16).

The king fasted that night and did not enjoy sleep but went immediately in the morning to the lions' den and called out:

> Daniel, O Daniel, servant of the living God, is thy God, whom thou servest continually, able to deliver thee from the lions? Then said Daniel unto the king, O king, live for ever.
>
> My God hath sent his angel, and hath shut the lions' mouths, that they have not hurt me: forasmuch as before him innocency was found in me; and also before thee, O king, have I done no hurt.
>
> Then was the king exceeding glad for him, and commanded that they should take Daniel up out of the den. So Daniel was taken up out of the den, and no manner of hurt was found upon him, because he believed in his God. (Dan 6:20–23)

We gain from this celebrated story insight into the process by which the Lord watches over the faithful with His protecting care.

MODERN PROPHETS SPEAK

Joseph Fielding Smith:

> Now there is a great blessing and promise the Lord makes to the members of the Church, protection, guidance, to give unto them his laws and direct them in righteousness and truth, and they will be called Zion, which is the pure in heart. I cannot stop the reading of this at this point because the Lord says something more, what he adds to what I have read is the part that troubles me and I want to do my part, as far as I can, to keep our people in the paths of righteousness and truth that they may be the pure in heart and have the protecting care of our Father in heaven and his Son Jesus Christ. (*Take Heed to Yourselves* [Salt Lake City: Deseret Book, 1971], 252)

Harold B. Lee:

> As one studies the Lord's commandments and the attending promises for compliance therewith, one gets some definite ideas as to how we might "stand in holy places," as the Lord commands—how we will be preserved with such protection in accordance with His holy purposes, in order that we might be numbered among the "pure in heart" who constitute Zion (see D&C 97:21). (*The Teachings of Harold B. Lee* [Salt Lake City: Bookcraft, 1996], 411)

Spencer W. Kimball:

> Should we be protected always from hardship, pain, suffering, sacrifice, or labor? Should the Lord protect the righteous? Should he immediately punish the wicked? If growth comes from fun and ease and aimless irresponsibility, then why should we ever exert ourselves to work or learn or overcome? If success is measured by the years we live, then early death is failure and tragedy. If earth life is the ultimate, how can we justify death, even in old age? If we look at mortality as a complete existence, then pain, sorrow, failure, and short life could be a calamity. But if we look upon life as an eternal thing stretching far into the pre-earth past and on into the eternal post-death future, then all happenings may be put in proper perspective.
>
> Is there not wisdom in his giving us trials that we might rise above them, responsibilities that we might achieve, work to harden our muscles, sorrows to try our souls? Are we not permitted temptations to test our strength, sickness that we might learn patience, death that we might be immortalized and glorified? . . .
>
> If mortality be the perfect state, then death would be a frustration, but the gospel teaches us there is no tragedy in death, but *only* in sin.
>
> *We* know so little. *Our* judgment is so limited. We judge the Lord often with less wisdom than does our youngest child weigh our decisions. (*TSWK,* 38–39)

Ezra Taft Benson:

> "Don't worry," says the devil; "the Lord will protect you, and besides, the world is so corrupt and heading toward destruction at such a pace that you can't stop it, so why try?" Well, to begin with, the Lord will not protect us unless we do our part. This devilish tactic of persuading people not to get concerned because the Lord will protect them no matter what they do is exposed by the Book of Mormon. Referring to the devil, it says: "And others will he pacify, and lull them away into carnal security, and they will say: All is well in Zion; yea, Zion prospereth, all is well—and thus the devil cheateth their souls, and leadeth them away carefully down to hell" (2 Ne. 28:21). (*God, Family, Country: Our Three Great Loyalties* [Salt Lake City: Deseret Book, 1974], 387–88)

Howard W. Hunter:

> I promise you in the name of the Lord whose servant I am that God will always protect and care for his people. We will have our difficulties the way every generation and people have had difficulties. But with the gospel of Jesus Christ, you have every hope and promise and reassurance. The Lord has power over his Saints and will always prepare places of peace, defense, and safety for his people. When we have faith in God, we can hope for a better world—for us personally, and for all mankind. The prophet Ether taught anciently (and he knew something about troubles): "Wherefore, whoso believeth in God might with surety hope for a better world, yea, even a place at the right hand of God, which hope cometh of faith, maketh an anchor to the souls of men, which would make them sure and steadfast, always abounding in good works, being led to glorify God" (Ether 12:4). (*That We Might Have Joy* [Salt Lake City, Deseret Book, 1994], 94–95)

DOCTRINES AND PRINCIPLES

The Lord in His infinite goodness provides protection for His children according to His good will and pleasure, so that the power of God might be manifest here upon the earth and His children be blessed in all things according to their righteousness. We know that there must be opposition in all things, or else the great plan of salvation would be frustrated:

> For it must needs be, that there is an opposition in all things. If not so, my first-born in the wilderness, righteousness could not be brought to pass, neither wickedness, neither holiness nor misery, neither good nor bad. Wherefore, all things must needs be a compound in one; wherefore, if it should be one body it must needs remain as dead, having no life neither death, nor corruption nor incorruption, happiness nor misery, neither sense nor insensibility.

> Wherefore, it must needs have been created for a thing of naught; wherefore there would have been no purpose in the end of its creation. Wherefore, this thing must needs destroy the wisdom of God and his eternal purposes, and also the power, and the mercy, and the justice of God. (2 Ne. 2:11–12)

In the cauldron of opposition, we experience the tests and trials of life. In faith and humility, we place ourselves in the hands of the Lord as we follow the counsel of the Prophet Joseph Smith: "But thy word must be fulfilled. Help thy servants to say, with thy grace assisting them: Thy will be done, O Lord, and not ours" (D&C 109:44). When we yield to the will of the Lord, we merit His protecting hand as we learn, grace for grace, and line upon line, how to transcend the challenges of life and rise in thanksgiving to a higher plane of spirituality. In this quest, we depend on the Lord fully to protect our families in their mortal sojourn:

> And the Lord will create upon every dwelling place of mount Zion, and upon her assemblies, a cloud and smoke by day, and the shining of a flaming fire by night: for upon all the glory shall be a defence.
>
> And there shall be a tabernacle for a shadow in the daytime from the heat, and for a place of refuge, and for a covert from storm and from rain. (Isa. 4:5–6)

UNIVERSAL GOSPEL: JONAH

MOMENT OF TRUTH

The story of Jonah is among the most famous in the Old Testament, probably because of the extraordinary undersea mode of travel that the prophet was subjected to for fully three days and three nights. But there are also multiple lessons of a spiritual nature to be learned from this account.

The details are familiar: Jonah was called of the Lord to preach repentance to Nineveh, the great Assyrian capital city. However, Jonah preferred not to participate and fled on a ship bound for Tarshish. In response, the Lord sent a fierce storm, and the crew cast Jonah into the sea for fear of being lost. In the midst of the deep, Jonah was swallowed by a whale: "Now the Lord had prepared a great fish to swallow up Jonah. And Jonah was in the belly of the fish three days and three nights" (Jonah 1:17). Jonah repented of his wrong and prayed for deliverance: "Then I said, I am cast out of thy sight; yet I will look again toward thy holy temple" (Jonah 2:4). The Lord accepted his change of heart and rescued him. Jonah fulfilled his prophetic office in Nineveh and delivered a message of impending destruction to the people because of their wickedness. Much to his surprise, the people responded to his call for repentance and, therefore, the Lord withheld the decreed judgments.

However, Jonah was displeased with the action of the Lord in sparing Nineveh in mercy, so, as a lesson, the Lord prepared a gourd to shelter the vexed Jonah, brooding on the outskirts of the massive city. Jonah was pleased with the gourd, but the Lord destroyed the gourd the next day to instruct Jonah in an important truth:

> Then said the Lord, Thou hast had pity on the gourd, for the which thou hast not laboured, neither madest it grow; which came up in a night, and perished in a night:

> And should not I spare Nineveh, that great city, wherein are more than sixscore thousand persons that cannot discern between their right hand and their left hand; and also much cattle?" (Jonah 4:10–11)

In this way, the Lord taught His prophet a grand principle—that all people are the Lord's and that He will extend His invitation to all that they might have a chance to repent and embrace the saving truths of the gospel.

MODERN PROPHETS SPEAK

James E. Faust:

> I speak of service to others, service to our callings, service to our profession, and service to our community and country. Most of our expanding horizons involve service and dedication. Members of the Church should be the leaven of the world, and if we are not serving the world, how can we provide the yeast?
>
> We do not always choose for ourselves the horizons in life where we will render service. The word of the Lord came unto Jonah, saying, "Arise, go to Nineveh" (Jonah 1:2). You will recall that Jonah recoiled from that idea; he went to Joppa, then on to Tarshish, to get away from the presence of the Lord (see Jonah 1:3). He found that the Lord had other ideas for him, and three days and three nights in the belly of the great fish that swallowed him changed his mind about a number of things (see Jonah 1:17–3:3).
>
> I bear my testimony to the divinity of this work and to the reality of Jesus of Nazareth, our Divine Redeemer, who should be our constant companion as we seek out and discover formerly lost horizons. ("Lost Horizons," *Ensign,* Aug. 1999, 5)

DOCTRINES AND PRINCIPLES

In the story of Jonah, many eternal truths and doctrines are exemplified so that we can liken it to our own lives and to those around us:

> *The Lord cares for all His children*—The Lord truly cares about all people, for all are the children of God. The gospel is a universal gospel. The people of Nineveh, though enemies to Israel, deserved the opportunity to repent. The Lord knows our names and He knows our hearts and He loves us. Heavenly Father and our Savior seek immortality and eternal life for all (see Moses 1:39).
>
> *The message of the prophets since the beginning of time has been to call people to repentance*—The message of the prophets is always one of repentance and the call to come unto the God of Israel, even the Lord Jesus Christ. The greatest thing we will ever do in regard to our exaltation is to repent and help others repent (see D&C 15:6; 58:42–43).

We are to be faithful in performing our duty—Jonah had been called to declare repentance, but at first he shirked his duty because of "lying vanities" (see Jonah 2:8). Let us learn our duty and do it, lest we be counted unworthy (see D&C 107:99–100).

We cannot escape the Lord and must always call upon Him in prayer—Jonah learned that he could not hide from the Lord. Finally, through the power of the prayer of faith unto repentance, he was delivered by the Lord out of the big fish after three days and three nights. Similarly, we will all be brought down into humility as needed by the power of God or by His word (see Alma 32:16; 48:20).

Jonah is a sign of the atonement—The Lord used the experience of Jonah to be symbolic of the verity that He would be three days in the tomb prior to His coming forth in the resurrection (see Matt.12:39–40; Luke 11:29–32).

True repentance brings gratitude and change—Jonah showed gratitude and a commitment to the Lord with sacrifice and thanksgiving; he went to Nineveh and warned them of their destruction if they did not repent—and they repented. When one repents, the first concern is to show gratitude to God by caring for and blessing His children with the gospel of Jesus Christ (see Mosiah 28:3; Alma 29:9–10; 36:24).

The Lord is merciful—As often as we repent, the Lord will forgive us. Oh, how we ought to be merciful and forgive all people who sin or even appear to do so (see Matt. 5:7).

Vengeance is the Lord's—Jonah's heart was anxious for the sinner to be punished. We ought to have joy over the sinner who repents, even as the Lord does. Lest we forget: vengeance is the Lord's, and we are to forgive everyone (see Morm. 8:20).

The Lord is tender in teaching us so that we might see and understand—The Lord raised up the gourd to shade Jonah. Jonah was pleased, and at its demise, he was filled with pity. Then the Lord tried to show Jonah the parallel of the value of people compared to a plant. We must never forget that people count more than things, statistics, and programs—people are precious.

TITHES *and* OFFERINGS: MALACHI

MOMENT OF TRUTH

Malachi taught the people of his day—and ours—that we should honor God (Mal. 1:5), bring a "pure offering" before Him in righteousness (Mal. 1:11; 3:3), give glory to His name (Mal. 2:2), walk with God "in peace and equity" (Mal. 2:6), remain faithfully within the covenant bounds in marriage (Mal. 2:11), care for the poor and needy (Mal. 3:5), return unto God (Mal. 3:7), pay our tithes and offerings (Mal. 3:10), fear God and always keep Him in our thoughts (Mal. 3:16), avoid pride (Mal. 4:1), and (under the influence of the sealing power of the Priesthood) cultivate a godly and eternal disposition of oneness among families, both fathers (parents) toward their children, and children toward their fathers (Mal. 4:5–6).

So important are the words of Malachi that the Lord brought many of them (Mal. 3–4) to the ancient–American Saints at Bountiful during His post-resurrection visit there:

> And it came to pass that he commanded them that they should write the words which the Father had given unto Malachi, which he should tell unto them. And it came to pass that after they were written he expounded them. And these are the words which he did tell unto them, saying: Thus said the Father unto Malachi—Behold, I will send my messenger, and he shall prepare the way before me, and the Lord whom ye seek shall suddenly come to his temple, even the messenger of the covenant, whom ye delight in; behold, he shall come, saith the Lord of Hosts. (3 Nephi 24:1)

MODERN PROPHETS SPEAK

Lynn G. Robbins:

> The Lord often teaches using extreme circumstances to illustrate a principle. The story of the widow of Zarephath is an example of extreme poverty used to teach the

doctrine that mercy cannot rob sacrifice any more than it can rob justice. In fact, the truer measure of sacrifice isn't so much what one gives to sacrifice as what one sacrifices to give (see Mark 12:43). Faith isn't tested so much when the cupboard is full as when it is bare. In these defining moments, the crisis doesn't create one's character—it reveals it. The crisis is the test. . . .

Elijah understood the doctrine that blessings come *after* the trial of our faith (see Ether 12:6; D&C 132:5). He wasn't being selfish. As the Lord's servant, Elijah was there to give, not to take. . . .

One reason the Lord illustrates doctrines with the most extreme circumstances is to eliminate excuses. If the Lord expects even the poorest widow to pay her mite, where does that leave all others who find that it is not *convenient* or easy to sacrifice?

No bishop, no missionary should ever hesitate or lack the faith to teach the law of tithing to the poor. The sentiment of "They can't *afford* to" needs to be replaced with "They can't afford not to."

One of the first things a bishop *must* do to help the needy is ask them to pay their tithing. Like the widow, if a destitute family is faced with the decision of paying their tithing or eating, they should pay their tithing. The bishop can help them with their food and other basic needs until they become self-reliant. ("Tithing—a Commandment Even for the Destitute," *Ensign,* May 2005, 34–35)

Joseph F. Smith:

By this principle [tithing] the loyalty of the people of this Church shall be put to the test. By this principle it shall be known who is for the kingdom of God and who is against it. By this principle it shall be seen whose hearts are set on doing the will of God and keeping his commandments, thereby sanctifying the land of Zion unto God, and who are opposed to this principle and have cut themselves off from the blessings of Zion. There is a great deal of importance connected with this principle, for by it it shall be known whether we are faithful or unfaithful. In this respect it is as essential as faith in God, as repentance of sin, as baptism for the remission of sin, or as the laying on of hands for the gift of the Holy Ghost. For if a man keep all the law save one point, and he offend in that, he is a transgressor of the law, and he is not entitled to the fulness of the blessings of the gospel of Jesus Christ. But when a man keeps all the law that is revealed, according to his strength, his substance, and his ability, though what he does may be little, it is just as acceptable in the sight of God as if he were able to do a thousand times more. (*Gospel Doctrine: Selections from the Sermons and Writings of Joseph F. Smith* [Salt Lake City: Deseret Book, 1939], 225)

Joseph F. Smith:

The law of tithing is a test by which the people as individuals shall be proved. Any man who fails to observe this principle shall be known as a man who is indifferent to the welfare of Zion, who neglects his duty as a member of the Church and who does nothing toward the accomplishment of the temporal advancement of the kingdom of God. He contributes nothing, either, toward spreading the gospel to the nations of the earth, and he neglects to do that which would entitle him to receive the blessings and ordinances of the gospel. (*Gospel Doctrine: Selections from the Sermons and Writings of Joseph F. Smith* [Salt Lake City: Deseret Book, 1939], 226)

DOCTRINES AND PRINCIPLES

It is fitting to consider the law of tithing in the same context with the subject of preparing for the Second Coming. In our day, the Lord has said:

> Behold, now it is called today until the coming of the Son of Man, and verily it is a day of sacrifice, and a day for the tithing of my people; for he that is tithed shall not be burned at his coming.
>
> For after today cometh the burning—this is speaking after the manner of the Lord—for verily I say, tomorrow all the proud and they that do wickedly shall be as stubble; and I will burn them up, for I am the Lord of Hosts; and I will not spare any that remain in Babylon.
>
> Wherefore, if ye believe me, ye will labor while it is called today. (D&C 64:23–25)

Elsewhere, He stressed the importance of having one's name "enrolled with the people of God" so that "he may tithe his people, to prepare them against the day of vengeance and burning" (D&C 85:3). It is the same message that Malachi sounded in his day: "For I am the Lord, I change not; therefore ye sons of Jacob are not consumed" (Mal. 3:6). And why are they not consumed? Because their names are kept in a "book of remembrance . . . for them that feared the Lord, and that thought upon his name" (Mal. 3:16). Malachi's universal question echoes with power down through the centuries: "But who may abide the day of his coming?" (Mal. 3:2). And, once again, the answer is lucidly clear for all of us who live in a time already well beyond the promised return of Elijah the prophet: "Wherefore, if ye believe me, ye will labor while it is called today" (D&C 64:25).

We give temporal offerings to the Lord, in particular our tithes—one tenth of our increase—and our fast offerings. Tithing is a commandment of God (see D&C 119). Payment of an honest tithe is a requirement for obtaining a temple recommend. Payment of tithes brings resultant blessings from our Heavenly Father, both temporal and spiritual. We cannot rob God in any of our tithes and offerings or else we shall be cursed (see Mal. 3:8–9).

Offerings to the Lord are given in many forms. We offer sacrifices unto the Lord of a broken heart and contrite spirit (see 3 Ne. 9:20). We offer our devotions to the Lord in all kinds of service. The important thing to remember is that we owe our Heavenly Father everything; therefore, we should not withhold our oblations from our Heavenly Father.

> And it pleaseth God that he hath given all these things unto man; for unto this end were they made to be used, with judgment, not to excess, neither by extortion.
>
> And in nothing doth man offend God, or against none is his wrath kindled, save those who confess not his hand in all things, and obey not his commandments. (D&C 59:20–21)

CHAPTER ONE

"THIS IS MY WORK *and* MY GLORY"

Reading Assignment: Moses 1.

And the great purposes of the Lord, the great purposes of the Father, were declared to Moses: ". . . this is my work and my glory—to bring to pass the immortality and eternal life of man" (Moses 1:39).

How can we, as members of this Church, forget that great principle? How can we fail to keep his commandments and to go forward as he has directed, for that will bring to us the immortality and eternal life which God promised. (J. Reuben Clark, Jr.)

THEMES *for* LIVING

1. The Nature of God and Our Divine Parentage
2. Humility, the Heavenly Virtue
3. Spiritual Strength in the Face of Opposition
4. Courage through Prayer and Priesthood Power
5. Divine Mission

INTRODUCTION

What Moses learned on the mount and later recorded for humankind by divine decree, is an unparalleled enrichment of the canon of spiritual truth. His face-to-face experience with God enabled him to gain an eternal view of the human condition and illuminate at least five supernal "moments of truth" that apply to our lives. It is our choice to embrace these truths of the gospel as we strive to achieve our potential of spiritual liberty according to the grand plan of heaven. The details of these points are given in the paragraphs that follow.

1. THE NATURE OF GOD AND OUR DIVINE PARENTAGE

THEME: God is endless and infinite in His wisdom and His works. He is our Father in Heaven. We are His children, and He knows us personally. We have a personal relationship with God.

> *Behold, I am the Lord God Almighty, and Endless is my name; . . . all things are present with me, for I know them all.* (Moses 1:3, 6)

> *Behold, I am the Lord God Almighty, . . . And, behold, thou art my son.* (Moses 1:3–4)

MOMENT OF TRUTH

As God spoke with Moses face-to-face, Moses came to understand the character and the attributes of God. We can also come to know these truths through study, prayer, and by the witness of the Holy Ghost. This knowledge of His goodness and power is necessary for one to act with faith, to show love, and to be obedient. The Prophet Joseph taught these quintessential principles to the School of the Prophets in Kirtland in the form of *The Lectures on Faith*. Understanding the nature of God will help us come to know Him: "And this is life eternal, that they might know thee the only true God, and Jesus Christ, whom thou hast sent" (John 17:3). Some have wondered about the wording: "but there is no God beside me" (Moses 1:6). In Moses' day idolatry was rampant, with many gods of all descriptions. The Lord wanted to be sure that Moses knew that there was ONE GOD to worship. This was reiterated later in the Ten Commandments (see *Messages of the First Presidency* 4:270–71; also 1 Cor. 8:5–6).

We, like Moses, are the literal children of our Heavenly Father (Rom. 8:16). Each of us is a divine being having a mortal experience to prove ourselves worthy of returning to our Heavenly Father's presence (Abr. 3:25). We have the potential to become perfect like our Heavenly Father and our Savior Jesus Christ and receive of Their fullness (3 Ne. 12:48; D&C 84:38). This knowledge should fill our souls with faith, hope, and charity. Knowing that Heavenly Father loves us makes **charity** abound in our hearts (John 3:16). We have **hope** of life eternal which God promised before the world began (Titus 1:2). We will be able to exercise our **faith** in Heavenly Father and our Savior because we have come to know of Their character and attributes (*Lectures on Faith* 1; 2). When we come to truly understand our relationship to God, we will be humble. We will be moved to action, recognizing our capacity and our potential. We have a divine destiny, for we are the children of God.

MODERN PROPHETS SPEAK

Hugh B. Brown:
> The vital and dynamic message of Mormonism is that there is a personal God in the heavens. He is omnipotent, omniscient, and omnipresent. He has not abated His power, He has not surrendered His sovereignty, He has not diluted His love, He changes not and His plans never fail. (*The Abundant Life* [Salt Lake City: Bookcraft, 1965], 282–83)

Joseph Smith:
> Without the knowledge of all things God would not be able to save any portion of his creatures; for it is by reason of the knowledge which he has of all things, from the beginning to the end, that enables him to give that understanding to his creatures by which they are made partakers of eternal life; and if it were not for the idea existing in the minds of men that God had all knowledge it would be impossible for them to exercise faith in him. (*Lectures on Faith* 4:11)

Joseph F. Smith:
> Man is the child of God, formed in the divine image and endowed with divine attributes, and even as the infant son of an earthly father and mother is capable in due time of becoming a man, so the undeveloped offspring of celestial parentage is capable, by experience through ages and aeons, of evolving into a God. (*Improvement Era,* Nov. 1909, 75–81)

ILLUSTRATIONS FOR OUR TIMES

Who Are You?
I will never forget the day my son Steven told me about a new couple who had moved into our ward. He said, "Guess who moved into that house? President Hugh B. Brown's daughter. Can you believe that, right here in our neighborhood—a daughter of a member of the First Presidency!"

I asked, "Who are you?"

He replied, "Big deal. Ed Pinegar's boy." I smiled and gave him a 'give me a better answer' look, and he said, quietly, "Oh, yes. I'm Heavenly Father's son."

This knowledge is imperative for all of us, and especially our children, to understand and appreciate. Then we will think and act as true children of God. Naomi W. Randall's famous song, "I Am a Child of God," speaks volumes concerning our divine parentage, our lives, and our future.

2. HUMILITY, THE HEAVENLY VIRTUE

THEME: We are dependent on the Lord for strength. Man, on his own, is nothing. Without God, we are nothing. With God, we have the promise of unending blessings. Humility gives us strength in the Lord.

Now, for this cause I know that man is nothing, which thing I never had supposed.
(Moses 1:10)

MOMENT OF TRUTH

Moses came to realize the greatness of God after having a magnificent spiritual experience on the mount. His strength was gone. It took hours before he could return to his "strength like unto man" (Moses 1:10). Moses had been a prince in Egypt, brought up in the courts of Pharaoh, surrounded by worldly splendor and power. Now, in the tutelage of the Creator, he learned the truth about mankind—that enduring strength comes only through God, and that man is totally dependent on divine power for his vitality and his very being. This knowledge gave Moses an understanding of the virtue of humility. Without humility, there is no growth. Humility is the beginning virtue of exaltation (Matt. 23:12), a quality that brings into our hearts a love of our fellow men and a feeling of connectedness to all mankind. Humility causes us to relate to God in prayerful gratitude and love because we realize that we are His children and acknowledge our dependence on Him. Moses learned on the mount—as we must learn—that we need an enduring attitude of humility if we are to succeed in helping to build up the kingdom of God (D&C 12:8).

MODERN PROPHETS SPEAK

Ezra Taft Benson:

> The Lord has made it very clear that no man can assist with this work unless he is humble and full of love (see D&C 12:8). Humility does not mean timidity. Humility does not mean fear. Humility does not mean weakness. You can be hum-

ble and still be courageous. You can be humble and still be vigorous and strong and fearless . . . .

Humility is an acknowledged recognition of our dependence on a higher power. (*TETB,* 119, 369)

Spencer W. Kimball:

One can be courageous and humble . . . . If the Lord was meek and lowly and humble, then to become humble one must do what he did in boldly denouncing evil, bravely advancing righteous works, courageously meeting every problem, becoming the master of himself and the situations about him and being near oblivious to personal credit. Humility is not pretentious, presumptuous, nor proud. It is not weak, vacillating, nor servile . . . . Humble and meek properly suggest virtues, not weaknesses. (*TSWK,* 232)

ILLUSTRATIONS FOR OUR TIMES

Royalty in Disguise

They were often very limited in their resources—even poor by any standard of measurement—but these humble German families often took us in as missionaries and regaled us with the best they could afford. I remember one elderly sister who watched with delight as we consumed the small clump of beef she had meticulously divided between us. When we asked about her portion, she replied that she did not care for any. We knew that she had willingly sacrificed her part so we could have more. We thanked her for her thoughtfulness, and we saw the joy of service reflected in her eyes.

Another family was excited to offer us baked rabbit one day after they had caught the animal nearby in a thicket. It was delicious—not so much because of our fondness for rabbit—but because of the atmosphere of charity and generosity in which it was prepared and given to us. They had nothing else to offer but that rabbit—and their loving kindness.

After all of these decades, I can still see that same family in my mind's eye when I met them unexpectedly at the Swiss Temple many months later. They looked resplendent in their temple clothing, complete with the glow of happiness about their countenances. It occurred to me then, and still remains a valued conviction, that this family all along was royalty in disguise. In the House of the Lord, they had set aside the homely and simple everyday clothing of their poverty for the robes of spiritual abundance. They had appeared as what they were all along—sons and daughters of God endowed with the capacity to be royal servants of the Almighty. Truly, humility is the heavenly virtue.

3. SPIRITUAL STRENGTH IN THE FACE OF OPPOSITION

THEME: We are free to choose between good and evil. That is our moral agency. With the help of God, we can resist temptation and overcome evil. We become what we are through our choices.

> *Satan came tempting him, saying: Moses, son of man, worship me.* (Moses 1:12)

> *And I can judge between thee and God; for God said unto me: Worship God, for him only shalt thou serve.* (Moses 1:15)

MOMENT OF TRUTH

What is the level of our spiritual vitality in the face of temptation and opposition? Moses, like all mankind, even Christ, had to be tempted. There is opposition in all things. It is a test of life. We must overcome the adversary. Moses was able to overcome temptation because he knew the glory of God, and so can we. He had a portion of the Spirit, therefore he could judge righteously (D&C 11:12), and the Spirit could show him all things to do (2 Ne. 32:5); we, too, can enjoy spiritual guidance and choose righteousness (1 Ne. 22:15, 26).

Opposition in all things is part of the divine plan; without it, there could be no happiness (2 Ne. 2:11). Temptation is a part of opposition in all things. The gift of God called agency gives us the power to choose. Because it is moral agency, there will be blessings or consequences according to our choices. For the gift of agency to work, there must be (1) eternal laws, (2) knowledge of good and evil, (3) opposition in all things, (4) power to choose, and (5) consequences of our choices here and hereafter. Recognizing these elements of agency gives us the perspective to choose righteousness.

MODERN PROPHETS SPEAK

Jeffrey R. Holland:

> A life without problems or limitations or challenges—life without 'opposition in all things' (2 Ne. 2:11), as Lehi phrased it—would paradoxically but in very fact be less rewarding and ennobling than one which confronts—even frequently confronts—difficulty and disappointment and sorrow. As beloved Eve said, were it not for the difficulties faced in a fallen world, neither she nor Adam nor any of the rest of us ever would have known 'the joy of our redemption, and the eternal life which God giveth unto all the obedient' (Moses 5:11.) So life has its oppositions and its conflicts, and the gospel of Jesus Christ has answers and assurances. ("The Peaceable Things of the Kingdom," *Ensign,* Nov. 1996, 84)

ILLUSTRATIONS FOR OUR TIMES

Tears of Joy

As a bishop, I have witnessed young people choosing to repent after grievous sins. The joy is beyond compare because of the Atonement of our Savior Jesus Christ and its cleansing power. As a temple sealer, I have seen the happiness of beautiful young couples kneeling at the altar in the House of the Lord amid tears of joy shed by loved ones. Every choice affects us now and in eternity.

A Towering Example

In our ward, we have a frequent visitor from the stake high council who cuts a rather unusual figure—if you can call a towering, 340-pound gentleman unusual. In his mild and humble way, he carries out his business on the Lord's errand with dispatch and self-deprecating modesty. But Eli Herring is special. As a former BYU senior offensive lineman with a 3.5 grade-point average, he declined a potentially lucrative deal with the Oakland Raiders in 1995 because he chose not to play professional football on Sunday. Instead, he decided to become a high school coach and teacher and carry on his service to the Lord in ways aligned more closely with his deeply held values.

When I asked him one day from what source he drew the strength to make such a far-reaching decision, he mentioned four things: (1) his mother, (2) the scriptures and the words of modern prophets, (3) prayer and the strength of his wife (since they had made this decision together), and (4) the example of other men in similar situations. What impact does this spiritual giant have on the youth of our stake and many others as well? He engenders profound respect for the kind of courage that enables one to uphold principles that one considers to be inviolate.

4. COURAGE THROUGH PRAYER AND PRIESTHOOD POWER

THEME: When we pray for the Spirit of the Lord to be with us, we shall not fear.

> *Moses began to fear exceedingly. . . . Nevertheless, calling upon God, he received strength . . . saying . . . In the name of the Only Begotten, depart hence, Satan. . . . and he departed hence.*
> (Moses 1:20–22)

MOMENT OF TRUTH

What is your disposition in the face of evil threats? Moses was tempted and tried by Satan face-to-face. In this world, with all its iniquity, we are continually being bombarded by the adversary and the hosts of Heaven who were cast down to the earth. Moses would not cease to call upon God, yet for a time he had fear. Fear is deeply destructive if we do not confront it with positive action. We must have *faith in God* (Matt. 8:26), *perfect love* (1 Jn. 4:18), *preparation* (D&C 38:30), *knowledge* (Prov. 24:5), *experience* to build confidence, and above all we must *pray to God always* (Moses 1:20). One can truly overcome fear in the strength of the Lord. Moses, being strengthened through prayer and inspired by the Holy Ghost, dismissed Satan by the power of the priesthood of God. Heavenly Father has been gracious to share His authority and power with His children for the purpose of blessing their lives. The priesthood operates only upon principles of righteousness (D&C 121:36) and through Christlike attributes (D&C 121:41–42), especially faith and responsiveness to the Holy Ghost.

MODERN PROPHETS SPEAK

Richard G. Scott:

> He is your Father; pray to him. If your life is in disarray and you feel uncomfortable and unworthy to pray because you are not clean, don't worry. He already knows about all of that. He is waiting for you to kneel in humility and take the first few steps. Pray for strength. Pray for others to be led to support you and guide you and lift you. Pray that the love of the Savior will pour into your heart. Pray that the miracle of the Atonement will bring forgiveness because you are willing to change. I know that those prayers will be answered, for God loves you. His Son gave his life for you. I know they will help you. ("True Friends That Lift," *Ensign*, Nov. 1988, 77)

Bruce R. McConkie:

> And the extent to which we become like him is the extent to which we gain his faith, acquire his power, and exercise his priesthood. And when we have become like him in the full and true sense, then we also shall have eternal life. Faith and priesthood go hand in hand. Faith is power and power is priesthood. After we gain faith, we receive the priesthood. Then, through the priesthood, we grow in faith until, having all power, we become like our Lord. Our time here in mortality is set apart as a time of probation and of testing. It is our privilege while here to perfect our faith and to grow in priesthood power. ("The Doctrine of the Priesthood," *Ensign*, May 1982, 32).

ILLUSTRATIONS FOR OUR TIMES

The Prayer of Faith

Enos had a concern—the welfare of his own soul. He prayed all day and into the night. His sins were forgiven, and his guilt was swept away. How can this happen? Because of faith in Jesus Christ (Enos 1:4–8). Our prayers, like the power of the priesthood, operate on the power of faith. All things are available to us through this magnificent principle. It is truly the foundation of all righteousness. Pray always in gratitude (D&C 59:21), or for direction, confirmation of a decision, or for a seemingly overwhelming need. We should always call upon our Heavenly Father.

A Great Calm

The storm had come up suddenly. The waves on the main channel of Lake Powell were surging, causing the boat to pitch and roll threateningly as we made our way past towering cliffs toward the marina. Then, without warning, the engine started to sputter and cut in and out. If we lost our power, we would have no way to prevent ourselves from drifting over against the rock cliffs where the waves were crashing like demons in the tempest. I ordered my family members to go down into the lower cabin and make sure their life preservers were securely fastened, then I frantically fought the engine to keep it going as long as possible. The safety of the marina was still miles away. It was late afternoon and the darkness of the storm was closing in around us. Could we make it?

As I fought to see clearly through the rain-spattered windshield, I heard a little voice calling me from the stairwell of the cuddy. "Dad," said the little voice. I looked down from the captain's chair and saw my young seven-year-old son, Matt, peering up at me through the darkness. He was smiling—smiling at a time of such ominous danger. "Don't worry, Dad," he said. "We're going to make it. I prayed to Heavenly Father."

I was suddenly enveloped in a spirit of comfort and reassurance. The faith of a child had prevailed. We were going to make it. And we did! Since then, the words of the Savior have echoed in my mind repeatedly as I have pondered this experience: "Peace, be still," He said. From the record, we know what happened next: "And the wind ceased, and there was a great calm" (Mark 4:39).

5. DIVINE MISSION

THEME: God's entire mission is centered on the well-being of all His children. Knowing this should fill us with gratitude and love for God and His Son. Each of us has an important role to play in the grand plan of Heaven, and each one of us can help God to complete His work. That is our task and mission in life.

> *For behold, this is my work and my glory—to bring to pass the immortality and eternal life of man.* (Moses 1:39)

> *And I have a work for thee.* (Moses 1:6)

MOMENT OF TRUTH

Moses was taught that the purpose of our Heavenly Father and our Savior is to bring about the immortality and eternal life of man. This is the work and glory of God—the happiness of His children. He loves us and wants us to return home to His presence to live forever. We, like Moses, have a work to do. We are disciples of Jesus Christ and are here to build up the kingdom of God. Our work then is our Heavenly Father's work: the immortality and eternal life of our brothers and sisters.

We can choose to follow the Lord's plan as outlined in the scriptures. Moses was commanded to write the things the Lord revealed to him. All the prophets have written the word of the Lord as it has been given to them. In our day, the Lord said through the Prophet Joseph Smith: "For you shall live by every word that proceedeth forth from the mouth of God" (D&C 84:44). The word of God will tell us plainly what we should do (2 Ne. 32:3). The Prophet Joseph received modern-day scriptures, including the Book of Mormon, which restored again the written word of the gospel of Jesus Christ. By committing to daily scripture study and aligning our walk with the principles of truth, we can, like Moses, find on our "mount" of transcendence the faith, strength, and courage to participate with the Lord in His divine mission to "bring to pass the immortality and eternal life of man" (Moses 1:39).

MODERN PROPHETS SPEAK

Gordon B. Hinckley:

> We are living in a wonderful season of the work of the Lord. The work is growing ever stronger. It is expanding across the world. Each of us has an important part to play in this great undertaking. People in more than 160 nations, speaking a score of languages and more, worship our Father in Heaven and our Redeemer, His Beloved Son. This is their great work. It is their cause and their kingdom. ("May We Be Faithful and True," *Ensign,* May 1997, 6)

Jack H. Goaslind, Jr.:

> The life of God—the eternal, exalted life we all seek—is inherently concerned with the salvation of souls. It is the "work and . . . glory" of God to "bring to pass the immortality and eternal life of man" (Moses 1:39). It is by bringing about the conditions necessary for the salvation of his children that God glorifies himself, progresses, and expands his dominions (See D&C 132:31). ("Our Responsibility to Take the Gospel to the Ends of the Earth," *Ensign,* Nov. 1983, 32)

ILLUSTRATIONS FOR OUR TIMES

For All Tongues and Peoples

What better way is there to prepare for our mission to help God bring about the immortality and eternal life of man than laying the foundation of spiritual growth within the family? As a family, we love to read the scriptures together and look for that special passage that resonates with us on this particular day. Then we read that passage aloud once again in another language—typically French, German, or Spanish—to feel how people in other cultures must feel as they experience the depth of the Lord's word, spoken in plainness according to their understanding. This way our family tries to see things from multiple points of view. This experience helps us appreciate the fact that the scriptures are for all kindreds, tongues, and peoples, and that the Lord's invitation is extended to every one of His children.

Learning to Love the Word of God

Helping Heavenly Father complete His mission begins with knowing His word. I will never forget when we started regular early-morning scripture study. The children thought I had become a religious fanatic. Who gets up so early in the morning to search the scriptures? The older children had a harder time getting used to it, but the younger children just thought that was the way of life . . . scripture study early in the morning. They just thought it was the thing to do. (That's a lesson within itself.) When our daughter Kelly spoke at her missionary farewell, she explained how she had learned to dislike my high, raspy voice as I would wake her up early in the morning for scripture time. Then she paused and began to cry, saying, "But that's when I learned to love the word of God." Needless to say, we were all happy.

SUMMARY

The five glorious doctrines from Moses 1 discussed here contribute immeasurably to our knowledge of God and reinforce our first steps for exercising faith and understanding our great dependence upon Him. Knowing of His goodness and mercy toward all the "children of men" (Moro. 10:3) builds a relationship of trust. Understanding the nature of God and our divine parentage raises our inner eye toward a vista of returning one day to our heavenly home. Similarly, humility is key not only to living a Christlike life but is also the cardinal virtue that will give us access to the promptings of the Spirit and help us be worthy to gain eternal life. Moreover, by continually seeking and applying spiritual strength in the face of opposition, and through constant prayer and the righteous exercise of priesthood power, we can overcome fear and become worthy servants of God in bringing about the salvation and eternal life of His children. And finally, understanding the divine mission leads to parental joy in seeing the growth and success of our children.

CHAPTER TWO

"THOU WAST CHOSEN *before* THOU WAST BORN"

Reading Assignment: Abraham 3; Moses 4:1–4.

Additional Reading: Isaiah 14:12–15; Revelation 12:7–9; Alma 13:3–5; D&C 29:36–39; 138.

> *Every man who has a calling to minister to the inhabitants of the world was ordained to that very purpose in the Grand Council of heaven before this world was. I suppose that I was ordained to this very office in that Grand Council.* (Joseph Smith, *JD* 24:01)

THEMES *for* LIVING

1. Godly Vision
2. Intelligence
3. Foreordination
4. Purpose for the Creation
5. Earth: A Testing Time
6. Doing the Father's Will
7. Avoiding Pride

INTRODUCTION

One of the most sublime and reassuring aspects of revealed truth is the knowledge that our spiritual roots reach back into the premortal halls of glory, where we were schooled in the principles of righteousness by our Father in Heaven and His Son personally, just as Abraham was. These "first lessons in the world of the spirits" (D&C 138:56) prepared us for our experience in mortality.

1. GODLY VISION

THEME: Whatever the Lord conceives, He brings inevitably into existence. Therefore, as children of God, we must learn to envision only that which is noble, godly, and righteous.

> *There is nothing that the Lord thy God shall take into his heart to do but what he will do it.* (Abr. 3:17)

MOMENT OF TRUTH

Abraham was given many visions from the Lord and received many truths that enlightened his mind and soul. He could clearly see things as they were, as they are, and as they would be. He had a vision of life and the work of the Lord. We need a clear vision, too. How can we as mortals have the vision of life and the things we need to do? We learn from Proverbs that "Where there is no vision, the people perish" (Prov. 29:18). We must have a vision of who we are and what we can do. Through faith and obedience, we can see and envision the work and glory of God—and our role is to help bring this about. This is the vision for our life.

MODERN PROPHETS SPEAK

Thomas S. Monson:
> Vision without effort is daydreaming; effort without vision is drudgery; but vision coupled with effort will obtain the prize. (*Conference Classics* [Salt Lake City: Deseret Book, 1984])

Gordon B. Hinckley:
> This is the business of the Church—to open the vision of men to eternal verities and to prompt them to take a stand for equity and decency, for virtue, sobriety, and goodness. (*Be Thou an Example* [Salt Lake City: Deseret Book, 1981], 17)

ILLUSTRATIONS FOR OUR TIMES

The Vision of Life

I will not forget when I came to realize the "vision" of life and its meaning as well as my role in it. I could see that I was Heavenly Father's "boy," yes, His literal son, just like all of you are His sons and daughters. Having this vision brought not only purpose to life but it brought self-esteem to my very soul. This vision has sustained me throughout my life.

Seeing with the Inner Eye

In our family, we have the extraordinary privilege of being parents to a special child with a complex array of multiple physical and mental challenges. One challenge he does not have, however, is spirituality; for here is a worthy son of God if ever there was one.

As parents, we can look back and envision this young man, with our inner eye, as a royal prince in the courts of our Father in Heaven during the premortal phase of life—stalwart, faithful, sound of spirit and capacity, perfectly willing to come to this earth despite the enormous adversity faced by all autistic children who must go through life in virtual communicative isolation. We can also look forward and envision his glorious assured future as a valiant servant in the kingdom of God throughout the eternities, restored through the resurrection to his complete, unrestricted potential for service and the abundant spiritual life.

What a comfort it is to understand the panorama of the plan of salvation, the magnificent view given by our Heavenly Father about where we have come from, why we are here, and where we will be going following this mortal experience. What a transcending thought to know that we can be with this special child in the hereafter, in all his maturity and radiance, as well as with all of our children and our children's children, provided we live faithful to those first lessons received in the spirit world and re-learned here through the scriptures and the teachings of modern-day prophets.

2. INTELLIGENCE

THEME: Intelligence is an eternal attribute of God and His spirit-children. We must therefore look to our Father in Heaven as the source of the highest intelligence and wisdom, and strive to magnify the intelligence with which we have been endowed.

> *I am the Lord thy God. I am more intelligent than they all. . . . my wisdom excelleth them all.* (Abr. 3:19, 21)

MOMENT OF TRUTH

Abraham was shown the intelligences "that were organized before the world was" (Abr. 3:22) and was taught that God was more intelligent than all of them. "The glory of God is intelligence" (D&C 93:36). Intelligence is light and truth. Light and truth are attributes of God; they are through and in all things created by the Lord. This light enlightens all things. Christ is the light, the way, the truth, and the life of the world. When our eye is single to the glory of God, we will be filled with this light and comprehend all things (D&C 88:67). Truth is eternal, and the truths of the gospel are absolute. The Holy Ghost is the "Spirit of Truth," and if it is not of this Spirit it is not of God (D&C 50:17–22). The intelligence we acquire on earth will rise with us in the resurrection and will be to our advantage in the hereafter (D&C 130:18–19).

MODERN PROPHETS SPEAK

Neal A. Maxwell:
> As we ponder intelligence, a summational strength and attribute of Jesus, it is vital that we understand that intelligence includes more than raw IQ; it includes judgment—and not only in the judicial sense. He who has intelligence, or the light of truth, will forsake completely "that evil one" (D&C 93:36–37). To forsake the evil one, as Jesus did, is an act of high intelligence and superlative wisdom. (*Even As I Am* [Salt Lake City: Deseret Book, 1982], 29)

Joseph Smith:
> The spirit of revelation is in connection with these blessings. A person may profit by noticing the first intimation of the spirit of revelation; for instance, when you feel pure intelligence flowing into you, it may give you sudden strokes of ideas, so that by noticing it, you may find it fulfilled the same day or soon; (i.e.) those things that were presented unto your minds by the Spirit of God, will come to pass; and thus by learning the Spirit of God and understanding it, you may grow into the principle of revelation, until you become perfect in Christ Jesus. (*HC* 3:381)

ILLUSTRATIONS FOR OUR TIMES

The Quest for Intelligence

My wife, Carol Lynn, often speaks about her vivid childhood memories of seeing her father so often seated in his easy chair, reading and pondering the scriptures. This image of her father, faithfully exercising his capacity to broaden his understanding and open up channels of pure intelligence through the word of God, is an enduring source of inspiration and comfort to her. She remembers fondly the frequent times when he noticed her there, and called her to his side to read a passage to her—most often from the Book of Mormon—and offer his commentary and feelings about it. "Is that not beautiful?" he would say, often with a tear in his eye. This made a lasting and wholesome impression on his daughter.

It generates in turn the question: How many of us present a similar image to others who may be watching? How many of us teach by example the principle of enlarging our spiritual boundaries and seeking after pure intelligence?

Missionary Example

The young missionaries often exemplify striving to gain more light, truth, and pure intelligence. They become so engrossed in the scriptures and studying that they literally "feast upon the word," and they can't get enough of it. I recall missionaries writing and telling me how much they love the Book of Mormon. They would get up at five a.m. just so they could read an extra hour and a half a day. Yes, their bodies would be filled with light. Their eye was single to the glory of God. They lived by the Spirit and were magnifying their calling.

3. FOREORDINATION

THEME: In the premortal realm, God chose many noble leaders to guide His work on the earth. Each of us was chosen to fulfill an important calling of service and love.

> *And God saw these souls that they were good, and he stood in the midst of them, . . . and he said unto me: Abraham, thou art one of them; thou wast chosen before thou wast born.*
> (Abr. 3:23)

MOMENT OF TRUTH

Abraham was one of the noble and great premortal spirits. He was called to lead a dispensation of time. His posterity would be blessed forever through his lineage. What did Abraham and others do premortally to be foreordained? "Being called and prepared from the foundation of the world according to the foreknowledge of God, on account of their exceeding faith and good works; in the first place being left to choose good or evil; therefore they having chosen good, and exercising exceedingly great faith, are called with a holy calling, yea, with that holy calling which was prepared with, and according to, a preparatory redemption for such" (Alma 13:3). Everything is predicated on obedience. Blessings and opportunities come to those who choose to follow the Lord. We were prepared during the premortal phase of our existence for our mortal experience today, as we learn from latter-day revelation: "Even before they were born, they, with many others, received their first lessons in the world of spirits and were prepared to come forth in the due time of the Lord to labor in his vineyard for the salvation of the souls of men" (D&C 138:56).

MODERN PROPHETS SPEAK

Harold B. Lee:

> Now a further word about this matter of foreordination. The Prophet Joseph Smith taught that "Every man who has a calling to minister to the inhabitants of the world was ordained to that very purpose in the grand council of heaven before this world was" (*Joseph Smith's Teachings,* 365). So likewise declared the Apostle Paul, "For whom he did foreknow . . . them he also called" (Rom. 2:29–30). But do not misunderstand that such a calling and such foreordination pre-determine what you must do. A prophet on this western continent has spoken plainly on this subject, "Being called and prepared from the foundation of the world, according to the foreknowledge of God on account of their exceeding faith and good works; in the first place being left to choose good or evil" (Alma 13:3). This last passage makes the others preceding more understandable. God may have called and chosen men in the spirit world or in their first estate to do a certain work, but whether they will accept that calling here and magnify it by faithful service and good works while in mortality is a matter in which it is their right and privilege to exercise their free agency to choose good or evil. (*Decisions for Successful Living* [Salt Lake City: Deseret Book, 1973], 168–69)

Bruce R. McConkie:

> The greatest and most important talent or capacity that any of the spirit children of the Father could gain is the talent of spirituality. Most of those who gained this talent were chosen, before they were born, to come to earth as members of the house of Israel. They were foreordained to receive the blessings that the Lord promised to Abraham and to his seed in all their generations. This foreordination is an election, Paul tells us, and truly it is so, for those so chosen, selected, or elected become, in this life, the favored people. Though all mankind may be saved by obedience, some find it easier to believe and obey than others. Hence the concept, taught by Jesus, that his sheep know his voice and will not follow the dissident voices of the world. (*A New Witness for the Articles of Faith* [Salt Lake City: Deseret Book, 1985], 512–13; see also Bruce R. McConkie, *The Millennial Messiah: The Second Coming of the Son of Man* [Salt Lake City: Deseret Book, 1982], 234–35)

Neal A. Maxwell:

> With the Restoration, however, we are blessed to understand that individual intelligences were organized before the world was (see Abr. 3:22; see also D&C 138). "Man

was also in the beginning with God," and thus man is co-eternal, but certainly not co-equal, with God (see Abr. 3:18,19; D&C 93:23, 29). The foreordination of some, based on God's foreknowledge, was and is a reality. "Before I formed thee in the belly I knew thee; and before thou camest forth out of the womb I sanctified thee, and I ordained thee a prophet unto the nations" (Jer. 1:5; see also Eccl. 12:7; John 9:2; Eph. 1:4; Heb. 12:9). "And this is the manner after which they were ordained—being called and prepared from the foundation of the world according to the foreknowledge of God" (Alma 13:3). "Among the great and mighty ones who were assembled in this vast congregation of the righteous were Father Adam, the Ancient of Days and father of all, And our glorious Mother Eve, with many of her faithful daughters who had lived through the ages and worshiped the true and living God" (D&C 138:38–39). (*If Thou Endure It Well* [Salt Lake City: Bookcraft, 1996], 82)

ILLUSTRATIONS FOR OUR TIMES

A Blessing from Heaven

When we read our patriarchal blessings, we come to know in a real sense the expectations and blessings we can look forward to if we are true and faithful. Sometimes there are indications of blessings that we can receive at this point in our lives. Why do we receive those blessings? We, like Abraham, lived premortally and received blessings according to our exceeding faith and good works.

4. PURPOSE FOR THE CREATION

THEME: As children of God, we stand in awe of the knowledge that this earth was created specifically as a mortal home for us. This truth should fill us with humble gratitude to our Father in Heaven for His eternal love.

> *And there stood one among them that was like unto God, and he said unto those who were with him: We will go down, for there is space there, and we will take of these materials, and we will make an earth whereon these may dwell.* (Abr. 3:24)

MOMENT OF TRUTH

Jehovah, the God of the Old Testament, even Jesus Christ our Savior, was the creator of our earth (John 3:3). The earth, with all its beauty and variety, was made for our dwelling place—our home. When one contemplates the goodness of the Lord in providing this earth for us, surely our hearts are filled with gratitude and thanksgiving. Its beauty is awe-inspiring and causes us to reflect on the divine plan of happiness and its blessings in our lives. Taking care of this earth is our responsibility and privilege.

MODERN PROPHETS SPEAK

Mark E. Peterson:

> The special creation of this earth was a vital part of the plan of salvation. It had a particular purpose. It was no afterthought. Neither was it an accident of any proportion, nor a spontaneous development of any kind. It was the result of deliberate, advance planning and purposeful creation. The Divine Architect devised it. The Almighty Creator made it and assigned to it a particular mission. . . . Do we appreciate what this earth really means to us? Do we see why it was made? Do we understand its purpose? Do we see that there was nothing accidental or spontaneous about its origin? Do we see that its creation was literally and truly, completely and exclusively, an act of God? ("Creator and Savior," *Ensign,* May 1983, 63–64)

James E. Talmage:

> Every created thing has been made for a purpose; and everything that fills the measure of its creation is to be advanced in the scale of progression, be it an atom or a world, an animalcule, or man—the direct and literal offspring of Deity. (*Jesus the Christ* [Salt Lake City: Deseret Book, 1983], 299)

ILLUSTRATIONS FOR OUR TIMES

A Living Gift

The earth is our home. Within the earth the power of God is manifest. It has all of the resources to sustain life. It provides a symbiotic state for plants and animals. We, as Heavenly Father's children, are the beneficiaries. The plants are self-perpetuating through their seeds. Animals propagate from their own kind and feed upon the earth. Plants and animals are for the benefit of mankind. The earth was created to sustain life for Heavenly Father's children. It is a gift from God. When we fully understand and appreciate this fact, we will surely take better care of this important creation of the Lord.

5. EARTH: A TESTING TIME

THEME: The purpose for our earthly existence is to prove ourselves worthy, through our own agency and obedience to the laws of heaven, to return to our Heavenly Father.

> *And we will prove them herewith, to see if they will do all things whatsoever the Lord their God shall command them.* (Abr. 3:25)

MOMENT OF TRUTH

Abraham learned from the Lord that earth life is a test. We came here to be tested and prove ourselves worthy to return to our Heavenly Father's presence. The test is hard, but we agreed to it, then shouted for joy premortally (Job 38:7). The test is primarily one of obedience. Will we do what the Lord commands? In this test we will have opposition in all things, be tempted by the devil, and be willing to submit to whatever the Father sees to inflict upon us. Sometimes it appears to be unfair. Some will be victims and have to endure extremely difficult circumstances. Others seemingly will have less difficult tasks. Heavenly Father knows best, and He and our Savior will judge us perfectly. It is simply our duty, and hopefully our joy, to obey His word and keep His commandments, thus enjoying the blessings of the Holy Spirit, happiness, and eternal life.

MODERN PROPHETS SPEAK

Ezra Taft Benson:

> I know, as I know that I live, that there is a God in heaven; that he is perfect and all powerful; that we are his children; that he loves us; and that we are eternal beings. I also know that life is a testing time in man's eternal existence, during which he is given his free agency—the right to choose between right and wrong—and that on those choices hang great consequences, not only in this life, but, even more important, in the life to come. There are boundaries beyond which Satan cannot go. Within those bounds, he is presently being permitted to offer an unrighteous alternative to God's righteous principles, thus allowing men to choose between good and evil and thereby determine the station they shall occupy in the next life. (*God, Family, Country: Our Three Great Loyalties* [Salt Lake City: Deseret Book, 1974], 402)

Neal A. Maxwell:

> Mortality without the dimension of temptation or trial would not be a full proving; it would be a school with soft credits and no hard courses. (*The Neal A. Maxwell Quote Book* [Salt Lake City: Bookcraft, 1997], 45)

Neal A. Maxwell:

> The tests given to us here are given not because God is in doubt as to the outcome, but because we need to grow in order to be able to serve with full effectiveness in the eternity to come. . . . The relentless love of our Father in Heaven is such that in His omniscience He will not allow the cutting short some of the brief experiences we are having here. To do so would be to deprive us of everlasting experiences and

great joy there. What else would an omniscient and loving Father do, even if we plead otherwise? He must at times say no. (*The Neal A. Maxwell Quote Book* [Salt Lake City: Bookcraft, 1997], 26)

ILLUSTRATIONS FOR OUR TIMES

Mortality is part of our progression to eternal life. In this condition, we often fail to remember the goodness of God and our daily purpose of preparing to return to His presence. Recognizing this fact, we need to provide ways to remember, so as to do well in our test of life.

The Lesson of the Hands

The Lord's special memory device for bringing to our minds the promises of obedience we make to Him is the sacrament of the Lord's supper. To partake of the sacrament we must, of course, use our hands. Should we not also think of our hands as a constant, ever-present lesson in remembering who we are and how we should behave?

I recall many years ago being assigned to visit the Hampstead Branch of the Baltimore Stake. Being seated on the stand during sacrament meeting, I had a clear view of the deacons along the front row waiting to pass the emblems to the congregation. That day, the sacrament hymn was the beautiful and tender song that begins "While of these emblems we partake, in Jesus' name and for his sake." As we continued with the words—"Let us remember and be sure our hearts and hands are clean and pure"—I happened at just that moment to be looking down at one of the young deacons. There he was, holding both of his open hands out in front of him, palms upward. He was gazing upon them intently as if to find reassurance that he was, indeed, a worthy servant of the Lord about to participate in a sacred ordinance.

I shall never forget that image of the young man and his extended hands. Our hands are, indeed, a constant reminder that we should be continually engaged in the Lord's errand, ever intent on keeping His commandments, ever vigilant that our hearts and hands remain unsullied by the world's ungodly practices, ever committed to that which is ennobling and edifying.

6. DOING THE FATHER'S WILL

THEME: The supernal prototype of godly obedience is the Savior, who, in perfect and humble submission to the will of the Father, offered Himself as Redeemer. To follow the Lord valiantly, we, too, must continue to submit humbly to God's will throughout our mortal probation, just as we chose to do in the premortal realm.

Father, thy will be done, and the glory be thine forever. (Moses 4:2)

MOMENT OF TRUTH

Moses was taught that our beloved brother Jesus Christ was chosen from the beginning to be the Savior of the world. The Savior demonstrated two magnificent attributes: (1) Obedience—"Thy will be done," and (2) Humility—"The glory be thine forever." When we seek to aggrandize ourselves, we become unrighteous (John 7:48). All good comes from God and the Holy Spirit, who leads us to do good and inspires all the good we do. We are always indebted to our Savior and our Heavenly Father for all things. We were "created in Christ Jesus unto good works" (Eph. 2:10), and we show our love by doing the will of our Father—even as the Lord Jesus Christ.

MODERN PROPHETS SPEAK

Gordon B. Hinckley:

> [The Church] expects that each of you will have a testimony of the living reality of God our Eternal Father and His Son, the Lord Jesus Christ. This is the beginning of all wisdom. It is the beginning of all faith. It is your duty and your obligation to acquire that knowledge. It is the only knowledge which will bring you salvation. Jesus said, "If any man will do his will, he shall know of the doctrine" (John 7:17), and that is the way you acquire a testimony—by doing the will of the Father. (*TGBH,* 404)

Neal A. Maxwell:

> Since the natural man is inclined to hold back his talents, his time, or his possessions, there will also be enhancing experiences to teach us, if we will, the need to let our wills be swallowed up in the will of the Father. (*Lord, Increase Our Faith* [Salt Lake City: Bookcraft, 1994], 42)

ILLUSTRATIONS FOR OUR TIMES

When You Do His Will

The young, enthusiastic father and husband sat across from my desk. It was his first time at our Baltimore Ward meetings since his family had joined the Church, and he was seeking counsel about a principle of the gospel new to him—tithing.

"Bishop," he said, "I believe in tithing, but our family budget is so tight that if I paid my tithing right now, there would not be enough left over for food."

In response, we opened the scriptures and reviewed together the wonderful promise in Malachi where the Lord invites us to "prove Him" with respect to this principle, and determine "if I will not open you the windows of heaven, and pour you out a blessing, that there shall not be room enough to receive it" (Mal. 3:10).

I looked him in the eyes and asked, "Do you have the faith to do the Lord's will?"

He swallowed hard and then replied, in all sincerity, that he would go and do what the Lord commanded. I then promised him that the Lord would bless him for it. He smiled, shook my hand, and left my office.

The following Sunday, he came back for another conversation, even more enthusiastic than the previous week. "You will not believe what happened this past week," he said. "The principal of the school where I teach physical education came to me and gave me a raise—equal exactly to the tithing I paid the Lord!" That young father went on to grow in the gospel grace upon grace, line upon line, until not too many years later he became the bishop of that same ward. Yes, the Lord blesses those who do His will. "I, the Lord, am bound when ye do what I say; but when ye do not what I say, ye have no promise" (D&C 82:10).

The Transformation

Submission to Heavenly Father's will becomes the great blessing in our lives. We not only prove ourselves worthy, but we become stronger because of our obedience. The more we obey—the more we have the Spirit—the more direction we have in our lives—the more righteous we become—the greater capacity to serve and bless others—the more we can build up the kingdom of God—the greater the level of happiness—the more charity we possess—the more we will be like our Savior.

7. AVOIDING PRIDE

THEME: The ultimate example of prideful rebellion is Lucifer, who shows all discerning onlookers the pattern of behavior that inexorably leads to a fall from the grace of God.

Behold, here am I, send me, I will be thy son, and I will redeem all mankind, that one soul shall not be lost, and surely I will do it; wherefore give me thine honor. (Moses 4:1)

MOMENT OF TRUTH

It was revealed to Moses that Satan wanted to be sent as the son of God, that he professed that he would redeem all mankind, and that he wanted the glory. First, he was not chosen. Second, he sought to take away our agency. Third, he wanted to usurp the glory of the Father. Satan was full of pride, and he rebelled against three eternal verities: (1) Heavenly Father chooses His servants. (2) Agency is eternal—and Satan seeks to destroy it. (3) Avoiding pride is essential to salvation. Pride is the universal sin. It is the primary motivation or attribute of those who are carnal, sensual, and devilish. Because of pride, some choose not to repent and thus refuse to put off the "natural man," as King Benjamin referred to it (Mosiah 3:19). In doing so, they effectively suspend their own progress toward a higher spiritual destiny. Only by overcoming pride can we become like the Savior and rise to the hope of eternal life.

MODERN PROPHETS SPEAK

Ezra Taft Benson:

> Pride is the universal sin, the great vice. It manifests itself in competition, selfishness, contention, power-seeking, backbiting, living beyond our means, coveting, climbing the ladder of worldly success at the expense of others, and in a multitude of ways that "pit our will against God's" and limit our progression. Pride affects all of us at various times and in various degrees. . . . Pride is the stumbling block to Zion. The antidote for pride is humility—meekness, submissiveness. Members can choose to humble themselves by conquering enmity toward others, receiving counsel and chastisement, forgiving others, rendering selfless service, going on missions and preaching the word that can humble others, going to the temple more frequently, and by confessing and forsaking sins and being born of God. ("Beware of Pride," *Ensign,* May 1989, 4–6)

Thomas S. Monson:

> Unfortunately, prosperity, abundance, honor, and praise lead some men to the false security of haughty self-assurance and the abandonment of the inclination to pray. Conversely, turmoil, tribulation, sickness, and death crumble the castles of men's pride and bring them to their knees to plead for power from on High. (*Be Your Best Self* [Salt Lake City: Deseret Book, 1979], 26)

ILLUSTRATIONS FOR OUR TIMES

The Emissary of Humility

The avuncular, silver-haired gentleman of kindly disposition who was assigned to visit me from the high council, was among the least prideful persons I have ever known. He would come to our Johns Hopkins University student-housing apartment from time to time, always with a gentle spirit, always with an uplifting thought for the new young bishop and his wife. His quiet and humble demeanor belied his influential station in the highest leadership circles in Washington, D.C., for Rosel H. Hyde was at the time the Chairman of the Federal Communications Commission. But you would not know it from his modest deportment. I can still see his pleasant smile as he graced our sparse apartment with his presence, truly a servant of the Lord. The specifics of his messages have long since left my memory, but the image of him as an emissary of humility and meekness remains forever.

SUMMARY

As students of the scriptures, we are permitted to go with Abraham into the circle of the Lord where resplendent truth is unfolded to our senses. With Moses we walk into the mount to learn firsthand the saving principles of the gospel as taught by the Master Himself. What a singular blessing that the Lord has seen fit to preserve the record of these priceless teaching moments and allow us to participate in the visions of grandeur that confirm in such a vivid and compelling way the purposes of life and the mission of the Savior.

By studying these scriptures faithfully and prayerfully, we can rekindle in our memories the comforting assurance that we, too, were once in the halls of glory with our Father in Heaven and His Son, where "the first lessons in the world of spirits" were taught us in preparation for our sojourn on earth. It was there that we first learned how to see with godly vision, how to magnify our divinely-endowed intelligence, how to prepare for the future mortal tasks assigned us there, how to honor and cherish the earth that had been prepared specifically as our temporal (and eventually spiritual) home, how to strengthen ourselves in anticipation of our probationary earth life, how to follow the will of the Father and the Son in all respects and at all times, and how to cultivate humility and meekness as antidotes to pride. Through the promptings of the Spirit, we can look forward to the blessings that follow the covenant promises, and see with our inner eye the time when we can return once again to the presence of the Maker from whom all blessings flow.

CHAPTER THREE

"AND BEHOLD, ALL THINGS WHICH I HAD MADE WERE VERY GOOD"

Reading Assignment: Moses 1:27–42; 2–3.

Additional Reading: Abraham 4–5; Genesis 1–2.

The Lord never created this world at random. He has never done any of His work at random. The earth was created for certain purposes; and one of these was its final redemption and the establishment of His government and kingdom upon it in the latter days, to prepare it for the reign of the Lord Jesus Christ. (Wilford Woodruff, *JD* 15:8)

THEMES *for* LIVING

1. The Savior as Creator
2. The Majesty of the Creation and the Plan of Life
3. In the Image of God
4. Man and Woman Together and as Parents
5. Agency
6. Day of Rest

INTRODUCTION

The creation is perfect; the plan behind it is perfect; the majestic ebb and flow of life attests to the perfection of the Maker. In this chapter, we identify six interdependent and indispensable aspects of the creative signature: the Savior's central role in all of it; the goodness and glory of the plan of creation; man's creation in the image of God; the harmony and unity of man and woman in the grand scheme of life; the principle of agency; and the everlasting covenant pattern of Sabbath rest as the crowning seal upon the creative act. Without these six fundamental truths, the Creation could not be complete and could not bear the signature of divine approval.

1. THE SAVIOR AS CREATOR

THEME: The Savior is the steward of all life, under the Father, being both Creator and Redeemer, the Beginning and the End.

> *And worlds without number have I created . . . and by the Son I created them, which is mine Only Begotten.* (Moses 1:33)

MOMENT OF TRUTH

Moses was taught that Jesus Christ is the Only Begotten Son of God the Father, also known as Jehovah, God of the Old Testament, Creator and Redeemer of the world. He did everything the Father asked Him to do. Concerning the actual temporal creation, the Lord said, "For I, the Lord God, created all things . . . spiritually, before they were naturally upon the face of the earth" (Moses 3:5). Jehovah, under the direction of the Father, and along with other noble spirits, including Michael, to be known later as Adam, created the earth (see Abr. 3:22–24; John 1:1–3).

MODERN PROPHETS SPEAK

Ezra Taft Benson:
> Jesus Christ was and is the *Lord God Omnipotent.* (See Mosiah 3:5.) He was chosen before He was born. He was the all-powerful Creator of the heavens and the earth. He is the source of life and light to all things. His word is the law by which all things are governed in the universe. All things created and made by Him are subject to His infinite power. (*Come unto Christ* [Salt Lake City: Deseret Book, 1983], 128)

Joseph B. Wirthlin:

> Jesus is the head of our church, the Creator of the universe, the Savior and Redeemer of all mankind, and the Judge of the souls of men. Who he is and what he does affected each of us before we were born and will affect us each day of our mortal lives and throughout the eternities. Much of what he is and does is beyond finite human ability to comprehend, but the Holy Ghost has borne witness to my soul of his reality. (*Finding Peace in Our Lives* [Salt Lake City: Deseret Book, 1995], 23)

ILLUSTRATIONS FOR OUR TIMES

The Dandelion

Pick up and closely examine a dandelion at your next opportunity. It is a homely plant, much reviled by lawn keepers and much loathed by landscape tenders. But the Savior created it. There is a bit of glory captured in its simple golden crown. There is something of the flight of majesty in its delicate airborne seedlings. In its own simple way, it testifies plainly and clearly about the Creation and about the abundance of life. It has nothing of the effulgent wonder of the orchid or the captivating spell of the rose. But He created it, nevertheless. And it speaks a quiet lesson. We may not value its encroaching presence in our garden, but its aliveness, in and of itself, is a thing of no little beauty to those who can perceive the invisible hand at work in His world. It is, in its own unpretentious way, a tender reminder that "without him was not anything made that was made" (John 1:3), and that all aspects of the Creation are a witness of God at work. Perhaps we, too, in our own spiritual infancy, in our own nothingness before the perfection of God, seem as dandelions from the higher perspective. Perhaps we, too, have a little of the crown of glory upon our heads. He created us. And as potential sons and daughters of God, we have within us the potential of flight, of transcendence to a higher level of spirituality, where we will ultimately see ourselves to be in His own image.

2. THE MAJESTY OF THE CREATION AND THE PLAN OF LIFE

THEME: Looking at the Creation from the Lord's perspective, we can see the grand scope and divine goodness of the plan of life, and can appreciate our world as a manifestation of the power and glory of God at work.

> *And I, God, saw everything that I had made, and, behold, all things which I had made were very good.* (Moses 2:31)

MOMENT OF TRUTH

Moses and Abraham were granted visionary insight into the creative process, as recorded in the history of the creation of heaven and earth. We learn from the Hebrew that the word "create" refers to "organize." Matter has always existed. The earth and firmament were organized in six periods of time. The Creation was concluded in the crowning moment when Adam and Eve were placed upon the earth. The knowledge and methodology used in creating the earth have not yet been made known to mankind; we are finite mortals, and in this state it would be impossible to comprehend such truth (Isa. 55:8–9). The time will come, if we are true and faithful, when all things will be made known to those who honor the oath and covenant of the priesthood: "All that my father hath shall be given unto him" (D&C 84:38; 121:26–32). The earth in all its splendor and beauty has a singular purpose—to be a place for Heavenly Father's children to live, be tested, and prepare to reside in the celestial kingdom if found worthy. This earth was made for us.

MODERN PROPHETS SPEAK

Gordon B. Hinckley:

> I have looked at majestic mountains rising high against the blue sky and thought of Jesus, the Creator of heaven and earth. I have stood on the sand of an island in the Pacific and watched the dawn rise like thunder—a ball of gold surrounded by clouds of pink and white and purple—and thought of Jesus, the Word by whom all things were made and without whom was not anything made that was made. I have seen a beautiful child—bright-eyed, innocent, loving and trusting—and marveled at the majesty and miracle of creation. What then shall we do with Jesus who is called Christ? (*TGBH*, 273)

Bruce R. McConkie:

> If there had been no temporal creation, this earth would not exist as an abiding place for man and all forms of life. If Adam had not fallen, there would have been no mortality either for man or for any form of life. Rather, "All things which were created must have remained in the same state in which they were after they were created; and they must have remained forever, and had no end" (2 Ne. 2:22). And if there were no mortality, there could have been no immortality, no eternal life. Birth and death are as essential to the plan of holiness of the Father as is the very wonder of resurrection. Can we glory too much in the wonder of temporal creation, in the marvel of the peopling of our planet with mortal men, and in the heaven-sent revelation, to all who will receive it, of the plan of salvation? (*The Millennial Messiah: The Second Coming of the Son of Man* [Salt Lake City: Deseret Book, 1982], 14)

ILLUSTRATIONS FOR OUR TIMES

The Model

I recall reading a number of years ago about an incident from the life of a celebrated astronomer. He had constructed an intricate miniature model of the solar system to visually display its complex operation. A colleague of atheistic persuasion came to visit the great man in his laboratory and observed the superb model with admiration.

"Where did you get this?" he asked.

With a twinkle in his eye, the scientist responded, "It came together on its own."

"On its own!" exclaimed the visitor. "Something like this could not just happen. There has to be a craftsman."

"Just so," replied the astute and religious scientist. "And thus you see why the solar system as well had to have a Maker."

3. IN THE IMAGE OF GOD

THEME: Through the knowledge of our divine parentage, we can set our course to become perfect, even as our Father and His Son are perfect.

> *Let us make man in our image, after our likeness; and it was so.* (Moses 2:26)

MOMENT OF TRUTH

We are literally the spirit children of God, the Eternal Father, Elohim. Our first parents in mortality were Adam and Eve. They were created in the image and likeness of our Heavenly Father and our Savior, Jesus Christ. This knowledge brings the understanding that each of us, as a divine child of God, has the potential for limitless growth, the capacity to be even as our Heavenly Parents. It teaches us where we came from, why we are here, and where we are going. As parents, we must share this knowledge with our children so they can appreciate the image they carry within them.

MODERN PROPHETS SPEAK

Lorenzo Snow:

> As man is, God once was; as God is, man may become.

Gordon B. Hinckley:

> All human beings—male and female—are created in the image of God. Each is a beloved spirit son or daughter of heavenly parents, and, as such, each has a divine nature and destiny. Gender is an essential characteristic of individual premortal, mortal, and eternal identity and purpose. (*TGBH*, 264)

Gordon B. Hinckley:

> Our bodies are sacred. They were created in the image of God. They are marvelous, the crowning creation of Deity. . . . The ear and the brain constitute a miracle. The capacity to pick up sound waves and convert them into language is almost beyond imagination. . . . These, with others of our parts and organs, represent the divine, omnipotent genius of God, who is our Eternal Father. I cannot understand why anyone would knowingly wish to injure his body. (*TGBH,* 433)

ILLUSTRATIONS FOR OUR TIMES

"That was Christ"

I was attending the celebrated Passion Play at Oberammergau in southern Germany in 1960, along with a number of other missionaries. It was interesting to walk the streets of this quaint and beautiful village and observe the townsfolk, virtually all of whom participated onstage during the performances. To a man, woman, and child, they looked as though they had just stepped out of a period of time millennia old. At one point we entered the bookstore near the theater to purchase a copy of the text for the performance next day. As we were considering our purchase, we noticed a distinguished gentleman walk in. He had a pleasant countenance, with a prepossessing smile, a well-trimmed beard, and long, neat tresses. Everyone in the store fell silent at his approach. He made a purchase and then left. Noting our puzzled looks, the saleswoman leaned over and whispered to us in hushed tones, "Das war der Christus" ("That was Christ").

It gave us a chill to think that we had come so close to "Christus"—even though in this case he was only a surrogate, an actor, albeit one who commanded great respect in the village, even reverence. Then we pondered the lesson flowing out of this brief encounter: "Beloved, now are we the sons of God, and it doth not yet appear what we shall be: but we know that, when he shall appear, we shall be like him; for we shall see him as he is" (1 Jn. 3:2). There will come a time, for all mankind, when the encounter with the Son of God will be literal. For the faithful and obedient, it will be a moment of glory and peace; for the disobedient and nonvaliant, a moment of profound remorse. And when we see Him, we will also see the Father, for Christ is "the brightness of his glory, and the express image of his person" (Heb. 1:3). As we are created in the image of God and His Son, we are reminded to honor this heritage and rise spiritually to meet the awesome potential that is ours.

4. MAN AND WOMAN TOGETHER
AND AS PARENTS

THEME: Marriage is a divinely ordained institution. Parenthood is also a divinely ordained institution, and a sublime means to participate in the ongoing creativity associated with God's work and glory. The family is the proper place for the gospel to be taught and practiced.

> *And I, the Lord God, said unto mine Only Begotten, that it was not good that the man should be alone; wherefore, I will make an help meet for him.* (Moses 3:18)

> *And I, God, blessed them, and said unto them: Be fruitful, and multiply and replenish the earth.* (Moses 2:28)

MOMENT OF TRUTH

The Lord taught Moses that it is crucial in the eternal plan of Heavenly Father that man and woman be together, that they be one, and have joy in their posterity by multiplying and replenishing the earth. Man is not whole without the woman, and neither is woman whole without the man; "and they shall be one flesh" (Moses 3:24). Eternal marriage is necessary in order to receive all the blessings of God (D&C 131). Eve was created to be a helpmeet or helpmate, a companion—a partner—an equal partner with Adam. As husband and wife, we are commanded to multiply and replenish the earth, to give mortal birth to the spirit children of Heavenly Father. Mortality was part of the plan. To receive a body is essential for our eternal progress. Some may wonder about the word "replenish." The Hebrew verb for replenish is *mole,* meaning to fill, or make full. It does not refer to filling up again, as is the common use in the English language.

MODERN PROPHETS SPEAK

The Family: A Proclamation to the World:
> We, the First Presidency and the Council of the Twelve Apostles of The Church of Jesus Christ of Latter-day Saints, solemnly proclaim that marriage between a man and a woman is ordained of God and that the family is central to the Creator's plan for the eternal destiny of His children.

Boyd K. Packer:
> Marriage is not without trials of many kinds. These tests forge virtue and strength. The tempering that comes in marriage and family life produces men and women who will someday be exalted. (*That All May Be Edified* [Salt Lake City: Bookcraft, 1982], 294)

ILLUSTRATIONS FOR OUR TIMES

The Blessing
My parents were as devoted to one another as any parents, I am sure, who ever lived upon the earth. I am told they enjoyed acting in plays together and attended many

parties with their friends in our small Canadian town. But I can recall seeing them leave the home together on only two occasions. One was when Dad took Mom, at that time expecting her third child, to get her patriarchal blessing. Even though she was in her young womanhood, she had never received her patriarchal blessing, and she was excited as she left us kids for a short while to take care of this important task. When she returned, she was quiet and somewhat downcast. The patriarch had, under inspiration, declared her lineage, but left the rest of the page virtually blank. She wondered at that. Shortly thereafter Dad took her to the hospital for the blessed event. That was the second time I recall them leaving home together. She never returned. Complications in giving birth to my brother resulted in her passing away.

We were all grieved. I saw in my father's profound mourning and lament a monument to his undying love and devotion to his mate; in his stoic courage in the face of such a loss, I saw a monument to his acceptance of the Lord's will in all things. Now we knew why her patriarchal blessing had been so sparse: the patriarch, in his vision of the future, had seen to the end of the book of her life, and the end was now. She left behind for me—I was ten at the time—a set of the standard works, inscribed, which I still have and treasure. And therein lies a lesson: it is through obedience to the word of the Lord that the children show the highest devotion to their parents, and it is by faithfully following the parents' example of togetherness and love for one another that the children help to write the rest of the book of life. When Dad finally passed away, still a widower, some 40 years after that event, I was secure in the comforting thought that he and his eternal mate were overjoyed at their grand reunion. Truly the man and the woman belong together in the Lord.

5. AGENCY

THEME: From the very beginning, it was God's purpose to grant unto us the right to choose, based on His law and in accordance with the consequences thereof.

Nevertheless, thou mayest choose for thyself, for it is given unto thee. (Moses 3:17)

MOMENT OF TRUTH

As Moses recorded the words of the Lord concerning Adam, a transcending eternal verity was given: "Thou mayest choose for thyself." Agency was at the heart of one of the premortal conflicts. Satan sought to destroy our will by insisting that his way would save all—forced obedience, no free will. On earth his tactics are more subtle—your choices don't really matter; sin a little; you will still be saved. This "moment of truth" is the defining factor as it relates to our eternal reward—damnation or exaltation. We are what we choose to be, because our Savior Jesus Christ has already done His part and continues to bless us. It is now up to us.

MODERN PROPHETS SPEAK

Spencer W. Kimball:

> If all the sick for whom we pray were healed, if all the righteous were protected and the wicked destroyed, the whole program of the Father would be annulled and the basic principle of the gospel, free agency, would be ended. No man would have to live by faith. If joy and peace and rewards were instantaneously given the doer of good, there could be no evil—all would do good but not because of the rightness of doing good. There would be no test of strength, no development of character, no growth of powers, no free agency, only satanic controls. (*Faith Precedes the Miracle* [Salt Lake City: Deseret Book, 1972], 97)

Gordon B. Hinckley:

> I should like to suggest three standards by which to judge each of the decisions that determine the behavior patterns of your lives. These standards are so simple as to appear elementary, but I believe their faithful observance will provide a set of moral imperatives by which to govern without argument or equivocation each of our actions and which will bring unmatched rewards. They are: Does it enrich the mind? Does it discipline and strengthen the body? Does it nourish the spirit? (*TGBH*, 54)

ILLUSTRATIONS FOR OUR TIMES

The Choice

My father died on Mother's Day 1947. I was a 12-year-old boy, the baby of the family. My mother, a living angel, became the true matriarch of the family. She taught me to live by high principles, including never taking anything into my body that would be harmful. I remember making a promise to her and to Heavenly Father that I would never do anything to hurt her or bring shame to her. It was sealed in my mind and my heart.

I went through the teenage years without too many problems. I recall the time when values and standards that my mother had taught were put to the test; I had a choice to make. Our high school football team, on which I played end, had just won a game, and we were having a party at a friend's house. We were having a great time and no one was doing anything wrong. A friend asked the host for a drink of water. He was directed to the kitchen cupboard for a glass. As he was getting a drink, he noticed a big dark bottle of sherry cooking wine. It was almost full. He suggested we should all have a sip of alcohol to prove ourselves. They all came in for a little drink. Something in my heart and mind (my conscience) said, "Don't do it," and then I became bold and told them, "Don't do it." They said one little drink wouldn't hurt. I told them no, and if they did, I would leave the party. They said, "Go ahead. We don't like babies anyway."

So I left. I was hurt because of their standards and their apparent lack of concern for me as their supposed friend. As I walked home, a good feeling came over me. I had listened to my conscience; I had made the right choice. I had obeyed the inner voice—my conscience. It had saved me from disappointing my mother. The memory lingered. Choose the right and let the consequences follow. Obeying your conscience brings peace to the soul.

6. DAY OF REST

THEME: We must honor God's decree that the seventh day is a day of rest, and help to keep it a holy day. We will be blessed as we keep the Sabbath according to the Lord's commandment.

> *And I rested on the seventh day from all my work, . . . And I, God, blessed the seventh day, and sanctified it.* (Moses 3:2, 3)

MOMENT OF TRUTH

Moses learned early in this revelation that the seventh day, the Sabbath day, was a sanctified day of rest. It is ordained of God that we should rest from our temporal duties on the Lord's day, the holy day, and make sure that we consecrate our lives to the God who gave us life.

MODERN PROPHETS SPEAK

Gordon B. Hinckley:
> The Sabbath is such a precious thing. It represents the great culmination of the work of Jehovah in the creation of the earth and all that is found therein. When that was completed He looked upon it and saw that it was good and He rested on the Sabbath day. Now, I make a plea to our people to refrain from shopping on Sunday. (*TGBH,* 559)

Joseph Fielding Smith:
> This commandment is quite definite and in this dispensation the Lord gave further instruction as follows: "Thou shalt thank the Lord thy God in all things. Thou shalt offer a sacrifice unto the Lord thy God in righteousness, even that of a broken heart and a contrite spirit. And that thou mayest more fully keep thyself unspotted from the world, thou shalt go to the house of prayer and offer up thy sacraments upon my holy day; For verily this is a day appointed unto you to rest from your labors,

and to pay thy devotions unto the Most High; Nevertheless thy vows shall be offered up in righteousness on all days and at all times; But remember that on this, the Lord's day, thou shalt offer thine oblations and thy sacraments unto the Most High, confessing thy sins unto thy brethren, and before the Lord. And on this day thou shalt do none other thing, only let thy food be prepared with singleness of heart that thy fasting may be perfect, or, in other words, that thy joy may be full. Verily, this is fasting and prayer, or in other words, rejoicing and prayer" (D&C 59:7–14). (*AGQ,* 1:101)

ILLUSTRATIONS FOR OUR TIMES

The Home Game

He was a bright young man, pleasant and articulate, with a charming wife and growing family—just the kind of brother you would want to have as one of your ward clerks. When the Spirit whispered a quiet confirmation, I went to visit him with the invitation. He was honored by the calling, but somewhat reserved in his response.

"Bishop," he said, "I want to be of help. But you know, there is something I need to explain."

Uh-oh, I thought to myself, preparing to hear a confession.

"Ever since I joined the Church a few years ago," he continued, "I have tried to do my duty and attend my meetings, but I have always had season tickets to see the Baltimore Colts play on Sundays. That's why you don't see me at the meetings sometimes."

I thought about his situation for a few seconds, then felt impressed to offer him a special arrangement. The Lord wanted him to be a part of our team. Therefore, he would complete his Church assignment to the best of his ability, and we would work around his schedule. When the team was in town with a home game, he would be away, and we would understand. He accepted the assignment, but I could see that he had a struggle going on inside—and that is just as it should be when one is learning.

For the next few months, every time my wife and I drove past Memorial Stadium on the way to our Church meetings, I thought of this young man's struggle. One Sunday when there was a home game, I was surprised when this young man showed up at my office. He was energized, with a kind of glow about him and a sparkle in his eyes. "Bishop," he said, "I have decided to give up my season tickets. The gospel is more important. I will always be here on the Sabbath."

I put my arm around his shoulder and bore witness to the strength and courage of his correct decision, and I thanked the Lord in my heart for the patient way the Spirit often works. The words of the Savior came to my mind: "If any man will do his will, he shall know of the doctrine, whether it be of God, or whether I speak of myself" (John 7:17). Then I thought: There is always a home game. It takes place within the heart of every individual as he or she engages in the choices of life, the choices that go to define character and honor and devotion to the cause of building up the kingdom of God.

SUMMARY

When the Lord looked upon the outcomes of the Creation and proclaimed, "And, behold, all things which I had made were very good" (Moses 2:31), He established the pattern for our own perspective. We, too, must look upon the divine creative process as transcendently "good." It is good because it bears the unmistakable signature of the Father of all goodness. It is good because the Savior is the Creator, the "author of eternal salvation unto all them that obey him" (Heb. 5:9). It is good because man and woman are created in the image of God, and being the product of goodness, belong together in the Lord as companions and parents to their children. It is good because it is based on the dignifying principle of agency, by which we can choose the way of immortality and eternal life through the Atonement of Christ. And it is good because it leads ultimately to the Lord's "rest." Just as the Sabbath was divinely instituted to be the crowning glory of the Creation and a day of rest, in just the same way we are striving to return, once again, through obedience and the grace of God, into His eternal rest—"which rest is the fulness of his glory" (D&C 84:24).

CHAPTER FOUR

"THIS IS *the* PLACE *of* SALVATION UNTO ALL MEN"

Reading Assignment: Moses 4; 5:1–15; 6:48–62.

Additional Reading: Genesis 2–3; 1 Corinthians 15:20–22; 2 Nephi 2:5–30; 9:3–10; Helaman 14:15–18; D&C 19:15–19; 29:34–44; A of F 1:2; Bible Dictionary, "Fall of Adam."

> *The Latter-day Saints believe . . . that Jesus is the Savior of the world; they believe that all who attain to any glory whatever, in any kingdom, will do so because Jesus has purchased it by His atonement.* (Brigham Young, *JD* 13:328)

THEMES *for* LIVING

1. The Fall
2. The Atonement
3. Mortality
4. The Joy of Life
5. Love of God, or Love of Satan and the World
6. Teach Your Children

INTRODUCTION

In His omniscience and infinite wisdom, the Lord saw from the beginning the pathway that man would have to follow in order to fulfill his potential as the bearer of the image of God. This pathway was marked by certain stations or crucial points of passage. Following the Creation itself came the fall of mankind through transgression, which the Lord anticipated as a necessary part of the journey. The grand counterbalance to the Fall was the atonement of Jesus Christ, through which mankind could once again be reconciled with God through faith and obedience, and return to His presence.

Between the Fall and the Atonement came the indispensable experience of mortality, through which Adam's posterity would receive mortal tabernacles and be granted a probationary opportunity. Even though the man and the woman were separated from their Maker for a time, they could still understand the purposes for life and have joy in their posterity. A central part of the mortal experience was the opportunity to exercise freedom of choice—to choose to love God and obey His will, or to love Satan and follow the byways of worldly enticements and sin. This ability to choose was God-given. It was a key part of the plan. All mortals were under strict command to teach their children the gospel plan, including the saving principles and ordinances. Those choosing the correct pathway would move upward toward a state where the Atonement would be operative in their lives and ultimately lead to deliverance from spiritual death. Each aspect is discussed in the ensuing pages.

1. THE FALL

THEME: The Lord anticipated the fall of mankind as a necessary part of man's journey toward immortality and eternal life.

> *And I, the Lord God, said unto mine Only Begotten: Behold, the man is become as one of us to know good and evil.* (Moses 4:28)

MOMENT OF TRUTH

The results of the Fall proved to be a blessing for all mankind. Because of the Fall, we now have a chance to grow and be tested and to prove ourselves worthy of returning to our Father's presence. Here are the outcomes:

- Beginning with Adam and Eve, the spirit children of God the Father are provided mortal tabernacles (Moses 5:11).

- All mankind would experience physical and spiritual death (2 Ne. 9:6).

- Opposition is necessary for our growth—trials and tribulations in all things (2 Ne. 2:11).

- We have the capacity to choose good or evil and receive the blessings or consequences (2 Ne. 2:27).

- The plan of redemption is revealed, which brings joy and eternal life if we follow it (Moses 5:10–11).

MODERN PROPHETS SPEAK

Joseph Fielding Smith:

> The fall of Adam and Eve was foreknown, and preparation for this restoration had been made long before they had been placed on this earth. In the grand council held in heaven, Jesus Christ voluntarily accepted the mission of Redeemer, to come in the due time of the Father and make the sacrifice that would bring to pass this restoration through the shedding of his blood. (*AGQ,* 1:181)

Bruce R. McConkie:

> Thus, Creation is father to the Fall; and by the Fall came mortality and death; and by Christ came immortality and eternal life. If there had been no fall of Adam, by which cometh death, there could have been no atonement of Christ, by which cometh life. (*A New Witness for the Articles of Faith* [Salt Lake City: Deseret Book, 1985], xvi)

ILLUSTRATIONS FOR OUR TIMES

Eternal Truths

The Fall of Adam was and is essential for our eternal progression. It has provided for us the opportunity to prove ourselves worthy to return to the presence of our Heavenly Father. As I sit at my computer and the screen comes alive, allowing me to communicate with others, to write, to search the gospel questions and doctrines from the Church's website, and to send thousands of people a thought for the day to live by, I marvel that it works so well and does all these wonderful things, and I am grateful. I do not understand how it works, but by its fruit I accept it and use it. With this very simple analogy I can surely accept all of the doctrines of the gospel of Jesus Christ, for the fruit is delicious and good. They are eternal truths that bless me and my family every day. And they can do the same for all of us.

No Word Was Said

He was a tall, impressive young man, one of the stalwarts in the ward. And now I had the task of trying to comfort him at the unexpected loss of his sweetheart. What can a young bishop (no older, in fact, than the bereaved) say in circumstances like that? The answer: nothing. I stood eye-to-eye with this noble brother, clasping his hand, and we just shed a few mutual tears together. The Spirit did the talking. It said simply that this mortal experience sometimes involves great trials and always involves death, sometimes sooner than expected. It is part of the plan. It will be all right. There will be a reunion. The Atonement provides the way for life to be restored and couples to be together. Through faithfulness and devotion, families are forever. No word was said on that occasion. But we both knew the truth.

2. THE ATONEMENT

THEME: The mission of the Savior assures the resurrection for all and opens the way for the obedient and faithful to return to God's presence.

> *Ye must be born again into the kingdom of heaven, of water, and of the Spirit, and be cleansed by blood, even the blood of mine Only Begotten; that ye might be sanctified from all sin, and enjoy the words of eternal life in this world, and eternal life in the world to come, even immortal glory.* (Moses 6:59)

MOMENT OF TRUTH

As a result of the Fall, man became mortal. In this fallen state it was necessary to provide a way for us to return to the presence of our Heavenly Father. Jesus Christ, Jehovah, the God of the Old Testament and Firstborn of Heavenly Father, became our Savior. It was through the plan of redemption and His gospel that we were provided with the way back, if we would follow Christ. Without the Atonement, we are left to be subjected to the devil and his angels (2 Ne. 9). We would be nothing without the Atonement of our Lord and Savior.

MODERN PROPHETS SPEAK

Jeffrey R. Holland:

> As noted throughout the Book of Mormon, the timeless, infinite, eternal nature of the Atonement provides promise of a remission of sins to the faithful, whether they live before Christ's advent, during his earthly ministry, or after his death and resurrection. This is a reminder of the eternal reach of the Atonement, each dispensation (including those before Christ's advent) making their covenants, obtaining their

blessings, and working out their salvation. These prophets, priests, and teachers labored to teach people the intent for which the Law of Moses had been given, "persuading them to look forward unto the Messiah, and believe in him to come as though he already was" (Jarom 1:11). (*Christ and the New Covenant: The Messianic Message of the Book of Mormon* [Salt Lake City: Deseret Book, 1997], x; see also 62)

Neal A. Maxwell:

> Can we, even in the depths of disease, tell Him anything at all about suffering? In ways we cannot comprehend, our sicknesses and infirmities were borne by Him even before they were borne by us. The very weight of our combined sins caused Him to descend below all. We have never been, nor will we be, in depths such as He has known. Thus His atonement made perfect His empathy and His mercy and His capacity to succor us, for which we can be everlastingly grateful as He tutors us in our trials. There was no ram in the thicket at Calvary to spare Him, this Friend of Abraham and Isaac. (*Even As I Am* [Salt Lake City: Deseret Book, 1982], 116)

ILLUSTRATIONS FOR OUR TIMES

A New Heart

I recall as a young bishop the long hours of interviews and visits with the young adults. Some had strayed from the straight and narrow path. They had a desire to confess and forsake their sins. They wanted to repent; they wanted to "feel good" again. They wanted to be free from sin, holy and pure without spot. As the visit would continue, they would explain their feelings of godly sorrow and how it happened. We often cried and prayed together for their forgiveness and well-being. We discussed the things they needed to do that would help them become clean and pure. "Becoming" was more than a list—it was a change of heart. It was a disposition to abhor sin, to stay off the road to sin, to have a desire to do good continually. It was truly a change of heart. When the visit ended, they would always feel a little better. They had started on the way back. They had started the process of repentance. After a length of time commensurate to the sin and proving oneself worthy, the blessings of the gospel and kingdom of God were restored. They were in full fellowship. Their countenance had changed. They were different. They were full of light. The Atonement of the Lord Jesus Christ had healed them . . . it was a miracle. Every Sunday was a dynamic experience with the Atonement of the Lord Jesus Christ.

3. MORTALITY

THEME: Adam and Eve were cast out of the garden and began their life as mortals. They were given the right to choose good or evil.

After I, the Lord God, had driven them out, . . . Adam began to till the earth, and to have dominion over all the beasts. (Moses 5:1)

And it is given unto them to know good from evil; wherefore they are agents unto themselves. (Moses 6:56)

MOMENT OF TRUTH

Adam and Eve, having been cast out of the Garden of Eden, began to work and provide for themselves. They started their family and kept the commandment of multiplying and replenishing the earth. They called upon God in prayer, and the Lord gave them commandments to worship God and offer sacrifices. Adam did not understand why he offered the firstlings of the flock, but he obeyed. (That is a lesson itself: obey and then seek understanding, not the other way around.) Later, he would learn that sacrifice was in similitude of the Only Begotten Son of Heavenly Father. This would keep his posterity in remembrance of the atoning sacrifice of the Savior. Remember that Adam and Eve and their posterity had the gospel of Jesus Christ while they lived as mortals, and they made these things known to their children.

MODERN PROPHETS SPEAK

James E. Faust:
> It is an inevitable fact of life that from time to time each of us suffers some of the troubles, challenges, and disappointments of this world. When we face the challenges of mortality, we wish there was a sure cure for heartache, disappointment, torment, anguish, and despair. The Psalmist stated, "He healeth the broken in heart, and bindeth up their wounds" (Ps. 147:3). The healing is a divine miracle; the wounds are a common lot of all mankind. (*Finding Light in a Dark World* [Salt Lake City: Deseret Book, 1995], 25)

Neal A. Maxwell:
> God has repeatedly said He would structure mortality to be a proving and testing experience (see Abr. 3:25; Mosiah 23:21). He has certainly kept His promise and carried out His divine intent. Thus even our fiery trials, said Peter, should not be thought of as "some strange thing" (1 Pet. 4:12). Hence enduring is vital, and those who so last will be first spiritually! Enduring is more than lasting, however: we are to "endure it well" and to endure it "valiantly" (D&C 121:8, 29). By taking Jesus' yoke upon us and enduring, we learn most deeply of Him and especially how to be like Him (see Matt. 11:29). Even though our experiences are micro compared to His, the process is the same. (*Men and Women of Christ* [Salt Lake City: Bookcraft, 1991], 68)

ILLUSTRATIONS FOR OUR TIMES

"You Haven't Lost Much"

Spiritual life based upon enduring gospel principles is steady and solid. By way of contrast, temporal affairs in our mortal lives are frequently characterized by a fleeting and impermanent nature. Our worldly empires, especially when we attach undue affection to them, often become "slippery" (Hel. 13:31) so that we cannot keep hold of them. I remember just such a time many years ago.

The stake president had invited me to his office to extend a priesthood calling. He inquired about my spiritual and temporal affairs. During the conversation, it became apparent to him that I was at the time going through a considerable dislocation with respect to professional matters, even to the point of losing everything. His observation was memorable and to the point. He looked me in the eye and said something I will never forget: "If you lose everything, but retain your testimony of the gospel of Jesus Christ, you haven't lost much."

And so it is. The one possession we have in mortality that will steady our course through all adversity and every challenge is the spiritual witness that God lives and remains in charge, that the gifts of the Spirit transcend any worldly goods, and that hope remains in Jesus Christ, our Redeemer. That is the foundation of spiritual wealth that families must build on during mortality and beyond. If one loses all else but this, then truly nothing of genuine worth has been lost.

The Dream Home

As young students in graduate school, my wife and I weren't very wealthy. In fact, we struggled. I borrowed in order to get through school. And for our dates, we would buy graph paper and draw our future dream house. This went on for nine years as we began our lives, did a stint in the military, and came back again. Then, finally, it looked like we were going to be in our dream home. My sweetheart drew the plans; she is so good at that. All those days we'd taken that graph paper and said, "When we move into our house, then we can really be happy. Then we can really be happy."

Around the tenth year, we began to move into our new home. It was beautiful, located on a mountain crest looking over the valley, under the shadows of the mountain peaks. It was wonderful, on a half-acre of land. Oh, our dreams came true. As we were moving in that day, I thought, "Wait, isn't this the day? Yes, this is the day we start being happy. We finally get to have our very own home." I was reflective, and I realized this physical presence of our house did not bring happiness. I had sought happiness in a possession that I thought would bring happiness.

"As my wife walked downstairs while we were moving some furniture and other items, I said, "How do you feel?"

She said, "Fine."

I said, "Do you feel any different than yesterday?"

"No, it's just fun to move in."

We had both missed the point. It's not moving into a new home that brings us happiness. Happiness is a journey—living a life according to principles based on happiness, not on things that are possessed, not on positions, or titles, or stations. Happiness is in the living, not in the getting.

4. THE JOY OF LIFE

THEME: The love of God brings blessings of enlightenment and joy to mankind through obedience to the commandments.

> *ADAM: Blessed be the name of God, . . . in this life I shall have joy, and again in the flesh I shall see God.* (Moses 5:10)

> *EVE: Were it not for our transgression we never should have had seed, . . . and the joy of our redemption, and the eternal life which God giveth unto all the obedient.* (Moses 5:11)

MOMENT OF TRUTH

Adam and Eve truly had the vision of life. They saw the joy that mortals can have because of the goodness of God, the plan of redemption, and the promised blessings through obedience. This moment of truth in their lives must also be part of our lives. Adam fell that we might have joy (see 2 Ne. 2:25)—now and in the life to come.

MODERN PROPHETS SPEAK

Gordon B. Hinckley:

> In matters of religion, when a man is motivated by great and powerful convictions of truth, he disciplines himself—not because of demands made upon him by the Church, but because of the knowledge within his heart that God lives; that he is a child of God with an eternal and limitless potential; that there is joy in service and satisfaction in laboring in a great cause. (*Be Thou an Example* [Salt Lake City: Deseret Book, 1981], 5)

James E. Faust:

> While few human challenges are greater than that of being good parents, few opportunities offer greater potential for joy. Surely no more important work is to be done

in this world than preparing our children to be God-fearing, happy, honorable, and productive adults. Parents will find no more fulfilling happiness than to have their children honor them and their teachings. That blessing is the glory of parenthood. John testified, "I have no greater joy than to hear that my children walk in truth" (3 Jn. 1:4). (*Finding Light in a Dark World* [Salt Lake City: Deseret Book, 1995], 89–90)

ILLUSTRATIONS FOR OUR TIMES

Blessed Problems

Years ago, while I was serving as a bishop in the BYU 4th Stake, one of the high councilmen was John Covey. He truly is a Saint. I recall the time we were visiting one day regarding one of his challenges. He said, "I'm so excited about this problem. I will grow so much because of this. Isn't it great?" I was overwhelmed with the concept and the perception of life that John had. He found joy in life's trials and tribulations. He was excited to overcome, anxious to achieve. He had not only the vision of life but the excitement and joy that can go with it. When we have the eyes to see the goodness of God and the purpose of mortality, we will find joy in life.

How Happy Can You Be?

He was a legend in the ward—a short, rotund gentleman, close to eighty years old, with thick metal-rimmed glasses, a high-pitched voice, and a perpetually disheveled appearance. Everyone loved Dorsey Decker, whose backwoods West Virginia drawl, unpretentious demeanor, and infectious enthusiasm endeared him to young and old alike. He never missed bearing his testimony on fast Sunday—and people looked forward to it, because they always felt good afterward.

Brother Decker, though poor in worldly goods, never left anyone in doubt that he was happy. He would lean his head back and peer through his thick lenses, looking for all the world more like a penguin in a dark suit than a mortal. Then he would grin and say the words—a line that everyone was listening for and knew would inevitably come. "I know the gospel is true," he would intone in all sincerity, "because it makes me happy. I am just as happy as a toad in a crock of buttermilk." Then everyone would chuckle and sigh, relieved that the truth had once more been revealed from the lips of one who was a master at being happy, and a master at infecting everyone else with the spirit of joy in life and gratitude for the blessings of the Lord.

My wife and I still frequently invoke the spirit of Brother Decker, and when we look at each other—as if to inquire "How happy are you?"—one or the other will say, "I am just as happy as a toad in a crock of buttermilk!"

5. LOVE OF GOD, OR LOVE OF SATAN AND THE WORLD

THEME: We can choose whom and how much we love and receive the blessings or consequences of our actions. The moment one chooses the world over God, he separates himself from God.

They loved Satan more than God. And men began from that time forth to be carnal, sensual, and devilish. (Moses 5:13)

MOMENT OF TRUTH

When Satan tempted the children of Adam and Eve, some of them chose to believe Satan instead of their parents concerning the plan of redemption. Cain and his wife were some of those who loved Satan more than God (Moses 5:28). Those who are carnal, sensual, and devilish are subject to the lusts and passions of the flesh. The world and the things of the world become their god. They are in a state of enmity with God (Rom. 8:7). They become a natural man and an enemy to God when they do not repent (Mosiah 2:38; 3:19).

MODERN PROPHETS SPEAK

Bruce R. McConkie:

But we must first set forth why there is so much evil in all the world. It is one of the signs of the times. It comes because of lust and carnality of the hearts of men. It comes because men love Satan more than God and choose to worship at his altars. We have seen that this was the case before the flood when the earth was cleansed by water, and now we see it in our day when the earth will soon be cleansed by fire. (*The Millennial Messiah: The Second Coming of the Son of Man* [Salt Lake City: Deseret Book, 1982], 367)

Gordon B. Hinckley:

The teachings set forth in modern temples give powerful emphasis to this most fundamental concept of man's duty to his Maker and to his brother. Sacred ordinances amplify this ennobling philosophy of the family of God. They teach that the spirit within each of us is eternal, in contrast with the body that is mortal. They not only give understanding of these great truths but also motivate the participant to love God and encourage him to demonstrate a greater neighborliness toward others of our Father's children. (*Be Thou an Example* [Salt Lake City: Deseret Book, 1981], 129–30)

ILLUSTRATIONS FOR OUR TIMES

Simple Truth

My wife was so pleased to accompany her friend to the stand where Ezra Taft Benson, then President of the Quorum of the Twelve, was receiving visitors. He had just spoken to a special gathering of Saints in the Washington, D.C., area, and my wife wanted her friend to meet him. This young woman had just that day—in the same stake center—been baptized a member of the Church, after many months of learning and being fellowshipped by my wife. So we stood in line, waiting for our turn to meet Elder Benson.

When we finally reached the place where the Apostle was standing, we greeted him, and then my wife introduced her friend as a new convert. He held the friend's hand and looked her straight in the eye. With a spirit of great kindness, but also soberness and firmness, he said to her, "The gospel is true. If you live it, you will be happy. If you don't, you won't."

What a rare blessing for a new convert to hear a personal witness from an Apostle of the Lord and receive such direct and penetrating counsel. My wife and I have spoken of this incident many times since, and the words echo in our minds and hearts as advice that all can benefit from: "If you live it, you will be happy. If you don't, you won't."

"If Only"

The friend was a good man. He had always provided for his family. In fact, he had provided extremely well. He was famous in his field for his lectures and seminars. It wasn't long before he was acclaimed throughout the world. He was gone from his home and family over 140 days in one year. He lamented the fact but still was involved with his "work." It wasn't long before his eyes began to wander on one of his extended trips. Then it happened . . . an illicit relationship . . . a divorce . . . a broken home . . . wayward children . . . a division of property . . . misery and sorrow . . . and the haunting words "if only."

We could debate the cause, but the results are clear—this family was destroyed and lives were ruined because he didn't put the kingdom of God first. The first and foremost calling in the Church is the family. It is our eternal role, never to be relinquished throughout all eternity. How can we say we love God and spend so much time on "mammon"? "No man can serve two masters: for either he will hate the one, and love the other; or else he will hold to the one, and despise the other. Ye cannot serve God and mammon" (Matt. 6:24). The family must be our first priority in terms of quantity and quality of our time as well as our concern for each member of the family. We cannot say we love God and neglect our family.

6. TEACH YOUR CHILDREN

THEME: The divine commission to teach your children in light and truth was instituted as an eternal law for all parents.

Wherefore teach it unto your children, that all men, everywhere, must repent, or they can in nowise inherit the kingdom of God. (Moses 6:57)

MOMENT OF TRUTH

"Teach your children" has been the clarion call to parents since the beginning of time. Adam and Eve were commanded to teach the gospel of Jesus Christ and the plan of salvation to their children (Moses 6:57–58) and to teach it "freely." The word "freely" is a multidimensional word. As we note in the dictionary of Noah Webster in 1828—this is the edition that was in circulation during the time of the Prophet Joseph Smith—the word "freely" connotes the following:

- Voluntary, yet under a moral agent accountable, he must act freely.

- Plentifully in abundance—always.

- Without scruple or reserve—with no doubt or hesitation.

- Without impediment or hindrance—with no obstruction or things of life getting in one's way.

- Spontaneously—anytime there is a teaching moment.

- Liberally and generously—truth of all things always.

- Gratuitously—free, with no claim of merit or compensation.

MODERN PROPHETS SPEAK

James E. Faust:

> Your role is not an accident nor a mistake. No doubt all of you were pleased and happy with your being a woman—a very special and unique being. Motherhood is a very special calling, as is fatherhood for men. It is a great privilege for you with your husband to be involved together in the greatest of all works—that of rearing and teaching his children. (*In the Strength of the Lord: The Life and Teachings of James E. Faust* [Salt Lake City: Deseret Book, 1999], 461)

James E. Faust:

> Surely we must begin in our homes. We must teach our children and grandchildren. The moral teachings of all our churches must have an honored place in our society. The general decline in the moral fabric of the citizenry places a greater responsibility on homes and churches to teach values—morality, decency, respect for others, patriotism, and honoring and sustaining the law. (*Finding Light in a Dark World* [Salt Lake City: Deseret Book, 1995], 67)

Gordon B. Hinckley:

> Let parents and children teach and learn together, work together, read together, and pray together. ("Saving the Nation by Changing Our Homes," BYU Management Society, Washington, D.C., March 5, 1994; see also *TGBH*, 675)

ILLUSTRATIONS FOR OUR TIMES

The Motivation of Love

Teaching children is tough. I recall the time my wife, Pat, said to me, "Sweetheart, why don't you put a little more into teaching the lesson for family home evening?" We had had good lessons and good times together, but she wanted a little more effort—you know, kind of like the Relief Society's lessons. So I went to the bookstore and bought some masonite, flannel material, characters for the story, Velcro, and colored pencils. I got the whole works. I made the flannel board, colored in the characters and things for the presentation, and prepared the lesson. I was ready to go.

Monday night came. I was on fire. I started the lesson, and the children were in rapt attention for a minute, then a child said, "How long will this last?"

"Just a few minutes," I responded, and on I went.

Not more than a minute went by when another child said, "Did you get the donuts for treats?"

I stopped and assured them that I had the donuts, then continued the lesson. And then it happened—one of the older children, realizing the lesson was geared to the little ones, said, "Dad, I've got homework. How much longer?"

That did it. I burst into tears and said, "I've worked for hours on this lesson and you don't even care. You can't even give me ten or fifteen minutes to help you."

Silence prevailed, and then my sweetheart said, "Look what you have done to Daddy."

Then they all started to cry. They said they were sorry. I told them I was sorry, too. I told them I wanted to teach them because I loved them. Heavenly Father had asked me to help them grow up in light and truth and know the gospel of Jesus Christ. We have never forgotten that day for the greater lesson that was taught: "Daddy and Mommy love us and want us to be happy, and that is why they spend so much time trying to teach us." The lesson was learned. Now all our children try to teach their children, our priceless grandchildren.

SUMMARY

The Fall was foreseen by God as a benign and indispensable aspect of life. The rise of mankind once again, based on freedom of choice, was likewise anticipated and empowered through the atonement of Jesus Christ. The resurrection was made universal through Jesus Christ as a victory over temporal death; but immortality and eternal life were to be the fruits of obedience to the principles and ordinances of the gospel. Mortality was the testing ground, and the challenge was to demonstrate an abiding love for God. Opposition provided another choice—the love of Satan and worldly institutions. But God's children were not left to wander the highways of life alone and without a spiritual compass. He would provide all that was needful for the journey home. It was, in all its aspects, a perfect opportunity for each of His children to overcome the world and qualify for eternal life. It was the plan of salvation.

CHAPTER FIVE

"IF THOU DOEST WELL, THOU SHALT BE ACCEPTED"

Reading Assignment: Moses 5–7.

Additional Reading: Genesis 4:1–16; 2 Nephi 2:25–27.

> *I need not remind you that this cause in which we are engaged is not an ordinary cause. It is the cause of Christ. It is the kingdom of God our Eternal Father. It is the building of Zion on the earth, the fulfillment of prophecy given of old and of a vision revealed in this dispensation.* (Gordon B. Hinckley, "An Ensign to the Nations," *Ensign,* November 1989, 53)

THEMES *for* LIVING

1. An Acceptable Offering
2. The Bondage of Darkness/The Freedom of Light
3. Zion: A Righteous People
4. An Interesting Note on Original Guilt
5. The Compassion of God
6. A Book of Remembrance

1. AN ACCEPTABLE OFFERING

THEME: When we follow the Lord's counsel, we are favored of Him; but He is displeased with those who reject his counsel.

And the Lord had respect unto Abel, and to his offering; But unto Cain, and to his offering, he had not respect. (Moses 5:20–21)

MOMENT OF TRUTH

The manner and type of sacrifice had been taught to Adam and his children. Cain, choosing to follow the counsel of Satan, offered the fruit of the field, which was not in similitude of the atoning sacrifice. Therefore, it was not done in faith; hence the Lord had no respect for Cain's sacrifice (*TPJS,* 58). The Lord counseled Cain that if he would but follow the Lord, he would be blessed, but if he didn't, then "sin lieth at the door" (Moses 5:23). If Cain were to continue on his misguided course, then he would be delivered up to Satan. Cain persisted in following Satan, "for he rejected the greater counsel which was had from God" (Moses 5:25). The Lord was still patient and implored him to repent, but Cain was angered and "listened not any more to the voice of the Lord" (Moses 5:26). Cain had chosen. He loved Satan more than God.

MODERN PROPHETS SPEAK

Jeffrey R. Holland:
> Jarom's great-great nephew Amaleki delivered his record to King Benjamin, "exhorting all men to come unto . . . Christ, who is the Holy One of Israel, and partake of his salvation, and the power of his redemption. Yea, come unto him, and offer your whole souls as an offering unto him" (Omni 1:25–26). (*Christ and the New Covenant: The Messianic Message of the Book of Mormon* [Salt Lake City: Deseret Book, 1997], 98)

Joseph B. Wirthlin:
> This leads us to the process of making covenants and participating in ordinances, which are sources of power as we realize the importance of the Lord's will in our lives and have faith in it. Such faith turns us toward the Savior, his life, and his unconditional love for us. As these truths sink into our hearts, we hear him requiring the sacrifice of a broken heart and contrite spirit. We must give up the ways of the world and accept and do his way. (*Finding Peace in Our Lives* [Salt Lake City: Deseret Book, 1995], 177)

ILLUSTRATIONS FOR OUR TIMES

Be Willing to Receive Counsel

A number of years ago I recall being in attendance at a regional conference of several BYU stakes in which Elder Boyd K. Packer of the Quorum of the Twelve was presiding. Because the meeting was taking place in the cavernous Marriott Center and the audience was occupying only a fraction of the seats, Elder Packer requested that all those seated higher up in the auditorium move down closer to the stage. Only a few of the attending students responded. Most did not move. The meeting continued, nevertheless, and good counsel was given by him and a number of other attending General Authorities and their wives.

During a subsequent meeting with the leaders of the stakes, Elder Packer shared enlightening detail concerning what had transpired. He told the leaders that the message which was intended to be delivered that day had been withheld because of the disobedience of so many in the congregation, and another message was given instead.

Thus, absent a broken heart and a contrite spirit on the part of so many there, the attendees had relinquished a grand opportunity to hear the exact words of counsel and receive the blessing that the Lord intended for them to have that day. The words of Alma echo strongly in the mind: "And they that will harden their hearts, to them is given the lesser portion of the word" (Alma 12:11). This experience was discussed widely throughout these stakes afterward, and many learned valuable lessons from it.

2. THE BONDAGE OF DARKNESS/ THE FREEDOM OF LIGHT

THEME: The gospel of light and love was sent to dispel the darkness of hate and the secret combinations of death. Revelation is the key to receiving knowledge from the Lord.

> *And thus the Gospel began to be preached, from the beginning, being declared by holy angels sent forth from the presence of God, and by his own voice, and by the gift of the Holy Ghost.* (Moses 5:58)

MOMENT OF TRUTH

The pattern for revelation has been the same from the beginning of time. God, angels, or living prophets, seers, and revelators, moved upon by the power of the Holy Ghost, have brought us the word of God. Adam preached repentance to his sons as the voice of God came unto him (see Moses 6:1). Enoch likewise preached repentance, having been commanded by a voice from heaven (see Moses 6:27). Of all the gospel themes, faith unto repentance has been preached the most. The purpose of revelation is to reveal the will of God to mankind, thus helping them return to His presence.

MODERN PROPHETS SPEAK

Ezra Taft Benson:

> The Lord will increase our knowledge, wisdom, and capacity to obey when we obey His fundamental laws. This is what the Prophet Joseph Smith meant when he said we could have "sudden strokes of ideas" which come into our minds as "pure intelligence" (see *TPJS,* 151).
>
> This is revelation. We must learn to rely on the Holy Ghost so we can use it to guide our lives and the lives of those for whom we have responsibility. ("A Principle with a Promise," *Ensign,* May 1983, 54)

Gordon B. Hinckley:

> God is the one sure source of truth. He is the fount of all inspiration. It is from him that the world must receive direction if peace is to come to the earth and if good-will is to prevail among men. This earth is his creation. We are his children. Out of the love he bears for us, he will guide us if we will seek, listen, and obey. "Surely the Lord God will do nothing, but he revealeth his secrets unto his servants the prophets" (Amos 3:7). (*Be Thou an Example* [Salt Lake City: Deseret Book, 1981], 92; see also *TGBH,* 555)

ILLUSTRATIONS FOR OUR TIMES

Inspired Dignity

At one time, the headquarters office of the West German Mission was located in a rather imposing building at Number 55 Bettinastrasse in Frankfurt. While serving in that office as a missionary under the leadership of President Theodore M. Burton, I observed firsthand how he was directed by inspiration to handle a challenging matter.

There was a metal plaque on the building identifying it as a "Mission"—which in German also implies services for those in need of temporal welfare and assistance. Therefore, we had a steady stream of homeless persons and indigents knocking on the door for aid. President Burton came up with an inspired solution to this problem. He would tell each such person that he was welcome to have a meal with us, provided he would be willing to accept an assignment working in the yard behind the building doing gardening and lawn care.

Mysteriously, this would seem to take care of the hunger of virtually all such candidates—except for one. I remember seeing one pleasant-looking, middle-aged man and his young son enthusiastically working for hours in the yard, then joining us for dinner. This man felt he was being treated with dignity to be engaged in productive work, and he was prompted by the Spirit to find out what sort of people we were. Subsequently he took the missionary discussions and, with his son, joined the Church. Thus the mission president was entitled to receive divine guidance in this matter, as well as in all other matters pertaining to his office and calling.

The Right to Revelation

The beloved Prophet Joseph asked and was given light and truth. He received revelation, and was the instrument of the restoration of the gospel (through the Book of Mormon), the priesthood of God, and the kingdom of God in these, the latter days. Joseph received revelation after revelation as the truths to help us return to the presence of our Heavenly Father. Mothers and fathers, priesthood leaders, missionaries, and individuals throughout time have received revelation for their stewardships. All have the right to receive light and truth. Lives have been preserved both temporally and spiritually as the Lord has revealed His truths and directions in the lives of His children. All have the right to revelation within their stewardships.

3. ZION: A RIGHTEOUS PEOPLE

THEME: To be of one heart and one mind with one another and with the Lord is to be a Zion people.

> *And the Lord called his people Zion, because they were of one heart and one mind, and dwelt in righteousness.* (Moses 7:18)

MOMENT OF TRUTH

The Lord called His people "Zion." They were His people because they were of one heart and one mind. The word "heart" in Hebrew is "leb" or "lebab." It refers to the inner man, his character, the whole man, the governing center of all his actions, the seat of his will, his emotions, his attention and reflection and understanding, his purpose and his desires. Today we often interchange the word "mind" as it relates to the word "heart" (see *The New Bible Dictionary*, J. D. Douglas). A Zion people became pure in heart. Enoch's people literally gave their heart and their will to the Lord.

MODERN PROPHETS SPEAK

Joseph F. Smith:

> Men may receive the visitation of angels; they may speak in tongues; they may heal the sick by the laying on of hands; they may have visions and dreams; but except they are faithful and pure in heart, they become an easy prey to the adversary of their souls,

and he will lead them into darkness and unbelief more easily than others. (*CR,* Apr. 1900, 40, 4; see also *Gospel Doctrine: Selections from the Sermons and Writings of Joseph F. Smith* [Salt Lake City: Deseret Book, 1939], 7)

Dallin H. Oaks:

To become pure in heart—to achieve exaltation—we must alter our attitudes and priorities to a condition of spirituality, we must control our thoughts, we must reform our motives, and we must perfect our desires. . . .

The degree of spirituality a person has achieved is a measure of his or her progress toward perfection. The acts and thoughts that make us more spiritual move us toward our goal of being pure in heart. (*Pure in Heart* [Salt Lake City: Bookcraft, 1988], 140, 144)

ILLUSTRATIONS FOR OUR TIMES

Walk with Him in Righteousness and Truth

Susan Kent Greene died on April 17, 1888, but her influence lives on. She has been a part of my strength and faith as I live my life and carry out the responsibilities placed upon me. On January 6, 1981, just prior to my 50th birthday, I was reading and pondering great-grandmother Susan's journal. I thought of her life, her faith, her endurance, and I was drawn to read and reread an entry she had made at age 59 on the front page of her journal, dated 3 February 1875: "I make this covenant to do the very best I can, asking God for wisdom to direct me in that I may walk with Him in all righteousness and truth. I much desire to be pure in heart that I may see God. Help me, Lord, to overcome all evil with good." Signed: Susan Kent Greene. (Barbara B. Smith, *Heroines of the Restoration* [Salt Lake City: Bookcraft, 1997], 87)

4. AN INTERESTING NOTE ON ORIGINAL GUILT

How does the concept of being pure in heart and having a pure and righteous nature square with the concept of "original guilt" so widely discussed in sectarian circles among many Christian religions and denominations? Here is what some LDS leaders and teachers have said concerning this theme:

In LDS teachings, the Fall of Adam made Christ's redemption necessary, but not because the Fall by itself made man evil. Because of transgression, Adam and Eve were expelled from Eden into a world that was subject to death and evil influences. However, the Lord revealed to Adam upon his entry into mortality that 'the Son of God hath atoned for original guilt'; therefore, Adam's children were not evil, but were "whole from the foundation of the world" (Moses 6:54). Thus, "every spirit of man was innocent in the beginning; and God having redeemed man from the fall, men became again, in their infant state, innocent before God" (D&C 93:38). (*Encyclopedia of Mormonism,* 561)

The "curse of Adam" is taken from children in Christ so that it has no power over them (see Moro. 8:8). What is called here the "curse of Adam" is presumably the effects of the Fall. In one sense, the curse of Adam, meaning an original sin or "original guilt" (Moses 6:54), is taken away from all men and women; that is, Adam and Eve's transgression in Eden was forgiven them (see Moses 6:53), and no person is held responsible for something our first parents did (see A of F 1:2). In another sense, the curse of Adam, meaning the fallen nature that comes as a direct result of the Fall (see 1 Ne. 10:6; 2 Ne. 2:21; Alma 42:6–12; Ether 3:2), is taken away from children as an unconditional benefit of the atonement of Christ (see Mosiah 3:16). (Robert L. Millet, *The Power of the Word: Saving Doctrines from the Book of Mormon* [Salt Lake City: Deseret Book, 1994], 254)

5. THE COMPASSION OF GOD

THEME: Though the heavens wept over the pervasive wickedness among mankind, there was a vision of joy through the mission of the Savior.

> *And behold, Enoch saw the day of the coming of the Son of Man, even in the flesh; and his soul rejoiced, saying: The Righteous is lifted up, and the Lamb is slain from the foundation of the world; and through faith I am in the bosom of the Father, and behold, Zion is with me.* (Moses 7:47)

MOMENT OF TRUTH

Enoch saw the day of the coming of our Savior Jesus Christ. He knew the condition of man. He comprehended the Fall, the Atonement, and the plight of man should there be no Atonement (see 2 Ne. 9). Because Enoch understood and appreciated the Savior's infinite atonement and His power of resurrection, he was filled with gratitude. This caused his attitude to be one of rejoicing, and his life reflected Christ in all he did.

MODERN PROPHETS SPEAK

Bruce R. McConkie:
> As members of The Church of Jesus Christ of Latter-day Saints, we seek salvation. We desire peace in this life and eternal life in the realms ahead. We have taken upon

ourselves the name of Christ, rejoice in the sure knowledge that he is the Son of God, and seek with all our hearts to be like him. He is the great prototype of saved beings. (*Sermons and Writings of Bruce R. McConkie* [Salt Lake City: Bookcraft, 1998], 357)

Ezra Taft Benson:

When we live a Christ-centered life, "we talk of Christ, we rejoice in Christ, we preach of Christ" (2 Ne. 25:26). We "receive the pleasing word of God, and feast upon his love" (Jacob 3:2). Even when Nephi's soul was grieved because of his iniquities, he said, "I know in whom I have trusted. My God hath been my support" (2 Ne. 4:19–20). (*TETB,* 11)

ILLUSTRATIONS FOR OUR TIMES

The Least I Could Do

The vision of gratitude and joy because of our Savior is demonstrated by the testimony of a young elder as he departed his mission. He stood and said with a quiver in his voice, "I have been a convert now for three years. After my conversion and baptism I came to realize the goodness of God and the magnificence of my Savior's sacrifice. I was so happy. The first year went by so slowly. I could hardly wait to get my mission call. It was the least I could do for my Savior." He expressed his joy over his Savior, the Atonement, and the feeling he had in preaching the word of God to his brothers and sisters. He had partaken of the joy of bringing souls unto Christ.

A Solemn Reminder

It was an unusual invitation. The leaders of some two dozen Utah stakes were asked to meet on a particular day at the Manti Temple for a solemn assembly with President David O. McKay and the other General Authorities. There was much conjecture about the nature and purpose of the meeting. What new policy or doctrinal innovation might be forthcoming that would require such a solemn gathering? I remember the sense of anticipation we felt as a bishopric while motoring down to the meeting.

The assembly room of the temple was packed with many hundreds of priesthood leaders, all of whom were honored to have the sacrament blessed and passed to them by General Authorities. Then there was rapt silence as the prophet arose, a tall and stately figure of leadership with his silver hair and white suit, and announced to us the reason he had brought us all together—simply to confirm that Jesus is the Christ, that He lives, and that He is at the head of this work.

It was a powerful reminder about what is of primary and pre-eminent importance in this world—the atonement of Jesus Christ and the reality of His life and mission.

All were edified to be thus filled with the word of inspiration. All rejoiced in the compassion of a just Father in Heaven and His Son to have opened the way for the faithful and valiant to return one day to Their holy presence. No one in attendance will ever forget the witness of the Spirit that day that God lives, that His Prophet speaks for Him, and that life is indeed full of joy and hope.

6. A BOOK OF REMEMBRANCE

THEME: Scriptures are the journals of God's prophets regarding their dealings with God and man. Keep a journal and write your personal history.

> *A book of remembrance we have written among us, according to the pattern given by the finger of God.* (Moses 6:46)

MOMENT OF TRUTH

Adam and his posterity kept a record—a book of remembrance that contained words written by inspiration in the language of Adam (see Moses 6:5). Abraham also recorded his history, "for the benefit of my posterity that shall come after me" (Abr. 1:31). The Lord has commanded His servants since the beginning of time to record the dealings of God with man. Christ, when visiting the American continent, reminded the people to record the words of Samuel the Lamanite, because they contained prophecies of our Savior. Under commandment of God the Father, the Savior also gave the Nephites the words of Malachi concerning Elijah and the work of family history and genealogy, for the Nephites had left Jerusalem prior to the ministry of the prophet Malachi (approximately 430 B.C.). It is imperative to leave the word of God with His children so they will have direction in their lives. Without it, they fall away (Mosiah 1:3–7).

MODERN PROPHETS SPEAK

Bruce R. McConkie:

> The thing which they [Adam and his posterity] first wrote, and which of all their writings was of the most worth unto them, was a Book of Remembrance, a book in which they recorded what the Lord had revealed about himself, about his coming, and about the plan of salvation, which plan would have force and validity because of his atonement. This was the beginning of the Holy Scriptures, than which inspired writing there is nothing that is more important. (*The Promised Messiah: The First Coming of Christ* [Salt Lake City: Deseret Book, 1978], 86)

Spencer W. Kimball:

> Those who keep a book of remembrance are more likely to keep the Lord in remembrance in their daily lives. Journals are a way of counting our blessings and of leaving an inventory of these blessings for our posterity. (*TSWK,* 349)

ILLUSTRATIONS FOR OUR TIMES

A Record of Providential Deliverance

I often think of the story my grandfather Harry Anderson Pinegar recorded in his journal. On December 3, 1899, he was to baptize his young daughter and the daughters of a neighboring family. As they traveled to the stream at Reynold's Mill, where the baptism was to take place, they were approached by three men on horseback who asked where they were going. Grandfather explained their intentions. The leader of the men threatened to bring a mob upon them if they went ahead with the baptismal service. Grandfather told them he intended to continue. As they made preparations for the baptism, they became aware that the men who had threatened them were near. Suddenly a large redbone hound owned by the leader of the mob bounded down near them. Grandfather Pinegar continued with the service.

At that point, the mob leader commanded his dog to attack Grandfather Pinegar. Then an amazing thing happened—the dog let out a low growl and turned on its master, knocking him to the ground. The mob fled in fear, followed by the dog. The Pinegar family and their neighbors thanked the Lord for their deliverance, and the baptismal service continued.

Later that evening, the mob appeared at Grandfather's gate and threatened him again. He commanded them in the name of the Lord Jesus Christ to leave. They departed and did not return. I am thankful for the loyalty, courage, and faith of my grandfather. I want to show my loyalty to him by also being loyal to the Lord. This story from my grandfather's life has changed me forever.

The Fifth Standard Work

I believe that everyone in the Church has what I like to call "The Fifth Standard Work"—a record of how the Lord has touched them in personal, spiritual ways. Sometimes this record is kept in the mind and the heart as a cherished memory of devotion and inspiration. Sometimes it is told to family members and friends in the form of uplifting stories. Sometimes it is written down where it can more readily be shared with a wider audience of appreciative family members and friends.

In my personal "Fifth Standard Work," I keep copies of sacred personal blessings that form the milestones of my life. One such is the father's blessing I requested and received just before I was married to my lovely and loving wife, still faithfully by my side after some forty years. One point in the blessing I share here only as an illustration of how a book of remembrance like this can preserve and convey powerful images for changing lives.

My father fasted for two days prior to giving me his blessing. After speaking many instructive and personal things, he said, "And now, my beloved son, as you journey forth into the uncertain world, reach up your hands to the lap of God. And if you will do this, He will lead you, He will guide you, save and exalt you in the eternal worlds." He later told me that the image of the young child kneeling in humility before the Father and reaching his hands up to the lap of God occurred to him in a dream one night after he had prayed long for guidance in giving the blessing. This image has stuck with me for all these years as a treasure from God, and continues to be a reminder of the correct attitude of humility we must cultivate if we are to be faithful servants of the Lord.

SUMMARY

By studying the holy scriptures, in this case the Pearl of Great Price and the words of the Old Testament prophets such as Moses and Enoch, we gain insight into the matchless gifts of love granted us by our Father in Heaven and His Son Jesus Christ. For these gifts we are asked only to bring a broken heart and a contrite spirit (2 Ne. 2:7). This offering can take a variety of forms in our daily lives. Immortality and eternal life can be ours if we bring an acceptable offering of obedience before the Lord. We are promised the light of the gospel if we follow the prophets and the Holy Spirit. We can be a Zion society if we will be unified and pure in heart. The blessings of the Atonement can transform our lives if we show our gratitude and thanksgiving through repentance and righteousness. We are given the holy scriptures as our guide, and asked only to follow them and to keep and share our own book of remembrance with our families and friends. By honoring and obeying the commandments of our Father in Heaven, we can have joy and peace in this life and eternal life in the world to come through the "merits, and mercy, and grace of the Holy Messiah" (2 Ne. 2:8).

CHAPTER SIX

"NOAH . . . PREPARED an ARK to the SAVING of HIS HOUSE"

Reading Assignment: Moses 8:19–30; Genesis 6–9; 11:1–9.

Additional Reading: Hebrews 11:7; Moses 7:32–36.

I promise you in the name of the Lord whose servant I am that God will always protect and care for his people. We will have our difficulties the way every generation and people have had difficulties. But with the gospel of Jesus Christ, you have every hope and promise and reassurance. The Lord has power over his Saints and will always prepare places of peace, defense, and safety for his people. When we have faith in God we can hope for a better world—for us personally, and for all mankind. (Howard W. Hunter, *Ensign*, October 1993, 72)

THEMES for LIVING

1. Noah: A Just Man
2. The Warning Voice of Prophecy
3. The Ark: A Symbol of Refuge Through the Covenant
4. The Scattering

INTRODUCTION

The Lord's pattern of dealing with His children is revealed in full clarity through the passages of scripture covered in this chapter. We see that He calls and empowers just and holy men like Noah to serve as His prophetic emissaries on earth. He then commands these servants to raise the voice of warning and preach repentance to the world. He provides places of refuge and resort to afford safety and security to His obedient Saints. From time to time, we see that He also scatters and re-gathers the people for their own protection or to diffuse prideful intent and bring about needful correction. Each aspect of this four-step pattern is discussed in the following pages.

1. NOAH: A JUST MAN

THEME: Noah, like all the Lord's chosen prophets, was a just and righteous man.

> *Noah found grace in the eyes of the Lord; for Noah was a just man, and perfect in his generation; and he walked with God.* (Moses 8:27; Gen. 6:9)

MOMENT OF TRUTH

In Moses 8:27, the description of Noah and some of his qualities and blessings are noted:

- Found grace in the eyes of the Lord.

- Was a just man.

- Was perfect in his generation.

- Walked with God.

These are transcendent truths with magnificent blessings. We should all seek to understand them and aspire to possess and emulate them.

AN EXPLANATION OF TERMS

Grace in the eyes of God. Noah found favor due to his righteousness. We can grow in grace and truth (see D&C 50:40) and can receive this grace through righteousness.

Just man. Many prophets have been described as just men. What does the adjective "just" really mean?

- Walks uprightly before God (see Alma 63:2).

- Performs miracles (see 3 Ne. 8:1).

- Teaches his children "in the nurture and admonition of the Lord (see Enos 1:1).

- Never deceives (see D&C 129:6).

- Is made perfect (see D&C 76:69).

- Walks in his integrity (see JST, Prov. 20:77).

- Is holy and fears God in all things. He is truly upright, honest, and obeys God with exactness.

Perfect in his generation. Noah was not an apostate like so many of his day. He truly was set apart from the people of his generation.

Walked with God. This phrase often refers to "walking in His ways" or "keeping His commandments." We, too, can walk with God in the same manner. "The just man walketh in his integrity: his children are blessed after him" (Prov. 20:7).

MODERN PROPHETS SPEAK

Joseph Smith:

> Noah . . . is Gabriel; he stands next in authority to Adam in the Priesthood; he was called of God to this office, and was the father of all living in his day, and to him was given the dominion. These men held keys first on earth, and then in heaven. (*HC* 3:385–86)

Harold B. Lee:

> And then concerning directly the working of miracles, which of course is an evidence of the wisdom of God working through men, the prophet Nephi declared, "And now it came to pass that according to our record, and we know our record to be true, for behold, it was a **just man** who did keep the record—for he truly did many miracles in the name of Jesus; and there was not any man who could do a miracle in the name of Jesus . . . save he were cleansed every whit from his iniquity" (3 Ne. 8:1). (*Ye Are the Light of the World: Selected Sermons and Writings of Harold B. Lee* [Salt Lake City: Deseret Book, 1974])

ILLUSTRATIONS FOR OUR TIMES

We Know Him

The guard at the international boundary peered into the car. "Who is that boy you have with you?" he asked.

"That is my nephew," I explained. "He is coming with me for a few days while I visit with my father."

The guard was not impressed. "How do I know you have permission from the boy's parents to take him out of the country?" he inquired.

I did not have an answer to that, because as a young BYU student returning home to Canada for a visit, it did not occur to me that having my young nephew along would be a problem. "This boy is my sister's son," I said. "Should I try to get her on the phone?"

"Wait a minute," said the guard. "Did you say you were going to visit your father?"

"Yes," I replied.

"Who is your father?" he then asked.

"John L. Allen of Raymond," was my response.

A smile crept across the guard's face. "John Allen," he said. "We know John Allen. He is a good and honest man. If you are the son of John Allen, then it will be all right." And he waved us through the border on our way home.

I have often thought about that incident and how it illustrates the power of a noble and righteous reputation.

2. THE WARNING VOICE OF PROPHECY

THEME: Knowing of the calamity that rampant wickedness was bringing upon his wayward children, the Lord gave them a chance to repent by sending His prophet Noah to speak plainly to them.

> *Believe and repent of your sins and be baptized in the name of Jesus Christ, the Son of God, even as our fathers, and ye shall receive the Holy Ghost, that ye may have all things made manifest; and if ye do not this, the floods will come in upon you.* (Moses 8:24)

MOMENT OF TRUTH

As has been the case with all of God's chosen prophets, those in the early dispensations called the people to repentance. In the time of Noah, wickedness had become epidemic. The whole earth had ripened in iniquity. This time the Lord warned the people through Noah to repent, or "I will destroy all flesh from off the earth" (Moses 8:30). Noah's time preceded the destruction of other nations for gross wickedness—

the Jaredites and the Nephites. In this state, the people did not yield to the warnings of Noah. Surely their hearts were "past feeling" (1 Ne. 17:45).

MODERN PROPHETS SPEAK

Joseph Fielding Smith:

> Much more could be written in detail regarding these conflicts, but what is written will suffice. It is, of course, a gloomy picture; but is it not the duty of the elders of Israel to speak of these things with a warning voice? Shall we close our eyes and our ears and seal our understandings simply because some things are unpleasant to the ear and to the eye? Shall we refuse to raise a warning voice when danger approaches, when trouble is near, when destruction is at our door? Such a course would be cowardly if we know the truth. We cannot cry "all is well" when danger lurks on every side. We must not lull the people to sleep in a false security. President Woodruff declared that "no man that is inspired by the Spirit and power of God can close his ears, his eyes, or his lips to these things!" (*DS,* 3:48)

Harold B. Lee:

> The field is not white alone with good grain, but it is white with tares or weeds along with the good grain. Ours is the responsibility not only to go to the honest in heart throughout the world, but our duty is to lift a warning voice to all people, that they may be left without excuse in the Day of Judgment. Now, we must get the concept of missionary work that the field to which the Lord made reference was a field just like those to which we are accustomed. We must not work alone with good grain, but grain filled with weeds and tares, all of which must be harvested in the manner in which the Lord speaks in the parable [of the wheat and tares] (see Matt. 13:25–40). (*The Teachings of Harold B. Lee* [Salt Lake City: Bookcraft, 1996], 594)

ILLUSTRATIONS FOR OUR TIMES

Listen to the Warning Voice

One of the tragic cases of not following the counsel of the Prophet Joseph Smith occurred in the attack at Haun's Mill. Brother Haun owned a grist mill, which took his name. A few days prior to the massacre he was appointed by those in the settlement to go to the city for advice to know what to do, as some of the brethren had already been murdered by mobs in the area. Brother Haun went to the city and first spoke with Captain John Killian of the Caldwell County Militia to ask his advice about what they should do. "Move into the city," was the prompt reply. Brother Haun then went to the Prophet Joseph and asked him the same questions and received the same answers word for word. "But we think we are strong enough to defend the mill and keep it in our hands," Brother Haun responded. "Oh well," replied the Prophet, "if you think you are strong enough to hold the mill you can do as you think best." His method had always been to give counsel when asked and let those parties who asked decide to receive or reject it. He could not take away people's agency. Brother Haun returned and reported that the Prophet had advised them to stay and defend the mill. The tragic results of that decision are now well known: on October 30, 1838, a mob rode into the Haun's Mill settlement, slaughtered seventeen men and boys, and severely wounded many others. (*The Juvenile Instructor,* Vol. 27, 1892.)

By contrast, Brother John L. Butler elected to follow the counsel of the Prophet Joseph and saved himself and his family from serious injury or possibly death. He saw the Prophet in Far West and the Prophet asked if he had removed his family from Haun's Mill. When he said he had not, the Prophet told him to go and remove them immediately and not sleep there another night. He followed the Prophet's counsel, packed his belongings and left by sunrise the next morning. Shortly after they left, the mob came and surrounded his home. Had he and his family been there, they would have been killed. He later said, "I then saw the hand of the Lord in guiding Brother Joseph Smith to direct me to move my family away, if he had not, why in all probability we should have been murdered" (*Autobiography of John Lowe Butler, 1808–1861,* 13).

"Up to this day God had given me wisdom to save the people who took counsel. None had ever been killed who abode by my counsel. At Haun's Mill the brethren went contrary to my counsel: if they had not, their lives would have been spared" (*HC* 5:137).

3. THE ARK: A SYMBOL OF REFUGE THROUGH THE COVENANT

THEME: According to divine instruction, Noah prepared an ark of safety for his family. The Lord established with him and his family a covenant whereby they might enjoy the spiritual safety of the gospel and the priesthood of God.

> *But with thee will I establish my covenant; and thou shalt come into the ark, thou, and thy sons, and thy wife, and thy sons' wives with thee.* (Gen. 6:18)

MOMENT OF TRUTH

The Joseph Smith Translation makes clear the covenant the Lord established with Noah's great-grandfather, Enoch, "that of thy posterity shall come all nations" (JST, Gen. 8:23). Noah and his sons and their wives would be saved from the flood. Covenants with the Lord truly save people. This concept is symbolized in the ark—a refuge from the flood.

MODERN PROPHETS SPEAK

Joseph F. Smith:

> In various dispensations there are various differences in regard to certain require-ments of the gospel. For instance, in the day of Noah, when he preached the gospel to the antediluvian world, he was given a special commandment to build an ark, that in case the people would reject him and the message sent unto him, **that him-self and all who believed on him might be saved from the destruction that await-ed them.** In this dispensation there is a principle or commandment peculiar to it. **What is that? It is the gathering of the people unto one place.** The gathering of this people is as necessary to be observed by believers, as faith, repentance, baptism, or any other ordinance. **It is an essential part of the gospel of this dispensation, as much so as the necessity of building an ark by Noah, for his deliverance, was a part of the gospel of his dispensation.** Then the world was destroyed by a flood, now it is to be destroyed by war, pestilence, famine, earthquake, storms and tem-pest, the sea rolling beyond its bounds, malarious vapors, vermin, disease and by fire and the lightnings of God's wrath poured out for destruction upon Babylon. The cry of the angel unto the righteous of this dispensation is, "Come out of her, my people, that ye be not partakers of her sins, and that ye receive not of her plagues" (Rev. 18:4). (*Gospel Doctrine: Selections from the Sermons and Writings of Joseph F. Smith* [Salt Lake City: Deseret Book, 1939], 104)

Neal A. Maxwell:

> We are Christ's kingdom builders. Those who build the heavenly kingdom have always made nervous the people who are busy building worldly kingdoms. Noah's ark-building was not politically correct. (*The Neal A. Maxwell Quote Book* [Salt Lake City: Bookcraft, 1997], 47)

ILLUSTRATIONS FOR OUR TIMES

Stay Away from the Precipice

After Mother passed away unexpectedly, Dad hired a series of housekeepers over the years to help out on the domestic home front and watch after us kids. One of these was Heddi Reithman, a very bright Swiss woman who was also a skilled mountain climber.

On one occasion Dad took the whole family mountain climbing in an area of the Canadian Rockies where there were few trails. As we passed over the summit of one high ridge, we spotted our destination in the valley far below: a beautiful lake renowned for its large rainbow trout. My friend and I were anxious to go fishing, so we started to run down the shale embankment toward the lake.

Heddi called us back. "Not that way," she said. "I think we should go around this other way."

"That would take longer," we objected.

But she insisted, saying, "I have a feeling it will be safer to go around the other way."

Dad concurred, so we all followed her advice and made our way along the ridge in a westerly direction, and then gradually descended down through the timber. After about fifteen minutes, we could look back through the trees and see why her instincts had been providential.

Unbeknownst to us while we were standing on the crest of that ridge, we were only a few hundred feet away from the edge of a sheer cliff that dropped down suddenly several thousand feet. Had we continued to run down that sloping embankment, we would likely not have been able to avoid lethal danger.

And so it is along the pathways of life. The prophets mark the course of safety. They warn about the cliffs and pitfalls of danger. They plead with us to stay back from the embankments that too easily roll down into the slippery slopes of evil and sin. How wisely should we listen and follow. Our very spiritual lives will depend on it.

4. THE SCATTERING

THEME: The vain ambition of the post-diluvian population gathering at Babel and wanting to make "a name" for themselves caused the Lord to intervene and thwart their conspiracy of pride by scattering them abroad. Noah and his family, plus the Jaredites, were preserved and guided by the Lord.

> *Go to, let us go down, and there confound their language, that they may not understand one another's speech. So the Lord scattered them abroad from thence upon the face of all the earth.* (Gen. 11:7–8)

MOMENT OF TRUTH

The people, who spoke one language, desired to reach heaven. Nimrod, the mighty hunter, began to build cities—Babel, Erech, Accad, and Calneh. It was in the city of Babel where the confounding of languages began and the people were scattered. The word "babel" has a similar Hebrew root, blal, which means to confuse or mix.

MODERN PROPHETS SPEAK

Joseph Smith:

> Behold, there are many called, but few are chosen. And why are they not chosen?
>
> Because their hearts are set so much upon the things of this world, and aspire to the honors of men, that they do not learn this one lesson—

That the rights of the priesthood are inseparably connected with the powers of heaven, and that the powers of heaven cannot be controlled nor handled only upon the principles of righteousness.

That they may be conferred upon us, it is true; but when we undertake to cover our sins, or to gratify our pride, our vain ambition, or to exercise control or dominion or compulsion upon the souls of the children of men, in any degree of unrighteousness, behold, the heavens withdraw themselves; the Spirit of the Lord is grieved; and when it is withdrawn, Amen to the priesthood or the authority of that man.

Behold, ere he is aware, he is left unto himself, to kick against the pricks, to persecute the saints, and to fight against God. (D&C 121:34–38)

Hugh B. Brown:

The historian Josephus, who relied on both Hebrew and Greek sources, says of the times immediately following the attempt to build the Tower of Babel: "After this they were dispersed abroad, on account of their languages, and went out by colonies everywhere, and each colony took possession of that land which they lit upon and unto which God led them; so that the whole continent was filled with them, both the inland and the maritime countries. There were some, also, who passed over the sea in ships and inhabited the islands." From a much more recent work we read, "All history demonstrates that from the central focus (Babylon) nations were propelled over the globe with an extraordinary degree of energy and geographical enterprise." (*Continuing the Quest* [Salt Lake City: Deseret Book, 1961], 97)

ILLUSTRATIONS FOR OUR TIMES

An Unseen Design

The Lord scatters and re-gathers His children for many reasons: sometimes for their own preservation (as in the case of Lehi or Alma or the Jaredites), sometimes to dilute the contaminations of pride (as in the case of the ambitious builders of Babel), and sometimes to suffuse the light of the gospel across the nations of the world (as in the case of missionary work). That same panorama is constantly playing out in the mind of our internal world. How often He blesses us to reach out into the far corners of our scattered thoughts and gather in the words of inspiration and truth that need to be applied that very moment to a lesson or a counseling opportunity (D&C 100:6). How often He blesses us with a benign "stupor of thought" (D&C 9:9) when our vain ideas and prideful ambitions need to be scattered into the purifying winds of oblivion. How often He sends us promptings of the need to render service to, or bear witness to, this particular person or that particular person whose footprints we just happen to find in the pathway ahead. I have experienced that many times in my own life. There is a divine purpose in how the Lord guides our steps and our thoughts. There is a spiritual pattern to life that we sometimes can only faintly discern through the overlay of worldly interests and interruptions that we all too readily allow to befog our view. Let us be grateful that the Lord, in His infinite wisdom, wisely resorts to the process of scattering and re-gathering as a means to train us up in celestial ways and bring about His divine purposes according to a carefully managed though unseen design.

SUMMARY

The Lord has a divine strategy for preserving the temporal and spiritual well-being of His children, while allowing them to exercise their agency. That strategy is built around the "word"—both the word of truth through angels and prophets, as well as the Word Himself, who is the Only Begotten. The message of the gospel of redemption is delivered through just and holy men like Noah and his prophetic colleagues throughout all the dispensations of time. Places of refuge are established, symbolized perfectly by the ark of old times. These places of resort may be lands of promise ordained to receive the faithful, or they may be stakes of Zion to which the faithful can flee for counsel and protection, or temples where saving ordinances are provided. When the covenant Saints obey and follow the will of the Lord, wherever it might take them, they are blessed with safety and His protecting hand. When they rebel and take counsel from their pride, the Lord often scatters them for correction and to dispel their prideful ambitions. Through prayer, study, and obedience, we can begin to discern the hand of the Lord in the tapestry of our lives.

CHAPTER SEVEN

"I WILL MAKE MY COVENANT *between* ME *and* THEE"

Reading Assignment: Abraham 1:1–4; 2:1–11; Genesis 12:1–8; 17:1–9.

Additional Reading: Genesis 15; D&C 132:19–24, 29–32; Bible Dictionary, "Abraham, Covenant of."

If there is anything calculated to interest the mind of the Saints, to awaken in them the finest sensibilities, and arouse them to enterprise and exertion, surely it is the great and precious promises made by our heavenly Father to the children of Abraham. (Joseph Smith, *HC* 4:128)

THEMES *for* LIVING

1. A Covenant of Righteousness
2. Promised Land/Promised Kingdom
3. Fruitful Lineage/Eternal Increase
4. Gospel Blessings: Now and Forever
5. Vessels of the Lord

INTRODUCTION

The covenant made by the Lord with Abraham and his posterity continues to inform the practices and operations of the restored Church. Through the Abrahamic Covenant, the Lord promises and extends grand blessings predicated upon worthiness, obedience, and service. The blessings commence in the mortal sphere and extend to the world hereafter, including divinely appointed places of gathering and repose, the unfolding of an immense posterity, and the enjoyment of redeeming truths here and in the eternities. Latter-day Saints have a sense of being among the "chosen people" (as in Deut. 14:2) from the standpoint that they are chosen to be servants on the Lord's errand. Each aspect of the covenant with its blessings and obligations is discussed in the pages that follow.

1. A COVENANT OF RIGHTEOUSNESS

THEME: The Lord established with Abraham and his posterity a covenant of righteousness, with an eternal promise of grand earthly and heavenly blessings based on obedience and service.

> *I am the Almighty God; walk before me, and be thou perfect. And I will make my covenant between me and thee, and will multiply thee exceedingly.* (Gen. 17:1–2)

MOMENT OF TRUTH

Abraham was a righteous man, even though his fathers had turned from their righteousness. He sought for the blessings of the Father, desiring to receive more knowledge and be a greater follower of righteousness (see Abr. 1:1–6). The Lord made a covenant with Abraham that He would multiply his seed exceedingly (this was Abraham's desire as well—see Abr. 1:2). Abraham would become the father of many nations. The Lord would covenant with Abraham and his seed, and He would be their God.

MODERN PROPHETS SPEAK

Joseph Fielding Smith:
> Because of Abraham's faithfulness, the Lord promised to make of him—through his posterity—a great nation and a blessing to all nations to the end of time. Said the Lord: "And I will bless them through thy name; for as many as receive this Gospel shall be called after thy name, and shall be accounted thy seed, and shall rise up and

bless thee, as their father" (Abr. 2:6–11; Gen. 17:1–14; 22:15–18; Acts 3:25; 7:1–8; 3 Ne. 20:25–28). The descendants of Abraham, the tribes of Israel, became the chosen people of the Lord according to the promise. The Lord honored them, nourished them, watched over them with a jealous care, until they became a great nation in the land the Lord had given to their fathers. Notwithstanding this tender care and the instructions and warnings this people received from time to time through their prophets, they failed to comprehend the goodness of the Lord and departed from him. Because of their rebellion they were driven out of their land and eventually were scattered among the nations. Their priesthood was lost and they were left in spiritual darkness (*Millennial Star,* vol. 90, 306–7). (DS, 1:165)

Joseph Fielding Smith:

In the past the descendants of Abraham, through Israel, have suffered greatly for their transgressions, and the blessings which were theirs by inheritance, based upon their faithfulness, have been withheld. They have been "scattered and peeled" as Isaiah said of them, and hated by all nations. Nevertheless the Lord has not forgotten them nor the covenant he made with their fathers. The nations that oppressed them have passed away, or are doomed to such a fate; but Israel is now being gathered and the Lord is renewing his covenants with them. Eventually they shall possess the land of their inheritance and the Lord will set his sanctuary in the midst of them forevermore. Much of the ordinance work now being done in the temples is in fulfillment of the covenant the Lord made with Abraham and his children. (*The Way to Perfection* [Salt Lake City: Genealogical Society of Utah, 1949], 90)

ILLUSTRATIONS FOR OUR TIMES

Point of Doctrine: The Law of Adoption

By the law of adoption, those who receive the gospel and obey its laws, no matter what their literal blood lineage may have been, are adopted into the lineage of Abraham (see Abr. 2:9–11). "The effect of the Holy Ghost upon a Gentile," the Prophet said, "is to purge out the old blood, and make him actually of the seed of Abraham." Such a person has "a new creation by the Holy Ghost" (*Teachings,* 149–50). Those who magnify their callings in the Melchizedek Priesthood are promised that they will be "sanctified by the Spirit unto the renewing of their bodies. They become the sons of Moses and of Aaron and the seed of Abraham" (D&C 84:33–34). Indeed, the faithful are adopted into the family of Christ; they become "the children of Christ, his sons, and his daughters"; they are "spiritually begotten," for their "hearts are changed through faith on his name," thus being "born of him," becoming "his sons and his daughters" (Mosiah 5:7). (*MD,* 23)

2. PROMISED LAND/PROMISED KINGDOM

THEME: The Abrahamic Covenant embraces the divine promise to grant unto the faithful special gathering places of refuge upon the earth, as well as an ultimate home among the mansions of the Father on high.

> *And I will give unto thee, and to thy seed after thee, the land wherein thou art a stranger.* (Gen. 17:8)

> *For he who is faithful and wise in time is accounted worthy to inherit the mansions prepared for him of my Father.* (D&C 72:4)

MOMENT OF TRUTH

From time to time, the Lord sets apart certain lands and locations as ordained gathering places for His covenant people. In the Middle East, it was the Holy Land; in the Book of Mormon context, it was the Americas; in the latter days, it is the stakes of Zion, and eventually the New Jerusalem. All of this mortal geography is but a type and symbol for the eternal abode of the righteous in the eventual heavenly courts of the Father and Son.

MODERN PROPHETS SPEAK

Joseph Smith:

> It would be nonsense to suppose that He [God] would condescend to talk in vain: for it would be in vain, and to no purpose whatever [if the law of God were of no benefit to man]: because, all the commandments contained in the law of the Lord, have the sure promise annexed of a reward to all who obey, predicated upon the fact that they are really the promises of a Being who cannot lie, One who is abundantly able to fulfill every tittle of His word. . . . And though we cannot claim these promises which were made to the ancients for they are not our property, merely because they were made to the ancient Saints, yet if we are the children of the Most High, and are called with the same calling with which they were called, and embrace the same covenant that they embraced, and are faithful to the testimony of our Lord as they were, we can approach the Father in the name of Christ as they approached Him, and for ourselves obtain the same promises. These promises, when obtained, if ever by us, will not be because Peter, John, and the other Apostles, with the churches at Sardis, Pergamos, Philadelphia, and elsewhere, walked in the fear of God and had power and faith to prevail and obtain them; but it will be because we, ourselves, have faith and approach God in the name of His Son Jesus Christ, even as they did; and when these promises are obtained, they will be promises directly to us, or they will do us no good.

They will be communicated for our benefit, being our own property (through the gift of God), earned by our own diligence in keeping His commandments, and walking uprightly before Him. If not, to what end serves the Gospel of our Lord Jesus Christ, and why was it ever communicated to us? (*HC* 2:12, 21–22)

ILLUSTRATIONS FOR OUR TIMES

Four Holy Places

On one occasion, circumstances took me out of state and away from the family over the Christmas holidays. It was a lonely time of temporary separation, but there was comfort in the gospel concept of "standing in holy places"—no matter where we might be. In pondering the blessings of God, I came to the conclusion that the Lord's injunction to "stand in holy places" (D&C 45:32; 87:8; 101:22) has at least four major dimensions: (1) to take refuge within our own person (heart and mind) as we purify ourselves and make ourselves a fit place for the Spirit to abide (as in the hymn "Abide with Me!"); (2) to gather within our own families and homes as we work diligently to make them sanctuaries of safety that are hospitable to the Spirit; (3) to gather in our wards and stakes as covenant children of our Father in Heaven; and (4) to gather for spiritual refuge in the temples of God. As I pondered these thoughts during that lonely Christmas, I was reminded of the blessings that come from standing in holy places of faith.

3. FRUITFUL LINEAGE/ETERNAL INCREASE

THEME: The Abrahamic Covenant embraces the divine promise of the abundance of "seed" (posterity) upon the earth, as well as eternal increase in the hereafter through the blessings of eternal marriage.

> *And I will make of thee a great nation.* (Abr. 2:9)

> *This is eternal lives—to know the only wise and true God, and Jesus Christ, whom he hath sent. I am he. Receive ye, therefore, my law.* (D&C 132:24)

MOMENT OF TRUTH

The blessing of an abundant posterity to Abraham brings to fruition the original commandment to Adam and to Noah of multiplying and replenishing the earth. In this case, it has even greater connotations. The covenant blessings include becoming a mighty nation in the mortal sphere, plus the exalted gifts of eternal marriage in the temples of God, leading to eternal increase ("eternal lives") in the hereafter. Abraham's lineage would bless the entire earth.

MODERN PROPHETS SPEAK

Brigham Young:

> Abraham was faithful to the true God; he overthrew the idols of his father and obtained the Priesthood after the order of Melchizedek, which is after the order of the Son of God, and a promise that of the increase of his seed there should be no end; when you obtain the holy Priesthood, which is after the order of Melchizedek, sealed upon you, and the promise that your seed shall be numerous as the stars in the firmament, or as the sands upon the seashore, and of your increase there shall be no end, you have then got the promise of Abraham, Isaac, and Jacob, and all the blessings that were conferred upon them. (*Discourses,* 106)

Joseph Fielding Smith:

> Thus through this scattering the Lord has caused Israel to mix with the nations and bring the Gentiles within the blessings of the seed of Abraham. We are preaching the gospel now in all parts of the world, and for what purpose? To gather out from the Gentile nations the lost sheep of the house of Israel. It is by this scattering that the Gentile nations have been blessed, and if they will truly repent they are entitled to all the blessings promised to Israel, "which are the blessings of salvation, even of life eternal." (*AGQ,* 2:57)

ILLUSTRATIONS FOR OUR TIMES

An Understanding Moment

There is no greater feeling than to have joy in the goodness and success of others (see Alma 29:14). A "fruitful lineage," which is not only great in numbers but in right-eousness, is quintessential joy. A father or mother pleased with a child's performance has a feeling of satisfaction. The feeling of observing a righteous decision or act in a child simply transcends all understanding. As parents, we literally live for this. As a father and grandfather, I now understand my sweet angel mother. I would ask, "Mom, what do you want for Christmas? What do you want for your birthday? What do you want for Mother's Day?"

The answer, always the same, was, "Oh, Ed, I have everything I need. Just be good, Ed—just be good."

Now I understand more fully the blessings of a righteous posterity. And I under-stand Heavenly Father's purpose more fully—to help His children be fruitful and enjoy eternal increase, even immortality and eternal life.

4. GOSPEL BLESSINGS: NOW AND FOREVER

THEME: The central blessing for those who participate in the Abrahamic Covenant is to have the fullness of the gospel of Jesus Christ while on earth, including all the essential saving doctrines and the associated blessings of the priesthood, plus the hope and promise of immortality and eternal life in the hereafter.

> *And in thy seed after thee . . . shall all the families of the earth be blessed, even with the blessings of the Gospel, which are the blessings of salvation, even of life eternal.* (Abr. 2:11)

MOMENT OF TRUTH

The core doctrine of the Abrahamic Covenant is the gospel of Jesus Christ, which offers ordinances and covenants of salvation, of purification, of sanctification and justification through the Lord and Savior Jesus Christ. The foundation of the Church is the gospel of Jesus Christ (see 3 Ne. 27:8–11). Through Abraham's seed, the whole earth will be blessed with the gospel.

MODERN PROPHETS SPEAK

Joseph Fielding Smith:

> When the Lord called Abraham out of Ur, the land of his fathers, he made certain covenants with him because of his faithfulness. One promise was that through him and his seed after him all nations of the earth should be blessed. This blessing is accomplished in several ways: Through Jesus Christ who came through the lineage of Abraham; Through the priesthood which was conferred upon Abraham and his descendants; Through the scattering of Israel among all nations by which the blood of Israel was sprinkled among the nations, and thus the nations partake of the leaven of righteousness, on condition of their repentance, and are entitled to the promises made to the children of Abraham; and . . . In the fact that the Lord covenanted with Abraham that after his time all who embraced the gospel should be called by his name, or, should be numbered among his seed, and should receive the Holy Ghost. All of these promises were made to Abraham because of his faithfulness. No person who is not of Israel can become a member of the Church without becoming of the house of Israel by adoption. . . . This doctrine of adoption, or grafting in of the wild olive branches into the tame olive tree, was understood by the prophets of Israel. It was taught by John the Baptist and by the Savior and is expressed most emphatically and beautifully in the parable of the tame olive tree in the 5th chapter of Jacob, in the Book of Mormon. (*DS,* 3:246)

Joseph Fielding Smith:

> Abraham, who because of his faithfulness was promised that the blessings of the gospel and the priesthood should descend through his lineage to the latest times, was a stockman, tending herds and flocks for his support and the support of those who depended upon him. It may be thought that Abraham's concern was solely with his

family, but a more careful reading of the scriptures will reveal that he was at the head of a great company, and from it he was able to muster a force large enough to defeat the invading kings and rescue Lot from them. It was the same with the prophets in Israel. We do not read of any of them being employed with a salary, but they labored with their hands. The Lord commanded Moses to teach the Israelites to be industrious and show them the way. (*AGQ, 3:77*)

ILLUSTRATIONS FOR OUR TIMES

Joy in Gospel Blessings

The family had lived a life full of the world's offerings. They were living life as they knew it. They had trials and tribulations like all families. They struggled and life became unfulfilling. There seemed to be no relief in sight. Life started to take its toll. Then it happened—the gospel of Jesus Christ was introduced into their lives. Answers to life's most perplexing challenges seemed to come from the missionaries and the book they had read—the Book of Mormon. As they related their conversion story to me, I could see the power of the gospel of Jesus Christ in their lives. Their countenances were different; they were full of light. Their attitude was one of hope, and their family interaction was positive and upbeat. They had never known such happiness. It was like living in the dark and suddenly the light burst forth, giving them hope and direction in all their trials and tribulations. After a year, they went to the temple. Their response was one of thanksgiving and gladness—a fullness of joy because of the blessings of the gospel of Jesus Christ. They had tasted of the joy (see Alma 36:24).

5. VESSELS OF THE LORD

THEME: The solemn obligation associated with the Abrahamic Covenant is to be worthy spiritual servants to the world, delivering to all nations, kindreds, tongues, and peoples the blessings associated with the kingdom of God upon the earth, including the priesthood in all its saving functions.

> *They shall bear this ministry and Priesthood unto all nations.* (Abr. 2:9)

> *Go ye therefore, and teach all nations, baptizing them in the name of the Father, and of the Son, and of the Holy Ghost.* (Matt. 28:19)

MOMENT OF TRUTH

We, as the seed of Abraham, have the obligation of being worthy emissaries of the Lord Jesus Christ, with the responsibility to carry the gospel message, along with all of the priesthood and temple blessings, to every nation, kindred, tongue, and people. The Book of Abraham has made it clear, as have all the scriptures and present-day prophets, that we must take the gospel to all the world.

MODERN PROPHETS SPEAK

Bruce R. McConkie:

> In the providences of the Lord, there has come to us in the Book of Abraham a broader and more carefully delineated account of the Abrahamic covenant, which includes these words: "And I will make of thee a great nation, and I will bless thee above measure, and make thy name great among all nations, and thou shalt be a blessing unto thy seed after thee, that in their hands they shall bear this ministry and Priesthood unto all nations." It is the seed of Abraham who themselves hold the same priesthood held by their noble forebear who will take salvation to all the nations of the earth. (*The Millennial Messiah: The Second Coming of the Son of Man* [Salt Lake City: Deseret Book, 1982], 263)

Spencer W. Kimball:

> We are not interested in numbers. They are secondary. We are interested in warning the nations of the world. I believe we have not scratched the surface. We are like the person who said, "Pull up the ladder; I'm aboard." Our goal is nothing less than the penetration of the entire world. Our new office building is a world building with four giant maps, each showing a particular part of the globe. We are not promised that the whole world will believe. Evangelization of the world does not mean that all men will respond, but all men must be given the opportunity to respond as they are confronted with the Christ. (*TSWK,* 545)

ILLUSTRATIONS FOR OUR TIMES

A Common Bond of Love

Having served as a mission president and as president of the Provo Missionary Training Center, I have seen the "vessels of the Lord," these mighty warriors, young and old alike, preparing to go forward to preach the gospel. There are not enough pages to tell of their goodness, devotion, and desire in regard to serving the Lord as His disciples and ambassadors throughout the world. I have seen those struggling to prepare, having overcome many problems. I have witnessed their tears as they say they are prepared and ready to serve. I have knelt on bended knee and shined the shoes of missionaries and expressed my love and gratitude for their willingness to serve. I have interviewed thousands of missionaries from every country throughout the world and witnessed the common bond of love. I have seen the joy of the missionaries as they expressed through their weekly letters the happiness they have found in serving the Lord and bringing His children into the waters of baptism. I have taught at the Senior MTC several years and have met thousands of couples and senior sisters. Some have sold all in order to serve. One man, eighty-four years old, expressed his joy at going on his eighth mission. My heart is filled with joy as I see them preparing to serve the Lord. The responsibilities are heavy, the joys are exhilarating.

My Missionary Commission

> I am called of God. My authority is above that of kings of the earth. By revelation I have been selected as a personal representative of the Lord Jesus Christ. He is my master and He has chosen me to represent Him—to stand in His place, to say and do what He Himself would say and do if He personally were ministering to the very people to whom He has sent me. My voice is His voice, and my acts are His acts; my doctrine is His doctrine. My Commission is to do what He wants done; to say what He wants said; to be a living modern witness in word and in deed of the divinity of His great and marvelous Latter-day work. How great is my calling! (Bruce R. McConkie, *How Great Is My Calling*)

SUMMARY

On April 3, 1836, as part of a magnificent sequence of heavenly manifestations in the newly completed Kirtland Temple, Joseph Smith and Oliver Cowdery experienced a visitation by Elias, who "committed the dispensation of the gospel of Abraham, saying that in us and our seed all generations after us should be blessed" (D&C 110:12). Thus the continuity of the Lord's ancient covenant program was assured in the latter days. The Lord delights in blessing His children. He gives them places of refuge in this world (lands and gathering places, such as the stakes of Zion). He gives them hope for eternal mansions on high. He makes them fruitful in their posterity and gives them the hope of eternal increase through the blessings of temple marriage. He provides the fullness of the everlasting gospel of Jesus Christ and the priesthood of God, with its ennobling and redeeming power to grant immortality and eternal life for the valiant who endure to the end. For all of these extraordinary blessings, He asks only that we walk in righteousness and obey his commandments, sharing our witness to the world through His missionary program.

CHAPTER EIGHT

"THEY SHALL KEEP *the* WAY *of the* LORD"

Reading Assignment: Genesis 13–14; 18–19.

Additional Reading: Genesis 12; JST, Genesis 14:25–40; Genesis 19:9–15.

The gospel of Jesus Christ is the power of God unto salvation, and it is absolutely necessary for every man and woman in the Church of Christ to work righteousness, to observe the laws of God, and keep the commandments that he has given, in order that they may avail themselves of the power of God unto salvation in this life. (Joseph F. Smith, *CR*, Oct. 1907, 2)

THEMES *for* LIVING

1. Abraham: Portrait of Righteousness
2. Melchizedek: A Second Portrait of Righteousness
3. Avoiding the Allure of Worldliness
4. Sodom and Gomorrah: Portrait of Wickedness

INTRODUCTION

Scriptural accounts provide compelling illustrations of the full range of righteousness among the children of God, from the sterling, unflinching examples of Abraham and

Melchizedek, to the wavering and partial commitment of Lot, the reluctant mindset of Lot's wife, and the fully rebellious lifestyles of the kings and inhabitants of Sodom and Gomorrah. Each element of this range of obedience is discussed in the pages that follow.

1. ABRAHAM: PORTRAIT OF RIGHTEOUSNESS

THEME: The righteous life of the patriarch and prophet Abraham serves as a worthy example for all the covenant people of the Lord.

For I know him, that he will command his children and his household after him, and they shall keep the way of the Lord, to do justice and judgment. (Gen. 18:19)

MOMENT OF TRUTH

Abraham sought after a happier and more peaceful place to live. The land of the Chaldeans was fraught with wickedness and idolatry. He wanted the blessings of the fathers. He was a follower of righteousness, and had a desire to gain great knowledge and receive direction from the Lord and keep the commandments. Abraham was a righteous man (see Abr. 1:1–2).

We later learn from the Lord that Abraham was a righteous father and leader, for he taught his family and his household in the ways of the Lord. They learned that the Lord is full of mercy and justice; thus, if they followed in the ways of the Lord, they would be blessed. Conversely, if they chose evil, the judgment of God was the result.

Abraham's classic demonstration of "peacemaking" is an example to us all. The herdsmen of Lot and Abraham had strife one with another over the land. Abraham, full of wisdom and charity, suggested that there be peace. Since there was adequate land available, he suggested, "if thou wilt take the left hand, then I will go to the right; or if thou depart to the right hand, then I will go to the left" (Gen. 13:9). In effect, he was saying that it didn't matter to him, but let there be peace, "for we be brethren" (Gen. 13:8). Lot chose the plain of Jordan, and Abraham then took Canaan. This is where the real win-win principle began. If it is good for you, then it is good for me (see Gen. 13:6–12).

Abraham, like all the righteous, paid his tithes and offerings to the high priest Melchizedek (see Gen. 14:20). He would not even partake of the spoils of war from the king of Sodom (see Gen. 14:23). Abraham's heart was pure, therefore he was a just man; hence his behavior was merely a reflection of his inner self. Because he was pure, he was righteous in his behavior.

MODERN PROPHETS SPEAK

Bruce R. McConkie:

The works of Abraham! The works of righteousness—for "Abraham believed God, and it was counted unto him for righteousness" (Rom. 4:3)—Abraham's works of righteousness were these: He had faith in the Lord Jehovah, whose gospel he believed and in whose paths he walked; he repented of his sins, was baptized, after the manner of his fathers, and received the gift of the Holy Ghost. Thereafter he endured in good works all his days—honoring the priesthood, living in the patriarchal order of matrimony, receiving visions and revelations and the gifts of the Spirit, and worshipping the Father in the name of the Son, as did Adam and all of the ancients. As to that celestial marriage practiced by Abraham and that eternal life which grows out of it, the revealed word to latter-day Israel is: "This promise is yours also, because ye are of Abraham, and the promise was made unto Abraham; and by this law is the continuation of the works of my Father, wherein he glorifieth himself. Go ye, therefore, and do the works of Abraham; enter ye into my law and ye shall be saved" (D&C 132:31–32). (*The Mortal Messiah: From Bethlehem to Calvary* [Salt Lake City: Deseret Book, 1979–81], 3:163)

Gordon B. Hinckley:

No other written testament so clearly illustrates the fact that when men and nations walk in the fear of God and in obedience to his commandments, they prosper and grow, but when they disregard him and his word, there comes a decay that, unless arrested by righteousness, leads to impotence and death. The Book of Mormon is an affirmation of the Old Testament proverb, "Righteousness exalteth a nation: but sin is a reproach to any people" (Prov. 14:34). (*Be Thou an Example* [Salt Lake City: Deseret Book, 1981], 100)

ILLUSTRATIONS FOR OUR TIMES

Righteousness Has an Aura

I had been asked by a friend to accompany him to receive his endowments. He had previously been baptized during a semester when he attended my Book of Mormon class. I remembered him saying, "Brother Ed, will you come with me when I receive my endowments?" I was honored, and responded with excitement and joy. Then he said, "By the way, Steve's grandpa will be there, too."

I said, "Great!"

He continued, "Do you know who Steve's grandpa is?" A slight pause, and he said, "President Kimball." Needless to say, the excitement rose even higher.

The big day came, and following the session, we all sat visiting with President and Sister Kimball. The boys introduced their teacher, "Brother Ed," to the prophet and Sister Kimball. I was thrilled—and that is when it all began. I knelt beside him while he was seated in a chair. He thanked me for teaching his grandson and his friend. All the while, I was feeling the presence of the prophet, my spirit was basking in the aura of this great man. I had an overwhelming desire to do good. I truly wanted to be righteous. I wanted to be like my Savior. The power of President Kimball's righteousness, even the image of Christ in his countenance (see Alma 5:14), affected my very being. Personal righteousness does have power wherever we are.

The Joys of the Gospel

Many years ago, while I was serving on the faculty of the Johns Hopkins University in Baltimore, a colleague asked me a most interesting question. He said, "What are the joys of being a Latter-day Saint?" Every representative of the Church longs for such a question, and though my spontaneous answer may have lacked the eloquence this question deserves, I was able to identify for my friend at least five key reasons why I personally feel so much joy in the gospel. They include: (1) the joy of raising a forever family, knowing that through the sacred sealing work of the temples of God, the family can and will, like love, endure beyond this life; (2) the joy of being able to follow righteous men of God called, like Abraham of old, to be prophets in these latter days; (3) the joy of knowing that each of us is created in the image of God, endowed with latent capacities of infinite potential, the development of which permits endless opportunities for service to our fellow beings; (4) the joy of knowing something of the magnitude and beauty of God's plan of salvation, which answers the age-old questions of where we came from, why we are here on the earth, and what our ultimate destiny can be—especially the revealed truth that God's mission is to bring to pass the immortality and eternal life of man (Moses 1:39); and (5) the joy of being able to share these restored truths with others who may be seeking answers to life's questions. Then I bore testimony to my friend (using Lehi's words) that "men are, that they might have joy" (2 Ne. 2:25), i.e., through learning and doing the will of our Father in Heaven.

2. MELCHIZEDEK: A SECOND PORTRAIT OF RIGHTEOUSNESS

THEME: The "King of Salem" was an exemplary prophetic leader whose faith and nobility of character were so perfect that the higher priesthood was named in his honor.

> *And this Melchizedek, having thus established righteousness, was called the king of heaven by his people, or, in other words, the King of peace.* (JST, Gen. 14:36)

MOMENT OF TRUTH

From the Joseph Smith Translation, we learn more of the prophet-king, Melchizedek. He blessed Father Abraham. He was a man of faith and was righteous even as a child. He reverenced the Lord. He was favored and approved of the Lord. He was called and ordained to the holy priesthood—the power to act for God. Melchizedek, like his forebear, Enoch, made this covenant and was given power to do all things by faith (see Moro. 7:33). He, like Enoch, established peace and was thus called the Prince or King of peace. Melchizedek blessed father Abraham—or rather, through Melchizedek God blessed Abraham according to the covenant (see JST, Gen. 14:25–40).

MODERN PROPHETS SPEAK

John A. Widtsoe:

> Paul, the apostle says, "this Melchizedec, . . . first being by interpretation King of righteousness, and after that also King of Salem, which is, King of peace." (Heb. 7:1,2.) The accepted Hebrew meaning of Melchizedek may then be taken as king of righteousness or peace. But, students of language suggested that the word is a title rather than a name, a title implying a high position of spiritual leadership. Linguists, dissecting the word and finding the syllable "el" in it, the Hebrew for God, interpret Melchizedek to mean a servant or king of the supreme God, a "King-priest." Paul tells the Hebrews to "consider how great this man was." (Heb. 7:4.) Through the ages Melchizedek has been a somewhat mystical figure, but one to whom the highest respect is given. (*Evidences and Reconciliations* [Salt Lake City: Improvement Era, 1960], 231–32)

ILLUSTRATIONS FOR OUR TIMES

Steps to the Master

Melchizedek Priesthood holders today can trace their priesthood authority in short steps back to the Master. The Savior called and ordained Peter, James, and John as a presidency over the higher priesthood in their day (John 15:16). In turn, they were sent in 1829 to the Prophet Joseph Smith and Oliver Cowdery to restore the keys of the Melchizedek Priesthood and authorize once again the administration of the saving gifts and ordinances in the kingdom of God upon the earth (see D&C 27:12–13). From that point, the line of priesthood authority went from Joseph Smith to the Three Witnesses (*HC* 2:187–188), and from them to Brigham Young, who was ordained an Apostle on 14 February 1835. In my own case, the line of authority extended forward by way of Brigham Young, Joseph F. Smith, Joseph Fielding Smith, and then Marion G. Romney, who ordained Theodore M. Burton a high priest on 27

January 1945. In turn, Theodore M. Burton ordained me a high priest on 3 October 1961, during the time he was an Assistant to the Council of the Twelve. Thus in only nine steps, the line of authority extends back to Jesus Christ. What a solemn and profound feeling comes over one to know that he has the same fundamental authority to act in God's name that Abraham, Melchizedek, Joseph Smith, and all holders of the higher priesthood have enjoyed and do enjoy as a blessing from the Almighty. Through obedience and righteousness, priesthood holders can render an indispensable service to their families and many others among God's children.

3. AVOIDING THE ALLURE OF WORLDLINESS

THEME: We must exercise extreme caution, while living in the world, not to partake of worldly practices.

Lot dwelled in the cities of the plain, and pitched his tent toward Sodom. (Gen. 13:12)

MOMENT OF TRUTH

Many readers do not pick up on the subtle significance of Lot's pitching his tent toward Sodom, a city of sin. We should abhor sin and avoid the road to it. Having pitched his tent toward Sodom, it wasn't long before Lot lived there (see Gen. 14:12). As is often the case when people ripen in iniquity, the result was war and bloodshed. Lot was caught up in this and lost everything. Abraham came to his rescue and saved Lot, his family, friends, and his possessions.

MODERN PROPHETS SPEAK

Harold B. Lee:

> How I wish I could impress you who must daily walk out on the swaying bridge of worldliness and sin which flows as a turbulent stream below you, how I wish that when you have twinges of doubt and fear that cause you to lose the rhythm of prayer and faith and love, may you hear my voice as one calling to you from further along on life's bridge, "Have faith—this is the way—for I can see further ahead than you." I would fervently pray that you could feel the love flowing from my soul to yours, and know of my deep compassion toward each of you as you face your problems of the day. The time is here when every one of you must stand on your own feet. The time is here when no man and woman will endure on borrowed light. Each will have to be guided by the light within himself. If you do not have it, you will not stand. (*Decisions for Successful Living* [Salt Lake City: Deseret Book, 1973], 234)

Spencer W. Kimball:

> In our journey toward eternal life, purity must be our constant aim. To walk and talk with God, to serve with God, to follow his example and become as a god, we must attain perfection. In his presence there can be no guile, no wickedness, no transgression. In numerous scriptures he has made it clear that all worldliness, evil and weakness must be dropped before we can ascend unto "the hill of the Lord." The Psalmist asked: Who shall ascend into the hill of the Lord? or who shall stand in his holy place? And he answered the question: He that hath clean hands, and a pure heart; who hath not lifted up his soul unto vanity, nor sworn deceitfully (Ps. 24:3–4). (*The Miracle of Forgiveness* [Salt Lake City: Bookcraft, 1969], 26)

ILLUSTRATIONS FOR OUR TIMES

Virtue over Glamour

The young women of the ward wanted to put on a fashion show—and that was all right. But the leaders came to me (the bishop) with a problem. It seemed that some of the girls insisted on having one segment of the show featuring swimwear, such as they had seen on "real" fashion shows on television. How could they talk the girls out of this idea without seeming to be prudish? After giving it some thought, I suggested they first organize a private dress rehearsal in the cultural hall. So that's what happened. These lovely young girls looked beautiful and confident walking out in their dresses, but when they came out in their swimwear, they seemed hesitant and embarrassed. The girls came up afterward and said to us, "We don't think the swimming suit part is going to work. It doesn't seem right." It was a teaching moment. We congratulated the girls for deciding to uphold the principle of modesty, and we said a quiet prayer of thanksgiving in our hearts that the Spirit of the Lord had illuminated for them the pathway of virtue in a world where alluring enticements can all too subtly dampen the desire to do good.

4. SODOM AND GOMORRAH: PORTRAIT OF WICKEDNESS

THEME: The Lord will guide His saints away from the destructive forces of evil.

Escape for thy life; look not behind thee. (Gen. 19:17)

MOMENT OF TRUTH

Abraham bargained with the Lord to spare Sodom and Gomorrah if there was an element of righteousness remaining there. Lot chose to be in proximity with worldliness and its beauty and at first seemed reluctant to leave. Angels of the Lord retrieved the only righteous souls and then destroyed the wicked. We need to heed the warnings of the prophets to flee Babylon and not look back as did Lot's wife (Gen. 19:26), whose commitment to righteousness was apparently imperfect.

MODERN PROPHETS SPEAK

Brigham Young:

> When you get up in the morning, before you suffer yourselves to eat one mouthful of food, call your wife and children together, bow down before the Lord, ask him to forgive your sins, and protect you through the day, to preserve you from temptation and all evil, to guide your steps aright, that you may do something that day that shall be beneficial to the Kingdom of God on the earth. Have you time to do this? Elders, sisters, have you time to pray? (*Discourses,* 44)

James E. Faust:

> In addition to the legacy of faith bequeathed by those who crossed the plains, they also left a great heritage of love—love of God and love of mankind. It is an inheritance of sobriety, independence, hard work, high moral values, and fellowship. It is a birthright of obedience to the commandments of God and loyalty to those whom God has called to lead this people. It is a legacy of forsaking evil. Immorality, alternative lifestyles, gambling, selfishness, dishonesty, unkindness, and addiction to alcohol and drugs are not part of the gospel of Jesus Christ. (*Finding Light in a Dark World* [Salt Lake City: Deseret Book, 1995], 54)

POINTS OF DOCTRINE

Ripened in Iniquity
Wickedness has a price. When a person or group becomes so wicked that their iniquity is virtually full, the Lord does not allow them to live upon the earth unless they repent. There are dramatic cases where the Lord has destroyed the wicked, such as during the time of Noah, toward the end of the Jaredite period, the final chapter of the Nephite chronicle, and at other isolated times and places (Sodom and Gomorrah). On an individual basis, when people do not repent, they become "chained" to the devil (see Alma 12:9–11).

Interesting Note
Did Lot really offer up his own daughters to distract the depraved citizens of Sodom (see Gen. 19:8)? Just the opposite was the case. The Joseph Smith Translation makes

clear that Lot made an impassioned attempt to *protect* his daughters from the mob (see JST, Gen. 19:9–15).

A Pillar of Salt
What is meant when it says that Lot's wife "became a pillar of salt" (Gen. 19:26)?

> Luke 17:32: "Look not back to Sodom and the wealth and luxury you are leaving. Stay not in the burning house, in the hope of salvaging your treasures, lest the flame destroy you; but flee, flee to the mountains." Luke 17:33: "Seek temporal things and lose eternal life; sacrifice the things of this life and gain eternal life." (*Doctrinal New Testament Commentary* [Salt Lake City: Bookcraft, 1965–73], 1:645)

"But verily, thus saith the Lord, let not your flight be in haste, but let all things be prepared before you; and he that goeth, let him not look back lest sudden destruction shall come upon him" (D&C 133:15). It seems clear that the turning back was a symbol of her lack of faith and devotion to the Lord . . . hence she returned to that type of life and perished.

SUMMARY

The Lord has given us a chronicle of righteousness in preserving the record of the lives of His chosen prophets, such as Abraham and Melchizedek. We can savor the witness of the goodness of God in studying the example of these individuals. At the same time, we can view the consequences of permitting the alluring enticements of the world to encroach upon our environment and displace the solid anchor of principle and righteousness. Lot looked with longing toward the great, indulgent cities of the plain; he pitched his tent toward Sodom and came narrowly close to the precipice. His wife apparently could not overcome her devotion to worldly values, which are as fleeting and ephemeral as the walls of Sodom and Gomorrah amidst the cleansing firestorms of a just God. We must be watchful and prayerful, valiant and humble, devoted and grateful, ever willing to follow in the footsteps of the prophets.

CHAPTER NINE

"GOD WILL PROVIDE HIMSELF *a* LAMB"

Reading Assignment: Abraham 1; Genesis 15–17; 21–22.

Additional Reading: Hebrews 11:8–19; James 2:21–23; Jacob 4:5; D&C 132:34–36.

Trust in the Lord with all thine heart; and lean not unto thine own understanding. In all thy ways acknowledge him, and he shall direct thy paths. (Proverbs 3:5–6)

THEMES *for* LIVING

1. All These Things Shall Give Thee Experience
2. All Things Are Possible with God
3. The Lord Requires the Heart and a Willing Mind
4. The Lord Will Provide the Means Whereby We Can Obey

INTRODUCTION

We can see reflected in the life of Abraham an exemplary pattern of spiritual growth. From his early youth, he was schooled by experiences of adversity and oppression, and the lessons of obedience and valor he learned carried him through life on the wings of divine support and blessing. Never losing the vision of his destined calling, he set an unequaled example of one willing to do everything asked of him by God, without hesitation and without question. In many ways, Abraham's life journey shows that our mortal environment is like a dwelling with four chambers, each of which we visit in cycles: the trials we encounter in life (chamber 1) lead to opportunities for exerting our faith through obedience and godly behavior (2), which in turn leads to an outpouring of blessings from our Father in Heaven (3) and a multiplicity of valuable lessons learned (4). Then the whole sequence is repeated once more.

As we go through this cycle again and again, our progress is traced by a spiral that carries us higher and higher, according to our diligence and willingness to keep the commandments. The motion is an upward cycle, ever closer to the objective of being more like our Father in Heaven and His Son, Jesus Christ. We will see in the following pages three of Abraham's spiritual cycles: the preparations of his youth, the challenge that he and his wife faced in their old age to fulfill the Lord's promise for a son, and the requested sacrifice of Isaac. All of these experiences taught Abraham, as they teach us, that the Lord will provide a way for us to follow His will in all things.

1. ALL THESE THINGS SHALL GIVE THEE EXPERIENCE

THEME: Abraham survived a youth fraught with abuse and danger. Similarly, the challenges and adversities of life give us training and experience in those qualities of faith, persistence, resilience, and problem-solving that make us better able to carry out the Lord's errand.

> *And as they lifted up their hands upon me, that they might offer me up and take away my life, behold, I lifted up my voice unto the Lord my God, and the Lord hearkened and heard.* (Abr. 1:15)

MOMENT OF TRUTH

Abraham had within his heart the vision of future service to God; however, his circumstances stood at odds with this hope and yearning to be a valiant servant. Abuse, evil, ignorance, cruelty, superstition, false gods—all of these conspired to thwart his mission. Thus, he had to depend on faith and on the Lord for his own safety and deliverance. His experiences were to prepare him for future challenges and tests that established him as the father of many nations and the great patriarch of coming generations. Just like Joseph Smith in our day (see D&C 122:7–9), Abraham had to tread the same path of sacrifice that the Savior so willingly trod in bringing about the Atonement.

MODERN PROPHETS SPEAK

Neal A. Maxwell:

> Concerning all of these challenges, a loving God said of us, as we stood on the edge of this mortal experience, "We will prove them herewith, to see if they will do all things whatsoever the Lord their God shall command them" (Abr. 3:25). Should this stern reminder not be adequate concerning how serious God is about schooling and stretching us, then let us ponder what the Savior said to the Prophet Joseph Smith, who was in the midst of being proved: "All these things shall give thee experience, and shall be for thy good" (D&C 122:7). Furthermore, in the succeeding words of that revelation (which are unfortunately quoted far less often), the Lord said to His suffering prophet, "Hold on thy way, . . . fear not what man can do, for God shall be with you forever and ever" (D&C 122:9). "Hold on," "fear not"—these are the words of Him who has passed perfectly through "all these things," and who now seeks to bring us lovingly and safely through our own individually designed experiences. (*All These Things Shall Give Thee Experience* [Salt Lake City: Deseret Book, 1979], 5)

Ezra Taft Benson:

> To press on in noble endeavors, even while surrounded by a cloud of depression, will eventually bring you out on top into the sunshine. Even our master, Jesus the Christ, while facing that supreme test of being temporarily left alone by our Father during the Crucifixion, continued performing His labors for the children of men, and then shortly thereafter He was glorified and received a fulness of joy. While you are going through your trial, you can recall your past victories and count the blessings that you do have with a sure hope of greater ones to follow if you are faithful. And you can have that certain knowledge that in due time God will wipe away all tears (Rev. 7:17) and that "eye hath not seen, nor ear heard, neither have entered into the heart of man, the things which God hath prepared for them that love him" (1 Cor. 2:9). (*TETB,* 396)

ILLUSTRATIONS FOR OUR TIMES

The Picture

She was frail and gaunt, but eager to participate in the sacrament service that our youth had prepared for the residents of the Orem, Utah, nursing home that day. She sat at the back of the room, clutching in her hand a small object. When I passed by to greet her after the meeting, she smiled and reached the object up for me to see.

Although unable to communicate in words, she spoke with her eyes and her smile. It was a small photograph that she was holding. She pointed to a little girl in the picture, standing next to a pleasant-looking woman with her hands around the girl in a gesture of motherly tenderness. Then she pointed to herself. Clearly the photograph was a snapshot from her youth, a reminder of a tender time with her mother. Now the picture, like her frame, was bent; and like her countenance, the image was wrinkled. But there was little doubt that fond memories were at work in her heart—memories of love that kept the flame of life alive until the Lord in His wisdom should deem the battle over, the mission complete. In the wrinkles and folds of adversity are hidden the seeds of faith. In the often lonely struggles of life are found the nurturing seed beds where faith can sprout anew again and again, and the spirit can rise in majesty toward destinies of everlasting life.

2. ALL THINGS ARE POSSIBLE WITH GOD

THEME: The Lord will fulfill all of His promises to His children, despite every challenge or obstacle.

Is any thing too hard for the Lord? (Gen. 18:14)

MOMENT OF TRUTH

The Lord had promised Abraham that he would multiply and be the father of many nations (see Gen. 17:1–4). The Lord, through holy men, reminded Abraham and his wife that Sarah would bear a son (see Gen. 18:10). And the Lord said, "Is any thing too hard for the Lord? At the time appointed I will return unto thee, according to the time of life, and Sarah shall have a son." Sarah bore a son, and Abraham named him Isaac (see Gen. 21:2–3).

MODERN PROPHETS SPEAK

George Q. Cannon:

> It is time, with the experience we have had now as a Church, that we should be a people of unbounded faith, willing to believe that all things are possible with God and that when He commands us to do anything, we should go to with our might and with unyielding determination to accomplish that end according to the mind and will of God. This is the kind of people God expects us to be. If we are going to build up Zion in power and in great glory upon the earth, it will be by this principle of faith, by putting our trust in God, listening to His word, receiving it in the

proper manner from that authority which He has placed on the earth to give His word unto His people. Zion cannot be built up in any other way. (*Gospel Truth: Discourses and Writings of President George Q. Cannon* [Salt Lake City: Deseret Book, 1987], 115)

Spencer W. Kimball:

> When a true consciousness of guilt finally settles down upon the one who has sinned and he feels the heaviness of it—its throttling force and crushing power—only then can the sinner begin to realize how powerless he is on his own to rid himself of his transgressions. Only then can he begin to understand how futile are his unaided efforts to wash away the stains so indelibly stamped on his life and character. In his anguish he must come to lean heavily upon the Lord and trust in him, acknowledging that "with God all things are possible." (*The Miracle of Forgiveness* [Salt Lake City: Bookcraft, 1969], 339)

ILLUSTRATIONS FOR OUR TIMES

Invisible Sources

One of the first assignments I was given as a young bishop in Baltimore was to get the financial obligations of the ward in order. The stake president indicated that the ward was considerably in arrears with its welfare and other assessments to the stake, and that I should see to it that all was brought current. It was a great ward, with many faithful Saints, but in general, the families were of modest means. The leaders of the ward were concerned when I proposed sending our meager reserve fund to the stake to satisfy the debt, but they were supportive nevertheless. We paid the bill based on faith, not knowing how we would replenish our accounts. Within one week, all of that money had mysteriously been regenerated from unexpected sources. One rather inactive but sympathetic brother, for example, felt impressed to donate a significant sum for the support of Church activities. Others came through as well.

It taught me a powerful lesson that the law of tithing, which is based on the principle of faith, operates even above the level of individuals. In fact, I can recall a meeting many years ago where Ezra Taft Benson (who served eight years as Secretary of Agriculture under Dwight D. Eisenhower) visited the mission home of the West German Mission and expressed his opinion to us during a meeting that the generosity of the American people in giving foreign aid to other countries was one reason America had been blessed so much by the Lord with ongoing prosperity. Truly all things are possible with God when faith is exerted and obedience practiced, whether by individuals, wards, or even entire countries.

An Observance

In the late 1960s, I was a young practicing dentist, and my friend, Joseph Bentley, invited me to a special meeting. He was asking people to contribute to the general missionary fund of the Church. My practice was just beginning, and I would classify myself as beginning a practice with moderate success. Needless to say, I was not wealthy. New equipment and the overhead always made it a challenge at first to make all the payments. The Lord was good to us, so we always had "enough." Brother Bentley asked each of us to donate and, feeling the Spirit, I said yes. I made a pledge for the following year, not knowing where the money would come from.

Later that month I received a letter from President Alvin R. Dyer's office thanking me for the pledge to the missionary fund and indicating that it would start that year. I was shocked and worried—here it was November, and the amount I would need would be Christmas for the family. I talked with my sweetheart, and we decided we would donate the money and charge Christmas for the children.

Right or wrong, that's what we did, and I felt good about it. As the bills came due in January and February, a miracle happened. A man whom I had helped years earlier called and said he could pay me his debt now. It was just the amount I had donated to the Church—a miracle to me. I thanked the Lord and went on with my life. Each year, I needed the same amount of money, for I had made a five-year pledge. The following year I wrote my first book, *You, Your Family and the Scriptures.* Lo and behold, the royalty check was just what I needed for the donation. I hand-carried the donation to President Dyer's office and told the stories to his secretary. She responded, "I can hardly wait till next year to see how the Lord gives you the money."

I smiled and thought, *I wonder.*

That summer, our water bill was higher and higher. I couldn't understand it. I had complained to the water department for six to seven years, wondering why my bill was so much higher than my neighbors' were. They sent engineers to check it, and everything seemed fine. I pleaded for one more inspection and asked, "Please look inside the water meter." To their chagrin, they found the problem. One of the little cogs was two or three times too small. The result was two or three times the normal water bill. I asked what they would do now. The water department returned the money, plus interest. When I gave the money to President Dyer's secretary, we laughed a little and thanked the Lord a lot.

With two years left on the pledge, I was now full of faith and my confidence had waxed strong. A friend asked me to help him sell his property. He said, "If you get me a buyer, I'll give you so many thousands of dollars."

I said, "I'll try."

Well, you know what happened—one of my friends bought the property, and I had enough money for the last two years of the pledge. Yes, there is nothing too hard for the Lord. From the least to the greatest need, He provides.

3. THE LORD REQUIRES THE HEART AND A WILLING MIND

THEME: Abraham was commanded to offer up the thing most dear to his heart—his own son. Only through a commitment to sacrifice all that we have, if required to do so, can we manifest to the Lord that our love for Him and His divine cause is perfect.

> *Take now thy son, thine only son Isaac, whom thou lovest, and get thee into the land of Moriah; and offer him there for a burnt offering.* (Gen. 22:2)

MOMENT OF TRUTH

God did tempt (prove) Abraham by commanding him to sacrifice his only son. Abraham took Isaac and two other young men on the journey to Moriah, where he was to offer Isaac as a burnt offering, even a sacrifice to the Lord. On the third day, Abraham and Isaac went to worship. Isaac carried the wood as they journeyed. Isaac asked about the sacrifice, and Abraham replied, "My son, God will provide himself a lamb for a burnt offering" (Gen. 22:8). Abraham bound Isaac and laid him on the altar, preparing for the ultimate sacrifice. As he took the knife, an angel of the Lord forbade him and said, "For now I know that thou fearest [i.e., showest reverence to] God, seeing thou hast not withheld thy son" (Gen. 22:12). A ram was provided for the burnt offering. The Lord then promised Abraham that, "in thy seed shall all the nations of the earth be blessed" (Gen. 22:18).

MODERN PROPHETS SPEAK

Thomas S. Monson:

> Remember the qualifying statement of the Master: "Behold, the Lord requireth the heart and a willing mind" (D&C 64:34). A latter-day minister advised: "Until willingness overflows obligation, men fight as conscripts rather than following the flag as patriots. Duty is never worthily performed until it is performed by one who would gladly do more if only he could" (Harry Emerson Fosdick). (*Be Your Best Self* [Salt Lake City: Deseret Book, 1979], 59)

Joseph Smith:

> Remember that all your hopes of deliverance from danger and from death, will rest upon your faithfulness to God; in His cause, you must necessarily serve Him with a perfect heart and a willing mind. (*HC* 2:192–93)

ILLUSTRATIONS FOR OUR TIMES

An Apostle's Blessing

I was teaching early-morning seminary in southern California in 1960. The subject was the Old Testament. We had two little children, Karie and Steven. I loved my children with all my heart. As I thought about Abraham and his willingness to sacrifice his son, I could hardly bear the thought—his only son. I loved Father Abraham, and my affinity for him grew because of his willingness to do all. Life went on, and I would say in my prayers silently, "Father, I will give all . . . I pray thee preserve my children."

The test did not come until October 18, 1986, when my son, Cory, was thrown from a car as it overturned. He suffered a severe brain concussion. We rushed to his side, having traveled from England where I was a mission president. He lay there, motionless—this future missionary, this boy who loved the Book of Mormon, this strong, vibrant outside linebacker on the football team—so strong, yet now so silent. I prayed with fervor and passion. I begged the Lord. I promised all and more, then concluded, "Father, if thou but sayest the words, I will command him to live." The answer was no.

The next day, I turned off the life support, and Cory died on October 21, 1986. I was devastated. I felt like I could never preach again. My whole insides felt as if they had been ripped from my body. President Monson spoke at Cory's funeral. He said, "Don't ask why. That is a negative comment." He went on to explain the master plan of God, and how Cory had left early for his mission. Then President Monson blessed our family with an Apostle's blessing of peace and comfort. It was miraculous. In less than two weeks, I was healed—I was at peace. The fervor of missionary work was back, and it was back stronger than ever before. All will be required to go through death. The question is, will we live for the Lord and give our heart and our mind willingly?

4. THE LORD WILL PROVIDE THE MEANS WHEREBY WE CAN OBEY

THEME: Abraham demonstrated complete devotion and obedience, and the Lord, in His mercy and goodness, provided the ram for the sacrifice. Thus it is for all the Lord's faithful children.

> *Lay not thine hand upon the lad, neither do thou any thing unto him: for now I know*
> *that thou fearest God, seeing thou hast not withheld thy son, thine only son from me.*
> (Gen. 22:12)

MOMENT OF TRUTH

The Lord provided a ram in the thicket for Abraham to offer as a burnt offering. The test was in Abraham's willingness; and then, as usual, the Lord provided a way—even prepared the way for the sacrifice to be completed. The Lord truly does provide the means to do all things He commands us. We simply must act with love and faith and do as He has commanded.

MODERN PROPHETS SPEAK

Thomas S. Monson:

> The Lord provided the counsel: "For behold, the Spirit of Christ is given to every man, that he may know good from evil; wherefore, I show unto you the way to judge; for every thing which inviteth to do good, and to persuade to believe in Christ, is sent forth by the power and gift of Christ; wherefore ye may know with a perfect knowledge it is of God. But whatsoever thing persuadeth men to do evil, and believe not in Christ, and deny him, and serve not God, then ye may know with a perfect knowledge it is of the devil" (Moro. 7:16–17). (*Be Your Best Self* [Salt Lake City: Deseret Book, 1979], 84)

Thomas S. Monson:

> Such knowledge will dispel that hidden and insidious enemy who lurks within and limits our capacity, destroys our initiative, and strangles our effectiveness. This enemy of whom I speak is fear: a fear to wholeheartedly accept a calling; a fear to provide direction to others; a fear to lead, to motivate, to inspire. In His wisdom, the Lord provided a formula whereby we might overcome the archvillain of fear. He instructed: "If ye are prepared ye shall not fear" (D&C 38:30). (*Be Your Best Self* [Salt Lake City: Deseret Book, 1979], 195–96)

ILLUSTRATIONS FOR OUR TIMES

Evidence from the Scriptures

The scriptures are replete with examples of the Lord providing the way. Here are just a few:

MOSES:	Deliverance of the Israelites
	Parting of the Red Sea
	Manna to eat
NEPHI:	Obtaining the brass plates
	Building the ship

	Bursting the bonds
	Fleeing from Laman and Lemuel
Alma the Elder:	Establishing the Church
	Praying through faith that God would bless his son, Alma, and bring him to repentance
Ammon:	Teaching Lamoni
	Doing all things
Moroni:	The Title of Liberty

The list could go on forever—stories from all the scriptures testify of the goodness of God in preserving and blessing His children so the work could go forward, and the blessing of His children that they might have immortality and eternal life.

A Miraculous Rescue

The family had emigrated to Canada under the sponsorship of one of my uncles. I can still remember as a young boy meeting them and hearing their remarkable story. During the Nazi oppression, many Germans were subjected to unspeakable abuse. This family recounted the time their home was being searched by the police. It was a terrifying experience. They had hidden their young daughters away in a closet to keep them from view. But the police, in searching all the rooms, discovered the girls. It was a moment of profound fear. Then the officer who made the discovery called out words to the effect that these were just old people and not of any interest. It was an unexplained misperception that saved the girls from harm. The family saw in it the hand of Providence. The Lord does work in mysterious and marvelous ways.

SUMMARY

The Lord made a covenant with Abraham and his posterity, as He had done earlier with the great prophets before him. In exchange for obedience and leadership in blessing the nations of the world, the people were promised a great lineage now and eternal increase in the hereafter, places of refuge on earth and mansions in heaven, the gospel and truth here and salvation in the world to come. Abraham passed all tests given, and the Lord blessed him mightily through lessons of truth and priesthood power. We are told that the Saints "must needs be chastened and tried, even as Abraham" (D&C 101:4). The lesson is clear: "Go ye, therefore, and do the works of Abraham; enter ye into my law and ye shall be saved" (D&C 132:32).

CHAPTER TEN

"WE SHALL BE FRUITFUL *in the* LAND"

Reading Assignment: Genesis 24–29.

> *It [celestial marriage] is one of the greatest blessings that ever was conferred upon the human family. It is an eternal law which has always existed in other worlds as well as in this world.* (John Taylor, *JD* 24:229)

THEMES *for* LIVING

1. Marriage in the Covenant
2. Portrait of Loyal Stewardship
3. Honor the Birthright
4. Personal Revelation

INTRODUCTION

In many ways, the jewel in the crown of salvation and exaltation is eternal marriage in the temples of God. The scriptural account of the marriage of Isaac, Jacob, and other personalities at the time of Abraham sheds light on this doctrinal "jewel" as it relates to the birthright and covenant issues of the gospel. There are four aspects of the doctrine that will be discussed in the following pages: (1) marriage in the covenant (temple marriage), (2) stewardship in the service of covenant duties and requirements,

(3) honoring the birthright obligations of obedience and righteousness, and (4) the role of personal revelation in following the commandments of God.

1. MARRIAGE IN THE COVENANT

THEME: In all dispensations of time from Adam on, eternal marriage has been the gateway to the highest covenant blessings of the Lord. Thus Abraham and his patriarchal successors, as well as all of God's chosen prophets, have taught the preeminence of celestial marriage and the wisdom of choosing mates who are worthy of this blessing.

> ABRAHAM: *Go unto my country, and to my kindred, and take a wife unto my son Isaac.* (Gen. 24:4)

> ISAAC: *Take thee a wife from thence of the daughters of Laban thy mother's brother.* (Gen. 28:2)

MOMENT OF TRUTH

Abraham labored diligently to prepare the way for his son Isaac to marry in the covenant. Isaac and Rebekah were saddened when Esau married out of the covenant (see Gen. 26:34–35) and took great pains to see that Jacob followed the ordained pathway of the Abrahamic Covenant in marriage (see Gen. 28:1–5). Marriage is a divinely ordained partnership of man and wife participating in the Lord's mission to bring to pass "the immortality and eternal life of man" (Moses 1:39). As such, marriage in the covenant (temple marriage) is essential as the foundation of "eternal lives" (see D&C 132:24). Great care must be taken in the selection of a mate.

MODERN PROPHETS SPEAK

Ezra Taft Benson:

> Marriage, designed to be an eternal covenant, is the most glorious and most exalting principle of the gospel of Jesus Christ. Faithfulness to the marriage covenant brings the fullest joy here and glorious rewards hereafter. The abuse of this sacred ordinance despoils the lives of individuals, wrecks the basic institution of the home, and causes the downfall of nations. (*TETB*, 533–34)

Harold B. Lee:

> Temple marriage is the key to a happy home. Mine has been the rich experience, for nearly twenty years, of being entertained each weekend in some of the most successful homes of the Church, and, by contrast, almost weekly I am permitted a

glimpse into some of the unhappy homes. From these experiences I have reached in my own mind some definite conclusions: First, our happiest homes are those where parents have been married in the temple. Second, a temple marriage is most successful if husband and wife entered into the sacred ordinances of the temple clean and pure in body, mind, and heart. Third, a temple marriage is most sacred when each in the partnership has been wisely schooled in the purpose of the holy endowment and the obligations thereafter of husband and wife in compliance with instructions received in the temple. Fourth, parents who themselves have lightly regarded their temple covenants can expect little better from their children because of their bad example. (*The Teachings of Harold B. Lee* [Salt Lake City: Bookcraft, 1996], 242)

ILLUSTRATIONS FOR OUR TIMES

The Decision

How does one come to make the commitment for eternal marriage? I recall as a young man asking this very question of my bishop long ago. His counsel is as good today as it was then: "Study it out in your mind. Fast and pray." Everyone who goes through this process should record the details of the experience, as it is truly one of the most far-reaching decisions of one's life. I share here a few excerpts from my journal only to illustrate how Heavenly Father blesses and guides us in these kinds of covenant decisions.

> Wednesday and Thursday, the twelfth and thirteenth of July, were set aside as special fast days. I had prayed all along that I might learn of the sanction of our continuing with our relationship. On Thursday morning as I was walking down the steps below the Joseph Smith Building [at BYU] en route to my music class on lower campus, I was struck by the beauty of the small garden and pool about fifty yards below the edge of campus hill. It was certainly a pleasant day and the comfort of the surroundings invited meditation. I stayed. Thoughts seemed to come quickly to mind from all areas. Was it the thing to do? Would Carol be happy with me? Should I ask her? When? . . . Factors came clearly and forcibly before my mind. . . . Things became logical and sound. I knew she was the one. No voice spoke and no light appeared—certainly no outward manifestation was given me on that beautiful morning—but the inward calm and peace, the heartfelt conviction that all areas of importance had been explored and successfully answered—this was indeed overwhelming.
>
> For anyone who has never experienced a prayer being answered in the way only the Lord can answer a prayer, this indeed would be hard to fathom. But I knew that the Lord would have it so, so Carol was to be my wife. Seldom have I been blessed with so powerful an outpouring of truth. What a joy to pray to the Lord, thanking

Him later for His attention to my problem, and for His testimony of prayer given to me. This I record with the hope that any who might peruse these pages will be able to share with me the profound knowledge we enjoy of God in the Church that prayer is based on very definite principles just as repentance or faith or sanctification or any doctrine in the gospel. One must pray always to God for guidance and help in decisions.

2. PORTRAIT OF LOYAL STEWARDSHIP

THEME: The portrait given in the scriptures of the loyalty and leadership of Abraham's chief steward is a remarkable illustration of faith, righteousness, obedience, and valor. His successful mission to obtain a wife for Isaac assured the continuity of the covenant lineage.

I being in the way, the Lord led me to the house of my master's brethren. (Gen. 24:27)

MOMENT OF TRUTH

Marriage customs and practices differed in Old Testament times from our current patterns. "In the choice of a spouse usually the parents of a young man chose his wife and arranged for the marriage" (J. D. Douglas, *The New Bible Dictionary*, 788). Thus was the case with Abraham. He, being old, sent his eldest servant on the errand to secure a wife for Isaac. Abraham commanded him to "not take a wife unto my son of the daughters of the Canaanites" (Gen. 24:3), but rather from his kindred (this was marrying in the covenant). Abraham assured his servant that the Lord would send angels before him, and the servant made an oath with Abraham to do as he requested. Upon arriving in Nahor with his camels, he waited outside the city by the well. The servant prayed to know who might be the right one—could it be the one who assisted in the watering of the camels (which would be no small task)? Rebekah drew the water, and then the servant gave her some gifts and asked for lodging. She explained who she was and that there was room for him to lodge. The servant worshipped the Lord and offered a prayer of gratitude. The household welcomed the servant and his companions most graciously. The servant explained his errand, that of obtaining a wife for Isaac, the son of Abraham in great detail. Laban and Bethuel agreed, and Rebekah was given to marry Isaac. Following this, the servant gave gifts. Rebekah agreed to go to become the mother of thousands of millions—the wife of Isaac. Isaac greeted the traveling party, and they were united in love and marriage.

MODERN PROPHETS SPEAK

M. Russell Ballard:

> To be most effective, women need to learn to work effectively with and under the direction of the priesthood. Sisters, be prepared both mentally and spiritually to discuss the needs of those who fall within your stewardship. Be bold. Be assertive. Feel confident about raising weighty issues and concerns. You have as much right to input and inspiration as any other council member. (*Counseling with Our Councils: Learning to Minister Together in the Church and in the Family* [Salt Lake City: Deseret Book, 1997], 94–95)

Gordon B. Hinckley:

> Every bishop is a man who has been called by the spirit of prophecy and revelation and set apart and ordained by the laying on of hands. Every one of them holds the keys of the presidency of his ward. Each is a high priest, the presiding high priest of his ward. Each carries tremendous responsibilities of stewardship. Each stands as a father to his people. (*TGBH*, 88)

ILLUSTRATIONS FOR OUR TIMES

The Nourishment of Stewardship

It was after eleven P.M. on a Sunday evening as I drove past the chapel on my way home from a stake presidency assignment in a neighboring city. There were lights still burning in the bishop's office. Concerned, I stopped by the chapel and walked down the hall to the office. Muffled voices were faintly audible within. I knocked on the door. There was silence, and then I heard, "Come in."

Opening the door, I was treated to an unforgettable sight. Here was the entire bishopric poring over their books and assignments—each person sheepishly holding a peanut butter sandwich in his hand! The bishop himself, the curator of the "bread of life" for the local congregation, was still holding the knife used for spreading the treat. We had a good chuckle at the incongruous situation of a bishop's office furnished with an open peanut butter jar. There were a few joking comments about a year's supply of food—and then I felt profound admiration and gratitude for these men. Here were the loyal stewards of the Lord, being nourished by the spirit of devotion and commitment to their duties—with a little supplement of peanut butter for their late-evening hunger. They probably hadn't even been home yet. So I encouraged them to join their families, and thanked them for their valiant service in building up the kingdom of our Father in Heaven.

A Grand Example

The account of how Abraham's chief steward obtained the hand of Rebekah for his master's son is remarkably complete (see all of Gen. 24). We find demonstrated here all the qualities of stewardship that a servant of the Lord in our day would do well to emulate: allegiance, resourcefulness, prayerfulness, faith, thoroughness, strict obedience to commandments, thoughtfulness, gratitude, unwavering devotion to the cause, and wisdom. This attitude and devotion is the example for all those who have stewardships—and this includes all of us, especially parents who are guiding their children to marry in the temple and honor their birthright. We shall have an accounting of our stewardships given us here upon the earth. There are eternal roles and callings. Each requires accountability.

3. HONOR THE BIRTHRIGHT

THEME: Every child of God needs to live up to the divine lineage of being a son or daughter of God, created in His image. In a special way, all those who participate in the Abrahamic Covenant must be true to their birthright and calling as servants of the Lord, commissioned to be exemplars of obedience and righteousness in carrying the gospel to the world.

> *And Esau said, Behold, I am at the point to die: and what profit shall this birthright do to me?* (Gen. 25:32)

MOMENT OF TRUTH

Esau had confused priorities and valued his temporal comforts above his spiritual birthright. Thus the Lord saw to it that the birthright blessings fell to Jacob, the younger son. We must have the faith and the humility to follow the Lord's counsel by seeking first His kingdom, and then He will bless us and multiply our gifts in righteousness and justice.

MODERN PROPHETS SPEAK

David O. McKay:

> But there came with these thoughts appreciation of parenthood. It is a wonderful thing to have an inheritance, though it carries great responsibility, and I share with you appreciation for my birthright. You have yours, and it is your responsibility to bring honor to that heritage. Every young man and every young woman carries this responsibility. (*Man May Know for Himself: Teachings of President David O. McKay* [Salt Lake City: Deseret Book, 1967], 310)

Thomas S. Monson:

> This is a fundamental doctrine, a foundation scripture, an eternal truth. To have been created in the image of God brings to each of us a sense of profound humility, and a very real responsibility toward our birthright. (*Be Your Best Self* [Salt Lake City: Deseret Book, 1979], 89)

ILLUSTRATIONS FOR OUR TIMES

The Noble Birthright

He was a bright and capable young man with a young family. He had a responsible position as choir director with one of the local Christian congregations. He was affiliated with a prestigious local conservatory of music. We had talked several times about the gospel and the restored Church. He was reading the Book of Mormon and sent me a note in which he bore witness that he knew he had found the truth. His interest was keen and searching. I felt that the Spirit was working with him to bring about a "mighty change of heart," as among the people of King Benjamin. He was attending some of our Church meetings. But there was a hesitation—questions about this doctrine or that aspect of Church history. I knew that his focus was being distracted by some other issue. What was it? And then I discerned what his concern might be. He was sensing that a commitment to the gospel could very well result in a dislocation for his career. He could lose his job. We encouraged him to move forward with faith, but he gradually drew back. My later correspondence to him was unanswered. He came so close to embracing the noble birthright. Maybe in time he will return to the pathway and join in singing anthems of praise to the true and living God.

4. PERSONAL REVELATION

THEME: We are not left alone in a world of confusion and shadows. The Lord has prepared a way to guide the prayerful at decisive moments through His Holy Spirit.

> *If it be so, why am I thus? And she went to enquire of the Lord.* (Gen. 25:22)

MOMENT OF TRUTH

Revelation is given to all mankind. There is a requirement, and Rebekah fulfilled that requirement—she asked. The Lord gave her revelation concerning Jacob and Esau. So likewise has the Lord revealed truth to all His children since time began. It is the pattern for giving knowledge to His children. We must ask with a sincere heart, with faith, having done our part according to our role and stewardship. One does not receive revelation for others outside one's stewardship.

MODERN PROPHETS SPEAK

Joseph F. Smith:

> I believe that every individual in the Church has just as much right to enjoy the spirit of revelation and the understanding from God which that spirit of revelation gives him, for his own good, as the bishop has to enable him to preside over his ward. Every man has the privilege to exercise these gifts and these privileges in the conduct of his own affairs, in bringing up his children in the way they should go, and in the management of his farm, his flocks, his herds, and in the management of his business, if he has business of other kinds to do; it is his right to enjoy the spirit of revelation and of inspiration to do the right thing, to be wise and prudent, just and good in everything that he does. I know that this is a true principle, and I know that I know it, too; and that is the thing that I would like the Latter-day Saints to know. (*CR,* Apr. 1912, 9–10; see also *Gospel Doctrine: Selections from the Sermons and Writings of Joseph F. Smith* [Salt Lake City: Deseret Book, 1939], 34)

Lorenzo Snow:

> There is a way by which persons can keep their consciences clear before God and man, and that is to preserve within them the Spirit of God, which is the spirit of revelation to every man and woman. It will reveal to them, even in the simplest of matters, what they shall do, by making suggestions to them. We should try to learn the nature of this spirit, that we may understand its suggestions, and then we will always be able to do right. This is the grand privilege of every Latter-day Saint. We know that it is our right to have the manifestations of the Spirit every day of our lives. (*CR,* Apr. 1899, 52; see also *The Teachings of Lorenzo Snow* [Salt Lake City: Bookcraft, 1984], 111)

ILLUSTRATIONS FOR OUR TIMES

Examples of Revelation in Our Day:

- The Prophet Joseph was seeking the knowledge of the true church. He followed James 1:5–6. Result: the First Vision.

- The Prophet Joseph sought the word of the Lord repeatedly. Result: The Book of Commandments (The Doctrine & Covenants).

- President Joseph F. Smith had some concerns with passages in the book of Peter in the New Testament. Result: Doctrine & Covenants 138.

- President Gordon B. Hinckley, the First Presidency, and the Quorum of the Twelve were concerned over the destruction of the family. Result: The Proclamation on the Family.

- Mothers and fathers, priesthood leaders, and members of the Church at large all ask for confirmation and direction. Result: The Lord reveals by the power of the Holy Ghost the confirmation, the direction, or the very words we need to say (see 2 Ne. 32:5; D&C 100:5–6).

Blessings in Reserve

It was my privilege on one occasion to set apart several stake missionaries who had been called to serve. After having set apart one middle-aged sister, I noticed that she was in tears. Following the session, I asked her if all was well. She told me the story behind her emotion. She had been called to serve on a full-time mission many years previous to that, but circumstances had prevented her from going. She had always felt that she had relinquished important blessings from her Heavenly Father, since a mission call had originally been mentioned in her patriarchal blessing. Her tears today were tears of joy, since the setting apart blessing included statements that were, as she put it, "word-for-word" from her patriarchal blessing. Thus she knew that her Father in Heaven loved her and had reserved for her the very blessings He wanted her to have through faithful service. Truly the Lord watches over us and wants us to know, through the Spirit, of His love and concern.

SUMMARY

If we are faithful in abiding by the new and everlasting covenant of marriage, entered into in the temple of God, we qualify ourselves for the highest gifts of exaltation and eternal lives. Our personal and family stewardship, as well as our stewardship within the Church and kingdom of God, is anchored in the celestial marriage covenant and relationship. There is no more solemn duty for parents than to teach these principles to their children, and to use their ordained stewardship to prepare the way for their children to follow in the footsteps of those who honor their birthright and covenant obligations. Through obedience and humble prayer, the gift of personal revelation will illuminate the way for these divine decrees to be obeyed.

CHAPTER ELEVEN

"AND *the* LORD WAS *with* JOSEPH"

Reading Assignment: Genesis 34; 37–39.

For behold, thou art the fruit of my loins; and I am a descendant of Joseph who was carried captive into Egypt. And great were the covenants of the Lord which he made unto Joseph. (Lehi to his son Joseph, 2 Ne. 3:4)

THEMES *for* LIVING

1. The Wages of Envy
2. Portraits of Moral Weakness
3. Portrait of Leadership and Virtue

INTRODUCTION

In the contrast between the character of Joseph and the character of his brothers, we see played out in the starkest terms the victory of integrity over envy, honesty over jealousy, and (in the case of some of the brothers) virtue over moral laxity. Joseph built his life upon a foundation of enduring principles and a commitment to follow the guidance of the Spirit. His moral courage and leadership reflect the kind of strength, discipline, and stability that a great leader must always have. By way of contrast, those who succumb to unchecked greed or lust display a wavering instability from which harmony, peace, and lasting happiness can never flow.

1. THE WAGES OF ENVY

THEME: Envy, jealousy, and greed exact dire penalties. When Joseph's brethren conspired to destroy the lad, they provided a bleak memorial to the consequences of sibling rivalry and wickedness.

And they rent the coat of many colours, and they brought it to their father. (Gen. 37:32)

MOMENT OF TRUTH

Joseph, being favored of Jacob "because he was the son of his old age" (Gen. 37:3), became a target of malice on the part of his older brothers. Joseph was not reluctant to share his dreams regarding his future leadership and hence contributed to his brothers' feelings of jealousy. When Joseph was sold into slavery by his brothers, the stage was set for a future reunion in the courts of Pharaoh when his brethren would confess their sins and admit that Joseph was indeed divinely chosen to be the leader of the family and the patriarchal standard-bearer for many future nations. The rent "coat of many colors" became a lasting symbol of the ultimate preservation of the Lord's chosen lineage (see Alma 46:23–34). The story of Joseph, who was sold into Egypt, shows the results of jealousy, envy, greed, and hatred, yet shows the power of God in all things.

MODERN PROPHETS SPEAK

Gordon B. Hinckley:

> Ours is the duty to walk by faith. Ours is the duty to walk in faith, rising above the evils of the world. We are sons and daughters of God. Ours is a divine birthright. Ours is a divine destiny. We must not, we cannot sink to the evils of the world—to selfishness and sin, to hate and envy and backbiting, to the "mean and beggarly" elements of life. (*TGBH,* 7)

David O. McKay:

> Jealousy, hatred, envy, animosity—all such evils you must overcome by suppression. That is where your control comes in. Suppress that anger! Suppress that jealousy, that envy! They are all injurious to the spirit. (*Gospel Ideals: Selections from the Discourses of David O. McKay* [Salt Lake City: Improvement Era, 1953], 356)

ILLUSTRATIONS FOR OUR TIMES

The Strength Is in You

Overcome envy, jealousy, greed, and hatred by doing the following:

- Build on a foundation of gospel values and unconditional love. Prioritize your life.

- Recognize that happiness is within, and not based on possessions or external gratification.

- Recognize your own divine nature and seek to improve yourself. That is the only true victory—overcoming the world and temptation, not in besting others.

Envy and jealousy are concerns for everyone because of their power to destroy the souls of men.

2. PORTRAITS OF MORAL WEAKNESS

THEME: Preserved in the scriptures are candid accounts of the moral lassitude and debauchery of several of Jacob's sons or associates. The painful consequences of their misdeeds serve as valuable lessons about the importance of following the commandments of God.

> *And Judah acknowledged them [the personal pledge gifts he had left with Tamar, his daughter-in-law], and said, She hath been more righteous than I.* (Gen. 38:26)

MOMENT OF TRUTH

When Jacob's daughter, Dinah, was defiled by Shechem, a Hivite prince, Jacob arranged to redress the situation by bringing all the Hivites under certain provisions of the covenant. However, Simeon and Levi destroyed the offenders and their community, thus laying the groundwork for lasting enmity in the land. "Ye have troubled me to make me to stink among the inhabitants of the land," said Jacob (Gen. 34:30), reminiscent of what Alma said to his son, Corianton: "When they saw your conduct they would not believe in my words" (Alma 39:11). Furthermore, Reuben and Judah committed serious moral sins that cast shadows over the landscape of this unfolding record of the work of the Lord. In the case of Reuben, he lost his birthright as the oldest son to Joseph (see 1 Chron. 5:1–2). The lesson overshadowing these chronicles of moral turpitude is the fact that the Lord's purposes are not defeated, for Joseph's sons inherited the birthright, and thus his lineage carried on the leadership role under the Abrahamic Covenant. Similarly, the Savior would come from the preserved lineage of Judah as the light and life of the world. No matter what some of the Lord's children do in defiance of His laws, the Lord is still in charge of the process whereby the plan of salvation can unfold to its ultimate destiny.

MODERN PROPHETS SPEAK

Ezra Taft Benson:

> Yes, one can repent of moral transgression. The miracle of forgiveness is real, and true repentance is accepted of the Lord. But it is not pleasing to the Lord prior to a mission, or at any time, to sow one's wild oats, to engage in sexual transgression of any nature, and then to expect that planned confession and quick repentance will satisfy the Lord. (*Come, Listen to a Prophet's Voice* [Salt Lake City: Deseret Book, 1990], 6)

Gordon B. Hinckley:

> There is in each of us that sense of modesty and morality to which this writer refers. . . . The Lord has made it clear, and the experience of centuries has confirmed it, that happiness lies not in immorality, but rather in abstinence. The voice of the Church to which you belong is a voice pleading for virtue. It is a voice pleading for strength to abstain from that which is evil. It is a voice declaring that sexual transgression is sin. It is contrary to the will of the Lord. It is contrary to the teachings of the Church. It is contrary to the happiness and well-being of those who indulge in it. (*TGBH,* 48)

ILLUSTRATIONS FOR OUR TIMES

A Story

I remember hearing a story told by my neighbor. It had to do with an attorney who was handling an adoption case involving a sixteen-year-old girl who had made a mistake, but decided not to marry the young man. Instead, she came to live with the attorney's family during the time of her pregnancy. The attorney's wife took this frightened and confused young lady under her wing and cared for her like a daughter. In due time, the girl gave birth to a beautiful little boy. Under provisions of the adoption rules in the hospital where the son was born, the young mother had to take the child from the arms of the nurse and present it to the attorney, who would then take the child from the room and give it to the adopting parents waiting nearby. It was not an easy thing to do.

After this ritual was finished and the baby was gone, the young girl said to her surrogate mother, "My boyfriend lied to me when he said no one would get hurt. He said that because we loved each other, whatever we did was good and right. But I know he didn't love me, and that's why I couldn't marry him, because he was not good enough to be the father of my little boy. It was all a lie, and I can't live a lie. If I had only known at the time of my mistake how it would feel to give up my baby!"

Here was a young girl who did not see ahead to the consequences of what she was about to do for a mere momentary pleasure. It is so important to see the big picture, to realize that some things are too sacred and far-reaching to be ignored and left out of the picture. Life is sacred. Lasting relationships are what matter. Peace and harmony do not flow from fleeting gratification. Honor and long-term happiness are at stake. We must live by principle or we will bring sadness to others and ourselves.

The Courage to Return

It took courage. It took faith. But he returned. The young husband and father had slipped, and for his confessed moral indiscretion, he had lost his membership in the Church. He had been one of the most popular among the youth leaders of the ward. Our own son thought highly of him. And now he was back, sitting with his family and participating each week. He was humble, but his head was held high. He was on the road back. People accepted him—even respected him for his courage in rebuilding what he had lost. Before long, he was serving again with the young people. They loved him. They loved his family. They valued his testimony and his example. He was a living example of the gospel of repentance at work. I have often thought about this young man and his spiritual resiliency. With God, nothing is impossible. How grand it would be if all of us were as anxiously engaged in the process of daily repentance as he was. It would be a better world, and we would be closer to a Zion society.

3. PORTRAIT OF LEADERSHIP AND VIRTUE

THEME: Joseph's example of moral uprightness in Egypt is among the most celebrated instances of strength of character in all of scripture.

> *The Lord was with him, and that which he did, the Lord made it to prosper.* (Gen. 39:23)

MOMENT OF TRUTH

Joseph's flight at the adulterous overtures of Potiphar's wife stands in stark contrast with the moral weakness of some of his brothers. The story of his strength of character is a beacon of light that still shines today in our world of moral relativity characterized by the loss of the anchor of enduring principles. Moreover, Joseph's resiliency, positive leadership, and creative problem-solving caused him to be elevated in stature and office in his Egyptian setting, thus laying the groundwork for his future role as preserver of his heritage under the Abrahamic Covenant.

MODERN PROPHETS SPEAK

Boyd K. Packer:

> If you are involved in a liaison, no matter how innocent it may appear, break it up right now. Some things tie you to this kind of temptation. Quit them. Avoid the very appearance of evil. This may be very painful if you are entangled in a relationship with deep emotional ties. Cut those ties and encourage the other person to do likewise. Get it done soon, and get it done completely and finally. (*That All May Be Edified* [Salt Lake City: Bookcraft, 1982], 197)

Spencer W. Kimball:

> Illicit sex is a selfish act, a betrayal, and is dishonest. To be unwilling to accept responsibility is cowardly, disloyal. Marriage is for time and eternity. Fornication and all other deviations are for today, for the hour, for the "now." Marriage gives life. Fornication leads to death. (*Faith Precedes the Miracle* [Salt Lake City: Deseret Book, 1972], 156)

ILLUSTRATIONS FOR OUR TIMES

Interrupting the Pattern

I recall vividly a stake priesthood leadership meeting at which Elder Boyd K. Packer was the presiding authority. He had come to reorganize the stake and train the new leadership. His speech at the leadership meeting included an impassioned call to repentance. He raised the specter of priesthood brethren possibly being tempted to initiate improper liaisons at work and stated emphatically the awful dangers of such behavior. He said, with great emphasis, speaking as if directly to those who might be allowing themselves to be in such circumstances: "Stop it! Stop it! Stop it! Stop it!" By repeating himself forcefully a number of times, he etched this command indelibly in the minds of all attendees. His message was unmistakable: We must avoid even the appearance of evil. Joseph in Egypt is the preeminent example of a leader with the courage to remove himself immediately from the alluring clutches of immoral entanglements. Any invitation to moral compromise must be rebuffed without hesitation. In Joseph and all of God's chosen leaders we have the example of righteous living, nourished and sustained by the Spirit of our Father in Heaven.

SUMMARY

When Lehi was blessing his young son Joseph, he told him of his namesake, Joseph of Egypt, and said,

> Wherefore Joseph truly saw our day. And he obtained a promise of the Lord, that out of the fruit of his loins the Lord God would raise up a righteous branch unto the house of Israel: not the Messiah, but a branch which was to be broken off, nevertheless, to be remembered in the covenants of the Lord that the Messiah should be made manifest unto them in the latter days, in the spirit of power, unto the bringing of them out of darkness unto light—yea, out of hidden darkness and out of captivity unto freedom. (2 Ne. 3:5)

Thus Joseph, son of Israel, was blessed by the Lord to foresee the time when his posterity would be broken off and directed to flee the wickedness of Jerusalem so that a righteous branch of the House of Israel could be preserved according to the purposes of the Lord. He foresaw the coming forth of the Book of Mormon at the hands of another Joseph to be raised up in the latter days with the mission to restore the record of Joseph as a witness to the truth of the Bible (the record of Judah). And the two mighty witnesses would stand side by side as a testimony of the divinity of the Savior and the truthfulness of the gospel. Joseph of Egypt knew of his role and destiny in this divine plan. He was anchored in a clear vision of the Lord's design for His covenant people. Because of Joseph's moral integrity and leadership, he stood the test and laid the foundation for a continuation of the covenant blessings to millions upon millions of people in the future.

CHAPTER TWELVE

"FRUITFUL *in* *the* LAND *of* MY AFFLICTION"

Reading Assignment: Genesis 40–45.

Additional Reading: 2 Nephi 2:2; D&C 64:8–11; D&C 122:5–9.

And if your eye be single to my glory, your whole bodies shall be filled with light, and there shall be no darkness in you; and that body which is filled with light comprehendeth all things. (D&C 88:67)

THEMES *for* LIVING

1. The Gifts of God
2. Redeeming Love
3. The Hand of God

INTRODUCTION

The traits of faith, hope, charity, love, being committed to the welfare of the covenant people, seeking the interest of others, and being filled with light are all abundantly epitomized in the life of Joseph. What does one see when one has an eye single to the glory of God, as did he? One discerns, first of all, how to deploy the spiritual gifts that God has imparted for the blessing of the Saints. Next, one discerns continually the daily opportunities to exercise forgiving love of the kind shown by the Redeemer. Third, one discerns with the spiritual eye the hand of God outstretched over the affairs of men, leading and guiding His people in the unfolding of the plan of salvation.

1. THE GIFTS OF GOD

THEME: Joseph was richly blessed with gifts of leadership and the ability to discern the patterns of divine intervention in human affairs. He used his gifts for the glory of God and the preservation of his people.

> *What God is about to do he sheweth unto Pharaoh.* (Gen. 41:28)

> *Can we find such a one as this is, a man in whom the Spirit of God is?* (Gen. 41:38)

MOMENT OF TRUTH

All leaders must be visionary. From his youth, Joseph had the ability to interpret spiritual phenomena, such as inspired dreams. He combined this gift with an uncanny understanding of how to rise in favor with those over him, whether it was the warden of the prison or the pharaoh of the land. Moreover, he had an unerring sense of confidence in devising and carrying out practical solutions to challenging problems, such as the coming famine in the land. As a leader among men—politically as well as spiritually—Joseph showed a better way, one that gave glory and honor to God and followed the principles of harmony, love, forgiveness, productivity, and the Redeemer's touch.

Following Joseph's interpretation of Pharaoh's dream, the monarch praised Joseph as one with the Spirit of God. Pharaoh gave Joseph the power to rule the people of Egypt. Joseph's interpretation was fulfilled; after seven years of plenty, the seven years of famine began.

MODERN PROPHETS SPEAK

Parley P. Pratt:
> What have not dreams accomplished? Dreams and their interpretation brought the beloved son of Jacob from his dungeon, made him prime minister of Egypt, and the savior of a nation, and of his father's house. Dreams, and the interpretation of dreams, raised a Daniel from slavery or degrading captivity in Babylon, to wear a royal chain of gold, and to teach royalty how to rule, whilst he presided over the gov-

ernors and presidents of more than a hundred provinces. Dreams, and the interpretation of dreams, have opened the future, pointed out the course of empire through all the troublous times of successive ages, till Saints alone shall rule, and immortality alone endure. (*Key to the Science of Theology/A Voice of Warning* [Salt Lake City: Deseret Book, 1965], 123)

James E. Talmage:

He manifests His powers through the graces of the Spirit, as seen in gifts of revelation, prophecy, tongues and their interpretation, by inspired dreams and visions, by healings, and by a diversity of gifts called by man miracles. (*The Parables of James E. Talmage* [Salt Lake City: Deseret Book, 1973], 62)

ILLUSTRATIONS FOR OUR TIMES

The Use of the Gifts of God

Joseph used his gifts to bless and preserve the house of Israel. All of us have gifts—love, faith, spiritual gifts, and blessings of the priesthood. Each gift, and each person who is blessed with these gifts, has one purpose—to bless people's lives. Prophets, priesthood leaders, and those who are called to serve seek to bring happiness to others. Parents, above all, have this responsibility to bless their children with the gifts they have been given. Just as Joseph blessed his people, each of us has this responsibility, too. The question is clear: what gifts do we have, and what gifts can we magnify in order to bless all mankind? Seek the best gifts that we might be instruments in the hand of God to bring souls unto Christ.

Gifts of the Kingdom

He was somewhat older than the average missionary, but his enthusiasm to preach the gospel was no less vibrant and energetic. He arrived with a group of new missionaries at the Frankfurt mission home. It was the custom in those days to take new missionaries to a street meeting soon after their arrival in order to introduce them directly to proselyting work. So without delay we accompanied these new elders, none of whom could speak German, to our favorite place near a large protestant church located on the *Hauptwache*—the main intersection in the center of the city. There, next to the wall of the church, we would hold our meetings for small gatherings of curious passersby and pass out tracts about the restored Church. Our practice was to have the new missionaries bear their testimony in English, then have the veteran missionaries translate for the German listeners, and that is what happened on this occasion. However, when it was this older missionary's turn to speak, he smiled with a particularly glowing countenance and said, "I won't need you to translate." Then he proceeded to bear his testimony in German, speaking very fluently and expressively, giving his witness to the truthfulness of the gospel and the restored Church to an attentive audience. We were all amazed. Afterward, I asked him whether he had ever studied the German language, and he told me that he had heard some of his relatives speak a few words years earlier. On this occasion, however, he felt inspired to speak to the people in their own language—and so he did. It was a heartwarming display of the gifts of God at work in a faithful and humble servant of God. Years later, I came across the passage in the *History of the Church* where the Prophet Joseph Smith explained that the gift of tongues "was particularly instituted for the preaching of the Gospel to other nations and languages" (*HC* 2:162)—a phenomenon in widespread evidence among the many tens of thousands of missionaries who are on the Lord's errand in countries where they need to teach the word of truth in a foreign tongue.

2. REDEEMING LOVE

THEME: Joseph is the unsurpassed paragon of brotherly kindness and love of parents in all of holy writ. Can one find, outside the example of the Savior, a greater demonstration of genuine love for one's family members, and a deeper compassionate concern for their welfare, than in the life of Joseph? When one has charity, as did Joseph, he or she will truly act like Christ.

> *God be gracious unto thee, my son.* (Gen. 43:29)

> *I am Joseph; doth my father yet live?* (Gen. 45:3)

> *There will I nourish thee.* (Gen. 45:11)

> *He kissed all his brethren, and wept upon them.* (Gen. 45:15)

MOMENT OF TRUTH

The dramatic account of the interaction between Joseph and his brothers, who came seeking food to preserve their families' lives, never loses its capacity to rivet the reader and generate unforgettable images of greatness of character. Joseph's leadership and integrity, forgiving nature, and genuine love combine to make the reader want to be better, want to improve, want to emulate such a Christlike example. We have, on the one hand, the deep and profound yearning of the father, Israel, who waits anxiously in his homeland to know of the safety and preservation of all his sons—even those whose youthful indiscretions had caused him untold grief. On the other hand, we have the outbound love of Joseph for his father and brethren. The two forces of love arch toward each other in this account, and provide the moving and memorable setting in which this divine family story plays itself out.

MODERN PROPHETS SPEAK

Hugh B. Brown:

> The abundant life is the joyous life. One must be healthy to be happy. The Lord's law of health promises physical fitness and radiant living. It is the teachable life, the life of awareness and appreciation; therefore, education helps to determine its quality. One prepares for more abundant living by gaining knowledge, and intelligence will be his glory. A candidate for this life must be spiritually responsive and in tune. It requires diligence, faith, virtue, knowledge, temperance, patience, godliness, brotherly kindness, charity—if his life is to be abundant rather than barren. (*The Abundant Life* [Salt Lake City: Bookcraft, 1965], 8)

Harold B. Lee:

> Before we can receive a testimony, we must have a trial of our faith in patience. We must have a trial of our faith in knowledge—that means studying the scriptures. We must have a trial of our faith in temperance—that means keeping the Word of Wisdom, primarily. We must have a trial of our faith in virtue, in charity, in brotherly kindness. (*The Teachings of Harold B. Lee* [Salt Lake City: Bookcraft, 1996], 134)

ILLUSTRATIONS FOR OUR TIMES

The Key to Life's Burdens

I sat down next to my seven-year-old son, Nathan, in the Primary opening assembly and leaned over to whisper something to his teacher to the effect that we, his parents, should be more involved during the class itself as well as the assembly. "It is quite a burden for you," I said, meaning the task of handling her regular class plus this young boy with challenging autistic behaviors. Her response was one that I shall never forget. She whispered back, "It is no burden when you love."

3. THE HAND OF GOD

THEME: Joseph's vision of heavenly workings in the affairs of mankind allowed him to overlook the petty intrigues of his brethren, though they conspired to exile him in a strange land. Though he started out as a prisoner in Egypt, he was never confined to a negative world of grudge-bearing, recriminations, and blame. Instead, Joseph had the miraculous power to see the good in all that transpired, and to become a partner with God in bringing about divine purposes.

Be not grieved, nor angry with yourselves, that ye sold me hither: for God did send me before you to preserve life. (Gen. 45:5)

And God sent me before you to preserve you a posterity in the earth, and to save your lives by a great deliverance. (Gen. 45:7)

MOMENT OF TRUTH

Joseph clearly saw the hand of God in all that transpired. He was at once the nourisher, the forgiver, the guide, the mentor, the man of grace, the uniter, the family man. In Joseph, we see a prototype of the Savior Himself, who provides the bread of life at times of spiritual famine, the water of life at times of spiritual thirst. Joseph is the purveyor of peace, the harbinger of spiritual harmony. He is the theme of life, the essence of restored vitality. Like the Savior, he is easy to love and easy to follow. Jacob, now Israel, said it best: "It is enough; Joseph my son is yet alive: I will go and see him before I die" (Gen. 45:28).

MODERN PROPHETS SPEAK

Ezra Taft Benson:

> Having declared America to be a land of liberty, God undertook to raise up a band of inspired and intelligent leaders who could write a constitution of liberty and establish the first free people in modern times. The hand of God in this undertaking is clearly indicated by the Lord himself in a revelation to the Prophet Joseph Smith in these words: "I established the Constitution of this land, by the hands of wise men whom I raised up unto this very purpose" (D&C 101:80). (*God, Family, Country: Our Three Great Loyalties* [Salt Lake City: Deseret Book, 1974], 344)

ILLUSTRATIONS FOR OUR TIMES

Coming to an Understanding

With the vision of purpose clearly in mind, Joseph of Egypt took his adversity, recognizing that God sent him ahead to preserve the posterity of Israel. This vision, while recognizing the power and strength of God in one's life, is what gives one the power of love, the power to forgive; and in forgiveness you free yourself from the baggage of vengeance. Remember that vengeance is the Lord's. For unto us we are commanded to forgive all. It is the responsibility of others to repent. Should we fail to show love and give freely of forgiveness then we too have sinned, and condemnation then rests upon us. Joseph truly is the illustration and example of love unfeigned, and forgiveness.

The Hand of God

When the fourteen-year-old lad—the namesake of Joseph of old—entered the grove that spring morning, the preparations of eons of time were being fulfilled. It was no coincidence, no happenstance of fate. It was the culmination of a grand design set in place before the foundations of the world.

The sectarians, then as now, protest: "Why should we heed the story of an untutored boy who professes to have opened the heavens that we know to be sealed? Why should the kingdom of God spring accidentally into existence because of the vain imaginations of some young upstart amateur?" Untutored? Accidental? Here was a prophet of God lovingly tutored in eternal principles by the hand of God in the premortal world, guided by the hand of God in his youth to inquire after truth, nurtured by the hand of God to bring forth priceless blessings for mankind, sustained by the hand of God to lay once again the foundations of the Kingdom of God upon the earth, magnified by the hand of God to transcend daunting challenges and complete his earthly mission with honor and then seal his testimony with his blood.

By the hand of God, this valiant servant rose up to commence a work that is blessing our lives and the lives of our families, and will yet bless the lives of countless millions in this, the last dispensation of time.

SUMMARY

To act with an eye single to the glory of God, as Joseph did, means we must humbly seek after the best gifts and use them in the service of our fellow beings. We must learn to kindle the Redeemer's love in our daily lives; we must look for and discern the hand of God at work in our lives and give Him heartfelt thanks for the gospel of Jesus Christ. When we begin to do this, we begin to catch the vision of God's covenant plan.

CHAPTER THIRTEEN

"SEE *the* SALVATION *of the* LORD"

Reading Assignment: Exodus 1–3; 5–6; 11–14.

Additional Reading: Exodus 4; 7–10; 15.

> *If you want to know how to be saved, I can tell you: it is by keeping the commandments of God. No power on earth, no power beneath the earth, will ever prevent you or me or any Latter-day Saint from being saved, except ourselves.* (Heber J. Grant, *Improvement Era* 48:123)

THEMES *for* LIVING

1. God Hears Our Prayers
2. Divine Calling/Divine Power
3. Freedom and the Atonement
4. Remember the Covenant
5. Guiding Light of the Gospel

INTRODUCTION

The story of the Exodus is a story of deliverance through the power of God. The liberation of Israel from Egyptian bondage is parallel to our own deliverance from the consequences of sin through the process of faith, repentance, baptism, and the gift of the Holy Ghost—the atoning principles and ordinances established for our blessing through the redemption of the Savior. Spiritual liberation involves a number of aspects, five of which are featured in this chapter: (1) the prayer of faith, (2) the calling of prophets to declare the will of the Lord (just as we, too, receive callings in the Church as a blessing for ourselves and others), (3) bringing about the effects of the Atonement through our obedience, (4) remembering our covenants in ways the Lord has prescribed (in particular the sacrament), and (5) receiving constant nourishment and guidance through the Holy Spirit.

Each aspect of these steps in the process of moving toward spiritual freedom is discussed in the coming pages.

1. GOD HEARS OUR PRAYERS

THEME: Just as the Lord heard the cries of ancient Israel suffering from their bondage, He will also listen to our sincere prayers for strength and guidance to overcome the challenges of mortality and lead our families to spiritual well-being.

> *I have surely seen the affliction of my people which are in Egypt, and have heard their cry by reason of their taskmasters; for I know their sorrows.* (Ex. 3:7)

MOMENT OF TRUTH

After the deaths of Joseph and Pharaoh, the Israelites began to suffer under successor regimes. Their burdens became heavy, their oppression painful. They cried to the Lord for relief, and He heard their prayers and intervened to bring a new situation into their lives and redress the wrongs that had befallen them.

Prayer has great power in our lives. Here are a few examples:

- Blessing of the Holy Ghost: 3 Ne. 19:9; D&C 19:38; 42:14.

- Avoid and overcome temptation: 3 Ne. 18:15–18; D&C 31:12.

- Receive strength: Moses 1:20.

- For others: Matt. 5:44; Mosiah 27:14.

- Receive forgiveness: Enos 1:4–6; JS—H 1:29.

- For all things: Mark 11:24; Alma 34:17–28.

• Gain faith and humility: Hel. 3:35.

• Express gratitude: Dan. 6:10.

• Receive knowledge and understanding: James 1:5–6.

• Receive Charity: Moro. 7:48.

MODERN PROPHETS SPEAK

Marvin J. Ashton:

> In D&C 23:6, Joseph Knight was counseled to pray: "Behold, I manifest unto you, Joseph Knight, by these words, that you must take up your cross, in the which you must pray vocally before the world as well as in secret, and in your family, and among your friends, and in all places." Sometimes we are given crosses so we can be taught to pray. Crosses become lighter and more manageable when we learn to pray and when we learn to patiently wait for the answers to our prayers. (*Be of Good Cheer* [Salt Lake City: Deseret Book, 1987], 36)

James E. Faust:

> Of all that we might do to find solace, prayer is perhaps the most comforting. We are instructed to pray to the Father in the name of his Son, the Lord Jesus Christ, by the power of the Holy Ghost. The very act of praying to God is satisfying to the soul, even though God, in his wisdom, may not give what we ask for. President Harold B. Lee taught us that all of our prayers are answered, but sometimes the Lord says no. The Prophet Joseph Smith taught that the "best way to obtain truth and wisdom" is "to go to God in prayer." Prayer is most helpful in the healing process. (*Finding Light in a Dark World* [Salt Lake City: Deseret Book, 1995], 30–31)

ILLUSTRATIONS FOR OUR TIMES

The Lost Needle

As parents, we had always prayed together as a family and encouraged our children to pray for all things—for help and in gratitude. Karie Lyn, our oldest daughter, was six years old and wanted to sew with a needle and thread with her friend, Cindy. My sweetheart, Pat, had suggested that if they played with a needle and thread they must be careful, because Karie's little sister was playing in the same room and was learning to crawl. Karie continued to plead, so finally Pat relented and warned them to be very careful, because if Kristi swallowed the needle it would be horrible.

They were excited and began to sew. As fate would have it, within a minute the tiny needle was lost. Karie Lyn was panicked. She quickly went to her bedroom and pleaded with the Lord, "Please help me find the needle." Hurrying back to the sewing area, she and Cindy began to search. Her prayer was answered—through another, as the Lord often does. Cindy exclaimed, "I've found it! I've found it!" Joy was felt—the needle and thread and material were returned to Mother, and Karie went directly to her bedroom and offered a prayer of gratitude. Yes, prayers are answered.

A Prayer in the Dark

A dense fog descended upon the countryside as our family was en route to a neighboring city one evening for a night at the movies. We crept along the deserted highway, scarcely able to see more than a few feet ahead of the car. The headlights made an eerie glow in the impenetrable fog. Suddenly two figures loomed into view directly before us, standing in the middle of the road. My father slammed on the brakes—but too late. A sickening thud signaled the tragic collision. In shock, we stumbled out of the car to view the two bodies lying by the side of the road. The fog covered everything like a blanket of death. There was panic. The two men who had been hit were still alive but seriously injured. What to do? I signaled my friend to follow me up the road embankment. We were perhaps eleven years old at the time. Faintly visible were two other vehicles a few yards away, apparently having earlier collided with each other. Moments later, several other vehicles hurtled along the highway and crashed into the abandoned cars. Then silence. It was a scene of mass confusion. People were wandering around. I suddenly had the urge to pray. So my friend and I knelt on the embankment and offered a prayer to our Heavenly Father to watch over the injured and protect all the rest from further harm. We prayed that all would be well. We prayed for help. Seconds later, the lights of some vehicles came into view on the highway. The vehicles stopped, including one police car. Help had arrived. Things were quickly brought under control. Flares were deployed. An ambulance retrieved the injured and delivered them to the hospital. We later learned they would be all right. It was a night never to be forgotten, and two young boys learned firsthand the power of prayer.

2. DIVINE CALLING/DIVINE POWER

THEME: When the Lord extends a calling, He supplies the power and guidance to carry it out.

> *Who am I, that I should go unto Pharaoh, and that I should bring forth the children of Israel out of Egypt?* (Ex. 3:11)

> *Certainly I will be with thee.* (Ex. 3:12)

MOMENT OF TRUTH

When God called Moses to liberate His people, Moses was at first reluctant to accept, feeling inadequate to influence worldly powers and events to bring about divine purposes. But God made clear that He was all-powerful and that Moses was to go forward with inexorable power to perform the commissioned deeds. The Lord is able to soften hearts and cause enemies to feel favor toward His people. He is also able to intervene with awesome force, if necessary, to open the way for His will to be carried out. We need have no fear of answering a call from the Lord, for He will fight our battles for us and provide means for us to carry out any assignments.

MODERN PROPHETS SPEAK

Thomas S. Monson:

> When we come to the temple let us come with the spirit of prayer, with the spirit of inquiry, with the spirit of acquiescence to the Spirit of the Lord and He will give us the power to fill any position that comes to us. He who the Lord calls, the Lord qualifies. ("A New Temple Is Dedicated," *LDS Church News,* 1 Sept. 1990).

Gordon B. Hinckley:

> We are here to assist our Father in His work and His glory, "to bring to pass the immortality and eternal life of man" (Moses 1:39). Your obligation is as serious in your sphere of responsibility as is my obligation in my sphere. No calling in this church is small or of little consequence. All of us in the pursuit of our duty touch the lives of others. To each of us in our respective responsibilities the Lord has said: "Wherefore, be faithful; stand in the office which I have appointed unto you; succor the weak, lift up the hands which hang down, and strengthen the feeble knees" (D&C 81:5). "And in doing these things thou wilt do the greatest good unto thy fellow beings, and wilt promote the glory of him who is your Lord" (D&C 81:4). . . . You have as great an opportunity for satisfaction in the performance of your duty as I do in mine. The progress of this work will be determined by our joint efforts. Whatever your calling, it is as fraught with the same kind of opportunity to accomplish good as is mine. What is really important is that this is the work of the Master. Our work is to go about doing good as did He. ("This Is the Work of the Master," *Ensign,* May 1995, 71); see also *TGBH,* 65)

ILLUSTRATIONS FOR OUR TIMES

Who Is In Charge?
It is an overwhelming assignment to be called as a bishop—especially in a large, diverse ward with many complex challenges, and especially when you are a twenty-seven-year-old

graduate student with a young family. But after sincere prayer, and with the support of a loving wife, I humbly accepted, despite great feelings of inadequacy. It was an act of sheer faith. Following the sustaining vote that Sunday, I was shaking hands with a line of well-wishers outside the chapel and came to one member known somewhat for his candid method of expression. He was a merchant seaman who had seen many a dangerous campaign in his career. Looking directly into my eyes, he said, in all seriousness, "I just cannot understand how they could put an ensign in charge of the ship." There was a moment of silence as I searched for any kind of satisfying response. Then a light suddenly came on, and the Spirit whispered the words (which I dutifully announced): "An ensign is not in charge of the ship. The Lord is in charge of the ship." The brother listened and paused, then nodded his approval, and subsequently became one of my most stalwart supporters. It is always good to sail on a ship where the Lord is in charge.

3. FREEDOM AND THE ATONEMENT

THEME: Just as the Lord liberated the captive Israelites from Egyptian bondage, He has also put in place the saving truths, ordinances, and powers to bless our lives with redeeming grace through the atonement of Jesus Christ.

Let my people go. (Ex. 5:1)

MOMENT OF TRUTH

The historical Israelite deliverance and exodus is a pattern for the journey of liberation that each of us must complete as we accomplish our "exodus" from the bondage of sin and worldly entanglements toward a state of spiritual freedom. The journey toward the Promised Land is symbolic of our passage toward Zion, where we can raise our families in truth and light, and taste the joys of the gospel through obedience and righteousness. Just as the Lord liberated Israel through the shedding of the blood of the firstborn of the Egyptians, so He liberated us through the shedding of blood of His Only Begotten, that we might not perish, but have everlasting life. The consequences of sin pass over us through the process of faith, repentance, baptism, and the gift of the Holy Ghost.

MODERN PROPHETS SPEAK

Bruce R. McConkie:

And because it is the power of God that saves men, it includes both what the Lord does for us and what we must do for ourselves to be saved. On his part it is the atonement; on our part it is obedience to all that is given us of God. Thus the gospel includes every truth, every principle, every law—all that men must believe and know. Thus it includes every ordinance, every rite, every performance—all that men must do to please their Maker. Thus it includes every priesthood, every key, every power—all that men must receive to have their acts bound on earth and sealed eternally in the heavens. (*The Millennial Messiah: The Second Coming of the Son of Man* [Salt Lake City: Deseret Book, 1982], 98)

Gordon B. Hinckley:

I cannot be grateful enough for the Atonement wrought by my Savior and my Redeemer. Through His sacrifice at the culmination of a life of perfection—that sacrifice offered in pain unspeakable—the bonds of death were broken, and the resurrection of all became assured. Beyond this, the doors of celestial glory have been opened to all who will accept divine truth and obey its precepts. ("My Testimony," *Ensign,* Nov. 1993, 52; see also *TGBH,* 27–28)

ILLUSTRATIONS FOR OUR TIMES

Coming to an Understanding and Appreciation of the Atonement

The Passover symbolized and embodied the future sacrifice of our Lord and Savior Jesus Christ (see 2 Ne. 11:4):

The firstborn male lamb	The Only Begotten Son
The blood of the lamb saved	The blood of the Lord purified the faithful Israelites
No bones to be broken	As with the Lord (see John 19:31–36)
Partake of unleavened bread (no yeast)	The bread of life. As we partake of Him (taking His name upon us), we can be purified
This bread couldn't spoil or mold	It symbolized a repentant and purified person
Partake in haste	Respond enthusiastically to the offer of the Lord

The children of Israel were in slavery; Egypt held them in bondage. Likewise, we are in slavery and bondage to Satan because of sin. When the final plague was instituted during the Passover, the firstborn sons of Pharaoh and the Egyptians were taken and Israel was granted its freedom. We, likewise, are made free by the atoning blood of the Lord Jesus Christ.

4. REMEMBER THE COVENANT

THEME: Just as the Lord remembered His covenant promises to Abraham, Isaac, and Jacob by delivering Israel, so must we show through our daily obedience that we remember His goodness and honor His commandments.

> *Remember this day, in which ye came out from Egypt, out of the house of bondage; for by strength of hand the Lord brought you out from this place.* (Ex. 13:3)

MOMENT OF TRUTH

The Lord remembered Israel. He kept His covenant promises. To help the Israelites remember His miraculous intervention on their behalf, He instituted the Passover, with detailed rules and observances that reminded the people of His blessings to them and pointed to the atoning sacrifice of the Son. Following the infinite sacrifice of the Savior, the sacrament was instituted as a lasting memorial to His atoning redemption and as a means for us to remember our covenant promises and renew our commitment to obey the Lord's commandments. We must teach our children to remember always the goodness of the Lord and the necessity of living gospel principles.

MODERN PROPHETS SPEAK

Orson F. Whitney:

> This sacred memorial, a reminder to God's people of what he had done, and would yet do, was observed in Israel, by divine appointment, until the coming of Christ. The night before he was sacrificed, he, the great Paschal Lamb, after partaking of the ancient feast with his disciples, instituted in its stead the Lord's Supper, commanding them to observe it thenceforth. The Supper and the Passover were both designed to commemorate the Savior's atonement; but in the Passover the pointing was forward, to an event yet to come, while in the Supper the indication is backward, to an event that has already taken place. It was about the same hour of the day when the paschal lamb was offered in the temple at Jerusalem, that Christ died on Calvary, the substance and the shadow thus corresponding. (*Gospel Themes* [Salt Lake City: n.p., 1914], 113–14)

Joseph Fielding Smith:

> Partaking of the sacrament is one of the most sacred ordinances given to the Church. It is given in order that we may be brought in closer communion with the spirit of

the Lord and thus renew three most sacred covenants. They are: first, that we will take upon us the name of Jesus Christ; second, that we will always remember him; third, that we will always keep his commandments which he has given us. We are promised if we will do this that we will be blessed with the constant companionship of his spirit. If we have violated any one of these covenants, then there should be sincere repentance through which we receive forgiveness of the Church before we partake of the sacrament. (*AGQ,* 1:85)

ILLUSTRATIONS FOR OUR TIMES

The Doctrine of "Remember"

"Behold, I would exhort you that when ye shall read these things, if it be wisdom in God that ye should read them, that ye would remember how merciful the Lord hath been unto the children of men, from the creation of Adam even down until the time that ye shall receive these things, and ponder it in your hearts" (Moro. 10:3). Our spiritual growth cycle begins when we recognize and remember the goodness of God. There are many ways to "remember." As a young bishop, I tried to remember to do the things that the Lord would have me do. And it seemed like life was full, for I could never do everything I wanted to do. My mind would wander to the cares of the world. So to get away from the things of the world, I put a little penny in my shoe. Six years wearing that penny in my shoe helped me remember that it is the power of the Holy Ghost by which we learn to be ever mindful of the things of the Lord. "But the comforter, which is the Holy Ghost, whom the father will send in my name, he shall teach you all things and bring all things to your remembrance, whatsoever I have said unto you" (John 14:26).

King Benjamin taught that as we come to a knowledge of the glory of God, and have tasted of His love and received a remission of our sins, we should always remember the greatness of God and His goodness and long-suffering toward us, and we should humble ourselves and call upon His name daily. He promised if we will do this we will always rejoice and be filled with the love of God, and retain a remission of our sins; and we will grow in the knowledge of God and of that which is just and true (see Mosiah 4:12).

As a penny in the shoe was a reminder to me of the things of God, so can little notes at home or at work become little signs and reminders. One word—where I dress, or in the car, or above the dental intercom—would be a reminder. Yes, just one word—"remember." As soon as I would see the word, it would cause me to think: "I must keep Heavenly Father's commandments." "I must remember the goodness of God." "I must stay on the straight and narrow path." If I but remember—the word, the process, the action. Remembering becomes the key to motivation, because in remembering we become mindful of the love of God. Nephi said, "And I, Nephi have written these things unto my people, that perhaps I might persuade them that they would remember the Lord their Redeemer" (1 Ne. 19:18).

King Benjamin, in his great address, counseled many times that the people remember: "I say unto you, I would that ye should remember to retain the name written always in your hearts, that ye not be found on the left hand of God, but that ye hear and know the voice by which ye shall be called, and also, the name by which he will call you" (Mosiah 5:12).

All the covenants we have entered into with the Lord, whether baptism, priesthood or temple, rely upon the sacrament and the commitment and covenant we make at that time. In that prayer, the word *remembrance* or *remember* is mentioned twice. Remembrance becomes a key. At the sacrament table we not only recognize the goodness of God, but also remember it. Why? . . . That we might have His Spirit with us. "Remember [interesting to use that word in this verse] the worth of souls is great in the sight of God" (D&C 18:10). As we recognize and remember the goodness and tender mercies of God, we will begin to deepen our trust, our respect, and our love for God. We will begin to look to God and live.

The orthodox Jews wore phylacteries on the left hand or on the head (called a frontlet). Inside the pouch were scriptures written on parchment. The purpose was to help them remember. The orthodox Jews interpret their use in a highly spiritual way. As these are put on in the morning, they meditate in their morning service (see J. D. Douglas, *The New Bible Dictionary*).

In the book of Helaman we are told that when the people prosper and are rich in the things of the world, when they are delivered out of the hands of their enemies and when the Lord is doing all things for their welfare and happiness, they forget the Lord their God because of their ease and their great prosperity. It then becomes necessary for the Lord to chasten His people with terror, famine, pestilence, and death so that they will remember Him (see Hel. 12:2–3).

Sacrament in the Alps

Many years ago, at the conclusion of our mission experience in Germany, a friend and I were privileged to be invited by F. Enzio Busche, then one of the priesthood leaders in the West German Mission, to accompany him on a brief motor tour through southern Germany and Switzerland. He and his wife and sister picked us up in Frankfurt on 7 April 1960, and we headed south. Before long, the magnificent peaks of the Alps came into view on the southern horizon. It was not long thereafter that we were surrounded by these lofty reminders of God's creative hand. One of the most memorable hours during this pleasant journey came the next morning at Grindelwald in the heart of the Swiss Alps. It was Sunday, and since there was no branch of the Church to visit, we did the next best thing, as my journal recounts:

> We took the chairlift halfway up the Firstberg, and there, in a small protected hollow high above the valley floor overlooking those massive peaks—including among others the Eiger-Nordwand and the Jungfrau—we held a Sunday School. Although the sun was hot and we were sunburned, we had a spiritual feast—songs, speeches, lessons, and the sacrament. My companion and boyhood friend, Thomas Wood, conducted. Sister Busche opened with prayer. Fräulein Busche (Brother Busche's nonmember sister) and I gave short two-and-a-half minute talks, hers on impressions of Mormonism and mine on peace and brotherly kindness. Sister Busche led the song practice, I blessed and Tom passed the sacrament, Brother Busche led a discussion on love, and I closed with prayer. . . . You couldn't pick a more beautiful tabernacle. It reminded us of the words of Zenos as quoted in Alma 33 about worship being valid both in the fields and in the house, in closets or congregations, when it is sincere. Being in the midst of those peaks we thought, too, of the quotation in D&C 88:41–48 about the order of the universe and nature being kingdoms of God and testimonies of His majesty and power.

That worship session in the tops of the Swiss mountains is among my most prized memories of taking the sacrament, and a lasting reminder that the Author of life and salvation must always remain vividly in our minds and hearts, no matter where we are. By the way, Brother Busche's sister later joined the Church and continues to be our good friend. I will ever be grateful to the Busches for this experience long ago.

5. GUIDING LIGHT OF THE GOSPEL

THEME: The Lord provided means to guide the Israelites in their journey out of Egypt. Similarly, He provides for us the light of the gospel and the voice of prophecy so we might find our way safely back into His presence.

> *And the Lord went before them by day in a pillar of a cloud, to lead them the way; and by night in a pillar of fire, to give them light.* (Ex. 13:21)

MOMENT OF TRUTH

The Lord supplied miraculous means for marking the path of liberation and showing the Israelites the way to safety. No less miraculous are His blessings to us today, leading us from one milestone to the next in our journey for spiritual liberation. We have the scriptures, including the Book of Mormon; we have the voice of living prophets; we have the priesthood to provide authorized ordinances of salvation; we have the sealing ordinances of the temple; we have the Holy Spirit to illuminate our souls. Our blessings are overwhelming. Who are the pillars of light in the family? They are the parents of Zion who raise their children in light and truth and remind them always of the goodness of God in the past, the covenants of the present, and the hope of the future through the Atonement of Jesus Christ.

MODERN PROPHETS SPEAK

John Taylor:

> Associated as we are with the kingdom of God, we may reasonably expect, so long as we do our duty before the Lord, to have continual developments of light, truth, and intelligence that emanate from the great God, for the guidance, direction, salvation, and exaltation of this people, whether it relates to time or to eternity. (*The Gospel Kingdom: Selections from the Writings and Discourses of John Taylor* [Salt Lake City: Improvement Era, 1941], 39–40)

Spencer W. Kimball:

> President Heber J. Grant related an example of the revelations of the Lord to him. For twenty-two years he had felt the inspiration of the living God directing him in his labors. He wrote: "From the day that I chose a comparative stranger [Melvin J. Ballard] to be one of the apostles, instead of my lifelong and dearest living friend, I have known as I know that I live, that I am entitled to the light and the inspiration and the guidance of God in directing His work here upon the earth." (*TSWK,* 448)

ILLUSTRATIONS FOR OUR TIMES

Angels on Earth

We were discouraged that night. First of all, we were in a new environment far away from our extended families. Second of all, the matchbox student apartment was rather Spartan, bleak, and noisy. And third of all, there had been some minor misunderstanding between us, long since forgotten. My wife and I sat glumly pondering our options. Suddenly there was a knock on the door. Who could that be? A look through the peephole revealed Dick Byrne, our home teacher. He exuded his normal, jolly enthusiasm. "I was just driving along St. Paul Street," he said, "and had the feeling I should stop by! How are you?" Since melancholy cannot long survive in an atmosphere of sincere friendship, we quickly fell in with the spirit of rejuvenation.

"I had the feeling I should stop by!" The gospel is like that. In moments where you are staring downward, the Spirit suddenly illuminates your soul and you are able to look up instead—with hope and cheer. In moments where the shadows are gathering, the light suddenly enters your heart and fills you with radiance. In the Lord's plan, there are unseen angels who bear you up, just as there are angels on earth who just happen to stop by when the Spirit whispers to them that you have a need. The light of the gospel is strong enough to break through all of life's challenges with its warmth and peace. Thank heaven for that.

A Mother's Inspiration
The Lord is ever there to guide us and direct us in our lives. My mother was led like Nephi as she saved my older brother's life. It was during the busy berry-picking season. My brothers, Glen and James, were playing together under a tree in the front yard. After checking on the boys, my mother went into the house for a moment to finish making the beds. When she came back Glen was still there, but James was missing. One of the berry pickers told my mother he had seen James go toward the front gate. She ran to search for him there, and as she did, she noticed that there was water in the ditch. It should have been empty at that time of the week, but someone hadn't wanted their allotted water and had turned it down the ditch. She frantically searched the ditch and even felt around in the water where it went under the culvert, but didn't find James there. After a few more moments of searching, she returned to the ditch and saw James's shoes protruding from the culvert. She pulled his lifeless body from the water and put him over her arm with his head and feet down and her arms locked together. As she ran toward the road, water gushed from his mouth. She collapsed by the side of the road, and a neighbor came by in his car to take them to the fire station. The doctor met them at the fire station, and after examining James he said, "Take it easy, Mother, everything is all right. You saved your baby when you jolted the water out of him." The Lord was directing my mother that day as He inspired her to not only find James but to carry him over her arms in an unusual way, which saved his life.

SUMMARY

From the scriptural account of the Exodus, we renew our acquaintance with the miraculous way the Lord delivered Israel from bondage through the leadership of a great prophet. Similarly, we can be delivered from the bondage of carnality and sin through the redemption of Jesus Christ. The process of deliverance is simple and straightforward. Our Heavenly Father hears our sincere prayers of faith and declares His will through the scriptures and the words of living prophets. Through obedience to the principles of the gospel, and through the saving ordinances administered by authorized priesthood leaders, we are blessed with the effects of the Atonement in our lives. Partaking of the sacrament allows us to renew our covenants and our commitment to obedience.

CHAPTER FOURTEEN

"FOR I AM *the* LORD THAT HEALETH THEE"

Reading Assignment: Exodus 15–20; 32–34.

Addtional Reading: Psalm 78; 1 Corinthians 10:1–11; D&C 84:19–27.

> *Here, then, is eternal life—to know the only wise and true God; and you have got to learn how to be gods yourselves, and to be kings and priests to God, the same as all gods have done before you, namely, by going from one small degree to another, and from a small capacity to a great one; from grace to grace, from exaltation to exaltation.* (Joseph Smith, King Follett Discourse, *HC* 6:306)

THEMES *for* LIVING

1. Singing Songs of Praise and Thanksgiving
2. Divine Nurture
3. Stewardship and Accountability
4. The Commandments of God
5. Seek the Face of the Lord Always
6. The Lesser Order

INTRODUCTION

The experiences of the liberated Israelites in the wilderness, following their exodus from Egypt at the hand of God, provide valuable lessons for us today. In many respects, Israel was like a tender growth being transplanted to a new environment, or like seeds being placed into a strange new growth terrain or garden. Perhaps we can discern the following six aspects of "spiritual horticulture": (1) The freedom to grow is similar to the deliverance of Israel from foreign bondage, an event evoking the most heartfelt feelings of gratitude and praise. (2) The essential nutrients relate to the continual flow of divine nurture in our lives. (3) The caretakers of the garden are the prophets and stewards called to prepare the way and build up the kingdom of God. (4) The principles of vitality sustaining all natural growth are like the commandments of the Lord, which sustain our spiritual development and well-being. (5) The sunshine on which all life depends has its symbolic counterpart in the radiant image of God and His glorious presence—just as we are commanded to "seek the face of the Lord always" (D&C 101:38). (6) The indispensable moisture for the growing plants is similar to the doctrines of the priesthood, which distil upon our souls "as the dews from heaven" (D&C 121:45).

1. SINGING SONGS OF PRAISE AND THANKSGIVING

THEME: The successful exodus of Israel was marked with a universal celebration of praise and thanksgiving. Our relationship with our Heavenly Father and His Son is incomplete without our constant expression of gratitude and thanksgiving for blessings received.

I will sing unto the Lord, for he hath triumphed gloriously. (Ex. 15:1)

MOMENT OF TRUTH

Moses and the children of Israel celebrated their liberation with songs of praise and glory unto the Lord. We must remember to recognize the hand of the Lord in all things, and give Him praise and honor for the infinite blessings He bestows upon us.

MODERN PROPHETS SPEAK

Bruce R. McConkie:

> What then are the sacrifices of the true Christian? They are unending praise and thanksgiving to the Father who gave his Only Begotten Son as a ransom for our sins;

they are everlasting praise to the Son for the merits and mercies and grace of his atoning sacrifice; they are obedience to the laws of the Lord; these are the sacrifices that please God. Or as it was said by the Lord himself to his other sheep: "Ye shall offer up unto me no more the shedding of blood; yea, your sacrifices and your burnt offerings shall be done away, for I will accept none of your sacrifices and your burnt offerings. And ye shall offer for a sacrifice unto me a broken heart and a contrite spirit. And whoso cometh unto me with a broken heart and a contrite spirit, him will I baptize with fire and with the Holy Ghost" (3 Ne. 9:19–20). (*Doctrinal New Testament Commentary* [Salt Lake City: Bookcraft, 1965–73], 3:242)

Howard W. Hunter:

> We need to express gratitude. We need to be expressive of appreciation for the good things that come to us, both from the Lord who has blessed us abundantly and also from those who do things for us. A few years ago, the teacher of a seminary class gave each of the pupils several sheets of paper and asked them to write the names of all the people to whom they owed a debt of gratitude. This was an interesting experiment. They wrote feverishly for the first part of the hour and then commenced to gaze off into space, not because they had run out of names, but because they concluded that the task was insurmountable. There are thousands and hundreds of thousands of people to whom we owe debts of gratitude. Isn't that true? People we have never seen. People we have never heard of but who have made contributions to our lives. (*THWH,* 94–95)

ILLUSTRATIONS FOR OUR TIMES

Gratitude, a Cardinal Virtue

I recall a student of mine who was taking a missionary preparation class. He was a good boy, but very sufficient in his own way. He was in control. He had his "things," and life was okay. He was planning on a mission, more or less. Everyone around him was going on a mission. Then it happened—he read the Book of Mormon with real intent and fervor for an assignment to get extra credit. While reading a chapter over and over, something happened inside. He exclaimed the following week, "Brother Ed, it's true, it's true! The Book of Mormon is true! I've got to leave on my mission right now. I can't believe all the Lord has done for me. I can't wait. I've got to go now. I'm so thankful for all my blessings." The young boy was on fire. The Spirit had touched his heart. His whole soul was full of gratitude. The result? A desire to serve, born of gratitude for the Lord. When one can be moved through love and receive a feeling of gratitude, righteousness is always the result, just as forgetting and ingratitude will eventually result in sin.

A Father's Surprise

I remember one day, many years ago, leaning down on the front porch of our home to tie the shoes of my young son. He said simply, "Thank you, Dad." That should not be surprising to a father, but it was to me. I was thrilled and overwhelmed. These words came from a young man with daunting developmental/autistic challenges. He had never said these words to me spontaneously before in his life—not in all the years since the Lord, in His goodness and wisdom, had sent such a precious and perfect soul into our lives. Verbal communication of this kind or any kind was just not in his nature, but this day he spoke three words of gratitude. I hugged him for joy. He seemed pleased. It made me wonder how the Lord views His sons and daughters. We all have developmental challenges—of the spiritual kind. Not until we come closer to a Christlike nature do we feel true gratitude in our hearts for the blessings of the gospel. Maybe, on those all-too-rare occasions where we give sincere and humble utterance to the true feelings of thankfulness in our hearts, the Lord looks down and is surprised and pleased.

2. DIVINE NURTURE

THEME: Just as the Lord provided nourishment for the Israelites in the wilderness, He provides spiritual manna for all the faithful who hunger and thirst after righteousness.

And Moses said unto them, This is the bread which the Lord hath given you to eat. (Ex. 16:15)

MOMENT OF TRUTH

The Lord heard the murmuring of the Israelites wandering in the wilderness and provided water, quail, and manna for their nourishment. As long as they followed the counsel of His prophet, they were sustained on their journey toward the Promised Land. Moses turned to the Lord with each challenge he faced. With a tree He made the waters of Marah sweet. When they needed bread, the Lord told Moses He would "rain" bread from the sky and prove the people if they would be obedient. In the evening, the Lord would give them flesh—quail would be provided. Surely these temporal nourishments would provide a daily reminder of the goodness of God and their total dependence upon Him.

MODERN PROPHETS SPEAK

Joseph B. Wirthlin:

> First, we should plant and nurture the seed of faith in the Lord Jesus Christ, our Savior and Redeemer. We each should develop the faith of Nephi to do the things

the Lord has commanded (see 1 Ne. 3:7), knowing that all commandments are given for our good. Nephi expressed his faith in these words: "If it so be that the children of men keep the commandments of God he doth nourish them, and strengthen them, and provide means whereby they can accomplish the things which he has commanded them." When the Lord instructed Nephi to build a ship, his brothers called him a fool to think he could do it. He told them: "If God had commanded me to do all things I could do them. If he should command me that I should say unto this water, be thou earth, it should be earth" (1 Ne. 17:3, 50). (*Finding Peace in Our Lives* [Salt Lake City: Deseret Book, 1995], 215)

Jeffrey R. Holland:

As Jacob confronted and defeated Sherem, the first great anti-Christ in the Book of Mormon, his concluding testimony remains with us as an echo of the allegory of the olive tree. It is crucial counsel to all: "Behold, after ye have been nourished by the good word of God all the day long, will ye bring forth evil fruit, that ye must be hewn down and cast into the fire?" (Jacob 6:7–8). (*Christ and the New Covenant: The Messianic Message of the Book of Mormon* [Salt Lake City: Deseret Book, 1997], 72)

ILLUSTRATIONS FOR OUR TIMES

Manna for the Soul

On one occasion a number of years ago, I was in the study of my home, pondering spiritual matters in preparation for a series of Church meetings to begin the next day. I was feeling rather inadequate in the face of callings that could come, and in my own way somewhat in the mood of Alma the Younger when he was "harrowed up" in the remembrance of his sins (Alma 36:13, 17). In this penitent frame of mind, I said a prayer asking for forgiveness for weaknesses and requesting spiritual strength to meet the challenges of life. Then as I pondered further, I rather absentmindedly let the scriptures fall open to a page in the Doctrine and Covenants. The first words that came into view were these: "Behold, your sins are forgiven you; you are clean before me; therefore, lift up your heads and rejoice" (D&C 110:5).

The coincidence shocked me into focusing completely on the process of spiritual rejuvenation. I felt an overpowering sense of peace, and spent some sweet moments thinking about the sublime gift of the Savior in atoning for our sins. It was a moment of manna for the soul. In gratitude, I thanked my Heavenly Father for His infinite blessings upon me and my family, and made a commitment to do a better job in helping to build the kingdom. Spiritual manna takes many forms in our lives, but the peace that comes from forgiveness and renewal is one of the greatest. The words of Amulek spring to mind: "Yea, I would that ye would come forth and harden not your hearts any longer; for behold, now is the time and the day of your salvation; and therefore, if ye will repent and harden not your hearts, immediately shall the great plan of redemption be brought about unto you" (Alma 34:31).

3. STEWARDSHIP AND ACCOUNTABILITY

THEME: The kingdom of God is a kingdom of order, organized according to a structure of participatory teamwork and delegation, with a prophet at the head to carry out the will of the Lord.

> *Be thou for the people to God-ward, that thou mayest bring the causes unto God: . . . Moreover thou shalt provide out of all the people able men, such as fear God, men of truth, hating covetousness; and place such over them, to be rulers of thousands, and rulers of hundreds, rulers of fifties, and rulers of tens.* (Ex. 18:19, 21)

MOMENT OF TRUTH

In the battle against the offender, Amalek, the Israelites under Joshua prevailed as long as Moses' hands were outstretched on top of the hill, supported on either side by Aaron and Hur (see Ex. 17:9–13). Thus we see the importance of noble "counselors" in the grand program of God's kingdom. Similarly, Moses was able to sustain the awesome burden of presiding over so vast a people as the Israelites only because his father-in-law, Jethro, wisely taught him the art and practice of careful delegation and prioritizing of the work (see Ex. 18:17–26).

MODERN PROPHETS SPEAK

James E. Talmage:
> "Who then is that faithful and wise steward, whom his lord shall make ruler over his household, to give them their portion of meat in due season?" (Luke 12:42). The faithful steward is a good type of the apostles, individually or as a body. As stewards they were charged with the care of the other servants, and of the household; and as to them more had been given than to the others, so of them more would be required; and they would be held to strict accountability for their stewardship. (*Jesus the Christ* [Salt Lake City: Deseret Book, 1983], 409)

Joseph Fielding Smith:
> The Lord guarded these revelations with the greatest care. After the Prophet Joseph Smith had made copies and had compiled them for publication, he and Oliver Cowdery, John Whitmer, Sidney Rigdon and William W. Phelps were called by revelation to be

"stewards" over the revelations and commandments, and the Lord said that "an account of this stewardship will I require of them in the day of judgment" (D&C 70:3–4). This indicates the importance with which the Lord held his divine word. Precautions were taken in forwarding these revelations to Zion, which was the "seat and a place to receive and do all these things" (i.e. publish the revelations and do the printing for the Church) (see D&C 69:6). (*Church History and Modern Revelation* [Salt Lake City: The Church of Jesus Christ of Latter-day Saints, 1946–49], 2:25)

ILLUSTRATIONS FOR OUR TIMES

An Eternal Doctrine

Stewardship and accountability are eternal verities. God the Father, Elohim, created the earth through His firstborn Son, Jehovah, who later would be the Savior of the world as the Lord Jesus Christ. The example of acting for and in behalf of another is usually described as stewardship. The priesthood is the power and authority of God given to man on earth to act in His stead for the salvation of all mankind. The brethren who bear the priesthood of God will have an accounting of their stewardship as it pertains to the oath and covenant of the priesthood. Likewise, all people who have been chosen or called to any eternal or mortal calling will stand accountable before God. We must not only fulfill our personal stewardships, but in leadership roles we should require an accounting of everyone we have a responsibility for.

Spiritual Compounding

Over the years, I have enjoyed helping neighborhood youngsters improve their reading skills. One young deacon was about three grade levels behind. Somehow, reading didn't have quite as much allure as sports and other activities. So we tried something different. At the suggestion of one of my friends, a reading expert, we started keeping score. Every few days, he would spend an hour reading out loud to me from a book or article of interest to him—and above his current school reading level. There was a catch: he had to correct each and every error before going on. We timed each session carefully and calculated the number of words read. Then he plotted the score on a sheet of graph paper after each session. We set a goal and settled on an appropriate reward for success. He could see the line that his progress was tracing over time. His line started to rise consistently—even dramatically. A light went on. He was not accounting to his teachers anymore; he was accounting to himself. That was different. Being highly competitive, he became more tolerant of the exercise and actually took satisfaction from seeing his results improve rapidly. Over a span of just fourteen sessions he brought his reading skill up three grade levels—where he needed to be. His comprehension also improved significantly as his fluency rose. It was a matter of changing his perspective on things—and giving him a little self-confidence. It's called stewardship and accountability—line upon line. It works with anyone.

The same principle is central to the gospel. We all have roles and assignments in our different stewardships. We can measure and monitor our progress. We can seek the best gifts and apply our talents for the good of others with increasing skill. As we learn more, we can report our progress to our leaders and to the Lord. We can watch ourselves grow and take courage in our progress. We can build our self-confidence. Every management expert knows that progress that is measured regularly—and rewarded—expands. This is also true in the Church, where the spiritual blessings of stewardship and service are being compounded every day.

4. THE COMMANDMENTS OF GOD

THEME: Through His prophet, Moses, the Lord provided universal laws to govern all human behavior. The giving of these laws was a gift designed to bring peace, harmony, well-being, and rich spiritual blessings into the lives of God's children.

> *Now therefore, if ye will obey my voice indeed, and keep my covenant, then ye shall be a peculiar treasure unto me above all people: for all the earth is mine.* (Ex. 19:5)

MOMENT OF TRUTH

The Lord established his covenant with Israel, and the Ten Commandments were given. These commandments are repeated in the Book of Mormon (see Mosiah 12:33–36; 13:12–24), the Doctrine & Covenants (see D&C 42:18–27; 59:5–16), and the New Testament (see Matt. 5:17–37). These commandments deal with relationships of eternal significance—God, family, and fellow man. We are taught that eternal life is establishing a relationship with our Heavenly Father and our Savior (see John 17:3). The basic unit of the Church is the family. The Proclamation on the Family makes clear the role of family here and hereafter. The sealing ordinance makes clear the priority that marriage and family play in our eternal lives (see D&C 131, 132). The way we treat our fellowmen is truly a demonstration of our feelings for the Lord Jesus Christ (see Matt. 25:40). We should love God and our fellowmen because it does fulfill all the Law and the Prophets (see Matt. 22:36–40).

MODERN PROPHETS SPEAK

Mark E. Petersen:
> Some people have the idea that the Ten Commandments were first given by Moses when he directed the children of Israel and formulated their code of laws. This is not

the case. These great commandments are from the beginning and were understood in righteous communities in the days of Adam. They are, in fact, fundamental parts of the gospel of Jesus Christ, and the gospel in its fullness was first given to Adam (*DS,* 1:94–96). (*Adam: Who Is He?* [Salt Lake City: Deseret Book, 1976], 58)

Matthias F. Cowley:

It is erroneously supposed by many that the laws observed by Israel previous to Christ's atonement were almost entirely obliterated, being, as many think, all fulfilled in His mission on earth. A little reflection upon this subject will correct this error in the minds of all who are diligently and honestly seeking for the truth. The Ten Commandments themselves are pre-eminently a part of the Gospel of Christ. When the young man came to the Messiah to learn the way of salvation, he was enjoined to observe the commandments, "Thou shalt not kill, Thou shalt not commit adultery," etc. (Matt. xix;16–21.) Whatever was discontinued after the atonement was that which had been established to symbolize and teach the great atonement to come. The offerings of lambs and bullocks in sacrifice was dispensed with, as it had pointed to the coming atonement now fulfilled in the Messiah. It was replaced by the sacrament, the broken bread and the wine, both blessed and administered to the disciples and enjoined as a continuous ordinance to keep bright in memory the sufferings, atonement and resurrection of our Lord Jesus Christ. (*Cowley's Talks on Doctrine* [Chattanooga: Ben. E. Rich, 1902], 151)

ILLUSTRATIONS FOR OUR TIMES

The Ten Commandments Today

1. *Thou shalt have no other gods before me* (Ex. 20:3).

God is first and foremost, and His purpose is His family's happiness. Therefore, in putting Heavenly Father first, we build up the kingom of God first—hence we bless our brothers and sisters.

2. *Thou shalt not make unto thee any graven image* (Ex. 20:4–6).

Idolatry has been a problem with mankind since the beginning of time. We cannot put any other god, thing, material possession, position, station, fame, fortune, vocation, hobby, or cause before our devotion to God.

3. *Thou shalt not take the name of the Lord thy God in vain* (Ex. 20:7).

Reverence for God is demonstrated by not profaning the name of God, swearing, or making oaths in the name of God in a light-minded manner. We could also take His name in vain by not honoring our covenants.

4. *Remember the sabbath day, to keep it holy* (Ex. 20:8–11).

The Sabbath is the day we rest from our temporal affairs, renew our covenants with God, allow the Lord to sanctify us on His day, and prepare and renew ourselves for the coming week.

5. *Honour thy father and thy mother* (Ex. 20:12).

This is demonstrated by a reverential attitude toward our parents, by obedience to them in righteousness, and by bringing joy and honor to their names.

6. *Thou shalt not kill* (Ex. 20:13).

The wanton act of destroying the life of a child of God is wrong. To protect our homes, our religion, and our families is the right of each individual. The killing of an individual is not necessarily wrong (as in defensive response); the reason for the death as the result of another's actions is the factor in determining whether it is a sin or not.

7. *Thou shalt not commit adultery* (Ex. 20:14).

This is crystal clear with regard to what the sin is. The real problem is staying off the road toward adultery and fornication. This requires staying on the straight and narrow path, with absolutely NO flirtatious behavior.

8. *Thou shalt not steal* (Ex. 20:15).

This applies to all acts of integrity and honesty. One cannot claim another's possessions, ideas, or what is due another in any form.

9. *Thou shalt not bear false witness* (Ex. 20:16).

Lies, gossip, and rumors in any form must be stopped before they can be passed along. A good test: Is it kind? Is it true? Is it necessary?

10. *Thou shalt not covet* (Ex. 20:17).

When one becomes covetous, it can be the beginning of countless sins. The Ten Commandments, as well as all the commandments of God, are interrelated and interwoven to such an extent that in breaking one, we break another or are led to another sin. Such is covetousness.

5. SEEK THE FACE OF THE LORD ALWAYS

THEME: The Lord commanded Israel to seek Him and His presence, to be His peculiar covenant people (i.e., His "own"), and to be holy in their walk of life. To abdicate this divine directive would provoke the Lord and relinquish promised blessings.

> *And Moses said unto the people, Fear not: for God is come to prove you, and that his fear may be before your faces, that ye sin not.* (Ex. 20:20)

MOMENT OF TRUTH

The Lord commanded Moses to sanctify the people and prepare them to meet Him. But the Israelites were profoundly frightened at the prospect of encountering Him, and withdrew themselves for fear of their lives (see Ex. 20:18). Moreover, when Moses went to the mount to obtain the tables from the Lord, the Israelites persuaded Aaron to fashion a golden calf for them to worship. Thus their hardness of heart provoked the Lord, whose only design was to prepare them to come into His presence. His directive to the people in the meridian of time was: "Harden not your hearts, as in the provocation, in the day of temptation in the wilderness: When your fathers tempted me, proved me, and saw my works forty years. Wherefore I was grieved with that generation, and said, They do alway err in their heart; and they have not known my ways" (Heb. 3:8–10). And in our time He has commanded: "And seek the face of the Lord always, that in patience ye may possess your souls, and ye shall have eternal life" (D&C 101:38).

MODERN PROPHETS SPEAK

Bruce R. McConkie:
> Patience, also, involves an exercise of forbearance under provocation as illustrated in the celestial principle, "whosoever shall smite thee on thy right cheek, turn to him the other also" (Matt. 5:38–42; 3 Ne. 12:38–42). Patience in righteousness leads to perfection and eternal life. Thus Paul wrote that "by patient continuance in well doing" the saints "seek for glory and honour and immortality, [and] eternal life" (Rom. 2:7). And by revelation in our day the Lord commanded: "Continue in patience until ye are

perfected" (D&C 67:13); "And seek the face of the Lord always, that in patience ye may possess your souls, and ye shall have eternal life" (D&C 101:38; *MD*, 557–58). (*Doctrinal New Testament Commentary* [Salt Lake City: Bookcraft, 1965–73], 3:273)

Bruce R. McConkie:

> We shall write living words, words that flow from the pen of prophecy, dipped in the ink of inspiration. Our message shall be one of joy and rejoicing for those who treasure up revealed truth, who desire righteousness, who seek the face of the Lord. It will be one of weeping and mourning for those who "know not God, and that obey not the gospel of our Lord Jesus Christ" (2 Thes. 1:8). (*The Millennial Messiah: The Second Coming of the Son of Man* [Salt Lake City: Deseret Book, 1982], 3)

ILLUSTRATIONS FOR OUR TIMES

Facing Our God

The Lord was encouraging Israel to come unto Him, yet because of their lack of righteousness and faith, they could not bear the thought of being in His presence. Alma had these same feelings (see Alma 36:13–14). Alma made changes. Israel yielded to old beliefs and made a golden calf. A person often turns to his old ways when conversion to Christ is not internalized or complete. This was the case with Israel. I have witnessed this sad scenario time and time again when people attempt to make lasting changes. They start out so well with diligence and determination, then it happens—one day they get discouraged, they feel hopeless, and an old friend comes by with questioned values and standards. The rest is history, and sin is the result. Israel, in their moment of trial, succumbed to the traditions and sins of the past. We often do the same unless we are prepared through faith, prayer, the word of God, and the Spirit. Then we will choose to "face our God" and keep his commandments.

The Custodian

One of my earliest recollections of Church as a young child growing up in southern Alberta was learning that the chapel was the house of God. There was a faithful and loyal older brother who served as the custodian of the building, and I would often see him on Sundays, silver-haired and patriarchal, coming up and down the stairs and walking the halls as he went about his duties. Somehow, a few of us junior members got the impression, because he had a room in the chapel, that he was the Lord—especially since he appeared to us, with his wrinkles of authority and wisdom, rather grandfatherly, if a little stern. It took some gentle counsel from parents to convince us otherwise. Since then, I have often thought that the naïve innocence of the child's perspective is perhaps the best preparation for later life, for the whole purpose of life is to seek the face of the Lord—literally—and aspire to be worthy of His actual presence. There will be a time, as our experience in the temple confirms, that the faithful and pure will indeed be ushered into the presence of the Lord: "and the keeper of the gate is the Holy One of Israel; and he employeth no servant there" (2 Ne. 9:41). Perhaps it is not so naïve after all to think of the Lord as the spiritual custodian of our eternal home.

6. THE LESSER ORDER

THEME: The Lord imparts to us truth and blessings according to our willingness and capacity to receive, adding grace for grace, line upon line, "as the dews from heaven."

My presence shall go with thee, and I will give thee rest. (Ex. 33:14)

If now I have found grace in thy sight, O Lord, let my Lord, I pray thee, go among us; for it is a stiffnecked people; and pardon our iniquity and our sin, and take us for thine inheritance. (Ex. 34:9)

MOMENT OF TRUTH

The Israelites were unwilling to abide by the higher order (Melchizedek) and thus were given a lesser order of outward commandments, principles, and covenants called the Law of Moses. This was to be their schoolmaster until their hearts and minds were prepared to receive more light and truth. They were content to let Moses be their intermediary with Deity and noted with trepidation that his face shone with glory after he had spoken with the Lord.

MODERN PROPHETS SPEAK

Bruce R. McConkie:

> One of the greatest prophecies for which there has been a partial fulfillment up to this time, and which awaits a far grander and greater fulfillment in the days ahead, is given in these words: "Behold, the days come, saith the Lord, that I will make a new covenant with the house of Israel, and with the house of Judah: not according to the covenant that I made with their fathers in the day that I took them by the hand to bring them out of the land of Egypt; which my covenant they brake, although I was an husband unto them, saith the Lord." The Mosaic covenant, the law of carnal commandments, the lesser law, the preparatory gospel—all these shall have an end. They will be replaced with the gospel, the higher law, the eternal fullness that includes the covenant God made with Abraham. (*A New Witness for the Articles of Faith* [Salt Lake City: Deseret Book, 1985], 548)

Neal A. Maxwell:

> It should not surprise us that we need to be schooled in lesser laws on our way to acquiring the eternal attributes. For instance, as we strive for love or humility in relationship

to our fellowmen, we can commence by practicing the schoolmaster virtue of politeness. "Politeness is not really a frippery. Politeness is not really even a thing merely suave and deprecating. Politeness is an armed guard, stern and splendid, vigilant, watching over all the ways of men; in other words, politeness is a policeman." (*We Will Prove Them Herewith* [Salt Lake City: Deseret Book, 1982], 65)

ILLUSTRATIONS FOR OUR TIMES

Struck by Lightning

One of the earliest home teaching (actually "ward teaching") assignments I had as a young Aaronic Priesthood holder was with a grand old English gentleman of short stature who lived on the edge of our small Canadian prairie town and ran a garden nursery. He was the only person I have ever known who had reportedly been struck by lightning—and lived. He had a small hole above his nose and between his eyes as a memorial to the event, and I recall being keenly interested in his unusual appearance and the story behind it. We would do our rounds and give the lessons faithfully each month, hoping that our reminders to live the gospel would be a blessing to the families assigned to us.

Since then, I have often thought about how truth comes to us. The doctrines of the gospel typically do not come as bolts of lightning, but gradually, quietly, here a little and there a little. We are not customarily struck by the lightning of doctrine, but rather it distills upon our souls over many years of time, "as the dews of heaven" (see D&C 121:45; 128:19; Deut. 32:2; Prov. 19:12; Hosea 14:5). We can thank our Father in Heaven for His patience in allowing us to grow up with the gospel over time, as it often takes many years for the simplest of truths to take root in our hearts and souls.

SUMMARY

"For I am the Lord that healeth thee" (Ex. 15:26). This phrase aptly encapsulates all principles of spiritual growth. All vitality flows from the Lord, and all rejuvenation comes from divine sources. Through the liberating blessings of the gospel we are planted in fertile soil, enjoy the nurture of spiritual manna, benefit from the guidance of ordained prophets and stewards in the kingdom of God, find our daily anchor in the covenant commandments, bask in the prospect of seeking and finding the face of the Lord, and feel the enlarging and edifying distillate of pure doctrines upon our soul. Zion is the garden of the Lord. May we live worthy to grow and develop within its secure walls.

CHAPTER FIFTEEN

"LOOK *to* GOD *and* LIVE"

Reading Assignment: Exodus 11–14; 21:1–9.

Additional Reading: John 3:14–16; 1 Nephi 17:41; Alma 33:18–22; 37:46–47; Helaman 8:13–15.

> *Remember all thy church, O Lord, with all their families . . . That thy church may come forth out of the wilderness of darkness, and shine forth fair as the moon, clear as the sun, and terrible as an army with banners.* (Joseph Smith, Dedication of the Kirtland Temple, D&C 109:72)

THEMES *for* LIVING

1. Shared Leadership: Many Hands to Bear the Load
2. Humility versus Taking Authority unto Ourselves
3. Faith Does Not Murmur
4. Look to Christ and Live

INTRODUCTION

When the Israelite nation was liberated from Egyptian bondage, it must have presented an ominous and impressive spectacle as it moved across the wilderness toward the promised land. The ancient image of the army of God has been used in modern times as a reminder of the strength and forward thrust of God's purposes in establishing His kingdom in the latter days: "But first let my army become very great, and let it be sanctified before me, that it may become fair as the sun, and clear as the moon, and that her banners may be terrible unto all nations" (D&C 105:31; see also D&C 5:14, 109:73). The idea of Israel's banners is well established in the scriptures. Isaiah exclaims: "Lift ye up a banner upon the high mountain, exalt the voice unto them, shake the hand, that they may go into the gates of the nobles" (Isa. 13:2). General Moroni lifted up the banner (title) of liberty (Alma 46:12–13, 36). Moses lifted up the brass image of a fiery serpent to remind the Israelites to think of the Savior and be saved (Num. 21:9). We might also suppose that the liberated Israel had flags and banners hoisted during its march. If so, what those banners may have depicted is unknown; however, if we allow our imagination some license, we could suppose that such banners would represent some of the principles that should govern the movement of the army of God. These might include (1) *teamwork* (everyone bearing a fair part of the load), (2) *loyalty* (rather than pridefully finding fault with leaders or usurping their power), (3) *faith* (rather than murmuring and complaining), and (4) *vision* (keeping our eyes focused on the Savior, as on the brazen serpent that Moses lifted up on the pole).

1. SHARED LEADERSHIP: MANY HANDS TO BEAR THE LOAD

THEME: The kingdom of God is an effective matrix of organized leadership with a prophet at its head and many inspired workers to move the work forward.

> *Would God that all the Lord's people were prophets, and that the Lord would put his spirit upon them!* (Num. 11:29)

MOMENT OF TRUTH

Moses was weighed down with the responsibilities of leading the increasingly resistant and murmuring Israel. The Lord provided seventy elders to lighten his load. Joshua appealed to Moses to restrain two of the elders who were prophesying in the camp, but Moses saw it quite differently. He wished that all the Lord's people would be moved by the spirit of prophecy, for that is the way the Lord would have it. Spiritual teamwork is one hallmark of a Zion society.

MODERN PROPHETS SPEAK

M. Russell Ballard:
> We spend many hours in various meetings talking about them and planning how
> we can bless their lives. Can you see the potential power of the priesthood and

auxiliaries working together to systematically reach out to families and individuals? I believe that the answers to the activity problems facing our wards and stakes can be found in the priesthood and auxiliary councils. (*Counseling with Our Councils: Learning to Minister Together in the Church and in the Family* [Salt Lake City: Deseret Book, 1997], 7)

L. Tom Perry:

The next friendships in my life were those with my missionary companions. We developed a real closeness from working together for a common purpose and being on our knees together so many times during the day. There is something special about friendships that develop from engaging in service. Do you remember the example of the Savior as he met with the apostles at the Last Supper? He wanted to serve them, so he girded himself with a towel and went to each of them and washed their feet. Then after washing their feet, he said, "Ye call me Master and Lord: and ye say well; for so I am. If I then, your Lord and Master, have washed your feet; ye also ought to wash one another's feet. For I have given you an example, that ye should do as I have done to you" (John 13:13–15). (*Living with Enthusiasm* [Salt Lake City: Deseret Book, 1996], 50–51)

ILLUSTRATIONS FOR OUR TIMES

That All Might Be Profited

On one occasion when I was serving in a stake presidency, a young man came to me to complain that various leaders in his ward were giving him conflicting advice when he asked them for help on a challenging marital situation. He felt that the Relief Society president had the most valuable counsel to give, and was troubled that the bishop hadn't come up with any better solutions himself. I assured him, first of all, that it was the individual's responsibility to prayerfully consider all options and then make a decision based on correct principles. Next, I reminded him that each one of his mentors would look at his situation with a different level of empathy and understanding, viewed from a unique set of personal experiences—and thus diversity of opinion is inevitable. But my main point can best be understood through the following excerpt of the letter I wrote to him a few days later:

A bishop is the common judge in Israel, which means that he must decide on matters of serious moral consequence and must issue temple recommends as well as monitor progress of priesthood brethren as to their advancement. The bishop is also the presiding high priest in the ward and is responsible for receiving the funds contributed. The bishop is nearly always a loving and concerned man, is frequently a radiant and warm individual, and typically an effective counselor.

He is almost *never* the single and ultimate font of wisdom for all members of his ward in all matters and at all times. . . . It seems to me that the Lord intended his Church to be a community of mutual support and mutual trust. There is a natural tendency for us to look to the leaders for guidance and direction; surely this is proper. However, the Church—if I understand 1 Corinthians 12 and D&C 46 correctly—is a complete network of resources where even the humblest and least visible member is of value and worth. In fact, it might be from the most unlikely source that inspiration might flow to one in need (not just from the bishop or Relief Society president). The reason that not all have all gifts is, it seems to me, so that we might have a need to depend on one another, "that all may be profited thereby" (D&C 46:12).

2. HUMILITY VERSUS TAKING AUTHORITY UNTO OURSELVES

THEME: The priesthood of God operates on principles of humility and meekness. Pride and arrogance have no place in spiritual leadership.

> *Now the man Moses was very meek, above all the men which were upon the face of the earth.* (Num. 12:3)

MOMENT OF TRUTH

Miriam and Aaron complained against Moses and claimed for themselves equal prophetic gifts. They were rebuked by the Lord, and Miriam was exiled for a week with leprosy. The Lord upheld his servant Moses as the chosen prophet and extolled his greatness as one who can speak face to face with the Lord. We must avoid finding fault with the Lord's anointed and instead sustain and uphold our ordained leaders with faith and humility.

MODERN PROPHETS SPEAK

James E. Faust:

> With faith in the Lord and humility, a priesthood leader may confidently expect divine assistance in his problems. . . . Brethren, we can learn, we can study, we can comprehend the basic things we need to know as members of God's holy priesthood. We can learn the giant truths and teach them with intelligence and understanding to those who come to learn. We can also lean upon the strengths of others whose talents are greater than our own. (in Russell M. Nelson, *The Power within Us* [Salt Lake City: Deseret Book, 1988], 179)

Neal A. Maxwell:

> Another example is Aaron, who, though he erred significantly, still has one of the Holy Priesthoods named after him, and his calling by a prophet is still cited as a model. How generous and merciful is our God! It is interesting to read how each time Aaron erred, a loving and meek Moses mediated for him and prayed for him, reflecting the growing compassion and mercy Moses had. Now Aaron has the veneration of generations, for the Lord tutored him and magnified him. (*Even As I Am* [Salt Lake City: Deseret Book, 1982], 89)

ILLUSTRATIONS FOR OUR TIMES

Things Will Work Out

The middle-aged ward member came into my office, took a seat, and proceeded to outline in some detail an account of certain failings of another ward member, counseling the bishop that it should be attended to.

"That is a concern," I responded. "Wait just a minute. That member is still here after the meeting. Let me go and have that person join us right now so that we can get things cleared up." My visitor looked surprised, so I added, trying to repress the twinkle in my eye, "It's always best, when there is a concern, to get the parties together and talk things out."

"Well," the member said, "I suppose things will work out." Then the person stood up and left my office, never to complain to me about anyone again.

3. FAITH DOES NOT MURMUR

THEME: The Lord's choicest blessings are reserved for the faithful. Murmuring and fear are not qualities of the righteous.

> *The Lord is with us: fear them not.* (Num. 14:9)

MOMENT OF TRUTH

The children of Israel displayed a chronic tendency to murmur, find fault, focus on memories of the abundance of their former Egyptian life, and complain against Moses and the Lord. In his wrath, the Lord plagued them with a surfeit of meat so they would be consumed in their greed. When their twelve captains were sent to spy out the promised land, ten of them succumbed to fear in the face of the enemy and brought back news of hopelessness. Only Joshua and Caleb had the faith to see Israel victorious with the help of the Lord. The Lord swears that the murmuring people will not enter the promised land.

MODERN PROPHETS SPEAK

Marvin J. Ashton:

> I am acquainted with a wife and mother who is chained securely at the present time to a life-style of murmuring and criticism. She is the first to point out faults in her husband or to repeat neighborhood gossip. How damaging is a habit that permits fault-finding, character assassination, and the sharing of malicious rumors! Gossip and caustic comments often create chains of contention. These chains may appear to be very small, but what misery and woe they can cause! (*Be of Good Cheer* [Salt Lake City: Deseret Book, 1987], 66)

Ezra Taft Benson:

> In 1492 Christopher Columbus set sail from Spain in three small ships with eighty-seven men. For seventy days they sailed across the uncharted sea. As early as the seventeenth day the men began to murmur in fear. From the twentieth day on, Columbus was hard put to restrain them from mutiny, but when we read the log that he kept, we are struck by the force of three words appearing again and again at the end of the day's events: "We sailed on." What courage, what trustworthiness, what faith these words reveal! (*God, Family, Country: Our Three Great Loyalties* [Salt Lake City: Deseret Book, 1974], 210)

ILLUSTRATIONS FOR OUR TIMES

Love Conquers Murmuring

Doubt and fear, with the trailing problem of murmuring, are the most devastating tools the devil uses to destroy missionary work. I have witnessed this many times. I have seen missionaries overcome this doubt and fear with love, faith, knowledge, preparation, and experience. They became mighty instruments in the hands of the Lord. As they open their mouths, the Spirit speaks for them and they realize that their faith in God has given them strength to do all things.

The Business of Saving Souls

When we first moved into the ward, we soon became aware of a controversy that was fomenting a good deal of discussion in hallway and classroom alike. It seemed that an evergreen tree near the chapel's front entrance had originally been planted somewhat too close to the building during the construction phase in 1937. Now the mature tree was growing at a considerable angle to the wall, which was of concern to many. The ward seemed to be divided into factions. One of them wanted to remove the tree, another insisted on doing nothing, and a third voted to trim the tree aesthetically. I noted that priesthood meetings were not infrequently given over to debating the issue.

Finally, we came to church one Sunday and found that the tree had completely disappeared. It seems one resourceful brother, having had his fill of the bickering and murmuring, had come on Saturday and taken the tree out all by himself, removing all the debris as clean as a whistle. He showed up at the meetings that day with a peaceful and satisfied look on his face, and many if not most of us said a silent prayer of thanks in our hearts that someone had had the wisdom to exorcise the spirit of contention and arguing over inconsequential matters. After that, it seemed much easier to get back to the business of saving souls.

4. LOOK TO CHRIST AND LIVE

THEME: By keeping our vision focused on the Savior and His gospel, we will have the sure guidance needed to complete our mortal journey successfully.

When he beheld the serpent of brass, he lived. (Num. 21:9)

MOMENT OF TRUTH

The Lord responded to the faithless murmuring of the Israelites by sending fiery serpents to humble them. He commanded Moses to set up a token of safety in the form of a brass serpent—signifying the Redeemer—so that all who would focus their eyes on this sign would live. The symbolism, which has endured over the millennia, is a powerful reminder that we must take upon ourselves the name of Christ and live by all the principles and ordinances of the gospel if we are to have the hope of salvation.

MODERN PROPHETS SPEAK

Joseph Fielding Smith:

> In the third chapter of John, we have the account of the Lord's conversation with Nicodemus in which the Lord said: "And as Moses lifted up the serpent in the wilderness, even so must the Son of man be lifted up: That whosoever believeth in him should not perish, but have eternal life." Do you recall how in the wilderness when they came among the serpents, the Lord told Moses to put a brazen serpent upon a pole and they who looked upon it should be healed, for some of them were dying when bitten? That was done in the similitude of our Lord's being lifted upon the cross, so that all who believed in him should not perish. (*DS*, 1:22)

Orson Pratt:

> "They shall take up serpents, or if they drink any deadly thing it shall not hurt them." This promise of our Great Redeemer was also made to every creature in all the world who should believe the gospel. The use of this miraculous gift was to preserve life, in case any believer should accidentally be bitten by a poisonous serpent as Paul was (see Acts 28); or should unintentionally swallow a deadly poison, as the sons of the prophets did (see II Kgs. 4). Jesus promised that it should not hurt them. When the Israelites were bitten by poisonous serpents, they were healed by simply looking at a brazen serpent which the Lord commanded Moses to raise up in the wilderness; so the believers in Christ can prevail against deadly poisons by simply looking to Him in faith; for Jesus cannot fail to fulfill His promise to the believer. (*Orson Pratt's Works* [Salt Lake City: Deseret News Press, 1945], 85)

ILLUSTRATIONS FOR OUR TIMES

The Mission of the Church

The process of coming unto Christ is shown dramatically with the Israelites as they were compelled to humility; then, being teachable, they looked upon the brazen serpent (symbol of Christ) and were saved. This process is duplicated in everyone's life in order to be saved. We become humbled either by the situation or by the word (it is always better by the word). Then, with broken heart and contrite spirit, we come unto Christ by faith unto repentance. This process is duplicated every day as people give up the world, humble themselves before God, and come unto Christ. This is the mission of the Church and kingdom of God—to invite all to come unto Christ.

SUMMARY

We can learn a great deal from the lessons of liberated Israel. Many hands lighten the load of building the kingdom of God. When everyone learns his or her duty and acts in all diligence (D&C 107:99), progress is leveraged and productivity magnified. When we display loyalty and sustain our Church leaders, rather than finding fault or second-guessing, blessings are multiplied and the work is moved forward. When we act on faith, and replace the tendency to murmur or complain with an active display of enthusiasm and hope, the Lord blesses us with the spirit of courage and success. And above all, when we keep our vision focused obediently on the Savior as our model and exemplar, and keep His commandments faithfully, we are immunized against the fiery darts of temptation and the consequences of sin.

CHAPTER SIXTEEN

"ALL THAT *the* LORD SPEAKETH, THAT MUST I DO"

Reading Assignment: Numbers 22–24; 31:1–16

Each and every intelligent being will be judged according to the deeds done in the body, according to his works, faith, desires, and honesty or dishonesty before God; every trait of his character will receive its just merit or demerit, and he will be judged according to the law of heaven. (Brigham Young, JD 8:154)

THEMES *for* LIVING

1. The Honor of God
2. The Will of God
3. The Justice of God

INTRODUCTION

From the sad commentary about Balaam, a fallen prophet, we learn valuable lessons about motivation—both the kind that leads to destruction as well as the kind that will lead to great spiritual blessings. People who are spiritually motivated aspire to the honor of God and seek to do His will. They reject the kind of life where the heart and will are anchored in the world. They know that spiritual wealth is infinitely more glorious than worldly goods and titles. They fear God by respecting His justice; they love Him by keeping His commandments and striving to emulate His Son in all things. The honor of God, the will of God, and the justice of God are the interacting themes of the story of Balaam.

1. THE HONOR OF GOD

THEME: Great blessings flow when we aspire to the honor and glory of God, rather than to the honor and pride of the world.

I went out to withstand thee, because thy way is perverse before me. (Numbers 23:32)

MOMENT OF TRUTH

Balaam was outwardly committed to upholding the honor of God, but in his heart he heeded the beckoning enticements of worldly wealth and prestige. Thus his vision was impaired as he set out on his journey, and he could not at first see the angel of the Lord standing to prevent his own self-destruction. Allowing the entanglements of pride and vain ambition to take root in our hearts will obscure our view of heavenly objectives.

MODERN PROPHETS SPEAK

David O. McKay:

> And yet how common insincerity is. What a miserable old humbug of a world we are living in, full of trickery and dishonesty and deceit of every kind. Society is cursed with affectation, business is honeycombed with dishonesty. The political world abounds in duplicity and chicanery, there is sham and pretense and humbuggery everywhere. Some use big words they do not understand, and some lay claim to knowledge which they do not have, and some parade in dresses which they cannot pay for; the life of many a man and many a woman is one colossal lie. We say things which we do not mean, express emotions which we do not feel, we praise when we secretly condemn, we smile when there is a frown on the face of the heart, we give compliments when we are really thinking curses, striving a hundred times a week to make people think we are other than we are. It is a penitentiary offense to obtain money under false pretenses. . . . But how many other things are obtained, do you think, by shamming and pretending, for which there is no penalty but the condemnation of Almighty God? Yes, it is a sad, deceitful, demoralized world in the midst of which we find ourselves; but thank God there are hearts here and there upon which

we can ever more depend. We have tested them, and we know them to be true. (*Man May Know for Himself: Teachings of President David O. McKay* [Salt Lake City: Deseret Book, 1967], 142)

Dallin H. Oaks:

> As we seek to determine whether we have become true Latter-day Saints—inwardly as well as outwardly—it soon becomes apparent that the critical element is progress, not longevity. The question is not how much time we have logged, but how far we have progressed toward perfection. As Elder Neal A. Maxwell has said, "Life is not lineal, but experiential, not chronological, but developmental" (*Ensign,* December 1986, 23). The issue is not what we have done but what we have become. And what we have become is the result of more than our actions. It is also the result of our attitudes, our motives, and our desires. Each of these is an ingredient of the pure heart. (*Pure in Heart* [Salt Lake City: Bookcraft, 1988], 138)

ILLUSTRATIONS FOR OUR TIMES

I Brewed It Myself

As a graduate student at the Johns Hopkins University many years ago, I learned that keeping the honor of God and the honor of the world separate is much less difficult if you have wise allies looking out for you. My senior faculty advisor, Dr. Harold Jantz, world-renowned in his discipline, was also a careful student of human affairs and human values. He regularly convened seminars in his home, where he served the graduate students coffee and tea. At my first such event, he served all of my colleagues their coffee or tea, and then turned to me and handed me a cup of herbal tea. "It's rose hips," he said with a friendly twinkle in his eyes. "I brewed it myself from my rose plants. I know you don't drink coffee or regular tea, so this is for you." His generosity was matched only by his magnanimous respect for one's values and standards. Thereafter, at each such occasion, he hospitably prepared and served me a portion of delicious and nutritious rose-hip tea. With such a hospitable host and mentor, I couldn't have compromised my values—even if I had wanted to!

2. THE WILL OF GOD

THEME: The purposes of God cannot be thwarted or altered by the hand of man. Our mission is to align ourselves with full devotion to the will of God and do all in our power to carry it out faithfully.

Out of Jacob shall come he that shall have dominion. (Num. 24:19)

MOMENT OF TRUTH

Balaam, enticed by promises of worldly rewards, succumbed three times to the entreaties of Balak to seek from the Lord a cursing of Israel. Was Balaam expecting the Lord to alter His decreed purposes? Was he somehow expecting the Lord to let him "have his cake and eat it too"—as if divine approval could ever flow out of imperfect devotion? It was not to be. He had no recourse but to declare the word of the Lord as it was given.

MODERN PROPHETS SPEAK

Joseph F. Smith:

> It is true that we are in a measure of the earth, earthy; we belong to the world. Our affections and our souls are here; our treasures are here, and where the treasure is there the heart is. But if we will lay up our treasures in heaven; if we will wean our affections from the things of this world, and say to the Lord our God, "Father, not my will, but thine be done," then may the will of God be done on earth as it is done in heaven, and the kingdom of God in its power and glory will be established upon the earth. Sin and Satan will be bound and banished from the earth, and not until we attain to this condition of mind and faith will this be done. (*Gospel Doctrine: Selections from the Sermons and Writings of Joseph F. Smith* [Salt Lake City: Deseret Book, 1939], 261)

George Q. Cannon:

> While I say we are sinners, I believe it is possible for us to live so as to have no sin held against us. We should have the spirit of repentance constantly in our hearts. Our hearts should be touched and softened by it, so that we will be mellowed under its influence and that we shall have such a horror of sin and such a desire for righteousness that when we become conscious that we have thought or said or done anything contrary to the mind and will of God, we will instantly bow down and acknowledge our sins before the Lord and repent of them with all our hearts and obtain forgiveness for them. (*Gospel Truth: Discourses and Writings of President George Q. Cannon* [Salt Lake City: Deseret Book, 1987], 127)

ILLUSTRATIONS FOR OUR TIMES

Doctrine of Balaam Versus the Gospel of Jesus Christ

In the Revelation of John the Beloved, the residents of the branch of the Church at Pergamos were censured because of some who "hold the doctrine of Balaam, who taught Balak to cast a stumbling block before the children of Israel" (Rev. 2:14). Any leader who would act contrary to the will of God by deflecting the Saints from the principles of righteousness and toward worldly or carnal patterns of living can be said, therefore, to practice the doctrine of Balaam. By way of contrast, leaders who act in all holiness under the direction of the Spirit act in harmony with the gospel of Jesus Christ.

The will and ways of the Lord's ultimate plan cannot be frustrated or destroyed. Balaam, having refused to curse Israel, still within his heart wanted the things of the world. He asked the Lord three times and the Lord still told him "no." It is always dangerous to seek anything other than the will of the Lord, either out of greed or the fear of man. The beloved Prophet, Joseph Smith, attempted to appease Martin Harris, and the results are well documented—he never recovered the missing 116 pages, and he lost his privileges "for a season" (D&C 3:14).

3. THE JUSTICE OF GOD

THEME: There is always a consequence for action. Good follows good, and evil follows evil. The justice of God is inexorable.

And the Lord spake unto Moses, saying, Avenge the children of Israel of the Midianites.
(Num. 31:1–2)

MOMENT OF TRUTH

The inhabitants of the promised land, ripened in iniquity, were to be removed by the Israelites. Balaam, evidently behind a campaign to cause the Israelites to compromise their covenant promises, was destroyed along with the Midianites. His example of infamy lives on as the prototype of the prophetic figure who was "called" of God for a great work, but not "chosen," because of his lack of pure devotion and his inability to turn away from the temptations of worldly honor and glory. By heeding the warning footprints he left in the sands of time, we can go a different way that will lead to harmony, peace, and spiritual acceptance of the Lord.

MODERN PROPHETS SPEAK

Dallin H. Oaks:
> Our Heavenly Father knows the desires of our hearts and will judge us accordingly. He will punish evil desires and reward righteous ones. We can suppress evil desires and substitute righteous ones. This involves education and practice. President Joseph F. Smith taught that the "education . . . of our desires is one of far-reaching importance to our happiness in life" (*Gospel Doctrine* [Salt Lake City: Deseret Book,

1919], 372). Through our divinely granted willpower we have ultimate control over our desires. But the desires of our hearts are so deep-seated that it may take many years of practice for us to be sure that education and practice have perfected our desires to the point where all are entirely righteous. (*Pure in Heart* [Salt Lake City: Bookcraft, 1988], 149)

Neal A. Maxwell:

Do we always know, however, what consequences will flow from certain decisions? Many times, not. Part of living consists of learning, personally and vicariously, what actions produce what consequences. When we govern ourselves by correct principles, we also govern our consequences. (*But for a Small Moment* [Salt Lake City: Bookcraft, 1986], 130)

ILLUSTRATIONS FOR OUR TIMES

In God's Own Due Time

The justice of God works in "God's own due time." When we wish that the enemies of the Church would suffer the immediate retribution of a just God, we forget that the Lord has His own timetable, often conditioned on the concept of "ripened in iniquity" (Ether 2:9, 9:20; D&C 18:6) or being "ripe for destruction" (Alma 10:19). An interesting example is the case of President Martin Van Buren, whom the Prophet Joseph Smith visited on 29 November 1839 at the White House to seek redress for the persecution of the Saints in Missouri. The Prophet writes: "We found a very large and splendid palace, surrounded with a splendid enclosure, decorated with all the fineries and elegancies of this world. . . . [W]e met the President, and were introduced into his parlor, where we presented him with our letters of introduction. As soon as he had read one of them, he looked upon us with a kind of half frown, and said, 'What can I do? I can do nothing for you! If I do anything, I shall come in contact with the whole state of Missouri'" (*HC* 4:40). Van Buren refused to secure peace for the embattled Saints. By contrast, our Lord and King would never say to us, "Your cause is just, but I can do nothing for you" (*HC* 4:80). Instead, He says, "For behold, this is my work and my glory—to bring to pass the immortality and eternal life of man" (Moses 1:39). The Lord does *everything* for us, even giving His life that we may live and have eternal peace.

As to the justice of God in the case of Van Buren, the Prophet declared: "May he never be elected again to any office of trust or power, by which he may abuse the innocent and let the guilty go free" (*HC* 4:89). Subsequently, Van Buren was soundly defeated in the presidential election of 1840 (receiving only sixty electoral votes) and again in the election of 1848 (in which he did not receive a single electoral vote). It took a few years for the first effects of justice to be felt, the remaining effects being left once again in the hands of God until judgment day itself, as is the case for all of us.

SUMMARY

The best summary of the doctrine of this chapter is a statement made by the Savior: "But seek ye first the kingdom of God, and his righteousness; and all these things shall be added unto you" (Matt. 6:33; 3 Ne. 13:33). Furthermore, in the words of Paul: "Be not deceived; God is not mocked: for whatsoever a man soweth, that shall he also reap" (Gal. 6:7). Balaam placed the honor of God in second place after worldly honors; he put his own desires and longings before the will of God, and therefore experienced the justice of God. It is the same for us all. The eternal purposes of the Lord are inexorable; they will come about, with or without our participation. Far better for us to cultivate spiritual motivation and bring our will into harmony with the principles of righteousness and salvation.

CHAPTER SEVENTEEN

"BEWARE LEST THOU FORGET"

Reading Assignment: Deuteronomy 6; 8; 11; 32.

Additional Reading: Deuteronomy 4; 7:1–4; 13:1–8; 34.

> *The building up of Zion is a cause that has interested the people of God in every age; it is a theme upon which prophets, priests and kings have dwelt with peculiar delight; they have looked forward with joyful anticipation to the day in which we live; and fired with heavenly and joyful anticipations they have sung and written and prophesied of this our day; but they died without the sight; we are the favored people that God has made choice of to bring about the Latter-day glory.* (Joseph Smith, *HC* 4:609–10)

THEMES *for* LIVING

1. Remember Your Covenants—Fear God and Keep His Commandments
2. Avoid Pride and Self-Righteousness/Forgetting God
3. Beware of Negative Influences
4. Celebrate God's Goodness

INTRODUCTION

The message of Moses' final exhortation to the people of Israel has keen relevance for us today. He enjoined the Saints of his day to cultivate and maintain a spiritual environment where they would remember to keep their covenant promises, avoid prideful self-righteousness, protect themselves and their families from polluting influences, and express love and gratitude for the goodness of God.

1. REMEMBER YOUR COVENANTS—FEAR GOD AND KEEP HIS COMMANDMENTS

THEME: With salvation at stake, we must create a spiritual environment, cultivate a righteous walk, and assure that our hearts and minds are set upon the Lord and His goodness.

> *And thou shalt love the Lord thy God with all thine heart, and with all thy soul, and with all thy might. And these words, which I command thee this day, shall be in thine heart: And thou shalt teach them diligently unto thy children, and shalt talk of them when thou sittest in thine house, and when thou walkest by the way, and when thou liest down, and when thou risest up.* (Deut. 6:5–7)

> *All the commandments which I command thee this day shall ye observe to do.* (Deut. 8:1)

MOMENT OF TRUTH

In his last sermon, Moses provided for Israel his final instructions. He memorialized the pattern of godly living that would edify and save Israel. We must fear God by keeping His commandments and honoring our covenant promises. We must show our love for God through devotion and obedience. We must constantly remind ourselves to have an eye single to the glory of God. We must diligently teach our children these things.

MODERN PROPHETS SPEAK

Spencer W. Kimball:

> Too many of our wives and mothers prefer the added luxuries of two incomes to the satisfactions of seeing children grow up in the fear and love of God. We golf and boat and hunt and fish and watch sports rather than solemnize the Sabbath. Total morality is found neither among the people nor among the leaders of the state and

nation. Personal interests and ulterior motives block the way. Old Man "Rationalization" with his long beard is ever present to tell us that we are justified in these deviations, and because we are not vicious enough to be confined in penitentiaries we rationalize that we are not failing to measure up. The masses of the people are perhaps much like those who escaped destruction in the ancient days of this continent. The Lord said to them: O all ye that are spared because ye were more righteous than they [the slain ones], will ye not now return unto me, and repent of your sins, and be converted, that I may heal you? (3 Ne. 9:13). (*The Miracle of Forgiveness* [Salt Lake City: Bookcraft, 1969])

John A. Widtsoe:

How to Become Worthy. (1) Faith in God. Men make themselves worthy of receiving the Priesthood by fearing God. That means that candidates for ordination to the Priesthood must acknowledge the existence and overshadowing power of our Father in heaven. They must have learned to love Him to such a degree that they yield themselves to Him with all their strength. The fear of God is the love for God—a love so strong that men fear to offend by disobeying His will. (*Priesthood and Church Government* [Salt Lake City: Deseret Book, 1939], 49)

ILLUSTRATIONS FOR OUR TIMES

A Formula for Success

As Moses delivered the final words of the Lord to the Israelites, he made it clear that we must do the following: fear (reverence) our God; love our God; remember the covenants; keep His commandments, and teach these things diligently unto our children.

Moses' valedictory address truly encompasses all things that we should do. Within each of these main topics rests a multitude of doctrines, principles, and concepts that will illuminate the mind and heart and quicken the soul to action. All the prophets since Moses have declared the same teachings.

- **Reverence for our God** – Respect and esteem for all of His perfection in all things and His goodness to His children.

- **Love our God** – We express affection and gratitude to God for all things and demonstrate our love through obedience.

- **Remember the covenants** – We keep in our minds and our hearts the covenants made. When we put other things in their place we forget God and our covenants. It is imperative always to remember, thus having the blessing of the Spirit.

- **Keep the commandments** – passing the test in life is reflected in obedience to the commandments of God. Obedience brings righteousness and all of its trailing blessings.

- **Teach these things diligently to your children** – There is no greater role of parents than to teach their children. Teaching the word has a greater power, when received, to cause your children to do good than anything else.

Wise Leadership

Our daughter Stephanie has done a courageous thing. As a way of remembering the covenants and assuring a wholesome environment for her young growing family, she and her husband decided a year ago to forego television viewing in the home altogether. Instead, they are building up a library of uplifting and interesting video programs for the family to watch. With church, music lessons, gymnastics, sports, school lessons, and other active involvements occupying their time, they are finding that television programs—often inane and superficial at best, and degrading and violent at worst—are not missed. It is an admirable thing for parents to take leadership in controlling what influences come into the home. During the time of Moses, the Lord warned the people to reject the culture of idolatry and wickedness around them: "Neither shalt thou bring an abomination into thine house, lest thou be a cursed thing like it: but thou shalt utterly detest it, and thou shalt utterly abhor it; for it is a cursed thing" (Deut. 7:26). Modern communications technology has both a corrupting as well as an elevating and enriching dimension; parents are wise to take a firm stand in deploying the positive elements of modern culture and rejecting that which is intolerable to the Spirit and draws minds and hearts away from the fear and love of God.

2. AVOID PRIDE AND SELF-RIGHTEOUSNESS/ FORGETTING GOD

THEME: When we forget to recognize the hand of God in all things, and instead take credit for our own prosperity, then surely the days of our security are shortened, and destruction is at the door.

> *Beware that thou forget not the Lord thy God . . . And thou say in thine heart, My power and the might of mine hand hath gotten me this wealth.* (Deut. 8:11, 17)

MOMENT OF TRUTH

It is God's desire that we flourish spiritually and temporally. His covenant promises provide for an increase in our posterity, a gathering place for our security, and a bounteous outpouring of truth and enlightenment. But all is contingent on our obedience and faithfulness. God will have a humble people. When pride enters into the picture, instability and disharmony are inevitable consequences (the curse that Moses refers to in Deut. 11:26–28). We must avoid pride and instead give honor and glory to God as the font of all our blessings.

MODERN PROPHETS SPEAK

Harold B. Lee:
> "The worst fear I have about this people is that they will get rich in this country, forget God and his people, wax fat, and kick themselves out of the Church and go to hell. This people will stand mobbing, robbing, poverty and all manner of persecution and be true. But my greatest fear is that they cannot stand wealth" [Brigham Young]. Many years of experience have proved that statement to be a prophecy that has been fulfilled. (*Decisions for Successful Living* [Salt Lake City: Deseret Book, 1973], 212)

Joseph Smith:
> I then addressed them and gave much instruction calculated to guard them against self-sufficiency, self-righteousness, and self-importance; touching upon many subjects of importance and value to all who wish to walk humbly before the Lord, and especially teaching them to observe charity, wisdom and fellow-feeling, with love one towards another in all things, and under all circumstances. (*HC* 3:383)

ILLUSTRATIONS FOR OUR TIMES

I Did It Myself
In prosperity, we often forget God and think of our own efforts as the reason for our success—a big mistake. Pride and self-righteousness have led so many away from God. Pride destroyed the people of Noah's time, and the Jaredites and Nephites. Self-righteousness takes its toll a soul at a time. I have been saddened because people say, "I know this is best. The Lord told me personally to follow my own revelations," or, "I did it myself, therefore I want the honor and glory." Sound familiar? That is the step that leads people away from God.

3. BEWARE OF NEGATIVE INFLUENCES

THEME: With baseness rampant in today's world, it is imperative that we beware of negative influences and peer pressure.

> *If thy brother . . . son . . . daughter . . . wife . . . or thy friend, which is as thine own soul, entice thee secretly, saying, Let us go and serve other gods . . . Namely, of the gods of the people which are round about you . . . Thou shalt not consent unto him, nor hearken unto him.* (Deut. 13:6–8)

MOMENT OF TRUTH

As the Israelites were tempted by others to serve and worship other gods, the Lord was adamant that they should not listen to them. In fact, the Lord suggested that these people who were tempting them should be stoned to death. This seems rather harsh to our culture and our finite mortal minds. However, we should take a step back and realize that if we worship false gods and do not keep the commandments, we will have separated ourselves from God, and indeed we will die a spiritual death. We cannot take lightly the matter of worshiping and loving our God.

MODERN PROPHETS SPEAK

David B. Haight:

> I believe that our Father planted into our souls a special ingredient that, if used, will influence us toward heavenly things. Families or individuals wondering how to better share the gospel or to show deeper concern for new members, or missionaries wanting to touch the hearts of those they are teaching, have available to them this heavenly influence. It may bring to us our greatest joy. It can help us overcome fear, peer pressure, hatred, selfishness, evil, and even sin. This special ingredient, which is powerful beyond words, was explained by the Savior himself when he was asked which was the great commandment of the law. He said: "Thou shalt love the Lord thy God with all thy heart, and with all thy soul, and with all thy mind. This is the first and great commandment. And the second is like unto it, Thou shalt love thy neighbour as thyself. On these two commandments hang all the law and the prophets" (Matt. 22:37–40). Love is this divine ingredient. It alone describes what can be our perfect relationship to our Heavenly Father and our family and neighbors, and the means by which we accomplish his work. (*A Light unto the World* [Salt Lake City: Deseret Book, 1997], 124)

Neal A. Maxwell:

> Some have little faith which then fails, because they can't stand the peer pressure, the shame and scorn heaped upon them by the world. They simply cannot learn to "despise the shame of the world" (see 2 Ne. 9:18), and they let go of the iron rod and slip away. Learning to despise the shame of the world means coming to think nothing of it, just as in taking no heed of temptation (see D&C 20:22). (*Lord, Increase Our Faith* [Salt Lake City: Bookcraft, 1994], 99)

ILLUSTRATIONS FOR OUR TIMES

By Your Very Presence

My companion and I had been asked by the mission president, Theodore M. Burton, to open up some of the smaller cities in the state of Hesse, north of Frankfurt, Germany. One of these, Bad Wildungen, was a resort community with a somewhat aristocratic aura of self-sufficiency. Part of our strategy to gain acceptance in the city was to meet with the local high school officials and seek the opportunity to lecture to the students and give English lessons. The principal in charge demurred. We responded to his hesitation by saying that we would gladly agree not to make any mention of Church matters whatsoever. His response was memorable. "I understand that you will not present any doctrine here. However, by your very presence you may influence my students."

Thus he showed his clear understanding that the missionaries were conveying by their deportment, appearance, attitude, language, and spirit something of the message that their words were intended to convey, and he played into the hands of the adversary by blocking entry into his schools. Looking at things from an opposite perspective, how wise it would be if parents, teachers, and civic leaders would understand more fully the prodigious impact that peers can have on our children, and take steps more effectively to supplant negative influences with the positive influences of the gospel.

4. CELEBRATE GOD'S GOODNESS

THEME: It is imperative that we elevate our minds to God through edifying expressions of praise and celebration. Songs of glory, language of praise, poetry of honor, sayings of truth, artwork of beauty and dignity—all these are reminders of our divine heritage and our noble birthright.

> *And Moses came and spake all the words of this song in the ears of the people.* (Deut. 32:44)

MOMENT OF TRUTH

Moses taught the people to cultivate the highest form of expression in remembering and celebrating God's goodness. He taught them songs of praise that kept the covenant ideas and commitment alive in their hearts. He taught them to think in terms of the "Rock of their salvation" (Jesus Christ) (see Deut. 32:15, 18, 30–31). He used words that edified and lifted, and rehearsed God's triumph in unforgettable terms (see Deut. 32:10–12). Moses was also explicit in his images of warning for Israel, that they might be stirred up to remembering the Lord their God.

MODERN PROPHETS SPEAK

James E. Talmage:
> Prior to the construction of the Tabernacle in the wilderness, and indeed during the early stages of the memorable journey from Egypt, the people of Israel had a certain depository for sacred things, known as the Testimony. This is definitely mentioned in connection with the following incident. Under Divine direction a vessel of manna was to be preserved, lest the people forget the power and goodness of God, by which they had been fed. (*The House of the Lord* [Salt Lake City: Deseret Book, 1968], 16)

Neal A. Maxwell:
> Recollect the deepest moments of marital and familial joy, whether in rejoicings, reunions, or reconciliations, when "because of the great goodness of God" there was a "gushing out of many tears" (3 Ne. 4:33); when your "heart [was] brim with joy"(Alma 26:11). Yet this was but a foretaste of the ultimate homecoming, when our cups will not only be brim but will run over without ceasing. (*Not My Will, But Thine* [Salt Lake City: Bookcraft, 1998], 143)

ILLUSTRATIONS FOR OUR TIMES

Celebrate from the Heart

For years, my wife and I have cultivated a spiritual activity of a personalized kind that has generated many fond memories for us and our family. From time to time, both of us have put into poetic form our heartfelt feelings and musings about the gospel of Jesus Christ. On occasion, these are also set to music, and we have the joy of celebrating the blessings of our Father in Heaven in our own form of religious praise and thanksgiving. As an example, my wife was asked once by a friend, a Relief Society president in a nearby ward, to help her come up with a memorable idea for teaching service to the sisters of the ward. It turned out that my father-in-law had taken ill at the same time, and we were driving down to the hospital to visit him. On the way, my wife developed the idea of writing a poem about how faith, love, and service form an interlocking web of good deeds that make up the fabric of our gospel life. She wrote down her thoughts in a poem entitled "On the Loom of the Lord," which she shared, in its initial version, with her friend. The piece has particular relevance for our family, since it turned out that my wife's visit of service and compassion at the sickbed of her father was the last opportunity to show her love to him. He passed away the next morning.

Celebrate in the Goodness of Our God

We ought to be so excited, and, better yet, enthusiastic, for all that our Heavenly Father and our Savior have given us. We tend to be so negative when all around us are the blessings of our God. Lehi expressed it well: "But behold, the Lord hath redeemed my soul from hell; I have beheld his glory, and I am encircled about eternally in the arms of his love" (2 Ne. 1:15). Alma likewise suggested to us to sing the song of redeeming love: "And again I ask, were the bands of death broken and the chains of hell which encircled them about, were they loosed? I say unto you, Yea, they were loosed, and their souls did expand, and they did sing redeeming love. And I say unto you that they are saved" (Alma 5:9). "And now behold, I say unto you, my brethren, if ye have experienced a change of heart, and if ye have felt to sing the song of redeeming love, I would ask, can ye feel so now?" (Alma 5:26). Every day is a day of celebration if we but look to see our blessings, never forgetting the goodness of God in all things. The illustration of God's handiwork and nurturing of His children is ever present.

SUMMARY

The greatest agent of change is the purifying, ennobling influence of the Holy Spirit of God in our lives. Therefore, we should nurture a positive spiritual environment in our homes and communities where the Spirit can touch our lives with truth and reinforce our fervent desires to do good. Moses taught a comprehensive program of spiritual redemption centered on the coming atonement of Jesus Christ. The program can be summarized in four steps: (1) honor the covenant through obedience to gospel principles, (2) avoid pride and destructive self-righteousness, (3) defend against unrighteous influences, and (4) cultivate a life of gratitude and thanksgiving as expressed through a spiritual walk and celebratory expressions of praise and glory unto God. We can learn much from the chronicles of God's dealings with his ancient covenant people. All of the principles taught by the prophets of God in those days are eternal in nature and central to the restored gospel in our times.

CHAPTER EIGHTEEN

"BE NOT AFRAID . . . *for the* LORD THY GOD IS *with* THEE"

Reading Assignment: Joshua 1–6; 23–24.

Additional Reading: Joshua 7; 14.

> *Every man should be willing to be presided over; and he is not fit to preside over others until he can submit sufficiently to the presidency of his brethren.* (Joseph F. Smith, Improvement Era, 21:105)

THEMES *for* LIVING

1. The Lord Will Magnify His Leaders
2. Save Your Family by Sustaining Your Leaders
3. The Lord Will Fight the Battles of the Faithful
4. Choose to Follow the Lord

INTRODUCTION

The Old Testament portrait of Moses and his successors at work gives a fascinating and instructive view of the Lord's principles of leadership. The scriptural passages assigned to this chapter outline at least four such principles: (1) As in the case of

Joshua and his colleagues, the Lord magnifies His leaders, both in their strength and in the eyes of their followers, so that these leaders might be more effective in building the kingdom; (2) It is our obligation to sustain our leaders and avoid fault-finding and usurping of authority; (3) The Lord will fight our battles as needed if we remain steadfast, faithful, and obedient; and (4) We must choose the way of the Lord and thus emerge as leaders in our own roles and duties.

1. THE LORD WILL MAGNIFY HIS LEADERS

THEME: Each person, in his or her own way, plays a vital leadership role in the kingdom of God. The obedient and faithful are sustained by the Lord and magnified in the eyes of others—parents in their families, teachers in their classes, bishops in their wards, missionaries in the field, prophets in their callings—that all might be edified and prosper spiritually.

> *According as we hearkened unto Moses in all things, so will we hearken unto thee: only the Lord thy God be with thee, as he was with Moses.* (Josh. 1:17)

> *This day will I begin to magnify thee in the sight of all Israel.* (Josh. 3:7)

MOMENT OF TRUTH

The Lord magnified Joshua in the eyes of the people by giving him the spirit of obedience, righteousness, and priesthood power. The waters of the Jordan were turned back in miraculous fashion to allow Israel to pass over into the promised land. In no less miraculous fashion, the Lord's leaders in the homes, wards, and stakes of Zion can open the passageways of spiritual opportunity. There are miracles happening around us every day in the transformations of souls brought about through humble obedience to the Lord's commandments. As leaders show humility and prayerfully seek the Spirit, the way will be opened for them, too, to fulfill their callings successfully and be accepted by those who depend on their example and courage.

MODERN PROPHETS SPEAK

Marion G. Romney:

> In order to magnify our callings in the priesthood, three things at least are necessary: One is that we have a motivating desire to do so. Another is that we search and ponder the words of eternal life. And a third is that we pray. Over and over again the scriptures teach that men receive from the Lord according to their desires. ("Magnifying One's Calling in the Priesthood," *Ensign,* July 1973, 89)

Gordon B. Hinckley:

> That word *magnify* is interesting. As I interpret it, it means to enlarge, to make more clear, to bring closer, and to strengthen. . . . Jacob, the brother of Nephi, in speaking of the call which he and his brother Joseph had received, said: "And we did magnify our office unto the Lord, taking upon us the responsibility, answering the sins of the people upon our own heads if we did not teach them the word of God with all diligence" (Jacob 1:19). To every officer, to every teacher in this Church who acts in a priesthood office, there comes the sacred responsibility of magnifying that priesthood calling. Each of us is responsible for the welfare and the growth and development of others. We do not live only unto ourselves. If we are to magnify our callings, we cannot live only unto ourselves. As we serve with diligence, as we teach with faith and testimony, as we lift and strengthen and build convictions of righteousness in those whose lives we touch, we magnify our priesthood. To live only unto ourselves, on the other hand, to serve grudgingly, to give less than our best effort to our duty, diminishes our priesthood just as looking through the wrong lenses of binoculars reduces the image and makes more distant the object. . . . Every teacher has the responsibility to magnify his calling in teaching the word of God. Every officer has the responsibility to magnify his calling in teaching the order of God. . . .We magnify our calling, we enlarge the potential of our priesthood when we reach out to those in distress and give strength to those who falter. . . . We magnify our calling when we walk with honesty and integrity. . . . We honor our priesthood and magnify its influence when we walk in virtue and fidelity. . . . To each of us the Lord has said, "Magnify your calling." ("Magnify Your Calling," *Ensign,* May 1989, 46–47, 49)

ILLUSTRATIONS FOR OUR TIMES

A Dedicated Teacher

Many years ago, when I was serving as a missionary in the city of Worms, Germany, the local branch met in a small rented hall at the back of a commercial building. One day my companion and I stopped by the hall during the Primary hour, which took place in the late afternoon on a weekday. We opened the door a crack and saw one of the local sisters of the branch presenting a lesson. Not wanting to disturb her or the children, we quietly slipped into the back of room to listen. As we entered, we were amazed to see that the room—except for the teacher—was completely empty. She was teaching out loud to an empty classroom, not even holding back any of the visual aids that she had prepared. Noting our surprise, she made a comment that has stuck with me all my life. She said, "I have been given this calling by the Lord, and I must follow through if I am to be worthy of His blessings." This sister was truly a dedicated teacher. Who knows but what the angels of the Lord were nearby, edified by her faithful performance?

2. SAVE YOUR FAMILY BY SUSTAINING YOUR LEADERS

THEME: To follow the counsel of the prophet and protect and sustain the work of the kingdom is a spiritual insurance policy for your family.

Swear unto me by the Lord, since I have shewed you kindness, that ye will also show kindness unto my father's house. (Josh. 2:12)

MOMENT OF TRUTH

Just as the woman Rahab protected Israel's emissaries at Jericho, and thus secured for all her kindred the protection of the Lord, we can mark out a line of defense for our families as we keep the commandments. Cultivating a character of obedience and faithfulness sets up a bulwark of fortifications for our children. We can say, with the Savior, "And for their sakes I sanctify myself, that they also might be sanctified through the truth" (John 17:19). We can teach our children the saving principles of righteousness and prepare them for the challenges of life. We can set up memorials like Joshua did to remind the Israelites of their miraculous passage over Jordan, or of the covenant of obedience that Israel made with the Lord.

MODERN PROPHETS SPEAK

George Albert Smith:

> When the Lord sustains his leaders, we should sustain them also. Do you believe that this is The Church of Jesus Christ of Latter-day Saints? Do you believe that Joseph Smith was a prophet of the Lord? Do you believe that the man who stands at the head represents our Heavenly Father? He may make mistakes. The Prophet Joseph made his. Moses, the greatest leader of ancient times, made his mistakes. But I want to say that as long as the Lord sustains his leaders we should sustain them. Today the men who stand at our head are unselfishly giving of their time that not only we but also the world in general may be blessed. As long as the Lord gives them physical strength, mental power and spiritual light, if we are wise we will follow their advice and counsel. (*CR,* Oct. 1936, 76)

Joseph B. Wirthlin:

> We who have been taught the commandments know what to do: pray, study the scriptures, fast, pay our tithes and offerings, attend our meetings, partake of the sacrament, magnify our callings, serve others, sustain our Church leaders, do our

home teaching and visiting teaching, make and keep sacred covenants, share the gospel, be honest, true, chaste, benevolent, and virtuous. (*Finding Peace in Our Lives* [Salt Lake City: Deseret Book, 1995], 233)

ILLUSTRATIONS FOR OUR TIMES

Accept Assistance with a Grateful Heart

For a period of time it was my privilege to serve as a home teacher in the home of Elder A. Theodore Tuttle and his wife. My companion and I would dutifully give our spiritual message in a home where we had a sense that it was scarcely needed—but we were nevertheless always graciously treated and made to feel welcome. Then on one of the visits, Elder Tuttle was somewhat under the weather, so I called back later on the phone to ask whether I might bring over some hot chicken soup that we had prepared that day for our family. He thanked me, saying that it wouldn't be necessary, since they were well taken care of. I thought nothing more of it until the following fast and testimony meeting when Elder Tuttle stood up to bear his testimony. Referring to the home teachers who had offered to bring him soup for his illness, he apologized publicly for not have accepted the offer of service. He made the point that when service is extended, it is our obligation to accept it with gratitude. My admiration for this man of God, already high, was elevated immeasurably through his contrition and humility. My wife and I have often talked of this incident when we have had occasion to remind ourselves to accept with thankfulness any sincere offer of service, especially from one of our leaders.

3. THE LORD WILL FIGHT THE BATTLES OF THE FAITHFUL

THEME: When we put our shoulder to the wheel and join with the forces of righteousness, we will triumph, for the Lord will fight our battles and sustain our efforts.

As captain of the host of the Lord am I now come. (Josh. 5:14)

MOMENT OF TRUTH

The battle of Jericho is a lasting memorial to the guidance and protecting care of the Lord. As Israel did all that was asked by the Lord, she prospered and secured a place of refuge for her Saints. Today, as we follow the commandments and seek the face of the Lord always, we can have the hope of being led to places of refuge: sanctuaries of our own hearts when they are broken and humble, homes of sanctity and peace, stakes of Zion that afford strength in the face of the world's challenges, and temples of holiness before the Lord.

MODERN PROPHETS SPEAK

Brigham Young:

> We all believe that the Lord will fight our battles; but how? Will he do it while we are unconcerned and make no effort whatever for our own safety when an enemy is upon us? If we make no efforts to guard our towns, our houses, our cities, our wives and children, will the Lord guard them for us? He will not; but if we pursue the opposite course and strive to help him to accomplish his designs, then will he fight our battles. We are baptized for the remission of sins; but it would be quite as reasonable to expect remission of sins without baptism, as to expect the Lord to fight our battles without our taking every precaution to be prepared to defend ourselves. The Lord requires us to be quite as willing to fight our own battles as to have him fight them for us. If we are not ready for an enemy when he comes upon us, we have not lived up to the requirements of him who guides the ship of Zion, or who dictates the affairs of his Kingdom. (*Discourses,* 303)

Bruce R. McConkie:

> But Nephi comes forth with a clarifying pronouncement that gives an entirely new perspective to the scriptures that speak of the latter-day triumphs of Israel over the Gentile nations. "All that fight against Zion shall be destroyed," he declares. That is to say, Israel's triumph over her enemies will occur not because her marching armies defeat their foes in battle, but because her enemies will be destroyed, simply because every corruptible thing will be consumed at the Second Coming. In that day the Lord will truly fight the battles of his saints, for as he descends from heaven, amid fire and burning, all the proud and they that do wickedly shall be burned as stubble. (*A New Witness for the Articles of Faith* [Salt Lake City: Deseret Book, 1985], 562)

ILLUSTRATIONS FOR OUR TIMES

The Lord Watches Out for His Children

On the very day on which I was completing my writing tasks for this chapter, something occurred that greatly reinforced my faith that the Lord does indeed fight our battles for us. I had a strong impression that something was not quite right at the apartment where our multiply challenged adult son lives during the week. I called the apartment repeatedly and got no answer—a matter of some concern, since there should always be a staff person on duty at that time. Upon consulting with my wife, I learned that she too had had promptings that something was not right. We immediately drove down to our son's apartment, about five miles away, and found him standing outside the front door, locked out. He had been standing there for about three-quarters of an hour, unable to gain access to the house (as we later determined, based on information from the bus driver who had delivered him to the house at the end of the work day).

A miscommunication among the staff of the residential service had left the house unattended at a critical time, and our son (who is virtually non-communicative) would have been standing there for hours on a winter day had we not been prompted to come to his aid. My wife and I said a silent prayer of thanksgiving to our Father in Heaven for His direct and merciful intervention on behalf of someone we love. The following morning, my wife commented at our family breakfast devotional that she prays continually to Heavenly Father for His guardian angels to attend our children. We realized that, more often than not, *we* are those guardian angels—and this is just as it should be when the Lord fights our battles.

4. CHOOSE TO FOLLOW THE LORD

THEME: There is a fundamental choice in life whether to pledge allegiance to the Lord and follow in His pathways, or to cater to the patterns and behaviors of worldliness. The way of holiness is the way of peace, harmony, and salvation.

> *Choose you this day whom ye will serve; . . . but as for me and my house, we will serve the Lord.* (Josh. 24:15)

MOMENT OF TRUTH

Joshua, in his final testimony and counsel, entreated the Israelites to follow the Lord and charged them strictly to avoid the false gods of the indigenous peoples of Canaan. Israel made a covenant to choose the Lord and remain on the pathway of righteousness. Joshua set up a memorial to the sacred event as a reminder to Israel to honor their pledge forever.

MODERN PROPHETS SPEAK

Howard W. Hunter:

> We are free to follow or oppose the Lord's direction. We came to mortal life to encounter resistance. It was part of the plan for our eternal progress. Without temptation, sickness, pain, and sorrow, there could be no goodness, virtue, appreciation for well-being, or joy. The law of opposition makes freedom of choice possible; therefore, our Heavenly Father has commanded his children, "Choose ye this day, to serve the Lord God who made you" (Moses 6:33). He has counseled us to yield to his spirit and resist temptation. Free agency, of course, permits us to oppose his directions; thus, we see many who resist the truth and yield to temptation. (*THWH,* 78)

Marion G. Romney:

> The only path to unity is to find out the will of the Lord and then follow it. The way to find it out is, first, to be humble. We must not be hard of heart. We must assume our proper relationship to our Father in heaven, recognizing that in his infinite wisdom he knows what ought to be done. Therefore, we should be willing to subject our personal opinions and actions to his will. (*Learning for the Eternities* [Salt Lake City: Deseret Book, 1977], 150–51)

ILLUSTRATIONS FOR OUR TIMES

Taking Action on Principle

It is always refreshing to come across individuals who are taking a stand for righteousness. I remember, a number of years ago, interviewing a young man in Maryland who was concerned about his employment situation. He told me that his employer was asking him to deal with customers in ways that he felt were dishonest, and that he had therefore decided to change jobs. I commended him for his integrity and honesty. The following year he returned for an interview once more and said that he had changed jobs yet again for precisely the same reason. This young man was standing on principle—a rare thing in our society. How often do we rationalize away our promptings without responding decisively?

SUMMARY

Joshua, as the successor to Moses, was a great prophet-leader at a time when righteous leadership was especially needed among the Israelites. Like Joshua, we also have our Jerichos to conquer. We need to remember that God will sustain His leaders and magnify them to be equal to any test. To save our families in light and truth, we must sustain our leaders in their efforts to fulfill the Lord's errand, and thus open the way for the Lord to fight our battles on a daily basis. We must choose decisively to be on the Lord's side and emulate the Savior's mission: "And for their sakes I sanctify myself, that they also might be sanctified through the truth" (John 17:19). As we apply the Lord's leadership principles, He will bless and sanctify our hearts and minds so that we will not be afraid, but know that the Lord is with us.

CHAPTER NINETEEN

"SURELY I WILL BE *with* THEE"

Reading Assignment: Judges 2; 4; 6–7; 13–16.

Additional Reading: Bible Dictionary, "Judges, The"; "Judges, Book of."

We are here to cooperate with God in the salvation of the living, in the redemption of the dead, in the blessings of our ancestors, in the pouring out [of] blessings upon our children; we are here for the purpose of redeeming and generating the earth on which we live, and God has placed His authority and His counsels here upon the earth for that purpose, that men may learn to do the will of God on the earth as it is done in heaven. This is the object of our existence. (John Taylor, JD 21:94)

THEMES *for* LIVING

1. The Tests of Time
2. Beacons of Light
3. Gideon and Samson: Instruments of God

INTRODUCTION

The 200-year period of the judges—between Joshua and Samuel—was a time of great turmoil in Israel. It was a period that reflected many variations of the cycles of obedience and falling away, faithfulness and forgetting the covenants, sin and recovery, weakness and valor. The diverse portraits of leadership emerging from this period are mixed; at times they give us encouragement and inspiration, at other times they sound the warning voice. The message is clear: when we remember the Lord and His commandments, all will be well. But when we venture into forbidden pathways, we relinquish peace, harmony, and the favor of God.

To guide us along the way, the Lord provides beacons of light in the form of angels, prophets, teachers, mentors, and leaders of all kinds (in this case judges). To exemplify courage and strength, He raises up individuals of uncommon stature, such as Deborah, Gideon, and even the controversial Samson. All of this serves to bring about His divine mission of perfecting the Saints.

1. THE TESTS OF TIME

THEME: The Lord gives us our agency, and allows us to be tested and tried through various influences—"thorns in your sides" (see Judg. 2:3) when we become forgetful—as a means of proving our faithfulness.

> *I may prove Israel, whether they will keep the way of the Lord to walk therein, as their fathers did keep it, or not.* (Judg. 2:22)

MOMENT OF TRUTH

Just as the Lord allowed segments of the Canaanite civilization to be preserved in proximity to Israel as a standing test of loyalty and fidelity, similarly He allows us to make our journey through the world's highways and byways in order that we might have the opportunity to choose the right according to His precepts and commandments, and remain free of worldly taint.

MODERN PROPHETS SPEAK

George Q. Cannon:

> We will show the world that we have principles that can stand the test of time and can withstand all the evil influences that can be brought against us. If we must rear our children in the midst of these, then let them rise superior to them. We cannot enclose our children in glass houses. We cannot exempt our children . . . from the temptations of the world. . . . They have to rise above them. . . . I am looking forward for such a development of wisdom, strength and skill . . . and power that the development and training of our children will be a matter almost of perfect safety in the midst of all hostile influences. Still, we have to contend against these wicked

things, the literature of the age and all the evils that abound—we have to contend against these and to teach our children to shun them. (*Gospel Truth: Discourses and Writings of President George Q. Cannon* [Salt Lake City: Deseret Book, 1987], 302)

Brigham Young:

If we do not take the pains to train our children, to teach and instruct them concerning these revealed truths, the condemnation will be upon us, as parents, or at least in a measure. Teach your children from their youth, never to set their hearts immoderately upon an object of this world. Parents, teach your children by precept and example, the importance of addressing the Throne of grace; teach them how to live, how to draw from the elements the necessaries of life, and teach them the laws of life that they may know how to preserve themselves in health and be able to minister to others. Bring up your children in the love and fear of the Lord. Teach your children honesty and uprightness, and teach them also never to injure others. If parents will continually set before their children examples worthy of their imitation and the approval of our Father in Heaven, they will turn the current, and the tide of feelings of their children, and they, eventually, will desire righteousness more than evil. (*Discourses,* 207–8)

ILLUSTRATIONS FOR OUR TIMES

Overcoming the Tentacles of the World

Some years ago, Elder Ezra Taft Benson, then President of the Quorum of the Twelve, contacted the presidency of the Silver Spring Maryland Stake and commended them for the notable advancement of some 19% of the prospective elders in the stake during the previous one-year period of time. Elder Benson asked them to research the reasons for the success, and I was privileged to receive that assignment as a member of the high council. All of the elders quorum presidencies and groups were interviewed in depth, and we were able to respond to Elder Benson's request by identifying the two strategies that proved overwhelmingly to be the most effective in reactivating almost 100 prospective elders that year: (1) the influence of faithful and interested home teachers (and in some cases Relief Society visiting teachers), and (2) getting the prospective elders to be involved in opportunities for serving in the quorum and ward. It is not surprising that home teaching and personal callings (whether in the ward choir, on a welfare project, teaching a class, or as a member of a home teaching team) were the decisive factors, since these are both divinely appointed functions (see D&C 20:42, 46, 51, 53–55; 107:99).

In many cases, the tenacious tentacles of inactivity were overcome by the more tenacious outreach of love on the part of devoted leaders. One member of a bishopric traced an inactive brother through four successive changes of address until he had located him and invited him and his family to participate in Church programs. This man responded and became active, ultimately being called to the quorum presidency. Another home teacher, newly assigned to visit an inactive family, felt impressed to talk about the concept of the temple on his first visit—precisely the theme that the family had a hunger to know more about. They responded and overcame their inactivity. In yet another case, the activity among LDS midshipmen at the Naval Academy in Annapolis rose sharply as a result of a concerted self-contained home teaching program, plus a sponsor program in which each midshipman was assigned to a local family in the area.

I was able to interview approximately three dozen of the reactivated brethren in a number of the wards following the initial research for Elder Benson. I asked the question, "What was the most difficult thing you had to overcome in returning to activity?" The predominant answer was very interesting. The majority said the most challenging factor was overcoming the feeling (whether within themselves or somehow conveyed by members) that one had to be "perfect" to be welcomed at church. It is a reminder that all of us need to open our minds and hearts to those around us who have a desire to become active but find that inertia or the tentacles of the world are holding them back.

2. BEACONS OF LIGHT

THEME: The Lord provides sources of light and leadership to keep us on the straight and narrow—prophets, angels, and righteous civil leaders (judges), according to the circumstances—all to kindle and keep alive the fire of righteousness in our lives.

> DEBORAH TO BARAK: *"Is not the Lord gone out before thee?"* (Judg. 4:14.)

MOMENT OF TRUTH

During this period of time, the Lord raised up a sequence of wise leaders—judges—to maintain some sense of godly order among the tribes of Israel. He also sent angels and prophets from time to time to stir the Israelites up to a sense of their commitments, and to remind them of the marvelous blessings that were part of their heritage. For the most part, the judges worked righteousness and brought about progress in the quality of life. Deborah stands out as an example—a beacon of light, friendship, and courage in a sometimes confusing and unstable historical terrain. She reflects the strength and power of divine leadership.

MODERN PROPHETS SPEAK

John Taylor:
> I would rather have God for my friend than all other influences and powers outside.
> (*The Gospel Kingdom: Selections from the Writings and Discourses of John Taylor* [Salt Lake City: Improvement Era, 1941], 343)

L. Tom Perry:

> I have found that the right friends have a powerful influence on our lives. Choose your friends wisely! Make certain they will complement your life goals and help to build within you the right values and standards. How do we develop better friendships? A Church tract printed many years ago gives us several ideas. It lists the following helps:
>
> > 1. Be sincere.
> >
> > 2. Become thoroughly acquainted by learning their names and other important things about them, being a good listener, and discussing their interests. Show interest in them, their hobbies, their work, their children.
> >
> > 3. Be unselfish.
> >
> > 4. Show brotherly love and concern for them. Meet their needs by giving them helpful service.
> >
> > 5. Graciously let them be of service to you when they offer.
> >
> > 6. Smile and be positive. (*Living with Enthusiasm* [Salt Lake City: Deseret Book, 1996], 54)

ILLUSTRATIONS FOR OUR TIMES

The Beacon of Friendship

One of the rare jewels in my library is a book of letters about my mother compiled by one of her thoughtful friends and co-workers in the Church and community. Mother passed away when I was ten, and these forty-seven letters from her friends and associates, recounting stories about her remarkable character and record of service, have preserved for her three children the priceless memory of her exemplary accomplishments as viewed by her contemporaries. In the colorful panorama of fleeting recollections and vignettes, one captures the essence of a life that reflected the spirit of joy, harmony, compassion, and pure friendship. Here are a few examples:

> *From a co-worker on the stake Primary and Sunday School boards:* "Some people are satisfied if they are happy. Others are concerned with the happiness of friends and relatives. A few are anxious to find the stranger or lonely person and make them happy too. Your mother belonged to this last group."

From her visiting teacher: "She was always happy and cheerful in the discharge of her duties, no matter where you met her, on the street, at church, or in her home. In visiting her home as a Relief Society teacher, we were always made welcome. In making our last visit just before the day she went to the hospital, she was very pleasant and optimistic."

From another sister: "To me, the one priceless gem in her crown of character was that she never found fault with, or criticized anyone or ever spoke evil of anyone. If she was in the company of anyone doing it, she always had something good to say about them or make excuses for their behavior."

From a friend: "Years later I stood, one evening, in a strange crowd of people, feeling very much alone. A hand touched mine and a cheery voice said, 'My, I'm glad you came!' Yes, it was Amy. She had sensed my loneliness, and in her natural, sweet way made me feel at home."

From a colleague and close observer: "Your mother had an abundance of charm. She had the ability to sit quietly and listen to all our joys and sorrows, aches and pains, and send us away feeling so much better. Your mother loved people of all ages and kinds—she could talk a child's language as easily as an adult's. She could laugh and giggle with the young girls and boys as well as with those her own age. She made people feel important by treating them that way."

From a mother: "I remember when I heard she passed away my little son Max said, 'I'm going to her funeral because she surely liked me.'"

From a neighbor sister: "She was one of the first to come with a scrub pail after a fire we had in our home. I cherish my association with her as one of the fine things of my life."

From a young lady hired to help in her home: "The first quilt I ever helped on was with Amy; this to my notion was not so good, but everything was appreciated and fine for Amy. She always told you how nice the work looked, and how the floor shined when you finished it, and how fast you did it."

From the last person she ever spoke to at the hospital: "We were both at the hospital together where our babies were born . . . That morning she had been so very sweet and kind to me by insisting that I sit down by her, and she fixed my hair very nice. She came in my room after dinner and sat, and we talked and laughed together for a long time. Then she was taken in to the case room, and soon a little new life was here on earth, but Amy had been called home."

3. GIDEON AND SAMSON: INSTRUMENTS OF GOD

THEME: To be worthy instruments in the hands of God, we must honor our covenant promises and be true to the principles of righteousness. Once committed, Gideon was a faithful servant of God. As with Samson, those who deviate from the appointed pathway will fail to measure up to the potential within them. Nevertheless, the Lord strives mightily with men and women, giving them every opportunity to overcome their weaknesses and bring about good results.

> THE ANGEL OF THE LORD TO GIDEON: *"The Lord is with thee, thou mighty man of valour."* (Judg. 6:12)

> *And the woman bare a son, and called his name Samson: and the child grew, and the Lord blessed him.* (Judg. 13:24)

MOMENT OF TRUTH

Gideon became an instrument in the hand of the Lord. The Lord used him and directed him to do things the Lord's way. When Gideon realized the Lord was not only with him but would insure the victory, he was full of faith. His men shared that faith and also became instruments in the hand of the Lord. Samson, on the other hand, presents a mixed portrait of great promise and power as well as weakness and appetite. As long as the Spirit of the Lord remained with him, he was poised to be a productive instrument in the hands of God. When he deviated from the course, however, then carnal desire, rancor, anger, and the spirit of vengeance flourished and overcame his spiritual motivation. We can learn great lessons from his example as we strive to cultivate harmony, balance, humility, and spirituality in our lives.

MODERN PROPHETS SPEAK

Ezra Taft Benson:

> Ours is a gospel of work—purposeful, unselfish and rendered in the spirit of the true love of Christ. Only thus may we grow in godly attributes. Only thus may we become worthy instruments in the hands of the Lord for blessing others through that power which can lead to changing the lives of men and women for the better. (*TETB,* 484)

Russell M. Nelson:

> Without a strong commitment to the Lord, an individual is more prone to have a low level of commitment to a spouse. Weak commitments to eternal covenants lead

to losses of eternal consequence. Laments later in life are laced with remorse—as expressed in these lines: For of all sad words of tongue or pen, The saddest are these: "It might have been!" [John Greenleaf Whittier, "Maud Muller," *The Complete Poetical Works of Whittier* (1892), 48]. (*Perfection Pending, and Other Favorite Discourses* [Salt Lake City: Deseret Book, 1998], 131)

ILLUSTRATIONS FOR OUR TIMES

Instruments of Joy

In the example of Gideon and Samson we see the power of faith, strength gained through honored covenants, and the sorrow of sin through temptation. The stories of Gideon and Samson are known by all. We recognize the faith and exact obedience of Gideon. We are saddened as Samson yielded to temptation, yet he returned in a sense to be an instrument in the hand of the Lord. The Lord wants all of us to be willing, faithful, pure, prepared, and devoted instruments in His hands. And what do instruments do? "I know that which the Lord hath commanded me, and I glory in it. I do not glory of myself, but I glory in that which the Lord hath commanded me; yea, and this is my glory, that perhaps I may be an instrument in the hands of God to bring some soul to repentance; and this is my joy. And behold, when I see many of my brethren truly penitent, and coming to the Lord their God, then is my soul filled with joy; then do I remember what the Lord has done for me, yea, even that he hath heard my prayer; yea, then do I remember his merciful arm which he extended towards me" (Alma 29:9–10). Our joy and glory is to be used in the service of our God and to bless our fellowmen.

Modern-day Gideons

In our day, the restored kingdom of God is emerging in glory and unity as never before. Local leadership has been placed in the hands of faithful stake presidents and bishops—pillars of Church government acting under the inspired direction of the General Authorities of the Church. In a sense, the local and regional leaders are the modern-day Gideons—righteous judges who set the tone of obedience and act in the defense of the Saints.

Such a modern-day Gideon was my own grandfather, Heber Simeon Allen, one of the pioneering settlers in southern Alberta, who was called in 1902 by President Joseph F. Smith as stake president there, and served faithfully in that capacity for thirty-four years. A successful merchant and businessman, he always put the Lord first and served with devotion and dedication in all dimensions of his calling.

His testimony came early, as his journal recounts:

> When we were children, our parents were opposed to the old custom of hanging up our stockings at Christmastime. They preferred that we set a plate on the table to

receive what presents were to be given us. One Christmas, when I was about twelve or thirteen years of age, Father put a Book of Mormon on my plate. He wrote on the flyleaf of the book: "Read and remember. And be kind to all people." It was, I think, the first book I ever owned except my school books, and I prized it greatly. . . . Soon after receiving the Book of Mormon from my father, I read it carefully. I knew very little of its contents before reading this sacred record, but when I read the words of Moroni and his promise as contained in Moroni 10:4–5, I received a strong testimony of the truthfulness of the book and the inspiration of it. My whole being was thrilled with a heavenly influence. I also received a testimony of the divine mission of the prophet Joseph Smith, and this fervent testimony I bore to my mother, who was in the room with me when I read this chapter in the record. This testimony is as bright today as it was at the time I received it in my mother's living room.

SUMMARY

To meet the tests of time and complete the journey of life with honor and allegiance to heavenly principles is to earn the crown of glory in the mansions of the Father: "And whoso is found a faithful, a just, and a wise steward shall enter into the joy of his Lord, and shall inherit eternal life" (D&C 51:19). We can count our blessings when we discern the hand of the Lord in our everyday lives: the scriptures containing the fullness of the gospel, living prophets, and other devoted teachers—the beacons of light and instruments of God who are placed along our pathway as guides and mentors—and above all, the inspiration of the Spirit. If we are faithful, the Lord's message to Gideon will be His message to us: "Surely I will be with thee" (Judg. 6:16).

CHAPTER TWENTY

"GO *in* PEACE: AND *the* GOD *of* ISRAEL GRANT THEE THY PETITION"

Reading Assignment: Ruth, 1 Samuel 1

> *It is impossible to speak of the abundant life without speaking of life as a continuum. This life, this narrow sphere we call mortality, does not, within the short space of time we are allowed here, give to all of us perfect justice, perfect health, or perfect opportunities. Perfect justice, however, will come eventually through a divine plan, as will the perfection of all other conditions and blessings—to those who have lived to merit them.* (Spencer W. Kimball, *Ensign*, July 1978, 3)

THEMES *for* LIVING

1. Devotion and Loyalty: Hallmarks of True Friends
2. Kindness and Love
3. Joy after Sorrow
4. The Universal Gospel
5. Child of the Temple

INTRODUCTION

The Savior said, "I am come that they might have life, and that they might have it more abundantly" (John 10:10). The word of the Lord contained in Ruth and the first chapter of 1 Samuel is a handbook on the abundant life, as seen many centuries before the coming of Christ. We see in these pages of scripture many of the building blocks of the abundant life, including the loyalty and devotion of Ruth, the kindness and love of Boaz, the effulgent joy Naomi experienced when her emptied home filled again with loved ones, the tolerance and respect the Israelites learned to cultivate for one of their Moabite adoptees, and the fulfilled faith of Hannah in bringing a "child of the temple" into the world. These building blocks of the abundant life are still efficacious in our day and age, and the same principles apply to our challenges and tests.

1. DEVOTION AND LOYALTY: HALLMARKS OF TRUE FRIENDS

THEME: For millennia, the story of Ruth's devotion to her mother-in-law, Naomi, has inspired those who value the jewel of loyal friendship as among the greatest of human character traits.

> *For whither thou goest, I will go; and where thou lodgest, I will lodge: thy people shall be my people, and thy God my God.* (Ruth 1:16)

MOMENT OF TRUTH

Naomi and her family sought food among the Moabite community during a time of famine. When Naomi's husband and two sons passed away, she was left with her sorrow and the care of her two Moabite daughters-in-law. She determined to send them back to their own cultural setting, but one of them, Ruth, decided out of friendship and loyalty to remain with her. In Ruth, Naomi found spiritual support and sustenance to help her through the years after her bereavement.

MODERN PROPHETS SPEAK

Hugh B. Brown:

> The prerequisite to ideal marriage and a happy home is deep and abiding love. If this holy relationship is to continue, there must be purity of thought, word, and action. The pillars of the home are devotion, loyalty, sacrifice, integrity, fidelity, honesty, and again unsullied virtue. (*The Abundant Life* [Salt Lake City: Bookcraft, 1965], 58)

Gordon B. Hinckley:

> Treat your wives with kindness. You will never have a greater asset in all of this world
> than the woman with whom you joined hands over the altar in the temple and to
> whom you pledged your love and loyalty and devotion for time and all eternity. . . .
> Be an example to your people of those who walk the path of faith. God bless you as
> leaders to set an example before your people. (*TGBH,* 311)

ILLUSTRATIONS FOR OUR TIMES

Only Two Were Fully Loyal

The chronicles of the restoration of the gospel and kingdom of God on the earth in the
latter days are replete with examples of how loyalty and genuine friendship were put to
the test. The crucible of trial and sacrifice is the place where the elements of true character emerge. Joseph Smith was magnanimous in his outreach of friendship and trust,
but not all who were embraced by his spirit of greatness measured up to the opportunity to forge bonds of lasting loyalty and service. On one occasion toward the end of
his mortal career, the Prophet gave a poignant perspective on this topic: "Of the Twelve
Apostles chosen in Kirtland, and ordained under the hands of Oliver Cowdery, David
Whitmer and myself, there have been but two but what have lifted their heel against
me—namely Brigham Young and Heber C. Kimball" (*HC* 5:412). All the rest had
occasion from time to time to compromise their allegiance and loyalty to the Prophet,
some treacherously so. In the final analysis, it is authentic loyalty, no matter what the
circumstances, that serves as the abiding touchstone of pure friendship.

2. KINDNESS AND LOVE

THEME: The traits of kindness and love, so enduringly reflected in the story of the
relationship of Boaz and Ruth, add a glow of the divine to our temporal lives of challenge and trial.

> *And now, my daughter, fear not; I will do to thee all that thou requirest: for all the city
> of my people doth know that thou art a virtuous woman.* (Ruth 3:11)

MOMENT OF TRUTH

The gleaner Ruth worked tirelessly to provide food for herself and the widow Naomi.
The landholder Boaz, a kinsman to Naomi's deceased husband, took note of Ruth's
love and industry and had compassion and admiration for her. He was as kind and
loving a person as Ruth was, and through the advice of Naomi, Ruth was able to facilitate the developing relationship. Boaz worked through long-standing social customs

to lay the foundation for a proper and community-sanctioned marriage with Ruth. It is one of the great happy-ending stories in all of literature, biblical or otherwise.

MODERN PROPHETS SPEAK

Gordon B. Hinckley:

> How much more beautiful would be the world and the society in which we live if every father looked upon his children as the most precious of his assets, if he led them by the power of his example in kindness and love, and if in times of stress he blessed them by the authority of the holy priesthood. And how much more beautiful would be our world and our society if every mother regarded her children as the jewels of her life, as gifts from the God of heaven who is their Eternal Father, and brought them up with true affection in the wisdom and admonition of the Lord. (*Be Thou an Example* [Salt Lake City: Deseret Book, 1981], 40)

John A. Widtsoe:

> Those who have authority should not be rulers, nor dictators; they should not be arbitrary; they should gain the hearts, the confidence and love of those over whom they preside, by kindness and love unfeigned, by gentleness of spirit, by persuasion, by an example that is above the reproach and above the reach of unjust criticism. In this way, in the kindness of their hearts, in their love of their people, they lead them in the path of righteousness, and teach them the way of salvation, by saying to them, both by precept and example: Follow me, as I follow our Head. This is the duty of those who preside. (*Priesthood and Church Government* [Salt Lake City: Deseret Book, 1939], 68–69)

ILLUSTRATIONS FOR OUR TIMES

A Small Miracle

The elevator was crowded with harried people anxious to get to their destinations. My wife and I were pressed against the back wall, holding our two-year-old daughter, Stephanie, in our arms. Then the car groaned to a stop on yet another floor en route to the lobby, and everyone sighed at the thought of taking on still another passenger. This time the rider was a very large man in scruffy coveralls. He was covered with dirt and grease from head to toe. In his hand was a heavy toolbox; on his face was an ominous grimace. As he stepped into the elevator, it creaked and dipped slightly under the added 300-plus pounds of weight. His scowl repelled everyone backwards as they made ample way for the invader and retreated into an unspoken covenant of protection against the enemy. The aroma he brought with him was certain proof that hard physical work had been successfully completed. Everyone fell silent, hoping beyond hope that the situation would be short-lived. There was palpable enmity for this encroacher.

Then a miracle occurred. Everyone saw it and heard it at the same time. Our little Stephanie, in her pink outfit, had taken the workman into her gaze. She looked intently at him, then, as only a two-year-old can do, she leaned toward him smiling broadly and said, with utter sincerity and disarming warmth, "Hi!" The world was suddenly transformed. The victim of her charms was captivated. He broke into a wide grin and returned the favor with his own "Hi." A bond of friendship had been forged instantly between the biggest and smallest of the pack. There was nothing left for all the rest to do but join in the celebration. People nodded in cheer. Others echoed the best greetings of the day. There was general tumult. Feet shuffled as the line of defense melted away. Somehow a selection of disparate lives, brought together this day through the wiles of fickle chance, had been united in a holy union of loyalty and friendship—all because a little girl had demonstrated the simple truth that everyone is worthy of our courtesy, respect, and kindness. Did Alma not say, "little children do have words given unto them, which confound the wise and the learned" (Alma 32:23)? Here was a case where the tipping point was one single word of wisdom spoken by a child. My wife and I shall never forget the lesson in tolerance and human decency taught by our two-year-old.

3. JOY AFTER SORROW

THEME: Life is full of adversity and trials, but we have within us the ability to respond with courage and hope, knowing that in time spring will follow winter, sunshine will follow rain, and the blessings of the Lord will prevail over the burdens of our worldly sojourn if we remember our covenants and live by faith.

> *Blessed be the Lord, which hath not left thee this day without a kinsman, that his name may be famous in Israel. And he shall be unto thee a restorer of thy life, and a nourisher of thine old age.* (Ruth 4:14–15)

MOMENT OF TRUTH

Naomi lost her husband and both of her sons. She became the prototype for all widows everywhere, and suffered greatly because of her loss and her sorrow. Added to that was the burden of having to support herself and her daughter-in-law, Ruth. But Ruth was the source of sunshine in her life, and eventually the marriage of Ruth and Boaz brought harmony and stability into their family circle. In time, sorrows pass and things improve. Moreover, the fruit of the new marriage was a continuation of the covenant lineage, leading to David, and beyond, to Christ Himself.

MODERN PROPHETS SPEAK

Hugh B. Brown:

> If we would find joy in sorrow, strength in weakness, light in darkness; if we would learn how to bear adversity and scorn and how to fight life's battle courageously; if we would find the best way of living, the noblest way of thinking, the most comfortable way of growing, it would be well for us to consult God's chart and steer our lives by it. It will show us where the harbor is and how to reach it without running on the rocks, and will keep us from the bottom of the sea. (*The Abundant Life* [Salt Lake City: Bookcraft, 1965], 106)

Neal A. Maxwell:

> It follows, then, that you and I cannot really expect to glide through life, coolly air-conditioned, while naïvely petitioning: "Lord, give me experience but not grief, a deeper appreciation of happiness but not deeper sorrow, joy in comfort but not in pain, more capacity to overcome but not more opposition; and please do not let me ever feel perplexed while on thine errand. Then let me come quickly and dwell with thee and fully share thy joy." (*If Thou Endure It Well* [Salt Lake City: Bookcraft, 1996], 4)

ILLUSTRATIONS FOR OUR TIMES

But for a Small Moment

In our time, few have felt the anguish of frequent separation from hearth and family as acutely as the Prophet Joseph Smith. While on an expedition to New York for the Church in October 1832, he was alone in the boarding house with time to feel the homesickness of being away from his children and from Emma, who was then expecting their fourth child. He wrote to her during this hour:

> After beholding all that I had any desire to behold, I returned to my room to meditate and calm my mind, and behold the thoughts of home, of Emma and Julia [an adopted daughter], rush upon my mind like a flood and I could wish for a moment to be with them. My breast is filled with all the feelings and tenderness of a parent and a husband and could I be with you I would tell you many things, yet when I reflect upon this great city like Nineveh not discerning their right hand from their left, yea, more than two-hundred-thousand souls, my bowels are filled with compassion toward them and I am determined to lift up my voice in this city and leave

the event with God who holdeth all things in his hands and will not suffer an hair of our heads unnoticed to fall to the ground. . . . I feel as though I wanted to say something to you to comfort you in your peculiar trial and present affliction. I hope God will give you strength that you may not faint. I pray God to soften the hearts of those around you to be kind to you and take the burden off your shoulders as much as possible and not afflict you. I feel for you, for I know your state and that others do not, but you must comfort yourself, knowing that God is your friend in heaven and that you have one true and living friend on Earth, your husband. (*The Personal Writings of Joseph Smith* [Salt Lake City: Deseret Book, 1984], 253; spelling and syntax modernized)

Later, in March 1839, from his confinement in Liberty Jail, he writes to his wife:

My dear Emma, I very well know your toils and sympathize with you. If God will spare my life once more to have the privilege of taking care of you, I will ease your care and endeavor to comfort your heart. I want you to take the best care of the family you can, [and] I believe you will do all you can. I was sorry to learn that Frederick was sick, but I trust he is well again and that you are all well. I want you to try to gain time and write to me a long letter and tell me all you can and even if old major [their dog] is alive yet and what those little prattlers say that cling around your neck. Do you tell them I am in prison that their lives might be saved. (408)

Joseph, like many of the founding leaders of the restored Church, placed the will of God and His purposes ahead of personal will and comfort. The suffering occasioned by loss and separation, the anxiety about longed-for relief and supplicated triumph was destined to last "but for a small moment" (D&C 122:4). The reward of these leaders will be eternal lives in the hereafter and the joy of immortality and eternal togetherness with loved ones. Their example is timeless and still reverberates in the hearts of the grateful heirs to their completed ministry.

4. THE UNIVERSAL GOSPEL

THEME: From the beginning, God's chosen people were to be a royal lineage with a special divine mission of bringing the blessings of the gospel to all the world. Through the process of adoption, all peoples everywhere are welcome to become part of God's family by accepting and living the gospel principles.

BOAZ TO RUTH: *"The Lord recompense thy work, and a full reward be given thee of the Lord God of Israel, under whose wings thou art come to trust."* (Ruth 2:12)

MOMENT OF TRUTH

Ruth was of the Moabite lineage, one of the indigenous cultures remaining in the Holy Land after the return of Israel from Egypt. The original Moab was the son of Lot's oldest daughter (see Gen. 19:37), and thus the Moabites were akin to the Israelites, but represented a different way of life and religion. Ruth represented the local culture at its best, being a pure and virtuous individual with the highest aspirations and character, and she wholeheartedly embraced the Israelite way of life. She was welcomed into her new environment and became instrumental in continuing the promised lineage via David to the Savior himself. It is a fitting unfolding of history that the Author of universal salvation should have come from a line that combined Ruth and Boaz—the confluence of two cultures, one Israelite and the other non-Israelite, but both from the same Maker and Creator. It is a reminder that converts to the Church and kingdom of God are welcome from all kindreds, nations, tongues, and peoples.

MODERN PROPHETS SPEAK

Joseph Fielding Smith:

> All blessings are based on worthiness of the individual. We are taught that it is he who endures to the end that is saved. Naturally, the Lord will judge each individual according to opportunities to know and obey his commandments. Thousands of those who died without the knowledge of the gospel and therefore failed to keep the commandments and covenants of the gospel while in mortality will enter the celestial kingdom. It is for this class of people that we do temple work and thus perform vicariously the ordinances of the gospel according to the revelation given to the Prophet Joseph Smith. (*AGQ,* 5:63)

Bruce R. McConkie:

> Abraham alone is the father of us all, speaking after the manner of the flesh, and all who receive the blessings of the gospel are either natural or adopted sons in his everlasting family. Thus, also, Nephi says: "As many of the Gentiles as will repent are the covenant people of the Lord; and as many of the Jews as will not repent shall be cast off; for the Lord covenanteth with none save it be with them that repent and believe in his Son, who is the Holy One of Israel" (2 Ne. 30:2). (*The Millennial Messiah: The Second Coming of the Son of Man* [Salt Lake City: Deseret Book, 1982], 245)

ILLUSTRATIONS FOR OUR TIMES

The Blessings of the Lord

The gospel is not only universal in its teachings, but universal in giving blessings to all of Heavenly Father's children who obey. The joy of converts and their friends is exclaimed all over the world every day. Hundreds of thousands of Heavenly Father's children come into the kingdom of God every year, and the joy is fulfilling.

I have seen families come into the Church. I have seen families welcome back a wayward child. I have seen husbands and wives resolve their differences and return to their love for each other. I have seen families cry with tears of joy as they leave their sons or daughters in the MTC. I have seen families at the airport welcoming home their beloved children who have served with honor. I have seen little families surrounding the altar in the temple of our God, being sealed for time and all eternity. And in all of this I have seen the blessings of God poured out to all of His children who simply choose God over the world. All have the opportunity to receive all that the Father has if we but accept His plan of happiness and endure to the end.

All Are Alike unto Him

It was my honor and privilege to make the acquaintance of a remarkable black investigator of the restored Church a few years ago. He and his family had operated a well-known business not far from the Oakland Temple for many years, and he had often gazed upon the transcendent beauty of the temple and wondered about its purpose and place in the religious life of its patrons. He even had a member of the Church in his employ, but the gentleman had never sought to talk with him about the gospel. It was later my opportunity to be among a series of priesthood brethren who shared their testimony with this good man and participated in missionary discussions with him. Having come from a family line with a long and distinguished history of pastors and churchmen, his faith was remarkably strong. At one point he was diagnosed with cancer, but told the doctors that his "Physician in Heaven" would watch out for him, and he miraculously survived the ordeal.

One of his heroes was Joseph Johnson of Ghana, Africa, who was touched by the spirit of the Joseph Smith story long before he had the opportunity to receive the missionary discussions, and long before the Official Declaration of 30 September 1978, making the priesthood available to all worthy male members of the Church without regard for race or color. Brother Johnson waited faithfully and patiently for the time when he could receive all the blessings of the restored gospel. "I used to walk fifty miles a day [teaching others about the truth] and wasn't bothered about it," he wrote. "Whenever I walked, I reflected on the early missionaries, and I gained strength because it seemed as if I was following in the footsteps of the pioneers. Their example inspired me—the way some died in the snow and the way they toiled to bring the truth. They were great people" (*Ensign,* Dec. 1999, 47). Brother Johnson's dream of being baptized a member of the Church was realized in 1978, and he has continued to help build up the kingdom of God in that part of the world, serving most recently as a patriarch in the Cape Coast Ghana Stake of the Church. His admirer, my black friend referred to above, has the dream one day of extending his business connections to Africa so that he, too, may be instrumental in furthering the work of the gospel among his ancestral forebears who are seeking for the truth.

5. CHILD OF THE TEMPLE

THEME: Everyone has deep-seated longings and desires to have a life of fulfillment and productivity. Like Hannah, who longed to be a mother, we can take our hopes and aspirations to the Lord, especially in the temples of God, and ask in faith and love that He might grant the righteous desires of our heart. As we give ourselves to the Lord, He will bless us in all things.

> *For this child I prayed: and the Lord hath given me my petition which I asked of him: Therefore also I have lent him to the Lord.* (1 Sam. 1:27–28)

MOMENT OF TRUTH

Hannah's heartfelt desire was to become a mother. Her devotion and pleading before the Lord at His temple were heard, and the Lord's servant promised her that her prayers would be answered. She conceived and bore Samuel, the future prophet of the Lord, and was filled with joy and thanksgiving, pleased to dedicate her son to the service of holiness.

MODERN PROPHETS SPEAK

Gordon B. Hinckley:

> Children are so very important. I never get over the thought that every man, good or bad, was once a little boy, and that every woman was once a little girl. They have moved in the direction in which they were pointed when they were small. Truly, "As the twig is bent, so the tree is inclined." The time to mold the pattern of virtuous youth and faithful adults is childhood. ("A Friend for Every Child," *Improvement Era,* Dec. 1970, 98; see also *TGBH,* 50–51)

James E. Faust:

> Whatever the era, whatever the times, one thing will never change: Fathers and mothers, if you have children, they must come first. You must read to your children and you must hug your children and you must love your children. Your success as a family, our success as a society, depends not on what happens in the White House but on what happens inside your house. (*Finding Light in a Dark World* [Salt Lake City: Deseret Book, 1995], 90)

ILLUSTRATIONS FOR OUR TIMES

In the Lord's Due Time

Virtually all parents have a deep-rooted longing to see the unfolding of vital blessings that will bring their children harmony, peace, light, truth, and joy. I remember many years ago a special experience that came to me on the occasion of the twenty-sixth anniversary of my wedding to my wife. I was pondering how very much I loved her and how happy I was to be enjoying her companionship. I thought about our four children, our gifts from God, and about the special one among them—our Nathan—who came to us with challenging handicaps. What happened then is best told in the contemporaneous words of my journal: "How sad, I said to myself, that he will not ever enjoy this type of deeply felt companionship that only a happy marriage can bring." It was a moment of true lament and sorrow. Then all at once a rush of positive energy swept over me, and a message, as clear as any I have ever received, quietly presented itself to me, saying, almost as if by a voice, "Don't worry about this. Nathan will have a companion in the eternities—a dear and lovely soul who lived a handicapped life in her earthly existence—and he will know the same happiness you now feel." I cannot help but conclude that all such challenged persons will, in the Lord's own due time, enjoy all the blessings of the gospel reserved for the choice spirits that have come from the mansions on high to complete their mortal sojourn and move onward and upward to the next phase of their existence.

SUMMARY

The purpose of the gospel is to bring about the abundant life for God's children, even eternal life and exaltation. We learn line upon line, precept upon precept. We build the edifice of our evolving spiritual life one block at a time. We learn to be loyal, kind and loving, hopeful, tolerant, and full of faith, even as the Father and Son epitomize these same qualities to us. We discern in the preserved records of our forebears the spirit of these building blocks of spiritual abundance at work. Just as Ruth, Naomi, Boaz, and Hannah exemplified these qualities, we too, by the grace of God, can leave behind for our posterity a legacy of obedience and honor. Let us open our hearts to receive the guidance of the Spirit in fulfilling such a calling: "For unto him that receiveth it shall be given more abundantly, even power" (D&C 71:6).

CHAPTER TWENTY-ONE

"THEM THAT HONOUR ME I WILL HONOUR"

Reading Assignment: 1 Samuel 2–3; 8

> *There is no substitute for the home. Its foundation is as ancient as the world, and its mission has been ordained of God from the earliest times. . . . The home then is more than a habitation, it is an institution which stands for stability and love in individuals as well as in nations. . . . A Latter-day Saint who has no ambition to establish a home and give it permanency has not a full conception of a sacred duty the gospel imposes upon him.* (Joseph F. Smith, *Juvenile Instructor*)

THEMES *for* LIVING

1. Favored of God: The Goodness of Samuel and the Wickedness of Eli's Sons
2. Principles and Responsibilities of Parenthood
3. Honoring the Lord's Call
4. Earthly King/Heavenly King

INTRODUCTION

Within these passages of scripture is a checklist of indispensable items for all parents and leaders in Zion to internalize and teach their children. First, we find persuasive evidence that the favor of God is drawn toward those who seek diligently to follow His will. Next, in the contrast between the faithful commitment of Samuel's parents and the unwise fatherly indulgence of Eli the priest, we perceive the pathway that parents are to follow in teaching their children the boundaries of safety and wise behavior. Third, the remarkable calling of Samuel reinforces the doctrine that the Lord has a mission for each of us to perform—in most cases many missions. An important part of the parental commission is to teach children to prepare for and accept such callings with enthusiasm and thanksgiving. Finally, these passages reinforce the truth that the Lord is our King and our Liege—and that any allegiance to worldly patterns of living rather than heavenly principles will lead away from the pathways of peace, harmony, and enduring joy that we all seek in life.

1. FAVORED OF GOD: THE GOODNESS OF SAMUEL AND THE WICKEDNESS OF ELI'S SONS

THEME: Those who seek after the principles of integrity, service, and holiness are favored of the Lord. He withdraws His hand of sustaining power from those who dishonor His word and His institutions. This is amply illustrated in the contrasting lives of the young Samuel and the sinful sons of Eli.

> *And the child Samuel grew on, and was in favour both with the Lord, and also with men.*
> (1 Sam. 2:26)

> ELI TO HIS SONS: *"And he said unto them, Why do ye such things? for I hear of your evil dealings by all this people."* (1 Sam. 2:26)

MOMENT OF TRUTH

Hannah gave praise to the Lord for His goodness as her son Samuel grew and prospered, ministering before the Lord and increasing in favor and righteousness. By way of contrast, Eli's two sons, Hophni and Phinehas, exercised unrighteous dominion as priests of God, being both greedy and immoral, thus bringing shame upon their family and calling forth the justice of God.

MODERN PROPHETS SPEAK

Neal A. Maxwell:

> Our choice is to seek to establish His righteousness or to rebelliously continue to walk in our own way. We are free to choose, to obey or not to obey, to come to terms or not to come to terms with the Lord. But we cannot revise the terms. (*Notwithstanding My Weakness* [Salt Lake City: Deseret Book, 1981], 76)

Hugh B. Brown:

> Brethren of the priesthood, let us never exercise unrighteous dominion. Let us honor the priesthood in our own homes, in our attitudes toward our wives and children, for there as elsewhere "when the Spirit is withdrawn, Amen to the priesthood or the authority of that man." The Spirit will not always strive with man but we should always strive to retain His Spirit in our homes, in our businesses, in all that we undertake to do. (*The Abundant Life* [Salt Lake City: Bookcraft, 1965], 192)

ILLUSTRATIONS FOR OUR TIMES

When the Saints Fall Short of Perfection

Nothing is quite so destructive as leaders who violate the laws of God. Such actions can be devastating to another's testimony and Church activity. Where possible, we must always separate the truthfulness of the gospel and kingdom of God from the imperfections and sins of others, and that includes those in leadership positions as well.

The sad story begins as the words were muttered: "I'll never darken the door of this church as long as that man is the bishop." The person had made a judgment that this leader was not worthy to serve as bishop. In reality, there could be several situations:

1. He (the leader) could have wrongfully done something and would not admit his mistake.

2. He could have made an honest mistake unknowingly.

3. The person could have misperceived the situation or been given wrong information.

4. The person was too quick to judge.

5. The person didn't have all the facts and did not inquire to get the correct information.

6. The person could not separate the frailties of man and the sin of an individual from the Church.

Recognizing each of the above scenarios leads one to the principle of mercy rather than judgment. The question arises, why would anyone let the behavior of another mortal keep him or her from God? Rather, why not pray for them, go to them to resolve the concern, or take the information (only if accurate) to your other leaders? Whatever the case, it is important to bless rather than condemn.

What's in a Name?
I was named after Richard R. Lyman—before this mighty Apostle of God stumbled on the stones of life's pathway and had to pick himself up once again. Those named after Matthew or Peter or John, or any of God's chosen who endured to the end, may think they have an advantage because of the luster of their namesake's exemplary walk of life— and perhaps they do. But I rather think I have an advantage of a special kind, for every time I think about my own name, I am reminded of the need for constant vigilance, continuous care, unending caution, and a watchful disposition—lest there be an occasion to stumble. I am also reminded of the infinite Atonement, that "bringeth about means unto men that they may have faith unto repentance" (Alma 34:15), and I say a silent prayer of thanks in my heart for the "merits, and mercy, and grace of the Holy Messiah" (2 Ne. 2:8), who made it possible for all mankind to rise above their weaknesses by renewing their hearts and humbly doing His will, as He did the will the Father.

2. PRINCIPLES AND RESPONSIBILITIES OF PARENTHOOD

THEME: Parents should illuminate the pathway of progress for their children, using the light of gospel truths. At the same time, they should mark clearly the boundaries and limits for appropriate behavior, and restrain their children from crossing the mark.

Wherefore kick ye at my sacrifices . . . and honourest thy sons above me? (1 Sam. 2:29)

Ye make the Lord's people to transgress. (1 Sam. 2:24)

MOMENT OF TRUTH

Eli learned of his sons' wicked behavior and reproved them, but not with sufficient sharpness. The Lord sorely chastised him for honoring his sons above Him, and for indulging in the abundance of the priest's office without restraint. The Lord condemned the family and shortened its tenure.

MODERN PROPHETS SPEAK

Spencer W. Kimball:

> Can anyone truthfully claim that he did not know stealing was wrong? Possessiveness seems to be a basic impulse in humans, but while a child may want other children's toys he soon comes to know that they are not his. Small thefts grow into larger ones unless the desire is curbed. Parents who "cover up" for their children, excuse them and pay for their misappropriations, miss an important opportunity to teach a lesson and thereby do untold damage to their offspring. If the child is required to return the coin or the pencil or the fruit with an appropriate apology, it is likely that his tendencies to steal will be curbed. But if he is lionized and made a little hero, if his misappropriation is made a joke, he is likely to continue in ever-increasing thefts. Most burglars and hold-up men would not have become so if they had been disciplined early. (*The Miracle of Forgiveness* [Salt Lake City: Bookcraft, 1969], 50)

Ezra Taft Benson:

> "I appeal to you parents, take nothing for granted about your children," said President J. Reuben Clark, Jr. "The great bulk of them, of course, are good, but some of us do not know when they begin to go away from the path of truth and righteousness. Be watchful every day and hour. Never relax your care, your solicitude. Rule kindly in the spirit of the gospel and the spirit of the priesthood, but rule, if you wish your children to follow the right path." Permissive parents are part of the problem. (*God, Family, Country: Our Three Great Loyalties* [Salt Lake City: Deseret Book, 1974], 224–25)

ILLUSTRATIONS FOR OUR TIMES

Hidden Windows of Possibility

In the brightly lit classroom of the private Bethel Pre-School Nursery, well-behaved, neatly-dressed children assembled for opening devotional each morning. Only one stood out, not because of her behavior, dress, or stature, but because of her radiant, golden-blonde hair. Her young Jewish and Israeli classmates considered her somewhat of an honored celebrity, and Adrienne, our four-year-old daughter, always rose to the occasion and savored the special treatment afforded her that year. The following year when she attended the public school kindergarten, the children put on the story of "Goldilocks and the Three Bears," and it was predictable who was chosen to play Goldilocks among the young candidates in the mostly Jewish neighborhood of northwestern Baltimore where we lived.

Here was a situation where a young person had a unique quality that was readily apparent to all. But there is a parable hidden in this reality, for not all qualities and potentialities of children are so manifest. Parents have to be geologists of the soul, often penetrating through many layers to find that which is uniquely special about each child. Each is equipped with a different set of gifts that needs to be unwrapped with care and devotion through the compassionate and tender assistance of the Spirit. Love and restraint, firmness and forgiveness, guidance and correction—all of these are part of the eternal recipe. Our Father in Heaven knows these children better than we, and we must continually invoke His blessing as we strive to be worthy parents in Zion.

The Most Rewarding but Difficult Role

In parenting, nothing is so difficult as to chastise in righteousness. Like Eli, we often talk about the problem, but never resolve the concern. No action is an action of indecision or passive acceptance. The result is that our children think it must not be really important. As parents, we are often afraid of confrontation because we think our relationship will suffer or our teenagers won't like us, so we acquiesce and become "permissive parents." Parents who fall into this category are inviting sorrow into their children's and their own lives.

The reality seems clear: parents are to teach, train, and then trust. Parents can never take agency away, for it is God-given. Even when one requires a certain behavior and standard of conduct, the child is still free to respond—and we as parents should be prepared to give consequences. There are always blessings or consequences for all our actions. Ideally, the consequence will be a natural one rather than contrived. The bottom line is that parents must be involved. They must love their children. The children must understand what is expected. Hopefully, with D&C 121:41–44 as our guide we will know the way to nurture, admonish, and even chastise in love. Parenting is the most rewarding yet most difficult role in all the world.

3. HONORING THE LORD'S CALL

THEME: We must be prepared to receive the Lord's callings to consecrate our time, gifts, and resources for the building up of His kingdom. Samuel's nocturnal commission is a prototype of humble acceptance.

> *And I will raise me up a faithful priest, that shall do according to that which is in mine heart and in my mind: and I will build him a sure house; and he shall walk before mine anointed for ever.* (1 Sam. 2:35)

> *The Lord called Samuel: and he answered, Here am I.* (1 Sam. 3:4)

MOMENT OF TRUTH

The boy Samuel received a divine commission during the night and began his role as a prophet of God by conveying the Lord's disapproval of Eli and his family for their unrighteousness.

MODERN PROPHETS SPEAK

Russell M. Nelson:

> "To my astonishment," he said, "when I looked at families there was a deficiency in some, there was a lack, for I saw families that would not be permitted to come and dwell together, because they had not honored their calling here." (*The Gateway We Call Death* [Salt Lake City: Deseret Book, 1995], 97–98)

John Taylor:

> We call upon you to honor your calling and priesthood and purge from your midst corruption of every kind. And we call upon the presidents of stakes and their counselors, upon the bishops and their counselors, and upon the priests, teachers and deacons, to magnify their offices, and not to be partakers of other men's sins. For as sure as I live and as God lives, if you do, God will require it at your hands. And therefore, I call upon presidents and men in authority, where men do not magnify their calling, to remove them from their positions of responsibility and replace them by men who will; and let us have correct principles and the order of God carried out in Zion. (*The Gospel Kingdom: Selections from the Writings and Discourses of John Taylor* [Salt Lake City: Improvement Era, 1941], 133–34)

ILLUSTRATIONS FOR OUR TIMES

An Awakening

God has called each of us. Some callings are eternal and were foreordained prior to earth life. Some callings are for this mortal existence and were foreordained prior to earth life. Some callings are for the spirit world (see D&C 138:58). This is a concept that must be rooted into our very soul. When called to a Church calling, we often accept it as a mere formality. When functioning in eternal roles (father, mother, husband, wife, brother, sister, son, daughter) we rarely take time to contemplate the significance as it relates to our being called of God. It usually takes an awakening to the realization that we truly have eternal callings in life—both as formal sustained callings and eternally endowed callings. Such an awakening happened to me.

I will never forget the day when I had just gotten home from work and I was tired. I sat down to read the evening paper for just a minute. All of a sudden my young four-year-old son came bursting into my room, wanting to make paper airplanes *now*. I said, "We'll do it later." He persisted and begged, and I still put him off. He kept at me until I made a mistake. I said, "Leave me alone. We'll do it when I'm ready." My son left with tears rolling down his cheeks. I threw down the paper and ran after my son saying, "We'll build them right now! We'll build them right now—this very minute!" A smile came over his face, and we built paper airplanes for a long time. We had fun. We were happy together. I felt great. I made a promise that day that when I come home, I am King Daddy, servant of all and friend to my children.

The realization or awakening must happen in all our roles and callings. We must come to know the Lord has called us to do all things, that His children may be blessed.

The Lord Had Made the Choice

As a stake presidency, we considered the assignment of selecting the new bishop a solemn and sacred task, not one to be accomplished without much prayer and fasting. The several candidates were interviewed, one after the other—all good and noble men with great talent and capability, all men of God. But the Spirit whispered clearly, not once but several times in a row: "Not these, but him." And the person identified was not on the short list at all. All three members of the presidency felt it independently. What a joy to disclose to each other after the interviews that the same prompting had come to each, and that the Lord had made the choice. We had but to obey. Subsequently, the good brother who had somehow been overlooked was dutifully called and served faithfully as a bishop in Zion. The Lord makes these calls. It is His Church. He looks upon the heart and reads the measure of talent and ability needed for a given mission. When the Lord extends the call, it is a divine call, attended with heavenly blessings of a very specific kind for His children: "According as his divine power hath given unto us all things that pertain unto life and godliness, through the knowledge of him that hath called us to glory and virtue" (2 Pet. 1:3).

4. EARTHLY KING/HEAVENLY KING

THEME: When a people supplant their Heavenly King with a preference for an earthly king, then adversity and oppression are at the door. We must seek the face of the Lord always, and honor Him as our King, Ruler, and Redeemer.

> *And ye shall cry out in that day because of your king which ye shall have chosen you; and the Lord will not hear you in that day.* (1 Sam. 8:18)

MOMENT OF TRUTH

Israel pled to have a king like other nations—one who would fight their battles. Samuel (himself a father with rebellious sons) resisted, but the Lord told him to indulge the Israelites' desire. Samuel described what manner of royal oppression the Israelites had to look forward to if they honored earthly institutions, but they insisted nevertheless. Thus Israel rejected the Lord and sought for earthly justice and power.

MODERN PROPHETS SPEAK

Marion G. Romney:

"O how you ought to thank your heavenly King!" said King Benjamin to his brethren. ". . . you should render all the thanks and praise which your whole soul has power to possess, to that God who has created you, and has kept and preserved you, and has caused that ye should rejoice, and has granted that ye should live in peace one with another" (Mosiah 2:19–20). (*Learning for the Eternities* [Salt Lake City: Deseret Book, 1977], 198)

Bruce R. McConkie:

"Therefore," that is, in the light of all I have told you about forgiveness, "is the kingdom of heaven likened unto a certain king," Jesus said, "which would take account of his servants." The kingdom of heaven here named is the Church, the Church of Jesus Christ; it is the kingdom of God on earth, the earthly kingdom that prepares men to inherit the heavenly kingdom. The King is the Lord himself—the heavenly King and the earthly King—the One who reigns supreme over all the creatures of his creating, but to whom the members of his earthly kingdom have sworn an especial and a particular allegiance. And his servants are the members of his church, perhaps more especially those members who have been called to positions of trust and responsibility. Though all his saints will be called to account for their stewardships, those who are appointed to lead and guide others have a fiduciary relationship with the King, a relationship that calls for the exercise of special trust. (*The Mortal Messiah: From Bethlehem to Calvary* [Salt Lake City: Deseret Book, 1979–81], 3:95)

ILLUSTRATIONS FOR OUR TIMES

Allegiance to the King of Heaven

A pall of gray hung over the streets of Washington, D.C., on that November morning in 1963 as Jacqueline Kennedy and her two little ones, dressed in solemn black, made their way down the east steps of the Capitol. My wife and I watched in silence, along with tens of thousands of other mourning onlookers. The endless, plaintive roll of the drums accompanied the caisson through the rain-drenched streets of the city as it bore the body of the fallen president to its resting place at Arlington National Cemetery. In our mortal experience, few events rival the profound grief that attends the unexpected loss of a national hero—a president, a king, a queen, a worldly leader of stature. The same kind of global shock and heartache was felt upon the death of Princess Diana. Herein lies a lesson. The most important event in all of the history of mankind took place when the King of Heaven gave His life for us and then took it up again through the Resurrection. From the foundations of the world, His death and Easter rising from the grave enabled and empowered God's children to transcend the temporal death and, through faith and obedience, achieve salvation and eternal life. No earthly king could do what the Heavenly King did for us.

Like Other Nations

A prophet-leader in all aspects of life—both temporal and spiritual—had led the Israelites. In a way, it was almost as if they practiced a theocracy, for a prophet of God led them in all things. Judges were put in place, but they too were righteous leaders, appointed by the prophets. In most countries we have separation of church and state. The sad part about the Israelites in this case is they now wanted a mortal king—not the King of Heaven and Earth, the Lord God Jehovah. With an earthly king they could do worldly things rather than the will of God. They wanted to be like the other nations. They honored the world and not God. All civilizations throughout time have eventually failed because of moral decay.

SUMMARY

Even though the Lord loves all of His children, His honor is reserved for those who honor Him, as the scriptures attest. We honor Him by keeping His commandments. We honor him by teaching our children to follow in His footsteps. As parents and leaders in Zion, we honor Him by infusing our lives with the light of the gospel. We consecrate our time, talents, and resources to the building up of His kingdom. We fulfill our missions with diligence and valor. We teach allegiance to the Heavenly King rather than to worldly practices not based on eternal principles. All of this brings glory to our Heavenly Father and blessings of light and truth into our family circles.

CHAPTER TWENTY-TWO

"THE LORD LOOKETH *on* *the* HEART"

Reading Assignment: 1 Samuel 9–11; 13; 15–17.

Additional Reading: 1 Samuel 12; 14.

> *I heard the Prophet Joseph say, in speaking the Twelve on one occasion: "You will have all kinds of trials to pass through. And it is quite as necessary for you to be tried as it was for Abraham and other men of God, and (said he) God will feel after you, and He will take hold of you and wrench your very heart strings, and if you cannot stand it you will not be fit for an inheritance in the celestial kingdom of God."* (John Taylor, *JD* 24:197)

THEMES *for* LIVING

1. The Lord Can Work with Willing and Renewable Hearts
2. The Nobility of Pure Obedience
3. The Consequences of Self-Justification
4. The Lord Looks upon the Heart
5. Victory in the Strength of the Lord

INTRODUCTION

The scriptural account of the early days of Saul and the calling of young David to become king of Israel is a study in aspects of the heart. We learn, as in the case of Saul, in the beginning, that the Lord can work with willing and renewable hearts that are humble and receptive. At the same time, we learn that such hearts must continue in reverence and pure obedience, lest the spirit of pride and arrogant self-containment supplant the commitment to do God's will. Saul is our witness of the danger of such a defection of heart, and the consequence of his self-justification is a sad commentary on what happens when we are no longer a person after the Lord's "own heart" (1 Sam. 13:14). At the same time, we learn from these scriptures that the Lord sees the heart, not the outward appearance, when He calls His servants on His errand, as in the case of the young David. We see, moreover, that the Lord gives courage to the faithful and the valiant, who do not experience fear in the face of the Goliaths of the world because they go in the power of God.

1. THE LORD CAN WORK WITH WILLING AND RENEWABLE HEARTS

THEME: Just as in the case of the young Saul, the Lord favors the humble and spiritually malleable, and blesses them in their callings by giving them a transformed and rejuvenated heart.

> SAMUEL TO SAUL: *"And the Spirit of the Lord will come upon thee, and thou shalt prophesy with them, and shalt be turned into another man."* (1 Sam. 10:6)

MOMENT OF TRUTH

When Israel rejected the Lord as their king and insisted on having a worldly king like the neighboring cultures, the Lord instructed the prophet Samuel to anoint the young Saul to be king of Israel. Saul had many good qualities, including (at the beginning) a humble nature. The Lord gave him "another heart" (1 Sam. 10:9)—i.e., Saul was illuminated by divine purpose and became spiritually committed. The Spirit of the Lord came upon him, and he prophesied with power. Samuel urged the Israelites and their new king to be obedient to the Lord's commandments, lest He reject them.

MODERN PROPHETS SPEAK

Neal A. Maxwell:

> Another cosmic fact: only by aligning our wills with God's is full happiness to be found. Anything less results in a lesser portion (see Alma 12:10–11). The Lord will

work with us even if, at first, we "can no more than desire" but are willing to "give place for a portion of [His] words" (Alma 32:27). A small foothold is all He needs. But we must desire and provide it. (*If Thou Endure It Well* [Salt Lake City: Bookcraft, 1996], 51)

Marin J. Ashton:

Do I have a willing heart? Let us look again to the scriptures for guidance: "Behold, the Lord requireth the heart and a willing mind; and the willing and obedient shall eat the good of the land of Zion in these last days" (D&C 64:34). A willing heart describes one who desires to please the Lord and to serve the Lord's cause first. He serves the Lord on the Lord's terms, not his own. There are no restrictions to where or how he will serve. As one who has tendered calls to serve to many, I am always pleased to see members willing to give their time, energy, and effort to the upbuilding of the Church. They do so primarily for one reason: to serve the Lord with all their heart, might, mind, and strength. (*The Measure of Our Hearts* [Salt Lake City: Deseret Book, 1991], 4)

ILLUSTRATIONS FOR OUR TIMES

The Willing Convert

There have been so many opportunities in the Church for my wife and myself to interact with people having remarkably saintly dispositions. While we were living in Maryland a number of years ago, we invited a young woman over to our home one day to talk about the gospel. She had been referred to us by a previous stake president as one having considerable interest in learning more about the Church. My journal account of this experience gives the details:

If anyone was converted, she was. She spent several hours with us, and toward the end of her stay she asked whether it was not so that Mormons paid tithing. I said yes, and asked what her understanding of that might be. She replied that it was her understanding that this meant one-third of one's income. Somewhat surprised, I asked her whether she would be willing to pay this much to the Lord. "Certainly," was her response, and she had the most sincere and warm spirit about her. I then explained what the law of tithing meant, and complimented her on her humble devotion and willingness to do whatever the Lord asked of her.

This young woman soon thereafter joined the Church and rendered much service in the spirit of humility and obedience. To this day, my wife and I remain impressed with her angelic faith and acceptance of the will of the Lord. She, for one, exemplified the principle taught by the Lord: "Verily I say unto you, all among them who know their hearts are honest, and are broken, and their spirits contrite, and are willing to observe their covenants by sacrifice, yea, every sacrifice which I, the Lord, shall command—they are accepted of me" (D&C 97:8).

2. THE NOBILITY OF PURE OBEDIENCE

THEME: When we begin to govern our lives according to our own desires and judgment rather than acting in the spirit of our commission as servants of God, we begin to falter and lose favor with the Lord. Only by obedience to the commandments and the will of God can we hope to have the blessings of heaven and prosper in our duties and service.

> *Hath the Lord as great delight in burnt offerings and sacrifices, as in obeying the voice of the Lord? Behold, to obey is better than sacrifice, and to hearken than the fat of rams.* (1 Sam. 15:22–23)

MOMENT OF TRUTH

Soon after assuming the role of king in Israel, Saul began to forget the Lord and attribute to himself the abilities of righteous judgment and priesthood authority. When Samuel delayed his arrival to offer sacrifice to the Lord, Saul took it upon himself to perform the priestly duties and was rejected by the Lord as no longer "a man after his own heart" (1 Sam. 13:14). Later, Saul disobeyed the Lord by saving the spoils from the battle with the Amalekites, thus sealing his rejection by the Lord as king over Israel. Thereafter he was plagued with an evil spirit, and only the music of young David could give him relief.

MODERN PROPHETS SPEAK

Gordon B. Hinckley:
> And so I repeat, do not let pride stand in your way. The way of the gospel is a simple way. Some of the requirements may appear to you as elementary and unnecessary. Do not spurn them. Humble yourself and walk in obedience. I promise that the results that follow will be marvelous to behold and satisfying to experience. (*Be Thou an Example* [Salt Lake City: Deseret Book, 1981], 68)

Jeffrey R. Holland:
> The essence of his earthly mission: Obedience and loyalty to the will of the Father, however bitter the cup or painful the price. That is a lesson he would teach these Nephites again and again during the three days he would be with them. By obedience and sacrifice, by humility and purity, by unflagging determination to glorify the Father, Christ was himself glorified. In complete devotion to the Father's will, Christ had become the

light and the life of the world. "And . . . when Jesus had spoken these words the whole multitude fell to the earth" (3 Ne. 1:8). (*Christ and the New Covenant: The Messianic Message of the Book of Mormon* [Salt Lake City: Deseret Book, 1997], 251)

ILLUSTRATIONS FOR OUR TIMES

The Spiritually Centered Life

The eventual disharmony reflected in the life of King Saul—his outward show of religiosity not anchored by a genuine inward faith (1 Sam. 15)—brings to mind an experience from my own past. Several years after the completion of the Washington D.C. Temple, I invited two good nonmember friends and university colleagues to drive down with me to the visitors' center at the temple for a tour. One was a young sociology professor, and the other was a Catholic priest who taught courses in comparative religion. They listened and observed carefully. Following the tour, my Catholic friend made a significant statement, which I recorded in my journal. He noted, in general, that many clergy have two religions, one that they "carry in their pocket," and one that they present in public. "Often there is a considerable gap between the two," he said, implying that they might be more "religious" outwardly than inwardly. "With the Mormons it is different," he observed. "The gap, in their case, seems to be rather small." With this compliment, he was articulating his own perspective that members of the Church typically live by their convictions, and since they seem to accomplish much practical good, they must therefore, he believed, have a strong, genuine faith. He was right. Such is indeed the case with Latter-day Saints who abide by the teachings of the Master and strive to make their lives consistently centered in spiritual ways—outwardly as well as inwardly. They are the good seed about which Jesus spoke: "But that on the good ground are they, which in an honest and good heart, having heard the word, keep it, and bring forth fruit with patience" (Luke 8:15).

The Lessons of Obedience

We lived on a farm during World War II. We had plenty of food, but we were still required to go to the store for additional items. During the war, everyone had a little book—a ration book. The ration book allowed each family to purchase so much food for each member of the family. I can still remember going to the store and helping my mother. We could buy only the amount of food we had coupons for. I learned that there was only so much food for every family, so food was important. That's where the story begins. You see, my father was a big man—6' 3" and 250 pounds—and when he spoke, we obeyed. When he said eat, we ate. I remember my parents liked to eat cooked cauliflower, cooked spinach, and cooked cabbage—and I couldn't stand any of them. I learned something as an eight-year-old boy: I could chew my food while holding my breath and taking a big drink of milk, and I couldn't even taste it. I was able to cope with all this horrible food my parents were eating. My angel mother always gave me just a small portion, knowing of my great dislike. Yet we had to eat—we had to obey.

Years went by. I got married, and we were getting ready to have another little baby. I was thirty-eight years old. It was our last child. My wife asked me if I would go to the store and buy the groceries. She gave me the list, and I was off. On the list was "cooking vegetables." I could choose anything I wanted—corn, peas, artichokes, squash. Consider this—I was the big man in the market, and I could buy what I wanted. I was alone with the list and the money. As I walked down through the produce section, I noticed a beautiful head of cabbage, which I took, along with a beautiful bag of spinach and a large white head of cauliflower. I stopped in amazement. I couldn't believe it. I had bought the very food I thought I hated. I learned to love these foods through obedience. Even to this day, I think of spinach steamed and hot with a little butter, a twist of lemon and sprinkles of pepper, and I feel like Pavlov's dog. I love cooked spinach, cabbage, and cauliflower, and I learned to love them through obedience. I would hate to think of never being able to enjoy these foods. Yes, obedience to any rule or law always has a blessing.

3. THE CONSEQUENCES OF SELF-JUSTIFICATION

THEME: The Lord "requireth the heart and a willing mind" (D&C 64:34). When we rationalize our misbehavior and sins and justify our unrighteous behavior, the Lord is displeased and we relinquish great spiritual blessings. Willing obedience makes all rationalization unnecessary and brings greater harmony, peace, and confidence into our lives.

> *Rebellion is as the sin of witchcraft, and stubbornness is as iniquity and idolatry.* (1 Sam. 15:23)

MOMENT OF TRUTH

When Saul disobeyed the Lord by saving out the spoils of war after battle, Samuel called him to repentance. Disobedience is a terrible sin. But Saul went even further; he justified his behavior at first by laying the blame on his people, and then by claiming to want to use the spoils as a sacrifice to the Lord. Saul's response in the face of the truth has become the enduring prototype of the self-justifying act, and stands as a memorial to the dire consequences of unrighteous rationalization.

MODERN PROPHETS SPEAK

Spencer W. Kimball:

> Self-justification is the enemy of repentance. God's Spirit continues with the honest in heart to strengthen, to help, and to save, but invariably the Spirit of God ceases to strive with the man who excuses himself in his wrongdoing. Practically all dishonesty owes its existence and growth to this inward distortion we call self-justification. It is the first, the worst, and the most insidious and damaging form of cheating—to cheat oneself. (*Faith Precedes the Miracle* [Salt Lake City: Deseret Book, 1972], 234)

Gordon B. Hinckley:

> The violation of his commandments in this age, as in any other, brings only regret, sorrow, loss of self-respect, and in many cases tragedy. Rationalization and equivocation will not erase the cankering scar that blights the self-respect of a person who disobeys the law of chastity. Self-justification will never mend the heart of a person who has drifted into moral tragedy. (*Faith: The Essence of True Religion* [Salt Lake City: Deseret Book, 1989] 83)

ILLUSTRATIONS FOR OUR TIMES

Trust in the Lord

In the story of Saul, we see a human trait that we all sometimes fall prey to—self-sufficiency and self-justification, an "I know best" attitude, impatience—"I want it done now." We become casual in our behavior, stubborn and slow to listen, afraid of others' opinions, complacent in exact obedience . . . and the list goes on.

I recall the sad tale of a friend who had served in many positions in the Church. He was a good man, but like Saul was suffering from some of the above symptoms—in fact, almost all of them. He mentioned how he would like to confront the devil and let him know "what's what." I was nervous as he expressed this desire. It was not long until he was divorced and not in full fellowship in the Church. I watched and tried to help, but was unable. I learned from this sad experience that you never take things for granted, that you flee from sin and temptation, trust in the Lord, take counsel from the Lord in all things, and rely on the Lord and not your own understanding.

This situation had a more joyous ending, for the man came back into full fellowship, and I was full of joy, and surely the Lord was pleased. Thank God for the power of the Atonement and the doctrine of repentance and forgiveness.

Each Gift Is Vital

After many decades of counseling in Church callings of various kinds, I have probably heard just about every conceivable variation of what we call a "rationalization"—and have caught myself using a few of them on occasion. It would be fairly easy to develop a "top ten" list of our favorite excuses for not doing better in our Church callings. But, there is one universal rationalization that perhaps more than any other, places at risk the forward momentum of the kingdom: "What I do or don't do will not make any significant difference."

Years ago, I read or heard a parable that has stuck with me. Perhaps you have heard it, too. In a certain village during the Middle Ages, the village fathers called for a grand harvest celebration. Each family was asked to contribute a measure of their finest wine as part of the refreshments. A massive empty wine barrel was placed in the market square, and each family brought its contribution the evening before the celebration and poured it into the barrel. The next day the wine was to be distributed as part of the hearty repast. But when the cask was tapped, out flowed only clear water. Each family had evidently decided that one pitcher of water would not be noticed in the wine mix, and therefore they had seen fit to give only water.

It is no different in the Church. Every member has a role to play. Every contribution is indispensable. In the totality of the gifts brought to the banquet celebration is made manifest the glory of God through untold blessings for the community of Saints. What each of us does (or does not do) always has significant consequences, both individually and collectively. The Apostle Paul explained that all callings, taken together, constitute the kingdom: "For the perfecting of the saints, for the work of the ministry, for the edifying of the body of Christ: Till we all come in the unity of the faith, and of the knowledge of the Son of God, unto a perfect man, unto the measure of the stature of the fulness of Christ" (Eph. 4:12–13).

4. THE LORD LOOKS UPON THE HEART

THEME: While mankind tends to evaluate based on outward appearances and temporal standards, the Lord discerns one's potential for doing good and judges by the heart (the desire and capacity for righteous service).

> *For man looketh on the outward appearance, but the Lord looketh on the heart.* (1 Sam. 16:7)

MOMENT OF TRUTH

When Samuel was sent to prepare the way for a new king in Israel, he went at first according to standard protocol by considering the oldest of Jesse's eight sons. But the

Lord guided him to discern the individual chosen for the throne—David, the youngest. Thus we learn how the Lord makes His selections—by looking at the heart and seeing with the inner eye of spiritual vision.

Samuel, having been inspired to do so, anointed David king of Israel prior to the death of Saul. David was called to play the harp for Saul, that he might be relieved of an evil spirit. David found favor in the sight of Saul and became his armor bearer.

MODERN PROPHETS SPEAK

Melvin J. Ballard:

> The Lord looks upon the hearts of men and women, and their intent, and they shall be judged according to their will and their desires. (in Bryant S. Hinckley, *Sermons and Missionary Services of Melvin J. Ballard* [Salt Lake City: Deseret Book, 1949], 206)

Joseph Fielding Smith:

> In the great plan of salvation nothing has been overlooked. The gospel of Jesus Christ is the most beautiful thing in the world. It embraces every soul whose heart is right and who diligently seeks him and desires to obey his laws and covenants. Therefore, if a person is for any cause denied the privilege of complying with any of the covenants, the Lord will judge him or her by the intent of the heart. (*AGQ*, 267–68; see also Dallin H. Oaks, *Pure in Heart* [Salt Lake City: Bookcraft, 1988], 62)

ILLUSTRATIONS FOR OUR TIMES

Quickening the Pace

Some callings, like that of father and mother or husband and wife, are eternal. Others are shorter callings that are really subsets of a greater and never-ending mission to help build the kingdom of God. Our family once lived in a ward where the bishopric used an unusual strategy that seemed to help the members focus with an uncommon degree of devotion on the callings they received. Each December, all of the callings in the ward were changed; that is, each member received a new calling—of precisely one's year duration. The entire ward family was therefore reorganized once each year. This had several consequences (apart from adding considerably to the leadership responsibilities of the bishopric): (1) the interest around roles and duties was heightened, (2) people tended to accelerate the pace of learning their new duties, since they had a shorter time in which to have a positive impact, (3) the energy level seemed to be higher, and (4) there was a lot of networking and discussion behind the scenes about correlation and cooperation. I am not sure the bishopric continued the practice for more than several cycles, as we moved on to another setting, but during the time it lasted, people did lengthen their stride and gain a keener sense of unity. We are indeed a unified body of

Christ where talents, gifts, and resources must be shared interdependently and with great devotion and commitment if there is to be an optimization of the gospel "harvest." What if we were to regard each calling as if it lasted only one day—*today*—and thus made this and every day of our involvement a shining example of our most noble and valiant contribution toward building the kingdom?

Judging by the Heart

The calling of David to be king teaches a doctrine of perception and judgment. The Lord, as should we, looks upon the heart. This transcending truth, when understood, can and will change one's life. It will help us become nonjudgmental and look for the good in all.

I remember the day, years ago, when this truth was taught on a pioneer trek that I took with the youth of our stake. We had been asked by the leaders of the trek to take our scriptures and go off on a "solo" experience to ponder and pray. Following this time alone, we returned and later had a testimony meeting. I will never forget one young, popular "cool cat" teenager as he stood to bear his testimony. He stood slowly, went to the front, and started to speak. His voice quivered, and tears welled up in his eyes as he started to express gratitude to the members of his "family group." He bore a fervent and strong testimony, and as he concluded he told us of this wonderful truth he had learned. He said, "I cannot believe how I have misjudged so many people in my life. Here I am, 'Mister Cool,' and I didn't even have the eyes, the mind, and especially the heart to see the good in others. I could tell right off what people were like simply by checking out the style of their clothes, the labels—whether they were the best or not, the hair style, the people skills, and could they play ball. Yes, I knew everything that made a person 'cool.' Then I met Tim (we'll call him that) here on the pioneer trek. You all know Tim—the short kid with the funny hair who has a weird personality." They all laughed. Then he stopped and said, "You need to know that Tim is my dear, close friend now. These few days I have gotten to know him. He is the greatest. He laughs at my jokes. He is nice to everyone in our group. He is simply the best. Everyone in our group loves Tim. We had the time, and we were together, and we got to know each other—long talks, shared concerns with life, and in all we got to know each other's heart. I am so grateful for this experience, for I have learned how good everyone is and how you should never, ever judge another by how he or she looks. Oh, I'm so happy. I love all of you."

There weren't many dry eyes as he slowly walked back to his place. That day, we all learned more deeply about taking the time to know, to appreciate, and to love each other.

5. VICTORY IN THE STRENGTH OF THE LORD

THEME: When we go about the Lord's errand by relying upon His power and following His Spirit, we are assured of ultimate victory, for the purposes of the Lord cannot be thwarted or compromised.

> *Thou comest to me with a sword, and with a spear, and with a shield: but I come to thee*
> *in the name of the Lord of hosts, the God of the armies of Israel, whom thou hast defied.*
> (1 Sam. 17:45)

MOMENT OF TRUTH

All the mighty men of Israel quaked at the Philistine hordes and shrank at the defiant strength of the giant, Goliath. But the anointed youth, David, going in the strength of the Lord, used his inspired skill to thwart the arrogant enemy at his one place of weakness. The story of David and Goliath is perhaps the supreme example in all of world literature of how the weak things of the earth can vanquish the strong through the help of the Lord. No story has so inspired the hearts of people everywhere—especially young people—to take courage in carrying out their mortal assignments with hope and faith.

MODERN PROPHETS SPEAK

George Q. Cannon:
> However weak he might be himself, he knew that in the strength of the Lord he could accomplish whatever might be required of him. (*The Life of Nephi: Faith-Promoting Series, no. 9* [Salt Lake City: Juvenile Instructor Office, 1883], 36–37)

Joseph Fielding Smith:
> Never in the history of the world has this truth been so greatly manifest as in the preaching of the Gospel by the weak and humble elders of the Church. They have gone forth into strength which the Lord promised them and they have confounded the wisdom of the wise and the understanding of their prudent men has been hid (Isa. 29:14). Think of the Prophet Joseph Smith, who was without training or education, only in the simple grades, so far as the learning of the world is concerned. Yet the Lord called him and educated him and he has confounded the entire religious world and brought to naught their false doctrines. (*Church History and Modern Revelation* [Salt Lake City: The Church of Jesus Christ of Latter-day Saints, 1946–49], 1:149)

ILLUSTRATIONS FOR OUR TIMES

A Missionary such as David

Man's strength is insurmountable when combined with the strength of the Lord. I will never forget a "righteous, humble, David-like" missionary.

He was just a medium-sized, quiet, soft-spoken missionary. His letters were difficult to read. His writing skills were in need of help. When he read, it was haltingly at best. He had struggled all his life in school, but he was now an anointed disciple of Jesus Christ. He was a full-time proselyting missionary in the London South Mission. I watched as his letters improved and his reading skills were enhanced. He was made a district leader. There was a missionary who was struggling and wanted to go home. The Lord inspired me to put him with this district leader before his scheduled departure to leave early from his mission. I would check regularly on how things were going. One day I suggested that this district leader give him a blessing to stay. He said, "Okay," and then added, "Will this take away his agency? If I bless him with the priesthood, he will stay."

I replied, "Don't worry, Elder, that's what the Lord wants. He wants him to stay, and so do I."

The district leader gave him a blessing. At the next zone meeting, I interviewed the struggling missionary and asked how he felt. He said, "You know, President, I've been thinking. I really want to stay now. Is that okay?" With joy in my heart I assured him it was fine. He stayed, and he was a good missionary. The Lord blessed us greatly, as this seemingly "regular" district leader became a powerful instrument in His hands. The odds were almost insurmountable against us, but with faith and the power of the priesthood, a life was blessed.

It Shall Be Given You What to Say

A member of the Church who takes up his or her cross in the spirit of the Lord's errand is magnified by the Spirit beyond earthly capacities. I recall from the mission field a young elder who, with his companion, felt impressed to attend a lecture on the "Mormons" given by a minister in one of the large Protestant churches in the city of Kassel, Germany. As the two missionaries sat in the back of the crowded cathedral listening, they became increasingly concerned with the untruths being promulgated about the restored Church. Finally, it was more than they could endure. As the young elder later described it, he felt as though he was literally lifted up by unseen hands and transported down the central aisle of the church to a position directly below the elevated pulpit where the minister was speaking. There, before a large congregation of mesmerized citizens, he engaged the minister in a discussion in which he corrected the misinformation and bore fervent testimony (all in fluent German) about the truthfulness of the restored gospel and the mission of the Prophet Joseph Smith. The minister was rendered speechless. Afterwards, the missionaries were able to distribute thousands of tracts on the steps in front of the cathedral, and found a more welcome entrance into the homes by virtue of their enhanced reputation. The elder later took no credit for the remarkable performance, but instead gave credit to the Lord. It was a wonderful confirmation of the charge and promise given in the Doctrine and Covenants: "Therefore, verily I say unto you, lift up your voices unto this people; speak the thoughts that I shall put into your hearts, and you shall not be confounded before men; For it shall be given you in the very hour, yea, in the very moment, what ye shall say" (D&C 100:5–6).

SUMMARY

Among many other lessons of the gospel in the passages we have been reading from the Old Testament are these: No matter our circumstances, no matter the task at hand, the Lord can work miracles with us if we will only have a willing and contrite heart, easily entreated and open to the promptings of the Spirit. Furthermore, we will maintain God's favor and ongoing support if we guard against pride and place our trust in Him rather than in man and the things of the world. Nothing will so quickly ensnare us and lead us astray as our own self-justification in sin and the rationalization of misbehavior. We must remember that the Lord sees all—our thoughts, our intent, our every desire and motivation. He makes His callings based on the heart, not on the trappings of outward glory and honor. He reserves His choicest blessings of courage and strength to those who go, like the young David, in the power of His service and in the glory of His name. Let us truly be people after the Lord's "own heart" (1 Sam. 13:14).

CHAPTER TWENTY-THREE

"THE LORD BE *between* THEE *and* ME FOR EVER"

Reading Assignment: 1 Samuel 18–20; 23–24.

Additional Reading: 1 Samuel 14:1–16; 2 Samuel 1.

> *Ever keep in exercise the principle of mercy, and be ready to forgive our brother on the first intimations of repentance, and asking forgiveness; and should we even forgive our brother, or even our enemy, before he repent or ask forgiveness, our heavenly Father would be equally as merciful unto us.* (Joseph Smith, *HC* 3:383)

THEMES *for* LIVING

1. Covenant Friendship: Jonathan and David
2. The Treachery of a Jealous Mind
3. The Forgiveness of a Magnanimous Heart

INTRODUCTION

The friendship of Jonathan and David is rightly celebrated as one of the most exemplary brotherly relationships recorded in the holy scriptures. They were carrying on the covenant lineage from Abraham, who was characterized, because of his faith and righteousness, as "a friend of God" (James 2:23, see also Isa. 41:8). Friendship between and among individuals united on the basis of the covenant always reflects faith and righteousness—faith that nothing can detract from, or interfere with, the loyalty and all-weather support of true friends; and righteousness based on principles of truth and love. In our dispensation of time, the Lord established a greeting of friendship for use in the School of the Prophets: "Art thou a brother or brethren? I salute you in the name of the Lord Jesus Christ, in token or remembrance of the everlasting covenant, in which covenant I receive you to fellowship, in a determination that is fixed, immovable, and unchangeable, to be your friend and brother through the grace of God in the bonds of love, to walk in all the commandments of God blameless, in thanksgiving, forever and ever. Amen" (D&C 88:133). Friendship of this kind cannot be eclipsed by the envy, greed, or malice of others (such as that which King Saul harbored for the forgiving David).

1. COVENANT FRIENDSHIP: JONATHAN AND DAVID

THEME: The bonds of friendship established through a mutual covenant of love and respect endure all the tests of life, including threat to life and limb. In the example of Jonathan and David, we see exemplified the kind of friendship that edifies and exalts.

> *The soul of Jonathan was knit with the soul of David, and Jonathan loved him as his own soul.* (1 Sam. 18:1)

MOMENT OF TRUTH

Jonathan loved David as much as Saul hated him. Time and again, Jonathan defended, protected, and rescued the son of Jesse from the king's assassination plots. Never for a moment stooping to jealousy or envy, Jonathan saw in David the future king of Israel (see 1 Sam. 23:17), and did all in his power to facilitate his preservation for that destined role.

MODERN PROPHETS SPEAK

Harold B. Lee:

> President George Albert Smith was a disciple of friendship and love. He was indeed a friend to everyone. My gaze at his likeness seemed to give me a warmth of that radiance which made every man his friend. (*Decisions for Successful Living* [Salt Lake City: Deseret Book, 1973], 238)

Gordon B. Hinckley:

> You will learn the importance of friendshipping and fellowshipping. Now is the time to practice these principles, to reach out with appreciation and kindness to others. Many a young man has come into this Church because of the friendship of a high school associate. I earnestly hope that no boy within the sound of my voice will ever do anything to prejudice an associate against the Church or its people. (*TGBH,* 222)

ILLUSTRATIONS FOR OUR TIMES

Bodyguards of the Soul

I remember when a student in one of my institute classes stood up to bear her testimony. In essence she explained how she had been adrift in life, with no direction or goals established. Then a friend, a true protector of her eternal life, said, "You simply have to come to institute with me." She gave all the reasons why she couldn't, but her friend persisted. Finally she relented and said she would come with her. From that moment on, her spirit was lifted and inspired. She wanted to do good. She set goals and made plans to be fully involved with the institute and the Church, and made a commitment to live the gospel of Jesus Christ. Her friend had truly been her guardian angel. Her life would be changed forever. Her friend had been a true friend, a life-saving friend, a proactive friend who truly cared for her soul. Real friends are involved as true "bodyguards" of the soul.

Your Neighborhood Prophet

If you want an interesting exercise in counting your blessings, make a list (as I just did) of all the bishops in your life. If you are young, there may be only a few; if you are maturing in age, there may be a dozen or more. In any case, write down a quality that you remember about each one of them.

For example, I recall one bishop in a ward in which my wife and I lived for several years who never failed to call each of us and our children on our respective birthdays to extend greetings and best wishes. He did this for every member of his ward, including even the very young, and thus permanently fixed in our minds a picture of the kind and sensitive person whose example could wisely be emulated.

Another bishop was humility personified; because of a condition he had, he found it difficult to stay awake at times on the stand and would often ask the ward's forgiveness for his weakness. We shall never forget his example as the confessional leader who asked for help to overcome his difficulties—and somehow that made it easier for the rest of us to confess our sins and make improvements in our lives.

It would be easy to construct a collective portrait of my lifelong "bishop" consisting of just one quality from each of these brethren. To kindness and humility (qualities just referred to), I would add these: positive attitude, penitence, overcoming adversity, honorable and truthful, service-minded, wise, skilled in leadership, articulate in the word of faith, gracious, prayerful, and having a sense of humor. No bishop is a perfect embodiment of all these qualities, but your current bishop has special gifts and abilities that can add greatly to the blessings of your life if you will regard him as your friend. Thank heaven for our bishops—our covenant friends and the local "prophets" in our lives.

2. THE TREACHERY OF A JEALOUS MIND

THEME: Pride and arrogance of the type that consumed King Saul are the fuels of lethal envy and jealousy. Only by cultivating a life of humility and penitence can we hope to avoid such a destructive state of pride and greed and qualify for the spirit of harmony, peace, and joy.

> *And Saul saw and knew that the Lord was with David, . . . And Saul was yet the more afraid of David; and Saul became David's enemy continually.* (1 Sam. 18:28–29)

MOMENT OF TRUTH

Saul was plagued by the spirit of jealousy and continually plotted the death of David. But David deftly followed the course of safety opened up for him by the Lord, and thus repeatedly escaped harm. Saul had been abandoned by the Lord, just as David had been taken into the Lord's favor; thus it was inevitable that David would ultimately ascend the throne of Israel.

MODERN PROPHETS SPEAK

Gordon B. Hinckley:
> I have . . . reflected much on the power of Christ to heal and bless. It was he who said, "I am come that they might have life, and that they might have it more abundantly" (John 10:10). In a world of sickness and sorrow, of tension and jealousy and greed, there must be much of healing if there is to be life abundant. (*Faith: The Essence of True Religion* [Salt Lake City: Deseret Book, 1989], 30)

Neal A. Maxwell:
> It should not surprise us if some questions are repeated from dispensation to dispensation: "Behold, are ye stripped of pride?" "Behold, I say, is there one among you who is not stripped of envy?" (Alma 5:28, 29). And in 1831 the Lord said, "Strip yourselves from jealousies . . . and humble yourselves before me, for ye are not suf-

ficiently humble" (D&C 67:10). (*Men and Women of Christ* [Salt Lake City: Bookcraft, 1991], 121)

ILLUSTRATIONS FOR OUR TIMES

The Antidote for Envy

The young man was shy and reserved. He did not comfortably blend into the sometimes competitive and outspoken assertiveness of his peers. But he had some unique qualities than were already shining through. He told me on one occasion that he felt envious of the others who found it so easy to take initiative in social settings. That was my opportunity to remind him of the gifts and talents that he had been given—different from those of his colleagues. There were things he could do that they could not so easily do, and these gifts from God would enable him to render valuable service.

I believe the plainest antidote to envy and jealousy is to focus on those gifts and talents we are given from time to time, and cultivate them for the building up of the kingdom. The Lord counsels: "And again, verily I say unto you, I would that ye should always remember, and always retain in your minds what those gifts are, that are given unto the church. For all have not every gift given unto them; for there are many gifts, and to every man is given a gift by the Spirit of God" (D&C 46:10–11). Since the Lord gives to everyone at least one of these spiritual gifts, we can gratefully cultivate our gift "for the benefit of the children of God" (v. 26) and "give thanks unto God in the Spirit for whatsoever blessing ye are blessed with" (v. 32). This being the case, there is no room in our hearts and minds for envy or jealousy, and we can instead 'practise virtue and holiness' before the Lord (v. 33).

A Change of Heart

Nothing is quite so devastating to the soul as is envy and jealousy. Envy is one of the most devastating feelings one can have. When you feel discontent or ill will over another's prosperity or success, you suffer from envy. Envy, which often leads to jealousy, should be avoided at all costs. Envious activities literally take captive those who participate in them, and they become prisoners of themselves—never free, for they are chained by their faults. Jealousy destroys the mind and heart, and allowed to fester and grow, destroys the freedom of the individual. It is so ironic as we seek for happiness that we should become jealous of another's prosperity and happiness. Happiness is from within, yet envy and jealousy seek it from without—externally— and that is a mistake. When will we ever learn that having things of the world or the gifts of another does not lead to joy or happiness? For even if we were to possess these things, there will always be others who have more. Envy and jealousy separate us from Deity. They create negative feelings and are truly debilitating to those who succumb to those feelings.

I have seen the effects of sadness within the souls of others when they succumb to envy and jealousy. Keeping up with the Joneses is simply not a worthy goal. This sort of attitude has caused so many problems in society. We must have a change of heart toward our fellow men and ourselves. This, however, takes time.

3. THE FORGIVENESS OF A MAGNANIMOUS HEART

THEME: Though repeatedly the target of Saul's murderous intrigues, David displays the spirit of ultimate forgiveness and becomes, with Joseph of Egypt, the prototypical practitioner of mercy and clemency among the Lord's chosen.

> *I will not put forth mine hand against my lord; for he is the Lord's anointed.* (1 Sam. 24:10)

MOMENT OF TRUTH

David has every reason to loathe Saul, who seeks repeatedly to kill him out of jealousy and treachery. However, David avoids even the hint of vengeance and chooses to spare Saul's life, even after the Lord has delivered the king into his hands, saying that he will leave judgment to the Lord.

MODERN PROPHETS SPEAK

Gordon B. Hinckley:

> Now, as we draw the curtain on 150 years of our history, it becomes us as a grateful people to reach out with a spirit of forgiveness and an attitude of love and compassion toward those we have felt may have wronged us. We have need of this. The whole world has need of it. It is of the very essence of the gospel of Jesus Christ. He taught it. He exemplified it as none other has exemplified it. In the time of his agony on the cross of Calvary, with vile and hateful accusers before him, they who had brought him to this terrible crucifixion, he cried out, "Father, forgive them; for they know not what they do" (Luke 23:34). None of us is called on to forgive so generously, but each of us is under a divinely spoken obligation to reach out with pardon and mercy. The Lord has declared in words of revelation: "My disciples, in days of old, sought occasion against one another and forgave not one another in their hearts; and for this evil they were afflicted and sorely chastened. Wherefore, I say unto you, that ye ought to forgive one another; for he that forgiveth not his brother his trespasses standeth condemned before the Lord; for there remaineth in him the greater

sin. I, the Lord, will forgive whom I will forgive, but of you it is required to forgive all men" (D&C 64:8–10). (*Be Thou an Example* [Salt Lake City: Deseret Book, 1981], 47)

ILLUSTRATIONS FOR OUR TIMES

Relief from the Burden of Bearing Grudges

True forgiveness is without a doubt the most difficult aspect of all human behaviors to achieve. It is an expression of godliness.

I remember a story told to me once concerning the price of not forgiving. A teacher once instructed each of her students to bring a clear plastic bag and a sack of potatoes to school. For every person they refused to forgive in their life's experience, they had to choose a potato, write on it the name and date, and put it into the plastic bag. Some of their bags were quite heavy.

They were then told to carry this bag with them everywhere for one week, putting it beside their bed at night, on the car seat when driving, next to their desk at work.

The hassle of lugging this around with them made it clear what a weight they were carrying spiritually, and how they had to pay attention to it all the time so as not to forget, and how they had to keep leaving it in embarrassing places. Naturally, the condition of the potatoes deteriorated to a nasty, smelly slime. This was a great metaphor for the price we pay for keeping our pain and heavy negativity! Too often we think of forgiveness as a gift to the other person, whereas it clearly is a gift for ourselves!

An Unexpected Visitor

A few years ago, I heard a knock at the door and found an old friend standing on the steps of my home. He told me he was just passing through the state and wanted to drop by. I was very pleased to see him and invited him in. During the course of our conversation, we brought each other up to date on happenings during the intervening years. Then, toward the end of our visit, much to my surprise, he handed me a check for a rather large sum of money.

"What is this?" I asked.

"It is the balance of the money you loaned me many years ago," he said. "Please forgive me for taking so long to return it to you."

Many years previous to that, I had indeed responded to a request from this brother to provide some relief at a time of need, but the resources had been given in the form of a gift, with the express understanding that it need not be returned. I had long since forgotten about the matter. Now here he was, sitting across from me, wanting to settle the account. He had regarded the money as an obligation, felt remiss at not having taken care of it sooner, and insisted that it be repaid in full. He sought forgiveness where it would ordinarily not even be needed. I admired his integrity, and have often thought how choice it would be if all men were as responsible and honorable as this man.

SUMMARY

David exemplified a forgiving spirit. The Lord has told us in our day, "I, the Lord, will forgive whom I will forgive, but of you it is required to forgive all men" (D&C 63:10). David was able to forgive even the one who continually plotted to have his life taken away. Saul, on the other hand, exemplified the basest form of envy, greed, pride, and malice. We have in the contrast an enduring lesson in how to conduct our lives so as to find favor with God. Additionally, David and Jonathan displayed an admirable quality of friendship that was able to survive every conceivable deterrent and twist of circumstance. As such, their story is a lasting monument to friendship based on faith and righteousness.

CHAPTER TWENTY-FOUR

"CREATE *in* ME *a* CLEAN HEART"

Reading Assignment: 2 Samuel 11–12; Psalm 51.

Additional Reading: 2 Samuel 2–10.

The second principle of the gospel of salvation is repentance. It is a sincere and godly sorrow for and a forsaking of sin, combined with full purpose of heart to keep God's commandments. (John Taylor, *The Mediation and the Atonement,* 182)

THEMES *for* LIVING

1. Heed the Early Warnings against Temptation
2. The Ominous Consequences of Sin
3. The Exquisite Pain of Repentance

INTRODUCTION

The Lord has promised us that our confidence in His presence will wax strong if we will faithfully let virtue "garnish" our thoughts unceasingly (see D&C 121:45). Such was not the case with David. The process of his fall is abundantly clear: he failed to heed the warnings against temptation and found himself ensnared in not just one but a chain of misdeeds that compromised his very exaltation. Thus he experienced the intense suffering of one who must contend with the ominous and harrowing reality of looking up from the deep pit of egregious moral transgression—"how sore you know not," said the Lord, speaking of this kind of ordeal, "how exquisite you know not, yea, how hard to bear you know not" (D&C 19:15). The agony of such suffering can only be matched in intensity by the joy of those who are able to avoid such missteps and remain valiant in the faith. Three themes in this process will be discussed in the pages that follow.

1. HEED THE EARLY WARNINGS AGAINST TEMPTATION

THEME: When circumstances present the opportunity for sin, we must, like Joseph of Egypt—and unlike David—flee to higher moral ground. Character is first displayed in the choice between principle and fleeting pleasure.

And the woman was very beautiful to look upon. (2 Sam. 11:2)

MOMENT OF TRUTH

David happened to observe Bath-sheba at a distance one evening and was enticed. Rather than turning back and putting away bad thoughts, he yielded to temptation. Though at the time triumphantly victorious on the field of battle against the enemies of Israel, he was tragically vanquished in the battle for his own soul—for he relinquished the power to heed early warnings against sin.

MODERN PROPHETS SPEAK

Hugh B. Brown:

> There are various types and degrees of infidelity, lewdness, and licentiousness, various ways in which men and women tempt themselves or permit themselves to be tempted to commit adultery. Lucifer uses all of them, even the secret thoughts of the mind and unclean conversation, as weapons in his arsenal to destroy mankind. Don't let anyone tempt you to believe that what you do is secret and won't get out. The devil will see that it does. Lucifer and his agents have unfortunately devised means by which men may partially protect themselves against the natural physical results of their indecency and have thereby led many into shameful acts by whispering the twin lies, "It is no longer dangerous," and "No one will ever know." With these false assurances, thousands who might have been deterred by fear of consequences have been lured into transgression. (*The Abundant Life* [Salt Lake City: Bookcraft, 1965], 66)

Gordon B. Hinckley:

> Your goodness must be as an ensign to your people. Your morals must be impeccable. The wiles of the adversary may be held before you because he knows that if he can destroy you, he can injure an entire ward. You must be wise with inspired wisdom in all of your relationships lest someone read into your observed actions some taint of moral sin. You cannot succumb to the temptation to read pornographic literature, to see pornographic films, even in the secrecy of your own chamber to view pornographic videotapes. Your moral strength must be such that if ever you are called upon to sit in judgment on the questionable morals of others, you may do so without personal compromise or embarrassment. (*TGBH,* 89)

ILLUSTRATIONS FOR OUR TIMES

Overcoming Temptation

Temptation is all about us. It is ever present. Sometimes it is happenstance, and sometimes knowing it is there we indulge ourselves thinking, "Surely this little bit won't matter." In the reality of life, every temptation indulged in will have an effect upon us. A man named Ted Bundy demonstrated one of the saddest results of the temptation of pornography.

Ted Bundy was a young boy of middle-school age—a good boy, according to his mother. He had come home one day and the neighbors were moving. All their garbage was outside on the curb. As he passed by, some provocative magazines caught his attention. He took some home and began to read them. He hid them under his bed, and each night it became his time to look at these magazines. As time went on, he started to go to bookstores and buy new ones, then some hard-core pornography, and it wasn't long before he just had to have some videos. He was addicted to pornography and all its vices. Soon it was XXX videos and shows, and then he wanted to act it out. He became a rapist and serial murderer . . . and it all started with a little glance at a magazine. This is the story Ted Bundy told prior to his execution. Needless to say, he had been tempted and succumbed like King David, only with even greater sin and sorrow. His lustful thoughts led him to a life of rape and murder.

Overcoming temptation becomes the challenge of life. Here are some things we can do:

- Pray (see 3 Ne. 18:15,18).

- Search the scriptures (see 1 Ne. 15:24).

- Exercise faith (see Alma 37:33).

- Live by the Spirit (see 2 Ne. 32:5; D&C 124:124).

• Keep the commandments (see 3 Ne. 18:25).

• Overcome pride (see D&C 23:1).

The Light of the Gospel

Here was a delightful young couple preparing for marriage—bright, faithful in Church participation, eager to do the right thing. But now there was a problem—a compromising of values and propriety. They were embarrassed and heartbroken as they sat across from me, wondering what to do. We counseled. We sorrowed together. We pondered the consequences. But we also took comfort together in the process of repentance empowered by the Atonement. Yes, there needed to be change. There needed to be prayerful, godly sorrow (2 Cor. 7:10–11) and faithful commitment to a better lifestyle. But, fortunately, they had caught themselves before going over the edge of the precipice, and they had recoiled under the strength of conscience. Now they wanted to do right before the Lord. They were good young people with the desire for righteousness. The Lord loved them and wanted them to have the fullness of His blessings. There needed to be some regular appointments for a few weeks to give momentum to the new commitments. But things went very well, so we came up with a plan—a code just between the bishop and these two. When we crossed paths each week thereafter at meetings, it took only a nod of the head and a twinkle in the eye as an indication that all was well. You can't disguise the light of the gospel in the eye. It is a sure sign that the Spirit is at work. And it was at work for them. They prospered. They rebounded. They rose to new heights, and once more the age-old story of the gospel transforming lives was repeated in a real-life setting. Thank heavens for the principles of the gospel. Thank heaven for the Atonement of Jesus Christ. "And how great is his joy in the soul that repenteth" (D&C 18:13).

2. THE OMINOUS CONSEQUENCES OF SIN

THEME: Sin draws the participant ever deeper into the quicksands of its captivity: one thing leads to another until salvation itself is placed at risk. The story of David's pitiful fall reminds all who aspire to the honor of God that sin cannot be hidden or dismissed. There is always a price to be paid, sometimes very dear.

> NATHAN TO DAVID: *"Thou art the man. Thus saith the Lord God of Israel, I anointed thee king over Israel, and I delivered thee out of the hand of Saul; . . . Wherefore hast thou despised the commandment of the Lord, to do evil in his sight?"* (2 Sam. 12:7, 9)

MOMENT OF TRUTH

After David yielded to temptation and crossed the threshold into the realm of immorality, he attempted to manipulate circumstances by bringing Uriah, Bath-sheba's husband, back from battle and into his family circle again, where he would appear to be the father of David's coming child. But Uriah's loyalty to his battle colleagues got in the way of David's strategy to hide his sin, so David felt constrained to plot the murder of the husband. This horrible deed completed, David found himself face to face with Nathan, a prophet of the Lord, sent to convey the awful truth that spiritual death would surely follow, for the Lord knows all and cannot be mocked. Thus David forfeited his exaltation (see D&C 132:39).

MODERN PROPHETS SPEAK

Boyd K. Packer:

> Lucifer in clever ways manipulates our choices, deceiving us about sin and consequences. He, and his angels with him, tempt us to be unworthy, even wicked. But he cannot—in all eternity he cannot, with all his power he cannot—completely destroy us; not without our own consent. Had agency come to man without the Atonement, it would have been a fatal gift. (*Let Not Your Heart Be Troubled* [Salt Lake City: Bookcraft, 1991], 80)

Spencer W. Kimball:

> But however he tries, a man cannot escape the consequences of sin. They follow as the night follows the day. Sometimes the penalties are delayed in coming, but they are as sure as life itself. Remorse and agony come. Even ignorance of the law does not prevent, though it may mitigate, the punishment. Remorse may be pushed aside with bravado and brainwashing, but it will return to prick and pinch. It may be drowned in alcohol or temporarily shocked into numbness in the increasing sins which follow, but the conscience will eventually awaken, and remorse and sorrow will be followed by pain and suffering and finally torture and distress in the exquisite degree spoken of by the Lord in the passage quoted previously in this chapter. And the longer repentance is pushed into the background the more exquisite will be the punishment when it finally comes to the fore. (*The Miracle of Forgiveness* [Salt Lake City: Bookcraft, 1969], 141–42)

ILLUSTRATIONS FOR OUR TIMES

The Process of Rebirth

The cleansing process requires facing up to the realities of one's choices. I recall an event from my high school days long before society so tragically began to let moral principle slip from its grasp. In those days, there was still a pervasive public sense of decorum and propriety concerning moral practice, and when someone slipped, it became a matter of community sorrow and suffering. I remember when a young man and a young woman in the community, children of prominent citizens, allowed themselves to slip and bring unhappiness to themselves, their families, and the whole community. I remember the day the high school principal had them stand in an assembly before the whole school and apologize for their actions. It was a sad occasion, and one that would be almost unthinkable in today's politically correct public institutions and environment. One can debate the propriety of so dramatic a public acknowledgment; but the fact remains that each of us must acknowledge our sins before the Lord, and in some instances before His chosen ecclesiastical leaders, in order to start back along the road of wisdom and righteousness. The noted psychologist Carl Rogers once said, "The facts are friendly." And indeed they are—even the painful ones—if they lead to repentance, recovery, rebuilding, restoration, and rebirth.

Stay off the Road to Sin

Sin separates us from God. When we break the laws of God we break ourselves. We lose the blessings of God: the Spirit, self-respect, self-esteem, and that most precious gift of hope. We become vulnerable to more sin. We lose the strength of the Lord. The consequences of sin have trailing vices of self-justification, lying, hypocrisy, rationalization, and a host of others. We literally become captives of the devil. Only through repentance can we break this cycle of sin. Alma describes this feeling of the consequences of sin vividly in the following verses:

> But I was racked with eternal torment, for my soul was harrowed up to the greatest degree and racked with all my sins. Yea, I did remember all my sins and iniquities, for which I was tormented with the pains of hell; yea, I saw that I had rebelled against my God, and that I had not kept his holy commandments. Yea, and I had murdered many of his children, or rather led them away unto destruction; yea, and in fine so great had been my iniquities, that the very thought of coming into the presence of my God did rack my soul with inexpressible horror. Oh, thought I, that I could be banished and become extinct both soul and body, that I might not be brought to stand in the presence of my God, to be judged of my deeds. And now, for three days and for three nights was I racked, even with the pains of a damned soul. (Alma 36:12–16)

Yes, sin has consequences. Oh, that we might be like the people of King Benjamin: "And they all cried with one voice, saying: Yea, we believe all the words which thou hast spoken unto us; and also, we know of their surety and truth, because of the Spirit of the Lord Omnipotent, which has wrought a mighty change in us, or in our hearts, that we have no more disposition to do evil, but to do good continually" (Mosiah 5:2). Or as Jacob, the younger brother of Nephi: "Behold, my soul abhorreth sin, and my heart delighteth in righteousness; and I will praise the holy name of my God" (2 Ne. 9:49). Flee from sin—stay off the road to sin.

3. THE EXQUISITE PAIN OF REPENTANCE

THEME: Repentance is a divine gift empowered through the Atonement of Jesus Christ—but it must be done in the Lord's way, and thus must always include godly sorrow and the pain of contrite transformation and renewal. Like David, all who sin—meaning, in effect, all accountable mortals—must go through the process of repenting for their sins if they are to become pure before God and worthy of His choicest blessings.

> *The sacrifices of God are a broken spirit: a broken and a contrite heart, O God, thou wilt not despise.* (Ps. 51:17)

MOMENT OF TRUTH

David's pain at the consciousness of his sin and its consequences was acute. He is the prototype of the fallen man, the archetype of the harrowed sinner. His poetry of contrition captures forever the awful state of one who cannot retrieve the lost innocence, who cannot undo the fateful deed. At best, he can present his story of tragic pain as a warning message to others that it need not have been so, that following the commandments of God is the indispensable choice in life: "Then will I teach transgressors thy ways; and sinners shall be converted unto thee" (Ps. 51:13).

MODERN PROPHETS SPEAK

James E. Faust:

> There is hope for all to be healed through repentance and obedience. The Prophet Isaiah verified that "though your sins be as scarlet, they shall be as white as snow" (Isa. 1:18). The Prophet Joseph Smith stated: "There is never a time when the spirit is too old to approach God. All are [in] reach of pardoning mercy" (TPJS, 191). After our full repentance, the formula is wonderfully simple. Indeed, the Lord has given it to us in these words: "Will ye not now return unto me, and repent of your sins, and be converted, that I may heal you?" (3 Ne. 9:13). In so doing, we have his promise that "he healeth the broken in heart, and bindeth up their wounds" (Ps. 147:3). (*Finding Light in a Dark World* [Salt Lake City: Deseret Book, 1995], 31)

ILLUSTRATIONS FOR OUR TIMES

The Key to Recovery

As a bishop, I have witnessed the repentance process over and over in the lives of people, as well as in my own life. When we are moved to godly sorrow and seek to come back more fully to Christ, we are in the process of repenting. Repentance is personified as we continue in righteousness and good works (see Hel. 12:24).

My mind cannot erase the picture of the young man with his head in his hands saying, "Why did I do it? Why? Why? Why? Will I ever be forgiven? How can I restore that which was lost?" The pain and sorrow for sin is excruciating (see Alma 36:12–16). This young man was feeling sorrow in the depths of his heart, as was Alma. In sin, we don't want to be in the presence of the Lord. As I worked with the young man, hope was restored (see D&C 58:42–43) through the Atonement of our Savior Jesus Christ. There is a way back, and it is through this most precious doctrine called repentance. When missionaries were afraid to confess and forsake their sins for fear of the repercussions, I often reminded them of the following: "For behold, I, God, have suffered these things for all, that they might not suffer if they would repent; But if they would not repent they must suffer even as I; which suffering caused myself, even God, the greatest of all, to tremble because of pain, and to bleed at every pore, and to suffer both body and spirit—and would that I might not drink the bitter cup, and shrink" (D&C 19:16–18). Repentance is the requirement to partake of the goodness of God and return to His presence.

God's Love for the Penitent

The Lord's love for His children, even those who are guilty of serious sin—perhaps especially such—is unfathomably deep and eternal, and we only get a hint at its depth and scope on those occasions where individuals have come face to face with issues of ultimate loss and recovery.

I recall a particularly striking illustration of this love of God on the occasion of one disciplinary council when I was serving as a high council member. The young man whose actions had brought him before the council was suffering terribly because of his choices. He had made others suffer, and he was still coming to terms with how he felt about all of this. His situation was reviewed according to the process outlined in the Doctrine and Covenants, Section 102, and then he was asked to wait outside the chamber for further word. After a lengthy process to evaluate all the facts and circumstances, the attitudes and spirit of the matter, the stake presidency came to a preliminary decision that, sadly, repentance in this case would require the loss of the young man's membership in the Church. The high council was unanimous in sustaining this decision. Then, according to practice, the stake presidency retired to seek the Lord's confirmation through the Spirit in prayer. Not long thereafter, the stake presidency returned. The president was ashen, almost visibly shaken. In a quiet voice, he announced to the high council that the decision would not stand, and that the young man would instead be placed on probation as he found his way back to God. The president said, as nearly as I can recall, "Brethren, we don't fully understand why it is to be so in this case, but we know that the Lord wants this young man to have a second chance. The Lord has spoken." Thereafter, the young man was ushered back before the council and told that the Lord had an especially deep love for him and wanted him to return. It was truly a message to him directly from the Lord. It was an unforgettable moment of very tender emotion as all in the room had a spiritual confirmation of the intense, all-encompassing, infinite love of the Lord for His children.

SUMMARY

David concluded, on the basis of his ordeal, that "The sacrifices of God are a broken spirit: a broken and a contrite heart" (Ps. 51:17). David certainly had such. We can learn from his experience, as we "liken all scriptures unto us, that it might be for our profit and learning" (1 Ne. 19:23). By heeding the warnings of the Spirit to avoid giving in to temptation, we can avoid suffering the consequences of serious transgression of the laws of God, and thus spare ourselves the exquisite pain and anguish of guilt and shame associated with such actions. Because the Lord suffered the anguish of universal sin, we can, through His Atonement, rise above such suffering. The pathway of faith, repentance, baptism, and the gift of the Holy Ghost leads to peace of soul, harmony of spirit, and confidence in the presence of the Lord.

CHAPTER TWENTY-FIVE

"THE LORD IS MY SHEPHERD"

Reading Assignment: Psalms

The Lord shall reign for ever, even thy God, O Zion, unto all generations. Praise ye the Lord. (Psalm 146:10)

THEMES *for* LIVING

1. The Messiah: The Good Shepherd
2. Winning the Battle Within: Redeeming the Soul
3. Winning the Battle Without: Defending and Building up Zion

INTRODUCTION

The Psalms are among the most revered and admired expressions of genuine poetic sentiment in all of world literature. But they are more than poetry and song; they are profoundly spiritual documents that capture much of the essence of the gospel and its enduring truths. Their central theme is "the Messiah: the Good Shepherd." David captured the chief moments of the Redeemer's mission as he looked forward with a prophetic eye to the coming of the Savior in the meridian of time, and His eventual return in glory and majesty at the end of the world's history and the beginning of the Millennium. A second theme is "Winning the Battle Within: Redeeming the Soul." David's prayers were rooted in his sense of sin, guilt, remorse, fear, anguish, and isolation—all emotions anchored in the experience of carnal weakness. But his prayers turned into songs of praise for the mercy, forgiveness, peace, freedom, healing, and atonement associated with the Master's touch. A third theme is "Winning the Battle Without: Defending and Building up

Zion." Once again, as David considered the situation of the Lord's covenant people, his prayers were rooted in a sense of oppression, iniquity within enemy ranks, ensnarement, captivity, pride, arrogance, affliction, reproach, and contempt—all emotions that flow from the burdens of Zion at the hands of her enemies. However, David's prayers turned to songs of praise as he celebrated God's gifts to Zion: His protection, defense, liberation, foundation, light, glory, blessings—all associated with love and compassion.

1. THE MESSIAH: THE GOOD SHEPHERD

THEME: At the center of our lives, as the focus of our continual praise and thanksgiving, is the Messiah, the good Shepherd, the Redeemer. David's psalms set the example for our devotion and our celebration. His words anticipate the coming of the Savior, just as our words can give thanks that He has already come to complete His mission of love.

> *What is man, that thou art mindful of him? and the son of man, that thou visitest him? For thou hast made him a little lower than the angels, and hast crowned him with glory and honour.* (Ps. 8:4–5)

> *I have said, Ye are gods; and all of you are children of the most High.* (Ps. 82:6)

> *Also I will make him my firstborn, higher than the kings of the earth.* (Ps. 89:27)

> *The stone which the builders refused is become the head stone of the corner.* (Ps. 118:22)

MOMENT OF TRUTH

David's several messianic songs of praise gave form and shape to his visions of the future mission of the Savior—"the Lord is my Shepherd" (Ps. 23). David's incomparable poetic imagery lifts our spirits and opens to our minds the visions of grandeur that David himself must have experienced in prophetic moods.

MODERN PROPHETS SPEAK

George Q. Cannon:

> The welfare, the future happiness and the prosperity of the people are to a great extent entrusted to those men who are called to be the shepherds of the flock of Christ. I often ask myself, how can I appear before the Lord Jesus, my Master, if He should call me to account for the charge that He has placed upon me; can I stand up and say I have not obstructed the work with which I am connected; I have not obscured the light of heaven; I have not acted in any way to divert the rays of

truth from shining in the midst of the children of men—I ask myself, can I stand in this position and look upon the face of God without feeling condemned and that my garments are unstained with the blood of this generation, that I have been a faithful minister of the Lord, a faithful shepherd of the flock of Christ, a watchman who has never slept at his post, who has never failed to utter the cry of warning when danger has menaced the Zion of God? This is a feeling it seems to me every man who bears the holy Priesthood ought to have. (*Gospel Truth: Discourses and Writings of George Q. Cannon* [Salt Lake City: Deseret Book, 1987], 210)

Howard W. Hunter:

The Lord, our Good Shepherd, expects us to be his undershepherds and recover those who are struggling or are lost. We can't tell you how to do it, but as you become involved and seek inspiration, success will result from efforts in your areas, stakes, and wards. (*THWH,* 218)

ILLUSTRATIONS FOR OUR TIMES

The Good Shepherd

The book of Psalms or "praises" to the Lord is filled with beautiful words of thanksgiving and gratitude. Some of them are literally compositions for music. Some of our most familiar hymns come from the Psalms—favorites like:

"The Lord is My Shepherd" (*Hymns,* 108; Psalm 23)
"The Lord is My Light" (*Hymns,* 89; Psalm 27:1)
"How Great Thou Art" (*Hymns,* 86; Psalms 8:3–9; 9:1–2)
"Praise to the Lord, the Almighty" (*Hymns,* 72; Psalms 23:6; 150)

The testament or witness of Christ is personified most beautifully in the twenty-third Psalm: "the Lord is my shepherd." Within the Church today, there are many roles that are like unto our true Shepherd—mother, father, older brother and sister, and Church leaders at every level, including home teachers and visiting teachers. To be a true shepherd, one must truly care for his flock—each individual. Following is the text of an address given by Elder John R. Lasater during general conference, April 1988.

Some years ago, it was my privilege to visit the country of Morocco as part of an official United States government delegation. As part of that visit, we were invited to travel some distance into the desert to visit some ruins. Five large black limousines moved across the beautiful Moroccan countryside at considerable speed. I was riding in the third limousine, which had lagged some distance behind the second. As we topped the brow of a hill, we noticed that the limousine in front of us had pulled off to the side of the road. As we drew nearer, I sensed that an accident had occurred and suggested to my driver that we stop. The scene before us has remained with me for these many years.

An old shepherd, in the long, flowing robes of the Savior's day, was standing near the limousine in conversation with the driver. Nearby, I noted a small flock of sheep numbering not more than fifteen or twenty. An accident had occurred. The king's vehicle had struck and injured one of the sheep belonging to the old shepherd. The driver of the vehicle was explaining to him the law of the land. Because the king's vehicle had injured one of the sheep belonging to the old shepherd, he was now entitled to one hundred times its value at maturity. However, under the same law, the injured sheep must be slain and the meat divided among the people. My interpreter hastily added, "But the old shepherd will not accept the money. They never do."

Startled, I asked him why. And he added, "Because of the love he has for each of his sheep." It was then that I noticed the old shepherd reach down, lift the injured lamb in his arms, and place it in a large pouch on the front of his robe. He kept stroking its head, repeating the same word over and over again. When I asked the meaning of the word, I was informed, "Oh, he is calling it by name. All of his sheep have a name, for he is their shepherd, and the good shepherds know each one of their sheep by name."

It was as my driver predicted. The money was refused, and the old shepherd with his small flock of sheep, with the injured one tucked safely in the pouch on his robe, disappeared into the beautiful deserts of Morocco.

As we continued our journey toward the ruins, my interpreter shared with me more of the traditions and practices of the shepherds of that land. Each evening at sundown, for example, the shepherds bring their small flocks of sheep to a common enclosure where they are secured against the wolves that roam the deserts of Morocco. A single shepherd then is employed to guard the gate until morning. Then the shepherds come to the enclosure one by one, enter therein, and call forth their sheep—by name. The sheep will not hearken unto the voice of a stranger but will leave the enclosure only in the care of their true shepherd, confident and secure because the shepherd knows their names and they know his voice.

The words of the Master Shepherd rang loudly in my ears:

"But he that entereth in by the door is the shepherd of the sheep.

"To him the porter openeth; and the sheep hear his voice: and he calleth his own sheep by name, and leadeth them out.

"And when he putteth forth his own sheep, he goeth before them, and the sheep follow him: for they know his voice.

"And a stranger will they not follow, but will flee from him: for they know not the voice of strangers" (John 10:2–5).

My dear brothers and sisters, there are great lessons to be learned from these stirring words of the Master Shepherd. Into our hands, as members of this great Church, has been given responsibility to be the true shepherds unto the flocks of

Israel. Do we understand the personal nature of the shepherd's call? Whether we go as home teachers or visiting teachers, whether we serve as auxiliary leaders or teachers, or priesthood leaders at whatever level, we have received a divine injunction from God, through a living prophet, to become personal shepherds and ministers. No, it is not a new call; it has always been so.

Do we know our sheep, each one, by name? Do they know our voice, or must they hearken unto the voices of strangers? Do they know us as true shepherds who love them, who willingly and freely give time and attention to their needs, and, in that marvelous process, instill the confidence and security so greatly needed in God's children today? Are we then able to lead them into full activity in the Church and onward to immortality and eternal life? Do we go before them, constantly reassuring and building confidence because they know our voice?

Or are we strangers unto many? I promise you that you will not be a stranger, that you cannot be if you come to know the voice of the Master Shepherd, for that voice will confirm what a prophet has declared, and the Spirit will direct your efforts. And then, and only then, you will become a true shepherd in Israel.

There can be no greater example of the very personal nature of a true shepherd's call than the events of that Easter weekend nearly two thousand years ago—the depth of the Master Shepherd's love, His willingness to give freely of Himself, His undeviating loyalty and devotion to the cause, and His constant attention to the needs of the one. Those same qualities must mark our ministries as the shepherds of Israel. (John R. Lasater, "Shepherds of Israel," *Ensign,* May 1988, 74)

A Personal Relationship

One of our prized possessions is a piece of artwork done by our daughter, Stephanie, depicting her young firstborn daughter Brittany (our first grandchild) seated on the lap of the Savior. She is comfortable there, smiling, just as He is smiling. It is clearly a personal relationship. The art is carefully detailed, as though it were a representation of reality—and of course it is just that, for the relationship between the Savior and His children is meant to be personal and real. As the First Vision burst upon the world in 1820, the truth of this kind of relationship was confirmed once again. In the words of the young Prophet: "When the light rested upon me I saw two Personages, whose brightness and glory defy all description, standing above me in the air. One of them spake unto me, calling me by name and said, pointing to the other—*This is My Beloved Son. Hear Him!*" (JS—H 1:17). To be called by name by Deity is to know that a relationship of divine character is personal in nature. It is a miracle to contemplate that the Savior calls us by name and seeks to cultivate with each of us a personal relationship. "And he numbereth his sheep, and they know him; and there shall be one fold and one shepherd; and he shall feed his sheep, and in him they shall find pasture" (1 Ne. 22:25).

2. WINNING THE BATTLE WITHIN: REDEEMING THE SOUL

THEME: Every mortal has occasion to feel the pangs of remorse for misdeeds and sins, and everyone who has reached the state of accountability must experience the motivating need to rise above the carnal self to a state more in keeping with one's innate potential as a son or daughter of God. We must also continually pray for forgiveness, just as David did. We must continually praise the Lord for His mercy and His atoning sacrifice on our behalf, just as David did.

Preserve me, O God: for in thee do I put my trust. (Ps.16:1)

Who shall ascend into the hill of the Lord? or who shall stand in his holy place? He that hath clean hands, and a pure heart. (Ps. 24:3–4)

Create in me a clean heart, O God. (Ps. 51:11)

MOMENT OF TRUTH

David's anguish over his carnality, his prayers for redemption, his praise of the Master's atonement—all set the tone and the example for our own prayers for forgiveness and praise for the Redeemer's mission of atonement and love. The Saints of God know the steps of faith, repentance, and the baptism of water and fire. Our prayers and songs of praise must reflect our heartfelt thanks for God's love and our commitment to keep His commandments and endure to the end.

MODERN PROPHETS SPEAK

Gordon B. Hinckley:
> Then the pressures begin to build. Sometimes these are social pressures. Sometimes they are personal appetites. Sometimes they are false ambitions. There is a weakening of the will. There is a softening of discipline. There is capitulation. And then there is remorse, self-accusation, bitter tears of regret. (*Be Thou an Example* [Salt Lake City: Deseret Book, 1981], 60)

Russell M. Nelson:
> Rich meaning is found in study of the word *atonement* in the Semitic languages of Old Testament times. In Hebrew, the basic word for atonement is *kaphar,* a verb that means "to cover" or "to forgive." Closely related is the Aramaic and Arabic word *kafat,* meaning "a close embrace"—no doubt related to the Egyptian ritual embrace. References to

that embrace are evident in the Book of Mormon. One states that "the Lord hath redeemed my soul . . . ; I have beheld his glory, and I am encircled about eternally in the arms of his love" (2 Ne. 1:15). Another proffers the glorious hope of our being "clasped in the arms of Jesus" (Morm. 5:11). (*Perfection Pending, and Other Favorite Discourses* [Salt Lake City: Deseret Book, 1998], 166)

ILLUSTRATIONS FOR OUR TIMES

Faith in the Parents

An unfortunate event that occurred many years ago still causes me deep anguish of soul. Our home has been blessed with the presence of a truly celestial being, a multiply-challenged young man whom we love dearly, just as we love all of our children. When he was of elementary-school age, he attended a regular school with a special classroom to accommodate the learning needs of children with unique requirements. As parents, we would deliver him to the school, which was not far from our home, and accompany him to his classroom each morning, then retrieve him after school. Eventually, he developed the independence to find his own way, and we would just drop him off at the curb and watch him until he had safely entered the school. For parents in this situation, it is always a matter of some trepidation to wave good-bye to a child with special burdens in life, and send him off into the care of other hands. One morning I took Nathan to school, gave him a hug, and watched him walk up to the doorway, passing by a number of other people milling about there. He disappeared into the building, just as on countless mornings before that.

Then I went about my professional duties. A few hours later I learned, quite by accident, that the school was not operating that day. In a panic, I rushed back to the school, a flood of fears and self-recriminations pouring through my mind. Saying one long, continuous prayer in my heart, I drove up to the curb and ran into the school building. There was our son, walking along one of the front halls of the school, alone. He was pleased to see me. I rushed to him and took him in my arms, saying how sorry I was that he had been there alone for so long. Being essentially non-communicative, he could not express his thoughts, but I could tell he was relieved. It turned out that the people I had seen earlier that morning were workers who were doing maintenance on the building. One of them said to me that he had noticed the boy wandering the halls, and had wondered about it. Certainly if there had been any danger, someone would have responded.

I have often thought about this event, always with a sense of remorse and agony, and always with a sense of relief that our son was preserved that day, and still is preserved day by day. What had he been thinking as he walked the hallways alone that morning? Would he be able to forgive me for my mistake? Would I be able to forgive myself? How must our Father in Heaven have felt, sending us from His presence into the pathways of mortality, knowing of the challenges and trials that inevitably must come if we are to learn independence and wisdom in the day of our probation? Even though "the morning stars sang together, and all the sons of God shouted for joy" (Job 38:7) at the glorious prospect of embarking on the journey of life and salvation, still our Heavenly Parents must feel continual concern for our well-being, especially when we stumble and fall short of our calling. Enoch was astounded to see, in vision, the heavens weeping over mankind. "How is it that thou canst weep," he asked the Lord, "seeing thou art holy, and from all eternity to all eternity?" (Moses 7:29). And the answer was clear: "Wherefore should not the heavens weep, seeing these shall suffer?" (v. 37). The Lord suffers with us when we fall, just as we suffer when our children, whether by our choices or theirs, are caused to suffer.

How much faith God has placed in the parents of the world to care for the little ones who are finding their way in life! How careful we must be not to add to their burdens. How sacred are the roles of father and mother in providing for their children an environment of love, safety, and righteous principles for living. We cannot remove all pain from our children—it would not be wise to do so, since learning must come line upon line, precept upon precept, always with effort and often with discomfort. But we can set a goodly example and not leave them alone unnecessarily in the mortal halls of learning.

The Lesson of Repentance and Hope

We all have need of repentance, and we all depend upon the redeeming power of the Lord's Atonement. I will never forget the young woman who taught me this principle in a visit I had with her. She said, "Every time I think of my chances of returning to my Heavenly Father, I think of my unworthiness, which makes me cry unto the Lord! In my prayers I come close to my Heavenly Father, and I am filled with hope because of my loving Savior, Jesus Christ. I know through repentance I will be forgiven, restored, and be able to return to His presence. Isn't that wonderful? I simply can't thank my Heavenly Father enough."

3. WINNING THE BATTLE WITHOUT: DEFENDING AND BUILDING UP ZION

THEME: We are all enlisted in the Lord's army in these latter days. Like David, we can sing the songs of Zion, pray for the Lord's protecting and guiding hand over the growth of His kingdom amid the threat from external enemies, and praise His glory and His matchless love for mankind.

The Lord is my rock, and my fortress, and my deliverer; my God, my strength, in whom I will trust. (Ps. 18:2)

Let all those that seek thee rejoice and be glad in thee: and let such as love thy salvation say continually, Let God be magnified. (Ps. 70:4)

MOMENT OF TRUTH

David was peerless in his ability to capture the essence of the Lord's role as defender, protector, and deliverer of Zion. In the contrast between the forces of iniquity and the forces of good, David set the stage for extolling the Lord's power to save Zion and remember the covenant promises to bring about ultimate victory.

MODERN PROPHETS SPEAK.

Bruce R. McConkie:

> True it is, as a general principle, that God sends disasters, calamities, plagues, and suffering upon the rebellious, and that he preserves and protects those who love and serve him. Such indeed were the very promises given to Israel—obedience would net them the preserving and protecting care of the Lord, disobedience would bring death, destruction, desolation, disaster, war, and a host of evils upon them. (*The Mortal Messiah: From Bethlehem to Calvary* [Salt Lake City: Deseret Book, 1979–81], 3:194)

Brigham Young:

> We are all the children of our common Father, who has placed us on the earth to prove ourselves, to govern, control, educate and sanctify ourselves, body and spirit, unto him, according to his will and pleasure. When all that class of spirits designed to take bodies upon this earth have done so, then will come the winding-up scene of this particular department of the works of God on this earth. It is his will that we should prepare ourselves to build up his Kingdom, gather the House of Israel, redeem and build up Zion and Jerusalem, revolutionize the world, and bring back that which has been lost through the fall. (*Discourses,* 57)

ILLUSTRATIONS FOR OUR TIMES

Bless Someone Today

The Lord protects His covenant people as we keep our covenants. As covenant people, we have responsibilities to live righteous lives and carry His gospel to all the world. As the Lord blesses us, so must we bless all those with whom we come in contact.

I know a person who understands this principle. She is constantly looking to bless and serve her fellowmen. She even writes down in her planner, "Bless someone today." She is fearless in sharing the gospel. She has a balanced life, and everything is in order, yet her priority with regard to honoring her covenants is at the forefront of her life. Sure, she has trials and tribulations, but it seems as if they are all, in her perspective, to make her better and more Christlike. Each of us can win this battle in life and build up the kingdom of God.

Holiness to the Lord

There are countless ways to sing praises to God for His protecting hand and merciful blessings. Some express their praise through the medium of painting or sculpture. Some through poetry or discourse. Some in the pages of books such as this. Some through quiet acts of selfless service when they "succor the weak, lift up the hands which hang down, and strengthen the feeble knees" (D&C 81:5).

I recall my mission president in Germany, Theodore M. Burton, telling of his Grandfather Moyle, who had been a skillful craftsman. The gentleman had lost his leg on a farm in Alpine, Utah, after being kicked by a cow, and had great difficulty hobbling about. But he nevertheless traveled twenty-eight miles each day to reach the construction site of the Salt Lake Temple, where his appointed mission was to chisel in the walls of granite the phrase, "Holiness to the Lord." That is a form of praise that has inspired countless thousands who visit the temple and its sacred grounds. Genuine praise for God, in all its forms, is a means to lift the one who praises, to edify the community of thanksgivers, and to magnify the joy of the gospel. It is a way to give utterance to the transcendent concept of "Holiness to the Lord."

SUMMARY

Shortly after the death of his father Lehi, Nephi gave expression to his spiritual feelings in a passage of scripture that some have referred to as the "Psalm of Nephi" (see 2 Ne. 4:15–35). All three themes we have been discussing in our review of the Psalms of David are reflected in Nephi's words as well: (1) the central place of the Savior in his life as the "rock of my salvation" (v. 30), (2) his sorrow over the temptations and sins "which do so easily beset me" (v. 18) and which he rebukes, and (3) his rejoicing over the protection of the Lord and His triumph over the enemies of goodness: "O Lord, wilt thou encircle me around in the robe of thy righteousness! O Lord, wilt thou make a way for mine escape before mine enemies! Wilt thou make my path straight before me!" (v. 33). This same pattern of praise and thanksgiving can infuse our daily lives. We can remember to make the Savior the anchor of our existence. We can demonstrate our love for Him by keeping His commandments and reordering our lives to become more like Him. We can remind ourselves and our children what great things the Lord has done to help our forebears in the past and to bring about the restoration of His kingdom for our sakes in these latter days. Nephi exclaims: "Awake, my soul! No longer droop in sin. Rejoice, O my heart, and give place no more for the enemy of my soul. . . . Rejoice, O my heart, and cry unto the Lord, and say: O Lord, I will praise thee forever" (2 Ne. 4:28, 30). Similarly, we can say with David, "I will sing unto the Lord as long as I live" (Ps. 104:33).

CHAPTER TWENTY-SIX

"LET YOUR HEART BE PERFECT *with the* LORD OUR GOD"

Reading Assignment: 1 Kings 3; 5–11.

Additional Reading: 1 Kings 2:1–12; 4:29–34; 7:13–51; 1 Chronicles 29; D&C 46.

The worst fear that I have about [members of this Church] is that they will get rich in this country, forget God and his people, wax fat, and kick themselves out of the Church and go to hell. This people will stand mobbing, robbing, poverty, and all manner of persecution, and be true. But my greater fear for them is that they cannot stand wealth; and yet they have to be tried with riches, for they will become the richest people on this earth. (Brigham Young, in Preston Nibley's *The Man and His Work*, 127)

THEMES *for* LIVING

1. Wisdom as a Gift of God
2. The House of the Lord—Eternal Symbol of Righteousness
3. Earthly Wealth in the Balance of Life: The Folly of Solomon

INTRODUCTION

One of the greatest tests of character is how we use the talents, gifts, and means with which the Lord has blessed us. The better part of wisdom is to aspire to outcomes of service and honor that will merit the reward cited by the Savior in His parable of the talents: "Well done, thou good and faithful servant: thou hast been faithful over a few things, I will make thee ruler over many things: enter thou into the joy of thy lord" (Matt. 25:21). Few in the history of the world have been blessed with gifts and means to exceed those of Solomon, the son of David. As long as he used these resources to bless the lives of others and further God's purposes, he prospered and enjoyed the blessings of heaven. When he lost balance in his life and elevated worldly goods and honors above the principles of heaven, he was supplanted. "Ye cannot serve God and mammon" (Matt. 6:24).

1. WISDOM AS A GIFT OF GOD

THEME: Just as Solomon sought for the best gifts to serve the people, we too should aspire to promoting the cause of salvation and bringing blessings into the lives of our loved ones.

> *And Solomon loved the Lord, walking in the statutes of David his father.* (1 Kgs. 3:3)

> *Lo, I have given thee a wise and an understanding heart.* (1 Kgs. 3:12)

MOMENT OF TRUTH

The Lord appeared to Solomon in a dream and offered to give him whatever he might desire. Rather than seeking after selfish gifts, Solomon asked for an understanding heart to judge the people effectively. The Lord was pleased and gave him the gift of unsurpassed wisdom, which Solomon used to cultivate peace and prosperity in Israel. As long as Solomon remained wise in spiritual matters, he flourished in his leadership.

MODERN PROPHETS SPEAK

George Q. Cannon:

> How many of you are seeking for these gifts that God has promised to bestow? How many of you, when you bow before your Heavenly Father in your family circle or in your secret places, contend for these gifts to be bestowed upon you? How many of you ask the Father in the name of Jesus to manifest Himself to you through these powers

and these gifts? Or do you go along day by day like a door turning on its hinges, without having any feeling upon the subject, without exercising any faith whatever, content to be baptized and be members of the Church and to rest there, thinking that your salvation is secure because you have done this? I say to you, in the name of the Lord, as one of His servants, that you have need to repent of this. You have need to repent of your hardness of heart, of your indifference and of your carelessness. There is not that diligence, there is not that faith, there is not that seeking for the power of God that there should be among a people who have received the precious promises we have. . . . If any of us are imperfect, it is our duty to pray for the gift that will make us perfect. Have I imperfections? I am full of them. What is my duty? To pray to God to give me the gifts that will correct these imperfections. . . . They are intended for this purpose. No man ought to say, "Oh, I cannot help this; it is my nature." He is not justified in it, for the reason that God has promised to give strength to correct these things and to give gifts that will eradicate them. . . . That is the design of God concerning His children. He wants His Saints to be perfected in the truth (Nov. 26, 1893, *DW* 48:34–35). The Lord has said in a revelation to the Church that the Saints should "seek ye earnestly the best gifts, always remembering for what they are given; for verily I say unto you, they are given for the benefit of those who love me and keep all my commandments" (D&C 46:8–9). How many Latter-day Saints are there who supplicate the Lord for the gifts which they need? . . . Every defect in the human character can be corrected through the exercise of faith and pleading with the Lord for the gifts that He has said He will give unto those who believe and obey His commandments. (*Gospel Truth: Discourses and Writings of President George Q. Cannon* [Salt Lake City: Deseret Book, 1987], 154–55)

ILLUSTRATIONS FOR OUR TIMES

First Things First

The delightful young Baltimore family had just joined the Church, and the parents were telling us about their very first experience watching general conference on television. "We were all assembled downstairs in front of the TV, waiting with great excitement—all except for our young son, who was still upstairs, busy with his playthings," they recounted. "We kept calling up to him to remind him, but he didn't come. And then when the broadcast started, we called once more, saying the Tabernacle Choir and General Authorities were coming on. In response, he called down, in all sincerity, 'When God comes on, let me know.'"

Here was a young man wise before the age of wisdom. Even though he had not yet learned much about the role of prophets in the Lord's kingdom, he was certainly putting his Father in Heaven at the top of his priority list, above everything else (even his toys). Would that all of us could have that kind of innocent focus and commitment.

The Gifts of God

Solomon's wisdom came as a gift from God. He sought a good gift that would bless others. So should we. Many of these good gifts are described in Moroni 10 and Doctrine and Covenants 46.

Truly the goodness of God is demonstrated in the gifts of the Spirit. I have had the great joy of witnessing these gifts. I have seen knowledge and wisdom demonstrated by young elders and sisters that astounds me to this day, saying and doing things beyond their mortal capability. I have participated in healings that are so sacred it is hard to express. Surely the power of the priesthood is evidenced in faith as directed by the Spirit. I have witnessed miracles in temporal things, and especially in spiritual things as hearts have been changed.

I have seen people receive the gift of prophecy within their own stewardship. I have witnessed the casting out of evil spirits by the power of the priesthood. I have seen young and old missionaries alike being blessed with speaking and interpretation of tongues.

These are gifts of the Spirit. They are available to those who seek to bless and serve God and their fellowmen. We must ask in the Spirit (being directed) and receive by the Spirit, that all might be blessed (see D&C 46:28–29).

2. THE HOUSE OF THE LORD—ETERNAL SYMBOL OF RIGHTEOUSNESS

THEME: We should look to the temple of God as the enduring icon of God's mission to bring about the immortality and eternal life of mankind. By keeping our eye on the temple and remembering our covenant promises, we prepare the way for great spiritual blessings in our lives.

I have hallowed this house, which thou hast built, to put my name there for ever; and mine eyes and mine heart shall be there perpetually. (1 Kgs. 9:3)

MOMENT OF TRUTH

The Lord had promised David that his son would build a house to the Lord. Solomon followed through with this destined project and erected a magnificent temple complex for sacred worship. The dedicatory program was replete with utterances importuning the Lord to accept His people as His own and prosper their way as long as they heeded His word and kept His commandments, looking toward the temple as a continual reminder of their covenant commitments. The temple edifice became renowned throughout the region, and rulers and potentates came from all around to admire it and bask in the opulence and wisdom of Solomon's court.

MODERN PROPHETS SPEAK

Joseph B. Wirthlin:

> We learn in the Doctrine and Covenants that a temple is a place of thanksgiving, "a place of instruction for all those who are called to the work of the ministry in all their several callings and offices; that they may be perfected in the understanding of their ministry, in theory, in principle, and in doctrine, in all things pertaining to the kingdom of God on the earth" (D&C 97:13–14). Doing temple work regularly can provide spiritual strength. It can be an anchor in daily life, a source of guidance, protection, security, peace, and revelation. No work is more spiritual than temple work. In the words of Hugh Nibley, "The temple is a scale model of the universe. The mystique of the temple lies in its extension to other worlds; it is the reflection on earth of the heavenly order, and the power that fills it comes from above" ("Nibley Considers the Temple in the Cosmos," *Insights,* March 1992, 1). As spirit children of our Heavenly Father, we should seek always to recognize the divine potential within us and never restrict our perspective to the limited scope of mortal life. (*Finding Peace in Our Lives* [Salt Lake City: Deseret Book, 1995], 135)

Neal A. Maxwell:

> In the renewal of our temple covenants we can be nurtured and encouraged by connecting the present with the past and the future. If we are deprived of these renewing opportunities over a sustained period of time, however, present cares can blur the past and cloud the future. (*If Thou Endure It Well* [Salt Lake City: Bookcraft, 1996], 112)

ILLUSTRATIONS FOR OUR TIMES

A Place of Peace

Within the House of the Lord are all the exalting ordinances, covenants, and blessings for the children of God. Surely all dispensations are blessed through the dispensation of the fullness of times. That time is now. Through the restoration of the keys of the priesthood by the prophet Elijah (see D&C 110) our hearts have turned to our fathers. It becomes our duty and our joy to bless all those who have gone before, as well as our immediate families.

The temple is matchless in its power. We learn of and make sacred covenants, which can bring us back into the presence of God. It is "a place of thanksgiving for all saints, and for a place of instruction for all those who are called to the work of the ministry in all their several callings and offices; that they may be perfected in the understanding of their ministry, in theory, in principle, and in doctrine, in all things pertaining to the kingdom of God on the earth, the keys of which kingdom have been conferred upon you. And inasmuch as my people build a house unto me in the name of the Lord, and do not suffer any unclean thing to come into it, that it be not defiled, my glory shall rest upon it; yea, and my presence shall be there, for I will come into it, and all the pure in heart that shall come into it shall see God" (D&C 97:13–16). The temple is a place of peace and revelation.

I had the privilege of serving in the temple for several years. I remember, as we would go into the sealing rooms to perform those sacred ceremonies, a feeling of peace that exceeded that of earthly experience. It was sublime in nature.

I sometimes attend endowment sessions with a concern or question or otherwise needed help in a certain area of my life. Often the witness comes with a power that is unparalleled. It is the temple that provides us opportunity of vicarious service for the dead. This work is vital to their, and our, salvation (see D&C 128:15).

A Place of Light

My wife and I were excited about the new home we were building. It would be a pleasant place to raise our two young daughters, and it was located only a short distance from one of the Lord's temples. That morning we stopped by the office of the architect to have him review the plans, but he asked for a little more time, since he had to present that day a plan for another kind of "home." With a twinkle in his eye and a glow on his face, he showed us the rendering he had just completed. It was magnificent—the artistic vision of the new Washington D.C. Temple. He was just on his way to show it to the First Presidency. Little did my wife and I realize at the time that our professional circumstances would soon thereafter take us from Utah to Maryland, a short distance from where the construction of the splendid new six-spired edifice was about to commence. It was our privilege over the next period of time to watch the temple rise in majesty from its spot of prominence on a hill overlooking the northern suburbs of Washington, D.C. We attended the dedication by a prophet of the Lord. We were able to participate over the years in the sacred ordinances of that house and feel the uplifting peace and tranquility of that holy place. So powerful in its community presence was the temple that the nighttime illumination had to be reduced so that motorists traveling along the beltway of the city would not be startled and transfixed as the imposing celestial structure came into view. Very few missionary initiatives could have had a greater influence for good than this temple, which opened up countless minds and hearts to the possibility of a power transcending the confines of this mortal world and a hope reaching beyond this life to an eternal kind of joy.

The temples of God are truly buildings of light and radiance. They are the architectural reminders that we, too, are temples of the Most High and places for the Spirit to abide. "Know ye not that ye are the temple of God, and that the Spirit of God dwelleth in you? If any man defile the temple of God, him shall God destroy; for the temple of God is holy, which temple ye are" (1 Cor. 3:16–17). Each one of us is the architect of his or her own life, and each must build that life and unfold it with a vision of the finished edifice being in the likeness of the master architect of our salvation, even the Lord Jesus Christ. We plan, we prepare, we work, and we gather into our house all the elements of vitality and growth. We dedicate that life to the glory and honor of God, and we invite the Spirit to visit often to give comfort and truth and peace to our life, just as in a temple of God. And when the final chapter of our life draws to a close, it will reflect the spirit of honor and righteousness to the same degree that we are able to align it with the motto on the walls of God's temples: "Holiness to the Lord."

3. EARTHLY WEALTH IN THE BALANCE OF LIFE: THE FOLLY OF SOLOMON

THEME: The consequence of allowing worldly influences to assume the upper hand in our lives is all too clear from the example of Solomon. When idolatry and moral decadence displace the statutes and ordinances of God, man falls from God's favor and destruction lurks at the gate.

> *So king Solomon exceeded all the kings of the earth for riches and for wisdom.* (1 Kgs. 10:23)

> *For it came to pass, when Solomon was old, that his wives turned away his heart after other gods: and his heart was not perfect with the Lord his God.* (1 Kgs. 11:4)

MOMENT OF TRUTH

The Lord had given Solomon the blessing of riches and honor, even though he had not asked for these (see 1 Kgs. 3:13). And therein was a test for Solomon, a test that he was not able to pass, giving in as he did to the idolatry of his wives and an intemperate (unbalanced) affection for material things. For this reason, the Lord was not pleased with Solomon and declared that a new situation would be introduced in Israel through the intervention of her enemies. The Prophet Ahijah informed Jeroboam that the kingdom would be rent in twain, and that he would become king of Israel, with the lesser part to remain with the lineage of David—"that David my servant may have a light alway before me in Jerusalem, the city which I have chosen me to put my name there" (1 Kgs. 11:36). Thus once again the forgetfulness of Israel would cause much dislocation and trial in the future, just as our own slowness to heed the commandments of God can bring difficulties into our lives.

MODERN PROPHETS SPEAK

Joseph Fielding Smith:

> Why, all these things are but temporary blessings. We eat to live. We clothe ourselves to keep warm and covered. We have houses to live in for our comfort and convenience, but we ought to look upon all these blessings as temporary blessings needful while we journey through this life. And that is all the good they are to us. We cannot take any of them with us when we depart. Gold, silver, and precious stones, which are called wealth, are of no use to man, only as they enable him to take care of himself, and to meet his necessities here. (*DS,* 1:68)

Spencer W. Kimball:

> The possession of riches does not necessarily constitute sin. But sin may arise in the acquisition and use of wealth. Paul implied this distinction in his statement to Timothy: "For the love of money is the root of all evil: which while some coveted after, they have erred from the faith, and pierced themselves through with many sorrows. But thou, O man of God, flee these things; and follow after righteousness, godliness, faith, love, patience, meekness" (1 Tim. 6:10–11). (*The Miracle of Forgiveness* [Salt Lake City: Bookcraft, 1969], 47)

ILLUSTRATIONS FOR OUR TIMES

Doing Good in the World

My grandfather, Heber S. Allen, along with Ira Card, was one of the principal settlers in the Church communities of southern Alberta in the late nineteenth century. Over a period of many years, he built up a prosperous mercantile business in the town of Cardston. His journal records this interesting passage:

> One day in 1902, Jesse Knight and Charles McCarthy were talking with me and suggested that I move to Raymond [a small community to the east of Cardston]. I replied that I was well satisfied where I was as I was making about $10,000 a year with the store, mill and other interests [a considerable sum in those days]. They replied, "We will get you." I replied: "There is only one person in the world who can get me to change my place of residence, and this is Pres. Joseph F. Smith."

Then he adds this telling phrase: "When the Taylor Stake was organized under the direction of President Smith in 1903, and I was called to be president, it became necessary for me to move to Raymond."

H. S. Allen served a total of thirty-four years in the capacity of stake president. His business interests continued to flourish, and he used his influence and means generously to help build the kingdom. In his farewell address, he made this observation:

> I have been accused at times of placing business before my church. I desire to say
> that this is not true—my first loyalty has always been to my church and the build-
> ing up of the Kingdom of God. I have enjoyed the confidence of hundreds of my
> fellow Canadians, many of them non-members of the church, and I have lived to
> see much of the prejudice and misunderstanding that has existed in the past,
> removed.

At the conference when President Allen was released in 1936, President Heber J. Grant presided and presented him with a signed commemorative card bearing the motto that best exemplifies how we should use our influence and means to do good in the world: "He that would be greatest among you, let him be the servant to all."

The Test of Wealth

Sometimes those of us without the so-called wealth of the world point fingers at those who have wealth, and in that we sin. Wealth can be difficult to handle.

Jacob has told us concerning the desire for wealth as well as its use:

> And the hand of providence hath smiled upon you most pleasingly, that you have
> obtained many riches; and because some of you have obtained more abundantly than
> that of your brethren ye are lifted up in the pride of your hearts, and wear stiff necks
> and high heads because of the costliness of your apparel, and persecute your brethren
> because ye suppose that ye are better than they.
>
> And now, my brethren, do ye suppose that God justifieth you in this thing?
> Behold, I say unto you, Nay. But he condemneth you, and if ye persist in these
> things his judgments must speedily come unto you. . . .
>
> Think of your brethren like unto yourselves, and be familiar with all and free
> with your substance, that they may be rich like unto you.
>
> But before ye seek for riches, seek ye for the kingdom of God.
>
> And after ye have obtained a hope in Christ ye shall obtain riches, if ye seek
> them; and ye will seek them for the intent to do good—to clothe the naked, and to
> feed the hungry, and to liberate the captive, and administer relief to the sick and the
> afflicted. (Jacob 2:13–14,17–19)

I know people in the Church who are good with the use of their monies. They truly are saints. They think of others first. It shows that people with money, when their priorities are pure, can and do live the gospel. This even occurred in Book of Mormon times:

> And the people of Nephi began to prosper again in the land, and began to multiply
> and to wax exceedingly strong again in the land. And they began to grow exceed-
> ingly rich.

> But notwithstanding their riches, or their strength, or their prosperity, they were not lifted up in the pride of their eyes; neither were they slow to remember the Lord their God; but they did humble themselves exceedingly before him.
>
> Yea, they did remember how great things the Lord had done for them, that he had delivered them from death, and from bonds, and from prisons, and from all manner of afflictions, and he had delivered them out of the hands of their enemies.
>
> And they did pray unto the Lord their God continually, insomuch that the Lord did bless them, according to his word, so that they did wax strong and prosper in the land. (Alma 62:48–51)

Wealth can be wonderful as we use it as the Lord and His prophets have described.

SUMMARY

The wisdom of Solomon is legendary. But through the grace, mercy, and merits of the Savior and His universal gospel, wisdom of a transcendent, godly nature is granted to every individual with a humble heart and a contrite spirit who seeks the face of the Lord always. Wisdom of a saving kind, unsurpassed by Solomon's gifts and splendor, is available to each one of God's children who fears God and honors the covenant promises, for "The fear of the Lord is the beginning of wisdom: and the knowledge of the holy is understanding" (Prov. 9:10). If we aspire to the best gifts in order to accomplish a higher level of service to others, if we stand in holy places such as devoted family circles, unified wards and stakes, and sacred temples, and if we are able, through the guidance of the Spirit, to maintain an eye single to the glory of God, then we can truly look forward to the day of judgment. On that occasion, the valiant will hear the Savior's words: "Well done, good and faithful servant; thou hast been faithful over a few things, I will make thee ruler over many things: enter thou into the joy of thy lord" (Matt. 25:23).

CHAPTER TWENTY-SEVEN

"BELIEVE *in* *the* LORD YOUR GOD, SO SHALL YE BE ESTABLISHED"

Reading Assignment: 1 Kings 12–14; 2 Chronicles 17; 20.

Additional Reading: 1 Kings 11:26–40; 2 Kings 17:20–23.

> *I am for the kingdom of God. I like a good government and then I like to have it wisely and justly administered. The government of heaven, if wickedly administered, would become one of the worst governments upon the face of the earth. No matter how good a government is, unless it is administered by righteous men, an evil government will be made of it.* (Brigham Young, *JD* 10:177)

THEMES *for* LIVING

1. Non-Covenant Leadership: The Consequences of Government Based on Worldly Pride and Idolatry
2. Covenant Leadership: The Consequences of Government Based on Divine Purpose

INTRODUCTION

It is abundantly clear from these passages of scripture that iniquity in the seat of government could have no wholesome outcomes for Israel. When the kings (like

Rehoboam or Jeroboam) followed a wicked agenda, the people suffered. The same was true on the American continent during Book of Mormon times. Righteous General Moroni had to hoist the title of liberty to rally the people against the evil onslaughts of the cunning Amalickiah. The message is clear for our times: "Thus we see how quick the children of men do forget the Lord their God, yea, how quick to do iniquity, and to be led away by the evil one. Yea, and we also see the great wickedness one very wicked man can cause to take place among the children of men" (Alma 46:8–9). At the same time, it is apparent that an upright leader of influence like Moses, Joshua, or Jehoshaphat—one who is anchored in righteous principles—has rather awesome power to bring about good for many, many people, sometimes for generations. We can see in the portrait honoring Captain Moroni, for example, a summary statement about the enduring truth concerning spiritual leadership: "Yea, verily, verily I say unto you, if all men had been, and were, and ever would be, like unto Moroni, behold, the very powers of hell would have been shaken forever; yea, the devil would never have power over the hearts of the children of men" (Alma 48:17).

1. NON-COVENANT LEADERSHIP: THE CONSEQUENCES OF GOVERNMENT BASED ON WORLDLY PRIDE AND IDOLATRY

THEME: When Israel's kings ignored principles of righteousness, the nation became divided and the people were led into iniquity. We can learn valuable lessons in proper leadership by studying these accounts.

> *My father made your yoke heavy, and I will add to your yoke: my father also chastised you with whips, but I will chastise you with scorpions.* (1 Kgs. 12:14)

> *And he made an house of high places, and made priests of the lowest of the people, which were not of the sons of Levi.* (1 Kgs. 12:31)

MOMENT OF TRUTH

After the death of Solomon, his son Rehoboam came to power in Jerusalem. Jeroboam, one of the leaders in Solomon's court, became the king of the separated tribes of Israel (all except Judah and Benjamin). Jeroboam's ascendancy had been foretold by the prophet Ahijah, the Lord promising him a "sure house" (1 Kgs. 11:38) if he would heed the covenant promises and commandments. Regretfully, he led the people astray, as did Rehoboam, who ignored the advice of the older men and increased the oppression on the people. Both of these kings—one over Judah and the other over Israel—failed to walk in the footsteps of their righteous predecessors among the rulers of the covenant people, and thus the Lord withdrew His support.

MODERN PROPHETS SPEAK

Bruce R. McConkie:

> When Solomon departed this life, Israel, who had been one people, divided into two kingdoms—Judah under Rehoboam and Israel under Jeroboam. And it was Jeroboam who led a whole nation into dire and evil apostasy. He made molten images, created his own priests, and caused his people to become as the aliens who dwelt in the land before them. In this setting Ahijah the prophet sent this word unto Jeroboam: "The Lord shall smite Israel as a reed is shaken in the water, and he shall root up Israel out of this good land, which he gave to their fathers, and shall scatter them beyond the river, because they have made their groves, provoking the Lord to anger. And he shall give Israel up because of the sins of Jeroboam, who did sin, and who made Israel to sin" (1 Kgs. 14:15–16). (*A New Witness for the Articles of Faith* [Salt Lake City: Deseret Book, 1985], 531)

Neal A. Maxwell:

> The unrighteous use of power—not just familial or ecclesiastical, but all expressions of it—carries certain consequences: "he is left unto himself" (D&C 121:38). This is not the loneliness of final responsibility felt in righteous leadership when decisions and actions devolve poignantly upon one's soul. Rather, unrighteous dominion brings an erring individual face to face with the echoing hollowness of soul. (*Meek and Lowly* [Salt Lake City: Deseret Book, 1987], 28)

ILLUSTRATIONS FOR OUR TIMES

Leadership Is a Choice

We witness on a daily basis carnal standards being lived by the world's leaders. This is sometimes a reflection of the values and standards of the people. Jeroboam and Rehoboam were such leaders. Examples are plentiful in today's world, from the atrocities of Hitler to the oppression of Mao Tse Tung. The results are death, sorrow, misery, and degradation of the human soul. Leadership has the power to do good or evil, and the people have a choice to accept or reject that leadership. In the United States, we fought the British for our freedom. We wanted self-rule. We took action, and as a result we have the many freedoms we enjoy today. Each individual must accept responsibility for his or her conditions and then take action. Mahatma Gandhi did, Mother Teresa did, Martin Luther King did—and so must we. We must get involved in our community. Volunteerism is a magnificent form of Christlike love. From mentoring a child to taking care of the homeless, individuals working with agencies throughout the world are making a difference. Consider what happened as a result of the Worldwide Conference on Families. As individuals and the Church became involved, we made a difference in the accepted values and standards for families throughout the world. The truth in leadership is that all can make a difference as they practice principles of leadership by dedicating their time and talents for the well being of others, and by so doing lead people to the Lord Jesus Christ.

God's Inexorable Will

No matter what reversals lie in the path, no matter what adversity will arise, the faithful Saints of Zion, under blessing from God, will prevail in their assigned mission to build the kingdom. From Liberty Jail in Missouri, suffering under the oppression of a misguided and miscreant civil leadership, the Prophet Joseph Smith penned these words: "How long can rolling waters remain impure? What power shall stay the heavens? As well might man stretch forth his puny arm to stop the Missouri river in its decreed course, or to turn it up stream, as to hinder the Almighty from pouring down knowledge from heaven upon the heads of the Latter-day Saints" (D&C 121:33; *HC* 3:297).

A few months earlier, on Wednesday, 31 October 1838, the scene at Far West was incendiary. How would you feel if your city were surrounded by a large and hostile army under orders from the state to exterminate you and your loved ones (as Governor Lilburn W. Boggs of Missouri had decreed on 27 October 1838)? Look at these consequences: on October 31st, the Missouri State Militia held the Mormon headquarters settlement of Far West under a state of siege. Tensions were extraordinarily high. The enemy command hoisted a peace flag. Church leaders feared for their lives; however, in the interest of protecting their families from forces outnumbering them five to one, they had no choice but to cooperate. Under pretext of wanting to facilitate the peace talks, Colonel George M. Hinkle (who was supposed to be guarding the Saints) induced Joseph Smith, Sidney Rigdon, Parley P. Pratt, and two others to leave the city and meet with General Lucas of the opposing militia. It was a treacherous, Judas-style betrayal. The Church leaders were taken prisoner and subjected during the night to severe abuse and an illegal court martial, where they were sentenced to be shot. In the words of Parley P. Pratt: "If the vision of the infernal regions could suddenly open up to the mind, with thousands of malicious fiends, all clamoring, exulting, deriding, blaspheming, mocking, railing, raging and foaming like a troubled sea, then could some idea be formed of the hell which we had entered" (*HC* 3:189). The next day the settlement was ransacked and the Saints forced to abandon their refuge for the fifth time in less than a decade. Joseph Smith and his colleagues were marched off to Richmond and eventually Liberty jail, where in March of the following year the Prophet wrote the stirring words given above, now part of D&C 121.

All of this is a solemn reminder of the need for citizens who believe in the principles of liberty and justice to encourage honorable leaders of integrity to seek civil offices in order to preserve inalienable rights and privileges. In our day, as always before, the faithful Saints are besieged on all sides from the invisible forces of evil far more ominous than any mob. Yet the kingdom of God will still roll forward according to the inexorable will of God.

2. COVENANT LEADERSHIP: THE CONSEQUENCES OF GOVERNMENT BASED ON DIVINE PURPOSE

THEME: When the people of Israel were led by God-fearing leaders, they prospered and enjoyed the favor of the Lord. Leadership based on faith, service, accountability to the principles of righteousness, and a willingness to follow the scriptures and living prophets leads to harmony, unity, peace, and well-being.

> *Thus saith the Lord unto you, Be not afraid nor dismayed by reason of this great multitude; for the battle is not yours, but God's.* (2 Chr. 20:15)

> *So the realm of Jehoshaphat was quiet: for his God gave him rest round about.* (2 Chr. 20:30)

MOMENT OF TRUTH

The great-grandson of Rehoboam, Jehoshaphat, provided a marked contrast to the leadership style of his wicked predecessors. He eliminated idolatry in his nation (Judah), sent Levite teachers among the people to teach the principles of the gospel from the scriptures, sought the Lord's advice in defending the land, and united the people against their common enemies from without. As a result, the Lord was willing to fight their battles for them and preserve their independence.

MODERN PROPHETS SPEAK

M. Russell Ballard:
> The Melchizedek Priesthood leaders who belong to the ward council—the high priests group leader and the elders quorum president—are responsible for the spiritual and temporal welfare of the men over whom they preside. Much of the work among the families of the ward that is currently being done by our bishops could appropriately be performed by quorum and group leaders, who are charged to "follow the Savior's

example of righteous leadership. . . . When priesthood leaders lead as the Savior did, they should help members develop greater love for God the Father and His Son; develop greater love for others; share the gospel, do temple and family history work, serve without thought of reward, assist the poor and needy, and minister to the lonely and distressed; receive ordinances and make covenants with the Lord that will lead to eternal life; obey the commandments; become more humble, repentant, and forgiving; pray and study the scriptures daily; attend church meetings regularly and partake of the sacrament worthily; achieve spiritual, emotional, and temporal self-reliance; [and] attend the temple regularly" (*Melchizedek Priesthood Leadership Handbook,* 1–2). (*Counseling with Our Councils: Learning to Minister Together in the Church and in the Family* [Salt Lake City: Deseret Book, 1997], 105)

Howard W. Hunter:

For a family to be successful in the way acceptable to the Lord, there must be dedicated leadership in the home and strong family organization. The Lord has prescribed a patriarchal order for the kingdom, and the family, being the basic unit of the kingdom, must, therefore, be patriarchal in its organization. Under this order the father becomes the head of the family, acting in the spirit of the priesthood, and the mother has the obligation to support, sustain, and be in harmony with that righteous leadership. (*THWH,* 151)

ILLUSTRATIONS FOR OUR TIMES

In His Strength

Elder Boyd K. Packer had presided over the reorganization of our stake, and now it was time for the new leadership to be set apart in a special session. The brother whom the Lord had called to be patriarch took his place on the designated chair, and the Apostle laid his hands on his head and began the ordination and setting apart with the words, "Brother [mentioning his name], you are *nothing* . . ." This last word received considerable emphasis, followed by a long pause—which gave everyone present the motivation for deep soul-searching. Then Elder Packer continued: "without the Lord." It was a profoundly powerful teaching moment about leadership.

No matter what our callings in the Church from time to time, we are truly "nothing without the Lord." It is the Lord, through His Spirit, who energizes our service. It is the Lord who kindles our desire, hope, and love—all essential for meaningful service. It is the Lord who activates within us the gifts and talents we must draw upon in order to contribute effectively to the building up of His kingdom. It is the Lord, through His Spirit, who sustains us, empowers us, guides us, and teaches us the correct way to proceed. We are truly nothing without the Lord. But *with* the Lord, the battle always moves toward eventual victory. He has promised the faithful: "I will fight your battles" (D&C 105:14).

Qualities of Leadership

Righteous leadership is multifaceted in scope and in the results it brings. Principles of good leadership were demonstrated by Jehoshaphat. Here are some things we might consider in becoming effective leaders in our lives and our families, as well as in school and the workplace:

- Vision—Leaders know what needs to be done and they share that vision.

- Values—Leaders are driven by values and standards, such as integrity, worth of souls, righteous causes, etc.

- Principles—Leaders always utilize correct principles.

- Enthusiasm—Driven by the inspiration of God (a contagious enthusiasm that engenders esprit de corps for success).

- Charity—Recognizes the value of people and their concerns, knowing that real success is always with people. A program is merely a tool, an organized way, to bless people's lives. Truly love the people you serve.

- Teacher—A team builder, trains, motivates, gives hope, listens and receives feedback, and counsels wisely.

- Gives "PIE"—**Praises** openly, genuinely and regularly in all sincerity. **Instructs** or informs, makes sure all understand their role, responsibility, accountability, follow-up, and report procedures. **Encourages** often, letting them know they care about them and what they are doing.

- Skills—Effective and affective skills that encourage trust and respect It gives credibility in leadership.

- Qualities—A character based on the principles of the gospel of Jesus Christ with this as a motto: "And know ye that ye shall be judges of this people, according to the judgment which I shall give unto you, which shall be just. Therefore, what manner of men ought ye to be? Verily I say unto you, even as I am" (3 Ne. 27:27).

- Relationships—With charity as the foundation, practice the advice in D&C 121:41–44: "No power of influence can or ought to be maintained by virtue of the priesthood, only by persuasion, by long-suffering, by gentleness and meekness, and by love unfeigned; by kindness, and pure knowledge, which shall greatly enlarge the soul without hypocrisy, and without guile—reproving betimes with sharpness, when moved upon by the Holy Ghost; and then showing forth afterwards an increase of love toward him whom thou hast reproved, lest he esteem thee to be his enemy; that he may know that thy faithfulness is stronger than the cords of death."

• Followership—Requires humility and dependence upon God for His strength and direction in all things. Maintain your relationship with God in all times and places, and call upon Him for that strength and direction.

• Servant—Leaders are always servant-leaders—one who looks upon their position as an opportunity to help rather than an opportunity to be.

Though this is not a complete or exhaustive list of leadership ideas, it nevertheless provides a beginning for things to consider in our divine roles and callings or positions we hold here upon the earth. Examples of successful leadership can be remembered by all. Our Savior was the perfect leader here upon the earth.

Jesus Christ, the Savior and Redeemer of the world, even the Creator of Heaven and Earth stands as the supreme example of leadership. His purpose was clear—the immortality and eternal life of man. He cared for individual souls and their happiness. The gospel of Jesus Christ was the way back to Father's presence. He was selfless and loving at all times. He cared about the one. He was the master teacher, the perfect example, as He implored, "Come follow me." He was always giving hope through His love and atoning sacrifice. In all things He was the true servant of God and His brothers and sisters. In true theocratic leadership, He followed the Father in every thought and deed throughout His life. Christ was the perfect leader.

SUMMARY

The Lord's summary word on leadership is given in these verses: "Wherefore, now let every man learn his duty, and to act in the office in which he is appointed, in all diligence. He that is slothful shall not be counted worthy to stand, and he that learns not his duty and shows himself not approved shall not be counted worthy to stand. Even so. Amen" (D&C 107:99–100). The stakes are high. Worthiness, learning one's duty, and diligent action are called for. The influence of each person extends in all directions to those responding to strong leadership. The Lord's chosen must demonstrate "a godly walk and conversation" (D&C 20:69). The covenant promises are contingent on obedience and righteousness. Spiritual leadership generates harmony, peace, unity, increased faith, and good works. We are indeed fortunate to have before us in the scriptures detailed portraits of great leaders—as well as models that we should avoid if we are to be true to our covenants before the Lord.

CHAPTER TWENTY-EIGHT

"AND AFTER *the* FIRE *a* STILL SMALL VOICE"

Reading Assignment: 1 Kings 17–19

As a result of the many miracles in our lives, we should be more humble and more grateful, more kind and more believing. When we are personal witnesses to these wonders which God performs, it should increase our respect and love for him; it should improve the way we behave. We will live better and love more if we will remember that. We are miracles in our own right, every one of us, and the resurrected Son of God is the greatest miracle of all. He is, indeed, the miracle of miracles, and every day of his life he gave evidence of it. We should try to follow after him in that example. (Howard W. Hunter, *THWH*, 115)

THEMES *for* LIVING

1. The Work of the Lord Is Sustained by Miracles
2. The Power of God/The Impotence of Baal
3. The Lord Is in Charge of His Program for Mankind

INTRODUCTION

Looking back on the ministry of the mortal Messiah, the Apostle Paul gave this summary of the organization of the kingdom of God: "Now therefore ye are no more strangers and foreigners, but fellowcitizens with the saints, and of the household of God; And are built upon the foundation of the apostles and prophets, Jesus Christ himself being the chief corner stone; In whom all the building fitly framed together groweth unto an holy temple in the Lord" (Eph. 2:19–21). We see in the mission of the prophet Elijah continuing evidence that the same foundation had been used in all earlier dispensations of time, with prophetic callings providing the central underpinning for the work of Jehovah in bringing about His agenda for mankind. "Surely the Lord God will do nothing," proclaimed Amos, "but he revealeth his secret unto his servants the prophets" (Amos 3:7). Upon this foundation of continuing revelation— the Savior Himself being the cornerstone—is layer upon layer of spiritual blessings and gifts provided for the faithful Saints engaged on the Lord's errand. Three of these will be discussed in the following pages: (1) the miracles of the Spirit that attend faithful service, (2) the manifestations of divine power that continually combat and overcome the forces of Babylon and Baal in the world, and (3) the constant, overarching presence of the hand of God at work in the building up of His kingdom.

1. THE WORK OF THE LORD IS SUSTAINED BY MIRACLES

THEME: When we come to our tasks with a prayerful and humble heart in the service of God, then miracles—both seen and unseen—sustain our efforts, just as they did the work of Elijah.

> *And Elijah said, See, thy son liveth.* (1 Kgs. 17:23)

> *And it came to pass, when Ahab saw Elijah, that Ahab said unto him, Art thou he that troubleth Israel? And he answered, I have not troubled Israel; but thou, and thy father's house, in that ye have forsaken the commandments of the Lord, and thou hast followed Baalim.* (1 Kgs. 18:17–18)

MOMENT OF TRUTH

Elijah the prophet, on the Lord's errand, sealed up the heavens in response to the pervasive wickedness of the leadership of Israel (Ahab had the distinction of being the most wicked of all the kings in a long line of succession—1 Kgs. 16:33). Elijah was sustained miraculously by ravens, and later by the widow whom the Lord had called into service. The meal and oil were multiplied. The son was restored to life. Elijah, who was ever unquestioning in his obedience, was able to prepare the way for the Lord's intervention in the idolatrous culture.

MODERN PROPHETS SPEAK

Jeffrey R. Holland:

> Preparatory faith is formed by experiences in the past—by the known, which provides a basis for belief. But redemptive faith must often be exercised toward experiences in the future—the unknown, which provides an opportunity for the miraculous. Exacting faith, mountain-moving faith, faith like that of the brother of Jared, *precedes* the miracle and the knowledge. He had to believe *before* God spoke. He had to act *before* the ability to complete that action was apparent. He had to commit to the complete experience in advance of even the first segment of its realization. Faith is to agree unconditionally—and in advance—to whatever conditions God may require in both the near and distant future. (*Christ and the New Covenant: The Messianic Message of the Book of Mormon* [Salt Lake City: Deseret Book, 1997], 18–19)

James E. Faust:

> I am persuaded that the miraculous and spectacular does not necessarily convert people to the gospel. Miracles are more to confirm a faith already held. After the ten lepers were healed by the Savior, only one even bothered to thank him, and I have found no convincing proof that even that one became a disciple. A quiet witness that Jesus is the Christ is more the product of a committed faith coming from dedication and sacrifice, an effort to keep God's commandments, and following the constituted priesthood authority of the Church. ("A Legacy of the New Testament," 12th Annual CES Religious Educators' Symposium, 12 Aug. 1988; see also *In the Strength of the Lord: The Life and Teachings of James E. Faust* [Salt Lake City: Deseret Book, 1999], 303)

ILLUSTRATIONS FOR OUR TIMES

Miracles Are All About Us

Miracles are defined as those things that are beyond the power of man. Elijah, by the power of the priesthood, performed many miracles. Sometimes we think that miracles have ceased or that they are not as prevalent today as in days gone by. Such is not the case. God is the same yesterday, today and forever (see 2 Nephi 27:23). Each of us have witnessed miracles. They are all about us. We only need eyes to see and hearts to recognize these blessings in our lives. Here are some examples:

- A mighty change of heart

- Healing the sick

- Casting out evil spirits

- The creation of the earth

- Life in all its forms

- The intricacies of the earth—its form, motion, and atmosphere

- Tempering of the elements

- Preaching of the word by the missionaries

- Healing the hearts of all mankind

- The miracle of forgiveness

The work of the Lord is all about us, and it is miraculous.

Victory for God

The miraculous drama of Elijah and the prophets of Baal plays itself out anew every day in the lives of individuals who are touched by the rejuvenating fire of the Lord's Spirit. Every time a young person says "no" to the insidious influence of harmful drugs, there is a victory for God and a defeat for the forces of Baal. Every time a modern Joseph flees the alluring enticements of immoral companionships or lascivious involvements, there is a victory for God and a defeat for the forces of Baal. When the conscious decision is made to depose the forces of dishonesty, greed, envy, or unrighteous pride, in any of their countless guises, there is a victory for God and a defeat for the forces of Baal. It can be as simple as turning the dial of the television set or Internet device to eliminate the influx of inappropriate material into the home. Or it can be as revolutionary as abandoning one's unfulfilling way of life in favor of membership in the Kingdom of God, with all of its saving ordinances and service opportunities.

The story is told of the time Elder Matthew Cowley felt impressed to call one of the more free-spirited Island brethren to be a branch president. He walked up to this brother's home and found him there with cigar in hand. When the call was extended, the brother said, "Does this calling apply to me *and* my cigar?" Elder Cowley replied, "No, just to you." Whereupon the brother immediately gave up his habit and took up his calling with full devotion. Another victory for God; another defeat for the forces of Baal. The prayer of Elijah is still at work: "Hear me, O Lord, hear me, that this people may know that thou art the Lord God, and that thou hast turned their heart back again" (1 Kgs. 18:37).

2. THE POWER OF GOD/ THE IMPOTENCE OF BAAL

THEME: No power of darkness, no force of iniquity, no influence of worldly honor or prestige can stand in the way of the Lord's agenda to bring about the building up of His kingdom and to establish Zion.

> *And when all the people saw it, they fell on their faces: and they said, The Lord, he is the God; the Lord, he is the God.* (1 Kgs. 18:39)

MOMENT OF TRUTH

Elijah, moved by the Spirit of the Lord, persuaded Ahab's governor, Obadiah, (who had secretly rescued one hundred of the righteous prophets from the hand of King Ahab and Queen Jezebel), to set up an audience with the king. Elijah ordered the king to assemble the prophets of Baal, and challenged them to a contest in which the Lord displayed His power miraculously. Elijah then eliminated the prophets of Baal, cleansing the land of their iniquitous influence, and caused the Lord to bring rain once again to the people.

MODERN PROPHETS SPEAK

Jeffrey R. Holland:
> "Mighty God" conveys something of the power of God, his strength, omnipotence, and unconquerable influence. Isaiah sees him as always able to overcome the effects of sin and transgression in his people and to triumph forever over the would-be oppressors of the children of Israel. (*Christ and the New Covenant: The Messianic Message of the Book of Mormon* [Salt Lake City: Deseret Book, 1997], 81)

Bruce R. McConkie:

> The sealing power! The apostolic power possessed by Adam and all the ancients; the heavenly endowment enjoyed by Enoch and Abraham and Elijah; the power of the Great God without which man cannot ascend to heights beyond the stars! Such now is resident with *all* of the Twelve—not with Peter only, to whom it was promised; not with the Chosen Three, who received it by angelic and divine conferral on the mount of Transfiguration, but with *all* of the Twelve. (*The Mortal Messiah: From Bethlehem to Calvary* [Salt Lake City: Deseret Book, 1979–81], 3:92)

ILLUSTRATIONS FOR OUR TIMES

In His Strength

When Joshua was preparing for the battle of Jericho, he saw nearby a man with sword drawn. Joshua went up to him and said, "Art thou for us, or for our adversaries?" The man replied, "Nay; but as captain of the host of the Lord am I now come." And Joshua dropped to the earth in a worshipful attitude of reverence, realizing this was an angelic person commissioned of the Lord to oversee the ensuing battle and assure the victory of Israel (see Josh. 5:12–15).

And so it is with us. No matter what our errand in the service of the Lord, if we proceed in His might and with His strength, we will enjoy success and untold spiritual blessings. Humility—openness to the guidance of the Spirit—is the foundation of righteous leadership. Ammon captured this truth perfectly: "Yea, I know that I am nothing; as to my strength I am weak; therefore I will not boast of myself, but I will boast of my God, for in his strength I can do all things" (Alma 26:12).

Faith as a Child

The omnipotence of God was displayed through the prophet Elijah. The Lord has power to do all things, and nothing can frustrate His work or His power. The power of the Lord is manifest through the priesthood—the power and authority of God delegated to His sons.

Priesthood blessings can and should be used to bless others. Fathers and priesthood leaders should prepare themselves for this great opportunity. All members should look to the priesthood to bless their lives and request blessings as moved upon by the Spirit.

In our family, we made a habit of giving blessings as the children were preparing for the school year and when illness was severe. Our little boy, Brett, in kindergarten, was sick with the flu, and he said, "Daddy, will you give me a prayer?" (That meant blessing.)

I replied, "Of course." That night I gave Brett a blessing.

The next morning, we gathered the children around for scripture time. Kristi said, "Brett, I thought you were sick."

He said, "Didn't you know? Daddy blessed me. I have to be well." Only the faith of a child could be so strong. Surely the power of God is exhibited as we exercise our faith.

3. THE LORD IS IN CHARGE OF HIS PROGRAM FOR MANKIND

THEME: The Lord in His almighty power stands waiting to bless mankind. It is His agenda that governs the flow of life upon the earth. Through fasting and prayer, we can learn of His will and see His hand at work as He manifests Himself and blesses His children. We can literally call down the powers of heaven through fasting and prayer.

> *And he arose, and did eat and drink, and went in the strength of that meat forty days and forty nights unto Horeb the mount of God.* (1 Kgs. 19:8)

> *Yet I have left me seven thousand in Israel, all the knees which have not bowed unto Baal, and every mouth which hath not kissed him.* (1 Kgs. 19:18)

> *And Elijah passed by him [Elisha], and cast his mantle upon him.* (1 Kgs. 19:19)

MOMENT OF TRUTH

In a still, small voice, the Lord called upon Elijah and comforted him in his isolation. Elijah had gone into hiding, fasting and praying, to avoid the treacherous hand of Queen Jezebel, and had been sustained by an angel. The Lord commanded Elijah to anoint Hazael to be king over Syria, Jehu to be king over Israel, and Elisha to be the prophet of the Lord. The mighty political forces were then to be unleashed to destroy the enemies of righteousness in their pervading and unremitting wickedness. Nevertheless, the Lord had identified in Israel the faithful few who were still willing to follow His counsel. He was able to comfort Elijah at this moment of crisis in Israel, and Elijah was able to render service during the transition of leadership. Elisha received the mantle of Elijah and learned that he must immediately take up his mission with full devotion to the cause of the Lord.

MODERN PROPHETS SPEAK

James E. Faust:

> I emphasize that fasting and prayer is a great way to receive the moral strength and spiritual strength to resist the temptations of Satan. But you may say this is hard and

unpleasant. I commend to you the example of the Savior. He went into the desert, where he fasted and prayed to prepare himself spiritually for his ministry. His temptation by the devil was great, but through the purification of his spirit he was able to triumph over all evil. (*In the Strength of the Lord: The Life and Teachings of James E. Faust* [Salt Lake City: Deseret Book, 1999], 302)

Gordon B. Hinckley:

> I would suppose that on this campus at least 20,000 people have been fasting and that you have accompanied your fasting with earnest prayer. I think that's a most remarkable phenomenon. Most of you, I assume, have fasted and prayed with a purpose—that you might find answers to perplexing personal problems or the needs of others, or that moisture might fall upon these arid western lands. I hope you haven't prayed for snow with the hope that you could go skiing on Sunday. I believe that the Lord will hear our earnest supplications, if we will back up our fasting and prayers with goodness in our lives. ("Forget Yourself," *BYU Devotional Speeches of the Year,* March 6, 1977, 43; see also *TGBH,* 217)

ILLUSTRATIONS FOR OUR TIMES

The Power of Prayer and Fasting

Prophets pay a high price to be the spokesmen for the Lord. Such was the case with Elijah. Yet in his hour of need, he taught us a great truth: through fasting and prayer we can be comforted, and the Lord will reveal the things we should do.

The power of prayer and fasting is demonstrated in the following verses:

• To overcome and avoiding temptation	3 Ne. 18:15,18
• To restore Alma the Younger's health	Mosiah 27:22
• To give thanks and worship	Alma 45:1
• To know the things of God	Alma 5:46
• To enjoy the spirit of revelation and prophecy	Alma 17:3
• To help those who know not God	Alma 6:6
• To gain faith and humility	Hel. 3:35
• To become sanctified	Hel. 3:35

The power of fasting and prayer has been shown throughout the scriptures. Today the Lord continues to bless us as we humble ourselves in prayer and fasting, pay our fast offerings, and seek blessings at His hand. Within our own families we should testify of the blessings that we have received through fasting and prayer.

SUMMARY

Elijah was a singularly imposing figure in a long line of extraordinary prophetic servants of the Lord. His influence was felt with compelling force among the Israelites and non-Israelites of his day, was called forth again on the Mount of Transfiguration (Matt. 17:1–11), and touches countless lives today through the restored keys of the sealing power for temple work placed in his charge (D&C 110:13–16). The story of Elijah is a dramatic confirmation of the fact that the Lord's work is always founded on prophetic ministry. As we take upon ourselves the assignment of being about the Lord's errand, we need to live worthy of all the blessings that attend faithful service, which include the sustaining support of miracles both seen and unseen, the power of God unto salvation, and the continual guidance of the Lord.

CHAPTER TWENTY-NINE

"THE MOUNTAIN WAS FULL *of* HORSES *and* CHARIOTS *of* FIRE"

Reading Assignment: 2 Kings 2; 5–6

Holy men and holy women have had heavenly visions, by the hundreds and by the thousands, yea by the tens of thousands since this gospel was restored to the earth in our day. (Heber J. Grant, *CR*, 92)

THEMES *for* LIVING

1. Mantle of the Prophet: Transition in Church Leadership
2. Great Blessings from Simple Acts of Obedience
3. Selfless Service Is the Pattern in the Kingdom of God
4. Vision of Faith

INTRODUCTION

The passages of scripture recounting the transition of prophetic authority from Elijah to Elisha, and detailing some of the miraculous happenings in the life of the latter, identify four of the many qualities that attend spiritual vision: (1) **spiritual desire**: At Elijah's bidding, Elisha revealed the desire of his heart in anticipation of receiving the awesome mantle of authority: "And Elisha said, I pray thee, let a double portion of thy spirit be upon me" (2 Kgs. 2:9). Along with this fundamental desire of righteousness is the need to practice (2) **humility**, something that the Syrian Naaman needed to internalize before he could be healed of his leprosy by completing a most simple task. In addition, the spiritual person needs to cultivate a motivation grounded solely in (3) **selflessness and love**. This was a hard lesson for Elisha's servant, Gehazi, to learn. Finally, being able to discern the hand of God at work in our lives (as another of Elisha's servants was able to do) is fundamentally a blessing from God, who alone can open our inner eye to view the "chariots of fire" that surround and guard the faithful. One must be (4) **open to this gift of God** and receive it in thankfulness.

1. MANTLE OF THE PROPHET: TRANSITION IN CHURCH LEADERSHIP

THEME: The Lord oversees the continuity of leadership in His kingdom. Just as the prophetic office passed smoothly from the translated Elijah to the younger Elisha, in our day there is a righteous transition of authority and leadership without worldly campaigning, dispute, or competition.

He took up also the mantle of Elijah that fell from him. (2 Kgs. 2:13)

And when the sons of the prophets which were to view at Jericho saw him, they said, The spirit of Elijah doth rest on Elisha. And they came to meet him, and bowed themselves to the ground before him. (2 Kgs. 2:15)

MOMENT OF TRUTH

When it came time for Elijah the prophet to be translated, provision was made for a transition of assignment to his student, Elisha. Elijah asked what gift might be bestowed upon the successor, and Elisha requested that "a double portion of thy spirit be upon me" (2 Kgs. 2:9). This transpired as Elijah was taken up by a chariot of fire, and Elisha thereafter performed mighty miracles just as his predecessor had done. When the people desired to seek after the departed Elijah, the new prophet counseled against this, but they were adamant and did not relent until he gave permission for the search. He later reminded them of the wisdom of his initial counsel. Similarly, we are well advised today to obey the counsel of the prophet right away.

MODERN PROPHETS SPEAK

Spencer W. Kimball:

> President McKay had been a man among men, a great prophet and a great leader,
> and a counselor to two Church Presidents, but now after he was ordained and set

apart as the President of the Church, I saw him rise to new pinnacles of power and authority and effectiveness. He began to speak with the voice of authority. The inspiration that came from him was contagious. His pronouncements were mature and all-encompassing. His leadership showed that unmistakably the mantle of his calling was upon him. I saw the mantle pass again when on the day following the funeral of President David O. McKay, President Joseph Fielding Smith was elevated to the first place. When our hands were taken from his head and he now not only held all the keys and authorities and powers, but was set apart as the President of the Church, we seemed to feel almost an immediate growth. Although he was a very old man, very aged as judged by the world, he seemed to freshen and liven and throw off much of his years. His sermons were an inspiration. His sweet spirit was everywhere manifest. He was impressive to visitor and member alike. (*TSWK,* 467)

George Q. Cannon:

On that occasion President Brigham Young seemed to be transformed, and a change such as that we read of in the Scriptures as happening to the Prophet Elisha, when Elijah was translated in his presence, seemed to have taken place with him. The mantle of the Prophet Joseph had been left for him. . . . The people said one to another, "the spirit of Joseph rests upon Brigham;" they knew that he was the man chosen to lead them, and they honored him accordingly. (*Gospel Truth: Discourses and Writings of President George Q. Cannon* [Salt Lake City: Deseret Book, 1987], 223)

ILLUSTRATIONS FOR OUR TIMES

People Are Rooted in Christ

As individuals, we often become attached not only to our leaders, but also to the people we serve. When I was released as a young bishop, I had this feeling of concern for my little BYU student ward. I loved them so much. Would the next bishop love them? Could he love them as much as I did? I felt ambivalent in my release. The counselor in the stake presidency had gone through this many times and could discern my feelings. He said, "Bishop Ed, I know how you are feeling. It's hard to let go. Remember the Lord is in charge, and it is His Church. The students will be fine. The new bishop will do a great job and take care of them, believe me."

Then it happened—I realized I was but an instrument in His hands. It was the Savior's Church, and the members were His children. He was the Shepherd, and I was the under-shepherd. It is His kingdom. I am a servant in the kingdom. Besides, people are rooted in Christ, not in mortals who are their present leaders. This is an imperative truth that all must understand. Don't be or not be a member because of some other mortal. Too many people become less active because of their relationship with others.

We have all seen changes in the presidency of the Church. I have witnessed nine of our Apostles become the Prophet, Seer, and Revelator. We must always remember that each one is different, but also that each one is the mouthpiece of the Lord. We must sustain each of our prophets with love, faith, and obedience.

2. GREAT BLESSINGS FROM SIMPLE ACTS OF OBEDIENCE

THEME: We can learn, with Naaman the Syrian, that simple acts of obedience in response to inspired counsel can lead to great benefits. The gospel is a system of simple truths and principles leading to immortality and eternal life.

> *If the prophet had bid thee do some great thing, wouldest thou not have done it? how much rather then, when he saith to thee, Wash, and be clean?* (2 Kgs. 5:13)

MOMENT OF TRUTH

When Naaman learned, through a young Israelite girl taken into domestic service in Syria, that the Lord's prophet could heal him of his leprosy, he came with his entourage to seek relief. But when Elisha instructed him to bathe seven times in the Jordan—a simple and non-elegant solution to his problem—Naaman was angry. Only through the wise counsel of his servant did Naaman think better of his impetuousness, and his obedience resulted in the desired cure. This event is rightly regarded as one of the most interesting examples of "spiritual leverage" in the scriptures.

MODERN PROPHETS SPEAK

Henry B. Eyring:

> He came to my office and said: "You told me that the Lord would someday let me know that I was forgiven. But I am going to the temple to marry a wonderful girl. I want to be the best I can be for her. I need to know that I am forgiven. And I need to know now. Tell me how to find out." I said I would try.
>
> He gave me a deadline. As I recall, it was less than two weeks away. Fortunately, during that period of time I went to Salt Lake City and found myself seeing Elder Spencer W. Kimball, then a member of the Quorum of the Twelve, at a social function. It was crowded, and yet he somehow found me. He walked up to me in that crowd and said, "Hal, I understand that you are now a bishop. Do you have anything you would like to ask me?"
>
> I said that I did, but I didn't think that was the place to talk about it. He thought it was. It was an outdoor party. My memory is that we went behind a shrub and there had our interview. Without breaking confidences, I outlined the concerns and the question of this young man in my ward. Then I asked Elder Kimball, "How can he

get that revelation? How can he know whether his sins are remitted?" I thought Elder Kimball would talk to me about fasting or prayer or listening for the still small voice. But he surprised me. Instead he said, "Tell me something about the young man." I said, "What would you like to know?" And then he began a series of the most simple questions. Some of the ones I remember were: "Does he come to his priesthood meetings?" I said, after a moment of thought, "Yes." "Does he come early?" "Yes." "Does he sit toward the front?" I thought for a moment and then realized, to my amazement, that he did. "Does he home teach?" "Yes." "Does he go early in the month?" "Yes, he does." "Does he go more than once?" "Yes." I can't remember the other questions. But they were all like that—little things, simple acts of obedience, of submission. And for each question I was surprised that my answer was always yes. Yes, he wasn't just at all his meetings: he was early; he was smiling; he was there not only with his whole heart, but with the broken heart of a little child, as he was every time the Lord asked anything of him. And after I had said yes to each of his questions, Elder Kimball looked at me, paused, and then very quietly said, "There is your revelation." (*To Draw Closer to God: A Collection of Discourses* [Salt Lake City: Deseret Book, 1997], 56)

Joseph B. Wirthlin:

I've been impressed recently with the thought that this life is made up of little things—little things that count a great deal. . . . I believe that the little things are of great importance in our relationship with ourselves, in our relationships with others, and in our relationship with God. . . . We must each take proper care to see that the little things regarding our personal life are in order. . . . These little things— which, in reality, become such big things—bring perspective to our lives as we learn to conquer them one by one in our effort to gain strength. And this we do in a spirit of humility and gratitude to our Heavenly Father. I testify to you that so-called little things really do count in the eternal perspective of what it is all about, and that is, to gain eternal life in the presence of our Heavenly Father. (*Finding Peace in Our Lives* [Salt Lake City: Deseret Book, 1995], 59, 70, 71)

ILLUSTRATIONS FOR OUR TIMES

The Great Divide

A few miles west of magnificent Lake Louise in Banff National Park, Alberta, there is a small stream that flows down the western slope of the mountain ridge and passes underneath the Trans-Canada Highway, where it soon encounters an outcropping of rocks and divides into two tiny streamlets, each one barely a foot across. One of them flows northward into the Bow River, and then eastward via major waterways into the Hudson Bay. The other flows southward into the Kicking House River, and from thence into the Columbia River and eventually into the Pacific Ocean. A droplet of water flowing down that stream would face the prospect, at the Great Divide, of going either toward the frozen expanse of the North, or toward the more hospitable waters of the Pacific.

As a young man, I used to drive a tour bus in that area to earn money for college. One of the most compelling sights for tourists was that stop near the large sign spanning the highway that identified "The Great Divide." The visitors would walk down a path along the small stream and peer with fascination at the spot where it divided into two. On one of the tours, I noticed a woman staring engrossed at the dividing stream for several minutes. "Why are you so interested in that stream?" I asked her.

"Because," she said quietly, "that's life."

And so it was—and is. Life is a series of small daily choices that define our ultimate directions. Out of the small choices of today will flow the mighty downstream rivers of tomorrow. In life, the small often defines the large; the seemingly insignificant frequently determines the big picture.

All of us come to the Great Divide every day of our lives. With the help of God, we can make those daily decisions that comprise fixing our gaze upon the Savior. We can decide to do the simple deeds of righteousness, kindness, and service that lead to eternal life.

Joy Depends on the Little Things

Obedience is a law that when obeyed in love brings one to a state of righteousness. Obedience has blessings associated with each commandment, whether great or small. The smallest, almost insignificant act or thing often has the greatest impact. Thus was the case with the Liahona. As Lehi's family exercised faith and diligence and gave heed to the writings they were directed in the wilderness. "And thus we see that by small means the Lord can bring about great things" (1 Ne. 16:29).

As a company of brethren was going to their missions, the Lord spoke the following to the Prophet Joseph, "Wherefore, be not weary in well-doing, for ye are laying the foundation of a great work. And out of small things proceedeth that which is great. Behold, the Lord requireth the heart and a willing mind; and the willing and obedient shall eat the good of the land of Zion in these last days" (D&C 74:33–34).

And again, the Lord said, "Let no man count them as small things; for there is much which lieth in futurity, pertaining to the saints, which depends upon these things. You know, brethren, that a very large ship is benefitted very much by a very small helm in the time of a storm, by being kept workways with the wind and the waves. Therefore, dearly beloved brethren, let us cheerfully do all things that lie in our power; and then may we stand still, with the utmost assurance, to see the salvation of God, and for his arm to be revealed" (D&C 123:15–17). It seems clear that little things make a big difference in our lives. Just a degree off course makes a huge difference at the end of the journey.

3. SELFLESS SERVICE IS THE PATTERN IN THE KINGDOM OF GOD

THEME: Unlike Elisha's servant, Gehazi, we can learn to avoid attaching material interests to spiritual service. The wages of obedience are harmony, peace, and spiritual wealth. We serve out of love, not self-interest.

> Naaman to Elisha: *"Behold, now I know that there is no God in all the earth, but in Israel: now therefore, I pray thee, take a blessing of thy servant. But he said, As the Lord liveth, before whom I stand, I will receive none."* (2 Kgs. 5:15–16)

> Elisha to Gehazi: *"Is it a time to receive money?"* (2 Kgs. 5:26)

MOMENT OF TRUTH

When the thankful Naaman wanted to give Elisha material rewards for his successful cure, Elisha refused any gratuity. But Gehazi, Elisha's servant, was not above the allure of material wealth, and arranged to appropriate some of Naaman's goods. When Elisha learned of this folly, he arranged to give to Gehazi something he had not anticipated receiving: Naaman's former leprous condition. The story thus becomes a vehicle for teaching that service rendered in the name of God has spiritual rewards associated with it. When the motivation is for material gain, the service loses its spiritual character.

MODERN PROPHETS SPEAK

Joseph B. Wirthlin:

> Stated simply, charity means subordinating our interests and needs to those of others, as the Savior has done for all of us. The Apostle Paul wrote that of faith, hope, and charity, "the greatest . . . is charity" (1 Cor. 13:13), and Moroni wrote, "Except ye have charity ye can in nowise be saved in the kingdom of God" (Moro. 10:21). I believe that selfless service is a distinctive part of the gospel. As President Spencer W. Kimball said, welfare service "is not a program, but the essence of the gospel. *It is the gospel in action.* It is the crowning principle of a Christian life." (*Finding Peace in Our Lives* [Salt Lake City: Deseret Book, 1995], 43)

Gordon B. Hinckley:

> I want to commend those of our people who give so willingly of their time in attending to the sacred work within the temples of the Lord. In temple work is found the very essence of selfless service. In my judgment, one of the miracles of our day is the great consecration of time and effort on the part of hundreds of thousands of busy

people in behalf of the dead. Those who are engaged in this service know that out of it all comes a sweet and satisfying feeling. This sweet blessing of the Spirit becomes literally a medicine to cure many of the ailments of our lives. From such experiences we come to realize that only when we serve others do we truly serve the Lord. (*Faith: The Essence of True Religion* [Salt Lake City: Deseret Book, 1989], 40)

ILLUSTRATIONS FOR OUR TIMES

The Motive Is Love

One of the miracles of the Church is its stability of leadership—with thousands of bishops, stake presidents, missionaries, and workers of every kind donating endless hours of time and devoted service for no other reason than love. It is the continuity of spiritual guidance and spiritual nourishment that keeps this miracle alive. In those rare instances where a leader allows his or her Church connections to cross over into professional interests, there is often disappointment and even anguish. My wife and I recall a time, early in our marriage, where a local Church leader quite innocently used his influence to facilitate the sale of a rather expensive product to a number of ward members. When the product turned out to be faulty, there was disappointment and concern. This leader told me of his grief over the outcome. Lessons were learned, forgiveness was asked, and new resolves were made. We should take up the Lord's errand out of love and selfless devotion, and for no other reason. Only then, when our eye is single to the glory of God, when our motives are pure, can the Spirit guide and direct without constraint.

4. VISION OF FAITH

THEME: By learning to look with spiritual eyes, we can perceive the "chariots of fire" representing the Lord's systems of power and support put in place to bring about His divine purposes and defend the interests of His faithful servants.

Fear not: for they that be with us are more than they that be with them. (2 Kgs. 6:16)

MOMENT OF TRUTH

Elisha gave wise counsel to the Israelite kings on how to conduct their war with Syria. Thus, the Syrians came seeking to destroy the prophet. When Elisha's servant fearfully viewed the surrounding hordes of the enemy, Elisha prayed that the Lord might open the servant's eyes to see the amassed forces of heaven ("chariots of fire"—2 Kgs. 6:17) arrayed against the enemy. The servant beheld and was filled with hope and courage. At the same time, Elisha prayed that the Lord would take away the sight of the Syrians so that he could lead them away and render them powerless. Thus the Lord, once again, brought about victory for His people.

MODERN PROPHETS SPEAK

James E. Faust:

> An article in *U.S. News and World Report* states that the earth is capable of producing food for a population of at least eighty billion, eight times the ten billion expected to inhabit the earth by the year 2050. One study estimates that with improved scientific methods, the earth could feed as many as one thousand billion people ("Ten Billion for Dinner, Please," *U.S. News and World Report,* 12 September 1994, 57–60). Those who argue for sustainable growth lack vision and faith. The Lord said, "For the earth is full, and there is enough and to spare" (D&C 104:17). That settles the issue for me. It should settle the issue for all of us. The Lord has spoken. (*Finding Light in a Dark World* [Salt Lake City: Deseret Book, 1995], 72–73)

Joseph Fielding Smith:

> Faith is knowledge that transcends ordinary boundaries. The range of the physical eye is sharply limited, it reaches only a part of the material world; but the vision of faith perceives the mystery of the invisible world and its limits are ever expanding. (*The Restoration of All Things* [Salt Lake City: Deseret News Press, 1945], 189–90)

ILLUSTRATIONS FOR OUR TIMES

The Miracle of Vision

The prophet Elisha's faith was evident throughout this moment in history. His prayer of faith brought spiritual "eyes" to his servant, allowing him to see the strength of the Lord as demonstrated by the "chariots of fire." This changed the servant's vision of the situation and gave him hope. Hope is integral to faith and charity; they cannot be separated in principle and doctrine. Faith, hope, and charity are intricately intertwined and become the basis of qualifying and assisting to serve God in this great work (see D&C 4:4; D&C 12:8). When we see only with our natural eyes, we are overwhelmed and can see no way to accomplish our goal.

While serving as president of the London South Mission, I would observe this fear—the lack of faith, hope and charity—among some of the missionaries as they served. They were wonderful young men and women. They just needed to see things as they really were. We had a special zone conference where we explained howthe power of God would be manifest if they would but open their mouths (see D&C 33:8–11, 84:85–88, 100:5–6). We demonstrated the power within them as they honestly prepared and paid the price to become true disciples of Christ with power and authority to do all things (see Alma 17:2–3; 26:11–12; 3 Ne. 5:13; D&C 38:30, 88:199).

Thus the vision of who they were and what they could do had empowered them to action. We gave them a new street dialogue that had been tested and proven successful. Following the meeting, we went to the town center and opened our mouths. A miracle happened. The mission found more people and made more appointments for "callbacks" in this zone conference by three times the number of people found in the entire week by all the missionaries working ten-hour days. They were astounded. Needless to say, their vision of missionary work changed. They became mighty instruments in the hands of the Lord. They thrust in their sickles and reaped great rewards, and they were happy in their work.

The Story of Elizabeth

When the new young family moved into our ward, my wife and I missed their introductory talks that first sacrament meeting because we were home tending a sick child. However, the next Sunday we met them in the hallway and extended greetings. Because we had missed their speeches, they told us briefly about their background, and mentioned a young daughter who had passed away some time before they had moved into the ward. Our son, about ten years old at the time, and now recuperated from his illness, looked at them and quietly spoke the word "Elizabeth." This amazed us as parents, since with his autistic disability he was essentially non-communicative. However, the impact on the new couple was profound. They both burst into tears, and when they had sufficiently gained their composure, they told us for the first time that the name of their deceased daughter was—Elizabeth. The following fast and testimony meeting, they stood to bear witness to the truthfulness of the gospel, recount the incident involving our son, and express gratitude that that Spirit of the Lord, though operating sometimes in mysterious ways, opens up from time to time a vision of the eternal brotherhood and sisterhood that exists among the Lord's children, on either side of the veil.

SUMMARY

Each person comes to earth with an immense storehouse of experiences and insights from the pre-mortal realm, softly blanketed with a filter of forgetfulness by a merciful Father who wants us to learn line upon line, precept upon precept, how to rise on the wings of obedience and faith to a state where we can return home again. From time to time, our inner eye allows us to catch a glimpse of the divine at work in our lives. Through faith, we can facilitate this kind of inner vision by cultivating a desire for righteousness (as did Elisha), by our humble willingness to abide by the simple and fundamental laws of the gospel, by giving selfless service based solely on love, and by accepting with grateful and contrite hearts the blessings of God.

CHAPTER THIRTY

"SANCTIFY NOW YOURSELVES, *and* SANCTIFY *the* HOUSE *of the* LORD"

Reading Assignment: 2 Chronicles 29–30; 32; 34.

Additional Reading: 2 Kings 18–19; 22–23; Isaiah 37:10–20, 33–38.

He [the Lord] will continue to feed us the bread of life as we need it from time to time, if we will but live in accordance with the teachings we have already received. (George Albert Smith, *CR,* Oct. 1912, 118)

THEMES *for* LIVING

1. The Lord Will Have a Pure House and Pure Servants
2. The Temple as a Fortress of Safety
3. The Scriptures as Protection for the Saints

INTRODUCTION

Renewal, reform, rejuvenation, rebirth—these are the governing principles in the reign of Kings Hezekiah and Josiah, whose contributions to spiritual progress under the covenant with God stand in marked contrast to the wickedness and idolatry of so many of their predecessors in the kingdoms of Israel and Judah. We see in the background the imposing influence of Isaiah and Jeremiah, two of the greatest of the Lord's prophets. The work of Hezekiah and Josiah and their righteous associates established once again a great spiritual defense bulwark for protecting the Israelites and securing not only their temporal safety but also their favor with the Lord through obedience to Him. Three grand designs are at play here: (1) the process of purification and sanctification, (2) the elevation once again of the temple as a visible symbol of the invisible covenant bonds and blessings, and (3) the reinstatement of the scriptures as an anchor and guide in the lives of the people.

1. THE LORD WILL HAVE A PURE HOUSE AND PURE SERVANTS

THEME: Just as Hezekiah, on his royal watch, stood for restoration and purification, so each one of us—as part of the "royal priesthood" (1 Pet. 2:9)—must commit to the cleansing principles of righteousness and honor in our homes and individual lives.

> *Now it is in mine heart to make a covenant with the Lord God of Israel, that his fierce wrath may turn away from us. My sons, be not now negligent: for the Lord hath chosen you to stand before him, to serve him, and that ye should minister unto him.* (2 Chr. 29:10–11)

MOMENT OF TRUTH

The twenty-nine-year reign of Hezekiah, king of Judah, beginning in 715 B.C. and extending to 686 B.C., stands out as a refreshing beacon of reform and righteousness in a long sequence of leaders (including his own father, Ahaz, desecrater and closer of the temple) who typically fell short of covenant standards and often supported idolatrous practices. In alliance with his older contemporary, the great prophet Isaiah, Hezekiah instituted sweeping reforms of religious practice and restored the temple to its state of sanctity. The people were able once more to praise the Lord with clean hands and a clean heart. Hezekiah (which means "God strengthens" in Hebrew) instilled in a significant segment of the populace a genuine respect for God and a realignment with the covenant walk of life. As a result, Judah was able to defend itself successfully before its enemies, the Assyrians, who had earlier succeeded, under King Shalmaneser in 721 B.C., in ravishing the northern kingdom of Israel and carrying the ten tribes into captivity.

MODERN PROPHETS SPEAK

Harold B. Lee:
> I suppose the greatest expectation of any of you is to stand one day in the presence of the Lord. How can you prepare yourself for that day? In one great, meaningful

statement, the Lord said this: "And if your eye be single to my glory, your whole bodies shall be filled with light, and there shall be no darkness in you; and that body which is filled with light comprehendeth all things. Therefore, sanctify yourselves that your minds become single to God, and the days will come that you shall see him; for he will unveil his face unto you, and it shall be in his own time, and in his own way, and according to his own will" (D&C 88:67–68). (*Decisions for Successful Living* [Salt Lake City: Deseret Book, 1973], 232)

Howard W. Hunter:

We must strive to be pure in thought and action. It is impressive to me that the primary requirement of the Lord for the work of his ministry is personal purity. To the first elders of the Church, the Lord said: "Sanctify yourselves; yea, purify your hearts, and cleanse your hands and your feet before me, that I may make you clean" (D&C 88:74). This implies more than just a chaste life. To those ordained to the ministry, the Lord said, "Strip yourselves from jealousies and fears, and humble yourselves before me" (D&C 67:10). We are further told that we cannot be pure in heart until we have acquired the pure love of Christ, which is charity, "that we may be purified even as he is pure" (Moro. 7:48). Purity of thought and action therefore requires us to take on the mind of Christ! As we ponder on the meaning of this thought, it is evident that spiritual promptings do not come to one who is covetous in heart, nor will they come to one who has an irritable disposition, one who is jealous, one who doubts, or one who constantly worries. (*THWH*, 75)

ILLUSTRATIONS FOR OUR TIMES

The Spirit Dwells in Pure Temples

While Hezekiah's reforms may not seem like much to modern Saints who live under the gospel covenant, those reforms engendered in the people of Judah far more righteousness than had existed for several years. Hezekiah explained to the priests and Levites that the Lord's past anger against Judah (and hence their political and social woes) were traceable to their forefathers' defilement of God's holy house (2 Chr. 29:6–9). The message, therefore, seems clear for every group in every dispensation which has placed itself in a covenant relationship to God through temple ordinances: community well-being depends on purity and exactness in temple worship (2 Chron. 29:10–11). (Kent P. Jackson, ed., *Studies in Scripture, Vol. 4: 1 Kings to Malachi* [Salt Lake City: Deseret Book, 1993], 76)

The temples of our God should not be defiled. As the children of God, we too are temples. The Lord has said, "Know ye not that ye are the temple of God, and that the Spirit of God dwelleth in you? If any man defile the temple of God, him shall God destroy; for the temple of God is holy, which temple ye are" (1 Cor. 3:16–17). We too must keep ourselves clean in order to receive the blessings of the Lord. The Spirit cannot dwell in unclean "temples." If we, through disobedience, defile ourselves, we lose the blessings of the Spirit.

The Most Desirable of All Things

A number of years ago, it was my privilege to serve in a branch presidency at the Missionary Training Center in Provo. You just had to love the young elders and sisters as they arrived and began the process of learning what it meant to give their "all" to the Lord as His ambassadors. One of the things we liked to watch for was what the new missionaries had to say about the people living in the areas to which they were being sent. Their feelings about these people gave an important clue about how they were equipping themselves spiritually for the errand of the Lord. Often you would find missionaries who would articulate their sincere love for these people—even though they had never met any of them. That was a sure sign that the missionaries were in tune with the Spirit, because, as Paul taught: "And hope maketh not ashamed; because the love of God is shed abroad in our hearts by the Holy Ghost which is given unto us" (Rom. 5:5). Others may also have felt this love budding in their hearts, but were still learning how to discern it, identify it, and express it to others. They were learning that "the fruit of the Spirit is love" (Gal. 5:22). A key part of becoming a missionary—in fact a key part of becoming a faithful Latter-day Saint—is to pray for this love to flourish in our hearts. Anyone who is called to service in the kingdom of God, who embraces this duty with humility and full purpose of heart, experiences an unfolding love for the people served. Thus Nephi understood the meaning of the tree in his father's vision: "Yea, it is the love of God, which sheddeth itself abroad in the hearts of the children of men; wherefore, it is the most desirable above all things" (1 Ne. 11:22).

2. THE TEMPLE AS A FORTRESS OF SAFETY

THEME: Just as Hezekiah taught his people to look once again to the temple as the emblem of divine light and protection, we too can find in our commitment to temple standards and temple activity a protection from the forces of evil abroad in the world.

> *Now ye have consecrated yourselves unto the Lord, come near and bring sacrifices and thank offerings into the house of the Lord.* (2 Chr. 29:31)

> *Now be ye not stiffnecked, as your fathers were, but yield yourselves unto the Lord, and enter into his sanctuary, which he hath sanctified forever: and serve the Lord your God.* (2 Chr. 30:8)

HEZEKIAH TO THE PEOPLE, CONCERNING THE INVADING ASSYRIAN KING: *"With him is an arm of flesh; but with us is the Lord our God to help us, and to fight our battles."* (2 Chr. 32:8)

MOMENT OF TRUTH

Hezekiah, having restored the temple as the tangible icon of God's power and guiding light, rallied his people around a unifying purpose of covenant fidelity—"And the Lord hearkened to Hezekiah, and healed the people" (2 Chr. 30:20). Hezekiah was therefore able, in concert with Isaiah, to seek the Lord's blessing in thwarting the siege of Jerusalem in 701 B.C. by the Assyrian King, Sennacherib, and his army. Hezekiah caused the waters of the spring Gihon to be diverted through a specially constructed tunnel ("Hezekiah's Tunnel," still in use today) into a pool within the city (2 Chr. 32:2–4), thus preserving his people and denying the besieging Assyrian army access to essential water. This tunnel can be seen as a symbol for accessing the "living water" of salvation (John 4:10–14), just as the temple is the source for the "living water" provided through the gospel's most sacred truths and ordinances. Thus, the temple stands as an invulnerable spiritual fortress of defense for the faithful and devout.

MODERN PROPHETS SPEAK

John A. Widtsoe:

> The vastness of meaning in temple worship makes it difficult at once for any person to remember and understand it. Only once are the endowments taken for himself by any one person. To refresh his memory, and to place him in close touch with the spirit of the work, a person may enter the temple as frequently as he desires and take endowments for the dead. In that way both he and the dead are benefited. The temples, then, are means whereby every member of the Church, of righteous conduct and sufficient age, may receive precious endowments and may be kept in refreshed memory of the Great Plan, under which he, with the rest of the human family, is living. Temple work is the safety of the living and the hope of the dead. (*A Rational Theology* [Salt Lake City: Deseret Book, 1937], 129)

Spencer W. Kimball:

> I am sure one could go to extreme in worshiping the cloth of which the garment is made, but one could also go to the other extreme. Though generally I think our protection is a mental, spiritual, moral one, yet I am convinced that there could be and undoubtedly have been many cases where there has been, through faith, an actual physical protection, so we must not minimize that possibility. (*TSWK,* 539)

ILLUSTRATIONS FOR OUR TIMES

Mountains May Come and Go

Edward J. Wood, first president of the Cardston Temple in Alberta, was a leader of legendary vision and spirituality during his many years of service in the House of the Lord. I recall as a young person hearing my father tell several times the story of the occasion when he and my mother were at the temple one day and she noticed in one of the corridors a painting of Chief Mountain, a famous landmark in southern Alberta and northern Montana. At the same time, she observed that this same craggy granite mountain peak is plainly visible through one of the temple windows to anyone who might choose to look at it.

President Wood happened to be passing by at the time, and she asked him the question, "Why would we have a painting of Chief Mountain hanging here in the temple when we can look through the window and see it in reality?"

Without hesitation, President Wood responded, "Because this temple is going to be here longer than that mountain, and we want to remember what it looked like."

His point, taken in the spirit of faith and hope, is that the temple is our most apparent evidence of the eternity of lives and the grand bonding that takes place among faithful families—present, past, and future—by virtue of the sealing powers of the priesthood of God. Families under the new and everlasting covenant of eternal marriage are intended to endure forever, far beyond the frontiers of mortality. Mountains may come and go, but the children of God and their covenant relationships are to be secured through sanctification and made to last forever.

A Place of Peace, Safety, and Joy

Temple service is vicarious service. It is service like that given by our Savior Jesus Christ. We become saviors on Mount Zion. "And now, my dearly beloved brethren and sisters, let me assure you that these are principles in relation to the dead and the living that cannot be lightly passed over, as pertaining to our salvation. For their salvation is necessary and essential to our salvation, as Paul says concerning the fathers—that they without us cannot be made perfect—neither can we without our dead be made perfect" (D&C 128:15). Within the walls of the holy temples are peace, safety and joy: peace as only the Lord can give, safety from the world and all of its vices, and joy in being instruments in the hand of the Lord to bless those who have gone on before.

As we keep the temple covenants, we will be safe from the world and all of its temptations. We will have the Spirit. We will desire to return to the House of the Lord in service to our kindred dead and feel that Spirit in the Lord's Holy House.

3. THE SCRIPTURES AS PROTECTION FOR THE SAINTS

THEME: We have the opportunity to "discover" anew each day the power of the scriptures to bring vitality, peace, inspiration, and saving truth into our lives and homes. Just as King Josiah caused the rediscovered "book of the law" to be read to his people, we too can make daily scripture study a foundation for our spiritual well-being and a protection for our families.

> *For great is the wrath of the Lord that is poured out upon us, because our fathers have not kept the word of the Lord, to do after all that is written in this book.* (2 Chr. 34:21)

> *And the king stood in his place, and made a covenant before the Lord, to walk after the Lord, and to keep his commandments, and his testimonies, and his statutes, with all his heart, and with all his soul, to perform the words of the covenant which are written in this book. And he caused all that were present in Jerusalem and Benjamin to stand to it.* (2 Chr. 34:31–32)

MOMENT OF TRUTH

King Josiah of Judah (641–610 B.C.), great-grandson of Hezekiah and younger contemporary of the prophet Jeremiah and of Father Lehi, cleansed the land of idolatrous practice once again—beginning when he was only fifteen or sixteen years of age—and repaired and reinstated the temple as the centerpiece of the Lord's program of religious worship for all of Israel. When Hilkiah the high priest discovered in the temple a book of the law of the Lord (scriptures as given through Moses; 2 Chr. 34:15), Josiah was profoundly impacted and caused these words to be read to the people so they could renew the Lord's standard of behavior within themselves, after their forefathers had allowed the covenant practices to be forgotten. The lost and rediscovered book became the key to reforms and a symbol of protection for the people of God. Josiah made a covenant of obedience to the Lord, and caused his people to stand by it.

MODERN PROPHETS SPEAK

Joseph Smith:

> Search the scriptures—search the revelations which we publish, and ask your Heavenly Father, in the name of his Son Jesus Christ, to manifest the truth unto you, and if you do it with an eye single to his glory nothing doubting, he will answer you by the power of his Holy Spirit. You will then know for yourselves and not for another. You will not then be

dependent on man for the knowledge of God; nor will there be any room for speculation. No; for when men receive their instruction from him that made them, they know how he will save them. Then again we say: Search the scriptures, search the prophets, and learn what portion of them belongs to you and the people of the nineteenth century. You, no doubt, will agree with us, and say, that you have no right to claim the promises of the inhabitants before the flood; that you cannot found your hopes of salvation upon the obedience of the children of Israel when journeying in the wilderness, nor can you expect that the blessings which the apostles pronounced upon the churches of Christ eighteen hundred years ago were intended for you. Again, if others' blessings are not your blessings, others' curses are not your curses; you stand then in these last days, as all have stood before you, agents unto yourselves, to be judged according to your works. (*Discourses of the Prophet Joseph Smith* [Salt Lake City: Deseret Book, 1977], 130–31)

Gordon B. Hinckley:

I promise you that if you will read the words of that writing which we call scripture, there will come into your heart an understanding and a warmth that will be pleasing to experience. "Search the scriptures; for in them ye think ye have eternal life: and they are they which testify of me" (John 5:39). Read, for instance, the Gospel of John from its beginning to its end. Let the Lord speak for himself to you, and his words will come with a quiet conviction that will make the words of his critics meaningless. Read also the testament of the New World, the Book of Mormon, brought forth as a witness "that Jesus is the Christ, the Eternal God, manifesting himself unto all nations" (Book of Mormon title page). ("The Miracle That Is Jesus," *Improvement Era,* June 1966, 531; see also *TGBH,* 572)

ILLUSTRATIONS FOR OUR TIMES

To Love the Word of God

The key to eternal life is to live by every word that proceeds from the mouth of God (see D&C 84:44). To apply the scriptures to our lives, each of us must:

- Read the scriptures carefully.

- Ponder them as they relate to you.

- Write down the main idea and how you are going to apply it to your life. (This should be a first-person statement such as "I will," "I must," and "I am going to.") I have had thousands of students testify of the power of doing such applications.

Simple Solutions

One of the scriptures of greatest impact in my life contains this advice: "Be thou humble; and the Lord thy God shall lead thee by the hand and give thee answer to thy prayers" (D&C 112:10). The earliest recollection I have of how the process can work in Church administration is a simple happening that took place while I was serving many years ago as president of the Young Men. The ward had asked the youth to put on a drama evening, so two groups were organized, each of which was to prepare a play for presentation on a certain evening. Each group invested significant time and energy over many weeks in rehearsing and preparing for the grand occasion. Everything was on schedule, until one of the groups asked for a week's postponement in order to bring their performance to a higher state of readiness (and allow their lead actress to recover somewhat from an illness). The other group demurred, saying that a week's delay would place them beyond their prime. What to do? The emotion on both sides began to run higher and higher. Each side began to act as though the performance date of their play was of overarching importance in the monumental flow of life. Feelings were heightened. Phone calls crisscrossed the valley. One irate actor even flagged me down on the highway to lobby for his position. Then I remembered that scripture about prayer in the Doctrine & Covenants.

I suggested that we all gather at a special prayer meeting and ask the Lord what to do. Everyone agreed. A time was scheduled. We came together, and one of the directors, a young man, was asked to say the prayer. Immediately after we had risen to our feet, an idea came into my mind. Why not have the group that was more prepared perform on schedule in a neighboring ward as a kind of dress rehearsal, then have both groups perform together for our ward a week later? Everyone was satisfied with this solution (including the neighboring ward, as it turned out). The other director, a young woman, in her closing prayer at the conclusion of our special meeting, thanked the Lord for His inspiration. This was a simple thing. But for the most part, life is a series of simple events that call for simple solutions based on the written and spoken word of the Lord.

SUMMARY

When Jesus spoke with the Samarian woman at Jacob's well and received from her hands a drink of water, he said, "Whosoever drinketh of this water shall thirst again: But whosoever drinketh of the water that I shall give him shall never thirst; but the water that I shall give him shall be in him a well of water springing up into everlasting life" (John 4:13–14). This same Jesus, who fulfilled His mission in the meridian of time, was Lord and Savior from the beginning. It was under His inspiration that

Hezekiah restored the sanctity of the temple and secured for the besieged people the "living waters" of Gihon (2 Chr. 32:2–4; compare John 4:11). It was under His loving guidance that the high priest Hilkiah found the missing book of the law of the Lord in the temple (2 Chr. 34:15), and that Josiah published it for the people once again. When we commit ourselves to the process of purification, make the temple covenants and ordinances the centerpiece of our spiritual lives, and establish our daily walk and conversation on the foundation of the written and spoken word of the Lord, we too will enjoy the blessings of the "living water" of life and the "true bread from heaven" (John 6:32).

CHAPTER THIRTY-ONE

"FOR *as* HE THINKETH *in* HIS HEART, SO IS HE"

Reading Assignment: Proverbs, Ecclesiastes

The best way to obtain truth and wisdom is not to ask it from books, but to go to God in prayer, and obtain divine teaching. (Joseph Smith, *HC* 4:425)

THEMES *for* LIVING

1. Trusting in God Is the Foundation of Wisdom
2. A Willingness to Be Entreated Is the Key to Cultivating Wisdom
3. The Flowering of Wisdom Is to Bring Forth Good Fruit
Unto the Lord
4. Pride Leads to Folly

INTRODUCTION

The proverbs of Solomon and the pronouncements of the "Preacher" in the book of Ecclesiastes comprise a veritable garden of wisdom and understanding in the form of cogent maxims for governing one's life. Some of the blossoms are miniature sermons on enduring principles of righteousness; others are more modest buds of practical advice. But all of these sayings follow the same organic pattern: they suggest that (1) trusting in God is the foundation of wisdom; (2) a willingness to be entreated and counseled is the key to cultivating wisdom; (3) the flowering of wisdom is to bring forth good fruit unto the Lord, and (4) by way of contrast, prideful and worldly living can only lead to folly. The message is that we must uproot the weeds of pride and iniquity in our lives and cultivate instead the flowers of wisdom, which alone can lead to lasting and eternal blessings.

1. TRUSTING IN GOD IS THE FOUNDATION OF WISDOM

THEME: When we trust in the Lord and fear Him—in the sense that we have profound respect for His eternal wisdom and thus yield to His will in all things—then we can strive daily to keep His commandments and always remember Him so we are worthy to have His Spirit attend us.

The fear of the Lord is the beginning of wisdom. (Prov. 9:10)

Every word of God is pure: he is a shield unto them that put their trust in him. (Prov. 30:5)

MOMENT OF TRUTH

Solomon was enormously prolific: "And he spake three thousand proverbs: and his songs were a thousand and five" (1 Kgs. 4:32). The underlying theme of his teachings is that we must fear God and place our trust in Him: "Trust in the Lord with all thine heart; and lean not unto thine own understanding. In all thy ways acknowledge him, and he shall direct thy paths" (Prov. 3:5–6). Only in this way can we hope to become spiritually wise. In the course of his own life, as it turned out, Solomon was better at conveying wisdom than at becoming its leading practitioner. Nevertheless, there is much in his legacy that can benefit and instruct the honest seeker after truth.

MODERN PROPHETS SPEAK

David O. McKay:
> Absolute trust in the Lord will awaken a desire, at least, to try to live in accordance with Christ's teachings, chief of which is to love, not hate one another. (*CR,* Oct. 1941, 55)

ILLUSTRATIONS FOR OUR TIMES

The Spiritual Wages of Fearing the Lord

A few years ago, as part of an assignment at the Missionary Training Center, I was privileged to work with a number of the new elders and sisters as they were preparing to go out into their assigned fields of labor. Reflected in their attitudes and disposition was a range of emotions, from exhilaration and enthusiasm to apprehension and, yes, even fear. We studied the subject of fear somewhat, and learned that fear is not contrary to the errand of the Lord, especially if it connotes a deep respect and honor for the majesty, work, and glory of God. We saw that the expression "fear the Lord" occurs 202 times in the scriptures. We asked ourselves what the expression means as it is used by the prophets, and how you can know if someone "fears the Lord."

By looking at the actions associated in the scriptures with fearing the Lord, we determined that the most frequently mentioned action was to *serve the Lord* (seventeen times, as in Josh. 24:14). *Keeping His commandments* is used thirteen times in conjunction with fearing the Lord (as in Eccl. 12:13). *Worshipping Him* is used seven times (as in 2 Kgs. 17:36), *praising Him* six times (as in Ps. 22:23), *trusting Him* six times (as in Ps. 115:11), and *heeding His words* six times (as in Deut. 6:10). There is also frequent mention of such actions as *sanctifying Him* (four times), *keeping His statutes* (three times), *giving glory to Him* (three times), and various additional manifestations of love and obedience to the Lord, including bearing testimony, paying tithing, acting in faith, rejoicing, and being unified. Thus "fearing" the Lord is synonymous with serving Him and keeping His commandments in the spirit of worship, praise, and trust.

It is also interesting to note the blessings mentioned in the scriptures that are associated with "fearing the Lord." The young elders and sisters came to realize that fearing the Lord in righteousness had profound consequences. Here are the most frequently mentioned ones: *wisdom* (mentioned twelve times in the scriptures in association with fearing the Lord, as in Prov. 1:7); *knowledge* (nine times, again as in Prov. 1:7); *salvation* (five times, as in Alma 34:37 and Morm. 9:27); *strength* (three times, as in 3 Ne. 4:10); *life* (three times, as in Prov. 14:27); *freedom from want* (twice, as in Ps. 34:9); and a variety of additional blessings that include learning the mysteries of the covenant, mercy, grace, glory, preservation, enduring forever, the protection of angels, confidence, refuge, prolonged days, and the comfort of the Holy Ghost.

Like the new missionaries, all of us have the opportunity in our own callings and Church activities to exemplify in our actions the spirit of "fearing the Lord" through obedience and trust. We can experience over time in personal ways how the Lord enhances our wisdom, knowledge, and strength as line upon line, precept upon precept, we advance along the pathway of salvation.

2. A WILLINGNESS TO BE ENTREATED IS THE KEY TO CULTIVATING WISDOM

THEME: Humility and meekness are qualities of spiritually-minded students of truth. Only those who are open to truth and understanding can be filled with the spirit of truth. Wisdom can be learned only by one who accepts the counsel of wise persons—especially the prophets of God who teach His will and reveal His commandments.

> *For whom the Lord loveth he correcteth; even as a father the son in whom he delighteth.* (Prov. 3:12)

> *For the commandment is a lamp; and the law is light; and reproofs of instruction are the way of life.* (Prov. 6:23)

MOMENT OF TRUTH

Pervasive in the writings of Solomon is the thought that one must be open to counsel, to entreaty, and to the chastenings of a loving Father. Solomon himself gradually closed his heart to the entreaties of the Lord: "And the Lord was angry with Solomon, because his heart was turned from the Lord God of Israel, which had appeared unto him twice, And had commanded him concerning this thing, that he should not go after other gods: but he kept not that which the Lord commanded" (1 Kgs. 11:9–10). Even though Solomon did not walk perfectly before God, we can still learn from his writings, as well as from the counsel of the Preacher, whose ultimate message is to keep the commandments of God.

MODERN PROPHETS SPEAK

Joseph Fielding Smith:

> If we will follow the spirit of light, the spirit of truth, the spirit that is set forth in the revelations of the Lord; if we will, through the spirit of prayer and humility, seek for the guidance of the Holy Ghost, the Lord will increase our light and our understanding so that we shall have the spirit of discernment; we shall understand the truth; we shall know falsehood when we see it, and we shall not be deceived. (*DS,* 1:285)

Joseph Fielding Smith:

> We rejoice in the words of the Lord to Joseph Smith: "The glory of God is intelligence." No better motto could be chosen, for it is filled with deep meaning and has

been, and still is, an incentive to members of the Church to seek after knowledge and wisdom, for "a good understanding have all they that do his commandments." That this saying came through revelation none can doubt when the full meaning of this thought is understood. (*The Way to Perfection* [Salt Lake City: Genealogical Society of Utah, 1949], 225–26)

Howard W. Hunter:

When we strive to be Christ-like, he is "formed" in us; if we open the door, he will enter; if we seek his counsel, he will counsel us. (*THWH,* 33)

Neal A. Maxwell:

Can we expect to become like Him, given our imperfections, unless we can learn to accept and apply needed reproof and correction . . . ? How essential our capacity to receive correction and reproof is, for "he that refuseth instruction despiseth his own soul: but he that heareth reproof getteth understanding" (Prov. 15:32). (*Even As I Am* [Salt Lake City: Deseret Book, 1982], 63)

ILLUSTRATIONS FOR OUR TIMES

A Voice from the Past

In a special file, I keep certain letters ready to be mailed in the future. Right now there are four such letters—one to be mailed on a specific date later this year, and three on specific dates next year. I have been holding these sealed letters now for some four or five years. No, these are not belated thank-you cards. Rather, they are personal letters that young people in our ward have written to themselves about the future—what they believed they were going to be doing with their lives at a distant point down the road of life, and what values, hopes, and involvements would be of paramount importance to them at that point in time. I hold these letters for a certain number of years, and then mail them on the requested date, usually on a future birthday. I do this exercise from time to time, knowing that the authors will forget all about these youthful predictions. They are typically surprised to see them show up once again in the mailbox, and they often learn valuable lessons by comparing their current lifestyle with the profile they had used in the letter.

Many years ago, I did this same exercise with another group of young people in Maryland. When one of the young men involved received his letter from the past, he came to me and asked if he could speak with me privately. He had been involved in various pursuits for a number of years, including the military, and had gone through something of an adjustment in his lifestyle. He told me that he had relaxed the principles his family had taught him. His walk in life had developed into something different from what he had hoped and dreamed for himself as a much younger person. He was stunned to realize from the letter he had written to himself that he had been gradually lowering his standards. He had allowed his mind to operate on a somewhat lower plane than he had been taught to use in the Church, and thus he was reaping an unintended harvest. "For as he thinketh in his heart, so is he" (Prov. 23:7). As a result of receiving his own letter, this young man changed his attitude and his behavior. He recommitted himself to a better way—a more "godly walk and conversation" (D&C 20:69). He was entreated by his own counsel from the past, and he listened. How appropriate it would be for all of us to respond day by day to the highest aspirations of our own hearts, the most noble dreams of our own minds, and the most righteous promptings of our own conscience as we work to heed the whisperings of the Spirit in conducting our lives.

A Mighty Instrument in the Hands of God
I recall a young man with dark black hair. He had an effervescent personality. Everyone liked him. He was lively and full of real enthusiasm—the enthusiasm associated with the Spirit of the Lord. He was preparing for his mission. I had the privilege of teaching him in a missionary preparation class. As each day brought him closer to departure, he wanted to know more . . . and know it faster and better. He was an outstanding student at the MTC, according to his teachers. He was like a sponge. He arrived in the Philippines and wrote a letter to me telling me how much he loved his mission, the people, and the Book of Mormon. He related how he would get up an hour and a half prior to the normal time just to study the Book of Mormon. He couldn't get enough of that book. He asked me to send him everything about the book and insights to the book. He wanted anything and everything to give him more knowledge about this magnificent record of God's dealings with some of His children. He simply could not get enough of that book. Missionaries who knew him would tell me about this missionary. He was a dynamic and powerful teacher, a devoted and loyal leader, a "missionary's missionary"—the ultimate compliment one could ever receive among his peers. Why? It all began with an insatiable desire to learn and grow and become a mighty instrument in the hands of God. This is the beginning of all wisdom.

3. THE FLOWERING OF WISDOM IS TO BRING FORTH GOOD FRUIT UNTO THE LORD

THEME: To be wise is to be obedient, cultivating a life of service. Wisdom is action motivated by love.

Wisdom is the principal thing; therefore get wisdom: and with all thy getting get understanding. (Prov. 4:7)

MOMENT OF TRUTH

The fundamental outcome advocated in Proverbs and Ecclesiastes is a life governed by wisdom—a life that is built on a foundation of obedience to God's laws and service to one's fellow beings. The wise person has confidence in the presence of God, because all pride and folly have been defeated. In place of rancor and deceit, there is peace and balance. The ultimate reward of a godly life is that a person has governed his or her thinking by bringing it into alignment with the will of God, and thus has become a son or daughter of God—a Saint in the true sense.

MODERN PROPHETS SPEAK

Gordon B. Hinckley:

> There is . . . incumbent upon you, you who are members of The Church of Jesus Christ of Latter-day Saints, the responsibility to observe the commandment to continue to study and to learn. Said the Lord: "Seek ye out of the best books words of wisdom; seek learning, even by study and also by faith" (D&C 88:118). (*TGBH,* 300)

John Taylor:

> We have learned this, that God lives; we have learned that when we call upon him he hears our prayers; we have learned that it is the height of human happiness to fear God and observe his laws and keep his commandments; we have learned that it is a duty devolving upon us to try and make all men happy and intelligent, which happiness and intelligence can only be obtained through obedience to the laws of God. (*The Gospel Kingdom: Selections from the Writings and Discourses of John Taylor* [Salt Lake City: Improvement Era, 1941], 30)

ILLUSTRATIONS FOR OUR TIMES

Follow the Prophet

The concept of wisdom in life brings one to the principle of its fruit. The pathway leading to the fruits of goodness and righteousness is strewn with acts of love and service. This is wisdom. This is what we must come to understand and appreciate. When we come to this point we will truly, like Solomon, recognize that wisdom is one of the greatest gifts of God (see 1 Kgs. 5:12). When this happens, the fruits of wisdom will change our attitude and behavior. Our approach and disposition to life will be: How can I better serve God and my fellowmen? How will my actions and conduct reflect the Lord Jesus Christ in my life? Will I be a true disciple who is pure in heart? Will I become even as He is?

As I contemplate wisdom in this dispensation of the fullness of time, my mind is drawn to fifteen men—fifteen prophets of God. Each prophet of God has had the wisdom of the Lord, for they have been the representatives of Christ here upon the earth—the mouthpieces of the Lord.

Today we are led by such a man, a true prophet of God, a man of action and love, a man who because of his wisdom—the wisdom of the Lord—has brought the fruits of the gospel to more people. An increase in the construction of temples is one visible effect of his leadership. His concern for the well-being of mankind is demonstrated in his teaching the necessity of conversion, retention, and activation. President Gordon B. Hinckley's fruits will remain, for he has the wisdom and the will of God in all things. We must sustain him with all of our hearts. We must remember that he speaks for the Lord. We must be wise and obey his words.

The Hidden Garden

The Washington D.C. Temple, located on a prominent wooded elevation in the Maryland suburbs north of the nation's capital, was dedicated on 19 November 1974. It has been an inspiring and beautiful addition to the landscape, with well-kept gardens and grounds to complement the whiteness of the imposing six-spired building. One day, as my wife and I were driving up the long approach road to the temple, I looked through the trees below the temple and caught site of a hidden garden a hundred feet or more off to the west of the road. It was a pleasant surprise. Someone had cultivated in a small clearing in the woods a magnificent little garden, complete with many varieties of beautiful flowers and shrubs. It was a secret jewel that delighted the eyes and lifted the spirits on the way up to the temple of God.

Wisdom is like that. It opens up within the undergrowth of the mind a better vista, a sanctuary of thoughts and aspirations cultivated by faith and nurtured by hope. It is the essence of the righteous life. It is the mentor of spirituality and the guarantor of joy. It illuminates the pathway leading to the House of the Lord, the ultimate place of rest in the eternities. One can delight in the wisdom of others, but only the wisdom cultivated in one's own life—through many years of listening, learning, doing, refining, building, and growing—can be the source of a spiritual harvest in the years to come. "Happy is the man that findeth wisdom, and the man that getteth understanding" (Prov. 3:13).

4. PRIDE LEADS TO FOLLY

THEME: In the garden of life, one must root out every noxious weed of pride, every instance of hardheartedness, in order to bring forth the growth of wisdom leading to the fruits of righteousness.

Pride goeth before destruction, and a haughty spirit before a fall. (Prov. 16:18)

MOMENT OF TRUTH

The opposite of the fear of God is pride—of leaning to one's own understanding. The chronicles and annals of the Israelites constitute a handbook of what happens when pride is allowed to flourish. Similarly, the Book of Mormon gives ample evidence of the destructive consequences of pride and hardness of heart. The Lord has warned us in our time to "beware of pride, lest ye become as the Nephites of old" (D&C 38:39). Wisdom cannot grow in a prideful soil; righteousness cannot flourish in a prideful heart. As we look toward the day of judgment, we need to remember, with the Preacher: "Rejoice, O young man, in thy youth; and let thy heart cheer thee in the days of thy youth, and walk in the ways of thine heart, and in the sight of thine eyes: but know thou, that for all these things God will bring thee into judgment" (Eccl. 11:9).

MODERN PROPHETS SPEAK

Dallin H. Oaks:

> Pride does not look up to God and care about what is right. It looks sideways to man and argues who is right. Pride is manifest in the spirit of contention. (*Pure in Heart* [Salt Lake City: Bookcraft, 1988], 96)

ILLUSTRATIONS FOR OUR TIMES

The Universal Sin

Having treated pride previously, we can remind ourselves that the Lord continually admonishes us against pride. Pride is the universal sin, as President Benson has taught us. It is the beginning and part of almost every sin. This enmity truly is at the root of all our problems. In breaking any of the Ten Commandments, pride is involved. In the repentance process, one will always see that within the sin is an element of pride. Lest we become so pleased with our humility, we must remember it is always easy to see pride in others, even though we ourselves suffer from pride. It would be wise to be merciful and humble in all things, thus allowing the strength of the Lord to magnify our souls.

SUMMARY

Fearing the Lord—in the sense that we trust in Him and obey His commandments—is the sustaining root system of wisdom as taught in Proverbs and Ecclesiastes. By listening to the whisperings of the Holy Spirit and following the advice of the prophets and other righteous teachers, we cultivate wisdom and facilitate the process described by Paul as coming "in the unity of the faith, and of the knowledge of the Son of God, unto a perfect man, unto the measure of the stature of the fulness of Christ" (Eph.

4:13). By striving for spiritual enlightenment, we emulate the pattern established by the Savior Himself: "And Jesus increased in wisdom and stature, and in favour with God and man" (Luke 2:52). When we dispel from our lives the spirit of pride, envy, contention, and deceit, we assure that the garden of our existence will be free of the weeds of folly and iniquity, leaving room for the kind of wisdom that saves and exalts. May we cultivate such wisdom in our lives.

CHAPTER THIRTY-TWO

"YET WILL I TRUST *in* HIM"

Reading Assignment: Job 1–2; 13; 19; 27; 42.

Additional Reading: Other chapters in Job; D&C 121:1–10.

> *The gospel embraces principles that dive deeper, spread wider, and extend further than anything else that we can conceive. . . . It "brings life and immortality to light," brings us into relationship with God, and prepares us for an exaltation in the eternal world.* (John Taylor, *JD* 16:369)

THEMES *for* LIVING

1. Transcending Adversity
2. Cultivating an Invincible Testimony
3. After the Trial of Faith Come the Blessings

INTRODUCTION

The book of Job is a book of light, for it focuses on the vision of hope and faith that shines through the shadows of adversity comprising every person's mortal experience. There is no spiritual image in the scriptures as pervasive as the image of light. The Savior is "the true Light, which lighteth every man" (John 1:9), the "light of the world" (John 8:12). "The Lord is my light and my salvation," sang the Psalmist (Ps. 27:1). The Savior is the "light which shineth in darkness, and the darkness comprehendeth it not" (D&C

6:21). On the day the Church was organized in this dispensation, the Lord gave a promise that He would "disperse the powers of darkness from before you" (D&C 21:6). In the ancient but still current message of Job, we begin to comprehend the divine mechanism for generating light in a world where even "the light is as darkness" (Job 10:22). We begin to see the illuminating power of the Spirit and the staying power of valiant testimony in the face of temporal adversity. The candle of Job sheds light on three aspects of spiritual victory: (1) transcending adversity through the help of God, (2) cultivating an invincible testimony, and (3) learning that after the trial of faith come divine blessings.

1. TRANSCENDING ADVERSITY

THEME: When our hope and faith are anchored in the Lord, then no loss of worldly goods, no interruption of temporal ease, no challenge to our physical well-being can conquer our spirit or our confidence in the saving grace and power of the Lord.

The Lord gave, and the Lord hath taken away; blessed be the name of the Lord. (Job 1:21)

MOMENT OF TRUTH

Job was one of the greatest estate holders of his time, with bounteous wealth and a large and devoted family. He was "perfect and upright, and one that feared God, and eschewed evil" (Job 1:1). When Satan was allowed to assail him and bring about the utter destruction of his temporal world, Job remained steadfast and resolute, maintaining his righteous way of living despite overwhelming adversity. He refused to curse God as the adversary had pledged to make him do. He thus became the timeless prototype of the indomitable spirit.

MODERN PROPHETS SPEAK

Neal A. Maxwell:
> God has told us that life itself passes away "as it were unto us a dream" (Jacob 7:26). Into the brief, fleeting time allotted to each of us must be crowded challenges that will help us, in our weaknesses, to develop the qualities we now lack. The presence of stress may be needed for their development. Otherwise, the adversary could taunt us as he did Job by saying that an insulated Job was an untested Job (see Job 1:8–12). The same availability to experience adversity will be ours, for "the Lord seeth fit to chasten his people; yea, he trieth their patience and their faith" (Mosiah 23:21). To expect immunity is naïveté! (*Notwithstanding My Weakness* [Salt Lake City: Deseret Book, 1981], 20–21)

Gordon B. Hinckley:

> Grant us faith to look beyond the problems of the moment to the miracles of the future. . . .
> Grant us faith when storms of adversity beat us down and drive us to the ground. In sea-
> sons of sickness may our confidence wax strong in the powers of the priesthood. . . .
> Lord, when we walk in the valley of the shadow of death, give us faith to smile through
> our tears, knowing that it is all part of the eternal plan of a loving Father, that as we cross
> the threshold from this life we enter another more glorious, and that through the atone-
> ment of the Son of God all shall rise from the grave and the faithful shall go on to exal-
> tation. ("'Lord, Increase Our Faith,'" *Ensign,* Nov. 1987, 53–54; see also *TGBH,* 195)

ILLUSTRATIONS FOR OUR TIMES

Steps for Overcoming Adversity

How can we gain a better perspective on adversity and learn to appreciate its role in our life so that we can grow from our experiences? The following ideas may help you view and respond to adversity in a positive manner.

Three things to remember and understand when dealing with adversity:

1. **Adversity is a universal experience.**

- We all face adversity. No one person has a monopoly on adversity— we are all in this together.

- Learning to overcome adversity is part of life.

- To wish away adversity will only make us weak. The result will be little or no growth.

- Great souls are those who handle adversity positively, maintain a good attitude, and have a proper perspective on life.

2. **We already have access to effective tools for overcoming adversity.**

- The Holy Spirit will show us all things to do (see 2 Ne. 32:5).

- The scriptures will tell us all things to do (see 2 Ne. 32:3).

- Prayer can strengthen us in all situations (see 3 Ne. 18:15–18).

- Faith and hope will enable us to endure and transcend adversity (Moro. 7, Ether 12, Alma 32, Heb. 11).

- Patience is a necessary and powerful tool for growth and overcoming adversity (see Alma 32:40–43).

- Family, friends, associates, and/or even caring strangers are there to lend support (D&C 108:7).

- In the heat of adversity, our minds and bodies will be filled with adrenaline, which will give us strength.

3. **There are great benefits that come through adversity.**

- Humility. Adversity cultivates humility, the virtue that truly blesses one's life.

- Sense of self-worth. Overcoming adversity brings great personal satisfaction and a sense of self-worth.

- Strength. Overcoming adversity brings an enduring kind of personal strength.

- Gratitude. Adversity is the teacher that helps us remember the good times and the blessings of God.

- Spirituality. From adversity, we often become closer to our Heavenly Father.

Remember:

- In the fiery furnace of adversity are forged the greatest of men and women.

- By serving, we can forget our problems and enhance our capacity to cope with adversity.

- Adversity is a cousin to opposition. It is to temper us, not consume us.

- In adversity, time is the great healer.

- The only difference between stumbling blocks and stepping stones is the way we use them.

• In overcoming adversity, we pass the test of life (see Abr. 3:25).

The Language of Transcendence

As I write this illustration on adversity, my thoughts go back to the Prophet Joseph Smith, and his inspired letter, written from Liberty Jail in Missouri, that would serve later as the basis for Sections 121, 122, and 123 of the Doctrine & Covenants. The Prophet and several colleagues had been held there under conditions of extraordinary deprivation for several months. In stark contrast to the squalid environment in which they were confined, Section 121 affords the most sublime language in holy writ concerning the effectual operation of the priesthood of God. He wrote, while suffering from monumental injustice at the hands of wicked men: "Let thy bowels also be full of charity towards all men, and to the household of faith, and let virtue garnish thy thoughts unceasingly; then shall thy confidence wax strong in the presence of God" (D&C 121:45). Section 122 is the source of unsurpassed inspiration in transcending adversity. The Prophet wrote the words of the Redeemer given to him: "all these things shall give thee experience, and shall be for thy good. The Son of Man hath descended below them all. Art thou greater than he?" (D&C 122:7–8). And the Prophet wrote (in what is now Section 123) an impassioned plea for the Saints to fulfill their duty to God and to their suffering families by bringing to light the facts around the injustices being heaped upon them. The coming forth of these treasures of wisdom, revealed from the depths of adversity, is a lasting memorial to the process of how the blessings of God flow "after much tribulation" (D&C 58:4). In the language of transcendence, the Prophet teaches us how to rise above adversity and tribulation with grace and thanksgiving.

2. CULTIVATING AN INVINCIBLE TESTIMONY

THEME: A testimony engendered by the Spirit, cultivated by devotion and obedience, nurtured by sacrifice, and mellowed by suffering is a priceless, inextinguishable beacon along the pathway of life.

> *He also shall be my salvation.* (Job 13:16)

> *For I know that my redeemer liveth.* (Job 19:25)

MOMENT OF TRUTH

Job's life, despite unspeakable challenges, was illuminated by his utter confidence in the living reality of the Savior and his indomitable assurance that he would one day return to the presence of his Maker. Job received enduring strength in the Lord to sustain his mission in life.

MODERN PROPHETS SPEAK

Joseph Smith:

> You have been indebted to other men, in the first instance, for evidence; on that you have acted; but it is necessary that you receive a testimony from heaven for yourselves; so that you can bear testimony to the truth of the Book of Mormon, and that you have seen the face of God. That is more than the testimony of an angel. When the proper time arrives, you shall be able to bear this testimony to the world. When you bear testimony that you have seen God, this testimony God will never suffer to fall, but will bear you out; although many will not give heed, yet others will. You will therefore see the necessity of getting this testimony from heaven. (*HC* 2:195)

Gordon B. Hinckley:

> If there are any lacking that testimony, you can get it; and you must get it. How? The Lord has said that he that doeth the will of the Father shall know of the doctrine, "whether it be of God, or whether I speak of myself" (John 7:17). That's the way you gain a testimony. You do the will of the Father, and as certainly as you do the will of the Father you will know of the truth of the gospel, including the knowledge that Jesus is the Christ, the Son of God. (*TGBH,* 648)

ILLUSTRATIONS FOR OUR TIMES

The Resonating Power of Testimony

Elder Alvin R. Dyer was known for his inspiring and motivating counsel about the process of spiritual conversion. I recall vividly the time he came to Frankfurt, Germany, at the beginning of his tenure as European Mission president many decades ago. He taught the missionaries what he had learned years earlier as president of the Central States Mission. While there, he had conducted extensive research with investigators and converts to determine when they had first obtained a conviction that the Church was true. Was it after having studied the Book of Mormon prayerfully? Was it after a certain period of activity in the Church? These factors were surely important, he learned. However, Elder Dyer discovered the startling truth that eighty-two percent of the converts knew the gospel was true the *very first time* they heard it presented. The first time the missionaries bore solemn testimony about its truthfulness of the gospel and the Church, the converts *knew* it was true. "My sheep hear my voice, and I know them, and they follow me" (John 10:27). This is persuasive confirmation of the resonating power of testimony spoken by individuals acting under the Spirit of God and received by honest seekers of truth responding to the same Spirit (D&C 50:17–22).

3. AFTER THE TRIAL OF FAITH
COME THE BLESSINGS

THEME: Our Father in Heaven delights in blessing His children. Though faith must precede the miracle and obedience the flow of the Lord's choicest blessings, His mission is to bring about the immortality and eternal life of man, with all attendant blessings of glory and joy in rich abundance.

Till I die I will not remove mine integrity from me. (Job 27:5)

So the Lord blessed the latter end of Job more than his beginning. (Job 42:12)

MOMENT OF TRUTH

Job lost everything but his testimony and his faith. And yet the Lord restored to this man in his sustained righteousness *double* what he had had before, and he received seven new sons and three new daughters to add to his ten children lost in the whirlwind. Thus his confidence in the Lord was confirmed and his happiness complete, for he had "spoken of me the thing that is right" (Job 42:7).

MODERN PROPHETS SPEAK

Joseph Fielding Smith:

> We learn from a study of the plan of salvation that every soul was given the gift of free agency. It is a divine law—and a very just law. . . . These divine laws have been in existence through the eternities. They have been tried and tested and proved to be just. No man can obtain salvation without a thorough trial of faith and obedience to the principles of eternal truth which have been established from the beginning for the salvation and exaltation of mankind. (*AGQ*, 4:149)

James E. Faust:

> The proving of one's faith goes before the witnessing, for, as Moroni testifies, "Ye receive no witness until after the trial of your faith" (Ether 12:6). This trial of faith can become a priceless experience. (*To Reach Even unto You* [Salt Lake City: Deseret Book, 1980], 99)

ILLUSTRATIONS FOR OUR TIMES

The Trial of Faith

Job lived according to the principle stated in Ether 12:6: "faith is things which are hoped for and not seen; wherefore, dispute not because ye see not, for ye receive no witness until after the trial of your faith." After his trial, he received not only a witness, but also a restoration of temporal blessings, even to the amount of double his previous holdings. Job was stripped down to the essence of those things that matter most—the things that bring one to eternal life: his faith, his testimony, and his individual righteousness. Job's faith was not in the things of the world. The three visitors did all they could to separate Job from God in a variety of insinuations, but Job never failed; instead, he still sought favor from God. Job passed the test. Satan could not tempt his testimony or his faith. The trial of faith was over. Job had sacrificed all, in a sense, and was rewarded with a multiplicity of blessings.

The Bookmark of Life

I have a small bookmark that I use to mark my place in the scriptures. It is something I devised many years ago to remind me of what I call the Eleventh Commandment: "Be of good cheer." It is especially important to remember this injunction when one is going through difficult times in life. The word "cheer," in its various forms, is used many places in the scriptures—thirteen times specifically, as in the statement "Be of good cheer." Why should one be of good cheer? The scriptures are very specific about this: We should be of good cheer because there is forgiveness if we are faithful and obedient; because the Lord fulfills his promises; because we can receive great spiritual wealth through our obedience; because the Lord will heal our spirits (and often our physical impairments); because the Savior is in charge in the storms of life; because there is safety in the Lord; because we can follow the prophet; because the Holy Spirit will tell us what to say and do; because we will be preserved until our mission is completed; because the Lord is with us; and because He has overcome the world. What grand and compelling reasons there are to sustain our commitment to "be of good cheer"! What overwhelming evidence is given in the scriptures to bolster our encouragement and buoy our spirits! We would do well to use this phrase "Be of good cheer" as a bookmark for our life. If we will place it faithfully between the pages of our temporal existence and lay it hopefully in the chapters of our probationary chronicle, then we can be reminded that the Spirit will whisper to us words of comfort, peace, and harmony to edify and lift us through the tests and trials of life.

SUMMARY

The Lord declares: "I have commanded you to bring up your children in light and truth" (D&C 93:40). An important dimension of that task is to display for our children and others the Job-like qualities of spiritual resilience, steadfast loyalty, and unassailable faith in the face of adversity. Through our patience in the Lord, the strength of our testimony in His goodness, and our long-suffering faith in His saving grace, we can overcome adversity and enjoy the enduring blessings of the gospel. We can emulate the example of the Savior: "Behold, I am Jesus Christ, the Son of the living God, who created the heavens and the earth, a light which cannot be hid in darkness" (D&C 14:9). We can be "the candle of the Lord" (Prov. 20:27) and say with Job, "yet will I trust in him" (Job 13:15).

CHAPTER THIRTY-THREE

"SALVATION IS *of the* LORD"

Reading Assignment: Jonah 1–4; Micah 2; 4–7.

> *There never was a dispensation on the earth when prophets and apostles, the inspiration, revelation and power of God, the Holy Priesthood and the keys of the kingdom were needed more than they are in this generation. There never has been a dispensation when the friends of God and righteousness among the children of men needed more faith in the promises and prophecies than they do today; and there certainly never has been a generation of people on the earth that has had a greater work to perform than the inhabitants of the earth in the latter days.* (Wilford Woodruff, *JD* 15:8)

THEMES *for* LIVING

1. The Compassion of the Lord Extends to All
2. From the Beginning, the Lord Envisioned the Restoration of Israel and Decreed the Ultimate Triumph of His Purposes

INTRODUCTION

When the Savior was asked to give a sign of His divinity, He referred to "the sign of the prophet Jonas [Jonah]. For as Jonas was three days and three nights in the whale's belly; so shall the Son of man be three days and three nights in the heart of the earth" (Matt. 12:39–40; see also Luke 11:29–30). The story of Jonah is a demonstration of the irrepressible force of divine love in the world. The love of God for all of His children is sufficiently powerful to break through any barriers and result in the eventual triumph of glory and salvation, for "Salvation is of the Lord" (Jonah 2:9). Nothing can restrain the effects of the love and grace of God—not death, not darkness, not worldly resistance or barriers, not the pride and stubbornness of the workers in Zion. God's purposes will be fulfilled. The Atonement extends in its reach to all mankind, and the work of the Lord is inexorable in its forward movement. "I will surely assemble, O Jacob, all of thee; I will surely gather the remnant of Israel" (Micah 2:12).

1. THE COMPASSION OF THE LORD EXTENDS TO ALL

THEME: The Lord sets His eternal agenda, and it is for us to obey. Jonah wanted to second-guess the Lord in His plan for the salvation of a heathen city-state, but the Lord's mercy was nevertheless extended to all whose hearts were contrite. In our callings, we should respond willingly and in alignment with the Lord's agenda of mercy and salvation.

> *Arise, go unto Nineveh, that great city, and preach unto it the preaching that I bid thee.*
> (Jonah 3:2)

MOMENT OF TRUTH

At first, the prophet Jonah was not valiant in his calling to preach repentance to the great cosmopolitan heathen city-state of Nineveh, capital of Assyria. Jonah tried to escape his mission, but found himself caught up in a learning situation where his own life was on the line. When the Lord gave him a second chance to function in his prophetic office, he fulfilled his calling with devotion—perhaps too much devotion! Even after his listeners repented, he was determined to see the Lord carry out the threatened destruction of the city, if for no other reason than to uphold his own reputation as a predictor of the future. But the Lord knew better, and in mercy saved the people. Using the parable of the gourd, the Lord then continued with Jonah's education by teaching him that if he was concerned about the vitality of a gourd, he should all the more be concerned about the well-being of a whole city of the Lord's children—even if they were of different extraction. Similarly, we must have compassion for all of God's children and willingly answer the call to serve.

MODERN PROPHETS SPEAK

Joseph Smith:

> Is it not also necessary to have the idea that God is merciful and gracious, long-suffering and full of goodness? It is. Why is it necessary? Because of the weakness and imperfections of human nature, and the great frailties of man; for such is the weakness of man, and such his frailties, that he is liable to sin continually, and if God were not long-suffering, and full of compassion, gracious and merciful, and of a forgiving disposition, man would be cut off from before him, in consequence of which he would be in continual doubt and could not exercise faith; for where doubt is, there faith has no power; but by man's believing that God is full of compassion and forgiveness, long-suffering and slow to anger, he can exercise faith in him and overcome doubt, so as to be exceedingly strong. (*Lectures on Faith* 3:20)

Neal A. Maxwell:

> One day, for instance, we shall know more about Jonah and his eagerness for vindication. A repentant Nineveh was mercifully not destroyed, which provided a great lesson not only in the tutoring of one prophet, but for us all, concerning the principle of mercy. Mercy rejoices in every step toward righteousness and is not offended by being pleasantly surprised. Though he acknowledged God's graciousness, mercy, and kindness, Jonah had not fully understood the application of these attributes. Has not God even referred to His Plan of Salvation as the *plan of mercy?* (Alma 42:15). (*Even As I Am* [Salt Lake City: Deseret Book, 1982], 51)

ILLUSTRATIONS FOR OUR TIMES

Souls Are Precious in the Sight of God

The compassion of the Lord is so evident in the story of Jonah. He gave Jonah a chance to repent and cared for the people of Nineveh that they might repent. Surely the worth of souls is great in the sight of the Lord (see D&C 18:13). The Lord desires that all might come unto Him and enjoy the blessings of eternal life just as Nephi explained so carefully: "For none of these iniquities come of the Lord; for he doeth that which is good among the children of men; and he doeth nothing save it be plain unto the children of men; and he inviteth them all to come unto him and partake of his goodness; and he denieth none that come unto him, black and white, bond and free, male and female; and he remembereth the heathen; and all are alike unto God, both Jew and Gentile" (2 Ne. 26:33). All souls are precious: nonmembers or members, active or less active, Jew or Gentile.

The feeling for the well-being of others is demonstrated by the sons of Mosiah. 'Now they were desirous that salvation should be declared to every creature, for they could not bear that any human soul should perish; yea, even the very thoughts that any soul should endure endless torment did cause them to quake and tremble" (Mosiah 28:3). They truly cared about all people—even their enemies. The Church has always sought to preach the gospel to every nation, kindred, tongue, and people (see Matt. 24:14), and prayed for those who know not God (see Alma 6:6). "And now, behold, I say unto you, that the thing which will be of the most worth unto you will be to declare repentance unto this people, that you may bring souls unto me, that you may rest with them in the kingdom of my Father" (D&C 15:6). Yes, souls are precious in the sight of God.

The Lost Sheep

A number of years ago, I made the acquaintance of a fine brother in one of the priesthood quorums of the Church. He was a choice person with a strong faith in the gospel and a pleasant disposition. As we got to know one another better, he shared with me something of his life's story, which had not been without its moments of adversity. There had been a period of time when his temporal existence had collapsed to the point where he actually found himself in a state of homelessness for several years, having to sustain himself from the dumpsters of grocery stores and fast-food restaurants. He would sleep on the streets of his city or in the hallways of public buildings.

I was touched deeply by his account of suffering, and even more by his resilient attitude and the way he had rebuilt his life. What shocked me, however, was to learn that the location of his homelessness was not half a mile from where I had lived in a previous ward. He had been too ashamed to reach out for help from others, and so had eked out his existence on his own. I will never forget the lesson of realizing that a good person had been homeless only a few blocks from the chapel where my family and our ward colleagues would worship each Sunday in comfort and fellowship with the Saints, oblivious to the dire need of a member so near. It was a stunning reminder to me that there is need for vigilant discernment of the opportunities to serve others all around us.

We are surrounded by our Ninevehs—enclaves of society or unseen circles of emptiness to which we sometimes fail to extend the hand of fellowship. We must watch and listen, being ready to share our resources, and bring the blessings of the gospel to all. "How think ye? if a man have an hundred sheep, and one of them be gone astray, doth he not leave the ninety and nine, and goeth into the mountains, and seeketh that which is gone astray? And if so be that he find it, verily I say unto you, he rejoiceth more of that sheep, than of the ninety and nine which went not astray. Even so it is not the will of your Father which is in heaven, that one of these little ones should perish" (Matt. 18:12–14). And why is it fair for the shepherd to bestow greater joy and compassion on the lost sheep than on those already safely in the fold? Because it is in the nature of life that each of us, at one time or another, will play the role of that lost sheep. We will have our hour of being alone and astray. Our circumstances will take us through pathways of adversity and distraction where we will need the searching eye of the Shepherd, the familiar voice of the Master, the saving comfort of the fold. And at those times we will sense profoundly the love of God, bestowed without discrimination, without reservation, without upbraiding, on all His children. He extends His choicest blessings to all who, with the sacrifice of a broken heart and a contrite spirit, accept the bread of life in all devotion. How important it is for us to assist Him in this universal work, for we are all homeless until we return once again to His presence and to His rest.

2. FROM THE BEGINNING, THE LORD ENVISIONED THE RESTORATION OF ISRAEL AND DECREED THE ULTIMATE TRIUMPH OF HIS PURPOSES

THEME: All the Lord requires is that we obey His commandments with humility, and He will establish us as His people once again through the process of gathering and restoration. He is the Savior foretold by prophets from the foundation of the world.

> *But in the last days it shall come to pass, that the mountain of the house of the Lord shall be established in the top of the mountains, and it shall be exalted above the hills; and people shall flow unto it.* (Micah 4:1)

> *And what doth the Lord require of thee, but to do justly, and to love mercy, and to walk humbly with thy God?* (Micah 6:8)

MOMENT OF TRUTH

Micah recorded his mighty vision of the latter days in which the Lord's kingdom will once again be established in power as the bastion of righteousness and salvation. Israel will be gathered and empowered to perform its divinely appointed mission of declaring the gospel message.

MODERN PROPHETS SPEAK

James E. Faust:

> We are announcing no new missionary programs. . . . We do not have any new organization to announce. The manuals, the guidelines, and the instructions are unchanged. Certainly, there is nothing new in the doctrine, nor in the covenants. . . . What we seek to do is to join with you in calling forth the Spirit of God upon our work. The

priesthood quorums, the auxiliary organizations, the stake missions, the member-missionary class are available. Everything is in place. It is felt at this time that no new changes in programs or organizations are needed. Perhaps the only change that is really needed is to change ourselves. Missionary work begins with each of us at home. It ought to be motivated more by fresh faith and conviction rather than obligation. It involves quiet living. If we do this, missionary work in the stakes and the wards will be fruitful. How can I change? I can certainly change my attitude. I can change *my* commitment. I can change my approach. Hopefully, with diligent study of the scriptures and obedience to saving principles, I can expand my soul. Missionary work is a natural manifestation of the pure love of Christ. We need to learn and teach the gospel doctrines—the requirements, principles and promises. Hopefully, like the sons of Mosiah, we will become "instruments in the hands of God in bringing many to a knowledge of truth" and "to the knowledge of their Redeemer" (Mosiah 27:36). (*In the Strength of the Lord: The Life and Teachings of James E. Faust* [Salt Lake City: Deseret Book, 1999], 371)

Gordon B. Hinckley:

Missionary work is concerned with searching and winnowing and gleaning and teaching with love and kindness. (*TGBH,* 374)

Gordon B. Hinckley:

You never can foretell the consequences of that which you do when you talk about the Church with another. This work is nothing of which we need be ashamed. It is something in which we can take great pride. The problem is that most of us are filled with fear. . . . Try it. Taste the sweet and wonderful joy of sharing your testimony of this work with others. (*TGBH,* 374)

Gordon B. Hinckley:

I wish I could awaken in the heart of every man, woman, boy, and girl here this morning the great consuming desire to share the gospel with others. If you do that you live better, you try to make your lives more exemplary because you know that those you teach will not believe unless you back up what you say by the goodness of your lives. Nobody can foretell the consequences of that which you do when you teach the gospel to another. (*TGBH,* 374)

ILLUSTRATIONS FOR OUR TIMES

Called to Serve

A number of years ago, I had the honor of serving in a branch presidency at the Missionary Training Center in Provo, Utah. It was in that capacity that I met a young elder who was on his way to his assigned mission field. He told me of a friend in his home stake who likewise had been called on a mission a year or two earlier. In that case, however, the calling had been to a mission in the western United States, whereas the friend had hoped for a foreign mission call. His feelings about it were so strong that the call was withdrawn for a time. Over the next year he was able to rethink his priorities, recover his spirit of missionary work, and once again seek the opportunity to serve a mission. A call was extended once more—to the same mission. This time he willingly responded. During his first days in the mission field, he and his companion were tracting in one of the neighborhoods and came across a man who invited them enthusiastically into his home. As recounted by my young colleague at the MTC, his friend was stunned to hear the investigator state, "I am so pleased that you have come to teach me the gospel. I had been praying to find the truth. A year ago I had a dream that young missionaries would call on me, but no one came—until now."

How important it is for all of us to respond willingly and forthrightly to the call to share our witness of the truthfulness of the gospel. Paul taught: "Preach the word; be instant in season" (2 Tim. 4:2). We cannot know how our service will play into the designs of our Father in Heaven for the ultimate blessing of His children. We cannot realize how our efforts may serve to gather specific individuals into the fold who are at present praying for guidance. We can only embark on the errand of the Lord with the faith that He will lead us to invest our talents and strength in ways that contribute to His work and glory. As He said, "For there are many yet on the earth . . . who are only kept from the truth because they know not where to find it" (D&C 123:12). We are the ones who can point the way.

The Kingdom Builders

The Prophet Joseph Smith declared that "the truth of God will go forth boldly, nobly, and independent, till it has penetrated every continent, visited every clime, swept every country, and sounded in every ear, till the purposes of God shall be accomplished, and the Great Jehovah shall say the work is done" (*HC* 4:540).

To do this work, all of us need to be missionaries at all times and in all places. Young men need to prepare earlier and better. Sisters who desire are welcome additions to the missionary force. There is a crying need for senior sisters and couples in every phase of missionary work. I have the privilege of teaching the senior missionaries every week. They are the most glorious and beautiful sight to see—grandmas and grandpas going out into the world to bless mankind. I am moved to tears as I look into their faces. Surely the Lord is pleased with their efforts. They are full of the excitement and enthusiasm of the Spirit. They will make a definite difference in the world.

The other day I was visiting with a semi-retired farmer who was around eighty years of age. He was so grateful to serve another mission. As we were visiting, a man came by and said, "This is their eighth mission." I was astounded. They were true Saints. They were kingdom builders. They loved their fellowmen. They believed in the Church poster, "If you love them . . . leave them," which is aimed at all the grandpas and grandmas. One by one, we all can make a difference. Every good deed lasts forever. Make a mission a part of your life today. Set a goal and make the plans and you will bless your family, yourselves, and especially your fellowmen. Missionary work, whether it be in our temples or in the field, is all part of the great latter-day work.

SUMMARY

Under the Abrahamic Covenant, all of Israel is called into service to carry the gospel of light and the blessings of the priesthood throughout the world. Micah foresaw the day when the Lord would consummate His plan to restore His kingdom once again and fulfill the covenant promises: "Thou wilt perform the truth to Jacob, and the mercy to Abraham, which thou hast sworn unto our fathers from the days of old" (Micah 7:20). Through the process of spiritual adoption, all mankind has access to the covenant blessings. The greatest joy is reserved for those who help in the gathering: "And now, if your joy will be great with one soul that you have brought unto me into the kingdom of my Father, how great will be your joy if you should bring many souls unto me!" (D&C 18:16).

CHAPTER THIRTY-FOUR

"FOR THERE IS NO SAVIOUR *beside* ME"

Reading Assignment: Hosea 1–3; 11; 13–14.

Additional Reading: The rest of Hosea.

> *Why did it need an infinite atonement? For the simple reason that a stream can never rise higher than its fountain. . . . A man, as a man, could arrive at all the dignity that a man was capable of obtaining or receiving; but it needed a God to raise him to the dignity of a God. (John Taylor, Mediation and Atonement, 145)*

THEMES *for* LIVING

1. The "Lovingkindness" of the Lord
2. The Perpetual Call to Return Home

INTRODUCTION

One of the Savior's similes for the Atonement was the reference to a hen desiring to gather her chickens under her wings (Matt. 23:37; 3 Ne. 10:4–6; D&C 10:65; 29:2; 43:24). This image is often used in the scriptures to convey the Lord's profound wish to nourish and nurture His sons and daughters, if only they would humble themselves and obey His commandments. The message of the prophet Hosea is the same—the deep compassion of the Lord for His people, very much like the love of a groom for his bride or the love of a father for his children. Israel was prone to waywardness and hardheartedness, but the Lord was ever ready to shower them with His mercy, even though "they knew not that I healed them" (Hosea 11:3). His message has been the same in all ages: "O Israel, return unto the Lord thy God" (Hosea 14:1). The interrelated themes of compassion and the call to return home are pervasive in the Book of Hosea. They form both sides of the same coin—the spiritual currency with which the Lord "buys" His ransomed children. As Paul said: "For ye are bought with a price: therefore glorify God in your body, and in your spirit, which are God's" (1 Cor. 6:20). Each of these two themes will be discussed in the following pages.

1. THE "LOVINGKINDNESS" OF THE LORD

THEME: Even though His children lapse into forgetfulness and sin, the Lord will remember them in mercy and love as they renew their commitment to follow in His ways. As we are merciful, we shall obtain mercy.

> *And I will betroth thee unto me for ever; yea, I will betroth thee unto me in righteousness, and in judgment, and in lovingkindness, and in mercies.* (Hosea 2:19)

> *When Israel was a child, then I loved him, and called my son out of Egypt.* (Hosea 11:1)

MOMENT OF TRUTH

Hosea is the only prophet of the northern kingdom whose pronouncements and writings have been preserved. He, like the prophet Amos, was active during the reign of King Jeroboam II of Israel (prior to 733 B.C.). Hosea's metaphorical style was filled with pathos over the rebellion and idolatry of the Lord's children during this period of decline and moral decay, and at the same time reflected the deep yearnings of the Lord for the recovery and reformation of Israel. At a time of moral decadence, not unlike the conditions in our own day, Hosea called for repentance and prophesied of a future time when the Lord's mercy would heal the returning flock.

MODERN PROPHETS SPEAK

James E. Talmage:

> We are prone to confound foreknowledge with cause: and this weakness of ours, absurdly inconsistent, illogical and childish though it be, is particularly manifest in our appraisement of Divine prophecy and its fulfillment. In mercy the Lord warns and forewarns. He sees the coming storm, knows the forces operating to produce it,

and calls aloud through his prophets, advises, counsels, exhorts, aye, even commands—that we prepare for what is about to befall and take shelter while yet there is time. (*The Parables of James E. Talmage* [Salt Lake City: Deseret Book, 1973], 50)

John A. Widtsoe:

> The Lord loves all alike, and desires for each of His children the highest possible destiny. To Him, the value of a human soul is very great, for it is the soul of His child. Throughout time and eternity He will reach out in help for every one of His children. The plan of salvation can not be fully completed until all the children of the Lord have had truth presented to them, and have had full opportunity to accept it. The mercy of the Lord is everlasting. (*Program of The Church of Jesus Christ of Latter-day Saints* [Salt Lake City: The Church of Jesus Christ of Latter-day Saints, 1937], 82–83)

ILLUSTRATIONS FOR OUR TIMES

The Pattern of Loving-kindness and Forgiveness in Our Lives

Israel's sins were forsaking and forgetting the Lord by worshiping false Gods. Israel looked to the world for its blessings and did not realize that the Lord was the giver of all blessings. The Lord, in His mercy, remembers His covenant in the bad times as well as the good. He seeks to reclaim Israel because He loves her. This loving-kindness has been and is continually demonstrated by the Lord. Those who find themselves required to forgive can demonstrate the ultimate Christlike attribute—that of forgiveness.

I recall a situation in the mission field. A sister missionary was having difficulty. Her companion mentioned how she cried a lot and had a difficult time functioning. When I would interview her, she was uneasy and sometimes would express her frustrations and feelings of depression. In one of her early interviews, she began to cry, and so I said, "That's okay. You relax here for a moment, and I'll just get a little drink of water." I was silently praying for inspiration.

As I started to stand up, I ran my fingers through my hair. She looked up at me as I did so, then shielded herself, thinking I was going to strike her. My heart sank. She had been abused. I stopped and sat back down. I expressed my love and my sorrow for her apparent fear. I asked, "Were you abused?"

She responded with a soft, "Yes."

I consoled her and expressed my anxiousness to help her in her trial. She truly was unable to cope with life because of this horrible past experience. We visited at length, and then I asked, "Would you be willing to try something?"

She responded with a nod of her head.

"Would you like to try to be happy?"

She sighed, "Of course. I can't stand this much longer."

As we visited, the Spirit was bold and these words came out of my mouth: "Tonight, call your father and tell him you frankly forgive him, and plead with him to see his bishop." I continued, "Will that be too hard to do? Could I help?"

She replied, "I'll do anything to get rid of these feelings—anything."

We concluded our visit with this agreement, and that evening she called home. She told me the next day that things went well. Her father begged for forgiveness and promised to see his bishop. Then the miracle continued. Her companion couldn't believe her countenance, her attitude, or her behavior. She was like a new missionary, full of hope and a desire to serve. She became an excellent missionary over the next year. Everyone loved to work with her. She returned home after her mission, married in the temple, and has two wonderful children. Her life changed because she was like Christ—in loving-kindness, she forgave and moved forward in her life.

Balm of Gilead

In the well-known hymn "Did You Think to Pray?" the final verse asks the searching questions, "When sore trials came upon you, Did you think to pray? When your soul was full of sorrow, Balm of Gilead did you borrow, At the gates of day?" I remember, as a young bishop many years ago, being approached by a new convert to the Church, a young father, who took me aside after a meeting and, in hushed tones, almost in the manner of supplication, asked me to explain to him the meaning of the phrase "balm of Gilead." His reverential attitude and quiet humility seemed to suggest that he felt it was time to be introduced to yet another of the grand mysteries of the gospel. Smiling, I explained that balm of Gilead was simply a traditional natural remedy from the Holy Land that had healing effects and was widely used by the Israelites. As such, it has become a symbol for the healing essence of the Atonement. He seemed almost relieved at the simplicity of the principle, and went his way with a smile on his face.

Since then, I have thought many times about his question concerning the balm of Gilead, for it is another way of asking, "What is the renewing essence of the gospel?" and "What is the mystery of the Atonement, that it should bring to mankind its miraculous healing influence?" When Joseph was betrayed by his jealous brothers, they sold him into the hands of itinerant Ishmaelite tradesmen who were en route from Gilead to Egypt with camels bearing "spicery and balm and myrrh" (Gen. 37:25). Gilead was a wooded highland region located to the east of Jordan, with many bushes that produced the resin used to make the healing gum or balm known throughout the area. Later, when it was time for Jacob to persuade the Egyptian viceroy—in reality his own missing son, Joseph—to provide food for his family in a time of dire famine, he thought to facilitate the bargain by sending the others back to Egypt with gifts of nuts, myrrh, and native balm (Gen. 43:11).

Because forgiveness was the governing nature of Joseph, son of Israel, he took compassion on his family in a time of need and readily forgave his brothers.

Similarly, because forgiveness is the essence of the divine nature, the Savior readily extends His "loving-kindness" to all and rescues them from ultimate temporal death, and through their faith and obedience, from the spiritual death that inevitably would come through universal weakness. Like the balm of Gilead in the temporal sphere, the balm of the Atonement is the healing power of salvation proclaimed from the foundation of the earth as the answer to the spiritual quest of mankind. Upon the administration of that kind of balm, there will be no remaining ailment, no enduring injury, for its renewing curative power is eternal, coming from the "Son of Righteousness," with "healing in his wings" (3 Ne. 25:2).

2. THE PERPETUAL CALL TO RETURN HOME

THEME: The Lord's continual entreaty to His children is to return home once again, to forsake the world and remember the covenant promises whose fulfillment will bring peace and everlasting rest.

> *O Israel, thou hast destroyed thyself; but in me is thine help.* (Hosea 13:9)

> *I will ransom them from the power of the grave; I will redeem them from death.* (Hosea 13:14)

> *O Israel, return unto the Lord thy God; for thou hast fallen by thine iniquity.* (Hosea 14:1)

MOMENT OF TRUTH

Hosea expressed the Lord's universal invitation to all mankind to return to the fold, to embrace the eternal principles of righteousness and spiritual vitality. Israel's eventual return was celebrated in prophetic visions of the restoration of life and the abundance of the Lord's blessings unto the faithful: "Ephraim shall say, What have I to do any more with idols? I have heard him, and observed him: I am like a green fir tree. From me is thy fruit found" (Hosea 14:8).

MODERN PROPHETS SPEAK

Ezra Taft Benson:

> With a shepherd's care, our new members, those newly born into the gospel, must be nurtured by attentive fellowshipping as they increase in gospel knowledge and begin living new standards. Such attention will help to ensure that they will not return to old habits. With a shepherd's loving care, our young people, our young lambs, will not be as inclined to wander. And if they do, the crook of a shepherd's staff, a loving arm and an understanding heart, will help to retrieve them. With a shepherd's care,

many of those who are now independent of the flock can still be reclaimed. Many who have married outside the Church and have assumed the life-styles of the world may respond to an invitation to return to the fold. (*TETB*, 231–32)

Gordon B. Hinckley:

> To any who may have such sons or daughters, may I suggest that you never quit trying. They are never lost until you have given up. Remember that it is love, more than any other thing, that will bring them back. Punishment is not likely to do it. Reprimands without love will not accomplish it. Patience, expressions of appreciation, and that strange and remarkable power which comes with prayer will eventually win through. (*Faith: The Essence of True Religion* [Salt Lake City: Deseret Book, 1989], 66)

ILLUSTRATIONS FOR OUR TIMES

Patience in the Lord's Work

Often the way home is illuminated for the lost and wayward by the patience, persistence, and long-suffering of good people who just never give up. A member of a bishopric in an area where we used to live meticulously tracked down an inactive priesthood holder through four successive address changes before finally finding him and facilitating his return to full activity. A sister I met in another area of the country had been working lovingly with an inactive friend. The two had enjoyed a close friendship that was somewhat disrupted when the ward they lived in was divided and the new boundary separated their two neighboring homes. The one sister was troubled by the change, and her attendance at meetings dropped. The other sister took it upon herself to stay in close touch with her friend. She called her on the phone. She visited with her in her home. But her main strategy was to write her a letter each and every week to keep the spirit of friendship alive. This went on for three years, until the sister writing the letters was called on a mission with her husband to another part of the country. The date for the missionary farewell was set, and, of course, the inactive sister was invited to attend. Would she come, or would this be like all the other times where she would choose to stay away from Church activities? The letter-writing sister prayed for her friend, as always, and on the day of the farewell, she was delighted to see that her friend showed up at church for the first time in a very long while, and seemed to enjoy it.

The husband of this persistent and loving sister told me that she had been writing each week not just to this one person, but to *nine* different people for years and years. They were young people who were lonely or without one or both parents, widows who were alone, people who were discouraged for one reason or another—even a young man they had met only once who needed an anchor in life. Her faithful ministering to these inactive or discouraged Saints calls to mind one of the passages that

President Gordon B. Hinckley often cites: "Wherefore, be faithful; stand in the office which I have appointed unto you; succor the weak, lift up the hands which hang down, and strengthen the feeble knees" (D&C 81:5).

In all of those years, there were only five occasions where any of the people she was serving seemed to be rekindled in their activity or show any positive response. But it was worth it, for the errand of the Lord takes patience and persistence and love. The devotion of this sister, like the persistence of the bishopric member in the earlier example, is repeated countless times throughout the Church every day by the "angels on earth" who remember the covenant obligation to gather in the Lord's elect and bring them home.

The Pathway of Repentance

The Lord wants us to repent, whether from minor or grievous sins. He seeks after us and encourages us to come back through His living prophets. The prophets' clarion message has always been repentance. This process requires of us godly sorrow (true remorse), confession to Heavenly Father and priesthood leaders when appropriate, forsaking sin, restitution and continued good works (see Hel. 12:24), which indicate our true feelings and the condition of our heart. Sometimes, due to the grievous nature of the sin, one must suffer disciplinary action. This action provides a way for a person to repent, and is not meant to drive them away. "Tough love" (true chastisement) is difficult, but sometimes necessary, if we truly care about the people we lead.

This is why the Lord was chastising the people of the Northern Kingdom—to help them come back. I have witnessed this above process time and time again. Surely the Lord loves those he chastises (see D&C 95:1–2).

SUMMARY

We can look to the philosophies of men for the solutions to life's problems; we can look to the wonders of modern science for the lifting of our burdens; we can look to our own devices and creativity for buoyancy in times of challenge. But until and unless we look to the eternal principles of the gospel of Jesus Christ for purpose and sustenance, until we accept the compassionate invitation of the Lord to return home, there can be no peace, no harmony, and no enduring vitality to our lives. "There is no saviour beside me" is the unmistakable message of the Lord (Hosea 13:4). In the words of the Book of Mormon: "And now, behold, my beloved brethren, this is the way; and there is none other way nor name given under heaven whereby man can be saved in the kingdom of God. And now, behold, this is the doctrine of Christ, and the only and true doctrine of the Father, and of the Son, and of the Holy Ghost, which is one God, without end. Amen" (2 Ne. 31:21).

CHAPTER THIRTY-FIVE

"SEEK *the* LORD *and* YE SHALL LIVE"

Reading Assignment: Amos 3; 7–9; Joel 2–3.

Additional Reading: D&C 1:14–28, 37–38; JS—H 1:41.

The distinction between this great Church and that of all other churches from the beginning has been that we believe in divine revelation; we believe that our Father speaks to man today as He has done from the time of Adam. We believe and we know—which is more than mere belief—that our Father has set His hand in this world for the salvation of the children of men. (George Albert Smith, *CR,* April 1917, 37)

THEMES *for* LIVING

1. God Acts Through Prophets to Guide His Work
2. Prophecy Is a Divine Blessing of Kindness and Love

INTRODUCTION

Amos has given us perhaps the most memorable phrase concerning the importance of the prophetic office: "Surely the Lord God will do nothing, but he revealeth his secret unto his servants the prophets" (Amos 3:7). And yet, we are *all* the servants of God, and we are *all* to play a role in actualizing the divine purpose, which is "to bring to pass the immortality and eternal life of man" (Moses 1:39). In that sense, the Saints of God themselves participate in the fulfillment of God's word. "Would God," Moses declared, "that all the Lord's people were prophets, and that the Lord would put his spirit upon them!" (Num. 11:29). Whenever we move forward along the pathway toward perfection—even a modest step—we are fulfilling the word of God, for He has promised that the faithful will participate with Him in building the kingdom. God imparts His word through prophets and confirms the truth of their words through the inspiration of the Spirit. This simple process is profoundly important in the plan of salvation, for without the blessings of the continuing word of God, we could not have hope for a better world to come, nor faith in the power of the Atonement.

1. GOD ACTS THROUGH PROPHETS TO GUIDE HIS WORK

THEME: Just as Amos clearly foretold the unfolding of events for the Israelites of his day, so the prophets of our day mark out the correct pathway with unmistakable clarity—the pathway of obedience, truth, and light in a world beset with growing iniquity and deepening darkness.

> *You only have I known of all the families of the earth; therefore I will punish you for all your iniquities.* (Amos 3:2)

> *Surely the Lord God will do nothing, but he revealeth his secret unto his servants the prophets.* (Amos 3:7)

> *And the Lord took me as I followed the flock, and the Lord said unto me, Go, prophesy unto my people Israel.* (Amos 7:15)

MOMENT OF TRUTH

Amos was a herdsman from a small community south of Jerusalem, called to speak the words of the Divine King to the worldly kings of Israel and Judah and the inhabitants of the Holy Land. He prophesied around the middle of the eighth century before Christ, during the reign of King Uzziah of Judah (who died around 740 B.C.) and King Jeroboam II of Israel (who died around 750 B.C.); thus Amos was active a few years earlier than the prophet Isaiah. His celebrated statement—"Surely the Lord God will do nothing, but he revealeth his secret unto his servants the prophets" (Amos 3:7)—is the seal and testament of the prophetic office, and a memorable reminder that God works through prophets in all ages of the world to bring about His work and His glory. Amos also foretold the coming joyous period of restoration for the scattered Israel.

MODERN PROPHETS SPEAK

Gordon B. Hinckley:

> God is the one sure source of truth. He is the fount of all inspiration. It is from him that the world must receive direction if peace is to come to the earth and if goodwill is to prevail among men. This earth is his creation. We are his children. Out of the love he bears for us, he will guide us if we will seek, listen, and obey. (*Be Thou an Example* [Salt Lake City: Deseret Book, 1981], 92)

Matthias F. Cowley:

> That there may be an authorized channel of communication between the heavens and the earth, the Lord has, whenever His Church has existed on the earth, appointed men to receive His will and make it known to the people. "Surely the Lord God will do nothing, but He revealeth His secrets unto His servants, the prophets" (Amos 3:7). This literally might be understood as equivalent to saying that where no prophet was, there the Lord was doing nothing that would result in man's salvation. Without being technical respecting the language of Amos, the history of the world from Adam down proves his statements true. When there has been no prophet there has been no revelation from God. When there has been no revelation or vision the people have wandered to and fro, have tossed upon the billows of clashing opinion, perished in darkness and have been buried in the great ocean of doubt and uncertainty. On the other hand, when authorized prophets have existed among men we may exclaim with the ancient Scriptures: "I have also spoken by the prophets, and I have multiplied visions, and used similitudes, by the ministry of the prophets. And by a prophet the Lord brought Israel out of Egypt, and by a prophet was he preserved" (Hosea 12:10, 13). And we affirm that without prophets Israel never was preserved and never will be. (*Cowley's Talks on Doctrine* [Chattanooga: Ben E. Rich, 1902], 85)

ILLUSTRATIONS FOR OUR TIMES

Listen to a Prophet's Voice

The word of God is given to us by His spokesmen—the prophets, seers, and revelators. When we truly believe this, we will be obedient to the words of the living prophets. I have watched new converts take notes at conference time, and then make a plan to do everything the prophets have asked. I have seen parents listen intently so as to know how to help their children. I have been the recipient of wonderful lessons as our home teachers taught us the words of our living prophets.

I remember a meaningful general conference that had a great impact upon our family. On April 1, 1989, President Benson spoke about pride. As a family, we studied his talk for sixty days, and we compiled forty pages of scriptures and statements by the Brethren to gain humility. We realized that we suffered from pride and made a conscious effort to do better.

When President Hinckley spoke of the need for fellowship in the Church, our stake made a new plan to insure that every member was instructed and motivated in regard to their duty in conversion, retention, and activation (see "Some Thoughts on Temples, Retention of Converts, and Missionary Service," *Ensign,* Nov. 1997, 49–52). It has made a difference. Convert baptisms are up. All of our converts in the last eighteen months residing in our stake are active, and we are working hard to bring back our less-active members. President Hinckley is so inspired that if we but choose to obey, the blessings are waiting for the obedient (see D&C 130:19–21).

Words for Today

The miracle of having the words of God written upon our hearts will allow the Spirit to call them forth in the very hour, even in the very moment, where they might be needed in order to strengthen and guide us (D&C 100:6). It might be instructive to ask ourselves what particular sentences spoken by the prophets in our day stand out with special force in our memory as governing principles particularly applicable to current conditions. In my own case, given the almost universal assault against the family by worldly forces, I find myself continually rehearsing President David O. McKay's famous declaration: "No other success can compensate for failure in the home." Always right behind that comes the equally celebrated observation of President Harold B. Lee: "The most important work you will ever do is within the walls of your own home." And then there is the related warning sentence from the concluding portion of the *Proclamation on the Family*: "Further, we warn that the disintegration of the family will bring upon individuals, communities, and nations the calamities foretold by ancient and modern prophets." By writing such words upon our hearts and abiding by the precepts upon which they are founded, we prepare ourselves with the correct and effective responses against the encroachments of temptation and evil, and we open the doorway to admit into our lives the enlightenment that comes only through the spirit of truth.

2. PROPHECY IS A DIVINE BLESSING OF KINDNESS AND LOVE

THEME: The prophetic word of the Lord is the refreshing moisture that quenches our spiritual thirst, and the bread of life that satisfies our soul's hunger for divine nourishment.

> *And it shall come to pass afterward, that I will pour out my spirit upon all flesh; and your sons and your daughters shall prophesy, your old men shall dream dreams, your young men shall see visions.* (Joel 2:28)

MOMENT OF TRUTH

Joel was called to prophesy during a period of severe drought in Judah. Although the time of his ministry is uncertain, his message was universal: the temporal droughts we experience in life are but earthly counterparts of the spiritual drought that drives the humble and the submissive in search of truth. It is the Spirit of the Lord that alone can satisfy such a thirst and hunger after righteousness. Joel foresaw the day when Israel would again be nourished by the outpouring of the Lord's Spirit of reformation and rejuvenation. His message focused on the love of God and His everlasting kindness. All who receive a testimony of the Savior through the confirmation of the Holy Spirit are endowed with the spirit of prophecy and revelation (see 1 Cor. 12:3; Alma 17:2–3).

MODERN PROPHETS SPEAK

Neal A. Maxwell:

> In such a climactic time as the last days, we shall see things both wonderful and awful. Joel and Zephaniah prophesied that the last times would be a "day of gloominess" (Joel 2:2; Zeph. 1:15). Even so, this is all the more reason for us to "shine as lights in the world" (Philip. 2:15). So illuminated, we can better help to gather the Lord's flock in "the last days" from wherever they have been scattered in the "cloudy and dark day" (Ezek. 30:3; 34:12). (*One More Strain of Praise* [Salt Lake City: Deseret Book, 1999], 17–18)

M. Russell Ballard:

> The tenth article of faith has to do with the prophetic destiny of the American continent and Christ's foretold millennial reign upon the earth. It affirms every scriptural prophecy regarding the second coming of Christ, including biblical prophecies relative to the gathering of Israel and the return of the Ten Tribes of Israel that became "lost" when the invading Assyrians deported them around 722 B.C. It is not my purpose here to explain such detailed doctrine. It suffices to say we believe that all that has been prophesied by God's prophets will eventually come to pass, and that Jesus Christ will return to earth in power and majesty to rule as King of Kings in reclaiming His people and ushering in a millennial era of peace. (*Our Search for Happiness: An Invitation to Understand The Church of Jesus Christ of Latter-day Saints* [Salt Lake City: Deseret Book, 1993], 97)

ILLUSTRATIONS FOR OUR TIMES

Fulfillment of Prophecy

Go back with me to Friday, 26 April 1839. A few minutes after midnight, a number of the Twelve Apostles gather with a few Saints at the temple site in Far West,

Missouri, for an unusual meeting. Among those present are Brigham Young, Heber C. Kimball, Orson Pratt, John E. Page, and John Taylor. These brethren ordain Wilford Woodruff and George A. Smith Apostles and then two others as Seventies. After prayers and a hymn ("Adam-ondi-Ahman"), the Twelve take leave of those assembled and depart into the night. Why this clandestine midnight meeting? Because the angry mobs that had driven the Saints away the previous fall had sworn that no such meeting would take place. They were well aware of the revelation given by the Lord through the Prophet Joseph Smith on 8 July 1838, announcing that the Twelve would "take leave of my Saints in the city of Far West on the twenty-sixth day of April next, on the building-spot of my house, saith the Lord" (D&C 118:5) to perform missionary duties in Europe. What better way to prove "Joe Smith" a false prophet than to prevent the gathering from taking place on that date? Imagine their shock when they learned later the same day that the event had already occurred, just as the Lord had commanded (see *HC* 3:336–40). Thus we see that the purposes of the Lord cannot be frustrated and will all be fulfilled: "and there is nothing that the Lord thy God shall take in his heart to do but what he will do it" (Abr. 3:17).

Guard Against Being "At Ease"

Amos was courageous in warning the people that evil would come upon them if they did not repent. He warned us about being at ease in the latter days (see Amos 6:1). When people are prosperous and at ease, they tend to forget their God and turn to the world (see Hel. 12:2). Nephi was even more explicit (see 2 Ne. 28:19–30). As the devil rages in the hearts of men, he will pacify, lull and flatter people to think all is well in Zion. The Lord counsels us,

> Therefore, wo be unto him that is at ease in Zion!
>
> Wo be unto him that crieth: All is well!
>
> Yea, wo be unto him that hearkeneth unto the precepts of men, and denieth the power of God, and the gift of the Holy Ghost!
>
> Yea, wo be unto him that saith: We have received, and we need no more! . . .
>
> For behold, thus saith the Lord God: I will give unto the children of men line upon line, precept upon precept, here a little and there a little; and blessed are those who hearken unto my precepts, and lend an ear unto my counsel, for they shall learn wisdom; for unto him that receiveth I will give more; and from them that shall say, We have enough, from them shall be taken away even that which they have. (2 Ne. 28:24–27, 30)

The message is clear. The prophets have prophesied for our day and we are left to embrace their words and act accordingly. If we don't, we are brought under condemnation. The Lord stands ready to show mercy, as Nephi recorded: "For notwithstanding I shall lengthen out mine arm unto them from day to day, they will deny me; nevertheless, I will be merciful unto them, saith the Lord God, if they will repent and come unto me; for mine arm is lengthened out all the day long, saith the Lord God of Hosts" (2 Ne. 28:32).

SUMMARY

The people are to be judged "according to the laws of the kingdom which are given by the prophets of God" (D&C 58:18). How important it is, therefore, to listen to the prophet's voice today and ponder the written word of the Lord preserved in the scriptures. The Lord has promised us peace: "Learn of me, and listen to my words; walk in the meekness of my Spirit, and you shall have peace in me" (D&C 19:23). To the extent we make ourselves worthy of achieving such spiritual peace, we are the living fulfillment of prophecy, for we will be enjoying the blessings of eternal life as promised through prophetic declarations since the beginning of the world. The counsel of Amos is as true today as it was when he first spoke it: "Seek the Lord, and ye shall live" (Amos 5:6).

CHAPTER THIRTY-SIX

"HOLY, HOLY, HOLY IS *the* LORD"

Reading Assignment: Isaiah 1–6.

Additional Reading: 2 Nephi 11.

> *Do you read the scriptures, my brethren and sisters, as though you were writing them a thousand, two thousand, or five thousand years ago? Do you read them as though you stood in the place of the men who wrote them? If you do not feel thus, it is your privilege to do so.* (Brigham Young, *JD* 7:333)

THEMES *for* LIVING

1. Isaiah the Prophet
2. Stand in Holy Places
3. Zion as the Fountain of Truth in the Wilderness of the World

INTRODUCTION

Isaiah captured with uncommon excellence the dramatic and compelling contrasts between the godly walk of the Saints in Zion and the staggering, uncertain meanderings of the misguided and prideful souls in Babylon, Sodom and Gomorrah, or any other worldly habitat. Three grand themes emerge from these early chapters of Isaiah:

first, the humility and yielding spirit of reverence that all of the prophets, including Isaiah, displayed in accepting their commission from the Lord; second, the prophetic message to "stand in holy places" (2 Chr. 35:5; Ps. 24:3; Matt. 24:15; D&C 45:32; 87:8; 101:22); and third, the appeal to flee from worldly entanglements and respond to the brilliant light of Zion's beacon upon the mount. These three themes are plainly visible in Isaiah's contrasting portraits of Zion and Babylon (or Sodom).

1. ISAIAH THE PROPHET

THEME: Isaiah willingly fulfilled his calling as a prophet of God. He was and is without equal in his prophetic utterances regarding the Messiah. We must do all we can to understand and apply his words to our lives. The Savior Himself has said:

> *And now, behold, I say unto you, that ye ought to search these things. Yea, a commandment I give unto you that ye search these things diligently; for great are the words of Isaiah.* (3 Ne. 23:1)

MOMENT OF TRUTH

Isaiah, the son of Amoz, the prophet most cited in subsequent scripture, was given by the Lord a profound gift to express with resounding impact, power, and clarity the message of the visions given him as the spokesperson for the Lord in his day. He wrote between 740 and 701 B.C., at a time when Israel had incurred the fierce anger of the Lord through her wanton behavior, pride, and idolatry. Isaiah's language soared and spiraled with the flight of thought and symbolism. He intermingled references to events of his own day with those of coming events that were to unfold in the future, using breathtaking sweeps that carry one from the distant past to the distant future and back again, often within the same passage. His declarations included the age-old prophetic message that "wickedness never was happiness" (see Alma 41:10), that Israel would suffer by persisting in her prideful and ungodly walk, and that good would eventually triumph in the last days as the faithful were gathered together in holy places of refuge. In no other passages of scripture can one find the word of the Lord expressed with greater power or more lasting influence than in the writings of Isaiah.

MODERN PROPHETS SPEAK

Mark E. Petersen:

> Again the words of the Lord to Isaiah identified the Christ: "Tell ye, and bring them near; yea, let them take counsel together: who hath declared this from ancient time? who hath told it from that time? have not I the Lord? and there is no God else beside

me; a just God and a Saviour; there is none beside me" (Isa. 45:21). Speaking of the divine Redeemer, who alone is Jesus Christ, Isaiah said this: "For thy Maker is thine husband; the Lord of hosts is his name; and thy Redeemer the Holy One of Israel; The God of the whole earth shall he be called. . . . In a little wrath I hid my face from thee for a moment; but with everlasting kindness will I have mercy on thee, saith the Lord thy Redeemer" (Isa. 54:5, 8). Note his frequent use of the titles "Redeemer" and "Savior," which are applicable only to Jesus of Nazareth. Can anyone mistake such scriptures? Did not Isaiah abundantly testify of Christ?

Is it any wonder that the Savior commanded us to read Isaiah, "For great are the words of Isaiah"? When it is realized that salvation comes alone through Jesus, and Isaiah was so vocal in declaring this fact, it becomes essential that all people understand and believe him. As Isaiah spoke of the Lord and his atonement, he taught clearly that mankind, through Him, may receive forgiveness of sins. He appealed to the people of his day in such terms and said: "Come now, and let us reason together, saith the Lord: though your sins be as scarlet, they shall be as white as snow; though they be red like crimson, they shall be as wool. If ye be willing and obedient, ye shall eat the good of the land: But if ye refuse and rebel, ye shall be devoured with the sword: for the mouth of the Lord hath spoken it" (Isa. 1:18–20).

He said further: "Fear not, thou worm Jacob, and ye men of Israel; I will help thee, saith the Lord, and thy redeemer, the Holy One of Israel" (Isa. 41:14). He revealed that the atonement paid the price of sin: "I, even I, am he that blotteth out thy transgressions for mine own sake, and will not remember thy sins" (Isa. 43:25). He spoke of the resurrection, which alone comes through Jesus, and said: "Thy dead men shall live, together with my dead body shall they arise. Awake and sing, ye that dwell in dust: for thy dew is as the dew of herbs, and the earth shall cast out the dead" (Isa. 26:19). He spoke repeatedly of the second coming of the Lord, of which the following is an example: "Behold, the Lord God will come with strong hand, and his arm shall rule for him: behold, his reward is with him, and his work before him" (Isa. 40:10). And he added: "For, behold, the Lord will come with fire, and with his chariots like a whirlwind, to render his anger with fury, and his rebuke with flames of fire. For by fire and by his sword will the Lord plead with all flesh: and the slain of the Lord shall be many" (Isa. 66:15–16). (*Isaiah for Today* [Salt Lake City: Deseret Book, 1981], 43)

ILLUSTRATIONS FOR OUR TIMES

Understanding the "Manner of Prophesying Among the Jews"
The words of Isaiah teach us of the mission and divinity of Jesus Christ (see Isa. 7:14; 9:6–7; 53:1–2), the fate and fortune of the house of Israel (see Isa. 2:1–5; 27:12–13; 44:1–4; 43:1–7; 1:25–27; 49:5–17), and the things we need to do to be worthy of the

blessings of God (see Isa. 58:1–14; 5:8–24). Isaiah is quoted extensively in the New Testament and numerous chapters in their entirety are found in the Book of Mormon. Still more phrases are found in the Doctrine and Covenants. Isaiah's message is just as important now as ever before, and God is the same "yesterday, today, and forever" (D&C 20:12).

We often don't fully understand the manner of prophesying among the Jews (see 2 Ne. 25:1). To understand the words of Isaiah, we must put forth the effort to comprehend the manner of his writing, as well as his prophesying. This can be done in many ways through diligent and prayerful study, but Nephi made the most useful recommendation:

> Wherefore, hearken, O my people, which are of the house of Israel, and give ear unto my words; for because the words of Isaiah are not plain unto you, nevertheless they are plain unto all those that are filled with the spirit of prophecy. But I give unto you a prophecy, according to the spirit which is in me; wherefore I shall prophesy according to the plainness which hath been with me from the time that I came out from Jerusalem with my father; for behold, my soul delighteth in plainness unto my people, that they may learn. (2 Ne. 25:4)

Nephi has made clear to us that we need the spirit of prophecy to understand Isaiah. The spirit of prophecy is a gift of the Spirit (see D&C 46:22). Knowing Jesus Christ is the Savior of the world comes by the spirit of prophecy (see Rev. 19:10). This is the gift that the sons of Mosiah possessed (see Alma 17:3), and it requires great effort on our part to be worthy. One cannot simply ask without putting forth effort, as Oliver Cowdery has demonstrated (see D&C 9:7–8).

My Grace Is Sufficient

It is instructive and characteristic that Isaiah, among all of the ancient prophets unsurpassed in the supremacy and mastery of his prophetic language, responded with contrition and meekness to his calling: "Then said I, Woe is me! for I am undone [i.e., overwhelmed by a sense of inadequacy]; because I am a man of unclean lips, and I dwell in the midst of a people of unclean lips: for mine eyes have seen the King, the Lord of hosts" (Isa. 6:5). Then, in the continuing heavenly vision, the Lord dispatches one of His angels to reassure the newly called prophet: "thine iniquity is taken away, and thy sin purged" (v. 7), whereupon Isaiah responds with humble words reminiscent of the Savior's own response in the premortal realm: "Here am I; send me" (v. 8; compare Abr. 3:27). This pattern of meekness in the face of a divine calling is not unlike the attitude of Moses on the mount (see Ex. 3:11–12; 4:10–12) or Jeremiah's deep feelings of inadequacy when he was called as a prophet (see Jer. 1:6–8). Similarly, Amos, a man of the field, rose to the stature of a prophet under guidance from the Lord (see Amos 7:14).

In Book of Mormon times, the prophet Moroni had grave reservations concerning his ability to fulfill the divine commission to preserve the written record of the Lord's dealings with the ancient American peoples (see Ether 12:23–24). But the Lord's response to this sense of inadequacy was the same as His response to Moses, Jeremiah, Isaiah, Amos, and all leaders called to serve: "And if men come unto me I will show unto them their weakness. I give unto men weakness that they may be humble; and my grace is sufficient for all men that humble themselves before me; for if they will humble themselves before me, and have faith in me, then will I make weak things become strong unto them" (Ether 12:27).

Thus the ancient records illuminate the key to service and the answer to feelings of inadequacy on the part of anyone called on the Lord's errand: His grace is sufficient to lift us above our weakness and infuse our souls with the strength and vision to succeed. It matters not that a person fearful of teaching be called to teach, or a person fearful of speaking be called to speak, or a person fearful of leading be called to lead. When the Lord extends a calling, He provides the grace, the power, and the ability to make one equal to the task. All of us, at one time or another, have confronted our own inadequacy when called to positions of service. I remember how overwhelming it was, many years ago, to be called as a bishop at age twenty-seven in a ward far away from my native roots. But when our roots are in the soil of faith, and when our spirit is contrite, we can remember the lessons taught by the prophets that the Lord will make up the difference. In the words of the Savior: "With men it is impossible, but not with God: for with God all things are possible" (Mark 10:27).

2. STAND IN HOLY PLACES

THEME: The righteous homes, congregations, and temples of Zion offer the only enduring refuge from the oppression and tyranny of iniquity and evil. The gospel of Jesus Christ is the only resort of eternal safety for all mankind.

> *And the Lord will create upon every dwelling place of mount Zion, and upon her assemblies, a cloud and smoke by day, and the shining of a flaming fire by night: for upon all the glory shall be a defence.* (Isa. 4:5)

MOMENT OF TRUTH

Isaiah, in his most beautiful imagery, taught us how the Lord can and will protect us as we "stand in holy places." Nothing is more prophetic or practical in protecting us from sin than to be in a safe place, sheltered and protected by the hand of God. His protection is enhanced as we do our part by being in the right place at the right time, doing the right thing.

MODERN PROPHETS SPEAK

Ezra Taft Benson:

> We will live in the midst of economic, political, and spiritual instability. When these signs are observed—unmistakable evidences that His coming is nigh—we need not be troubled, but "stand in holy places, and be not moved, until the day of the Lord come" (D&C 87:8). Holy men and women stand in holy places, and these holy places consist of our temples, our chapels, our homes, and stakes of Zion, which are, as the Lord declares, "for a defense, and for a refuge from the storm, and from wrath when it shall be poured out without mixture upon the whole earth" (D&C 115:6). We must heed the Lord's counsel to the Saints of this dispensation: "Prepare yourselves for the great day of the Lord" (D&C 133:10). (*TETB,* 106)

Howard W. Hunter:

> Our homes should be holy places in which we can stand against the world. Without doubt there are significant challenges facing the Latter-day Saints, both here and elsewhere in the world. We hope that you will not be overcome with discouragement in your attempts to raise your families in righteousness. Remember that the Lord has commanded this: "But my disciples shall stand in holy places, and shall not be moved" (D&C 45:32). While some interpret this to mean the temple, which surely it does, it also represents the homes in which we live. If you will diligently work to lead your families in righteousness, encouraging and participating in daily family prayer, scripture reading, family home evening, and love and support for each other in living the teachings of the gospel, you will receive the promised blessings of the Lord in raising a righteous posterity. In an increasingly wicked world, how essential it is that each of us "stand in holy places" and commit to be true and faithful to the teachings of the gospel of Jesus Christ. (*THWH,* 155)

ILLUSTRATIONS FOR OUR TIMES

Holiness to the Lord

Many years ago, when there were relatively few operating temples in the world outside of Utah, I had an experience that dramatically reinforced for me the spirit of peace and sanctity emanating from these sacred edifices. As a small group of Latter-day Saints, my party had visited an institution on the outskirts of Basel, Switzerland, where an art exposition on biblical themes was being shown. We found the display characterized (to quote from my journal) by "bright greens and yellows and hideous satanic characters and forms." The effect of these bizarre configurations combined with the strange asymmetrical structures of the edifice in which they were housed to produce a most constricting and unsettling feeling in us, and several members of our group became physically ill and had to leave the site. What happened next has become an enduring memory in my archive of cherished insights. The journal continues:

> We ourselves didn't realize what an impression it [the art exposition and gallery] had made on us until several hours later, when we approached a small town just outside of Bern and saw, through the trees, the spire of an unusual edifice. The contrast between what we had experienced and, now, the Swiss Temple, was so great that it really opened our eyes. Truly, this magnificent building, nestled among the trees overlooking the white Alps on the horizon, is a testimony of the order of heaven. What perfect symmetry and grace! We immediately felt a spirit of peace and serenity as we viewed the temple and read the inscription "Holiness to the Lord." How grateful we were to be members of His Church and possess the knowledge of His gospel! The peace and quiet within these walls is truly spiritually refreshing.

3. ZION AS THE FOUNTAIN OF TRUTH IN THE WILDERNESS OF THE WORLD

THEME: The scriptures—and particularly the words of Isaiah—make clear the striking contrast between the transitory fruit of worldly entanglements and the abundant and enduring fruit of gospel light and truth. Isaiah foresaw the time, dawning in our own day, when the brilliance and glory of Zion would again be an exalted ensign to the nations.

> *And it shall come to pass in the last days, that the mountain of the Lord's house shall be established in the top of the mountains, and shall be exalted above the hills; and all nations shall flow unto it.* (Isa. 2:2)

> *And he will lift up an ensign to the nations from far, and will hiss unto them from the end of the earth: and, behold, they shall come with speed swiftly.* (Isa. 5:26)

MOMENT OF TRUTH

Isaiah outlined in painstaking detail the misdeeds and treachery of the wayward people of the Lord, whose prideful and idolatrous behaviors would predictably lead to their being smitten and dispersed. In stark contrast were Isaiah's visions of the coming times of restoration, when the scattered remnants would be gathered in from the four quarters of the earth and the nations would look to Zion as the only dependable source of wisdom and truth.

MODERN PROPHETS SPEAK

Joseph B. Wirthlin:

> The scriptures are full of warnings against worldliness and pride because they too can lead us off course. The Lord explained to the Prophet Joseph Smith that many people veer from the path "because their hearts are set so much upon the things of this world" (D&C 121:35). (*Finding Peace in Our Lives* [Salt Lake City: Deseret Book, 1995], 198)

L. Tom Perry:

> Are we not simply repeating history? While these problems may manifest themselves in different ways, they are as prevalent today as they were at the time immediately preceding the fall of Rome. Moreover, they all represent direct violations of God's commandments. Isn't it time that we consider our ways? Shouldn't we contemplate our roles as spouses and parents, battle the worldliness and immorality that surrounds us, and work to deepen our religious beliefs? (*Living with Enthusiasm* [Salt Lake City: Deseret Book, 1996], 40)

ILLUSTRATIONS FOR OUR TIMES

The Word of God as Armor

Isaiah has warned us concerning those who will rebel against God, those who claim to worship yet are without real intent or faith, and those who worship the things of the world. He also warned against pride, disrespect, greed, oppression of others, feeling no guilt for sin, taking advantage of one another, failing to care for one another, caring more about appearances than righteousness, pleasure-seeking, rationalizing sin, self-sufficiency rather than trusting in the Lord, and despising the things of God, including His word and commandments.

The examples that stand out in my mind occur over and over again. Everyone thinks they are immune to sin or have the power to overcome it in any situation. Joseph of Egypt was right—he ran. We, in our self-sufficiency, think we can handle any situation, and that is where we err. Countless young people have said words like these to me: "We weren't planning to"; "We were just at the party"; " We didn't know everyone was going to be drinking"; "Just because some were doing drugs that didn't make us guilty"; "We were just at the wrong place at the wrong time"; "We were . . . ." And the stories go on. Each person always thinks he or she can handle the situation—and they are wrong. Many a good person has transgressed when there was no willful plan to sin; but because of failure to make correct choices, they were led to situations in the world which they could not handle. The result was sin.

The Courage to Change

I remember a neighbor telling me a number of years ago about a remarkable meta-morphosis he had gone through one evening while on a business trip far away from his young family. He was lying alone on the bed of his hotel room, staring at the ceiling, pondering his predicament as a senior officer under strict company orders to carry out policies that he felt were increasingly at variance with the fundamental principles of honesty taught by the gospel. He sensed the deep responsibility he had to provide for his wife and children, yet his growing uneasiness over the nature of his professional duties brought agony to his soul. Suddenly, while lying there in prayerful meditation, he had the distinct impression that he must change. Instantly he made a decision. Like Joseph of Egypt, he found within himself the courage to go in a totally different direction. He made some quick telephone calls to inform his superiors and bring the pleasant news to his family, then packed his bags and returned home. His pathway thereafter was marked by increased harmony, peace, and prosperity.

Another neighbor told me about his troubling experiences on the professional Hollywood music scene, and how he had decided one day to withdraw rather than compromise his standards any further. Still another neighbor recounted his decision to go through a fundamental professional transformation, giving up considerable equity and temporal advantage, in order to have more time with his family. The sto-ries of courageous transitions are legion. Those who look to the mountain of the Lord's house to obtain their bearings will not easily go astray, for "he will teach us of his ways, and we will walk in his paths" (Isa. 2:3). By seeking the face of the Lord always (2 Chr. 7:14; D&C 101:38), we can flee from Babylon and take refuge in the peace and rest of Zion.

SUMMARY

Like Isaiah, we can in all humility and devotion take upon ourselves the commitment to assist in the building up of Zion. We can cultivate a "godly walk and conversation" and stand firmly planted in the triad of holy places—home, congregation, and tem-ple—illuminated by the light of the gospel. Not only can we navigate in accord with the beacon of Zion that casts a spiritual glow over the landscape of worldly enterprise, but we can also contribute to that beacon by adding our own beam of righteous endeavor to the glory of God. We can then say, with Isaiah, "Holy, holy, holy, is the Lord" (Isa. 6:3).

CHAPTER THIRTY-SEVEN

"WE WILL BE GLAD *and* REJOICE *in* HIS SALVATION"

Reading Assignment: Isaiah 22; 24–26; 28–30.

When Jesus came, He came as a sacrifice not simply in the interest of Israel . . . but in the interest of the whole human family, that in Him all men might be blessed, that in Him all men might be saved; and His mission was to make provision by which the whole human family might receive the benefits of the everlasting gospel, . . . not alone those dwelling upon the earth, but those also in the spirit world. (Lorenzo Snow, 4 November 1882, Deseret Weekly News, 32:18)

THEMES *for* LIVING

1. Attributes of the Savior
2. As a Book Crying from the Dust

INTRODUCTION

Among the ranks of God's mouthpieces since the beginning of time, the prophet Isaiah is probably the most comprehensive delineator of the Messiah's divine qualities and attributes. Five of those special qualities are described in the passages of scripture for this chapter, using the unique tactile symbolic imagery so characteristic of Isaiah's style of expression. We see in our mind's eye his treatment of the visual symbols of the key, the nail, the feast, the crown, and the stone. In addition, we see in stark detail, the image of the book that he describes in chapter 29.

1. ATTRIBUTES OF THE SAVIOR

THEME: Isaiah's words are filled with statements that anticipate the Lord's coming mission as Savior and Healer of mankind. We see reflected in powerful symbols the qualities of redeeming grace central to the Lord's mission. Among them are: *the key* (author of salvation), *the nail* (executor of the Atonement), *the feast* (bringer of truth), *the crown* (sovereign of peace and glory), and *the stone* (foundation for the kingdom of refuge).

> *And the key of the House of David will I lay upon his shoulders.* (Isa. 22:22)

> *And I will fasten him as a nail in a sure place.* (Isa. 22:23)

> *And in this mountain shall the Lord of hosts make unto all people a feast of fat things.* (Isa. 25:6)

> *In that day shall the Lord of hosts be for a crown of glory, and for a diadem of beauty, unto the residue of his people.* (Isa. 28:5)

> *Therefore thus saith the Lord God, Behold, I lay in Zion for a foundation a stone, a tried stone, a precious corner stone, a sure foundation.* (Isa. 28:16)

MOMENT OF TRUTH

Isaiah, whose name means "the Lord is Salvation," wrote his mighty visions in the period from 740 B.C. to 701 B.C., during the early reign of King Hezekiah (715 B.C. to 686 B.C.), for whom he served as courtly advisor. His language, filled with powerful symbolism, continues to echo across time as if from a great altitude and overarching perspective. Isaiah painted his canvas with broad strokes of opposites—darkness and light, scattering and gathering, imprisonment and liberation, hunger and satiety, tearing down and building up, all contingent on man's obedience to the covenants of God. Under the inspiration of the Spirit, he saw the grand breadth of the earth's history from beginning to end and foreshadowed the coming day of judgment, when the wicked will shrink under the awesome burden of guilt and the righteous will rejoice in the salvation of the Lord.

MODERN PROPHETS SPEAK

Neal A. Maxwell:

> Therefore, let us become such and proceed to make our way, righteously and resolutely, notwithstanding our weaknesses, to the beckoning City of God. There the self-assigned gatekeeper is Jesus Christ, who awaits us out of a deep divine desire to welcome us as much as to certify us; hence, "He employeth no servant there" (2 Ne. 9:41). If we acknowledge Him now, He will lovingly acknowledge and gladly admit us then! (*Notwithstanding My Weakness* [Salt Lake City: Deseret Book, 1981], 124)

Jeffrey R. Holland:

> Even though there are some conditional aspects of the Atonement that require our adherence to gospel principles for the full realization of eternal blessings, the Book of Mormon makes clear that neither the conditional nor unconditional blessings of the Atonement would be available to mankind except through the grace and goodness of Christ. Obviously the unconditional blessings of the Atonement are unearned, but the conditional ones also are not fully merited. By living faithfully and keeping the commandments of God, we can receive a fuller measure of blessings from Christ, but even these greater blessings are freely given of him and are not technically "earned" by us. In short, good works are necessary for salvation, but they are not sufficient. And God is not obliged to make up the insufficiency. As Jacob taught, "Remember, after ye are reconciled unto God, that it is only in and through the grace of God that ye are saved" (2 Ne. 10:24). (*Christ and the New Covenant: The Messianic Message of the Book of Mormon* [Salt Lake City: Deseret Book, 1997], 236)

ILLUSTRATIONS FOR OUR TIMES

Everyday Reminders of the Redeemer

Isaiah has taught us the Savior's role and attributes. We, too, should seek to become as He is (see 3 Ne. 27:27). The question or thought should always be in our minds: "What can I do to remember to be like the Savior?" Devise a reminder so that you don't forget your Savior, and then make a plan to be Christlike in all of your doings. You might consider the following:

1. Pray with all the energy of your heart (see Moro. 7:48; 3 Ne. 18:15, 18).

2. When you hear a bell or look at the time, think, "It is time to choose the right and keep the commandments" (see D&C 20:77, 79).

3. Mark your scriptures as you study with those things you need to do to be like Christ (see 3 Ne. 27:27).

4. Make applications in the first person from the scriptures and general conference (see 1 Ne. 19:23).

5. Plan to do an act of charity (see Matt. 25:40).

6. Always seek to lift another (see D&C 81:5, 108:7).

2. AS A BOOK CRYING FROM THE DUST

THEME: The coming forth of the Book of Mormon in our day as a voice from the dust was foreseen by Isaiah in astounding detail, showing that the Lord's design for blessing His people with the fullness of the gospel was prepared with loving care and meticulous wisdom from the beginning.

> *Therefore, behold, I will proceed to do a marvellous work among this people, even a marvellous work and a wonder: for the wisdom of their wise men shall perish, and the understanding of their prudent men shall be hid.* (Isa. 28:16)

MOMENT OF TRUTH

Isaiah saw in vision the mission of Moroni as messenger and tutor to Joseph Smith, and the circumstances under which the Book of Mormon would be brought forth by unlearned hands as a "marvellous work and a wonder," confounding worldly wisdom and restoring the gospel to the earth.

MODERN PROPHETS SPEAK

Ezra Taft Benson:

> The Book of Mormon will change your life. It will fortify you against the evils of our day. It will bring a spirituality into your life that no other book will. It will be the most important book you will read in preparation for life's challenges. (*Come, Listen to a Prophet's Voice* [Salt Lake City: Deseret Book, 1990])

Ezra Taft Benson:

> As far as preaching the gospel is concerned, the Book of Mormon contains the clearest, most concise, and complete explanation. There is no other record to compare with it. In what record do you get such a complete understanding of the nature of the Fall, the nature of physical and spiritual death, the doctrine of the Atonement, the doctrine of justice and mercy as it relates to the Atonement, and the principles

and ordinances of the gospel? The Book of Mormon contains the most comprehensive account of these fundamental doctrines. (*TETB,* 56)

ILLUSTRATIONS FOR OUR TIMES

The Key to a Sealed Book

Many decades ago, as a graduate student, I attended a lecture on pre-Columbian transatlantic migrations to America, given by one of the faculty members at a well-known eastern university who was celebrated for his research on that topic. After the lecture, several attendees were questioning the professor about his theories, and one of the students asked him if he had ever heard of the Book of Mormon. His reply was interesting. He said that he regularly received several copies of the Book of Mormon each year, always with certain pages marked for his reading guidance. His opinion of the book—which betrayed his scant familiarity with its nature, mission, and merit—was that "anyone could have put together such material in a short period of time."

My mind immediately turned to the experience of Martin Harris in 1828 in showing to Professor Charles Anthon of Columbia College (now Columbia University) in New York a transcript of the Book of Mormon and its translation. The professor had issued to Martin Harris a certificate of authenticity concerning the characters, but later retracted it upon learning the divine origin of the material. His famous words, "I cannot read a sealed book" (*HC* 1:20) were almost a verbatim echo of Isaiah's prophecy, "Read this, I pray thee: and he saith, I cannot; for it is sealed" (Isa. 29:11).

It was clear that the learned university professor who lectured to us on transatlantic migrations that day was oblivious to the meaning of the record of Joseph. To him, as well as to all others who seek spiritual truth by any means other than through spiritual light, the Book of Mormon remained sealed. How easily that seal can be broken to release the abundance of spiritual blessings awaiting the honest seeker after truth: "Ask, and it shall be given you; seek, and ye shall find; knock, and it shall be opened unto you" (Matt. 7:7).

The Key to Changing Lives

I had the privilege of teaching the Book of Mormon for many years at BYU and at the Orem, Utah, Institute of Religion. I often would have my students read the Book of Enos and 2 Nephi, chapter 9, for as many as thirty days in a row. Some of them wondered about my reasoning. After two or three weeks, however, many of them would say what a dramatic effect it had had on them, how their lives had changed, how they wanted to repent, how much more they loved the Savior, and what a profound effect the book was having on their very being. That was the power of the word of God coming into their lives. The Book of Mormon truly can change us as we sup from its pages. I testify that it has changed my life forever. It is the key to knowing and loving our Heavenly Father and our Savior Jesus Christ. Ponder on Moroni 10:3–5, and you will have this assurance as well.

SUMMARY

When we seek humbly to learn of Christ and come to know of His goodness and attributes of perfection, we will want to become like Him. We will hope to take upon ourselves the qualities of His divine nature, including the ultimate attribute of charity and all of its attendant blessings (see 2 Pet. 1:3–12). As we come unto Christ, we partake of the fruit of the tree of life, and we are happy. One of the divinely appointed guides for this process is the Book of Mormon, the coming forth of which Isaiah saw in prophetic vision. When we pattern our lives after the teachings of this remarkable book, we cultivate the mission of helping all mankind come unto Christ and be perfected in Him—which is precisely our commission under the Abrahamic covenant. Thus the Book of Mormon is our action plan under this commission. As we "feast upon the words of Christ" (2 Ne. 32:3; see Jacob 3:2) and share this spiritual nourishment with others, "we will be glad and rejoice in his salvation" (Isa. 25:9).

CHAPTER THIRTY-EIGHT

"LOOK *unto* ME *and* BE YE SAVED"

Reading Assignment: Isaiah 40–49.

Jesus is the Redeemer of the world, the Savior of mankind, who came to the earth with a divinely appointed mission to die for the redemption of mankind. Jesus Christ is literally the Son of God, the only begotten in the flesh. (Heber J. Grant, *CR,* Apr. 1921, 203)

THEMES *for* LIVING

1. "And Beside Me There Is No Saviour"
2. The Lord Will Remember Zion and Cause her Faithful to Flourish
3. Latter-day Mission for the Covenant People

INTRODUCTION

The Prophet Nephi, who shared with his brethren and their families many of the words of Isaiah, spoke of the Redeemer's office in this way: "And he gathereth his children from the four quarters of the earth; and he numbereth his sheep, and they know him; and there shall be one fold and one shepherd; and he shall feed his sheep, and in him they shall find pasture" (1 Ne. 22:25). This concept of one Savior, one fold, one saving message, and one way back home was sounded again and again with the voice of grandeur by the prophet Isaiah. In the pages that follow, we will explore three themes of hope: (1) the doctrine that beside Jesus Christ there is no Savior, (2) the assurance that He will always remember Zion and cause her faithful to flourish, and (3) the declaration that the latter-day mission of the covenant people is to carry the unified gospel message to a waiting world.

1. "AND BESIDE ME THERE IS NO SAVIOUR"

THEME: The most important question in life is the one Isaiah asked repeatedly in endless variations: "Is there a God beside me?" (Isa. 44:8). The answer resounds for all the world to hear: There is no God beside the Lord, in whom all grace and glory and power of redemption reside. All other gods of man will perish in the dust of idolatry, leaving their worshipers abandoned at the feet of silent, empty figures of clay and wood and brass.

> *Lift up your eyes on high, and behold who hath created these things, that bringeth out their host by number: he calleth them all by names by the greatness of his might, for that he is strong in power; not one faileth.* (Isa. 40:26)

> *For I am the Lord thy God, the Holy One of Israel, thy Saviour.* (Isa. 43:3)

> *I am the first, and I am the last; and beside me there is no God.* (Isa. 44:6; compare 45:5, 18, 22)

> *Go ye forth of Babylon.* (Isa. 48:20)

MOMENT OF TRUTH

With unsurpassed literary mastery, Isaiah contrasted the divine supremacy of the Lord with the empty hollowness of human-fashioned idols. These passages lay naked the truth about the impotence of wooden or metallic gods and the folly of all those who call upon them for redemption. The Lord alone has the power to save. Only by fleeing Babylon and gathering to Zion can the people have hope of renewal and eternal life.

MODERN PROPHETS SPEAK

Neal A. Maxwell:
> Faithful and tried John Taylor candidly said we need to have faith in the plan, even when we do not have all the explanatory divine data: "I do not know why Jesus

should leave his Father's throne and be offered up a sacrifice for the sin of the world, and why mankind have to be put through such an ordeal as they have to pass through on this earth; we reason upon this, and the Scriptures say that it is because man cannot be made perfect only through suffering. We might ask why could not mankind be saved in another way? Why could not salvation be wrought out without suffering? I receive it in my faith that this is the only way, and I rejoice that we have a Savior who had the goodness to come forth and redeem us." (*Lord, Increase Our Faith* [Salt Lake City: Bookcraft, 1994], 43)

David O. McKay:

Christ is real; he lives! His life is real. He is the Son of God. The Babe of Bethlehem, The One Perfect Gentleman who ever lived—the Ideal Man whose character was supreme; our Brother, Our Savior, The "Anointed One." God help us to believe in him with all our souls to make him real in our lives! (*Man May Know for Himself: Teachings of President David O. McKay* [Salt Lake City: Deseret Book, 1967], 423)

ILLUSTRATIONS FOR OUR TIMES

A Name and an Aim

As a young high school student in Canada, I interviewed one of the faculty members for a feature article in the school publication. In the article, I quoted him as having said, "You have to have a name in life." He came to me afterward, rather upset, and said that his statement had actually been, "You have to have *an aim* in life." It was an honest misunderstanding because of how the words sounded, but he was anxious to be on record as saying that your name, or station by birth, is not as important as your inner motivation and will.

Since then, I have often thought about "name" and "aim" and have come to the conclusion that both are ultimately of equal importance. Who we are and what we do in life are intimately related. In the case of the Savior, he was the Only Begotten of the Father—a station by birth that was of paramount significance. At the same time, His eternal aim was to do the will of the Father, to carry out the mission assigned Him from before the foundations of the world. Thus His eternal nature by birth, as well as His eternal purpose in the Father, were both indispensable to His divine mission. His Atonement is clearly revealed in the proper names assigned Him: from the beginning He was called Jehovah, which implies "the Unchanging One" and "the Eternal I AM" (Ex. 6:3; Ps. 83:18, Isa. 12:2; 26:4). His aim is eternal and unchanging, centered in the blessing of God's children; thus He is also called "Jesus," which is the Greek form of the name Joshua or Jeshua, meaning "God is help" or "Savior." The angel Gabriel instructed Joseph to call his son by this very name—"Jesus" (see Luke 1:31; Matt. 1:21). Next, the Savior was to be called "Christ," which means "Anointed." Christ is the Greek form of the word "Messiah" in Hebrew. Thus it is not only in the Lord's nature and will to be the Savior, but He is also anointed of the Father to carry out this eternal mission. Finally, it was essential for the Savior to come down and live among mortals in order to complete His atoning sacrifice. In recognition of this condescension, He is called "Immanuel" or "Emmanuel," meaning "God with us" (see Isa. 7:14; 8:8). We see that Jehovah, the Unchanging One, the Eternal I Am, is at the same time the Saving One (Jesus), who was anointed of the Father (Christ, the Messiah) to come down among God's children (Immanuel) to complete His mission of love that alone could bring about the work and glory of the Father.

The Savior has both the name as well as the aim of divinity. If we are to fulfill our mission in life successfully, we too must remember who we are as sons and daughters of God, and at the same time do the will of the Father and the Son in living up to every holy commitment and promise that we make before God.

2. THE LORD WILL REMEMBER ZION AND CAUSE HER FAITHFUL TO FLOURISH

THEME: The covenant promises of the Lord will be fulfilled as He blesses His righteous servants with vitality, strength, fruitfulness, and spiritual enlightenment.

He shall feed his flock like a shepherd: he shall gather the lambs with his arm, and carry them in his bosom, and shall gently lead those that are with young. (Isa. 40:11)

But they that wait upon the Lord shall renew their strength; they shall mount up with wings as eagles; they shall run, and not be weary; and they shall walk, and not faint. (Isa. 40:31)

But thou, Israel, art my servant, Jacob whom I have chosen, the seed of Abraham my friend. (Isa. 41:8)

Fear thou not; for I am with thee: be not dismayed; for I am thy God: I will strengthen thee; yea, I will uphold thee with the right hand of my righteousness. (Isa. 41:10)

I will pour my spirit upon thy seed, and my blessings upon thine offspring. (Isa. 44:3)

I have chosen thee in the furnace of affliction. (Isa. 48:10)

MOMENT OF TRUTH

Isaiah inventoried in unforgettable fashion the qualities that characterize the Savior: He is the source of all strength, truth, and atoning grace. He nourishes us with His Spirit, counsels us when we are wanting, listens to our prayers, and keeps us "graven" upon the palms of His hands (Isa. 49:16). Isaiah used tactile imagery and concrete metaphors to edify the people's minds and teach them of infinite things. He spoke of streams and eagles, shepherds and mountains, refiner's fire, and waves of the sea—all with an eye to glorifying God and turning hearts to the ways of obedience.

MODERN PROPHETS SPEAK

Joseph Fielding Smith:
> The Lord promised that in the last days he would gather them and cleanse them. They could have been cleansed and retained their promised lands, but they turned from serving the Lord, and this great punishment came upon them. Now, in these last days, the Lord is remembering his promises to them, and the gathering has commenced both to the land of Zion, which is America, and to Jerusalem, or the land of Palestine. (*AGQ*, 2:180)

Spencer W. Kimball:
> I remember that the Lord was long-suffering with ancient Israel. For a long time he endured their pettiness, listened to their eternal complaining, revolted at their filthiness, groaned at their idolatries and their adulteries, and wept at their faithlessness, and yet finally forgave them and led the rising generation of them into the promised land. They had been the victims of four centuries of destructive background of servitude, but consistent now with their continued faithfulness, every door was opened to them toward immortality and eternal life. (*Faith Precedes the Miracle* [Salt Lake City: Deseret Book, 1972], 299)

ILLUSTRATIONS FOR OUR TIMES

The Strength of the Scriptures
All mortals traverse varied and shifting pathways. All of us find that the route of mortality passes through both rocky terrain as well as pleasant pastures, treacherous valleys as well as glorious summits. A number of years ago, I was facing a particularly challenging period requiring a great deal of faith and courage. The Book of Isaiah, with its sublime passages about the Lord's promises of comfort and deliverance, became a particularly helpful companion, and I often found occasion to derive

strength and spiritual sustenance from its pages. Certain passages began to stand out as particularly memorable formulas of transcendence and hope. I wrote these down in my journal and began to organize them into a pattern of phrases that I could rehearse again and again in moments of particular need. There was enormous strength and vitality that flowed from these quiet moments reviewing the prophet Isaiah's inspired writings. I would often walk in the early hours of the day before sunrise and in the late hours after sunset to ponder these comforting passages and seek guidance from the Spirit—guidance that would always come just when it was most needed. Each of us can turn to the scriptures and find in them personalized answers to our needs as sons and daughters of our Father in Heaven.

The Lord Does Not Forget Us

We are the reason for His sacrifice. He seeks to gather us even as a hen gathers her chicks. He remembers us, for we are engraven in His hand, and the faithful shall remember Him. This remembering will cause us to grow and flourish, for we will become even as He is.

Knowing that the Lord knows me and cares about me brings a sense of self-esteem and self-worth. He cares about all of His children. As we become faithful, He will endow us with blessings of success. These blessings are manifested in the growth of Zion—having a people who are pure in heart. We become part of His team. We can do our part. We are part of the whole body of Christ, and each has an important function.

I remember as a young boy trying out for various athletic teams, and there were always "cuts" made from the team, supposedly leaving only the "best" players on the team. This always caused me great anxiety. Would I make it? The beautiful part of the gospel of Jesus Christ is that all are needed. We just need to be worthy and willing, then we all can help. There is no competition with others, only ourselves. This is the key to helping Zion flourish—be pure in heart, be available and willing to serve. Always remember to give credit to the Lord. This way we will remember God, and we can flourish as instruments in His hands to bless others.

3. LATTER-DAY MISSION FOR THE COVENANT PEOPLE

THEME: Under the Abrahamic covenant, the Saints of God are to take the message of redemption to the world. Bolstered by the strength of Gentile support, Zion is to emerge from the wilderness and become a light to all nations in preparation for the Second Coming.

> *And the glory of the Lord shall be revealed, and all flesh shall see it together: for the mouth of the Lord hath spoken it.* (Isa. 40:5)

I the Lord have called thee in righteousness, and will hold thine hand, and will keep thee, and give thee for a covenant of the people, for a light of the Gentiles. (Isa. 42:6; compare 49:3)

I will place salvation in Zion for Israel my glory. (Isa. 46:13)

In the shadow of his hand hath he hid me, and made me a polished shaft; in his quiver hath he hid me; And said unto me, Thou art my servant, O Israel, in whom I will be glorified. (Isa. 49:2–3)

Sing, O heavens; and be joyful, O earth; and break forth into singing, O mountains: for the Lord hath comforted his people, and will have mercy upon his afflicted. (Isa. 49:13)

MOMENT OF TRUTH

Isaiah foresaw the restoration of the gospel and the establishment of the kingdom of God as a blessing to the world in its final hours. The Lord, he declared, would remember the remnants of Israel and gather His forces together as a standard for the nations. He would shape the events of human history to allow the coming forth of His Church: "Thus saith the Lord God, Behold, I will lift up mine hand to the Gentiles, and set up my standard to the people: and they shall bring thy sons in their arms, and thy daughters shall be carried upon their shoulders. And kings shall be thy nursing fathers, and their queens thy nursing mothers" (Isa. 49:22–23).

MODERN PROPHETS SPEAK

Matthias F. Cowley:
> They, knowing that the atonement of Christ and the principles of the Gospel must apply to those who lived before His coming as well as to all who came after, understood that the millions who died without the Gospel in this life must hear and obey in the life to come. Isaiah prophesied concerning the mission of the Son of God: "I, the Lord, have called thee in righteousness, and will hold thine hand, and will keep thee, and give thee for a covenant of the people, for a light of the Gentiles; to open the blind eyes; to bring out the prisoners from the prison, and them that sit in darkness out of the prison house" (Isa. xlii: 6, 7). (*Cowley's Talks on Doctrine* [Chattanooga: Ben. E. Rich, 1902], 125)

Boyd K. Packer:
> We are a covenant people. We covenant to give of our resources in time and money and talent—all we are and all we possess—to the interest of the kingdom of God upon the

earth. In simple terms, we covenant to do good. We are a covenant people, and the temple is the center of our covenants. It is the source of the covenant. (*The Holy Temple* [Salt Lake City: Bookcraft, 1980], 170)

ILLUSTRATIONS FOR OUR TIMES

The Covenant Duty

Something we might never have supposed is evident in our study of the Old Testament. We, the covenant people, the seed of Abraham, have the responsibility of taking the gospel to the world. Having discussed this, it seems only appropriate that we reemphasize the primary responsibility of missionary work as taught by the Prophet Joseph. He said, "After all that has been said, the greatest and most important duty is to preach the Gospel" (*HC* 2:478). Souls are precious, and the work and glory of our Lord are preeminent. This is the purpose of the Church—to invite all to come unto Christ. Missionary work is our dispensation's duty (see Jacob 5:70–71; Alma 13:3–7; 29:9–10; 36:24; Mormon 9:22; D&C 33:8–11; 88:81; 138:53–57; etc.).

The Bishop without a Collar

Many years ago, I had an experience that demonstrated how members of the Church are very much in the spotlight at all times. An interfaith gathering of ecclesiastical leaders was being sponsored by a community agency in a large city in the eastern United States where I was living with my family, and, as the bishop of the local ward, I decided to attend and represent our congregation. As it turned out, the circle of attendees was fairly small—several dozen—so the sponsoring group had us all introduce ourselves. There was a minister from one group, a pastor from another, and—since the area was predominantly Catholic—a wide variety of priests from different parts of the city.

When my turn finally came, I introduced myself simply as the bishop of our congregation. The reaction took me by surprise. All eyes immediately turned toward me in wonderment at how this young man in a suit, white shirt, and tie could possibly be representing such an august office. It was a teaching moment that allowed me to explain to a captive audience the office of a lay bishop in The Church of Jesus Christ of Latter-day Saints, with its several duties to organize a hundred or more volunteer workers to care for the needs of many hundreds of members of the group—just as in the primitive Church. Even a humble graduate student with a small family might well be selected to serve in the office and would willingly do his part for the building up of the kingdom of God.

All listeners received the instruction in the spirit of good fellowship and community cooperation, and I was able to convey my testimony of the truthfulness of the gospel in all sincerity while savoring the irony of being the youngest non-collared bishop the group had ever met. Thus was fulfilled once more the Lord's covenant promise, comfirmed in so many variations each day throughout the world, "That the fulness of my gospel might be proclaimed by the weak and the simple unto the ends of the world" (D&C 1:23).

SUMMARY

There is no other way back to Heavenly Father than in and through the Lord Jesus Christ. He is our Savior. This should become our goal: "Learn of me [Christ], and listen to my words; walk in the meekness of my Spirit, and you shall have peace in me" (D&C 19:23). The goodness of God and our Savior are always evident, for They never forget Their children. Therefore, we should always remember Them, thus gaining the Spirit in our lives and being able to bless others and ourselves as directed by that Spirit. In response to such a blessing, we have the opportunity to spread the gospel of Jesus Christ. It is our privilege to be saviors on Mount Zion (Obad. 1:21) and share the gospel of everlasting life. Thus we can personally see the fulfillment of the Lord's promise, "Look unto me, and be ye saved" (Isa. 45:22).

CHAPTER THIRTY-NINE

"FOR *the* LORD SHALL COMFORT ZION"

Reading Assignment: Isaiah 50–53.

Additional Reading: Mosiah 14–15.

> *I forewarn you therefore to cultivate righteousness and faithfulness in your-selves, which is the only passport into celestial happiness.* (Brigham Young, *JD* 2:132)

THEMES *for* LIVING

1. The Joy of Salvation
2. The Eternal Author of Salvation
3. The Sacred Responsibilities of Those Who Seek Salvation

INTRODUCTION

Isaiah's words are sustained by a vision of the transcendent and sublime mission of the Redeemer and the atoning power of the Father's plan of salvation. We hear the repeat-ed expressions of joy as Israel's faithful are gathered once again to the protecting care of Zion's resorts. We see in our mind's eye the unfolding of the earthly ministry of the Savior and His condescension in coming among the children of men with saving grace. We listen as Isaiah continually reminds us of our covenant obligations.

1. THE JOY OF SALVATION

THEME: No joy can compare with the comfort and peace that come to individuals and families through the mission of the Savior. The redeeming blessings He brings into the lives of the humble and obedient are sources of unending joy and thanksgiving.

> *For the Lord shall comfort Zion: he will comfort all her waste places; and he will make her wilderness like Eden, and her desert like the garden of the Lord; joy and gladness shall be found therein, thanksgiving, and the voice of melody.* (Isa. 51:3)

> *How beautiful upon the mountains are the feet of him that bringeth good tidings, that publisheth peace; that bringeth good tidings of good, that publisheth salvation; that saith unto Zion, Thy God reigneth!* (Isa. 52:7)

MOMENT OF TRUTH

Isaiah articulated with masterful imagery and dynamic expression the incomparable joy of the Saints at the enlivening, revitalizing power of the gospel.

MODERN PROPHETS SPEAK

Marvin J. Ashton:
> Good cheer is a state of mind or mood that promotes happiness or joy. . . . With God's help, good cheer permits us to rise above the depressing present or difficult circumstances. It is a process of positive reassurance and reinforcement. It is sunshine when clouds block the light. (*Be of Good Cheer* [Salt Lake City: Deseret Book, 1987], 1–2)

George Q. Cannon:
> Whence comes your enjoyment? Whence come the glorious feelings that you have when you feel the best? Do they come from the outside? Do external circumstances produce real happiness of the kind that I describe? Doubtless, they contribute to happiness; but the purest joy, the greatest happiness, that which is most heavenly proceeds from within. A man must carry the principles of happiness and the love of God in his own breast, or he will not be happy. It is not true enjoyment when it comes from any other source. Not from without, therefore, must we expect happiness and exaltation but from within. Deity is within us, and its development brings happiness and joy inexpressible. (*Gospel Truth: Discourses and Writings of President George Q. Cannon* [Salt Lake City: Deseret Book, 1987], 78)

ILLUSTRATIONS FOR OUR TIMES

A Lesson in Patience

On that Saturday morning, I said good-bye to my wife and young family and started the hour-long drive to the neighboring city to attend a stake leadership meeting. As I drove alone down the highway, I wondered how many such meetings I had attended in the past, and I lost count. A spirit of resentment came upon me, and I struggled to maintain my positive attitude. How I missed my family at that moment! I must not have been attending to the time adequately, for as I drove into the parking lot of the stake center, I noticed that the hour had already arrived. Hurriedly I gathered up my materials and rushed into the building. Then it happened. The strains of a familiar song greeted my ears. "O that I were an angel, and could have the wish of mine heart." These were the words of Alma I was hearing, set to a beautiful melody and sung by a chorus. As I neared the chapel doors and then took my place among the assembled crowd, I heard the rest: "O that I were an angel, and could have the wish of mine heart, that I might go forth and speak with the trump of God, with a voice to shake the earth, and cry repentance unto every people!" (Alma 29:1). It was the fervent prayer of the prophet Alma as he sought strength and guidance to bring his people closer to the Lord, "that there might not be more sorrow upon all the face of the earth" (v. 2). I remembered that his prayer was answered shortly thereafter as he found the inspiration to protect his flock from the treacherous mistruths of the antichrist Korihor. And his prayer was answered again as he found the inspiration to "try the virtue of the word of God" (Alma 31:5) in teaching the ostracized Zoramites one of the greatest lessons on faith ever uttered.

I repented that Saturday, having been reminded so dramatically of the need for prayerful preparation in carrying out our duties as Latter-day Saints. I repented for being jealous of a few hours of time, when the founding elders of the Church were often called upon to spend years away from their families in the building up of the kingdom of God. I repented for my narrowness of heart when the Lord was waiting to expand, edify, nurture, nourish, and exalt—if only the people would let Him. Isaiah articulated the feelings of the Lord regarding His penitent covenant people: "For a small moment have I forsaken thee; but with great mercies will I gather thee. In a little wrath I hid my face from thee for a moment; but with everlasting kindness will I have mercy on thee, saith the Lord thy Redeemer" (Isa. 54:7–8). That Saturday morning, I learned a lesson in patience: "Therefore it is expedient in me that mine elders should wait for a little season, for the redemption of Zion" (D&C 105:13). When we wait faithfully upon the Lord, we can look forward to the joy of salvation and the glory of eternal life.

2. THE ETERNAL AUTHOR OF SALVATION

THEME: The Lord Jesus Christ wrought His atoning sacrifice on behalf of all mankind, and thus became the Father of those whose salvation He purchased through His blood.

I gave my back to the smiters, and my cheeks to them that plucked off the hair: I hid not my face from shame and spitting. For the Lord God will help me. (Isa. 50:6–7)

And who shall declare his generation? for he was cut off out of the land of the living: for the transgression of my people was he stricken. . . . Yet it pleased the Lord to bruise him; he hath put him to grief: when thou shalt make his soul an offering for sin, he shall see his seed, he shall prolong his days, and the pleasure of the Lord shall prosper in his hand. (Isa. 53:8, 10)

MOMENT OF TRUTH

Isaiah foresaw in vivid detail the mission and sufferings of the Lord, who accomplished the will of the Father by offering Himself as the redeeming sacrifice for all mankind, and opening up the way of eternal life for all who obey His commandments.

MODERN PROPHETS SPEAK

David O. McKay:

Indifference toward religion is a dangerous state of mind. The most precious thing in all the world is to accept God as our Father, to accept his Son as our Redeemer, our Savior, and to know in one's heart that the Father and the Son appeared in this dispensation and gave the gospel of Jesus Christ for the happiness, salvation, and exaltation of the human family. To accept that as an eternal truth is to have the greatest possession that the human mind can possess. (*Man May Know for Himself: Teachings of President David O. McKay* [Salt Lake City: Deseret Book, 1967], 145)

Howard W. Hunter:

Without the Atonement there would be no hope of eternal life. Modernists dispute that the Master voluntarily offered himself to atone for the sins of mankind, and they deny that there was in fact such an atonement. It is our firm belief that it is a reality, and nothing is more important in the entire divine plan of salvation than the atoning sacrifice of Jesus Christ. We believe that salvation comes because of the Atonement. In its absence the whole plan of creation would come to naught. (*THWH*, 7)

ILLUSTRATIONS FOR OUR TIMES

A Christmas Story—Not for the Fainthearted

It was the morning of Christmas Eve on a clear, crisp winter day. The emergency came with no warning. The only sign of distress was word from our neighbors across the street that there was some difficulty with the sewer system running below and down the center of our street, and sludge was threatening to back up through the basement drains in their home. A utility expert was summoned, and he quickly determined that a major blockage had occurred in a shaft in the middle of the street not far from our home, causing the sewage to back up. Our home was in fact next in line, and if nothing was done, we faced the prospect of having the lower level of our home flooded with the noxious material. The shaft beneath the manhole cover appeared to be some eight to ten feet deep and was filling rapidly with sewage. The blockage was at the bottom of the shaft, and the workman was unable to dislodge the problem with his grappling tools. What could be done? We were only minutes away from a major flood in our home. I looked at the workman in utter helplessness.

Suddenly, I saw him swing into action. He removed his shoes and his jacket. "You are surely not going down into that shaft!" I exclaimed. His response was simply that it had to be done. I watched with horror as he wrapped a handkerchief across his mouth, took a deep breath, and disappeared into the muck, emerging a minute later covered with ooze from head to foot. I sprayed him off with the garden hose until finally I could plainly see his smile emerging from the debris. He had solved the problem. The slime in the shaft began to recede. Our home was saved! He had given us a Christmas present of incalculable value. Later that evening, I located his home in another part of the city, and my wife and I delivered a large box of candy and a thank-you card. His wife told us that this was not the first time her husband had sacrificed himself that way on behalf of utility customers.

I have told this story many times to smaller groups, always with the anticipated reaction of listeners who recoil in horror at the thought of a man submitting himself willingly to such a distasteful experience in order to protect the well-being of customers. But then they see the point. It is, after all, a Christmas story that echoes the sublime truth that another figure, a divine figure, accomplished on a cosmic scale the very same thing, submerging Himself willingly below the accumulated refuse of all the failings of mankind in all ages, diverting the poison of transgression, neutralizing the effects of sin—if only we would accept His sacrifice in the spirit of faith and obedience, and endure to the end. How the Savior accomplished His atoning sacrifice remains a mystery beyond our grasp. But He did it. "Though he were a Son, yet learned he obedience by the things which he suffered; And being made perfect, he became the author of eternal salvation unto all them that obey him" (Heb. 5:8–9). His sufferings were intense: "For behold, I, God, have suffered these things for all, that they might not suffer if they would repent: But if they would not repent they must suffer even as I; Which suffering caused myself, even God, the greatest of all, to tremble because of pain, and to bleed at every pore, and to suffer both body and spirit—and would that I might not drink the bitter cup, and shrink—Nevertheless, glory be to the Father, and I partook and finished my preparations unto the children of men" (D&C 19:16–19). How noble and inspiring is the story of the Atonement. How worthy of valiant obedience and humble thanksgiving.

The Atonement Is the Key to the Mighty Change

We must understand and appreciate the Atonement of the Lord and make it efficacious in our lives by obedience to the principles and ordinances of the gospel, then go forward with the message of salvation. When we understand this doctrine, when we appreciate it and apply it to our lives, we change. We become converted. And converted people are different people. They act differently. They are grateful. They feel indebted to the Lord for their very lives.

On one occasion while I was serving as president of the Missionary Training Center, a branch president called—he needed help quickly. One of the missionaries had threatened his companion, he was disruptive in class, and the district was losing the Spirit they felt because of him. He wasn't easily entreated. He wanted to go home. He hated his mission, and besides, he didn't want to be there in the first place. This missionary wanted to go home now, and the branch president was ready to have him go, too. The situation was critical. An interview was arranged, the missionary sat down, and our tender interview began.

"How do you feel, Elder?"

"Lousy. I want to leave now, but I knew I had to talk to you before I left, so here I am."

We visited a little to get acquainted, I tried to set him at ease, and then I invited the Spirit to attend us. We discussed home, family, and life in general. Then I asked him how he felt about Heavenly Father. He was frustrated and didn't fully understand his relationship with God or the many blessings he had received at His hand. So we began. We talked of God's goodness and tender mercy. We rehearsed how much He had done for us and how we should love Him for all of this. He began to become serious-minded as he caught hold of the meaning of some of the words. He became meek, lowly, and very teachable. The Spirit had touched his heart. We discussed the love of God and the infinite Atonement of Christ. We read portions of Jacob's sermon in 2 Nephi 9. I could see a change. The words were softening his heart and bringing a depth of understanding he had not known or felt before. The Atonement was beginning to make an impact on his heart and mind. He was filled with gratitude, and he wanted to do good. Tears welled up in his eyes. We cried together. He cried out, "Oh, President, I'm so mixed up. I want to stay. I love the Lord. I need help."

The lack of understanding and the magnitude of the change were too much all at once for him. We prayed and planned how he could gain strength to become the Lord's missionary. He did. He stayed and prepared to serve the Lord, and served his mission well. Understanding and appreciating the Atonement of our Savior made a difference in his life. This is coming unto Christ. When we apply the Atonement to our lives, we come unto Christ and can be perfected in Him. It is the Atonement that brings about this mighty change in the hearts of the children of men. We apply the atonement of Jesus Christ to our lives by partaking of the principles and ordinances of the gospel, and by enduring to the end. Then is the Atonement efficacious; then we remember the goodness of God, and our love for Him increases. As we depend on Him in all things and become truly humble, we are taught the doctrine of the Atonement and come to understand it, appreciate it, and bring it into our hearts.

3. THE SACRED RESPONSIBILITIES OF THOSE WHO SEEK SALVATION

THEME: The plan of salvation requires strict and enduring compliance with the covenant obligations. The sons and daughters of God must practice holiness before the Lord and honor and obey His law.

> *Who is among you that feareth the Lord, that obeyeth the voice of his servant, that walketh in darkness, and hath no light? let him trust in the name of the Lord, and stay upon his God.* (Isa. 50:10)

> *Awake, awake; put on thy strength, O Zion; put on thy beautiful garments, O Jerusalem, the holy city.* (Isa. 52:1)

> *Depart ye, depart ye, go ye out from thence, touch no unclean thing; go ye out of the midst of her; be ye clean, that bear the vessels of the Lord.* (Isa. 52:11)

MOMENT OF TRUTH

Isaiah gives a clear statement of what is expected of all who participate in the plan of salvation—obedience, honoring priesthood covenants, virtue and cleanliness, and living lives full of righteousness and joy.

MODERN PROPHETS SPEAK

Ezra Taft Benson:

> There are three great and important obligations, possibly overshadowing all others, which rest upon this people and upon this great Church of Jesus Christ of Latter-day Saints. The first of these, at least in the order of emphasis in this dispensation, is that of missionary work—the responsibility which rests upon this people to carry the message of the restored gospel to the people of the world. We have been engaged in that work ever since the Church was organized, yea, even before. Second, we have the responsibility of building up the stakes and wards and branches of Zion. This entails the providing of facilities—houses of worship, temples, seminary buildings—that are so necessary for us to carry on the spiritual part of the program. It entails taking care of our people—temporally, physically, culturally, and socially, as well as spiritually. And in the third place, we have the great responsibility of performing certain sacred ordinances in the temples of the Lord—a responsibility which rests upon every holder of the priesthood as well as upon the sisters of the Church. (*TETB,* 175)

Gordon B. Hinckley:

> Every young man seeking to please his Heavenly Father would be willing and anxious to give approximately a tithe of his life at the age of nineteen or twenty to go into the world to preach the gospel. He would save his money for this; he would plan his life's program around it; he would keep himself physically, mentally, and morally alert, as well as spiritually strong, to be prepared for this great and sacred responsibility. (*TGBH,* 346)

ILLUSTRATIONS FOR OUR TIMES

To Save the Children

Anyone would have done the same thing. I just happened to be looking out the window one afternoon and noticed that the neighbor's huge Alaskan Malamute dog was on the loose, moving stealthily toward a young boy across the street. I froze in horror as I saw the dog suddenly lunge toward the boy and bite him severely and repeatedly about the head. Instinctively, I rushed from the house toward the bloody scene, screaming at the top of my lungs. The dog backed off, and the boy was able to escape and run into his house. The outcome had a happy ending for the boy, who after a few stitches was soon on the road to recovery. Unfortunately, the dog had to be sacrificed in the interests of neighborhood safety. To this day, the boy—now a young man—considers me a hero, even though I did nothing more than what others would have done. When we see the immediate unfolding of danger around us, we normally take steps to thwart it. Parents are constantly pulling their children from harm's way, and friends often respond quickly when their associates are in danger. I recall once hiking in the Canadian Rockies with a young pal, who stepped too close to the edge of a precipice and would have fallen to his death had I not instinctively reached out and gently restored his teetering balance.

Such obvious need brings immediate and decisive response in all of us. But are we equally responsive to the duties of spiritual living? Do we take action of a decisive character on behalf of our families and friends when invisible forces and influences around them threaten their well-being? More everyday heroism of a spiritual kind is called for in the interests of saving the children of God. More hour-by-hour service is needed to emulate the character of Jesus Christ as Redeemer, Deliverer, Savior, Light of the World, and Good Shepherd. It takes a special kind of heroism to contribute a word of encouragement or warning at the right time, to turn off the television or turn on the computer filtering system as needed, to preserve the sanctity of the Sabbath by supplanting activities of a recreational kind with spiritual duties, to say no to illicit drugs, to draw the line on improper amusements and immodest dress, to clear one's life of pride and unwise priorities. Our homes need heroes of this kind. Our lives need the valor of spiritual heroism and more evidence of "a godly walk and conversation" (D&C 20:69), and our ears and hearts need to be more responsive to the prophet's voice: "For by doing these things the gates of hell shall not prevail against you; yea, and the Lord God will disperse the powers of darkness from before you, and cause the heavens to shake for your good, and his name's glory" (D&C 21:6).

SUMMARY

Happiness and joy come through obedience, which in turn leads to righteousness, which causes us to serve and bless others. This is joy. This is happiness. This is life eternal. The Atonement is at the core of the gospel, and only by applying it in our lives can we partake of the goodness of God and our Savior. The responsibility of each son or daughter of God is to become pure in heart, free from sin through repentance and the atonement of Jesus Christ. As we are converted, it is our duty to warn our neighbors (see D&C 88:81) and invite all to come unto Christ. In this way, we can help build the kingdom and open up avenues of peace and spiritual harmony for our families.

CHAPTER FORTY

"GREAT SHALL BE *the* PEACE *of* THY CHILDREN"

Reading Assignment: Isaiah 54–56; 36–65.

The world has had a fair trial for six thousand years; the Lord will try the seventh thousand Himself. . . . Satan will be bound, and the works of darkness destroyed; righteousness will be put to the line and judgment to the plummet, and "he that fears the Lord will alone be exalted in that day." (Joseph Smith, HC 5:64–65)

THEMES *for* LIVING

1. Strengthening the Stakes of the Kingdom
2. The Blessings of the Gathering of Israel
3. Waiting in Hope and Gratitude for the Second Coming and the Millennium

INTRODUCTION

The power and mission of the Redeemer, as He said, is to "draw all men unto me" (3 Ne. 27:14). Isaiah saw with transparent clarity the inexorable gathering power of the gospel of Jesus Christ. The gathering under divine decree is a convergence of many keys, influences, powers, and blessings. Three of these aspects are explored in great detail by

Isaiah: (1) the appointed *locus* of the gathering, i.e., the stakes of Zion worldwide; (2) the *aegis* of the gathering, i.e., in and through the holy name of the Lord Jesus Christ, who alone holds the power and authority to endow mankind with the blessings of salvation and exaltation; and (3) the culminating *purpose* of the gathering, i.e., to lay the foundation for the return of the Redeemer and the ushering in of the millennial reign.

1. STRENGTHENING THE STAKES OF THE KINGDOM

THEME: The tent of Zion, with its securing stakes and reinforcing cords, is the perfect image for the refuge afforded by the kingdom of God. Just as the temple is symbolized by the immovable mountain of the Lord, Zion itself, as a tent, is shown as agile and growing, flexible and expanding, lithe and unfolding. The Saints of Zion can thus internalize the fixed and unchanging character of eternal principles as well as the responsive and dynamic character of the expanding kingdom whose saving and protecting influence extends into all quarters of the earth.

Enlarge the place of thy tent, and let them stretch forth the curtains of thine habitations: spare not, lengthen thy cords, and strengthen thy stakes. (Isa. 54:2)

MOMENT OF TRUTH

Isaiah was given a prophetic view of the canopy of Zion, with its ever-expanding scope as the kingdom of God spreading throughout the world. His language perfectly captures the role of Zion's communities as the gathering places for the faithful. The message of Zion is one of spiritual stability in times of chaos and confusion.

MODERN PROPHETS SPEAK

Joseph Fielding Smith:
> The expression "stake of Zion," first used in the revelation given in November 1831 (Sec. 68) is taken from the expression in Isaiah: "Look upon Zion, the city of our solemnities; thine eyes shall see Jerusalem a quiet habitation, a tabernacle that shall not be taken down; not one of the stakes thereof shall ever be removed, neither shall any of the cords thereof be broken" (Isa. 33:20). Again: "Enlarge the place of thy tent and let them stretch forth the curtains of thine habitation: spare not, lengthen thy cords, and strengthen thy stakes" (Isa. 54:2). Isaiah speaks of Zion as a tent, or tabernacle, having in mind the Tabernacle which was built and carried in the wilderness in the days of Moses, and the cords are the binding cables that extend from the tent, or tabernacle, to the stakes which are fastened in the ground. Now, the Lord

revealed that Zion was to be built and surrounding her would be the stakes helping to bind and keep her in place. This figure of speech has almost been lost through the intervening years, but it retains its significance, or beauty. To speak of Zion, the new Jerusalem, or even that section where the city will be built as a stake of Zion is a sad mistake. Zion is the tent, the stakes of Zion are the binding pegs that support her. Zion, therefore, cannot be a stake, it would be as improper to call a tent a stake as to apply this term to Zion. (*Church History and Modern Revelation* [Salt Lake City: The Church of Jesus Christ of Latter-day Saints, 1946–49], 2:88)

Spencer W. Kimball:

The idea of "lengthening our stride" or "stretching our muscles" or "reaching our highest" has an interesting scriptural base. The second verse in the fifty-fourth chapter of Isaiah proclaims: "Enlarge the place of thy tent, and let them stretch forth the curtains of thine habitations: spare not, lengthen thy cords, and strengthen thy stakes." (*TSWK,* 175)

ILLUSTRATIONS FOR OUR TIMES

Senior Missionaries

Isaiah spoke not only Messianically, but he also spoke of kingdom building throughout his writings. Missionary work and perfecting the Saints in preparation for the Second Coming is admonished continually. Today, one of the greatest needs in the Church is senior missionaries. Here are some of the feelings of two senior missionary couples presently serving:

What could possibly be more exciting than to be able to serve the Lord and His people, our brothers and sisters? You may serve in your own stake and out of your own home, or from Salt Lake City to Mongolia! There must be over a thousand types of jobs to do. You can repair bicycles or proselyte in Spanish in Montreal!

Alma, Ammon, and others left their homes and went out to preach the gospel. Some even went directly to their "enemies." Think of how exciting it would be to do this in your own life. You can be an "Alma" today. And your wife can be "Sister Alma!"

We are on our second day in the Senior MTC, and it is already worth it. The Spirit is thick around us, and we are overwhelmed with the love of Jesus Christ. We will still travel and enjoy this great earth He created, but we will be so blessed to be able to serve Him. Even better than all the above: Our families will be blessed by our serving this mission.

There is no question. There is nothing more exciting than serving the Lord. We thank God for this opportunity and blessing and bear witness that Jesus is the Christ and has blessed us immeasurably.

B. Thomas & Rose Hopkins

From the very beginning of our marriage, my wife and I have planned to serve a mission together. Now our daughter (our last child) is in the MTC, and we are fulfilling our dream. I love my Heavenly Father and my Savior and I want to demonstrate that love by helping others of His children to come back home. When I contemplate their uncomprehendable sacrifice I feel a great need to give of myself to help make it effective in the lives of my brothers and sisters. How can I look upon the wounds of the atonement without shrinking if I have not given my best in His service? There is nothing to compare with the feeling here in the SMTC.

B. Gary Jespersen

The Seeds of Greatness

A number of years ago, while serving in the Young Men's organization of one of the wards, I had the privilege of developing a training retreat for the youth serving in leadership positions. One of the themes was to strengthen the wards and stakes by seeing the value of each person. As the youth leaders were assembling on the bus in preparation for the journey to the retreat site, they were reminded of the scripture from 1 Samuel 16:7: "man looketh on the outward appearance, but the Lord looketh on the heart." They were asked to watch for opportunities that day to serve others without regard to outward appearance.

A mile or two down the road, as it turned out, we passed a homeless person walking along the road, disheveled, unkempt, and tattered. We asked the driver to pull over and stop about half a block beyond the vagabond. "Should we interrupt our retreat to help this person?" was the question posed to the young people. Clearly some were wondering if that would be the appropriate thing to do—after all, the whole day was already planned around a fun program.

After some discussion, however, the group was unanimous in the decision to stop and help the homeless person. By then, he had caught up with the bus, and we opened the door and invited him to come in. With some difficulty, he mounted the steps of the vehicle and then stood there, somewhat embarrassed, under the silent, watchful gaze of several dozen young people. He began to express his appreciation for the help, and it did not take the young people long to discern that this was indeed a special person hidden under the dirty and torn rags of clothing he was wearing. In fact, it was the bishop himself—and his brief and loving remarks about seeing the value in every person cast a spiritual glow over the rest of the day. The apostle Paul asked, "Do ye look on things after the outward appearance? If any man trust to himself that he is Christ's, let him of himself think this again, that, as he is Christ's, even so are we Christ's" (2 Cor. 10:7). What greater way to strengthen wards and stakes than to perceive within all members of the body of Christ the seeds of greatness as sons and daughters of God?

2. THE BLESSINGS OF THE GATHERING OF ISRAEL

THEME: Even though the Lord's ways are higher than man's ways, and His thoughts higher than man's thoughts (Isa. 55:9), He nevertheless succors His people with mercy, grace, and a gathering hand.

> *Even unto them will I give in mine house and within my walls a place and a name better than of sons and of daughters: I will give them an everlasting name, that shall not be cut off.* (Isa. 56:5)

> *For mine house shall be called an house of prayer for all people.* (Isa. 56:7)

MOMENT OF TRUTH

Isaiah saw things from the heavenly perspective; thus he could reveal the broadness and scope of the Lord's plan to gather home the flock of His faithful and valiant servants—not only the covenant people by birth, but all those who are adopted into the fold through faith, repentance, and the baptism of water and fire.

MODERN PROPHETS SPEAK

Bruce R. McConkie:

> Thus, the gathering of Israel is both spiritual and temporal. The lost sheep gather spiritually when they join the Church, and they gather temporally when they come to a prepared place—that is, to Zion or one of her stakes. There they can strengthen each other in the Lord; there they can receive for themselves, in holy houses built for that very purpose, the covenant made in days of old with Abraham, Isaac, and Israel. There they can redeem their dead through the vicarious ordinances of the temples. Speaking of places and locales, Zion itself (the New Jerusalem) has not as yet been established in our day, but it will be in due course. For the present, the Lord's people, who are Zion, are called to gather in the stakes of Zion as these are established in the lands of their inheritance. (*A New Witness for the Articles of Faith* [Salt Lake City: Deseret Book, 1985], 569)

Bruce R. McConkie:

> Why is the Lord gathering Israel in these last days? It is to fulfil the covenant made with Abraham and renewed with Isaac and Jacob and others. What is that covenant? It is not the gathering of Israel per se, but something far more important than the mere assembling of a people in Jerusalem or on Mount Zion or at any designated place. It is not the

allocation of Palestine for the seed of Abraham, or the designation of the Americas as the inheritance of Joseph, though each of these arrangements has a bearing on the fulfillment of the covenant. The gathering of Israel, at whatever place Deity specifies, is a necessary condition precedent, something that makes possible the fulfilling of the ancient covenant. What, then, is the covenant itself? Jehovah promised—covenanted with—his friend Abraham that in him and in his seed, meaning the literal seed of his body, should "all families of the earth be blessed, even with the blessings of the Gospel, which are the blessings of salvation, even of life eternal" (Abr. 2:8–11). (*The Mortal Messiah: From Bethlehem to Calvary* [Salt Lake City: Deseret Book, 1979–81], 4:337–38)

ILLUSTRATIONS FOR OUR TIMES

When a Prophet Weeps for Joy

Go back with me to Wednesday, 12 April 1843. The steamer *Amaranth*—the first up the Mississippi River this season—arrives this day in Nauvoo about noon, at a time when a special three-day conference of the Priesthood (including most of the Twelve) is being conducted. While the conference is busy ordaining elders and sending near-ly ninety missionaries into the field (see *HC* 5:347–49), the ship is delivering some 240 immigrant convert Saints from England, under the leadership of Lorenzo Snow. The Prophet Joseph Smith greets them in person with great joy. A few hours later, at 5:00 P.M., the steamer *Maid of Iowa* arrives with around 200 more Saints from England, under the leadership of Levi Richards and Parley P. Pratt (whose thirty-sixth birthday happens to fall on this day). The Prophet notes in his journal:

> I was present at the landing and the first on board the steamer, when I met Sister Mary Ann Pratt (who had been to England with Brother Parley) and her little daughter, only three or four days old. I could not refrain from shedding tears. So many friends and acquaintances arriving in one day. . . . I was rejoiced to meet them in such good health and fine spirits; for they were equal to any that had ever come to Nauvoo. (*HC* 5:353–54)

Thus the fledgling Church sustains a beehive of activity, spreading the gospel and gathering in the Saints of Zion, as the Lord had commanded. These are the moments of truth that remind us to labor diligently to spread the "good news" so that others might also obtain the blessings of the gospel. "Remember the worth of souls is great in the sight of God; . . . And if it so be that you should labor all your days in crying repentance unto this people, and bring, save it be one soul unto me, how great shall be your joy with him in the kingdom of my Father! And now, if your joy will be great with one soul that you have brought unto me into the kingdom of my Father, how great will be your joy if you should bring many souls unto me!" (D&C 18:10, 15–16).

Following the Light

The Lord wants all of His children who are willing and obedient to come back into His presence (see 2 Ne. 26:33). His tender mercy is extended to all mankind:

- To those who know not God (see Alma 6:6; Isa. 53:3, 5–8)

- To those who repent (see Acts 2:38–39; Isa. 55:6–7; D&C 20:29)

- To those who seek God (see 3 Ne. 12:6; Isa. 55:1–3)

I remember when President Kimball asked us to pray so that the "iron curtain" would come down. We all prayed, and the miracle happened. We now have twenty-two missions in the former eastern bloc of countries and more to come in the near future. Could one ever imagine so great a miracle in our day? Thousands of new members come into the Church every year in that area. Little did Gorbachev realize he was an instrument in the Lord's hands.

Every day the process of repentance is practiced. Repentance is not an event, but rather is a process. As a bishop, my primary goal was to help people repent and to help people avoid temptation and sin. Every time a person started or continued in the process of repentance, I had a dynamic experience with the Atonement of the Lord Jesus Christ. The forgiveness of the Lord is there for all, if they but confess and forsake their sin (see D&C 58:42–43).

There are people throughout the earth who are seeking God . . . trying to find their way, but they are lost, not knowing where to find the truth (see D&C 123:12). We must be "finders." We must be missionaries to help those who seek the truth. We must open our mouths (see D&C 33:8–11, 24:12, 100:5–6). Some of my Book of Mormon students at BYU and the Orem Institute of Religion were nonmembers. They often said after their conversion and baptism, "I didn't know why I came here at the beginning, but now I do. It was to receive the gospel." Surely the Lord leads all of His children who are willing to follow His light.

3. WAITING IN HOPE AND GRATITUDE FOR THE SECOND COMING AND THE MILLENNIUM

THEME: The Millennium is to be ushered in with enormous upheaval and cataclysmic change—a nightmare for the wicked and a blessed dream come true for the faithful. The Son of Man is to return in power and sanctity to perform His final labors before the dawning of the Millennium of peace.

Wherefore art thou red in thine apparel, and thy garments like him that treadeth in the winefat? (Isa. 63:2)

Thou, O Lord, art our father, our redeemer; thy name is from everlasting. (Isa. 63:16)

For since the beginning of the world men have not heard, nor perceived by the ear, neither hath the eye seen, O God, beside thee, what he hath prepared for him that waiteth for him. (Isa. 64:4)

And it shall come to pass, that before they call, I will answer; and while they are yet speaking, I will hear. (Isa. 65:24)

MOMENT OF TRUTH

What vistas were afforded Isaiah as he saw to the ends of the earth and viewed the calamitous and earth-shattering events of the last hours, with the return of the red-mantled Savior to judge the inhabitants of the earth and receive the faithful in a cloud of angelic choirs! Today, His words plead with us to receive the blessings of salvation and exaltation through obedience to the covenant promises. The Lord is so full of mercy and kindness that He hears and answers our prayers even before they are uttered.

MODERN PROPHETS SPEAK

Neal A. Maxwell:

> Thus gospel hope is a very focused and particularized hope that is based upon justified expectations. It is a virtue that is intertwined with faith and charity, which virtues are not to be understood either when they are torn apart from each other or apart from the Lord Jesus Christ, without whom they are all vague virtues. Doubt and despair go together, whereas faith and hope are constant companions. Those, for instance, who "hope" in vain for (and speak of) the day of world peace when men "shall beat their swords into plowshares" ignore the reality that the millennial dawn will be ushered in only by the second coming of Jesus Christ. Neither secular rhetoric nor secular assemblies will succeed in bringing lasting peace to this planet. Secularists, meanwhile, have ironically appropriated the Lord's language of hope while denying Him! It is He and His ways alone that can bring about such desirable conditions. There will be no millennium without the Master. Paul's futuring focused on the Lord, giving us consolation by holding forth that which is to come, confirming hope. But this hope develops, as does faith, "line upon line, precept upon

precept; here a little, and there a little" (D&C 128:21). (*Notwithstanding My Weakness* [Salt Lake City: Deseret Book, 1981], 41–42)

Bruce R. McConkie:

> In our day we look forward with hope and joy to the Second Coming of the Son of Man, and to the setting up of the millennial kingdom of peace and righteousness, over which he shall assume personal rule for the space of a thousand years. We do not know and shall not learn either the day or the hour of that dreadful yet blessed day. We are expected to read the signs of the times and know thereby the approximate time of our Lord's return and to be in constant readiness therefore. (*The Promised Messiah: The First Coming of Christ* [Salt Lake City: Deseret Book, 1978], 457)

ILLUSTRATIONS FOR OUR TIMES

Hope Is Rooted in Christ

Isaiah truly prophesied of the Second Coming of the Lord Jesus Christ and of His peaceful millennial reign. As our minds reflect on these things, we feel a sense of hope, and above all, great gratitude for the Lord. Hope is a power that causes one to endure. Gratitude for the blessings of God is exemplified in the change of our attitude and behavior.

As a teacher for many years, I have witnessed the change of heart of many students. It comes as they embrace the gospel by making sacred covenants and receiving lifesaving ordinances that can bring them back to the presence of our Heavenly Father. This happens when they are full of hope, and the change occurs when gratitude is felt and then expressed through loving obedience to God and service to one's fellow men. This was my underlying goal for my students: be sure they leave the classroom with hope. Hope is rooted in Christ and in the anticipation of eternal life. You really can't exist on this earth and overcome temptation without hope. If one is hopeless, sin lies at the door. Hope is preceded by, and part of, our personal righteousness, for faith and hope are so intertwined they cannot be separated. They truly are the foundation of all righteousness. This is why as parents and teachers we must be positive. We must give people hope to carry on—hope for eternal life which God provided before the world began (see Titus 1:2).

Gratitude, the forgotten virtue, must be taught over and over, for failing to acknowledge the goodness of God and His hand in all that is good is a grievous sin and displeases our Heavenly Father (see D&C 59:21). As gratitude flows from understanding the doctrines, one is truly motivated to change. The words echo in my mind from hundreds of students, said in different ways but communicating the same idea: "I can do it now, Brother Ed. I'm so grateful for my Savior." It's a simple statement, but filled with transcending truth. Isaiah has given this doctrine throughout his work—gratitude to God and hope for a better life through obedience to the Lord and living a righteous life.

"The Seed of the Blessed of the Lord"

Behind the Iron Curtain, we were in the hands of the leadership of the Communist Youth Movement. Would we be subjected to heartless propaganda and find ourselves locked in a hard-nosed debate with our political foes? It didn't turn out that way at all. Our BYU Semester Abroad group was on tour to learn more about Eastern European mores and culture, and the consensus among our students, as well as the members of our young welcoming delegation, was that we should have a party and a dance. So that's what we did.

As I looked on peacefully with my wife and other faculty members, the young people from both sides simply related to each other as human beings, as young people seeking new friendships and new dialogue, as energetic, fun-loving citizens of one grand human family. They danced and laughed and shared insights about life and their hopes for the future. For an hour or two, all potential acrimony about important differences in principles of government was suspended—replaced by a dance. Hope flourished. Peace abounded. Friendship took root. It was, in a sense, an anticipatory microcosm of the millennial era, when borders would dissolve and the government would be in the hands of a divine Ruler with infinitely more wisdom than anyone on earth. "For, behold, I create new heavens and a new earth: and the former shall not be remembered, nor come into mind. . . . And I will rejoice in Jerusalem, and joy in my people: and the voice of weeping shall be no more heard in her, nor the voice of crying. . . . They shall not labour in vain, nor bring forth for trouble; for they are the seed of the blessed of the Lord, and their offspring with them. And it shall come to pass, that before they call, I will answer; and while they are yet speaking, I will hear" (Isa. 65:17, 19, 23–24).

SUMMARY

Where in the world can one obtain hope, peace, harmony, and security? Isaiah proclaimed the answer to this question in magnificent, flowing language imbued with the Spirit of revelation and prophecy. The hope of Israel is to be found in the process of gathering with the Saints of God in holy places, i.e., the homes, stakes, and temples of Zion. The peace of Israel is to be obtained in and through the "merits, and mercy, and grace of the Holy Messiah" (2 Ne. 2:8). The harmony of Israel will come with the preparations for, and the ushering in, of the millennial reign under the governance of the Lord Himself. And all of this affords the spiritual security that is the object of every honest seeker after truth.

CHAPTER FORTY-ONE

"AND THEY SHALL BE MY PEOPLE"

Reading Assignment: Jeremiah 1–2; 15; 20; 26; 36–38.

The Old and New Testaments, the Book of Mormon, and the book of Doctrine and Covenants . . . are like a lighthouse in the ocean or a finger-post which points out the road we should travel. Where do they point? To the fountain of light. . . . That is what these books are for. They are of God; they are valuable and necessary; by them we can establish the doctrine of Christ. (Brigham Young, *JD* 8:129)

THEMES for LIVING

1. Strength in Adversity
2. The Power of the Word of God

INTRODUCTION

Jeremiah was among the most courageous of the Lord's prophets in boldly completing his mission in the face of fearful abuse and life-threatening adversity. The Lord had planted in his mouth and heart the word of God, and he was charged to deliver it in its pristine purity and awesome power to the ears of the deviant princes of the covenant. Nothing could distract or deter him. The word of God—and only the word of God—has the power to save and exalt. These two themes—strength to carry out one's mission despite adversity, and the blessings and power of the word of God in our lives—form the essence of the message of Jeremiah to his contemporaries as well as to us in the latter days.

1. STRENGTH IN ADVERSITY

THEME: In the strength of the Lord, the Saints shall accomplish all that is required of them. The Church, in the face of all adversity and tyranny, shall fulfill its mission to strengthen God's children, preach the gospel to the world, and hasten the work of the temples. The devotion of every member shall be rewarded with blessings of strength, courage, and fortitude—just as in the case of Jeremiah and all of the Lord's holy prophets.

> *But the Lord said unto me, Say not, I am a child: for thou shalt go to all that I shall send thee, and whatsoever I command thee thou shalt speak. Be not afraid of their faces: for I am with thee to deliver thee, saith the Lord.* (Jer. 1:7)

> *For, behold, I have made thee this day a defenced city, and an iron pillar, and brasen walls against the whole land, against the kings of Judah, against the princes thereof, against the priests thereof, and against the people of the land. And they shall fight against thee; but they shall not prevail against thee; for I am with thee, saith the Lord, to deliver thee.* (Jer. 1:18–19)

MOMENT OF TRUTH

Jeremiah was called of the Lord to preach repentance to a wayward and idolatrous Israel. Unless the people would reverse their course of rejecting the Lord and His covenant in favor of impotent gods of their own devices, they would be overtaken by the Babylonians and taken into captivity. In the face of daunting torment and abuse, Jeremiah remained true to his calling and spoke the Lord's words with courage and great power. "Diminish not a word" (Jer. 26:2) was his charge, and he held back nothing from the ears of the Israelites. At the same time that Lehi and his family were fleeing Jerusalem by command of the Lord, Zedekiah retrieved Jeremiah from the dungeon where he was imprisoned and took him aside secretly, so the princes might not see it, and said, "Is there any word from the Lord? And Jeremiah said, There is: for, said he, thou shalt be delivered into the hand of the king of Babylon" (Jer. 37:17). That is precisely what occurred (see Jer. 39:5).

MODERN PROPHETS SPEAK

Dallin H. Oaks:

> Seen with the perspective of eternity, a temporal setback can be an opportunity to develop soul-power of eternal significance. Strength is forged in adversity. Faith is developed in a setting where we cannot see what lies ahead. (*Pure in Heart* [Salt Lake City: Bookcraft, 1988], 122)

Marvin J. Ashton:

> Adversity will surface in some form in every life. How we prepare for it, how we meet it, makes the difference. We can be broken by adversity, or we can become stronger. The final result is up to the individual. Henry Fielding said: "Adversity is the trial of principle. Without it, a man hardly knows whether he is honest or not." (*Ye Are My Friends* [Salt Lake City: Deseret Book, 1972], 96)

Marvin J. Ashton:

> Proper self-management and self-discipline in all of our trials can bring strength. If we are prepared, we can meet life's challenges victoriously. We become His disciples when we continue faithfully under all circumstances, including suffering and tragedy. C. S. Lewis shared a meaningful observation when he said, "I have seen great beauty of spirit in some who were great sufferers. I have seen men, for the most part, grow better not worse with advancing years, and I have seen the last illness produce treasures of fortitude and meekness from most unpromising subjects." (*Ye Are My Friends* [Salt Lake City: Deseret Book, 1972], 101–2)

ILLUSTRATIONS FOR OUR TIMES

Never Give Up; Never Give In; Never Give Out

Jeremiah was devoted to his calling regardless of the opposition. From the scriptures, as well as from the examples of those around us, we learn the importance of pressing forward with steadfastness, regardless of the difficulties.

I recall the story told by my sister-in-law, Shirley M. Pinegar, concerning her ancestors as they crossed the plains. One of her ancestors, Louisa Mellor, walked across the plains with the Martin Handcart Company. Louisa's family lived in Leicester, England. In April of 1844, Louisa's father heard two young Mormon elders preach. The next Sunday, he walked three miles to the church to hear them again. He was so impressed by their message that he walked home and brought his wife back to hear them. She, also believing the missionaries were preaching the truth, walked back and brought her mother to hear their message. Louisa's mother was baptized that afternoon, and her father was baptized the following week.

The family endured persecution because of joining the Church, and were happy when they were finally called to emigrate west with their seven young children, ranging in age from three to sixteen. While they were waiting in Liverpool for passage to America, Louisa's mother, Mary Ann, gave birth to twins, who both died. Mary Ann was so ill that initially the captain of the ship refused to let her come aboard because he feared she would die on the journey. But the missionaries blessed her and promised she would live to see her seed in Zion, and she was carried aboard on a stretcher.

After a five-and-a-half-week journey, they reached Boston Harbor on June 28, 1856. They traveled west in cattle cars to Iowa City, Iowa, where Louisa's father was able to find work and to secure two handcarts and food and clothing to make the journey across the plains. They left with the Martin Handcart Company on July 28, 1856. They endured many hardships on their journey. Both of Louisa's parents became ill. Food was scarce. They even resorted to boiling some of the rawhide used to tie the carts to make a thick, sticky mush for nourishment.

They suffered from illness, cold, hunger, fatigue, and frozen limbs. The campfire at night served three purposes: it cooked their food and kept them warm; frightened away the night creatures; and in the morning that spot was the only place where the ground was soft enough to dig graves for those who had died during the night.

The missionaries had passed them on the trail and had gone on ahead to advise President Brigham Young of their condition. President Young's relief party found them on October 31, 1856, camped at the edge of the Sweetwater River, about sixty-five miles east of Devil's Gate. It was like looking at death itself for them to try to cross that ice-choked river in their condition. Eighteen days earlier, they had crossed the icy North Platte River, and one-sixth of their party had died from that ordeal. Then three eighteen-year-old young men stepped forward, members of the rescue party, and they carried nearly every one of the company across the icy river. Later all three of these young men died as a result of this courageous act.

They arrived in the Salt Lake Valley in pitiful condition on November 30, 1856. After recovering from their long journey, the family went to live in Springville, where a son, John Carlos, was born on February 1, 1860—the fulfilment of the promise made to Louisa's mother that she would live to see her seed in Zion.

These courageous, faithful pioneers gave all they had, and suffered untold hardships for the gospel. Today, we also have adversity. As we think of the pioneers, may we gain courage from their lives, hope from their examples, and strength from their faith to live our own lives, knowing that with Heavenly Father's help all things are possible.

The Joy of Adversity

My brother-in-law, Homer Jensen, was a brilliant attorney with a successful practice and a wonderful young family. I recall distinctly hearing him say many years ago, in humble thankfulness to God, that things seemed almost too easy, that his success was almost too effortless. It was not long thereafter that he was unexpectedly called home. His family was devastated. We all reeled at the sudden loss. Even so, at the funeral, Elder Mark E. Petersen, beholding the inconsolable sorrow of the wife and children, counseled them to withhold their tears, to see from a higher perspective the plan of life, and take comfort and joy in the gospel of Jesus Christ that would eventually unite the family once again. Through that valley of adversity passed the route of courage and faith that my sister Shirley traversed as she led her little family forward in the steady knowledge of higher principle, and in the conviction anchored in the words, "For I know that my redeemer liveth." Were it not for that adversity, she and her little family could not have known the joy of personal triumph over suffering, the bliss of transcendence over sorrow, the peace of victory over life's shadows. I admire them for their example and positive attitude.

Take a map of your community. Put your finger down on the place where you now live. Draw a circle around that spot to encompass but a few blocks of dwellings. Within that circle is sufficient adversity in the experience of your neighbors—and perhaps your own family—for a lifetime of trials. Those who succumb and let the light of courage flicker out lose twice—once to the forces of misfortune, and once to themselves as they let the opportunity to rise above adversity slip from their grasp. Those who muster the courage to fight on and overcome win twice—once over the negative forces of circumstances and hardship, and once by taking control over inner attitude and personal conviction, no matter what might happen. Adversity is the lens through which we clearly see the joy of victory in doing the will of the Father and entering into his rest, "which rest is the fulness of his glory" (D&C 84:24). The Prophet Joseph Smith, himself one of the greatest students of adversity in the history of the world, put it memorably in his inspired dedicatory prayer for the Kirtland Temple in 1836: "Help thy servants to say, with thy grace assisting them: Thy will be done, O Lord, and not ours" (D&C 109:44). And that is the key to finding joy in adversity. It is through the grace of God that the battle for joy and peace and harmony is ultimately won.

2. THE POWER OF THE WORD OF GOD

THEME: The word of God, when written in the hearts of the Saints and infused in their thoughts, actions, and patterns of living, becomes the power of salvation and exaltation for all who will yield to the will of the Father and the Son.

Then the Lord put forth his hand, and touched my mouth. And the Lord said unto me, Behold, I have put my words in thy mouth. (Jer. 1:9)

Thy words were found, and I did eat them; and thy word was unto me the joy and rejoicing of mine heart: for I am called by thy name, O Lord God of hosts. (Jer. 15:16)

But his word was in mine heart as a burning fire shut up in my bones, and I was weary with forbearing, and I could not stay. (Jer. 20:9)

Take thee a roll of a book, and write therein all the words that I have spoken unto thee against Israel, and against Judah, and against all the nations, from the day I spake unto thee, from the days of Josiah, even unto this day. (Jer. 36:2)

Take thee again another roll, and write in it all the former words that were in the first roll, which Jehoiakim the king of Judah hath burned . . . . and there were added besides unto them many like words. (Jer. 36:28, 32)

MOMENT OF TRUTH

Jeremiah was given a great spiritual blessing to bear God's word to the nations. He was taught by the Lord that "whatsoever I command thee thou shalt speak" (Jer. 1:7). The word within Jeremiah was as a burning fire that he could not restrain. The princes sought to repress the word of God by consigning Jeremiah to prison and threatening to kill him, but he spoke the truth nevertheless. In all he did, Jeremiah was the paragon of obedience and strength in the Lord. He knew that a time would come, beyond the captivity of Israel, when the Lord would again restore His full word unto the people. Today, those who accept the restored word of God will find the living waters to quench their spiritual thirst: "Blessed is the man that trusteth in the Lord, and whose hope the Lord is. For he shall be as a tree planted by the waters, and that spreadeth out her roots by the river, and shall not see when heat cometh, but her leaf shall be green; and shall not be careful in the year of drought, neither shall cease from yielding fruit" (Jer. 17:7–8).

MODERN PROPHETS SPEAK

Joseph Smith:

> The Spirit of God accompanied the preaching of the word to the hearts of men. Whole households, on hearing the word, have received it into good and honest hearts, and gone forth and received the ordinances of the Gospel; and frequently we have baptized from eight to twelve the first time of meeting with the people in new places, and preaching the word of God to them. (*HC* 4:152)

Henry B. Eyring:

> Just as soil needs preparation for a seed, so does a human heart for the word of God to take root. Before he told the people to plant the seed, Alma told them that their hearts were prepared. They had been persecuted and cast out of their churches. Alma with his love and the circumstances of their lives, which led them to be humble, had prepared them. They were then ready to hear the word of God. If they chose to plant it in their hearts, the growth in their souls would surely follow, and that would

increase their faith. (*To Draw Closer to God: A Collection of Discourses* [Salt Lake City: Deseret Book, 1997], 186)

ILLUSTRATIONS FOR OUR TIMES

"Come, Follow Me"

I recall as a young boy hiking one day with my family in a remote part of the Canadian Rockies not far from where I grew up. We had chosen as a destination for our day-long adventure a small cluster of lakes known as Lineham Lakes. Because of their location above a daunting granite cliff at the end of a box canyon, these lakes were among the least accessible of the various crystal fishing lakes in Waterton National Park. Also because of their inaccessibility, the lakes were reportedly home to some of the largest rainbow trout in the area. Not wanting to risk the climb up and along the cliff, we chose instead to reach these lakes by climbing over a mountain ridge from the other side. The problem was that we had underestimated the time it would take to follow the circuitous indirect route, and it was already ominously late in the afternoon by the time we reached the lakes. Not having planned an overnight stay, we were faced with the unpleasant prospect of having to return to our car by traversing the cliff we had wanted to avoid in the first place. After spending an all-too-short period of time fishing, we faced our ordeal and ventured over to the place where the trail led to the beginning of the granite cliff.

The view was terrifying—perhaps several thousand feet straight down. What was called a trail was in fact nothing but a series of ledges used by the nimble mountain goats to cross over and down into the lower valley. In some sections, the trail was half a foot wide; in other parts it was barely an inch, and it invariable curved downward—toward the abyss. There were no trees to hold on to. Like the cliff, we were petrified. Even my father, no stranger to mountain adventures, seemed nervous. We looked down in silence as the evening sun disappeared behind the peaks.

Then something strange and unforgettable happened. We heard from somewhere in that isolated and lonely place the sound of happy whistling. We heard voices and laughter drawing nearer. Presently two men appeared from nowhere, carrying their fishing gear and wearing broad smiles. They must have sensed our forlorn spirits, for they joked and teased us with their banter. I can still hear the one fellow, whose name was Slim, saying in a kind of twang, "Anyone want a hardboiled egg?" No one in our party had much of an appetite at that moment, so he added, "We can take you down the cliff. Come follow us. And don't look down."

With that, Slim and his friend, whistling all the way, guided us painstakingly step-by-step across and down that cliff—one reach at a time—toward an enormous shale embankment located at what seemed like an endless distance away. I can still remember the fear of stepping from one goat ledge to another, sometimes reaching my foot around rock protrusions to gingerly test the foothold on the other side, all the while clinging with sweaty fingers to the face of the cliff and trying not to look down. But we made it, and when we finally reached the shale embankment, it was an easy thing to make our way down the rest of the incline toward the valley floor far below. Those experienced mountain guides were heroes in our eyes.

Since then, I have often thought of the words of those guides: "Come follow us." They knew the trail. They knew the dangers. They had cultivated both the techniques and the attitude of success. And they knew how to lead the inexperienced to safety. On the cliffs of life there are dangers lurking. There is an abyss of spiritual emptiness that yawns upward to the lonely traveler. But then the words echo: "Come, follow me" (Luke 18:22), and we know that the Shepherd is near and calls us toward pathways of safety and joy. He said, "My sheep hear my voice, and I know them, and they follow me" (John 10:27). The word of the Lord is the iron rod across the cliffs of life, the anchor to the fearful heart, the comfort to the weary, and the balance to the unsteady. Thank God for the word of truth to guide our steps and bring saving light into our lives.

The Word of God in Our Lives

In visiting with Elder Bruce R. McConkie when I was a young man, I asked him why the fullness of the gospel was not in the Book of Mormon. He said to me, "Oh, Ed, my brother, you don't understand. You see, the fullness of the gospel is in the lives of the people as they live the teachings from the Book of Mormon, or the word of God." That was the day I began to understand that the word of God becomes powerful in our lives as we apply it—when we recognize that the words of Christ will tell us all things we should do; when we recognize that it is the mind of the Lord, the will of the Lord, the voice of the Lord and the word of the Lord, and the power of God unto salvation; when we realize that the word of God will cause men to do good. Then all scriptures become our profit and learning. We take all scriptures personally that we may apply them to our lives. The word of God is for us to live today. The fullness of the gospel is in our lives as we live the word of God.

SUMMARY

The purpose of delivering the word of God to His children with courage and resolve despite all adversity, and of receiving the word of God in our lives at the hands of the prophets and servants of the Lord in faith and obedience, is expressed in this simple formula: "And they shall be my people" (Jer. 31:33). That is the whole matter put in its simplest terms—that we should become the covenant people of the Lord and keep his statutes in righteousness. "He hath shewed thee, O man, what is good; and what doth the Lord require of thee, but to do justly, and to love mercy, and to walk humbly with thy God?" (Micah 6:8).

CHAPTER FORTY-TWO

"I WILL MAKE *a* NEW COVENANT *with the* HOUSE *of* ISRAEL"

Reading Assignment: Jeremiah 16; 23; 29; 31.

Additional Reading: Jeremiah 3–9; 13; 30; 32:37–42; 33; 35.

> *When we have faith to understand that He must dictate and that we must be perfectly submissive to Him, then we shall begin to rapidly collect the intelligence that is bestowed upon the nations, for all this intelligence belongs to Zion. All the knowledge, wisdom, power, and glory that have been bestowed upon the nations of the earth, from the days of Adam till now, must be gathered home to Zion.* (Brigham Young, *JD* 8:279)

THEME *for* LIVING

1. The Lord Will Write His Law in Our Hearts

INTRODUCTION

The prophet Jeremiah was blessed with the gift of perceiving the majestic scope of the plan of God for His children from the foundations of the earth through the meridian of time and reaching forward to the latter days. He saw in the dispersal of Israel through the Babylonian conquest in 587 B.C.—and their return to their homeland after seventy years of repentance—a type for the broader dispersal of the covenant people and their eventual gathering in connection with the restoration of the gospel in the latter days.

Jeremiah also discussed other grand parallels operating through the agenda of the Lord. The law of God in Moses' day was written on tablets of stone, but in future days it would be written in the minds and hearts of the people. The kings of Israel and Judah were wont to lust after strange gods and pollute the righteous vessels of the Lord; but Jeremiah saw the coming of a righteous King (the Messiah) who would execute judgment in purity and holiness. Moreover, he saw the eventual gathering of the dispersed tribes through future fishers and hunters in an act of divine providence so grand as to equal and surpass the exodus from Egypt. Finally, the ancient covenant was broken by the promised people, but the new covenant would bring about a general reformation of spirituality to the extent that "they shall all know me" (Jer. 31:34).

THE LORD WILL WRITE
HIS LAW IN OUR HEARTS

THEME: For ancient Israel, the Lord wrote His law on the tablets of Moses; for Israel of the latter-day gathering, the Lord writes His law in their hearts and inward parts (Jer. 31:33). The greatest knowledge of all is the knowledge of the Lord and His ways, for to know the Lord and keep His covenant is to know joy and peace and have the hope of eternal life.

Behold, I will send for many fishers, saith the Lord, and they shall fish them; and after will I send for many hunters, and they shall hunt them from every mountain, and from every hill, and out of the holes of the rocks. For mine eyes are upon all their ways. (Jer. 16:16–17)

Behold, the days come, saith the Lord, that I will raise unto David a righteous Branch, and a King shall reign and prosper, and shall execute judgment and justice in the earth. In his days Judah shall be saved, and Israel shall dwell safely: and this is his name whereby he shall be called, THE LORD OUR RIGHTEOUSNESS. (Jer. 23:5–6)

Therefore, behold, the days come, saith the Lord, that they shall no more say, The Lord liveth, which brought up the children of Israel out of the land of Egypt; But, The Lord liveth, which brought up and which led the seed of the house of Israel out of the north country, and from all countries whither I had driven them; and they shall dwell in their own land. (Jer. 23:7–8; compare Jer. 16:14–16)

But this shall be the covenant that I will make with the house of Israel; After those days, saith the Lord, I will put my law in their inward parts, and write it in their hearts; and will be their God, and they shall be my people. (Jer. 31:33)

And ye shall seek me, and find me, when ye shall search for me with all your heart. (Jer. 29:13)

MOMENT OF TRUTH

The governing theme in these passages from Jeremiah is "covenant"—meaning the sacred relationship and formal bond between the Lord and His people. The word itself embodies the process, for covenant means, literally, "a coming together." Jeremiah was imbued with a sense of covenant in what he was given to perceive and discern through prophetic vision. He clearly saw the scattering and gathering as a sifting and learning process, a means to filter out idolatrous practices and bring people to a remembrance of the ancient promises embodied in the covenant with the Lord. He also perceived a time in the future when the Lord would make a new covenant with His people leading to universal spiritual knowledge.

MODERN PROPHETS SPEAK

Neal A. Maxwell:

> Thus great stress must be placed upon the need for intellectual meekness—"humbleness of mind." Meekness is not a passive attribute that merely deflects discourtesy. Instead, it involves intellectual activism. "For Ezra had prepared his heart to seek the law of the Lord, and to do it, and to teach in Israel statutes and judgments" (Ezra 7:10; see also 2 Chr. 19:3; 20:33). (*Meek and Lowly* [Salt Lake City: Deseret Book, 1987], 37)

Bruce R. McConkie:

> Other prophets also spoke of his coming. For instance, Haggai said, "The desire of all nations shall come" (Hag. 2:7). And scattered through the Psalms are great numbers of Spirit-inspired statements such as these: "Blessed be he that cometh in the name of the Lord" (Ps. 118:26), and "Then said I, Lo, I come: in the volume of the book it is written of me, I delight to do thy will, O my God: yea, thy law is within my heart" (Ps. 40:7–8). And it was of this great body of prophetic utterances that he himself spoke when, after his resurrection, he said to his apostles: "All things must be fulfilled, which were written in the law of Moses, and in the prophets, and in the psalms concerning me" (Luke 24:44). (*The Promised Messiah: The First Coming of Christ* [Salt Lake City: Deseret Book, 1978], 81)

ILLUSTRATIONS FOR OUR TIMES

Becoming His Sons and Daughters

When we choose to follow Christ, we give our hearts to the Lord. We literally give our will to do His will. We are easily entreated because of our broken heart and contrite spirit (our sacrifice). We yield to the enticings of the Holy Spirit. His law becomes our law. We love His law and want to keep it. The law can be a covenant, ordinance, statute, doctrine, principle, or commandment.

This process is called by many names: the mighty change, born again, conversion to Christ, becoming pure in heart, and becoming His sons and daughters, to name a few. We truly become Saints through the Atonement of Jesus Christ when we have faith unto repentance, receive baptism, take His name upon us, and then receive the gift of the Holy Ghost.

I have had the privilege of witnessing this process in our family, in young men and women at Church, students in seminary, BYU, and institutes of religion, in missionaries, and in converts in the mission field. This is the process of becoming. This is our goal in life—to become as He is.

I recall a most wonderful young student in my Book of Mormon class. He was a tennis star for BYU. He was a nonmember at that time, but was easily entreated and readily accepted the gospel of Jesus Christ. He served an honorable mission and married a beautiful daughter of God in the holy temple. He has raised magnificent children and has served in many callings in the Church. He recently changed professions to become a full-time institute teacher. He is the perfect example of diligently seeking the will of God and then doing it. His letters over the years have been a strength to me. His devotion to our Heavenly Father and our Savior is legendary in his ward, where he has served as bishop. These words will embarrass him, but they prove the point of Jeremiah's words: when we choose to be His people, His words will be written in our hearts and we will do His will. Russ Greiner is one who has done it with all of his heart.

When Charity Calls

How do you know when a person has the law of the Lord written in his or her heart? The Savior gave a telling answer to this question at the time He sent His latter-day servants into the world to proclaim the restored gospel: "Whoso receiveth you receiveth me; and the same will feed you, and clothe you, and give you money. . . . And he that doeth not these things is not my disciple; by this you may know my disciples" (D&C 84:89, 91). Those who have the law of the Lord written on their hearts seem to be blessed with the capacity to discern, and respond charitably to, the needs of others. Evidence of this kind of charity abounds.

My own mother-in-law, Lucille Hansen, told of the time she had the strong impression to write to one of her grandsons, then serving as a missionary in Nassau, the Bahamas, and provide some additional financial support. She was well aware that the missionaries received funds regularly through the contribution channels funded by missionary families and friends worldwide, but she could not shake off the feeling that something extra was needed. Finally she responded to the prompting and mailed off a letter containing a check.

Meanwhile, this missionary grandson and his companion were ministering to the needs of investigator families in a remote part of the islands. Poverty was rampant, and many families had insufficient food for their daily needs. One family was destitute, so the missionary companions took everything they had—all of their reserve funds—and gave everything to the family so that these poor people might have food for survival. The elders were acting on pure faith, for they did not know how they would be able to support themselves until the next regular mission payment came many days hence. When they arrived back at their dwelling that day they found the letter and check from Sister Hansen, and they gratefully thanked their Father in Heaven for His goodness and the faithfulness and responsiveness of the grandmother.

"And it shall come to pass, that before they call, I will answer; and while they are yet speaking, I will hear" (Isa. 65:24). Such are the signs of the latter days, when "I will put my law in their inward parts, and write it in their hearts; and will be their God, and they shall be my people" (Jer. 31:33). At his missionary homecoming, the grandson made mention of this incident and bore witness about the love of God for His people. You can clearly identify those who have the law of the Lord written in their hearts, because they walk the pathway of charity and respond to the promptings of the Spirit to minister to the needs of God's children.

SUMMARY

The Lord touches His prophets and imbues them with a sense of divine purpose. They have the law of the Lord written in their minds and hearts. This same process applies to each of God's children. His will is to touch them all and write His word of truth upon their inward being so that they might know Him and walk according to the tenets of the divine covenant. Only when we have accepted His will in all things are we made parties to the covenant of grace and mercy intended to govern our relationship with our Father in Heaven and His Son, Jesus Christ. Only then can we come to understand the sacred implication of the Lord's promise to Jeremiah: "I will make a new covenant with the house of Israel" (Jer. 31:31), for we will know at that time that this new covenant applies to us in a very personal way.

CHAPTER FORTY-THREE

"THERE SHALL BE SHOWERS *of* BLESSING"

Reading Assignment: Ezekiel 18; 34; 37.

Additional Reading: Ezekiel 2.

> *He had power, when all mankind had lost their life, to restore life to them again; and hence He is the Resurrection and the Life, which power no other man possesses.* (John Taylor, *The Mediation and the Atonement* [1892], 135)

THEMES *for* LIVING

1. The Shepherds of Israel
2. The Power of God to Restore Life and Hope
3. The Coming Together of the Word of God

INTRODUCTION

The vision of Ezekiel, like the visions granted to Jeremiah and all other prophets of ancient and modern times, projects the message of the covenant, or the message of "coming together." That is the ultimate objective of the scriptures of God—to bring mankind together in the fold of God. Out of that oneness of purpose flow the themes of this chapter: (1) the need for the shepherds of Israel to be diligently engaged in the cause of Zion; (2) the restorative, redeeming power of the gospel of hope; and (3) the ordained process of gathering the words of God as a combined latter-day testament of the divinity of Jesus Christ.

1. THE SHEPHERDS OF ISRAEL

THEME: The Lord gives His children their agency, causes them to be taught correct principles, and then holds every individual accountable for his or her own actions. At the same time, the Lord holds the shepherds of Israel—all who have stewardship over the flock at whatever level of responsibility—accountable to teach the principles of righteousness, shirking no opportunity to bring the sheep unto Christ. Shepherds are called to guide the Saints in the pathway of righteousness, and to restore any wayward and wandering souls to the fold.

> *Therefore I will judge you, O house of Israel, every one according to his ways, saith the Lord God. Repent, and turn yourselves from all your transgressions; so iniquity shall not be your ruin. Cast away from you all your transgressions, whereby ye have transgressed; and make you a new heart and a new spirit.* (Ezek. 18:30–31)

> *Son of man, prophesy against the shepherds of Israel, prophesy, and say unto them, Thus saith the Lord God unto the shepherds; Wo be to the shepherds of Israel that do feed themselves! should not the shepherds feed the flocks?* (Ezek. 34:2)

> *For thus saith the Lord God; Behold, I, even I, will both search my sheep, and seek them out.* (Ezek. 34:11)

> *And I will set up one shepherd over them, and he shall feed them, even my servant David; he shall feed them, and he shall be their shepherd.* (Ezek. 34:23)

MOMENT OF TRUTH

Ezekiel, who prophesied for some twenty-two years (from 592 until 570 B.C.), was the messenger of God's strong disfavor with the covenant people. The leaders of Israel were under condemnation for polluting the sacred principles of the covenant and desecrating their roles as "shepherds of Israel." Not heeding the warnings of Ezekiel and other prophets of God, the people were thus consigned to endure a state of captivity at the hands of the invading Babylonians under Nebuchadnezzar. Ezekiel could offer hope only to those who, in the future, would choose to obey the Lord's commandments and be restored to their place of favor with God and find peace under the leadership of the Good Shepherd (Jesus Christ).

MODERN PROPHETS SPEAK

Ezra Taft Benson:

> There are no *new* solutions to this *old* problem. The charge Jesus gave to Peter, which He emphasized by repeating it three times, is the proven solution: "Feed my lambs. . . . Feed my sheep. Feed my sheep." The answer, then, is found in shepherding the flock. In other words, priesthood watchcare. It is real concern by a true shepherd, not just the feigned concern a hireling might show. In discussing the concept of a true shepherd, it is recognized that the Lord has given this responsibility to priesthood holders. But our sisters also have callings of "shepherding" in their charitable and loving service that they give to one another, to youth, and to children. Here are some questions every true shepherd should ask:

> **Shepherds—home teachers:**

> • Are you watching over your families as you should?

> • Are you ministering to their needs?

> • Do you care enough about your families' welfare that you find out their interests, that you remember birthdays and special events, and that you continually pray for them?

> • Are you the first one to the home when the family needs assistance?

> • Does the head of the household call on you first?

> • Are you attentive to the needs of each member of the family?

> • When one of your assigned families moves, do you know where they have moved? Do you make an effort to obtain their new address? Do you check with neighbors, friends, and relatives?

> **Shepherds—stake presidents, bishops, quorum leaders:**

> • Are you welcoming into your ranks new converts?

• Do they feel your love and concern?

• Are new converts invited into your homes?

• Do they know what family home evening is and how to use it?

• Does the family feel welcome and comfortable in your midst?

• Do you ordain worthy male members to offices of the priesthood following baptism?

• Do you give them meaningful Church assignments?

• Do you leave the ninety and nine and search after the lost one?

• Do you call and appoint advisers and others who can reach impressionable youth and visit them on their "own ground"?

• Have you fully implemented the youth program, and are you using this program to meet the individual needs of each youth?

• Are you watchful over the young singles, the divorced, and those with special needs?

• Do you carefully and spiritually prepare those who enter military service?

• Are you especially attentive to young men between the transition period from Aaronic Priesthood to Melchizedek Priesthood?

• Bishops, do you make sure they come under the care of their new shepherd, the quorum president?

• Do you provide significant Church-service opportunities for our returned missionaries so that these young men and women do not drift into inactivity because they do not have occasion to serve as they have been doing for eighteen months?

• Do you use visiting teachers to augment home teaching?

• Are you teaching fathers their duties?

- Do you have temple preparation seminars to encourage prospective elders to prepare for the Melchizedek Priesthood and the temple?

- Do you have older prospective elders assigned to the high priests and invited to join those with whom they would feel most comfortable?

- Are younger prospective elders invited to participate with the elders quorums?

Some leaders say that some men are past hope, but, as the angel told Abraham, nothing is impossible with the Lord! One brother who was regarded by some as a hopeless case tearfully exclaimed to the temple worker at the sealing altar, "I don't know why I waited so long for this blessing!"

In a recent Saturday evening meeting of leaders I heard a determined brother state, "I've sure had a time with the devil since I started to become active. Prior to that time, I just went along with him."

- Are you helping the one who needs help because he has started on the way back to full activity?

- Are you attentive to the records of Church members under your charge—especially those who are not participating with you in meetings?

- Do you obtain forwarding addresses from home teachers when members leave your midst, or are you just relieved to get them off your records and send their records to the "address unknown" file?

Shepherds—fathers in Israel:

- Are you holding family prayer with your family, morning and evening?

- Do you hold a regular, consistent, inspiring family home evening once a week?

- Do you lead out in spiritual matters?

- Is your example what it should be before those whom you lead? Do you ask and pray for the welfare of your own?

- Do you love them?

- Would you give your life for them?

Shepherds—all who hold the priesthood:

- Let us solemnly evaluate our performance in relation to these matters.

- The Lord calls on us, as Paul did to the elders of Ephesus: "Take heed therefore unto yourselves, and to all the flock, over the which the Holy Ghost hath made you overseers, to feed the church of God, which he hath purchased with his own blood" (Acts 20:28; italics added).

- Today our Lord repeats the same charge He gave Peter. He repeats it with the same emphasis, the same repetition: "Feed my lambs. . . . Feed my sheep. . . . Feed my sheep!" (Come unto Christ [Salt Lake City: Deseret Book, 1983], 65–69)

ILLUSTRATIONS FOR OUR TIMES

Getting a New Heart and a New Spirit

The Lord truly is our shepherd. He leads us along the way. He has asked us to be shepherds of the flock, watchmen over His kingdom.

I recall riding home from a stake conference with Elder Hans Ringger. He was telling me of the precious nature of the Lord's flock. While serving as a bishop, he had two people who were not only struggling, but also becoming antagonistic toward the Church. It had become so bad that they wanted their names removed from the records of the Church. They were bothered by their home teachers and simply wanted nothing more to do with the Church. Elder Ringger pleaded with them and promised that no one would bother them anymore, then asked if it was okay if they simply left their names on the records of the Church. They reluctantly agreed. He simply became their friend, with only their welfare and well-being in mind. As he told the story, tears welled up in his eyes as he concluded by saying that now one of them was the Primary president and the other was the elders quorum president. He was a true shepherd. His love was Christlike. He never gave up on them. He exhibited the attributes of charity through his patience, kindness, and never-ending expression of love.

As shepherds in Israel, we must be strong. We must stand for truth and righteousness. When necessary we must warn and even chastise those with whom we have stewardships, so as to prepare a way for them to repent (see D&C 121:41–44; Ezek. 3:17–24).

Helping others get a new heart and spirit is part of the shepherd's duty. I remember one elder who had struggled at the MTC. He wasn't worthy and he wasn't prepared. His confession was belated and he needed to visit with his stake president. After I had visited with him and conferred with his stake president, it was decided that he should return home for a personal visit with his stake president and bishop. As I explained this to the elder, I could sense his anger and frustration. He didn't want to talk with them, and least of all return home. His disappointment was visible, and he became angered to such a point that he was threatening never to come back, and said he didn't care anymore. I did my best to counsel with him and show him love and concern. He left the following day to return home. My prayers were constant in his behalf.

A few weeks later, he returned to the MTC. I greeted him when he returned, and he seemed much better, but still troubled. A week went by and I was scheduled to visit with him again. As he walked in, I could discern a sweet spirit.

He said, "Oh, President, how can I ever thank you? I was so angry with you and my stake president that I could hardly stand it. I was mad at the whole world. Then I realized I had to change my heart and my mind and humble myself before God. While I was home, I came to realize my problem and that I needed to change. Day by day, I have become a new person. Everything I hear at the MTC I take notes on and make a plan to be like my Savior. I feel so good inside. I'm happy and grateful to serve a mission for the Lord. Oh, President, I love you." We cried together and prayed in gratitude for the goodness of God in his life.

This wonderful elder's experience proves that we can all make a mighty change in our heart as Ezekiel and Alma have taught us (see Ezek. 18:21–22, 27–28, 31; Alma 5:7–14).

2. THE POWER OF GOD TO RESTORE LIFE AND HOPE

THEME: God is omnipotent in His ability to restore and enliven all aspects of man's existence—including the ultimate restoration of the body and its reunion with the spirit in a resurrected state, the restoration of the spirit of hope to His struggling children, and the restoration of His chosen people to the promised land (in both the temporal as well as the heavenly sense).

> *Then he said unto me, Son of man, these bones are the whole house of Israel: behold, they say, Our bones are dried, and our hope is lost: we are cut off for our parts. Therefore prophesy and say unto them, Thus saith the Lord God; Behold, O my people, I will open your graves, and cause you to come up out of your graves, and bring you into the land of Israel. . . . And shall put my spirit in you, and ye shall live, and I shall place you in your own land: then shall ye know that I the Lord have spoken it, and performed it, saith the Lord. (Ezek. 37:11–12, 14)*

MOMENT OF TRUTH

Ezekiel was granted a remarkable vision of the "valley which was full of bones" (Ezek. 37:1). He saw in an extraordinary spectral drama how the bones were rejuvenated, given once again their fleshly embodiment, and enlivened through the spirit of life. It was a unique and memorable spiritual event with many harmonic overtones: a view of the resurrection, an insight into the restorative power of God to generate hope and faith within His children, and a renewal of the promise under the Abrahamic covenant to give the Lord's chosen a homeland on earth, as well as a place of rest in the hereafter.

MODERN PROPHETS SPEAK

Jeffrey R. Holland:

> Faith in Christ and hope in his promises of resurrected, eternal life can come only to the meek and lowly in heart. Such promises, in turn, reinforce meekness and lowliness of heart in that believer. Only thorough disciples of Christ, living as meekly as he lived and humbling themselves as he humbled himself, can declare uncompromised faith in Christ and have genuine hope in the Resurrection. These then, and only these, come to understand true charity—the pure love of Christ. (*Christ and the New Covenant: The Messianic Message of the Book of Mormon* [Salt Lake City: Deseret Book, 1997], 335)

Gordon B. Hinckley:

> I believe that through his atoning sacrifice, the offering of his life on Calvary's hill, he expiated the sins of mankind, relieving us from the burden of sin if we will forsake evil and follow him. I believe in the reality and the power of his resurrection. I believe in the grace of God made manifest through Jesus' sacrifice and redemption, and I believe that through his atonement, without any price on our part, each of us is offered the gift of resurrection from the dead. I believe further that through that sacrifice there is extended to every man and woman, every son and daughter of God, the opportunity for eternal life and exaltation in our Father's kingdom, as we hearken to and obey his commandments. (*Faith: The Essence of True Religion* [Salt Lake City: Deseret Book, 1989], 24)

ILLUSTRATIONS FOR OUR TIMES

Look Ahead to Joy

My wife and I have devised a saying that we rehearse together rather frequently. It simply says: "Don't look back on sorrow—look ahead to joy." When circumstances begin to cast a shadow over the pathway of life, and we begin to give voice to discouragement, then one or the other of us will retrieve that little saying and, with a smile, recite it. Then we will both nod with understanding and say it together, or sing it to a little tune we have developed: "Don't look back on sorrow—look ahead to joy." There is really no other choice in life. Through the hope of the gospel, we can indeed look forward to joy. The burdens of life—be they the result of a lapse of good judgment on the part of someone, or in relation to our willing sacrifices for the kingdom of God, or because of mere happenchance—can serve a constructive purpose: "all these things shall give thee experience, and shall be for thy good," the Lord said to the Prophet Joseph (D&C 122:7). At times, our spirit of courage can wane and our hope can slacken—almost as if we were without life. Those are the times when the Comforter can breathe new hope into our being. Truly the Lord can revive us on a daily basis, if we will allow Him to do so. Thank heaven for families and for loved ones who can serve together and make the pathway of life bearable. "Don't look back on sorrow—look ahead to joy. Hand in hand we'll go, finding our tomorrow, for we know we'll always go in love."

Running Home to the Savior

In the power of God lies the power to restore, to make whole, to be resurrected into a newness of life. Hope truly governs our attitude, which is reflected in our behavior.

It was Mother's Day 1947, and my daddy had just died of heart failure. I couldn't believe my daddy could die. He was so big—6'3," 250 lbs.—and so strong. I was twelve years old, and I had been to the funeral of my Grandma Pinegar. Death was so final. Death was the end of life as I knew it. I had been taught of the resurrection; I knew that when people died they went to the spirit world and later would be resurrected. I had the knowledge, but my understanding and appreciation came later. When I truly realized the goodness of God, His supreme power and concern for His children, my heart was filled with gratitude. Then, oh how I wanted to live a good life so I could enjoy the blessings of coming forth on the morning of the first resurrection. I love life and I want to live a long time, but I still treasure this thought.

As a little boy, I would run down the lane after school to our farmhouse, and there would be my mom, waiting for her boy. We would have a treat, and then she would ask me about my day at school.

I think of passing through the veil in the same light—running to my Savior and Heavenly Father, and them taking me in their arms and giving me their love. This fills my soul with the joy of eternal life. It gives me hope to live a life worthy of their presence. God loves His children, and His power is always used to bless our lives.

3. THE COMING TOGETHER OF THE WORD OF GOD

THEME: The agenda of God is to restore all spiritual things into one as a key function of the final dispensation of time, including all aspects of the word of God. Thus God's message to all of His children in all dispensations of time and in all locations, will be brought together into a grand whole, including the Bible, the Book of Mormon, and all other sacred writings.

> *Moreover, thou son of man, take thee one stick, and write upon it, For Judah, and for the children of Israel his companions: then take another stick, and write upon it, For Joseph, the stick of Ephraim, and for all the house of Israel his companions: And join them one to another into one stick; and they shall become one in thine hand.* (Ezek. 37:16–17)

> *And David my servant shall be king over them; and they all shall have one shepherd: they shall also walk in my judgments, and observe my statutes, and do them. . . . Moreover I will make a covenant of peace with them; it shall be an everlasting covenant with them: and I will place them, and multiply them, and will set my sanctuary in the midst of them for evermore.* (Ezek. 37:24, 26)

MOMENT OF TRUTH

Ezekiel was commanded to take a stick (or scroll) and write upon it "For Judah," and another stick and write upon it "For Joseph," and then to combine the two sticks together in one, that they might be unified. It is clear that the stick of Judah is the Bible—but where is the stick of Joseph? It is the Book of Mormon, just as the word of the Lord to other remnants of scattered Israel is doubtless preserved in scriptural accounts that will one day be restored to the central repository of the word of God (2 Ne. 29:12–14).

MODERN PROPHETS SPEAK

Jeffrey R. Holland:

> Latter-day Saint scholars consider the bringing together of the stick of Joseph with the stick of Judah, as prophesied by Ezekiel, one of the great contributions of the Book of Mormon, and so it is (see Ezek. 37:15–28; 1 Ne. 13:41; 2 Ne. 3:12). However, in the matter of bringing together disparate records, it is equally important to acknowledge what the Book of Mormon does to unite the Old Testament with the New Testament in a way that is not usually acknowledged and is, in fact, sometimes seen as impossible in other religious traditions. (*Christ and the New Covenant: The Messianic Message of the Book of Mormon* [Salt Lake City: Deseret Book, 1997], 13)

Neal A. Maxwell:

> A great deal of what we know about Jesus' role, atonement, and character and about the Father's plan of salvation comes to us from the precious Restoration scriptures. A major source is the Book of Mormon with its "convincing," Christ-centered content. The Book of Mormon, Another Testament of Jesus Christ, was also provided by the Lord as a tangible, enduring witness to the prophetic mission of Joseph

Smith. The coming forth of the Book of Mormon preceded all the other Restoration scriptures in providing refreshing, renewing, and convincing evidence about Jesus and about God's plan of salvation. Indeed, the substance of the Restoration scriptures responds to life's largest and most troubling issues. (*Lord, Increase Our Faith* [Salt Lake City: Bookcraft, 1994], 55)

ILLUSTRATIONS FOR OUR TIMES

The Power of the Word of God

One day in my Book of Mormon class, a student came up to me and lamented the fact that she and her roommates weren't getting along. She asked for counsel. I suggested that she take an assignment from me for extra credit and get everyone in her apartment to read aloud the Book of Mormon every night before bed, and then have a kneeling prayer. I suggested that she ask them to do this as a favor for her—just ten minutes a night. They agreed, and so the experiment upon the word began. A few weeks passed, and she reported how much joy she felt and how all the roommates loved each other. She explained how the spirit in the apartment was so wonderful. She told me how they had just come back from spring break, having stayed with one of their roommate's parents in California. She was so excited as she explained how they took sleeping bags and slept on the beach, and then she asked, 'Guess what we took to the beach? Two things, Brother Ed. What do you think they were?' I pondered, and before I could answer she said, "A flashlight and the scriptures. You see, Brother Ed, we can't go to bed without reading the Book of Mormon. It has changed our lives. We all love the Book of Mormon now. And you know what's great? We all love each other."

This is one example of the power of the word of God expressed in the lives of His children.

SUMMARY

When Ezekiel prophesied that "there shall be showers of blessing" (Ezek. 34:26), he was looking forward to a time in which the Lord would once more gather His people under the unifying banner of Zion: "And I will make with them a covenant of peace, . . . and they shall dwell safely in the wilderness, . . . And I will make them and the places round about my hill a blessing" (Ezek. 34:25–26). Before that day can come, we will need to learn line upon line, precept upon precept, "Till we all come in the unity of the faith, and of the knowledge of the Son of God, unto a perfect man, unto the measure of the stature of the fulness of Christ" (Eph. 4:13). Measuring up to that stature requires unity of service, unity of hope, and unity of testimony—all attributes of a Zion people to which we can aspire.

CHAPTER FORTY-FOUR

"THE GLORY *of the* LORD FILLED *the* HOUSE"

Reading Assignment: Ezekiel 43–44; 47.

Additional Reading: Revelation 22:1–3; 1 Nephi 8:10–11; 11:25.

These [Temple] ordinances have been revealed unto us for this very purpose, that we might be born into the light from the midst of this darkness—from death into life. (Joseph F. Smith, *JD* 19:285)

THEME *for* LIVING

1. The Temple of God as the Source for Healing Truth

INTRODUCTION

The last eight chapters of the book of Ezekiel constitute a visionary journey to the city of God and a visit to the glorious temple in its midst. Nothing was withheld from the prophet's view, including all of the details of the building's construction and appointments, together with the ordinances administered there. "And, behold, the glory of the God of Israel came from the way of the east: and his voice was like a noise of many waters: and the earth shined with his glory . . . . and, behold, the glory of the Lord filled the house" (Ezek. 43:2, 5). Flowing from below the threshold of the temple was a current of water that expanded in size and volume as it continued eastward, bringing healing and life-sustaining influences to all the realm. The river of abundance is a dynamic metaphor for the effulgent, everlasting flow of truth and light that enlivens the lives of all individuals who seek the Lord's endowment of eternal blessings through the work of the temples.

THE TEMPLE OF GOD AS THE SOURCE FOR HEALING TRUTH

THEME: Endless spiritual vitality flows from the institution, ordinances, endowments, and power of the temple in its function as the pivotal hub of a Zion society. As the Lord's house, the temple provides the key agenda for seeking the face of the Lord (see D&C 101:38).

> *Thou son of man, shew the house to the house of Israel, that they may be ashamed of their iniquities: and let them measure the pattern . . . . and write it in their sight, that they may keep the whole form thereof, and all the ordinances thereof, and do them.* (Ezek. 43:10–11)

> *And they shall teach my people the difference between the holy and profane, and cause them to discern between the unclean and the clean.* (Ezek. 44:23)

> *And it shall come to pass, that every thing that liveth, which moveth, whithersoever the rivers shall come, shall live: . . . and every thing shall live whither the river cometh.* (Ezek. 47:9)

MOMENT OF TRUTH

Like Jeremiah and Isaiah before him, Ezekiel received visionary insight into the full panorama of God's dealings with mankind, from the creation of the earth to the final battle that will usher in the millennial reign of the Good Shepherd. The remarkable images in which Ezekiel couched his message—the parchment roll of wisdom that he was required to eat, the watchmen of Israel, the wheels and cherubims about the throne of God, the withering vine of an idolatrous nation, the profligate sisters, the goodly tree of righteousness, the righteous shepherd, showers of blessings, the valley of bones, the stick of Judah and the stick of Joseph, and ultimately the great river of life flowing from the temple—all provided stark visual reinforcement for the universal call to repentance that undergirded his pronouncements and pointed to the final destiny of the faithful who would live forever in the city of God. Like John the Beloved, who saw in vision "a pure river of water of life, clear as crystal, proceeding out of the throne of God and of the Lamb" (Rev. 22:1), Ezekiel beheld the temple as the source of an almighty river of truth, nurturing the faithful in ever deeper immersions in the pools of divine wisdom. He foretold that the ultimate resting place of the Saints would be a city whose name revealed the nature of the glory within it: "And the name of the city from that day shall be, The Lord is there" (Ezek. 48:35). Against the bleakness of the landscape of iniquity, idolatry, and captivity characterizing Israel's plight at the time of Ezekiel's ministry, we see the blinding radiance of hope for a future restoration of Israel's covenant blessings—blessings that promise fruitfulness, a gathering place of rest, the refreshing abundance of truth, the sealing ordinances of the temple, and a heavenly home of eternal life in the presence of God and the Lamb.

MODERN PROPHETS SPEAK

Gordon B. Hinckley:

> Many have traveled that far and even farther to receive the blessings of temple marriage. I have seen a group of Latter-day Saints from Japan who had denied themselves food to make possible the long journey to the Hawaii Temple. In London we met those who had gone without necessities to afford the 7,000-mile flight from South Africa to the temple in Surrey, England. There was a light in their eyes and smiles on their faces and testimonies from their lips that it was worth infinitely more than all it had cost. (*Be Thou an Example* [Salt Lake City: Deseret Book, 1981], 138)

Ezra Taft Benson:

> We urge all who can to attend the temple frequently and accept calls to serve in the temple when health and strength and distance will permit. We rely on you to help in temple service. With the increasing number of temples, we need more of our members to prepare themselves for this sweet service. Sister Benson and I are grateful that almost every week we can attend the temple together. What a blessing this has been in our lives! (*Come, Listen to a Prophet's Voice* [Salt Lake City: Deseret Book, 1990], 73)

ILLUSTRATIONS FOR OUR TIMES

Messengers of the Lord

> I recall an incident in my own father's experience. How we looked forward to the completion of the Logan Temple. It was about to be dedicated. My father had labored on that house from its very beginning, and my earliest recollection was carrying his dinner each day as he brought the rock down from the quarry. How we

looked forward to that great event! I remember how in the meantime father made every effort to obtain all the data and information he could concerning his relatives. It was the theme of his prayer night and morning that the Lord would open up the way whereby he could get information concerning his dead.

The day before the dedication while writing recommends to the members of his ward who were to be present at the first service, two elderly gentlemen walked down the streets of Logan, approached my two young sisters, and, coming to the older one of the two placed in her hands a newspaper and said:

"Take this to your father. Give it to no one else. Go quickly with it. Don't lose it."

The child responded and when she met her mother, her mother wanted the paper. The child said, "No. I must give it to father and to no one else."

She was admitted into the room and told her story. We looked in vain for these travelers. They were not to be seen. No one else saw them. Then we turned to the paper.

The newspaper, *The Newbury Weekly News,* was printed in my father's old English home, Thursday, May 15th, 1884, and reached our hands May 18, 1884, three days after its publication. We were astonished, for by no earthly means could it have reached us, so that our curiosity increased as we examined it. Then we discovered one page devoted to the writings of a reporter of the paper, who had gone on his vacation, and among other places had visited an old cemetery. The curious inscriptions led him to write what he found on the tombstones, including the verses. He also added the names, date of birth, death, etc., filling nearly an entire page.

It was the old cemetery where the Ballard family had been buried for generations, and very many of my father's immediate relatives and other intimate friends were mentioned.

When the matter was presented to President Merrill of the Logan Temple he said, "You are authorized to do the work for those, because you received it through messengers of the Lord" (Melvin J. Ballard, *Three Degrees of Glory* [Salt Lake City: Magazine Printing, 1922])

Endowment of Truth

In February 1831 in Kirtland, Ohio, the Lord made a promise to the Saints through the Prophet Joseph Smith: "And ye are to be taught from on high. Sanctify yourselves and ye shall be endowed with power, that ye may give even as I have spoken" (D&C 43:16). On 27 March 1836, the Kirtland Temple was dedicated and became the site for profoundly important heavenly visitations a few days later on 3 April, including the appearance of the Savior and the bestowal of essential keys for the unfolding and operation of the latter-day kingdom of God on the earth. A significant aspect of that restorative process was the bestowal of keys for temple work. A few years later, on 4

May 1842, after the Saints had survived daunting dislocations and tribulations at the hands of their enemies, the Prophet Joseph Smith introduced the particulars of the sacred temple endowment for the first time in this dispensation. Present at this meeting, held in the upper story of the Prophet's red brick store in Nauvoo, were such prominent individuals as Hyrum Smith, Newel K. Whitney, Brigham Young, Heber C. Kimball, and Willard Richards. The instruction included

> all those plans and principles by which any one is enabled to secure the fullness of those blessings which have been prepared for the Church of the First Born, and come up and abide in the presence of the Elohim in the eternal worlds. In this council was instituted the ancient order of things for the first time in these last days. And the communications I made to this council were of things spiritual, and to be received only by the spiritual minded: and there was nothing made known to these men but what will be made known to all the Saints of the last days, so soon as they are prepared to receive, and a proper place is prepared to communicate them, even to the weakest of the Saints; therefore let the Saints be diligent in building the Temple. (*HC* 5:2)

From this humble beginning—a key phase of "the times of restitution of all things" (Acts 3:21)—temple work has unfolded and flourished until it now reaches into all corners of the world.

SUMMARY

Ezekiel drew from the celestial archives of the word of God the message of hope and a view of the ultimate state of the redeemed. Drawing from the same heavenly archive, the book of Revelation—of all New Testament books the one most similar in cadence and imagery to the majestic rhetoric of Isaiah, Jeremiah, Ezekiel, Daniel, and other Old Testament Prophets—spoke of a time of restoration when the righteous would be arrayed in white robes before the throne of the Lamb, worshipping with thanksgiving: "Saying, Amen: Blessing, and glory, and wisdom, and thanksgiving, and honour, and power, and might, be unto our God for ever and ever. Amen. . . . These are they which came out of great tribulation and have washed their robes, and made them white in the blood of the Lamb. Therefore are they before the throne of God, and serve him day and night in his temple: and he that sitteth on the throne shall dwell among them. They shall hunger no more, neither thirst any more; neither shall the sun light on them, nor any heat. For the Lamb which is in the midst of the throne shall feed them, and shall lead them unto living fountains of waters: and God shall wipe away all tears from their eyes" (Rev. 7:12, 14–17).

Relating the gospel of Jesus Christ to the living waters that sustain eternal life is a pervasive image in the pages of holy writ. Nephi also discerned clearly the meaning of these waters: "And it came to pass that I beheld that the rod of iron, which my father had seen, was the word of God, which led to the fountain of living waters, or to the tree of life; which waters are a representation of the love of God; and I also beheld that the tree of life was a representation of the love of God" (1 Ne. 11:25). In our day, the Lord re-emphasized this theme: "But unto him that keepeth my commandments I will give the mysteries of my kingdom, and the same shall be in him a well of living water, springing up unto everlasting life" (D&C 63:23).

For Ezekiel, the living water was inseparably connected with the temple, for the temple was the source of the river that nurtured the trees along its banks—trees of enduring verdure and never-ending fruit: "And by the river upon the bank thereof, on this side and on that side, shall grow all trees for meat, whose leaf shall not fade, neither shall the fruit thereof be consumed: it shall bring forth new fruit according to his months, because their waters they issued out of the sanctuary: and the fruit thereof shall be for meat, and the leaf thereof for medicine" (Ezek. 47:12). Blessed by water from the sanctuary, the faithful will never lack for spiritual nurture and healing grace, because the temple is the place where "the glory of the Lord filled the house" (Ezek. 43:5).

CHAPTER FORTY-FIVE

"THERE IS NO OTHER GOD THAT CAN DELIVER"

Reading Assignment: Daniel 1; 3; 6; Esther 3–5; 7–8.

Additional Reading: Esther 1–2; 6; 9–10.

> *We all know that no one ever lived upon the earth that exerted the same influence upon the destinies of the world as did our Lord and Savior Jesus Christ; and yet He was born in obscurity, cradled in a manger. He chose for His apostles poor, unlettered fishermen. More than nineteen hundred years have passed and gone since His crucifixion, and yet all over the world, in spite of all strife and chaos, there is still burning in the hearts of millions of people a testimony of the divinity of the work that He accomplished.* (Heber J. Grant in *Selections from the Sermons and Writings of Heber J. Grant*, 22)

THEMES *for* LIVING

1. Portraits of Covenant Character and Honor

INTRODUCTION

The chronicles of the captivity of Israel, beginning in 587 B.C. under the vanquishing leadership of Nebuchadnezzar of Babylonia, and lasting until the decree of liberation of Cyrus in 536 B.C. allowing the return of the Jewish people to Jerusalem, provide ample illustrations of exceptional courage and spiritual strength on the part of many of the Israelite expatriates. Some of the most notable were Daniel and his young colleagues, and Esther and her cousin Mordecai. What allowed them to stand firm in the face of life-threatening challenges to their standards and principles? What gave them courage to draw the line and reaffirm their commitment to the covenant promises of righteousness and faithfulness? It was the strength of the Lord, which they sought and obtained through mighty prayer and fasting, enabling them to perform their missions with exemplary valor. Character is always measured in the context of adversity and challenge.

PORTRAITS OF COVENANT CHARACTER AND HONOR

THEME: Character is measured when one faces the ultimate challenges of one's devotion and loyalty to divine purposes. Sooner or later, life brings to all of us the occasion of being "weighed in the balances" (Dan. 5:27). It is then that valor is assessed, and the depth of one's commitment to God evaluated.

> *But Daniel purposed in his heart that he would not defile himself with the portion of the king's meat, nor with the wine which he drank.* (Dan. 1:8)

> *As for these four children, God gave them knowledge and skill in all learning and wisdom.* (Dan. 1:17)

> *If it be so, our God whom we serve is able to deliver us from the burning fiery furnace, and he will deliver us out of thine hand, O king. But if not, be it known unto thee, O king, that we will not serve thy gods, nor worship the golden image which thou hast set up.* (Dan. 3:17–18)

> *Therefore I make a decree, That every people, nation, and language, which speak any thing amiss against the God of Shadrach, Meshach, and Abed-nego, shall be cut in pieces . . . because there is no other God that can deliver after this sort.* (Dan. 3:29)

Now the king spake and said unto Daniel, Thy God whom thou servest continually, he will deliver thee. (Dan. 6:16)

So Daniel was taken up out of the den, and no manner of hurt was found upon him, because he believed in his God. (Dan. 6:23)

And who knoweth whether thou art come to the kingdom for such a time as this? (Esther 4:14)

I also and my maidens will fast likewise; and so will I go in unto the king, which is not according to the law: and if I perish, I perish. (Esther 4:16)

If I have found favour in thy sight, O king, and if it please the king, let my life be given me at my petition, and my people at my request. (Esther 7:3)

MOMENT OF TRUTH

A life founded on enduring principles is a life imbued with truth and the glory of God. Daniel and his three young colleagues followed the principles of health and wholesome living (in opposition to the king's prescribed gourmet diet), and thus were rewarded with wisdom, comely appearance, brightness of mind, and opportunities for leadership. Later, his three young colleagues (renamed by their captors Shadrach, Meshach, and Abed-nego) followed the principle of worshiping the one true God and not idols, and thus ran afoul of the king's decree to worship his golden image. But again, as a result of following the principle of meticulous obedience to God's laws, they were attended by an angel of God in the fiery furnace, and emerged without even the odor of smoke upon their clothing. Likewise, Daniel followed the principle of continual, unremitting service to the God of Israel, despite life-threatening opposition at the hands of King Darius' nefarious princes, and thus emerged from the lions' den as an instrument for the preservation of true worship among his people.

Similarly, Queen Esther followed the principle of being a deliverer to her people by placing her own life at risk before King Ahasuerus, and through fasting and prayer thwarted the evil designs of Haman to bring about the extermination of the Jewish people in the land. Daniel and his three friends, as well as Esther and her cousin Mordecai, rose to places of prominence within the circles of their captors—much like their forebear, Joseph of Egypt.

Thus we see that the Lord, in His wisdom and eternal designs, prepares shepherds and stewards of the covenant by bringing them through the valley of adversity and trial. They then emerge as spiritual paragons endowed with power and wisdom, able to lead many in the paths of righteousness.

MODERN PROPHETS SPEAK

Dallin H. Oaks:

> A person earns no blessings for acts of service that are coerced or are performed with feelings of resentment. The Lord warned the children of Israel that they should serve him "with joyfulness, and with gladness of heart" (Deut. 28:47). In the present dispensation, the Lord has promised choice blessings to those who keep his commandments "with thanksgiving, with cheerful hearts and countenances" (D&C 59:15). That promise is even extended to those who serve and worship through song: "For my soul delighteth in the song of the heart; yea, the song of the righteous is a prayer unto me, and it shall be answered with a blessing upon their heads" (D&C 25:12). (*Pure in Heart* [Salt Lake City: Bookcraft, 1988], 29)

John A. Widtsoe:

> However, the main service of angels on earth is clearly to be helpers to humankind. They are watchmen, protecting and ministering to us in hours of need. John Taylor says, "The angels are our watchmen, for Satan said to Jesus: 'He shall give his angels charge concerning thee: and in their hands they shall bear thee up, lest at any time thou dash thy foot against a stone' (Matt. 4:6). It would seem from a careful perusal of the scriptures, that the angels, while God has Saints upon the earth, stay in this lower world to ward off evil" (*The Gospel Kingdom,* 31). The scriptures are replete with evidence, that these heavenly visitors are ministering angels for the righteous. Thus an angel brought courage to Hagar (Gen. 16:7), food to Elijah (1 Kgs. 19:5–8), protected Daniel against the lions (Dan. 6:22), and secured the release of Peter from prison (Acts 12:17). (*Evidences and Reconciliations* [Salt Lake City: Improvement Era, 1960], 402)

ILLUSTRATIONS FOR OUR TIMES

The Hand of the Lord Is Extended

Principles honored in adversity are in turn honored by God. The servants of God have been promised that, "I, the Lord, am bound when ye do what I say; but when ye do not what I say, ye have no promise" (D&C 82:10). He promised again, "And whoso receiveth you, there I will be also, for I will go before your face. I will be on your right hand and on your left, and my Spirit shall be in your hearts, and mine angels round about you, to bear you up" (D&C 84:88).

The missionaries were full of faith, exactly and courageously obedient, showed compassion and love, and were blessed by the Spirit, even as the sacrament prayers promised. Their lives had not been threatened like Daniel of old, or the Prophet Joseph, but honoring their covenants brought the blessings from God. They were seeking families to baptize, and had prayed and worked diligently. Surely the Lord could provide some of His elect families to hear His servants. They had just finished morning studies and were going to the town center to do some street contacting. As they drove down the street, the senior companion said, "There! That man! He's the one." The elders stopped the car and ran to the house and introduced themselves, and the man invited them back to teach his family that evening. Like so many times in so many missions, the hand of the Lord was extended. The missionaries were blessed, as were His children by the message of the Restoration—they were converted by the Spirit and were baptized. In all things, the Lord will honor His covenants as we honor ours.

Angels on Earth

The expression "angels on earth" is an apt reminder that brothers and sisters, mothers and fathers, extended family members, and caring friends and associates are continually involved in a "labour of love" (Heb. 6:10)—sometimes manifest, but often invisible—to support, encourage, sustain, heal, and guide in ways that promote our well-being and happiness. We do not often face the fangs of a caged lion as Daniel was forced to do, or the flames of a fiery furnace that licked at the faces of his three compatriots. Nor do we often have to face the potential wrath of a tyrant such as Esther did when she rose in nobility as a champion of the covenant people. But from time to time, life nonetheless presents to all of us occasions of trial and testing where the succor of "angels on earth," as well as unseen angels from heaven, provides balm to the troubled soul and rescue for the captive heart.

I had a sainted aunt who was devoted to the cultivation of family unity and well-being. During her long and productive lifetime, Aunt Grace would often supply me with family history materials to enlarge my understanding of the roots from which our branch of Israel had sprung. On one occasion many years ago, she related to me a story about a special kind of "angel on earth" who played an important role in opening up one of the genealogical channels that had long remained hidden. The family organization had retained a professional genealogist and dispatched her to Wales to see if a particular parish might hold the key for a breakthrough in research. Since the local curators of the records were rather particular about protocol, she had prepared the way by writing ahead concerning a particular volume of records she needed to see, knowing that she would be permitted to see only that which she had ordered ahead of time.

On the appointed day, she was ushered into the reading room, and the priceless volume was placed before her. However, when she examined it, she noted, much to her disappointment, that it was not the volume she had requested, but another one. As she pondered her predicament in coming so far without the opportunity to view the precious records, she looked about and caught the eye of an older gentlemen seated in a corner of the same room. He was smiling pleasantly at her, and his countenance seemed somehow to be familiar to her. Then, for an instant, she looked back at the volume before her and noted from its index that it was, though not the requested volume, precisely the one that contained the needed information. Overjoyed, she looked back toward the older gentleman, but he had disappeared. She smiled, knowing now who he was—a venerated member of the family organization who had labored long to further the cause of family history and temple work until his passing several years earlier.

"Have miracles ceased?" asked Mormon. "Behold I say unto you, Nay; neither have angels ceased to minister unto the children of men" (Moro. 7:29). And the Psalmist declared: "For he shall give his angels charge over thee, to keep thee in all thy ways" (Ps. 91:11).

SUMMARY

The lesson learned by Nebuchadnezzar—"There is no other God that can deliver" (Dan. 3:29)—is the same lesson that all of us must learn, preferably sooner than later. Darius learned it early on, saying: "Thy God whom thou servest continually, he will deliver thee" (Dan. 6:16). And so it was. The exemplary leaders of Israel confirmed time and time again through their experiences that the Lord glorifies honor, obedience, and righteous character with blessings of deliverance and compassion. It is a spiritual partnership of eternal consequence: "And I will betroth thee unto me for ever; yea, I will betroth thee unto me in righteousness, and in judgment, and in lovingkindness, and in mercies" (Hosea 2:19). To follow in the footsteps of Daniel, Esther, and their courageous and obedient fellow-travelers on the pathway of perfection is to invite the Lord's enduring blessings into our own lives and into the lives of our family members.

CHAPTER FORTY-SIX

"A KINGDOM, WHICH SHALL NEVER BE DESTROYED"

Reading Assignment: Daniel 2.

Additional Reading: D&C 65.

After a happy time spent in witnessing and feeling for ourselves the powers and blessings of the Holy Ghost, through the grace of God bestowed upon us, we dismissed with the pleasing knowledge that we were now individually members of, and acknowledged of God, "The Church of Jesus Christ," organized in accordance with commandments and revelations given by Him to ourselves in these last days, as well as according to the order of the Church as recorded in the New Testament. (Joseph Smith, HC 1:79)

THEME *for* LIVING

1. The Stone that Filled the Whole Earth

INTRODUCTION

Nebuchadnezzar, king of the Babylonian empire and captor of the hosts of Israel since 587 B.C., had a troubling dream one night about a stone hewn from the mountain without hands that destroyed a mighty image in human form. The king commanded his wise men to reveal its contents to him and interpret its meaning. Because they were helpless to perform their assignment, saying that only the gods could do so, the king ordered all such wise men—including the bright and visionary young Daniel—to be destroyed. But Daniel, being full of faith and wisdom, gained more time from the king so that a spiritual solution could be sought. Through prayer, Daniel was able to open up the channels of revelation from the Lord so that His eternal agenda, as it related to earthly kings and empires leading to the restoration of the Church in the latter days, might be made known to Nebuchadnezzar and all seekers of truth after him.

THE STONE THAT FILLED THE WHOLE EARTH

THEME: The stone "cut out of the mountain without hands" (Dan. 2:45) is the kingdom of God, which is to supercede all earthly kingdoms and fill the world with a heavenly dominion of truth and light under the supreme rulership of the Redeemer and Lord of Lords.

> *And in the days of these kings shall the God of heaven set up a kingdom, which shall never be destroyed: and the kingdom shall not be left to other people, but it shall break in pieces and consume all these kingdoms, and it shall stand for ever.* (Dan. 2:44)

> *The king answered unto Daniel, and said, Of a truth it is, that your God is a God of gods, and a Lord of kings, and a revealer of secrets, seeing thou couldest reveal this secret. Then the king made Daniel a great man, and gave him many great gifts, and made him ruler over the whole province of Babylon, and chief of the governors over all the wise men of Babylon.* (Dan. 2:47–48)

MOMENT OF TRUTH

Faced with certain death unless the king's dream could be revealed and interpreted, Daniel counseled with his three young companions—renamed by their hosts Shadrach, Meshach, and Abed-nego—and as a team they sought the "mercies of the God of heaven concerning this secret" (Dan. 2:18). It is instructive that when the answer came to Daniel "in a night vision" (v. 19), he immediately blessed the name of God and gave humble thanks and praise for the divine gift (v. 23). Daniel was able to save all condemned wise men in the kingdom by advising Nebuchadnezzar correctly concerning the dream, which foretold the coming of the restored kingdom of heaven to become "a great mountain" and fill "the whole earth" (v. 35). But the king refused to relinquish his idolatry, and a second dream depicting the king as a great and mighty tree that was hewn down at the behest of "an holy one coming down from heaven" (Dan. 4:23) was interpreted by Daniel to portend the king's death. Daniel counseled the king in all candor to "break off thy sins by righteousness, and thine iniquities by shewing mercy to the poor; if it may be a lengthening of thy tranquillity" (Dan. 4:27). But it was not to be: "The same hour was the thing fulfilled upon Nebuchadnezzar: and he was driven from men" (v. 33). From his deposed perspective, it was easy for the king, now stripped of his opulence, to confess: "I blessed the most High, and I praised and honoured him that liveth for ever, whose dominion is an everlasting dominion, and his kingdom is from generation to generation: . . . and those that walk in pride he is able to abase" (Dan. 4:34, 37).

The royal reveler Belshazzar, who succeeded his father as king of Babylon, did not fare much better after Daniel interpreted the celebrated and ominous writing on the wall of his chamber this way: "Thou art weighed in the balances, and art found wanting" (Dan. 5:27). That night, Belshazzar was deposed by Darius the Mede. Thus continued the unfolding of the certain prediction that a succession of earthly kingdoms would fall, one after the other, until, ultimately, the Lord would restore a heavenly kingdom to the earth.

MODERN PROPHETS SPEAK

Joseph Fielding Smith:

> This Gospel is decreed to "roll forth" until it shall eventually fill the earth. When Christ comes the wicked shall be destroyed, and righteousness will follow until it will cover the earth as the waters do the sea (Isa. 11:9). (*Church History and Modern Revelation* [Salt Lake City: The Church of Jesus Christ of Latter-day Saints, 1946–49], 2:16)

Gordon B. Hinckley:

> This was the final charge given by the Lord following his resurrection and before his ascension. It was repeated at the opening of this dispensation. Following the organization of the first Quorum of the Twelve in 1835, Oliver Cowdery, counselor in the First Presidency, delivered a charge to these men. That statement has become something of a charter for all members of the Twelve who have succeeded that first group. In that charge is the following counsel: "Be zealous to save souls. The soul of one man is as precious as the soul of another. . . . The Gospel must roll forth, and it will

until it fills the whole earth. . . . You have a work to do that no other men can do; you must proclaim the Gospel in its simplicity and purity; and we commend you to God and the word of His grace" (*HC* 2:196–98). (*Faith: The Essence of True Religion* [Salt Lake City: Deseret Book, 1989], 51)

ILLUSTRATIONS FOR OUR TIMES

The Greatest Good

From its humble beginnings on 6 April 1830, to over 12,275,000 members in 2004 (*Ensign,* May 2005, 25), the kingdom of God is rolling forth and covering the earth. The gospel is preached in over 120 nations and twenty-four territories and in over forty-five languages. The Book of Mormon has been translated into forty-five languages and selected portions in another forty-six languages. How has this happened?

> Wherefore, I the Lord, knowing the calamity which would come upon the inhabitants of the earth, called upon my servant Joseph Smith, Jun., and spake unto him from heaven, and gave him commandments;
>
> And also gave commandments to others, that they should proclaim these things unto the world; and all this that it might be fulfilled, which was written by the prophets—
>
> The weak things of the world shall come forth and break down the mighty and strong ones . . .
>
> That faith also might increase in the earth;
>
> That mine everlasting covenant might be established;
>
> That the fulness of my gospel might be proclaimed by the weak and the simple unto the ends of the world, and before kings and rulers. (D&C 1:17–19, 21–23)

The Lord will use the weak and simple of the earth—lay members of the Church, young men and women, mature couples and sisters. The time for the final gathering is now (see Jacob 5:70–71; D&C 138:53, 56). We are the ones to do the work. Presently over 60,784 missionaries are serving in 334 missions.

The name of Owen M. Sanderson means a great deal to the Pinegars, for he taught and baptized Harvey Anderson Pinegar in May of 1895. Each family owes a great debt of gratitude to those early missionaries for bringing the Church into their or their family's lives. Stories of conversion thrill each family as they read from the diaries and journals of their ancestors. It is our duty now to take the gospel to everyone in their own language. Remember, "Wherefore, seek not the things of this world but seek ye first to build up the kingdom of God, and to establish his righteousness" (JST, Matt. 6:38). Building up the kingdom by bringing our brothers and sisters to Christ will be the greatest good we can do.

"By Small Means the Lord Can Bring About Great Things" (1 Ne. 16:29)

To experience the magnificent new Church Conference Center north of Temple Square in Salt Lake City is to gain an inkling of the destiny of the stone cut out of the mountain without hands, rolling forth to fill the entire world. With translation capability for as many as sixty languages at a time, the 21,000 seat, 1.5-million-square-foot facility (about forty times the size of the Tabernacle) has a worldwide reach.

As I ponder this imposing edifice, my mind returns to a small garden house in a remote German city where my missionary companion and I once conducted Church services and taught the gospel. The garden house was really a tool shed, perhaps six feet by ten feet in size, with a small door and a few tiny windows. It was nestled in a beautiful orchard located behind the home of the only member family in the city. Because the owner was also the proprietor of a small neighborhood grocery store, she was fearful that her business would suffer should it become known by her intolerant neighbors that she was hosting Church services in her home. Therefore, she suggested that we use the garden house for meetings on Sundays, everyone coming up through the back of the property from different directions through the trees in order to avoid detection.

And that's what we did. My companion and I would teach the gospel in the garden house to a handful of investigators (typically two or three) who would crowd into this humble facility to learn true principles. I recall one session where it rained so hard that the noise of the water on the roof made it difficult to present the lesson on the Holy Ghost. But the Spirit nevertheless touched our hearts in that lowly setting. Testimonies were cultivated. Lives were changed. It was all part of the motion of that stone cut from the mountain without hands—the process by which the influence of restored truths was being felt once again, even in remote parts of the world.

When the Prophet Joseph Smith conducted that historic meeting on 6 April 1830, at the Peter Whitmer farmhouse in Fayette, New York, at which the kingdom of God was once more organized on the earth, beginning with just six souls, he very likely saw in his mind's eye the prophetic view of the inexorable destiny of that kingdom—how a small stone "became a great mountain, and filled the whole earth" (Dan. 2:35). The Great Architect knows the final design: "Wherefore, be not weary in well-doing, for ye are laying the foundation of a great work. And out of small things proceedeth that which is great" (D&C 64:33).

SUMMARY

In describing the kingdom of God on the earth, the Apostle Paul spoke of its members as having been "built upon the foundation of the apostles and prophets, Jesus Christ himself being the chief corner stone; In whom all the building fitly framed together groweth unto an holy temple in the Lord" (Eph. 2:20–21). The stone that rolls forth to fill the world is the gospel kingdom of Jesus Christ, in its fullness a mighty temple unto God. In a special and unique way, the stone is the Savior Himself: "Therefore thus saith the Lord God, Behold, I lay in Zion for a foundation a stone, a tried stone, a precious corner stone, a sure foundation: he that believeth shall not make haste" (Isa. 28:16). In referring to this word of prophecy, the Apostle Peter expressed it this way: "He that believeth on him shall not be confounded" (1 Pet. 2:6). Thus the foundation for the spiritual existence of the sons and daughters of God, for the salvation of all mankind and the exaltation of the faithful, is Jesus Christ. By doing our part to advance the cause of the "stone," we help build the kingdom of God.

CHAPTER FORTY-SEVEN

"FOR *the* LORD HATH MADE THEM JOYFUL"

Reading Assignment: Ezra 1–8; Nehemiah 1–2; 4; 6; 8.

Additional Reading: Haggai 1; Bible Dictionary, "Ezra"; "Nehemiah."

The principle of knowledge is the principle of salvation. This principle can be comprehended by the faithful and diligent; and everyone that does not obtain knowledge sufficient to be saved will be condemned. The principle of salvation is given us through the knowledge of Jesus Christ. Salvation is nothing more nor less than to triumph over all our enemies and put them under out feet. And when we have power to put all enemies under our feet in this world, and a knowledge to triumph over all evil spirits in the world to come, then we are saved, as in the case of Jesus, who was to reign until He had put all enemies under His feet, and the last enemy was death. (Joseph Smith, *TPJS*, 297)

THEME *for* LIVING

1. The Work of God Is to Edify, Renew, and Make Joyful

INTRODUCTION

When Cyrus overthrew the Chaldean dynasty and took control of Babylon, he was moved by the Spirit of the Lord (Ezra 1:1) and issued a decree in 537 B.C. (some fifty years after Nebuchadnezzar had sacked Jerusalem) allowing the captive Israelites to return to their city and rebuild the temple, as Jeremiah had foretold (see Jer. 25:11–12; 29:10). The work of rebuilding the temple and restoring the walls of the city provided a backdrop to the emergence of inspired leadership and the preservation of tales of courage and conviction in the face of sinister plots to thwart the work of God. It was a dramatic reminder that the Saints of God on the Lord's errand must rise in the majesty of His cause and His armor as they complete their ordained tasks.

THE WORK OF GOD IS TO EDIFY, RENEW, AND MAKE JOYFUL

THEME: To learn to keep the covenants of God is to learn how to become sanctified and make a holy offering unto the Lord in righteousness. The Spirit of the Lord induces the ongoing work of building—building joyful families, building temples, building a Zion society, building the kingdom of God. When we work in faithful obedience to secure our families, the Lord will fight our battles for us by softening the hearts of those who have influence over us (as He did in the case of the ancient kings) and by providing strength and leadership in support of the cause of truth.

> *Let us rise up and build.* (Neh. 2:18)

> *The God of heaven, he will prosper us; therefore we his servants will arise and build.* (Neh. 2:20)

> *Be not ye afraid of them: remember the Lord, which is great and terrible, and fight for your brethren, your sons, and your daughters, your wives, and your houses.* (Neh. 4:14)

> *In what place therefore ye hear the sound of the trumpet, resort ye thither unto us: our God shall fight for us.* (Neh. 4:20)

> *Now therefore, O God, strengthen my hands.* (Neh. 6:9)

> *For the joy of the Lord is your strength.* (Neh. 8:10)

MOMENT OF TRUTH

Ezra was a celebrated, God-fearing priest and scribe who helped with the return of many of the exiles from their Babylonian captivity. He has left us a record of the initial phase of the rebuilding of Jerusalem (from the edict of Cyrus in 537 B.C. down to the completion of the temple in approximately 515 B.C.), as well as the annals of his own personal mission some years later, beginning in 458 B.C., to assist in the return of many more Israelites to Jerusalem. He was a reformer who taught the people the principles of fasting and prayer, and caused the scriptures to be read publicly for their edification and understanding: "For Ezra had prepared his heart to seek the law of the Lord, and to do it, and to teach in Israel statutes and judgments" (Ezra 7:10). Nehemiah made a similar contribution by leading the movement to restore the walls of the city for strength and protection. An influential "cupbearer" at the court of King Artaxerxes of Persia (465–425 B.C.; see Neh. 1:11), Nehemiah was moved by the accounts of the sufferings of his compatriots at Jerusalem and launched a major campaign to restore the security of the city. For twelve years he labored as governor—against daunting odds and life-threatening plots by enemy forces—to complete the walls of the city: "They which builded on the wall, and they that bare burdens, with those that laded, every one with one of his hands wrought in the work, and with the other hand held a weapon" (Neh. 4:17). Thus Nehemiah and Ezra have left us stirring examples of restoration, rebuilding, fortifying, strengthening, and renewing—all to the glory of God and the service of establishing His kingdom upon the earth.

MODERN PROPHETS SPEAK

John A. Widtsoe:

> Conformity to law spells victory; opposition to law means defeat and eventual destruction. We must seek out law; and conform to it, whether in the material or spiritual domains, if we are to be winners in the race of life. (*An Understandable Religion* [Independence, MO: Zion's Printing and Publishing, 1944], 58–59)

Harold B. Lee:

> The purpose of your being on the earth. It is that you might obtain a fulness of joy. But remember as well the Lord has said that "in this world your joy is not full, but in (him) your joy is full" (D&C 101:36). A heart full of happiness is an evidence that you are building a heaven on earth that will last for eternity. At one stage in the world's history, the religious record tells the story of a people who had attained to this heavenly joy of which the Lord spoke: "And there were no envyings, nor strife, nor tumults, nor whoredoms, nor lyings, nor murders, nor any manner of lasciviousness;

and surely there could not be a happier people among all the people who had been created by the hand of God" (IV Ne. 1:16). (*Decisions for Successful Living* [Salt Lake City: Deseret Book, 1973], 153–54)

ILLUSTRATIONS FOR OUR TIMES

Restoring the Man

Ezra and Nehemiah were great examples of rebuilding. They were restorers, instrumental in the restoration of the Jewish nation and the temple. When people make righteous choices, like Ezra they literally become Saints. Truly converted Saints have an overwhelming desire to share the gospel, to be deliverers of the message and teachers of the word of God. This is a regular occurrence in the kingdom today—young men finally catching the vision. They have been estranged like the Jews. Their temple has broken down temporally and spiritually, but the light of the Lord is still there. They are still teachable. They want to be good, but simply have given into temptation. They seek the word of God, come to the institute, and are taught the statutes and commandments of God.

The story begins with a young man with longish hair and earrings attending a missionary preparation class. I looked at the young man and thought, "This young man needs empathy and love. He needs to be understood and accepted. He needs to feel the Spirit."

He was attentive in class and attended regularly. We became friends and visited in my office a few times. When the semester was about half over, he came to talk with me and had some questions on his mind. We visited and had a wonderful time together. As our visit was coming to a close, I asked him what he wanted in life. He responded, "I think I really want to serve a mission."

I was elated. Then the Spirit took over. I became bold. I said, "You mean you want to prepare to be a true disciple of the Lord Jesus Christ?"

"Yes," he replied.

"You really do? Well then, let's get started the right way. Do you look like a missionary?" He knew right off what I was getting at. He squirmed and mentioned something about not judging by appearances. I had him look at a picture of the prophet and asked, "Do you look like him? Will you follow his counsel?"

The Spirit was strong and he said, "I understand." He took out his gold earrings and threw them in the garbage can.

We rejoiced together as the Spirit had touched his nature. The next class period, he looked like a sharp missionary. He became even more attentive. He served a glorious mission for the Lord. He was rebuilt. He was edified. He was restored, for his heart was right. He sought the will of God, he kept the commandments, and he was full of joy in the service of his Savior and his fellow men.

Be Vigilant and Watchful in Protecting the Things of God

The story of Nehemiah's leadership in organizing the Israelites to rebuild the walls of Jerusalem, often under threat of attack from enemy forces round about, reminds me of an incident from Church history that occurred on Wednesday, 8 January 1834, in Kirtland, Ohio. On that day, guards were placed to protect the Kirtland temple as a result of persecution by detractors and the threat of violence at the hands of the gathering mob. Some workmen were seen armed with a hammer in one hand and a rifle in the other. Joseph Smith recorded in his journal: "On the morning of the 8th of January, about 1 o'clock, the inhabitants of Kirtland were alarmed by the firing of about thirteen rounds of cannon, by the mob, on the hill about half a mile northwest of the village" (*HC* 2:2). However, with the coming of dawn, it was determined that the temple had not been damaged. Of this period, Heber C. Kimball wrote in the *Times and Seasons* that: "we had to guard ourselves night after night, and for weeks were not permitted to take off our clothes, and were obliged to lay with our fire locks [rifles] in our arms" (*HC* 2:2). Do we ponder often enough upon the sacrifices and trials of our forebears—including our ancient brothers and sisters in Old Testament times—and upon their vigilance and endurance in securing for us the blessings that we enjoy so abundantly today? Are we prepared to stand up for righteous principles and guard the things of God with our lives as they did?

In the days of Nehemiah, as in the days of the Kirtland Saints, the righteous were constrained to carry on their labors with a tool in one hand and a weapon in the other. And so it is today—and at all times during the experience of mortality. The prudent and wise never venture forth in their pursuits without first providing themselves with divine armor. As Paul stated it: "Put on the whole armour of God, that ye may be able to stand against the wiles of the devil" (Eph. 6:11; see also D&C 27:15–18). The weapons of godly armament—truth, righteousness, preparations of the gospel of peace (as in the scriptures), faith, salvation (the principle of saving knowledge leading to victory over all one's enemies), and the Spirit—are more than pleasant images. They are real, potent, and highly effective defenses when used in the Lord's way.

I recall an incident from the life of my own son, Matthew, that illustrates the challenges that the youth of today must face in standing up for truth and right. When he was thirteen years old and completing the work toward his Eagle Scout Award, he decided as a project to conduct a neighborhood educational campaign about the dangers of drug abuse. As it turned out, I was at the time in the midst of a similar campaign with a national organization that was sponsoring a gala in the nation's capital for the purpose of adding momentum to the war on drugs. My wife and I decided to take Matthew with us on this occasion, and the thought occurred to us that it would be a memorable experience for him if arrangements could be made for him to say a few words about his project to the four or five hundred chiefs of police, senators, congressmen, and other dignitaries attending the event. So we approached one of the keynote speakers, Hyrum Smith, founder of the Franklin Planner organization, and asked whether he might include Matthew as part of his time on the program. Hyrum graciously consented, and at the appointed time Matthew stood up in all the majesty of his thirteen young years and made an impassioned case for honor and vigilance in fighting the war on drugs. The same thing occurs every day in the lives of all faithful youth—they stand up before their peers and before their detractors and say no to illicit drugs and any other pernicious influence that besets them. They don the whole armor of God and fight the battles of mortality in His strength and in His power. May the Lord bless the noble youth of His kingdom.

SUMMARY

The inspiring leadership of Ezra and Nehemiah echoes in the lives of God's leaders in all dispensations of time. The same call to service resounds with even greater urgency in our day as we prepare for the Second Coming and the ushering in of the millennial age. We are on the Lord's business to build His kingdom: "Wherefore, as ye are agents, ye are on the Lord's errand; and whatever ye do according to the will of the Lord is the Lord's business" (D&C 64:29). By putting on the whole armor of God, we can transcend the negative forces at work to thwart the designs of the Almighty. "And for this cause, that men might be made partakers of the glories which were to be revealed, the Lord sent forth the fulness of his gospel, his everlasting covenant, reasoning in plainness and simplicity—To prepare the weak for those things which are coming on the earth, and for the Lord's errand in the day when the weak shall confound the wise, and the little one become a strong nation, and two shall put their tens of thousands to flight. And by the weak things of the earth the Lord shall thrash the nations by the power of his Spirit" (D&C 133:57–59). Like the Saints at the time of Ezra and Nehemiah, we can don the whole armor of God and take comfort in the hope of Israel: "for the Lord had made them joyful" (Ezra 6:22).

CHAPTER FORTY-EIGHT

"BUT WHO MAY ABIDE *the* DAY *of* HIS COMING?"

Reading Assignment: Zechariah 10–14; Malachi.

Additional Reading: D&C 45.

> *You and I live in a day in which the Lord our God has set His hand for the last time, to gather out the righteous and to prepare a people to reign on this earth,—a people who will be purified by good works, who will abide the faith of the living God and be ready to meet the Bridegroom when He comes to reign over the earth, even Jesus Christ . . . and be prepared for that glorious event—the coming of the Son of Man—which I believe will not be at any great distant day.* (Joseph F. Smith, *Millennial Star* 36:220)

THEMES *for* LIVING

1. The Law of Tithing
2. Preparing for the Second Coming

INTRODUCTION

Two of the final voices from the prophetic quorum of Old Testament witnesses—Zechariah and Malachi—sounded ominous warnings about the coming day of judgment, when all individuals would need to account for the quality of their mortal choices. The view of these final two messengers was not only of the Messiah's ministry upon the earth just a few hundred years hence, where the majesty of His atoning sacrifice would stand out in stark contrast to the myopic blindness of the generation that would utterly reject Him, but of His eventual Second Coming in glory and power as the King of Kings and Lord of Lords before whom "every knee shall bow, and every tongue shall confess" (D&C 88:104).

The operant question is this: How should we prepare for this singularly important event and be able to "abide the day of his coming" (Mal. 3:2)? The answer is clear: choose the Lord (Zech. 13:9), worship Him (Zech. 14:17), make "holiness to the Lord" a pervasive dimension of life (Zech. 14:20), honor Him (Mal. 1:5), bring a "pure offering" before Him in righteousness (Mal. 1:11; 3:3), give glory to the name of God (Mal. 2:2), walk with God "in peace and equity" (Mal. 2:6), remain faithfully within the covenant bounds in marriage (Mal. 2:11), care for the poor and needy (Mal. 3:5), return unto God (Mal. 3:7), pay your tithes and offerings (Mal. 3:10), fear God and always keep Him in your thoughts (Mal. 3:16), avoid pride (Mal. 4:1), and (under the influence of the sealing power of the priesthood) cultivate a godly and eternal disposition of oneness among families, both fathers (parents) toward their children, and children toward their fathers (Mal. 4:5–6). Only then can we hope to enjoy the "spirit of grace and supplication" (Zech. 12:10) that the Lord will pour out upon His covenant people in the day of both rescue and retribution. Only then will the earth—already destined to endure a universal cleansing at the Lord's coming—be spared the curse of emptiness that would come if the eternal covenant principles would not in the end prevail.

1. THE LAW OF TITHING

THEME: The kingdom of heaven on the earth is to be built up with the tithes of the Lord's people. With His abundance, He will sustain the faithful Saints through their obedience to His laws and principles.

> *Bring ye all the tithes into the storehouse, that there may be meat in mine house, and prove me now herewith, saith the Lord of hosts, if I will not open you the windows of heaven, and pour you out a blessing, that there shall not be room enough to receive it.*
> (Mal. 3:10)

MOMENT OF TRUTH

Malachi, prophesying around 430 B.C., taught the lessons of spiritual abundance—that the Lord is prepared to open the windows of heaven in blessing the faithful who obediently support the unfolding of His kingdom through their sacrifice and consecrations. His promise is that "all nations shall call you blessed: for ye shall be a delightsome land, saith the Lord of hosts" (Mal. 3:12).

MODERN PROPHETS SPEAK

Ezra Taft Benson:

> One is blessed temporally for obedience to the law of tithing. But the greatest blessings of the Lord are, after all, spiritual in nature. Perhaps that is the deeper meaning to the expression, "I will open you the windows of heaven and pour you out a blessing, that there shall not be room enough to receive it" (Mal. 3:10). The late Elder Melvin J. Ballard, an Apostle, said that "the Lord has promised that the man and woman who pay their honest tithing shall be provided for, [but] He doesn't promise to make them rich, not in material things. The greatest blessings of the Lord are spiritual, and not material" ("Crusader for Righteousness," Logan, Utah, 6 December 1975, 124). (*TETB,* 472–73)

Gordon B. Hinckley:

> By way of personal testimony, while speaking of the financial resources of the Church, we reiterate the promise of the Lord given anciently through the prophet Malachi that he will open the windows of heaven upon those who are honest with him in the payment of their tithes and offerings, that there shall not be room enough to receive the promised blessings. Every honest tithe payer can testify that the Lord keeps his promise. ("The Miracle Made Possible by Faith," *Ensign,* May 1984, 47; see also *TGBH,* 654)

ILLUSTRATIONS FOR OUR TIMES

A Promise Fulfilled

I remember a story told once by Preston Nibley. Upon noticing that a branch president had regularly paid a large tithing, Brother Nibley remarked to him that he must have an outstanding testimony of the law of tithing. He replied that he did and related how that testimony came about.

He said that his wife and children had joined the Church in England some years before, but he hadn't been baptized at that time because he didn't have faith to pay his tithing and did not want to be a hypocrite. Some time later, shortly before one of the missionaries was being released to return home, the elder came to this brother and told him he wanted to baptize him before returning home. The brother refused, because he still wasn't paying his tithing. The missionary promised him that if he would be baptized and pay an honest tithe, he would be in America with his family within a year's time and be earning three times as much as he was then.

The brother took him up on his promise and was baptized. Shortly thereafter, he was able to be released from the two-year contract he had with the company that employed him and was sent to America to teach cloth makers how to make fabric dyes. Not only was he in America with his family within that one-year period of time promised by the missionary, but he was making *four* times his previous salary. The genuineness of this experience is attested by the faithfulness of this brother in paying his tithing following his baptism into the Church.

"Before They Call, I Will Answer"

I remember, as a small boy, paying my tithing for the first time. My parents had taught me that the Lord blesses those who pay tithing, so I carefully prepared a tithing slip covering the sixteen cents—a large sum indeed—and gave it to the bishop.

That afternoon I was invited to attend a family gathering in honor of a cousin who was celebrating her birthday. In those days, it was customary for the hostess to wrap small coins in wax paper and bake them in the birthday cake as a surprise to the celebrants. Sure enough, I was one of the fortunate ones to discover a dime hidden in my piece of cake. "It's working already," I said to myself, thinking of the tithing donation.

Following the party, as I was walking home, I looked down and discovered a small coin purse lying in the grass. Sure enough, it contained six cents. Upon inquiring around the neighborhood, I could not discover the owner of the lost purse, and so, in my young simplicity, I concluded that the Lord returns tithing immediately—penny for penny.

Since that time, I have repeatedly confirmed through personal experience that the Lord does indeed return blessing upon blessing for those who pay an honest and willing tithe. The blessings are often of a tangible and material nature—sometimes miraculously so—but always with a spiritual essence and connection. I recall, as a young graduate student at the Johns Hopkins University, counseling with my wife concerning the hospital bill for the birth of our second daughter, Adrienne. The question was whether we should we pay this bill or pay the tithing that was due, for it seemed improbable that our resources could cover both at the same time.

We decided prayerfully to pay our tithing and had a good feeling about it. The next day, I was called into the office of the Dean at the university, who informed me that I had been selected that year to receive a certain award pertaining to graduate teaching. It was to be bestowed at the graduation ceremonies a few days hence. I was surprised and most gratified at the honor, especially when he explained that it was unusual for the award to be going to someone in my department this year, since another colleague in the same department had received the award the previous year.

As I was leaving his office, he called me back to say, "By the way, there is a stipend that comes with the award." He then mentioned a figure that was almost exactly the same amount as the hospital bill. I was amazed and touched by the news, and I still thrill over the memory of it to this day. Upon receiving word later, my wife was also overjoyed at such an unanticipated blessing. Clearly this award had been under consideration by the university authorities for some time. "Before they call, I will answer," was the promise of the Lord recorded in Isaiah 65:24.

We found, moreover, that our employers had adjusted the terms of our employment unexpectedly to provide even more revenue than we were counting on. Thus we paid our hospital bill on time, and with money to spare. For that reason, my wife and I have often referred to Adrienne as our "tithing child," because she was paid for by the Lord. In fact, we are all paid for in a similar way through the Atonement: "For ye are bought with a price: therefore glorify God in your body, and in your spirit, which are God's" (1 Cor. 6:20). It was one more instance, among many others, where we learned the absolute nature of the promise inherent in the divine challenge to: "prove me now herewith, saith the Lord of hosts, if I will not open you the windows of heaven, and pour you out a blessing, that there shall not be room enough to receive it" (Mal. 3:10).

2. PREPARING FOR THE SECOND COMING

THEME: When He shall return, no man knows. But the Saints are well advised to make their walk and conversation each day an offering in righteousness and obedience, that all may be ready for His return.

> *And he shall purify the sons of Levi, and purge them as gold and silver, that they may offer unto the Lord an offering in righteousness.* (Mal. 3:3)

> *For I am the Lord their God, and will hear them.* (Zech. 10:6)

> *I will strengthen them in the Lord; and they shall walk up and down in his name, saith the Lord.* (Zech. 10:12)

> *And one shall say unto him, What are these wounds in thine hands? Then he shall answer, Those with which I was wounded in the house of my friends.* (Zech. 13:6)

I will say, It is my people: and they shall say, The Lord is my God. (Zech. 13:9)

Behold, I will send you Elijah the prophet before the coming of the great and dreadful day of the Lord: And he shall turn the heart of the fathers to the children, and the heart of the children to their fathers, lest I come and smite the earth with a curse. (Mal. 4:4–5)

MOMENT OF TRUTH

Zechariah prophesied in the period 520 B.C. to 518 B.C. concerning the earthly travails and destiny of the covenant peoples of God against the backdrop of the coming mission of the Savior in the meridian of time and His ultimate appearance in glory at the dawning of the millennial age. The forces of righteousness would triumph through the saving intervention of heaven, and the Zion people would once again emerge in the last days as the people of God, purified and sanctified through the redeeming grace of the re-enthroned Savior. Some hundred years after the ministry of Zechariah, Malachi, the last of the Old Testament prophets, intoned the same theme around 430 B.C., reproving the priests for their neglect of duty and the people in general for straying from the covenant principles. He called for a reform in anticipation of the coming of the Lord and reminded the people that the Lord would send Elijah the prophet once again to bring about the grand unifying work (the sealing enterprise of the temples) that would save the earth from a curse.

MODERN PROPHETS SPEAK

Neal A. Maxwell:

> Thus gospel hope is a very focused and particularized hope that is based upon justified expectations. It is a virtue that is intertwined with faith and charity, which virtues are not to be understood either when they are torn apart from each other or apart from the Lord Jesus Christ, without whom they are all vague virtues. Doubt and despair go together, whereas faith and hope are constant companions. Those, for instance, who "hope" in vain for (and speak of) the day of world peace when men "shall beat their swords into plowshares" ignore the reality that the millennial dawn will be ushered in only by the second coming of Jesus Christ. Neither secular rhetoric nor secular assemblies will succeed in bringing lasting peace to this planet. Secularists, meanwhile, have ironically appropriated the Lord's language of hope while denying Him! It is He and His ways alone that can bring about such desirable conditions. There will be no millennium without the Master. Paul's futuring focused on the Lord, giving us consolation by holding forth that which is to come, con-

firming hope. But this hope develops, as does faith, "line upon line, precept upon precept; here a little, and there a little" (D&C 128:21). (*Notwithstanding My Weakness* [Salt Lake City: Deseret Book, 1981], 41–42)

Bruce R. McConkie:

> In our day we look forward with hope and joy to the Second Coming of the Son of Man, and to the setting up of the millennial kingdom of peace and righteousness, over which he shall assume personal rule for the space of a thousand years. We do not know and shall not learn either the day or the hour of that dreadful yet blessed day. We are expected to read the signs of the times and know thereby the approximate time of our Lord's return and to be in constant readiness therefor. (*The Promised Messiah: The First Coming of Christ* [Salt Lake City: Deseret Book, 1978], 457)

ILLUSTRATIONS FOR OUR TIMES

The Clouds of Heaven

As a young boy growing up in a small town on the Canadian prairies, I recall inviting a neighborhood friend to go camping one summer day. After making all preparations, we set out on our adventure and set up the scout tent beneath an old tree at the edge of a wheat field not too far from the edge of town. All went well until we noticed water advancing up the furrows of the field. It was evidence of modern irrigation procedures at work, and it was an alarming threat to our hours of hard labor. What to do?

I had learned from my parents something of the importance of prayer, so I suggested that we kneel down and ask for God's help to save our little kingdom. After saying a fervent prayer, we watched in silence as the water continued to advance with relentless consistency up the field toward our campsite. When it came to within a few yards of our tent, we started to comprehend the contours of our fate. When it came to within a few feet of our tent, we saw the future with certainty. When it finally touched the fabric of our tent, we saw the wisdom of taking immediate action to locate a more secure campsite. And that's exactly what we did. Our prayer was answered; and the answer was "Move."

On that day I learned the meaning of a word that I wasn't even to hear for many years to come. It is the word *inexorable.* It comes from a Latin root *orare,* meaning to pray. If you put an *ex* in front of it, it means to pray "out," i.e., to pray earnestly. And if you put an *in* (meaning "not") in front of both, you get the basis for the word *inexorable*—that is, not capable of being changed by prayers or entreaties. Synonyms for the word would be *relentless* or *unyielding.* We sometimes speak of the forces of nature as being inexorable, since they seem from our human perspective bound to happen, regardless of our will.

There are aspects of the gospel of Jesus Christ that are inexorable. One of them is the ultimate day of judgment that dawns with the Second Coming. This will happen regardless of the will of mankind. It is destined to take place as an essential and indispensable chapter in the unfolding of God's work and His glory. The scriptures contain graphic images of ill-prepared people who earnestly desire to avoid their appointment at the bar of justice: "Enter into the rock, and hide thee in the dust, for fear of the Lord, and for the glory of his majesty," is the relevant expression found in Isaiah 2:10. The prophet Alma had this to say to the rebellious Zeezrom (charitably using the first person plural): "For our words will condemn us, yea, all our works will condemn us; we shall not be found spotless; and our thoughts will also condemn us; and in this awful state we shall not dare to look up to our God; and we would fain be glad if we could command the rocks and the mountains to fall upon us to hide us from his presence" (Alma 12:14). The writer of the book of Revelation beheld a compelling scene associated with the Second Coming where the mighty of the earth "said to the mountains and rocks, Fall on us, and hide us from the face of him that sitteth on the throne, and from the wrath of the Lamb: For the great day of his wrath is come; and who shall be able to stand?" (Rev. 6:16–17).

The behavioral response to the inexorable eventuality of the Day of Judgment is the same response that was inculcated into the hearts of the two young scouts facing the advance of the irrigation water in the field: "Move!" It is what the repentant Zeezrom did under the burden of his guilt—he "moved" and became a changed person and an effective teacher of gospel principles. It is what all the righteous Saints do in preparation for the Second Coming, the inexorable Day of Judgment when the Lord will come (as He declared) "in a cloud with power and great glory" (Luke 21:27).

It is our lot to "move" ourselves ever closer to the pathway of righteousness, and to prepare ourselves for this final coming, that we might be caught up in the "clouds of heaven" (D&C 45:16) on that inexorable day: "And then they shall look for me, and, behold, I will come; and they shall see me in the clouds of heaven, clothed with power and great glory; with all the holy angels; and he that watches not for me shall be cut off" (D&C 45:44).

The Turning of the Hearts

In the latter days, Elijah restored the sealing power and turned the hearts of the fathers and children toward each other. This work, the sealing of husbands and wives and families for time and all eternity, was essential in order that families be forever. This work had to precede the Second Coming. And if the turning of hearts to their fathers had not occurred, "the whole earth would be utterly wasted at his coming" (D&C 2:3). The stories are legend of how the Lord has inspired people, through the Holy Ghost, to do their family history, genealogical research, and temple work.

Elder LeGrand Richards has written,

> What evidence have we that the promise of Malachi has been fulfilled? If Joseph
> Smith and Oliver Cowdery had spoken a falsehood when they said Elijah came to
> them, then the hearts of the children could not have turned to their fathers. No one
> else has claimed that Elijah committed these keys to him. The hearts of the children
> were not turned to their fathers before the proclamation by Joseph and Oliver.
>
> It is well to know in this connection that in 1836 there were no genealogical
> societies in this land or in Europe. Save for the keeping of pedigrees of royal and
> noble families, very little attention was being paid to the records of the dead in any
> Christian country. The first organized effort to collect and file genealogies of the
> common people was made shortly after the coming of Elijah. This was the forma-
> tion of *The New England Historic and Genealogical Society.* In 1844, this society was
> incorporated. Its chief purpose is to gather and publish data in relation to American
> Families. *The New York Genealogical and Biographical Society* was incorporated in
> 1869. *The Pennsylvania Genealogical Society, the Maine Genealogical Society,* together
> with other like societies in Maryland, New Hampshire, New Jersey, Rhode Island,
> Connecticut and most of the other states of the Union, have all been organized since
> 1836. A great many societies have also been organized in Great Britain and on the
> continent of Europe, but all of them since the keys of the Priesthood were returned
> to the earth which planted in the hearts of the children the promises made to their
> fathers (Joseph Fielding Smith, *The Way to Perfection,* 168–69).
>
> Hundreds of thousands of genealogical records have been compiled. The spirit
> of turning the hearts of the children to their fathers has swept the whole earth since
> Elijah came to accomplish his promised mission. While this spirit cannot be seen,
> the operation thereof has touched the hearts of men and women the world over.
> They do not know why they are compiling genealogical records, yet this work has
> made rapid strides—really it is "a marvelous work and a wonder" in and of itself.
> (LeGrand Richards, *A Marvelous Work and a Wonder* [Salt Lake City: Deseret Book,
> 1950], 184–85)

The power of the Lord was manifested in the life of Wilford Woodruff. He said:

> I will here say . . . that two weeks before I left St. George, the spirits of the dead
> gathered around me, wanting to know why we did not redeem them. Said they, "You
> have had the use of the Endowment House for a number of years, and yet nothing
> has ever been done for us. We laid the foundation of the government you now enjoy,
> and we never apostatized from it, but we remained true to it and were faithful to
> God."

These were the signers of the Declaration of Independence, and they waited on me for two days and two nights. I thought it very singular, that notwithstanding so much work had been done, and yet nothing had been done for them. The thought never entered my heart, from the fact, I suppose, that heretofore our minds were reaching after our more immediate friends and relatives.

I straightway went into the baptismal font and called upon Brother McAllister to baptize me for the signers of the Declaration of Independence, and fifty other eminent men, making one hundred in all, including John Wesley, Columbus, and others. I then baptized him for every President of the United States, except three; and when their cause is just, somebody will do the work for them. (*JD*, 19:229)

SUMMARY

It is fitting to consider the law of tithing in the same context with the subject of preparing for the Second Coming. In our day, the Lord has said, "Behold, now it is called today until the coming of the Son of Man, and verily it is a day of sacrifice, and a day for the tithing of my people; for he that is tithed shall not be burned at his coming. For after today cometh the burning—this is speaking after the manner of the Lord—for verily I say, tomorrow all the proud and they that do wickedly shall be as stubble; and I will burn them up, for I am the Lord of Hosts; and I will not spare any that remain in Babylon. Wherefore, if ye believe me, ye will labor while it is called today" (D&C 64:23–25). Elsewhere, He stressed the importance of having one's name "enrolled with the people of God" so that "he may tithe his people, to prepare them against the day of vengeance and burning" (D&C 85:3). It is the same message that Malachi sounded in his day: "For I am the Lord, I change not; therefore ye sons of Jacob are not consumed" (Mal. 3:6). And why are they not consumed? Because their names are kept in a "book of remembrance . . . for them that feared the Lord, and that thought upon his name" (Mal. 3:16). Malachi's universal question echoes with power down through the centuries: "But who may abide the day of his coming?" (Mal. 3:2). And, once again, the answer is clear for all of us who live in a time already well beyond the promised return of Elijah the prophet: "Wherefore, if ye believe me, ye will labor while it is called today" (D&C 64:25).

IMPORTANT COMPARATIVE DATES RELATING TO THE OLD TESTAMENT AND PEARL OF GREAT PRICE

TRAD. DATING*	REVISED DATING**	EVENT	SCRIPTURAL REFERENCES THAT INCLUDE TIME FRAMES	SYNCHRONISMS FROM OTHER CULTURES
4000	—	Fall of Adam		
3870	—	Birth of Seth	Gen. 5:3–5	
3765	—	Birth of Enos	Gen. 5:6–8	
3675	—	Birth of Cainan	Gen. 5:9–11	
3605	—	Birth of Mahalaleel	Gen. 5:12–14	
3540	—	Birth of Jared	Gen. 5:15–17	
3478	—	Birth of Enoch	Gen. 5:18–20	
3313	—	Birth of Methusalah	Gen. 5:27	
	3150			Beginning of Hieroglyphic writing about this time; development of the calendar
3126	—	Birth of Lamech	Gen. 5:25	
3070	—	Death of Adam	Gen. 5:5; 2:17; 2 Pet. 3:8	
2958	—	Death of Seth	Gen. 5:8	
2957	—	Enoch translated	Gen. 5:23–24; Heb. 11:5–6	
2944	—	Birth of Noah	Gen. 5:28–31	
2860	—	Death of Enos	Gen. 5:11	
2778	—	Death of Cainan	Gen. 5:14	
2765	—	Death of Jared	Gen. 5:20	
2710	—	Death of Mahalaleel	Gen. 5:17	
	2600			The period of the pyramids of Egypt (ca. 2600–2500)
2442	—	Birth of Shem	Gen. 5:32; 11:10	
2349	—	Death of Lamech	Gen. 5:31	
2344	—	Death of Methuselah	Gen. 5:26–27; 7:6	
2344–2343	2340–2300	The Flood	Gen. 5:26–27; 7:6	
2343	—	Birth of Arphaxad, son of Shem	Gen. 11:10–11	
2307	—	Birth of Salah, son of Arphaxad	Gen. 11:12–13	
2277	—	Birth of Eber, son of Salah	Gen. 11:14–15	
2243	—	Birth of Peleg, son of Eber	Gen. 11:16; 10:25	

*Approximate dates B.C. from Biblical references
** Approximate dates B.C. from secular references

2243–2004	—	"... in his [Peleg's] days the earth was divided"	Gen. 10:25; 10:32; Deut. 32:8; Acts 17:26
2213	—	Birth of Reu, son of Peleg	Gen. 11:18–19
2181	—	Birth of Serug, son of Reu	Gen. 11:20–21
2151	—	Birth of Nahor, son of Serug	Gen. 11:22–23
2122	—	Birth of Terah, son of Nahor	Gen. 11:24–25
2052	—	Birth of Abram, son of Terah	Gen. 11:26
2042	—	Sarai is born (Abram's future wife)	Gen. 17:17
2004	—	Death of Peleg	Gen. 11:19
2004	2004	Tower of Babel	Gen. 11:1; 9
2003	—	Death of Nahor	Gen. 11:25
1997	—	Death of Noah	Gen. 9:28–29
1994	—	Departure of Abram and Lot from Haran	Gen. 12:1–5
1974	—	Death of Reu	Gen. 11:21
	1968?	Abram settles in Hebron; ministry of Melchizedek in this time frame; Abram pays tithes to Melchizedek	JST, Gen. 14:25–40
1967	—	Marriage of Abram and Hagar	Gen. 16:3–4
1966	—	Birth of Ishmael, son of Abram	Gen. 16:16
1953	—	God's covenant with Abram (Abraham)	Gen. 17:25
1952	—	Birth of Isaac, son of Abraham	Gen. 17:17
1951	—	Death of Serug	Gen. 11:23
1947	—	Ishmael and Hagar are cast out	Gen. 21:14
1917	—	Death of Terah	Gen. 11:32
1915	—	Death of Sarah	Gen. 23:1–2
1912	—	Marriage of Isaac and Rebekah	Gen. 25:20
1904	—	Death of Arphaxad (son of Shem, grandson of Noah)	Gen. 11:13
1892	—	Birth of Jacob and Esau, sons of Isaac	Gen. 25:26

1877	—	Death of Abraham	Gen. 25:7	
1874	—	Death of Salah	Gen. 11:14–15	
1852	—	Marriage of Esau and Judith	Gen. 26:34	
1842	—	Death of Shem	Gen. 11:11	
1829	—	Death of Ishmael	Gen. 25:17	
1816	—	Jacob asks for Rachel's hand	Gen. 29:18–21	
1813	—	Death of Eber	Gen. 11:16–17	
1809	—	Jacob is given Leah instead of Rachel (for whom he must work seven more years)	Gen. 29:25–30	
1808	—	Birth of Reuben, son of Jacob and Leah	Gen. 29:32	
1807	—	Birth of Simeon, son of Jacob and Leah	Gen. 29:33	
1806	—	Birth of Levi, son of Jacob and Leah	Gen. 29:34	
1805	—	Birth of Judah, son of Jacob and Leah	Gen. 29:35	
1802	—	Marriage of Jacob and Rachel	—	
1801	—	Birth of Joseph, son of Jacob and Rachel	Gen. 30:25–34	
1796	—	Jacob completes tasks for Laban and leaves	Gen. 31:41	
1795	—	Jacob's name changed to Israel	Gen. 32:28	
1788	—	Around this time Benjamin is born to Jacob and Rachel; Rachel dies	Gen. 35:17–20	
1784	—	Israel makes the coat of many colors for Joseph, who is sold into Egypt by his brothers	Gen. 37:2	
1783	—	Joseph begins working for Potiphar	Gen. 39:1–6	
1774	—	Joseph is made ruler over the house of Potiphar	Gen. 39:7–10	
1773	—	Joseph is imprisoned on the basis of false accusations	Gen. 40:5	
1772	—	Death of Isaac	Gen. 35:27–28; 41:46	

1771	—	Joseph interprets the dream of Pharaoh		
1770	—	Joseph made ruler over all of Egypt, next to Pharaoh	Gen. 41:39–40	
1762	—	Jacob moves to Egypt	Gen. 45:6–11; 47:9, 28	
1671	—	Death of Joseph	Gen. 50:26	
1669	—	Death of Levi	Ex. 6:16	
1630	—	Birth of Aaron	Ex. 7:7	
1627	—	Birth of Moses	Gen. 15:12–16	
1587	—	Birth of Joshua	Joshua 14:7	
1547	1547	The Exodus (when Moses was 80 years old)	Ex. 7:7, Gen. 15:16	
1507	—	Death (translation) of Moses; end of the Wandering; Joshua takes Israel into the promised land	Deut. 34:7–9; Numbers 32:13	
1506	—	Beginning of the wars with the nations of Palestine		
1502	—	Fifth year of the wars; period of rest begins	Joshua 14:10, 15	
1501	—	Joshua begins his tenure as judge only		
1477	—	Death of Joshua	Judges 2:8	
1468	—	Commencement of the period of the judges, beginning with Othniel	Judges 3:9–11	
1429	—	Death of Othniel	Judges 3:11	
1387	—	Tenure of Ehud as judge begins (Shamgar also acts as deliverer)	Judges 3:15, 31	
1331	—	Death of Ehud		
1310	—	Tenure of Deborah as judge and prophetess	Judges 4:4	
1271	—	Death of Deborah	Judges 5:31	
1263	—	Tenure of Gideon as judge	Judges 6:11–16	
1224	—	Gideon (Jerubbaal) refuses to be king of Israel	Judges 8:22, 28	
1223	—	Birth of Abimelech, son of Gideon	Judges 8:31–33	

	1190			Period of the legendary Trojan War
1157	—	Jephthah made captain of Israel's armies	Judges 11:1–11	
1152	—	Death of Jephthah	Judges 12:7	
1126	—	Tenure of Eli as judge occurs around this time; Samson acts as deliverer during this period as well	Judges 13–16	
1125	—	Birth of Samuel around this time; Samuel is soon placed in service to Eli	1 Sam. 2:18, 26	
1107	—	Samuel recognized as a prophet by the people	1 Sam. 3:20	
1096	1095	Birth of David occurs around this time; reign of Saul over the next period		Tiglath-pilesar I is king of Assyria around this time
1066	—	Death of Samuel and Saul. David made king over the house of Judah. David retrieves the ark out of Kirjathjearim.	2 Sam. 2:4; 1 Chron. 13:5–6	
	1063	David annointed by Samuel		
	1055	David made king in Hebron		
	1047	David made king in Jerusalem		
	1047	Ministry of the prophets Nathan and Gad		
1026	1015	Death of David. Ascension of Solomon	1 Kings 2:12	
1022	1012	Solomon commences building the temple	1 Kings 6:37–38	Hiram is king of Tyre in this time frame
1015	991	Temple completed and dedicated	1 Kings 6:38; 8:1–2, 65–66; 2 Chron. 7:9–10	

986	975	Commencement of reign of 22-year Jeroboam of Israel; revolt of the Ten Tribes from Rehoboam	1 Kings 14:20–21	Shishak is king of Egypt in this time frame
985	975	Commencement of 17-year reign of Rehoboam of Judah		
969	932	Commencement of 3-year reign of Abijah (Abijam) of Judah	1 Kings 15:1; 2 Chron. 13:21	
967	929	Commencement of 41-year reign of Asa of Judah	1 Kings 15:9	
965	927	Commencement of 2-year reign of Nadab of Israel	1 Kings 15:25	
964	925	Commencement of 24-year reign of Baasha of Israel	1 Kings 15:28, 33	
941	901	Commencement of 2-year reign of Elah of Israel	1 Kings 16:8	
936	897	Commencement of 12-year reign of Omri of Israel	1 Kings 16:23	
929	875	Commencement of 22-year reign of Ahab of Israel	Joshua 6:26; 1 Kings 16:29	
926	873	Commencement of 35-year reign of Jehoshaphat of Judah; beginning of ministry of the prophet Elijah; rebuilding of Jericho	1 Kings 22:41–42	
909	853	Commencement of 8-year reign of Ahaziah of Israel	1 Kings 22:51	
908	851	Commencement of 12-year reign of Jehoram of Israel; beginning of ministry of the prophet Elisha if the revised dating is correct	2 Kings 3:1	

904	848	Commencement of 8-year reign of Jehoram (Joram) of Judah	2 Kings 8:16	
898	844	Commencement of 8-year reign of Ahaziah of Judah	2 Kings 9:29	
897	843	Commencement of 28-year reign of Jehu of Israel	2 Kings 8:25–26	
897	843	Commencement of 6-year reign of Athaliah Queen of Judah	2 Kings 11:1–3; 2 Chron. 22:10–12	
891	837	Commencement of 40-year reign of Joash of Judah; the time of the prophecies of Joel	2 Kings 11:4; 12:1	
869	—	Commencement of 17-year reign of Jehoahaz of Israel	2 Kings 13:1	
855	798	Commencement of 16-year reign of Jehoash of Israel	2 Kings 14:1; 13:10	It is thought that the Greek poet Homer flourished sometime in the period 800 to 700
854	—	Commencement of 29-year reign of Amaziah of Israel	2 Kings 14:1; 2 Chron. 24:25; 25:1	
840	790	Commencement of reign of Jeroboam II of Israel	2 Kings 15:1	
	790–749	Ministry of Jonah occurred during this period		
825	—	Commencement of 52-year reign of Azariah of Israel	2 Kings 14:21	
794	—	Commencement of period of interregnum	2 Kings 15:8–17	
788	749	Commencement of brief reign of Zachariah of Israel	2 Kings 15:8	
787	748	Commencement of brief reign of Shallum of Israel, followed by 10-year reign of Menahem of Israel	2 Kings 15:13, 17	

776	—	Commencement of 2-year reign of Pekahiah of Israel	2 Kings 15:23	First Olympic games held in Greece (776)
774	—	Commencement of 20-year reign of Pekah of Israel	2 Kings 15:27	
773	740	Commencement of 25-year reign of Jotham of Israel	2 Kings 15:32–33	
758	734	Commencement of 16-year reign of Ahaz of Judah		
757	733	Commencement of 9-year reign of Hoshea of Israel	2 Kings 17:1	
750–740	—	It is probably in this general time frame that the prophet Hosea and the prophet Amos commenced their ministry	Book of Hosea; Book of Amos	Legendary founding of Rome around 750 by Romulus and Remus
755	728	Commencement of 29-year reign of Hezekiah of Judah	2 Kings 18:1; 2 Chron. 29:1	
740	—	Commencement of 39-year ministry of Isaiah (740–701)		
	728–699	The time frame for the ministry of the prophet Micah	Book of Micah	
721	722	End of the Northern Kingdom	2 Kings 18:9–10	Conquest of Israel by Shalmanesar of Assyria
693	697	Commencement of the 55-year reign of Manasseh of Judah	2 Kings 21:1	
	670			The Republic founded in Athens about this time
639	642	Commencement of 2-year reign of Amon of Judah; ministry of Nahum might well be around this time	2 Kings 21:17–19	
638	640	Commencement of 31-year reign of Josiah of Judah	2 Kings 21:23–26; 22:1–2	
639–608	640	Time frame for the ministry of the prophet Zephaniah	Book of Zephaniah	

626	628	Commencement of 23-year ministry of the prophet Jeremiah	Jer. 25:1–4	
625	—	Commencement of the Babylonian Empire		Nabopolassar defeats the Assyrians; Babylonian Empire launched
621	—	Law of Moses discovered in the temple	2 Kings 22:3; 23:22	
612	606	End of Assyrian Empire		Nabopolassar and Cyazares destroy Nineveh, effectively ending Assyrian Empire
608	609	Commencement of short reign of Jehoahaz of Judah	2 Kings 23:31–33	Nebuchadnezzar fights Assyrians; King Josiah killed
607	609	Commencement of 11-year reign of Eliakim (Jehoiakim) of Judah	2 Kings 23:34–37	
605	—	Ascension year of Nebuchadnezzar	Daniel 1:1; 2 Kings 24:12	Nebuchadnezzar comes into power
604	—	Many Jews taken captive to Babylon, including Daniel, during this time period		Nebuchadnezzar defeats Pharaoh Necho in the battle of Carchemish and then reigns 43 years as King of Babylon
604–600	—	During this period the prophet Daniel commences his ministry	Book of Daniel	
600	598	Perhaps the time frame for the ministry of the prophet Habakkuk	Book of Habakkuk	
597	598	Commencement of reign of Zedekiah of Judah (following brief reign of Jehoiachin, who is taken captive); commencement of the ministry of Lehi and also of his son Nephi	2 Kings 24:18; 1 Ne. 1:4; 5:12–13; Hel. 8:21	
592–593	—	Ministry of Ezekiel begins and lasts until 570	Ezekiel 1:1–2	
589	—	Siege of Jerusalem	2 Kings 25:1	Nebuchadnezzar lays siege to Jerusalem

587	—	Destruction of Jerusalem, including the temple	Jer. 44:30; 52:12–13; 2 Kings 25:8–10	Nebuchadnezzar destroys the city and takes many captive to Babylon
587	609?	Probably also the time frame for the ministry of the prophet Obadiah		
587–585	—	Jeremiah writes the Lamentations	Book of Lamentations	
562	—	Death of Nebuchadnezzar		
561	561	Release of Jehoiachin from prison by the Babylonians		Evil-merodach king of Babylon
	555			Belshazzar as co-regent of Babylon with Nabonidus
538	559	Babylon defeated	Jer. 27:6–7; Ezra 1:1; Isa. 44:26–28; 45:1–5	Cyrus (Darius) the Persian defeats Babylon and reigns 9 years
537	—	Decree of Cyrus (Darius) to allow the Jews to return to their land and rebuild the temple	Ezra 2:36; 3:12; 1 Chron. 24:11; 2 Chron. 31:15; Neh. 7:7; 12:1, 7, 10, 26	The Greek philosopher and mathematician Pythagoras flourished around this time
	536	Joshua as high priest		
	525			Birth of Greek playwright Aeschylus (525–456)
519–520	—	Time frame for the ministry of the prophet Haggai and the prophet Zechariah	Haggai 2:10–18; Zech. 1:12–17	
485	496			Birth of Greek playwright Sophocles (496?–406)
	486	Commencement of reign of Xerxes	Esther 1:1	Accession of Xerxes, King of Persia (ruled 21 years: 486–465)
479	—	Service of Esther takes place around this time	Book of Esther	
	470?–399			Life span of Socrates, Greek philosopher
463	—	Commencement of reign of Artaxerxes, son of Xerxes	Ezra 7:1	Accession of Artaxerxes, King of Persia (ruled 39 years)
	460?–400?			Life span of Greek historian Thucydides, chronicler of the Peloponnesian War

459	—	Repatriation of many of the captive Jews		
457	458	Ezra receives the order to rebuild the city and set up a government	Dan. 9:26, 25–27	
444	—	Ministry of Nehemiah on behalf of the Jews occurred around this time; he was appointed governor of Judaea	Neh. 2:1; 5:14	Parthenon in Athens completed around this time
	432	Nehemiah's second mission to Jerusalem		
430	432	Ministry of the prophet Malachi takes place		
	431–404			Peloponnesian War 431–404
	427			Birth of Plato (427?–347?)
	424			Accession of Darius II
	359			Accession of Philip, king of Macedon
	332			Alexander in Syria and Egypt
	330			Darius III slain; end of Persian hegemony
	323			Death of Alexander the Great

THEMES FOR LIVING INDEX

ABOUT THE AUTHORS

ED J. PINEGAR is a retired dentist and long-time teacher of early-morning seminary and religion classes at Brigham Young University. He teaches at the Joseph Smith Academy and has served as a mission president in England and at the Missionary Training Center in Provo, Utah. He has been a bishop, a stake president, and is a temple sealer. Ed and his wife, Patricia, are the parents of eight children and reside in Orem, Utah.

RICHARD J. ALLEN is a husband, father, teacher, and writer. He has served on several high councils, in several stake presidencies, and as a bishop. Richard's teaching assignments in the Church have included service as a full-time missionary, instructor in various priesthood quorums, gospel doctrine teacher, and stake institute director. He has served as a faculty member at both Brigham Young University and The Johns Hopkins University. Richard has coauthored many articles, manuals, and books and has served on a number of national educational boards. He and his wife, Carol Lynn Hansen Allen, have four children and five grandchildren.